Mastering Corel Draw 3

Chris Dickman

with Pawel Bodytko, Sherwood Fleming, Michael Kieran,
Stephen Roth, Steve Sagman, Steve Shubitz, Rich Zaleski

Peachpit Press
Berkeley, California

Mastering Corel Draw 3

Peachpit Press, Inc.
2414 Sixth St.
Berkeley, CA 94710
510 548-4393

Cover design: Ted Mader + Associates (TMA)
Cover illustration: Norbert Chausse
Book design: Peter Dako, Casual Casual

ISBN 1-56609-006-7

0 9 8 7 6 5 4 3 2 1
Printed and bound in the United States of America

For Sherwood, again.

Thanks

I like to create books the way I edit magazines — assemble a team of top-notch contributors and designers, poke and prod until light is shed on the darkest corners of the project at hand, enlist the support of hardware and software vendors who share my objectives, and market the daylights out of the result.

I thus owe a considerable debt to the many people who found this project valuable enough to contribute significant amounts of that most precious of commodities, time. My thanks, first of all, to Peachpit publisher Ted Nace, who has provided the freedom and encouragement to do my best work, through three editions.

The team of contributing authors for this edition, faced with demanding schedules, contributed chapters that are all I hoped they would be. Pawel Bodytko, Michael Kieran, Steve Sagman, Steve Shubitz and Rich Zaleski have all made invaluable contributions to the book in their areas of specialty, clarifying the obscure and in many cases documenting material for the first time.

Other material came from a wide variety of sources. Jim Phillips provided the text and illustrations for *Cartooning with Draw*, with additional images for this edition. *Service Bureau Strategies* contains material adapted from articles by Frank Braswell and Bob Hires that first appeared in the AISB *timeout* newsletter. This chapter also contains tips on blending and trapping adapted from the *ColorTips* booklet produced by the ColoRip Pre-Press service bureau. In addition, the *Getting the Best Scan* chapter was adapted from *ScanJet Unlimited* (Peachpit Press) by Steve Roth, Salvatore Parascandolo and myself. Full credit for the technical content of the chapter, however, must go to Steve.

The introduction to the *Choosing a Training Firm* chapter was adapted from an article by Sherwood Fleming. Sherwood also rigorously tested the tutorial chapters. Rosalyn Wosnick copy edited the manuscript, ably catching many a slip. Michael Lee Advertising & Design and Keith Donally kindly let me reproduce their work in the color section. Peter Dako single-handedly managed the book's design and production with aplomb, patiently incorporating my suggestions under a tight deadline.

Thanks are in order to the many authors of the programs on the Utility disk included with this book. Too numerous to name, those who create freeware and shareware programs are both to be commended and, if they request a donation, supported. However, special thanks is due to Costas Kitsos for providing his useful FONPRN utility exclusively for readers of this book. John Murdoch let me include his customized TRUMATCH palette. And the collection of Draw macros is supplied courtesy of Diane Byrd.

The Fonts disk marks what I believe is a publishing first — a book with an included disk of dozens of free, commercial-grade fonts. Shareware fonts can be of surprisingly good quality, but the disk of 26 fonts in TrueType format from the Castcraft OptiFonts type library is truly exceptional. These fonts are provided with no registration fee or payment request of any kind. I can only thank Lawrence Kreiter, of OptiFonts, for his continuing faith in this project. I hope the response exceeds his expectations.

NEC Canada supplied an NEC 5D monitor that I used for running Draw and Word for Windows while writing the book. Bill Neuenschwander, from LaserMaster, has provided continuing support through several editions and was responsible for supplying the Unity 1200 employed for creating final pages, as well as the WinPrinter 800, which was used for proofing. Agfa Canada was enthusiastic enough about the book to output the film for the last three pages in the color section on its SelectSet 5000 imagesetter. My thanks to Paul Panza and Bruno Carrer for their assistance in this.

Corel Corp. has provided support throughout three editions of the book. There are many at Corel to thank, but Arlen Bartsch and Fiona Rochester must be singled out for providing unflagging assistance and access to Corel's resources. Vivi Nichol, Kelly Fraser, Paul Coffin, Donna Hogan and Richard Pali, of Corel's technical support department, patiently and competently answered what must have sometimes seemed like a never-ending stream of questions. And thanks to Paul Klauninger for the updated version of the font of Draw's tools and icons used throughout the book.

Chris Dickman
Toronto, December, 1992

Table
of Contents

What You Can Do with CorelDRAW

I f you're new to CorelDRAW and its suite of companion applications, you may be unclear about just how far its capabilities extend. Is this for technical illustrators? Is it appropriate for manipulating clip art? Can you use it for creating presentation graphics? What about laying out ads? Will it help you clean up scanned images? Are business presentations something its designed to create? Or is it more suited to publications, such as newsletters or brochures? Can you create high-quality color separations with it? And what about specialized applications, such as cartography, product design, packaging, sign cutting or slide creation? In fact, Draw is being used for all of the above applications and many more besides.

The graphics horizon is virtually limitless

Modifying Clip Art

While CorelDRAW is a powerful tool in the hands of a graphic arts professional, most Draw users have little or no graphic arts background. Instead, they rely on clip art to illustrate their publications, using graphics either from the sizable library of images and symbols that accompanies Draw or from vendors who supply clip art in one of the many file formats supported by Draw. Such files, once imported into Draw, can be customized using the program's powerful arsenal of editing capabilities.

Creating Business Graphics

The included CorelCHART program is a very capable template-based presentation graphics application that lets even graphing neophytes quickly create impressive charts. These can be output right from Chart, or exported in a wide variety of industry-standard formats. Graphics created with Chart can also be moved into Draw for further modification, and Draw graphics can be incorporated into charts. The program's import capabilities, coupled with OLE support, can create dynamic links between a charts data and the originating application, such as a spreadsheet or word processor. The Autographix software included with Chart automates the task of sending completed images to a service bureau for slide output.

You could also import charts into Draw created in other charting applications, such as Harvard Graphics, and make use of its advanced object editing and fill capabilities, such as 3-D effects and textured fills.

Using Scanned Images

The ability to import, edit and export a wide variety of file formats is one of the keys to Draw's versatility. Bitmap images, such as those created with scanners, can be imported into Draw and either used as part of the final image or converted into editable vector form by manual or automatic tracing. The included CorelTRACE program can be used to quickly create finished artwork that closely resembles the scanned original. This could be a commercially printed clip art image or be one taken from any source that can be scanned. Graphic artists, on the other hand, often prefer to sketch their idea quickly and freely on paper, scan it and fine tune the image in Draw.

Scanned images can also be brought into CorelPHOTO-PAINT for pixel-based manipulations, such as cleanup, color correction or the application of special-effect filters, such as emboss and motion blur.

Making Presentations

Once youve created striking images in Draw, Chart or Photo-Paint, you can integrate them and add sound or animation clips with CorelSHOW. Designed for organizing on-screen presentations, its supplied with a wide variety of transition effects to tie your images together into a seamless show.

PC/Macintosh Exchange

Draw makes it easy to import files created from many PC applications, enhance them and export them in a format compatible with popular desktop publishing and word processing programs such as PageMaker, Ventura and WordPerfect. Since Draw can also import, edit and export files in the popular

Macintosh Adobe Illustrator format, files are moved between the PC and Macintosh platforms with relative ease. Draw also imports, edits and exports Macintosh PICT files. You could even import a chart created with Lotus 1-2-3 into Draw, for example, edit it, export it in .EPS format and then import it into the Macintosh version of PageMaker.

CAD Compatibility

While not designed to take the place of dedicated CAD programs such as AutoCAD, the greater ease of use of Draw, coupled with its superior type handling and the ability to import, edit and export AutoCAD files, makes it a natural companion to many CAD programs.

Color Output Options

Draw outputs to any Windows-supported printer, which includes such color devices as the HP PaintJet ink jet printer and the QMS ColorScript line of thermal color PostScript printers. Draw provides extensive control over color specification and creates full four-color film separations on a PostScript imagesetter. Slides are also an increasingly popular way to capture color images, using either in-house equipment or the facilities of a service bureau. Even color plotters can be driven by Draw, either with the Windows driver or by exporting to HPGL format.

Page Layout

Draw is normally used to create text and graphics effects that are then imported into page layout programs or word processors. But Draw will also allow you to create complete single-page documents. Large blocks of text can be imported and automatically placed in columns, with control over hyphenation, spell checking and inter-paragraph spacing.

Specialized Applications

Thanks to its flexibility, Draw also lends itself to more specialized applications. Some of the more unusual include glass cutting and woodworking design, label and package creation, cartography, sign and silkscreen film cutting, and rubber stencil cutting for tombstone engraving. Draw images are showing up in everything from modest club newsletters to four-color magazine covers and computer animations. As a judge in the annual Corel Design Contest, I can vouch for the astonishingly broad spectrum of applications for which Draw is used.

Working with Type

Draw's type handling capabilities are particularly strong. It's supplied with a library of over 150 TrueType fonts (with 100 more on the CD-ROM) that will output to virtually any printer and can be used with any Windows application. You can manipulate fonts directly on the screen by rotating, stretching and condensing them, or aligning them along a curve. You can even convert them to editable curve segments and play type designer — just the thing for creating logos and custom type treatments.

In addition, Draw lets you create your own TrueType or PostScript fonts, using any object you draw or import. This makes it possible to generate custom fonts of commonly used symbols, for example.

A Passionate Affair

As you may have guessed by now, there's very little of a graphical nature that *can't* be accomplished with Draw and its companion applications. In the nine years that I've been in-volved with personal computer-based publishing, I've tested dozens of graphics packages for the PC, Macintosh and Amiga platforms. And yet I continue to return to Draw for my design needs. After three and a half years of intensive use, it's an application I still feel passionate about. I can only hope that some of that passion is transmitted to you through the pages of *Mastering Corel Draw*.

This Book and How to Use It

You're holding a very special resource on learning to use CorelDRAW and its companion programs. *Mastering Corel Draw* was the first book about Draw to be published and it remains the only one ever to be endorsed by Corel Corporation. It's also the best-selling book of its kind and has been translated into many languages. So what's so special about it? Whether you're just beginning to work with Draw, or have picked it up on your own and are looking for a solid grounding and advanced techniques, this is the only Draw resource you'll need.

Guaranteed mastery (and fun while you're at it)

Mastering Corel Draw is intended as an adjunct to, not a replacement for, the supplied reference material. It is most definitely *not* a rehash of the Draw documentation. Over years of daily work with Draw, I have uncovered much undocumented and poorly understood material. It's my goal to not only help you become productive with Draw, but to share my tips and secrets. So I've flagged sections with graphical symbols to identify the tips or undocumented secrets I've uncovered through my years of working with Draw. There's much in this book you will find nowhere else. In fact, I've crammed everything I know about Draw between these covers — and it's my pleasure to pass it on to you.

Tip

In addition to the tutorial chapters, this book contains a number of sections providing coverage of key aspects of Draw. Topics include an introduction to the Windows environment, output device options, Draw loading strategies, using service bureaus, color separations, changing defaults and enhancing Windows performance. There are also sections on core topics such as scanning and color — vital for the effective use of not only Draw, but virtually any graphics or publishing application. A color section reproduces some of the ambitious color work being created with Draw.

Secret

An in-depth chapter on TrueType and PostScript font management provides essential information for making effective use of the extensive library of type supplied with Draw. It contains information on hardcore font installation, conversion and management strategies for both type formats.

Detailed tutorials have also been included on all the applications included with Draw. Turn to these for hands-on sessions with CorelTRACE, CorelMOSAIC, CorelCHART, CorelSHOW and CorelPHOTO-PAINT. Of course, all of these contain lots of tips and secrets of their own.

The extensive glossary of Draw and graphic arts terms should be consulted when you come across unfamiliar terms in the book, and a bibliography has been provided covering the graphic design and print production fields. I've also included a chapter on how to choose a training firm, which contains a directory of firms providing Draw courses.

What's on the Disks?

Two disks have been included with this book. While others have since followed suit, this was the first book on Draw to include a disk and the current edition has taken this idea to new levels. One disk is packed with Draw files and Windows utilities to make your illustration sessions more productive. Font management tools, a floating button bar for switching between applications, my favorite on-screen clock, new Draw color palettes, color reference cards — I've provided all kinds of goodies, including some exclusive to this book.

But even more significant is a disk holding over two dozen commercial-grade TrueType fonts from the Castcraft foundry. I've carefully picked these from the thousands of faces in the Castcraft type library, and I believe you'll find they complement the sizable library supplied with Draw. Unlike the fonts included with other books, these are not shareware fonts created by amateur type designers, with a requirement that you send in a fee of some sort. Thanks to an exclusive arrangement with Castcraft, these top-quality faces are yours to use. In addition, a coupon at the back of the book provides discounts on the purchase of more Castcraft fonts. Other coupons provide

AGENCY GOTHIC

Diode Vogue

Antique Bold

Einstein Black

OPTI ASIAN

Novel Gothic XBold Agency

Bauer Bodoni Bold

Globe Gothic

Runserif Regular

Goudy Bold Agency

Bernhard Gothic XHeavy

HUXLEY VERTICAL

BINNER

NEULAND INLINE CAPS

Bodoni Antiqua

Korinna XBold Agency

Caslon No. 2 Black

Latin Bold

Cheltenham Bold Condensed

Franklin Gothic Triple Condensed

Corvinus Skyline

Metropolis Bold

Craw Modern Bold

Koloss

Radiant Bold Condensed

Similunatix Heavy

discounts on a range of Draw-related products, such as type utilities, advanced Draw videotapes, newsletters and seminars.

What About the Tutorials?

The fastest way to master any domain is to begin taking action, guided by someone who has been there before you. *Mastering Corel Draw* is thus primarily in tutorial form. You'll find that simply reading the tutorial sections will not prove nearly as effective as firing up Draw, and its companion applications, and working your way through them.

No prior knowledge of Draw is assumed, but being comfortable with the Windows environment it runs under will make things go a little more smoothly. So if you're new to Windows, you should mouse your way through the section on Windows fundamentals that precedes the Draw tutorials. While a modest online tutorial is supplied with Draw itself, there's no need to work your way through it before beginning this book; you'll soon have progressed far beyond its limited scope.

The goal of the tutorial chapters in this book is to lead you through a series of exercises, building your familiarity not only with Draw's features but with the sequence of actions you must take to actually work effectively. For example, I'll lead you step-by-step through the process of wrapping text along a curved path, creating complex fill effects and manipulating clip art.

The tutorial chapters will prove most useful if worked through at a leisurely pace. Time permitting, the optimal way to use these chapters is to go through them twice. At frequent intervals the text will encourage you to experiment with variations of the current operation, something that's worth doing the second time through.

A quick first run-through to get an overview of the fundamental principles being covered and a second, slower reading, accompanied by an exploration of possible variations, will bring solid results. In the same vein, it's a good idea to finish reading a paragraph in its entirety before performing any of the actions it suggests.

Draw is a stable program on most systems, but any graphics application will hang on occasion. So I recommend regularly saving the file you're working on to avoid the loss of time going over old ground in the event of system crashes. You'll also find it useful to perform incremental saves by making copies of all or part of the image you're working on and placing it to the side of the page.

Don't overlook the reference material supplied with Draw. The manual is worth reading from cover to cover, and the online help provides additional material, such as a technical reference and documentation for CorelMOSAIC. There really is no substitute for methodically working your way through the documentation accompanying any software application you'll be using on a regular basis. And while working on the tutorials, you should keep Draw's documentation handy for a different perspective, or more detail, on the features being covered.

Will I Really Master Draw?

Yes. I guarantee that completing the tutorial chapters will turn you into a Draw guru of the first order. And you'll enjoy yourself along the way. I've tried to make the tutorial sections both fun and effective for mastering the creation of graphics with Draw. Many of the exercises have been forged in the red-hot crucible of the Draw classes I lead in Toronto, amplified by my own discoveries and discussions with other users. *Mastering Corel Draw* should enable you to do just that — master the use of Draw, and its companion programs, for the creation of just about any image you can imagine.

Windows Survival Skills

Corel DRAW is a Microsoft Windows application, which means you must have Windows installed to run it. Draw is in good company; virtually all PC graphics and publishing applications are now designed specifically for the Windows environment.

Windows can be thought of as an extension to the good old DOS operating system we know and love. Since it's putting a graphical face on such DOS operations as running programs and performing file operations, you'll use Windows (and Draw itself) more confidently if you're familiar with fundamental PC concepts, such as files and directories. If you feel less than confident in that area, a one-day course in PC fundamentals, and perhaps Windows, might be in order.

Failing that, there are many books available on both topics. While most of the Windows books I've encountered are basically windy rehashes of the manual, *The Little Windows Book*, from Peachpit Press, is designed as a tutorial that will let you quickly mouse your way through the basics. It would serve as an excellent next step after working your way through this chapter.

In the following pages, you'll learn the Windows skills you need to work your way through the tutorial sections of this book and make effective use of the material on the two included disks. If you're already a competent Windows user you can probably skip this section, but do check out the *Optimizing Windows* chapter further on. Run Windows now so you can mouse your way through this chapter. You'll be using the left mouse button exclusively throughout, although Draw itself does make use of the right button.

When you first run Windows, the Program Manager loads —

If Draw is your first Windows program, then this section is a must

unless you've replaced it with a third-party substitute, such as Norton Desktop. Program Manager displays a collection of *icons*, graphic representations of the programs on your hard disk. When you install Windows it creates collections of these icons in several areas, or *groups*: Main, Accessories, Applications, StartUp and Games.

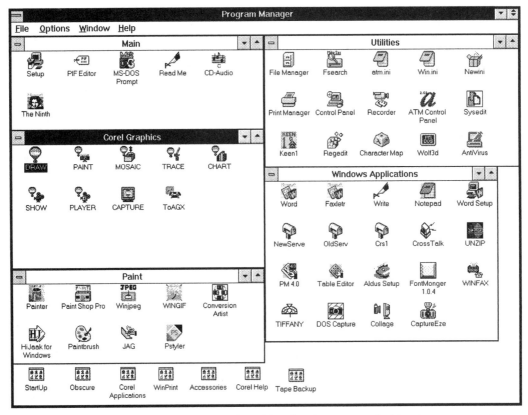

The Corel Applications group holds nine program icons

The icons in the Main group run several programs for configuring and controlling the Windows environment, as well as working with your files. The icons in the Accessories group run Write (a word processor), Recorder (a macro recorder), Character Map (a utility that provides quick access to special characters) and a number of other programs. Some of these can serve as useful adjuncts to Draw and will be covered briefly later in the book. In addition, the documentation included with Windows itself, the *Windows User's Guide*, performs a good job of covering these and the other accessories.

Moving program icons into the StartUp group runs those programs automatically when Windows is loaded. You'll make use of this later to auto-load some of the programs supplied on the two disks in the back of the book. Finally, the Games group

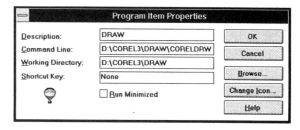

contains, well... games. You can always identify new Windows users: they're the ones playing Solitaire.

You might also have groups for other Windows applications you've installed, such as WordPerfect or PageMaker. In the Program Manager screen illustrated here I've created new groups and added many new program icons, organizing the icons and groups to suit the way I work.

When you installed Draw it created a Corel Graphics group and placed a number of program icons in it: CorelMOSAIC!, CorelTRACE!, CorelCHART!, CorelPHOTO-PAINT!, CorelSHOW!PLAYER, CAPTURE, ToAGX and CorelDRAW! itself. To see what function these icons actually perform, click just once on the CorelDRAW! icon and then click on Program Manager's File menu. Then click on Properties. The dialog box indicates what command is connected to the CorelDRAW! icon; in my case it loads Draw (CORELDRW.EXE) from the COREL3\DRAW subdirectory of the D: drive. Make a note now of the drive and directory of CORELDRW.EXE on your system — you'll need this information in a moment. When a dialog box is displayed, clicking on any other part of your screen simply produces a beep. You must close dialog boxes by clicking on OK or Cancel before you continue. Click on the Cancel button now to return to Program Manager.

DRAW

What happens if one of the Draw icons isn't displayed? Sometimes icons get deleted or moved to new groups, but generating a new icon is quite simple. It's a matter of finding the program file and attaching an icon to it. If you already have a CorelDRAW icon displayed, the

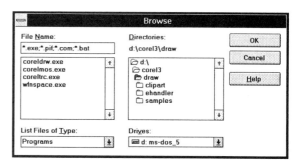

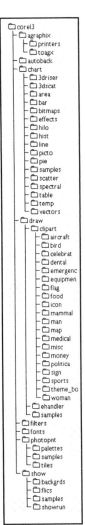

```
corel3
├─ agraphix
│  ├─ printers
│  └─ toagx
├─ autoback
├─ chart
│  ├─ 3driser
│  ├─ 3dscat
│  ├─ area
│  ├─ bar
│  ├─ bitmaps
│  ├─ effects
│  ├─ hilo
│  ├─ hist
│  ├─ line
│  ├─ picto
│  ├─ pie
│  ├─ samples
│  ├─ scatter
│  ├─ spectral
│  ├─ table
│  ├─ temp
│  └─ vectors
├─ draw
│  ├─ clipart
│  │  ├─ aircraft
│  │  ├─ bird
│  │  ├─ celebrat
│  │  ├─ dental
│  │  ├─ emergenc
│  │  ├─ equipmen
│  │  ├─ flag
│  │  ├─ food
│  │  ├─ icon
│  │  ├─ mammal
│  │  ├─ man
│  │  ├─ map
│  │  ├─ medical
│  │  ├─ misc
│  │  ├─ money
│  │  ├─ politica
│  │  ├─ sign
│  │  ├─ sports
│  │  ├─ theme_bo
│  │  └─ woman
│  ├─ ehandler
│  └─ samples
├─ filters
├─ fonts
├─ photopnt
│  ├─ palettes
│  ├─ samples
│  └─ tiles
└─ show
   ├─ backgrds
   ├─ flics
   ├─ samples
   └─ showrun
```

following procedure will create a duplicate, which you can later delete. Choose New from the File menu. Click on the Program Item button, if it isn't currently selected, and then click on OK. Now click on Browse in Program Item Properties to display the Browse dialog box.

Before you can find the program file you're after, you should be clear on how the hard disk of your computer is organized. Hard disks hold data and program files, and are anywhere from 20 to over 200 megabytes in size. To make it easier to find files, hard disks are divided into a number of areas, or *drives*, such as C:, D: and E: (in contrast, your floppy disk drives are A: and B:). If you're on a network, you may have many more drives available than this on a remote server. These drives in turn are subdivided into smaller areas, called *directories*, in which you can place related files. You have a WINDOWS directory, for example, holding Windows-related files. These directories in turn may contain *subdirectories*, which may in turn contain other subdirectories, and so on. Your WINDOWS directory, for example, has a SYSTEM subdirectory.

Windows follows the naming convention used by the Macintosh and calls directories *folders*. By all means use the file folder metaphor if it helps you visualize the organization of your hard drive, because visualize it you must if you want to avoid wasting time hunting aimlessly for lost files. This collection of drives, directories and subdirectories is said to make up the *tree directory structure* of your hard disk. The Browse dialog box is indicating your current drive and directory, probably C:\WINDOWS.

A CORELDRW directory was created when Draw was installed, as well as subdirectories for Draw, CorelCHART and the other supplied applications and files. You were given the option of changing the names of these directories, and as you can see in the directory listing from my hard disk I chose to call the main directory COREL3. It's time to move to Draw's directory, the one indicated earlier in the Properties dialog box. *Double-click* (click twice quickly) on the drive icon under Directories: (probably C:\ or D:\) to move to the top, or *root*, directory. You can also click once on a drive or directory icon and then click on OK if you're having trouble double-clicking.

If CORELDRW isn't displayed in the available list of directories, Draw must be installed on another drive. You can change drives by clicking on the current selection in the Drives: box and choosing another from the drop-down list. By default, Draw is installed in — what else? — a DRAW subdirectory of CORELDRW. On my system this is on the D: drive, since C: was getting full. Double-click on the DRAW directory icon to display the files it contains. The Browse dialog box doesn't display all the files it finds, just programs — primarily those that end in .EXE (for *executable*). In the Draw directory you should see a number of program files for CorelMOSAIC, CorelTRACE, WFNSPACE and Draw itself, CORELDRW.EXE. Double-click on CORELDRW.EXE to select it.

This returns you to the Program Item Properties dialog box. Click on OK to return to the page and a new icon will have been created for Draw. You'll use this procedure later to generate icons for the programs included on the disks with this book. Since you didn't name it, the icon has been given the name of the program file: CORELDRW. Choose Properties from the File menu, and in the Description box edit the name to something more civilized, like simply Draw. Since the existing description is already highlighted for you, simply type in a new name to take its place and click on OK.

If you now have two Draw icons, click on either one to select it and choose Delete from the File menu to zap it. Deleting an icon doesn't actually delete any files, so there's no chance of damaging any of the CorelDRAW programs by deleting their icons.

Control Panel

Now double-click on the Control Panel icon in the Main group. Control Panel displays a series of icons that let you customize your Windows environment. Many of these icons lead to arcane dialog boxes that rarely need to be altered. Others, such as Fonts, Printers and Mouse, let you control Windows attributes that relate directly to your work in Draw. Double-click on the Mouse icon.

Control Panel

This dialog box lets you alter the sensitivity of both the movement and buttons of your mouse, as well as switch the function-

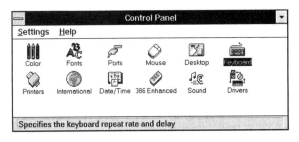

Mouse

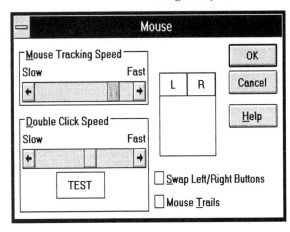

Printers

ality of the two buttons. (Switching the buttons might be appropriate if you're left-handed.) Since mice have varying resolutions, you should set the Mouse Tracking Speed to establish a comfortable relationship between mouse and cursor movement.

Click on the left scroll arrow to set the speed to Slow, for example, and move your mouse around the screen a bit. Now set it to Fast to observe the difference. If you're new to the world of mice, you may feel more in control with this set to a low value. Experienced Draw users typically set this to Fast, since it minimizes hand and wrist movement, and hence fatigue.

You've seen that Windows interprets two quick clicks as a double-click. If you've been struggling to get Windows to recognize your double-clicks, a solution is to make Windows more forgiving of your digital limitations. Set this value to Slow and double-click slowly on the Test button. It will change color to black or white if it recognizes your two clicks as a double-click. Conversely, change this to Fast and you may not be able to click fast enough for Windows to recognize your double-clicks, so somewhere in the middle is your best bet. When the mouse is set up to your satisfaction, click on OK.

Printer Configuration

As a Draw user, you'll be creating frequent printouts of your work. When Windows was first installed, you told it the output device to which you'd be printing. In the best of all possible worlds you never have to alter your printer configuration, but in the real world of Windows this necessity is bound to arise at some point. There's no need to venture too deeply into the black art of printer configuration at this point, but you need to know where to look when the time comes.

Double-click on the Printers icon to display a list of the installed printers. When you first install Windows it asks you what output devices you want installed, but you can later add new printers or update existing ones by installing a more current printer driver (the software that *drives* your output devices). Click on the Add button to display a list of the Windows-supported output devices. To install a new or updated driver you

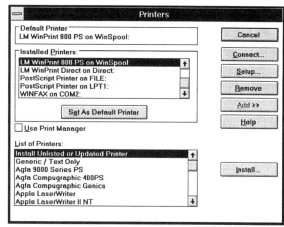

would select the appropriate device from the list, click on Install and insert a disk holding the printer driver file for your output device. If you need to install a printer that's not on this list, you'd leave Install Unlisted Or Updated Printer selected and click on Install. If you have several printers installed, Draw always prints to the default Windows printer. You can select any installed driver and click on the Set As Default Printer button to accomplish this.

Click on the Setup button, then on About. Here's a fact of life for Windows users you should keep in mind: all device drivers, whether for your mouse, monitor or printer, are in a state of flux. That is, they're constantly being upgraded to provide better performance, or to take into account the capabilities of new devices. A case in point is printer drivers. In the illustration you can see that I'm using the 3.52

version of the PostScript printer driver. How about you? Does it say 3.5? Ah, then you're using an old driver; the current version as I wrote this was 3.53. In fact, I just recently downloaded this new version from the DTP Forum on the CompuServe information service (type GO DTPFORUM), a typical place to ferret out new drivers. Drivers are typically free, but you have to know when they become available and where to get them.

Don't feel bad if you've got an old driver installed, but it *is* advisable to stay current. The 3.50 PostScript driver, for example, had some nasty bugs that were ironed out in later

---

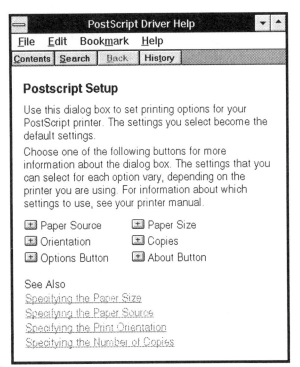

Postscript Setup

Use this dialog box to set printing options for your PostScript printer. The settings you select become the default settings.

Choose one of the following buttons for more information about the dialog box. The settings that you can select for each option vary, depending on the printer you are using. For information about which settings to use, see your printer manual.

⊞ Paper Source   ⊞ Paper Size
⊞ Orientation   ⊞ Copies
⊞ Options Button   ⊞ About Button

See Also
Specifying the Paper Size
Specifying the Paper Source
Specifying the Print Orientation
Specifying the Number of Copies

versions. When all else fails, call Microsoft and ask for a new driver — they'll usually provide it for a modest handling fee. Click on OK to close the About dialog box.

There are additional levels of printer dialog boxes to wander through, but now is not the time to explore them all. However, do click on the Help button. The PostScript and Hewlett-Packard printer drivers are supplied with generous online help that provides many useful tips. Click on any of the buttons for an overview of the available topics for the current dialog box. You can view help on any solid underlined topic simply by clicking on it; items that have a dotted underline provide a pop-up glossary when clicked on. Wander around for a while in help and then click on the Back button to return to the index. While not a replacement for the manual, online help can sometimes help you out when you're faced with printing problems. When you've finished poking around, click on the File menu and choose Exit. Click on OK to return to the initial Printers dialog box, and then on Close to return to Control Panel.

Fonts

Fonts

Double-click on the Fonts icon. This dialog box displays the currently installed TrueType and system fonts, and lets you remove them or add new ones. Unless you installed Draw from its CD-ROM, it was installed along with more than 150 fonts in TrueType format. Scroll down the list of fonts and click on a font name to see a preview of what it looks like. You'll be returning to this dialog box later to work with the Draw fonts, as well as to install the TrueType fonts included on the disks with this book. After you've looked at a few fonts, click on Close to return to Control Panel.

Control Panel has its own online help, which is worth a look.

Click on Help in its menu bar, choose Contents and scroll down the list of topics. Note that there is generic information here about configuring your printer. Close Control Panel's help when you've satisfied your curiosity about its contents. Then feel free to explore the other Windows configuration programs in Control Panel, by double-clicking on their icons. Click on Cancel to exit dialog boxes and avoid making changes to your Windows configuration. You can close Control Panel itself by choosing Exit from its Settings menu, but a quicker way to close any Windows program (including Draw) is to double-click on the small horizontal bar in the top-left corner of the application, called the Control menu box. Try closing Control Panel this way.

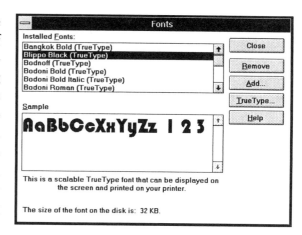

Now that you're back in Program Manager, you should take a look at the help available here. Click on Contents in the Help menu and choose from a list of topics about either Windows or Program Manager itself. There's even help available on how to use help! Close this after you've taken a look at it. If I've gone on about help, it's because I'm convinced that it's one of the great overlooked resources for Windows users. Nothing comparable now exists on the Macintosh, but all too often I find Windows users are oblivious to the existence of help. I'll remind you of this later when you're using Draw, which has its own context-sensitive help system.

The Print Manager

Whenever you print from Draw, or any Windows application, your document isn't sent directly to the printer. Instead, the Windows Print Manager is activated and the document is first printed to your hard drive before being sent to the printer. Print Manager is simply a *print spooler* that takes files being sent to the printer and stacks them up in a *first in, first out* print queue. Instead of twiddling your thumbs while printing a long document, you can continue working in your application.

Print Manager

Print Manager runs automatically when you print, at which time you can display its window to monitor the status of your print job. It can also be disabled by turning off Use Print Manager in the Printers dialog box. This can be useful, since complex files that refuse to output will sometimes print if the Print Manager is disabled. You can also run Print Manager directly by double-clicking on its icon in the Main group, a procedure that lets you display and change its default settings. Run Print Manager now by double-clicking on it.

You can change several aspects of how Print Manager operates. For example, click on the Options menu. Settings here let you control how much of your computer's resources is being used by Print Manager, versus your application. I prefer the default Low Priority, which allows Draw to run as fast as possible, at the expense of a slight increase in printing time. If you're in a rush to get pages out while you continue to work, however, you could set this to High. A tick mark next to a menu setting indicates it's currently active. Clicking on a tick mark disables it.

If something goes amiss while you're printing (a not uncommon occurrence), Print Manager can try to get your attention. I recommend choosing Alert Always, thereby instructing Print Manager to pop up a warning if a document fails to print. You could then take action to remove the offending publication from the print queue, add paper to your printer, or do whatever else was required.

When Print Manager is sent a file, it can display the time and date the file was sent to the printer, its print file size and a running percentage of how much of it has been printed. This can be useful information in the case of large Draw files, which take so long to output that it's wise to check Print Manager and

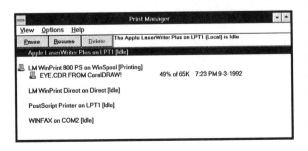

see if the files in fact are still being sent to the printer. So I recommend enabling both Time/Date Sent and Print File Size from the View menu. In the illustration you can see a typical Draw file being sent to a PostScript printer. Close Print Manager now by double-clicking on its Control menu box. (That's the small bar in the top-left corner of its window.)

File Manager

So far you've been using Program Manager to run applications. But equally important is the ability to perform file- and disk-related operations, such as creating subdirectories, formatting floppy disks, and copying, deleting and moving files. Double-click on File Manager in the Main group. As with the other elements of Windows you've already explored, File Manager has its own online help. Click on Help in the menu bar, then click on Index. Poke around a bit and then close Help by double-clicking on its Control menu box.

File Manager

All Windows applications, including File Manager, Draw and even Program Manager itself, run in their own *window*. Some basic skills in working with these windows are thus essential to ensure your efficient operation of Draw. For example, the File Manager window has sizing icons on the far top right of its title bar. Click on the up arrow to expand File Manager's window. You will usually want to run Draw with its window *maximized* in this manner. To return the window to its former size, click on the new icon containing both up and down arrows.

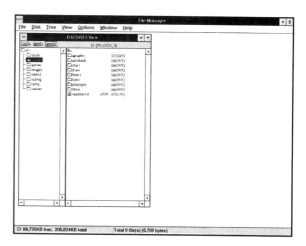

You can also *minimize* a window. Click on the down arrow and File Manager will vanish. It's still running, but it has been reduced to an icon on the Windows desktop, which is not currently displayed. To find out what applications are running, and to move between them, press the Control and Escape keys (on the left side of your keyboard) simultaneously. This displays the Windows Task List, which indicates that both Program Manager and File Manager are currently running. In the illustration, you can

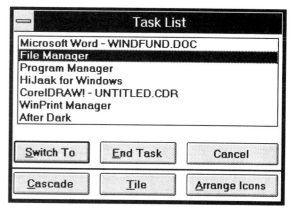

see that I'm running quite a few applications at once while I write this book.

Double-click on Program Manager to switch to it. Then press Control-Escape again and double-click on File Manager to redisplay it. The Task List provides a good way to find out what applications are running and to switch between them. Windows 3.1 also added another way, which is sometimes faster. Holding down the Alt key on your keyboard, tap once on the Tab key. A title bar of another running application will be displayed. Still keeping the Alt key down, tap again on Tab. If you have a third application running, its title bar will now be displayed. This is thus a way to cycle through all the currently running apps. If you let go of the Alt key while the title bar of the program to which you want to switch is displayed, the application will come to the front. Try this technique to move back and forth between File Manager and Program Manager, winding up with File Manager displayed.

File Manager uses *directory windows* to display information about the files on your hard drive and floppies. A directory window has its own set of arrow icons for maximizing and minimizing — experiment with these. If you minimize the directory window, it will display as an icon. You can then double-click on the icon to redisplay the window. The directory window can be moved around by clicking and dragging its title bar. You can also resize a window. Place the tip of your pointer on any of its borders and when it changes shape to a

two-headed arrow, click and drag to change its size. Later, you'll perform all these actions in Draw's own window.

File Manager begins with a graphical display of the subdirectories and files on your current drive (probably C). Other available drives are displayed as icons at the top of the display — A and possibly B, for floppy drives, and C, D and so on for the divisions of your hard drive. You can display the folders available on other drives by clicking on the drive icons.

The dilemma here is that you can currently only see the directories and files in one drive at a time. This makes it difficult to copy files from one drive to another. So here's a way of configuring File Manager to display two (or more) drives at once. Choose New Window from the Window menu; this creates a new window of your current drive. Then choose Tile from the Window menu to place the two windows side by side. You can now click on the icons in either window to change drives and view the contents of two drives simultaneously.

It's unfortunate that the two windows were tiled horizontally, since drives containing many directories won't have enough room to display all of them without scrolling. So I recommend you spend a bit of time now to change the windows to a vertical orientation. This will require a little mousing around.

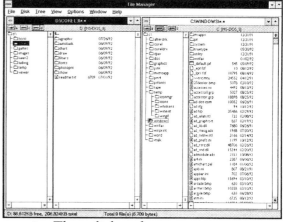

A thin double line divides each window into directory and file areas. Move the tip of your mouse cursor until it rests on this line in the top windows and you'll find it changes shape to a line with an arrow on either end. Hold down the mouse button and drag to the left, to decrease the directory area size until it resembles the illustration. Do the same for the other window. Now move your cursor to the far right of the top window, until it changes shape again. Then click and drag until the window occupies only about half the screen. Do the same from the left side of the lower window. Then drag the top and bottom of the windows until they're side by side and filling the screen, as shown in the illustration. Since you don't want to go through this procedure every time you run File Manager, choose Save Settings On Exit from the Options menu. This will capture your dual window setup when you close the program.

Knowing a few common file- and disk-related operations in File Manager will prove very useful in your later work with Draw. The drive on which all your Draw files are installed should contain a folder called CORELDRW, or something similar. Click once on that icon and the right side of the directory window will display any files in the directory, as well as any subdirectories it contains. Double-click on the DRAW folder to display the files in this folder and the subdirectories it contains, such as SAMPLES and CLIPART. Double-click on SAMPLES.

Each file in a directory has a small icon of its own. Click once on any file icon in SAMPLES to select it, and its size will be displayed in the Status Bar in the lower left corner of the screen. You can select multiple files by holding down the Control key while you click, with the Status Bar displaying the cumulative size.

Once selected, a number of operations can be performed on files. For example, you could simply press the Delete key to erase them. Or you could move or copy them by dragging the icons of the selected files and dropping them on top of the destination folder or drive icon. Dragging between folders on the same drive moves files, while dragging between drives copies them. You can force File Manager to always copy files by holding down the Control key while you drag. To force it to move them, hold down the Alt key. However, at this point you probably don't want to delete, move or copy any of the files in the SAMPLES window. So close the window now by double-clicking on its Control menu box.

An essential practice for organizing your hard disk is to create new folders in which to group your files. Click on your DRAW folder once to select it and then choose Create Directory from the File menu. Since you'll be working with traced scans later in the book, create a directory to hold these images by typing in TRACES and clicking on OK. Clicking on the TRACES folder will reveal an empty directory, ready for your new files.

```
┌─────────────────────────────────────────┐
│ ═          Create Directory              │
├─────────────────────────────────────────┤
│ Current Directory: D:\COREL3\DRAW   ┌────────┐ │
│                                     │   OK   │ │
│ Name:  ┌──────────────────────┐     └────────┘ │
│        │ TRACES               │     ┌────────┐ │
│        └──────────────────────┘     │ Cancel │ │
│                                     └────────┘ │
│                                     ┌────────┐ │
│                                     │  Help  │ │
│                                     └────────┘ │
└─────────────────────────────────────────┘
```

If you have a large hard drive holding hundreds or thousands of files, it's

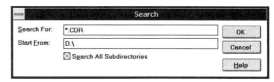

very easy to lose track of them. Most of us have experienced the annoyance of wandering through one directory after another in search of a stray file. Thankfully, File Manager provides a handy way to quickly find files that match your search criteria.

Choose Search from the File menu. If you knew the file name you were searching for, you could simply type it in and click on OK. But often you only know part of the name; in this case you can use DOS wildcards to cast a wide net. For example, if you knew a Draw file name began with the letter C, then C*.CDR would do the trick. Change Search For: to *.CDR, to instruct File Manager to hunt for all Draw files. Change Start From: to just the letter of the directory window's drive, such as C:\ or D:\. This ensures that the search will cover the entire drive. Now click on OK. When the search is finished, the Status Bar will indicate the number of files found that matched your search criteria, and their name and location will be displayed. You'll find Search a useful function for locating Draw files.

There's much, much more to both File Manager and Windows itself. But let me end with a tip that has a direct tie-in to Draw. Double-click on any of the .CDR files in the Search Results window. Draw will run and then open the file on which you double-clicked. File Manager is still running, as is Program Manager, and you can return to them at any time with Control-Escape or Alt-Tab. Close Draw by double-clicking on its Control menu box. Then close File Manager in a similar fashion. Running applications and opening files is a seldom-used feature of File Manager, but it reveals how much is lurking in Windows that can be missed by the casual user. I guarantee that time spent mastering Windows will pay dividends when you use Draw, or any Windows application.

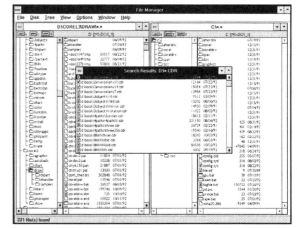

The CorelDRAW Environment

Y ou're no doubt itching to start creating dramatic text effects and colorful illustrations. But as with any graphics-based application, before jumping in and creating new material it's vital to first be comfortable with CorelDRAW's *environment.* Creating a solid foundation for your work will make all the difference between confidently using Draw's powerful abilities and simply flailing around. You'll find that mastering views, grids, rulers and guides is critical for working with speed and precision.

Mastering views, grids, guides and rulers is the first step

Draw makes excellent use of the Microsoft Windows graphical interface, so that much of its environment is actually that of Windows itself. As with other Windows applications, such as PageMaker, you work with Draw by choosing possible actions from menus, filling out dialog boxes, choosing tools from the toolbox on the left side of the screen and selecting and working with graphic objects and text in the editing window.

Each Draw file is composed of a single page. Choose Page Setup now from the File menu. Draw provides a number of standard sizes or you can click on the Custom button and enter a page size between 1 and 30 inches vertically or horizontally. Your choice here specifies the size of the Draw page, which may or may not be the same as the size of paper or film used by your output device. You can specify a Draw page size of 11 by 17 inches, for example, even though your laser printer uses 8 ½ by 11-inch paper. In this case, at print time you could tell

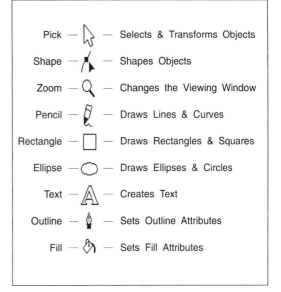

Pick	—	Selects & Transforms Objects
Shape	—	Shapes Objects
Zoom	—	Changes the Viewing Window
Pencil	—	Draws Lines & Curves
Rectangle	—	Draws Rectangles & Squares
Ellipse	—	Draws Ellipses & Circles
Text	—	Creates Text
Outline	—	Sets Outline Attributes
Fill	—	Sets Fill Attributes

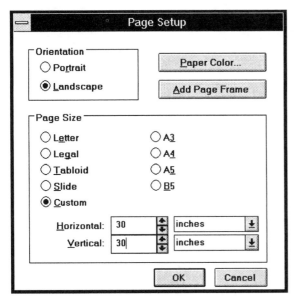

Draw to *tile* your drawing, and it would print as many pages as necessary to hold your oversize drawing, which you could then manually assemble into a single large page. So what you're specifying in this dialog box is the printable portion of Draw's editing window.

The ability to change measurement systems is available in many Draw dialog boxes. Define a Custom page size now by clicking on the Custom button and setting either of the page orientations in different measurement systems — make the vertical in inches, for example, and the horizontal in millimeters. Do this by clicking on 'inches' and choosing a different measurement system. Note that the size value has changed to reflect the new system of measurement. You can change numerical values in any Draw dialog box by double-clicking on an existing value to highlight it and then typing in the new value, or by clicking on the scroll arrows. Change the horizontal and vertical size values, then click on OK.

Verify the size of the new page by checking the rulers above and to the left of the page. No rulers displayed? Choose Show Rulers from the Display menu to turn on the rulers. If they were already on, choosing Show Rulers would turn them off — this is an example of one of the many *toggles* found on Draw's menus. A toggle is enabled if a check mark is displayed next to it.

You should notice something interesting about the rulers at this point: they're both using the same default measurement system, despite your having specified two different systems in the Page Setup dialog box. Draw is using the default ruler values of the last document created. If you want to change the units of measurement of the rulers themselves, you'll have to use a different dialog box.

There's a shortcut to call up the Page Setup dialog box. Place the tip of your cursor on any of the four borders of the page and double-click (click twice quickly) with the mouse. This double-click technique only works when you have the Pick ▶ or Shape ⨍, tools selected. Experiment with some of the other page sizes, such as the four metric sizes or Slide, which sets up a page with the correct proportions for slide creation.

If you've noticed that the illustrations of dialog boxes I'm using in the book look a bit different from those on your screen, that's because I've disabled a display option called *3-D Look*. Details on this procedure are provided in the *Customizing Draw's Defaults* chapter.

Opening Draw Files

Fundamental to the efficient creation of images in Draw is being comfortable with the different techniques of moving around the editing window. To explore this you first need an image on the page; you'll work with one of the sample files that comes with Draw. By the way, one of the best ways to master a drawing program is to pick apart the illustrations of other designers. If you have a CD-ROM player the Corel ArtShow CD contains hundreds of images from Corel's annual design contest. As one of the judges for this annual event, I can say with confidence that many of these make ingenious use of Draw's features and are worth a close look.

Choose Open from the File menu and click on No when asked to save changes. If you're not there currently, move to the SAMPLES subdirectory of your DRAW directory. Having trouble moving around your hard disk's subdirectories? Get in the habit of finding files by double-clicking on the drive and directory icons with the mouse — avoid typing in path names. If you're struggling with this and other aspects of working with files, run through the short tutorial in the previous chapter on using the Windows environment.

Click once on any file name in the SAMPLES directory and notice that a low-resolution preview of the file is displayed. Click on a few more, then double-click on EYE.CDR to open it (or click once on it and then on OK).

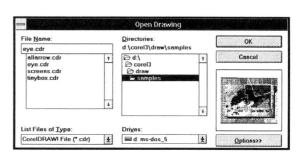

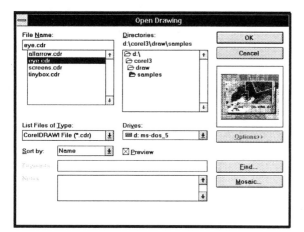

While this is the way you'll typically open files, there are a number of useful options when opening them that you should know about right at the beginning of your work with Draw. Choose Open again from the File menu and click on the Options button. The dialog box expands to provide additional information about the currently selected file and to let you retrieve files in a number of different ways. Note that the size of the currently selected file, as well as its time and date of creation, is displayed at the bottom of the dialog box. If it isn't displayed, try clicking once on a few other Draw CDR files. By default, the list of files is arranged in alphabetical order. Click on Name in the Sort By: drop-down list and then click on Date. Verify that the file display order has changed by clicking on several files in turn and observing the date of creation. This is handy when you need to select the most current version of a file from a large list.

Of course, this feature is only useful if your computer's clock is set to the correct time and date. If you're not sure, check this later by double-clicking on the Control Panel icon in the Main group of the Windows Program Manager, double-clicking on Date/Time and adjusting the date and time.

Later, I'll show you how to assign one or more keywords to a file when it's saved. You could then search for all the files that have particular keywords. This is a useful way to quickly find all the files associated with a given project or subject matter. You could also enter a note when saving a file; this can provide information on the file's contents when sending it to a service bureau for output or exchanging it with another Draw user.

Just Say Mosaic

Click on the Mosaic button. As well as displaying a list of files, which can be individually previewed and opened, you can also make use of the Mosaic utility to quickly preview all the CDR files in a directory. Mosaic provides many more functions than this, most of which, such as batch printing a number of Draw files, can only be accessed by double-clicking on the Mosaic icon directly from Program Manager. You'll explore these advanced options later in detail.

Because Mosaic doesn't fill the screen when it runs, if you click anywhere in the Draw window Mosaic will be sent behind it. This is also true of other programs supplied with Draw, such as Trace and Chart. If you 'lose' a running program, press the Control and Escape keys simultaneously to display the Windows Task List, then double-click on the application you wish to bring to the front. Or (in Windows 3.1) hold down the Alt key and tap on the Tab key until the title bar of the application you're looking for is displayed. Then release the Alt key to bring it forward.

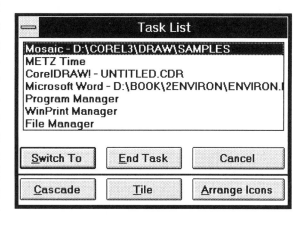

When Mosaic runs it begins by displaying the files in the directory that was used the last time the program was run. If you're not seeing preview, or *thumbnail*, representations of the CDR files in the SAMPLES directory choose Open Directory from the File menu. In this dialog box change directories and, if necessary, change List Files Of Type to CDR before clicking on OK.

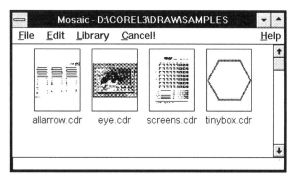

Draw and its accompanying programs can be customized in many ways to meet individual needs. You'll begin by customizing a number of Mosaic parameters. Choose Preferences from the File menu and experiment with different thumbnail orientations and widths. (Unfortunately, one thing you *can't* change is the 3-D Look of

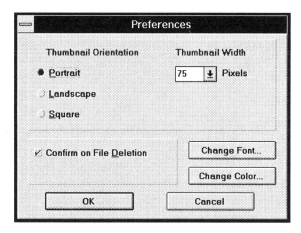

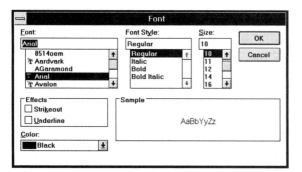

some Mosaic dialog boxes.) Then try changing the background color of the thumbnails and their title font. In the illustration I've chosen the Arial font supplied with Windows 3.1. The TT next to it in the dialog box identifies it as a TrueType font. Legibility is the key here, so resist the temptation to choose one of the really ornate Draw fonts, like Willow or Frankenstein (as the name would indicate, the latter is pretty monstrous).

MOSAIC

There's no point changing Confirm On File Deletion — you can only delete files with Mosaic when you run it from Program Manager. Now double-click on the thumbnail of EYE.CDR to open it. If it doesn't display in color, or in shades of gray on a monochrome monitor, choose Edit Wireframe from the Display menu.

Zoom, Zoom

Complex drawings such as this require you to constantly change your magnification, or *view*, of the page as you zoom in to work on a detail and then zoom out to view the entire image. Click on the Zoom ⊕ tool in the toolbox. You're currently displaying the EYE file in a view that corresponds to the ⬚ icon on the far right of the flyout menu; this displays the entire printable page.

While this gives you an overview of your illustration, it can't be trusted to accurately display detail. For example, the creator's name, Jeff Brice, appears to be in a sans serif face, perhaps Helvetica. Click on the ⊕ zoom-in icon, move your cursor onto the page and note that it's changed shape to that of the zoom-in icon. Click, hold down the mouse button and diagonally drag a dotted rectangle, or *marquee*, around Jeff Brice. When you release the mouse button, the area you've defined with the marquee will fill the display area.

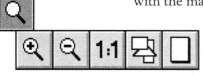

Now that you've zoomed in you can see that the type is far from being sans serif. In fact, it's set in a Draw font called Memorandum. Zoom in again by selecting the icon from the fly-out menu and drag a marquee over just the letter F. This time, your attempt at zooming in probably produced little effect, since you've reached the limit of how far you can zoom in. When fully zoomed in, one screen pixel represents .001 inch.

Zoom out by choosing the ⌕ tool and the ⌕ zoom-out icon. This takes you back to the view prior to the most recent zoom in. If there was no previous zoom in, or you changed views with one of the other zoom icons, you will zoom out by a factor of two. In handling views of your illustration, Draw thus works differently from most drawing or page makeup programs, which typically let you select 100%, 200% or a similar fixed percentage view. Draw never indicates the percentage at which you're displaying the page; you simply zoom in as much as required for the task at hand.

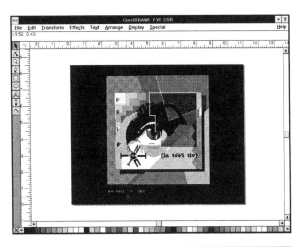

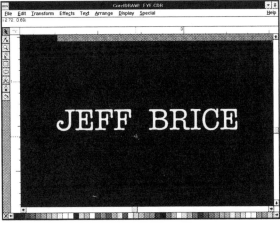

Zoom out several times to retrace your zooms until the full page is displayed. Zooming out one more time at this stage takes you out as far as you can go, but doesn't display the entire editing window. Use the scroll arrows on the edge of the screen to see how far the editing window extends on either side of the page. Objects placed on the area surrounding the page don't print but are kept with the contents of the page when you save a file. This is a good place to keep bits and pieces of text or graphics you might need later, or to store different versions of a work in progress.

There are two more views on the ⌕ menu worth investigating. If you choose the ⌕ tool and 1:1 from the fly-out menu, Draw will try to display the contents of your drawing at actual size. I say *try* because the success of its effort depends on your monitor. At 1,024 by 768 resolution on my own monitor, for example, an inch on one of Draw's rulers in this view actually measures almost 1 ¾ inches when I check it with a real ruler. Try this yourself.

Do Draw's horizontal and vertical rulers each display an inch as the same length on your monitor? Due to the differing aspect ratio of monitors, this is often not the case. It's somthing that should be kept in mind while designing. For example, a circle that prints perfectly round will look slightly oval on the screen. Frequent printouts, or an expensive monitor, are the only real solutions to this dilemma. So you'd do better to think of 1:1 simply as a zoomed-in view of your page, rather than as an accurate display of what will emerge from your printer.

The final view available from the Q flyout menu is $\boxminus$. This displays all the objects in a drawing (whether on or off the page) at maximum size. When zoomed in, this is a useful way to quickly locate objects you've tucked away in a dark corner of the editing window. You can also use this view to locate imported graphics that have wound up in unexpected places in the editing window.

Draw provides a healthy selection of keyboard shortcuts to speed the choice of commonly used commands. These are detailed in the cardboard reference card supplied with the program. One of the files on the disks supplied with this book is the TEMPLATE.CDR keyboard template. You can open this in Draw, modify it if desired and print out your own template for a quick reference to keyboard shortcuts.

Try using the function keys F2, F3 and F4 to choose the Q, Q or $\boxminus$ tool or view; holding down the Shift key and F4 chooses the $\Box$ view. Since you often want to zoom in or out, Draw provides the option of assigning this function to your right (secondary) mouse button. To enable, this choose Preferences from the Special menu, click on Mouse in the dialog box and you'll be presented with a number of actions you can assign to your right button. Click on 2x Zoom and then click on OK twice to return to the page.

Move your cursor to the area of the screen you want to zoom in to and click the right mouse button to zoom in by a factor of two. Draw thus works much like PageMaker or Ventura Publisher, both of which zoom in based on cursor location. You can zoom out by a factor of two by double-clicking the right mouse button. By using the right button and the function keys, you can usually bypass the slower ℚ menu. As with all settings in Preferences, a function assigned to the right button will be saved as a default when you exit Draw.

Finally, it's worth mentioning that instead of clicking and dragging, you can also simply click with the ℚ icon to achieve the same effect as clicking with the right mouse button. If you use this in conjunction with the F2 keyboard shortcut, you can repeatedly choose the ℚ icon and zoom in by a factor of two. This is handy if you've assigned your right mouse button to a function other than 2x Zoom.

While there are a lot of ways to zoom in and out, moving horizontally or vertically around the editing window is more straightforward, and simply follows the conventions used by all Microsoft Windows applications. You can use the scroll bars at the bottom and right of the screen by clicking either on a scroll arrow, or on either side of the gray scroll box in the middle of the scroll bars. You can also click and drag the scroll box itself.

Status Seeking

Draw provides a number of ways to orient yourself in the editing window. The *Status Line*, the area between the rulers and the menu bar, provides you with information about selected objects you've already created or those you're currently creating or modifying. As with the rulers, displaying the Status Line is a toggle, so check the Display menu to ensure that Show Status Line is enabled. You can investigate the nature of some

---

of the objects in the EYE illustration by using the Pick ⊀ , or selection, tool.

Click on the ⊀ tool in the toolbox. Now click inside one of the four triangles on the left side of the illustration to select it, and observe the Status Line. Selected objects display the eight sizing *handles* immediately familiar to users of such publishing applications as PageMaker and Ventura. When you click on another object or on a blank part of the page or editing window the object is deselected. Click on a few more objects. You'll be sizing, skewing, blending, extruding, enveloping and rotating the living daylights out of objects in short order. Before you dive into that, however, you should observe that the Status Line informs you that you're selecting different kinds of objects; text, a curve, an open path, a rectangle, a group. The top-right corner of the Status Line also indicates any fill or outline the selected object may contain.

You're currently working in Draw's *preview* window, which displays the fill and outline attributes of objects. Although you'll typically work in this view, it's sometimes simpler to select and work with objects when only their outlines are displayed. This speeds up screen redisplay and makes it easier to edit objects in complex illustrations. Choose Edit Wireframe from the Display menu (or press Shift-F9) to switch to the *wireframe* window. Select a few objects in turn by clicking on their outlines and note that in this view the Status Line also displays any fill or outline attributes of the selected object. Changing editing windows is another toggle, so use the mouse or keyboard to return to the preview window.

You can also display the image full-screen by pressing F9. Then press any key again to return to the previous window. This is a function that can be assigned to the right mouse button if you're partial to full-screen previews. When you close Draw, it saves many of the settings you've made in its menus or dialog boxes and uses them the next time you run the program. Changes you've made to the right mouse button function or the window you were in when you closed Draw are examples of defaults.

To begin to get a sense of how to use the Status Line when working with objects, click and drag one of the triangles to move it. (Be careful not to click and drag one of its handles or you'll resize it.) As you move the triangle, the Status Line provides four pieces of information: how far you've moved it horizontally (x axis) and vertically (y axis), the distance from where you began dragging to your current cursor location, and the re- sulting angle between the x axis of the object being moved and the line joining the beginning and current locations of the cursor.

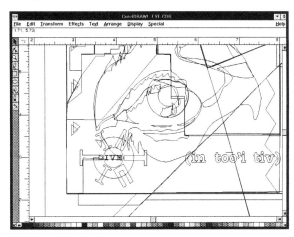

Choosing the appropriate view is critical to performing accurate work, and moving objects is a case in point. Moving an object a very precise amount with the mouse is difficult (sometimes even impossible) while displaying the entire page. Zoom in by clicking the right mouse button on a triangle once or twice and then move the triangle. You'll find you can move it in amounts as fine as .01 inch. Zoom out and try the same thing while keeping your eye on the Status Line. You'll find you can no longer move the object in smooth numerical increments.

Rulers and Grids

You've probably already observed that as you move your cursor around the drawing area, dotted lines in the rulers indicate your current location, taking the lower-left corner of the page as the default point of origin of the rulers. The left side of the Status Line also shows the current location of the cursor relative to the ruler origin. The first value indicates your location on the horizontal (x) axis and the second the vertical (y) axis. Move your cursor to the ruler origin on the lower-left page corner and note that the Status Line now indicates your loca- tion as 0,0. (You may have to zoom in quite a bit to get this to display exactly 0,0.)

You'll find the cursor-tracking abilities of the rulers and Status Line extremely useful when creating and manipulating objects. An equally useful control is Draw's grid feature, which also has

---

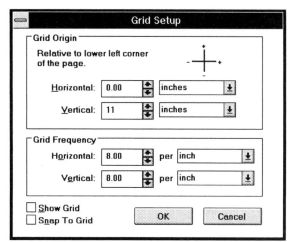

a connection with the rulers. Rulers and grids, coupled with the Status Line, let you create and position objects with precision. Choose Grid Setup from the Display menu. Draw lets you set not only the grid origin, but its horizontal and vertical frequency, its measurement system, and whether it displays on-screen and snaps objects to it.

Changing the grid origin from its default location at the lower-left corner of the page also changes the ruler origin. For example, to move the grid (and ruler) origin to the top-left corner of the page, enter 7.33 inches as the vertical grid origin. Click on OK and note that the rulers now measure from the top-left corner of the page. This is the ruler origin used by many page layout programs, such as PageMaker. If you use one of these programs, you may prefer to use a similar ruler origin in Draw.

Display the Grid Setup dialog box again, this time by using a shortcut — simply double-click on any ruler. Enter the appropriate horizontal and vertical values to move the ruler origin to the bottom-right corner of the page, using the rulers as your guide. How about the middle of the page? You can also enter negative values to move the point of origin left of, or below, the page. You'll find Draw often uses this coordinate method of specifying positive and negative values in the horizontal and vertical axes, so becoming comfortable with it now is important.

But there's another, more interactive, way to change the ruler and grid origin. Move your cursor to the area where the two rulers meet, just to the right of the ▶ tool. Click and drag your cursor onto the page. Using the rulers as a guide, move the crosshairs you're dragging to any corner of the page and release the mouse button.

Now check the Grid Setup dialog box to see how accurately you placed the crosshairs on the page corner. It should be evident that you can define new origins more precisely with the dialog box than by dragging the crosshairs. If you were a little off, enter the correct Grid Origin values for the corner you were shooting for.

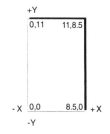

When creating grids, you can specify the number of grid increments per unit of measurement. Display the Grid Setup dialog box, click on the unit of measurement box of horizontal Grid Frequency and choose 'point' from the drop-down list, then change the number of horizontal increments to 1 per point and click on OK. Note that the horizontal ruler above the page is now displayed in points. Graphic artists and designers typically use picas and points to specify the size of objects and areas on a page, since these measurement units subdivide into each other nicely, but by all means stick with inches when working with Draw if that's what you're comfortable with. Zoom in as far as you can and you'll find that each increment on the horizontal ruler corresponds to 1 point ($\frac{1}{72}$ inch). This is as accurate as Draw's rulers get.

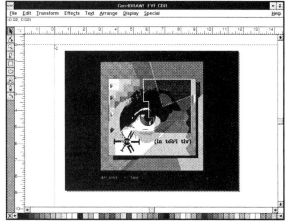

Don't overlook the rulers when working with objects, but keep in mind that when you move an object the rulers display the position of your cursor, not the object. Again, zooming in is often the key to using rulers effectively, since the more you zoom in the more increments (or *tick marks*) they display. When your rulers are in inches, for example, you'll find that Draw can display ticks every $\frac{1}{16}$ inch, but only if you've zoomed in quite a bit.

It's not mentioned in the Draw documentation, but when using different measurement systems for the horizontal and vertical rulers, as you're doing here, the two coordinates for the pointer location displayed in the Status Line always use the horizontal measurement system.

By redefining the grid frequency you've changed the rulers, but the grid isn't visible, nor is it affecting objects on the page. Zoom out to display the entire page, then return to the Grid Setup dialog box and ensure that the horizontal grid frequency is set to 1 per point and the vertical to 1 per inch. Click on Show Grid

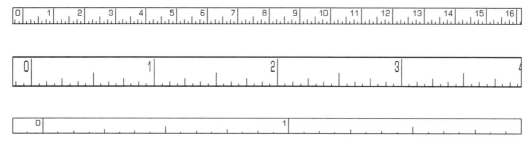

Draw's rulers at normal page view, 2X zoom and 4X zoom

and OK. The grid is now visible and it's displaying one grid mark for each inch vertically, but not for each point horizontally.

Click the right mouse button and you'll find the grid display becomes more accurate the more you zoom in. If you zoom all the way in, you'll find the best the grid can do is display one mark for every four points on the grid. The rulers at the top of the page are a little confusing here — they may be numbered 1, 2 and 3 but this corresponds to 10, 20 and 30 points. You can verify this by observing the location of your cursor in the Status Line while you move it with the mouse.

At this point the grid marks are simply providing a way of orienting yourself, but to make them perform useful work choose Snap To Grid from the Display menu. The Status Line should now indicate that Snap To Grid is enabled. Since you often want to turn this feature on or off, the keyboard shortcut Control-Y is worth remembering. Observe that as you move your cursor vertically on the page, the cursor location marker in the vertical ruler snaps to the inch tick marks. When you move the cursor horizontally it's snapping to each point, a grid so fine that its effect won't be noticeable unless you've zoomed in quite a bit.

To get a taste of the grid in action, try moving a triangle and notice how the borders of its *highlighting box* snap to the grid marks while you drag it. The grid can provide invaluable precision when creating, moving or modifying objects. If you like, experiment with other grid frequency settings.

Non-printing Guides

A final aid to placing and sizing objects with precision is the

---

ability to position horizontal and vertical non-printing guides anywhere in the editing window. Draw's guides work much like those in PageMaker, with the addition of a few novel abilities.

As with many operations in Draw, you can create and position guides either directly with the mouse or by using a dialog box. Place the cursor on the horizontal ruler at the top of the page, then click and drag a guide onto the editing window. As you drag the guide, the ruler at the left of the page indicates your vertical position, as does the rightmost numerical value on the Status Line. If Snap To Grid is on, the guide will snap to the grid and the ruler ticks marks as you drag — this is a more precise way of positioning it than by eye. Drag a few guides onto your page from both the vertical and horizontal rulers.

You'll find guides useful for providing an underlying structure to your documents but they also have a more active role if Snap To Guidelines, on the Display menu, is enabled. You'll be able to see the effect of this better if you switch to the wireframe window (Shift-F9). Click on the outline of one of the triangles, drag it and you'll find its highlight box snaps to the guidelines, even when a grid mark is nearby. If you want to position an object near, but not on, a guide either disable Snap To Guidelines or press the cursor (arrow) keys on your keyboard to nudge it, since nudging ignores the guides and grid marks.

Double-click on any guide to display the Guidelines dialog box. (You can also reach the Guidelines dialog box with the Display menu, if there are no lines in the editing window for you to double-click.) The horizontal or vertical orientation of the guide on which you clicked is indicated. Also shown is its position, relative to the ruler/grid origin, in the measurement system used by the grid for that orientation. In other words, if you've set up your horizontal ruler/grid in millimeters, horizontal guides will have their location in the Guidelines dialog box displayed in millimeters, even though the vertical ruler may be indicating their location in inches.

Click on the Next button repeatedly to cycle through all the guides on your page. You can delete the currently selected guide, add a new one at a location you specify or move it. You

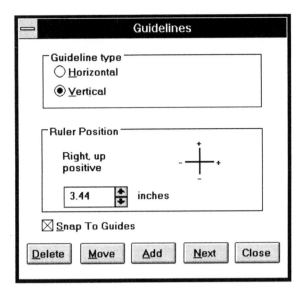

can also get rid of guides by dragging them right off the editing window. Using the dialog box to work with guides is slower than with the mouse but with Snap To Grid disabled it's more precise. If Snap To Grid is enabled, the dialog box will let you precisely position a guide anywhere on the page, not just on the grid marks.

You must create new guides one at a time with the mouse or with the dialog box — you can't automatically create a series of guides spaced an inch apart, for example. However, there are more powerful aspects of working with guides that can be tapped using Draw's *layer* feature, which is covered later in a chapter of its own. By using layers you can quickly create or delete multiple guides, create guides of any shape and even print them out.

Experiment until you're comfortable with the material in this first tutorial, since you'll build on it in the following chapters. If you're moving on to the next chapter now, choose New from the File menu to close the EYE drawing and create a fresh page. You'll be asked if you want to save the changes you've made to the drawing. Click on No to leave EYE as you found it.

To end your session and close Draw itself, choose Exit from the File menu to close the EYE drawing and shut down Draw. You can close Windows by choosing Exit from its File menu or simply by double-clicking on the Control menu box — the horizontal bar at the top-left corner of the screen.

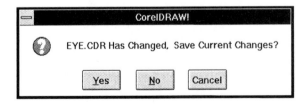

Working with Objects

3

Although CorelDRAW, as you'd judge from its name, is known as a drawing program, most users rely on it less to construct complex drawings from scratch than to manipulate type, symbols, clip art, images imported from other applications, such as CorelCHART, Lotus 1-2-3 and Harvard Graphics, or scanned images traced with CorelTRACE.

So before using the drawing tools to create fresh imagery you should first be comfortable working with existing objects. For example, Draw comes with about 3,000 symbols, relatively simple graphics that are grouped in *libraries*. A complete listing of these is provided in the clip art reference book supplied with Draw. You can employ these ready-made images as convenient raw material with which to explore object manipulations.

Choose New from the File menu to create a fresh editing window, then ensure that on the Display menu both Show Rulers and the Status Line are enabled, and that Snap To Grid is disabled. Click and hold down the mouse button on the Text 𝔸 tool in the toolbox until the ☆ icon is displayed, and then click on it. Move your cursor anywhere onto the page and click the mouse to display the Symbols dialog box.

If you've already worked with symbols the default selected library will be the last one you used. Otherwise, the default library is Animals, and the first symbol in the library (one of the more curious members of the animal kingdom) is previewed. Notice the small triangle in the lower-right corner of the symbol window. You'll encounter this triangle in other dialog boxes. Click anywhere in the symbol window and a scrollable menu of symbols in the Animals library will appear.

Scroll through the symbols to see what's available in the library

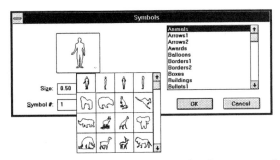

and then click on any symbol to choose it. Now choose a few different libraries in turn and explore their contents. If you've displayed a symbol menu and want to exit it without making a selection, press the Escape key. This technique works in all of Draw's scrollable popup menus. If you were using the printed reference guide, you could choose a symbol by number. For example, enter the number 115 as the Symbol # in the Geographic library, and you'll quickly choose the reindeer I used in the illustrations. When you've found a symbol you'd like to work with, make it two inches tall using the Size box and click on OK. The symbol will appear with its lower-left corner near where you clicked on the page.

You can also access the Symbols dialog box when the A tool is displayed. Click and hold on the ☆ tool and then click on the A tool. If you hold down the Shift key now and click on the page the Symbols dialog box will be displayed. You may find it faster in future to simply choose the A tool and Shift-click, rather than switch back and forth between the two tools. Return to the Symbols dialog box now and place a few more symbols on different areas of your page.

In Draw, as with most object-oriented, or *vector*, graphics applications, you must first select the object or objects with which you want to work. Then you perform some action, either with the mouse or by making a choice from a menu or dialog box. So it's important to be able to select objects efficiently.

Selecting Objects

Choose the Pick ▶ tool and the last symbol you created will be automatically selected. The Status Line indicates that you've selected a curve object and shows how many points, or *nodes*, the object contains. Soon you'll use these nodes to reshape symbols. In the previous chapter you saw that selecting a single object that's been given a fill is as simple as clicking anywhere on it. But if you're in Draw's wireframe window or if the object has no fill, as in the case of a symbol, you must click on its outline to select it. Select several symbols in turn by clicking on their outlines. To fill them, click on the scrollable color palette at the bottom of the screen. If this isn't currently displayed, choose Show Color Palette and Process Colors to display it.

You'll frequently want to select more than one object, to be able to move, delete, copy, fill, resize, rotate or otherwise work with all of them at once. There are two ways to select multiple objects with the mouse. One is to hold down the Shift key and click in turn on all the objects on the page. Note that the Status Line keeps track of how many objects are currently selected. In addition, the area enclosed by the eight handles expands to encompass all the selected objects. Now deselect all the currently selected objects by clicking anywhere on a blank part of the page. You can also deselect by pressing the Escape key.

Another method of selecting multiple objects, which is useful when there are more than a few, is to click anywhere on a blank part of the editing window and drag a dotted marquee to completely enclose the objects to be selected. This action is similar to dragging a marquee with the ⊕ tool. As when clicking on objects, you must have the ▶ tool selected when you drag a selection marquee.

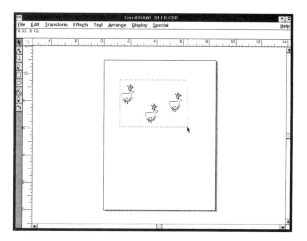

To select all objects in the editing window, choose Select All from the Edit menu. The Shift key is often used in conjunction with Select All, since with this held down you can also deselect just one object at a time. For example, this is handy when you want to work with everything on your page except a few objects. PageMaker users will find Draw's approach to object selection is virtually identical.

One of the most frequent actions you'll take is to delete objects; in this,

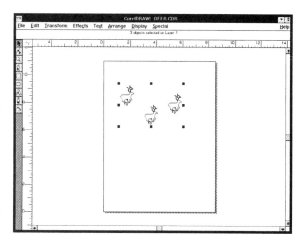

Draw works much like all Windows applications. Select just one of the symbols on the page and choose Delete from the Edit menu, or simply press the Delete key on your keyboard. If you've turned off the Num Lock key, the Delete key on the numeric keypad at the far right of the keyboard can be used, as well as the usual one above the cursor keys.

In Praise of Undo

But what if you accidentally delete that logo you've spent umpteen hours slaving over? As with most Windows programs, Draw provides a safety net in the form of Undo on the Edit menu, along with its alter ego Redo (which undoes an undo). These only undo or redo your most recent action, however — you can't undo a series of actions or one you performed before going on to other actions. Try moving an object, then choosing Undo and Redo.

Since it's easy to accidentally move or resize an object, you should get in the habit of undoing such a slip, rather than using the mouse to try to restore the object to the way it was before; Draw has a better memory than you do. The Alt-Backspace keyboard shortcut is thus worth remembering, since you'll have frequent recourse to it. Think of the Backspace key taking you *back* to an earlier version of your illustration.

Once multiple objects are selected you can perform the same operations on them as you can on a single object. As well as deleting them, for example, you can move them all by clicking and dragging any one of them. Try this now. All the object manipulations that follow in this chapter can be performed simultaneously on all the currently selected objects. I leave it to you to verify this as you go.

More Ways of Moving

While Draw is a mouse-based program, it uses the Control and Shift keys on the keyboard to modify the nature of certain actions you take. The Control key, which restricts, or *constrains*, whatever action is being performed, is ubiquitous. It can be used when performing a multitude of object and text manipulations with both the ▶ and Shape ⚲ tools. Hold down the Control key while moving an object, for instance, and you'll find that its movement is restricted to just the horizontal (x) or vertical (y) axes.

Most object manipulations in Draw can be performed either directly with the mouse — using the rulers, grid and Status Line as a guide — or by specifying numerical amounts in a dialog box. You've already encountered this when changing the ruler/grid zero point, for example. It also holds true when moving objects. Whether you use the hands-on or dialog box approach is a matter of personal preference, although dialog boxes often provide more accuracy.

Moving objects is a case in point. You can drag an object with the mouse or use a dialog box to move it either a specified distance from its current location, or to a particular location on the page. Drag a vertical and horizontal guide onto the page, make sure Snap To Guidelines on the Display menu is enabled, and drag an object until the lower-left corner of its highlight box snaps to the conjunction of the two guides. Then Choose Move from the Transform menu.

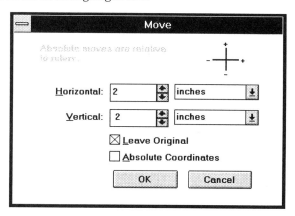

You can move objects in two different ways with this dialog box. By using the first technique, you can specify how far you want to move an object from its current location. Enter 2 inches for both the horizontal and vertical amounts, then click on Leave Original and OK. A duplicate of the object has now moved the distance you specified in relation to the lower-left corner of its selection box. Verify this by dragging the zero point (click and drag on the icon where the two rulers meet) to the conjunction of the guides at the lower-left corner of the original object, and then check the rulers to see where the duplicate object was moved. You could also drag horizontal and vertical guides over to the two-inch point of both rulers, as shown in the illustration.

Put the zero point back to its original location at the lower-left corner of the page, using the Grid Setup dialog box to reset Grid Origin to 0,0. Then select the original object and click on

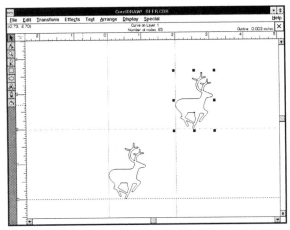

Absolute Coordinates in the Move dialog box. As you click on the nine check boxes that appeared, the horizontal and vertical numerical values in the dialog box will change, indicating the location of the selected part of the object in relation to the current zero point — in this case, the lower-left corner of the page. The Move dialog box in the illustration indicates that the lower-left corner of the highlight box of the currently selected object is positioned 5 inches horizontally and 6 inches vertically from the zero point.

Click on the middle check box to use it as a reference point and make both values 0 inches. When you click on OK your object should be centered on the lower-left corner of the page. Return to the dialog box, click on a different reference point, enter new distances to move the object from the zero point and click on OK. Do this several times, moving the object with different reference points.

You can make use of this ability to move an object to a particular page location in a number of ways. One approach is to move your cursor to the desired location and then enter the horizontal and vertical location values displayed on the Status Line in the Move dialog box. Another is to first move the ruler zero point to the desired location and then enter 0 for both the horizontal and vertical values in the Move dialog box. Try this, then use the following undocumented shortcut to reset your zero point to the lower-left page corner: simply double-click on the page border to open the Page Setup dialog box, then click on OK. Neat, I think you'll agree.

Earlier, you clicked on Leave Original in the dialog box to move the object while leaving the original intact, in effect making a copy of the object and placing it at a new location. You can accomplish the same thing using the mouse. While dragging an object, press and release the right mouse button. As you continue to drag you should see Leave Original on the right side of the Status Line. When you release the button, you'll have copies of the object at both the old and new locations. In fact, I recommend this as a way to quickly copy an object. And you can use the right button to leave behind the original when performing any of the operations in this chapter.

Finally, a technique you looked at briefly in the previous chapter will prove useful for situations in which you want to move an object a small distance in either axis. You can *nudge* a selected object a fixed distance by pressing one of the four cursor control (arrow) keys on your keyboard.

An object moves .01 inch with each key press, but this default can be changed in the Preferences dialog box of the Special menu. I usually set this value to 1 point, but you can nudge accurately as low as .5 point. Draw will let you set the nudge value to .1 point, but it actually moves objects an indeterminate amount at this setting. Use this if you want the smallest possible nudge, but don't expect accuracy. Zoom in and experiment with this way of moving objects, trying different nudge values. You'll find that nudge is a handy way of making small object movements, even when you're close to a guide or grid mark.

To quickly change your nudge values, you'll want to avoid continued mouse trips to the Preferences dialog box. Macro creation applications, such at the Recorder program supplied with Windows, can automate recurrent tasks such as this. You'll find some ready-to-run macros on the disks supplied with this book, as discussed in *The Draw Companion Disks* chapter. Recorder itself is covered in the *Optimizing Windows* chapter.

Transforming Objects

Draw provides a number of ways to modify the shape of an object. When using the ↖ tool these changes, or *transformations*, are applied to one or more selected objects. Later you'll use the ↗ tool to make changes to just part of an object by editing the line and curve segments of which it's composed. Knowing when to use either the ↗ or ↖ tool is critical to the efficient use of Draw.

One of the most common transformations to perform on an object is to resize it. When your cursor is placed over any handle of a selected object it changes to a plus sign. At this point click and drag one of the four corner handles of an object diagonally and note that the Status Line tells you how much you are proportionally *scaling* the size of the object either up or down. It's important to point out that if you perform multiple scale operations on an object, the percentage displayed in the Status Line is expressed not in terms of the original object, but rather according to its size before the current scaling operation.

Holding down the Control key will constrain scaled objects to multiples of their size, such as 100%, 200% and so on. The Shift key, on the other hand, scales the object out from its center. You can also hold both keys down to create an object that's scaled out from the center in multiples of its original size. And if you also hold the Alt and Tab keys... just kidding. You never have to hold down more than two keys when using Draw, thank goodness. Experiment with scaling using the Shift and Control keys before going further.

Have a Good Stretch

Dragging any of the four middle handles lets you resize, or

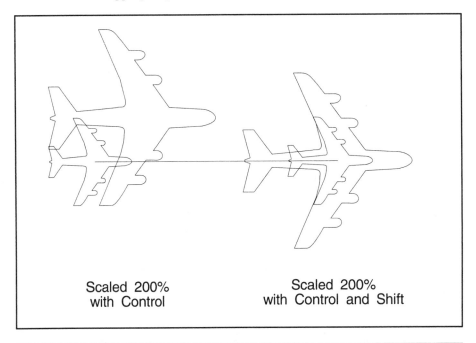

Scaled 200%
with Control

Scaled 200%
with Control and Shift

Original

Stretched 150%

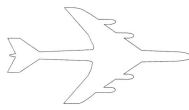

**Stretched 200%
with Control**

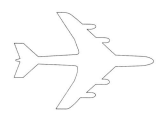

**Stretched 150%
with Shift**

**Stretched 200%
with Control and Shift**

stretch, an object non-proportionally in either the x or y axis. The Control and Shift keys work their expected magic during this operation.

You can create a mirror image by dragging a middle handle into an object, going right across it and continuing on until the Status Line registers a negative scale value. This flips the object on the axis in which you're dragging, and also moves it. Since you typically want the mirror image to be the same size as the original, hold down the Control key to constrain the mirror image to 100%. And if you want to leave behind the original, tap the right mouse button while you're dragging.

The Draw manual doesn't mention it, but you can also leave behind the original object by pressing and releasing the + key on the far right of your keyboard while dragging a handle. This was the only way to accomplish this in older versions of Draw, before Corel added the more elegant right mouse button method.

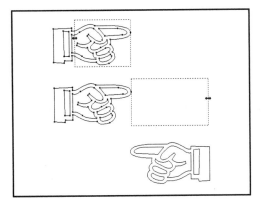

Now create a mirror image by dragging one of the corner handles, which has the effect of mirroring in both the horizontal and vertical axes simultaneously. Again, use the Control key to constrain the object's size. When mirroring, the Shift key has the interesting effect of flipping the object in place, rather than moving it to a new location. It can be used in conjunction with the Control key and right mouse button to scale the object from its center while you mirror it and leave behind an original. Take the time now to experiment with some of these key and mouse combinations.

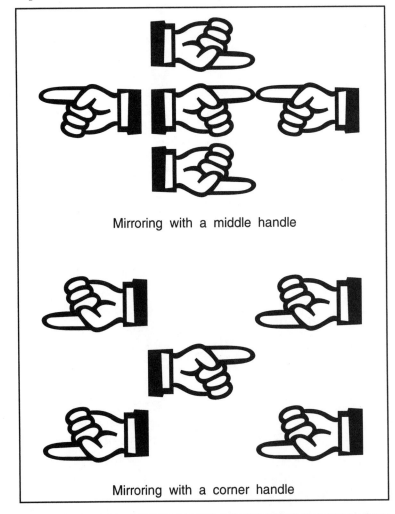

Mirroring with a middle handle

Mirroring with a corner handle

Working with Objects

As well as scaling and stretching objects directly on the screen, you can also perform these actions using precise numerical values. Select an object and choose Stretch & Mirror from the Transform menu. Enter positive values to stretch or scale the object, negative numbers to mirror it.

To reduce the object's size by half, for example, enter 50% for both values, or to double it enter 200%. If you simply want to mirror the object and keep its size the same, click on either the horizontal or vertical mirror buttons, or both. This has the same effect as mirroring the object

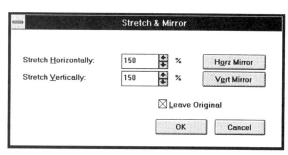

with the mouse, by dragging the side or corner handles with the Shift and Control keys held down. Either way, the mirrored object will have the same center point as the original. Clicking on the Leave Original check box corresponds to pressing the right mouse button when scaling, stretching or mirroring on the page.

Finish off this section by stretching, scaling and mirroring objects with both Snap To Grid and Snap To Guides enabled. I leave this to you to investigate.

Rotating Objects

Since most page layout programs, such as Ventura or PageMaker, currently provide only limited abilities to rotate objects, this feature alone makes Draw a valuable companion to these applications. Select an object with the ▶ tool and click on it again to enter rotate mode; the eight sizing handles will be replaced by lines with arrows on either end. Click on the object several times to become comfortable toggling between the rotate and selection modes, then wind up in rotate mode.

You can still move an object while it's in rotate mode by clicking on it and dragging it, although this will toggle it back to selection mode when you complete the move. However, you can nudge it with the cursor keys (as well as change its fill or outline) and remain in rotate mode.

Rotating an object is as simple and direct as placing your cursor over one of the four corners of an object that's in rotate mode, which changes the cursor shape to a plus sign. Then click and drag clockwise or counter-clockwise and the object will rotate around its center, with the angle of rotation displayed in the Status Line in .1° increments. As with most object manipulations using the mouse, you'll find you can do this more accurately when zoomed in, otherwise the rotation angle will jump between large increments. Be careful not to click until your cursor changes shape to a plus sign, or you'll deselect the object and have to begin again.

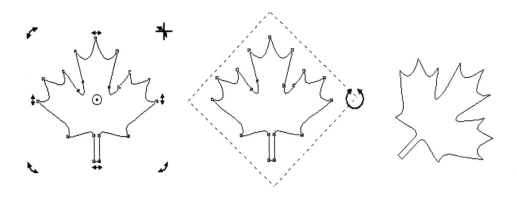

 I wasn't exaggerating when I promised earlier that the Control key will keep popping up during object movements and transformations. Hold it down while rotating and the object will rotate in steps of 15°, the default constrain value. Choose Preferences from the Special menu, click on the Lines & Curves button and change the Constrain Angle to a value between 1° and 90°, in .1° increments. Unfortunately, you can't specify a constrain amount below 1°. Now hold down the Control key and observe the Status Line while rotating. As with stretching and scaling, if you perform multiple rotations on an object, the angle displayed in the Status Line is not the cumulative amount of rotation but the current one. Guides and the grid have no effect on the object being rotated.

You're not restricted to rotating an object around its center point. Put an object in rotate mode, drag its round center point icon to a new location outside the object and then rotate it around the new center of rotation. If you deselect an object that's had its rotation moved, Draw remembers the location of the rotation point. So if you later select this object and put it in rotate mode, the custom rotation point is still displayed.

You can use a variation of this technique to place a variety of objects around a common center of rotation. You'll construct a circle of 10 different symbols rotated around a common center.

Create a clean page by choosing Select All from the File menu and pressing the Delete key. Zoom out, if necessary, to see the entire page (Shift-F4). Assuming your ruler origin is the bottom-left corner of the page (reset the zero point there if necessary), drag a horizontal guide down to 5 inches and a vertical guide over to 4 inches. In the Symbols dialog box choose the Dixieland symbol library, double-click on the Symbol # box, type in 202 to select the symbol of the number 1 in a circle, and make it an inch high.

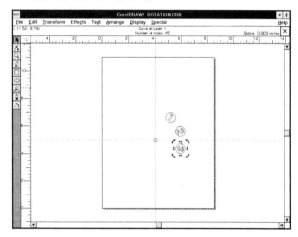

You need to center the symbol on the vertical guide, something easily performed with the Move command. With the symbol selected choose Move from the Transform menu. Click on Absolute Coordinates, click on the center check box and change the horizontal value to 4 inches and the vertical to 7 inches. Click on OK to move the symbol.

Since you want to place 10 objects around a 360° circle, you need to place them every 36°. Set the constrain angle in Preferences to this amount to make placement faster and more accurate than using the Status Line. You'll make use of the center point icon's ability to snap to guides when dragged. Make sure Snap To Guidelines on the Display menu is enabled, click on the symbol to put it into rotate mode and then drag its rotation point until it snaps to the intersection of the guides. Now rotate the symbol clockwise by dragging a corner handle, using the Control key to snap it to -36°.

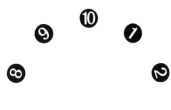
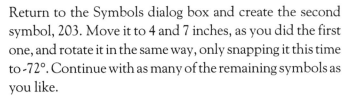

Return to the Symbols dialog box and create the second symbol, 203. Move it to 4 and 7 inches, as you did the first one, and rotate it in the same way, only snapping it this time to -72°. Continue with as many of the remaining symbols as you like.

As you might expect, pressing the right mouse button while rotating an object leaves behind a copy of the original. This is especially useful when coupled with the Repeat command, which can be used for creating multiple rotated versions of the same object.

Because Draw remembers the last action you've taken, it can not only undo it but repeat it. You can use this ability to repeat many Draw operations, including moves and object transformations. Select an object, put it in rotate mode, drag its center point a few inches in any direction and while rotating the object 30° press the right mouse button. Then use the Repeat command (Control-R) 10 times to construct a circle of objects. In the illustration, I used the star symbol 72 from the Dixieland library.

Experiment with the Repeat command after moving, stretching and scaling an object, both with the mouse and the corresponding dialog boxes. For example, you could drag an object one inch to the right (keeping an eye on the Status Line as you go) while holding down the Control key to prevent movement up or down. Before releasing the mouse, tap the right mouse button to leave behind the original. Then use the Repeat command to

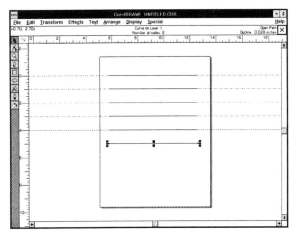

create multiple, identically spaced objects. You could also perform the move-and-leave-behind operation in the Move dialog box and then repeat as desired. In the illustration, I used this technique to create multiple lines spaced one inch apart.

You can even repeat an operation you've performed by selecting one or more different objects and then choosing Repeat from the Edit menu. Try this out by moving or resizing an

---

Working with Objects

object, selecting a different object and then using the Repeat command. As another experiment, with an object selected open the Stretch & Mirror dialog box and set the horizontal and vertical values to 101%. Then use the Repeat command multiple times to slowly increase the size of the object.

Applying repeated rotations to a second object is a little trickier. Begin by rotating any object on the page, then select a second object and apply the Repeat command. Yes, the second object rotated, but probably not the way you expected. Just what's happening here is undocumented, but there is a way to predict how the rotation will be applied.

Make a copy of any object on the page by dragging it with the mouse and tapping the right button as you go. Rotate the copied object, then click on the first object twice to put it in rotate mode and press Control-R. The secret is now revealed. The first object has taken on the rotation point of the copy and then been rotated to a similar angle. Since it began in a different location on the page than the copied object, moving the rotation point before rotating had the effect of moving the first object.

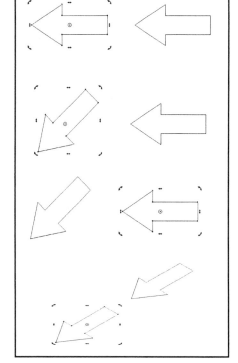

This shifting of the rotation point has another effect that may also be unanticipated. To see this, make another copy of an object. Then put the copy in rotate mode and drag its rotation point outside the object. Select the original object and rotate it, then select the copy, put it in rotate mode again and press Control-R. So far everything looks the same as in the previous exercise. But deselect the copy and then click on it again. You should see that the rotation point is back to its original position in relationship to the object. It made use of the other object's rotation point during the rotation, and rotated using its angle, but its own rotation point remained intact for subsequent manipulations.

Since this is rather an unusual way to combine the Repeat command and rotations, you may want to go through this sequence several times. Granted, this isn't a feature you're going to make use of every day. But I want to deal with as many potentially confusing aspects, obscure features and undocumented tips as possible during your rigorous exploration of Draw in these tutorial chapters.

As you've seen, an object rotates by default around its center, unless you've dragged its rotation point to a new location. However, you can also rotate an object precisely around one of its corners or midpoints, by first holding down the Control key and then dragging the rotation point until it snaps to one of eight possible locations. Give this a try. If you're in an experimental mood, you'll find that rotating an object 180° by dragging one of its corners produces the same result as mirroring it both horizontally and vertically.

Even more possibilities for controlling rotation become available when you combine it with Draw's Snap To Object feature. While the Draw documentation discusses Snap To Object in detail, it's strangely silent on the topic of using it while rotating. I'll return to Snap To Object in future chapters, to ensure you work with it in a number of contexts. For now, the principle to keep in mind is that every object has at least two *snap points*. These act much like grid points, in that your cursor will snap to them when moving or transforming an object. Rectangles, for example, have nine snap points at their centers, corners and midpoints, while circles have five at their centers and at the conjunction of the four arcs of which they're constructed.

You've probably already noticed that when you select a symbol the Status Line displays the number of points, or *nodes*, connecting the object's line and curve segments. These nodes can all function as snap points when moving, rotating or performing other object transformations with the mouse. Enable Snap To Objects on the Display menu and put a symbol in rotate mode. Now drag its rotation point and you'll find it snaps to the object's nodes. Snap it to any node and then rotate the object with mouse, tapping the right mouse button as you go to leave behind the original. Repeat this several times by snapping to different nodes. I've followed this procedure in the illustration using symbol 25 from the Arrows1 library.

Working with Objects

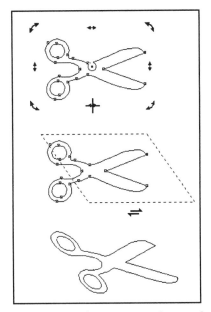

Rotate mode is more accurately described as rotate/skew mode, since it also lets you stretch objects diagonally. Click on an object until it's in rotate/skew mode and drag any of the four straight arrowed lines displayed on its midpoints. Don't overlook the use of the right mouse button and Control key while skewing, although the Shift key currently has no effect. As with rotating, the guides and grid have no effect when skewing.

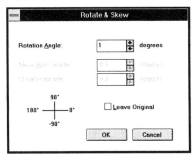

Draw also provides a dialog box for entering numerical values for rotating and skewing objects. Select an object and choose Rotate & Skew from the Transform menu. Negative values rotate clockwise, while positive values rotate counter-clockwise. Draw lets you either skew or rotate each time you visit the dialog box, leaving behind an unmodified original if desired.

There is currently no way to rotate an object repeatedly a predefined amount, as you can with the nudge feature when moving. You could rotate a small amount, say 1°, with the mouse or Rotate & Skew dialog box, then use the Repeat command (Control-R) multiple times to continue rotating this amount. In fact, you can enter values in the dialog box as low as .1° degree. But Draw rotates objects inaccurately when using Repeat, so you should use it with caution when precision is important. In the illustration, I rotated the horizontal line 1° and then used the Repeat command 89 times. As you can see, minute positioning errors are cumulative when using Repeat, with the result that the line is improperly positioned.

And finally, what should you do when you make a complete hash of an object? What's needed here is an undo of major

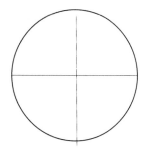

proportions, which is what choosing Clear Transformations from the Transform menu provides. Draw discards any scales, stretches, mirrors, rotations or skews performed on an object, returning it to its pristine, as-created state.

In this chapter you explored the fundamental techniques of moving and transforming objects. Up next is creating new objects with the Pencil ℓ, Rectangle □ and Ellipse ◯ tools and editing them with the ⸏ tool. In later chapters I'll ask you to save your work, but there's no need for that now. If you've created something worth saving at this point, however, choose Save from the File menu and specify a drive, directory and name for your file.

Creating and Editing Outlines

4

CorelDRAW provides just three tools for the creation of new graphic objects: the Pencil ✐ , Rectangle ☐ and Ellipse ⬭ tools. But with these seemingly limited resources there is in fact virtually no limit to what you can create with Draw. This, then, is a core chapter in which you will build skills essential for creating and editing the content of your Draw illustrations. It is also one of the more demanding chapters. My recommendation is to set aside several hours for its completion. You may be wise to complete it in several sittings, to avoid overloading yourself with new material.

Choose New from the File menu to create a fresh editing window, choose the Display menu and enable the rulers and the Status Line. Also on the Display menu, make sure Snap To Grid is turned off.

Time to begin drawing. Choose the ☐ tool, click anywhere on the page and drag the mouse. Keep an eye on the Status Line as you drag to create an object one inch square, and observe that it's displaying the object's current width and height, as well as the horizontal (x) and vertical (y) coordinates of its start, end and center points. As always, the location of the cursor is also displayed on the far left of the Status Line.

When you release the mouse, the Status Line now displays the type of object you created, as well as its width, height and center point location. (On the far right, it also displays the default fill and outline.) As when moving or transforming an object, this numerical information is displayed in the measurement system of the horizontal ruler. Don't struggle too long to get it exactly one inch square — I'll show you a shortcut

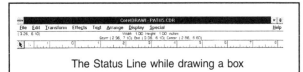

The Status Line while drawing a box

---

to accomplish this in a minute. Although the object you just drew doesn't display any selection handles, it *is* selected. For example, you could use the dialog boxes on the Transform menu to move, resize, mirror, rotate or shear it.

To display the selection handles of the object you just drew either click on the Pick ⟍ tool or press the Spacebar. Either way, press the Spacebar again to return to the ☐ tool. This is a quick way to toggle between the ⟍ tool and the current drawing tool. You can also select the ☐ tool by pressing the F6 function key. What if you find you can't create a box exactly one inch square? Zoom in — you should then be able to draw objects to an accuracy of .01 inch as you drag.

Drawing with the Grid

In addition to the Status Line, you can use the rulers as a reference when creating and resizing objects. And the grid is yet another powerful tool that can help you create objects with precision. Choose Grid Setup from the Display menu and set the horizontal and vertical Grid Frequency to 1 per inch. In the same dialog box enable the grid with Snap To Grid and click on Show Grid. Choose the ☐ tool and as you move your pointer onto the page, note that it snaps to the inch increments of the ruler, matching the grid frequency you just defined.

Earlier, without the grid enabled, you probably found it difficult or impossible to draw a box exactly one inch square while in the ☐ view. Try drawing it now, using either the rulers or the Status Line as your guide. Drawing with a grid makes it possible to avoid constantly zooming in and to remain in the ☐ view while still creating objects with precision. Such relatively modest time-savers can add up to a significant number of saved mouse clicks.

The drawback to this approach is that you're limited to the creation of objects that are multiples of the grid frequency. So whether you'll find grids useful depends on the nature of the drawing on which you're working. Use the Control-Y keyboard shortcut to quickly toggle Snap To Grid on and off; the Status Line lets you know if it's enabled. Make sure grid snap is off before you move on to the next section of the tutorial.

Back to the Keyboard

You've seen in the previous chapter that while Draw is a mouse-based program, it makes use of the Control and Shift keys to modify the nature of certain actions. Hold down the Shift key while drawing a rectangle, for example, and you'll find that it's now being drawn out from the center. Holding down the Control key, on the other hand, lets you draw perfect squares, and both keys can be held down at once if desired.

The process of drawing circles and ellipses is the same as for squares and rectangles. Choose the ○ tool and verify that it works much like the □ tool, right down to the operation of the Shift and Control keys. No surprises here. Create some ellipses with and without Snap To Grid enabled.

At this point your page is probably filling up with objects. Before you move on in the tutorial, choose the ▸ tool, choose Select All from the Edit menu and then Delete, also from the Edit menu. A faster alternative would be to simply press the Delete key on your keyboard. Follow this procedure whenever you need to get rid of everything on your page.

Drawing Lines and Curves

While the □ and ○ tools let you draw basic shapes, it's hard to create much of interest with a repertoire of just boxes and circles. To go beyond this you must resort to the Pencil ℓ tool, which is used for creating both straight lines and curves.

You can draw with the ℓ tool in two modes, Freehand or Bézier, with Freehand being the default mode. Click on the Freehand ℓ tool now. If the Bézier ℓ tool is currently displayed in the toolbox, click and hold on it to display the flyout menu, then click on the ℓ tool. The Status Line should indicate you're drawing in Freehand mode. You can also use the F5 function key to choose whichever version of the tool is currently displayed.

To create a straight line click anywhere on the page, release the mouse button and move the mouse. Don't hold down the mouse button while you move it or you'll be drawing curves — simply click, release and move the mouse.

As you move the cursor, the Status Line provides valuable information about the straight line you're creating, such as the distance you've moved in both the x and y axes, the total length of the line (distance), the angle between where you clicked and the cursor's current location, and the x and y position of the start and end of the line. As you'd expect, the coordinates for the end of the line are the same as the cursor coordinates displayed at the left of the Status Line. Click a second time anywhere to end the line.

Drawing is a Snap

Beyond its ability to create the lines that constitute your objects, the ℓ tool can also be used to measure angles and distances between objects on the page. Test this by drawing a line between two points on the page, observe the distance indicated on the Status Line and then delete the unneeded line. But what if you want to precisely measure the distance between particular nodes of two objects?

Draw two boxes on the page and enable Snap To Objects, under the Display menu. Choose the ℓ tool and click near, but not on, a corner of one of the boxes. Release the mouse button, without

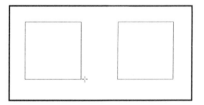

moving the mouse, and the left corner of the Status Line will change from Snap To Objects to read Snapped To Rectangle. As with guides and grids, as long as you click within a certain distance of an object's snap point, the *gravity effect* will snap the object you're creating or manipulating to the snap point.

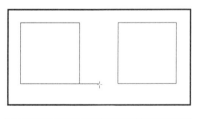

Now drag the mouse to draw the line, and as you go observe that the Status Line has reverted to simply Snap To Objects. However, continue the line over to the second rectangle and you'll find that the end of your line snaps to its corners, midpoints and center. As it does so, the Status Line indicates this by displaying Snapped To Rectangle. If you were using this technique to measure the distance between two objects, you'd then simply delete the line. But it's also great for accurately drawing lines between objects. Experiment by drawing lines between the snap points of rectangles, ellipses and lines. You could also place

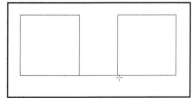

Creating and Editing Outlines

an object on the page from Draw's symbol libraries and snap lines to it. The tricky part here is that you can't see the nodes to which you're snapping.

Since I often make use of Snap To Objects when drawing, I usually leave it enabled. Unfortunately, there's no keyboard shortcut to quickly toggle it on and off, but you could create a macro to accomplish this with Windows Recorder. (I've included one on the Utility disk included with the book.) Another way to get around Snap To Objects without disabling it is to zoom in. Since the gravity effect is a fixed amount of distance on the screen, when you've zoomed in you're able to begin or end lines slightly to one side of the snap points without their snapping.

The rulers, the grid and the Control key can all be used when creating straight lines. Holding the Control key down restricts lines to the constrain angle defined in Preferences, a handy technique when drawing horizontal or vertical lines. Draw some lines using first the rulers as a guide, then with Snap To Grid and finally Snap To Guidelines enabled. As always, zoom in if you need more accuracy — to be able to draw lines .01 inch longer or shorter, for example.

When you click a second time to finish drawing a line, the segment you drew displays a node on either end. These nodes indicate that the line is selected and can be deleted without shifting to the ⬚ tool. You can also continue adding new lines to any selected segment. If you want to add new lines to a line that isn't currently selected, select it first with the ⬚ tool, then choose the ⬚ tool. To draw a second line connected to one you just drew, click on a node at either end of the line and move the mouse to create a new connected line segment. You can't connect a line to a node that already has two lines connected to it, although it may *look* connected. When it comes to nodes, three's a crowd.

To quickly draw an object composed of a number of connected straight lines, just double-click to end one line segment and begin another. Try this technique, then select one of the polygons you've drawn with the ⬚ tool. The Status Line informs you that the selected object is a curve with an open path.

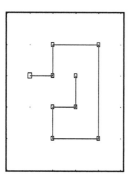

Remember, the Spacebar toggles you back and forth between the three drawing tools and the ▶ tool. To draw a new line and ensure that it's *not* connected to a line you just drew, press the Spacebar twice to switch to the ▶ tool and back to the ℓ tool.

If you have Snap To Grid enabled while you draw lines it's very easy to click on an end node that rests on the grid, but the grid can prove limiting. As long as you click within 5 pixels of a node, whether the grid is enabled or not, Draw assumes you're adding a line to an existing object, rather than starting a new one. If you're having trouble connecting new to existing lines, either zoom in, or in Preferences click on Curves and increase the AutoJoin value from its default 5 pixels up to 10. All the values in this dialog box can be set from 1 to 10.

Conversely, if you're creating a drawing from scratch using a more free form technique with many tightly spaced lines, you should decrease the AutoJoin value to 1 to increase your control over which lines are actually joined. To put it another way, the smaller the setting, the closer you must click for lines to be automatically joined. It's instructive to zoom in as much as possible and watch AutoJoin in action by clicking slightly off an existing selected end node with the ℓ tool and creating a new line. Try this with both Snap To Objects and Snap To Grid disabled, using different AutoJoin values.

Since the functions of AutoJoin and Snap To Objects overlap, their respective roles when drawing a series of connected lines need clarification. AutoJoin is always active, so even if Snap To Objects isn't enabled this feature will help you create a series of connected lines. However, unlike Snap To Objects, you can specify the gravity effect of AutoJoin. If you set it lower than the corresponding setting for Snap To Objects (an unknown amount), then it will take precedence when drawing. The big difference is that Snap To Objects can be used for operations besides drawing.

To get a sense of how Snap To Grid, AutoJoin and Snap To Objects relate, make sure both snaps are enabled, zoom in and create a polygon (a series of connected lines) such as the zigzag object in the illustration, double-clicking to end one node and begin another on the grid marks. If you then press the Spacebar

Creating and Editing Outlines

to select what you've just drawn, the Status Line will indicate the number of nodes in the lines that make up this one object.

Create a similar object, this time double-clicking not on, but to one side of, the grid marks — try to click almost halfway between them. When you've finished, click on each line in turn with the ▶ tool and you should find that each line segment is a separate object. It looked like you were creating a series of connected lines, thanks to Snap To Grid, but if you clicked outside the range of both AutoJoin and Snap To Objects, you wound up with unconnected lines.

The Nature of Objects

A collection of connected segments, whether straight lines, curves or a mix of the two, is called a *curve object*. Such segments are typically joined end to end, forming a *path*. As you'll see, a curve object can also be composed of a number of separate paths, or *subpaths*, that aren't actually joined at their ends but are linked together with the Combine command.

Select the first zigzag object you drew. Because the beginning and endpoints of the object aren't joined, the Status Line indicates that the path is currently open. The path of a curve object must be closed before it can be filled with a color.

Now add some straight line segments with the ℓ tool to close the object. You'll find that AutoJoin will snap the new nodes you create to the open end nodes of the zigzag object. Not only will it snap them to the same location, but it will actually join them, as would Snap To Objects. When you return to the ▶ tool with the Spacebar, note that the Status Line indicates that the object now has the current default fill. If an ✕ is displayed, it indicates the default fill is transparent, or None. Fill your object with something more colorful by clicking on the Color Palette at the bottom of the screen with your left mouse button. (If no palette is available, choose Show Color Palette and Process Colors from the Display menu.) Press Shift-F9 to switch to preview mode if your fill isn't displayed.

Create some more connected straight line segments with the ℓ tool. Now's the time to perform some of the transformations you explored in the last chapter, such as stretching and rotating, on the objects you've drawn. After such transformations you can return to the ℓ tool and continue to add line segments to a selected open curve object.

Draw depicts all objects, whether text or graphics, in terms of a path composed of straight lines and curves. An object you draw with the ☐ tool is thus simply four straight lines connected at 90° angles, while an ellipse is four connected arcs. No matter how you resize or transform these objects, Draw remembers their basic structure, unless you use a special command for breaking down such *structured* objects, including text, into their component parts for editing.

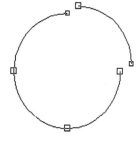

The complex objects you create with the ℓ tool are still no more than collections of lines and curves connected by nodes. In Freehand mode Draw follows the movement of the mouse when you click and drag. When you release the mouse button, Draw converts what you've drawn into the curve and line segments that make up a curve object. You can then modify the object using the transformations available with the ▶ tool or edit individual line and curve segments with the Shape ⚲ tool.

Select the ℓ tool, click and drag on the page to create a curve object and release the mouse button. (If it feels awkward drawing curves with a mouse, you've got company — a mouse is in fact a rather poor drawing tool. If you'll be creating most of your drawings from scratch, you'll find a drawing tablet equipped with a cordless stylus — such as those supplied by Wacom, Kurta or Summagraphics — more responsive.) There are a few differences between drawing straight lines and curves. One is that the Control key has no effect while drawing curves. Another is that you can erase as much of the curve object that you're currently drawing as desired by holding down the Shift key and retracing your path with the mouse.

Draw a closed freehand curve object now by clicking and dragging the mouse. The Status Line tells you that you've created a curve object with the default fill. When you used a straight line to close a curve object, you had to select the object with the ▶ tool to see its fill displayed in the Status Line. When you close it with a curve, however, the fill is displayed without leaving the ℓ tool. Strange, but true.

Creating and Editing Outlines

Curve Object Parameters

Draw uses a number of parameters to interpret the path your mouse follows before converting it to an object composed of lines and curves. Choose Preferences from the Special menu and click on Curves. The Freehand Tracking value determines how closely Draw follows your mouse. With a low value you'll wind up with a path composed of a large number of line segments, since Draw will assiduously note your every twitch of the mouse. A higher number results in fewer nodes and a smoother (though possibly less accurate) path.

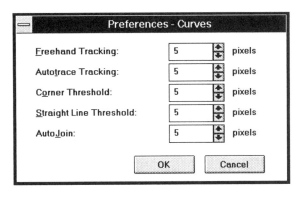

The brand of mouse you draw with, its resolution, state of repair and the surface on which you use it, can all make a big difference in how much control you have over the lines you draw. Cleaning out the mouse once in a while isn't a bad idea. Neither is adjusting its sensitivity using the Windows Control Panel. The illustration shows the dialog box for the driver supplied with a Microsoft mouse, which provides control over both sensitivity and acceleration.

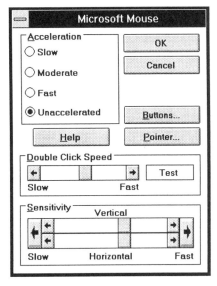

As the accompanying figure shows, when I traced a circle drawn using the ◯ tool with Freehand Tracking set to 1, 5 and 10 pixels, the resulting objects wound up with 38, 23 and 18 nodes, respectively. A *pixel*, by the way, is a unit of measurement tied to the resolution of your monitor, and therefore also to the current view of your document. You've seen that Draw becomes more accurate as you zoom in. In the same way, the greater number of pixels of a high resolution monitor provides subtler control of object creation, movement and manipulation.

Duplicate the experiment by drawing a perfect circle with the ◯ tool and Control key, then zooming in until it fills the screen and tracing around it using different Freehand Tracking values. You'll find the number of nodes created (displayed in

---

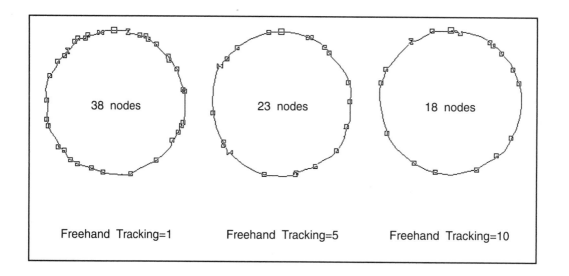

38 nodes	23 nodes	18 nodes
Freehand Tracking=1	Freehand Tracking=5	Freehand Tracking=10

the Status Line) is a function both of how smoothly you draw and the Freehand Tracking value.

Node Types

Many of Draw's tools perform multiple functions. The ∕◆ tool, for example, is employed to edit the line and curve segments that make up curve objects, as well as to perform text manipulations and crop imported bitmap images. Select one of your circle tracings with the ∕◆ tool and zoom in to display just a few of the nodes connecting the segments.

All curve or straight line segments are connected by one of three types of node. As you select different nodes by clicking on

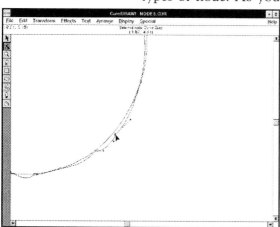

them, the Status Line indicates the location of the node and the nature of the curve or line segment associated with the selected node: either a cusp, symmetrical or smooth curve, or a cusp or smooth line. To find out which segment is associated with a node, click on a segment to select its node. Selected curve nodes will display as solid black, while those with straight line segments will be hollow. The exception is the first node of a curve object, which always displays larger and in solid black when selected. You will have to click directly on this node to select it.

You're going to use the curve object editing abilities of the ⚲ tool to more accurately fit your trace to the circle. Click and drag a node that's currently off the circle back onto its diameter. Note that the Status Line provides the same information when a node is moved as it does when moving an object with the ⬉ tool. Not surprisingly, the Control key performs a similar vertical and horizontal constrain function. Nodes being moved also respond to Snap To Grid, Snap To Guidelines and Snap To Objects, if they're enabled.

You'll find that simply moving the nodes back onto the circle is only part of the battle. The angles of the curve segments connecting many of the nodes are wrong, and some nodes may be connected with straight line segments. Converting straight line segments to curves is simple enough. Double-click with the ⚲ tool on a straight line or its associated node and when the Node Edit menu appears choose toCurve. Can't find a straight line segment? Convert a curve segment to a straight line and back again.

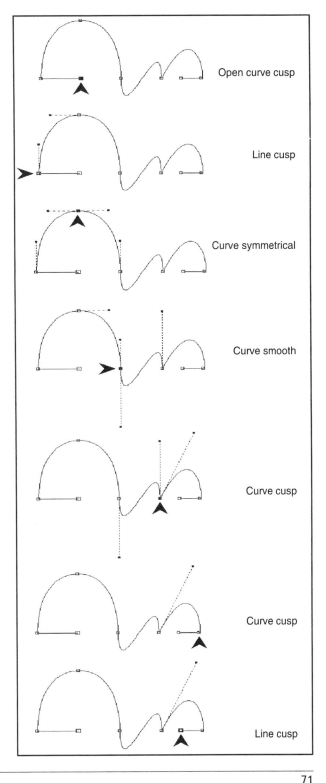

Open curve cusp

Line cusp

Curve symmetrical

Curve smooth

Curve cusp

Curve cusp

Line cusp

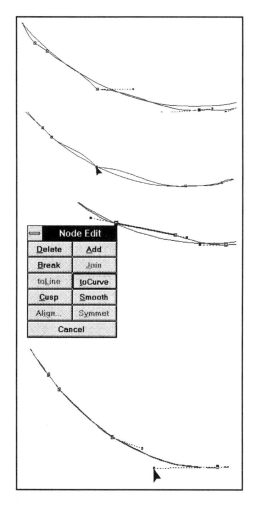

Be careful not to move the mouse when double-clicking or you'll shift the position of the node. Resting the palm of your hand on the mouse pad when you double-click on a node is a good way to minimize accidental node movement. If you do accidentally shift a node, then cancel the Node Edit menu and choose Undo from the Edit menu.

You can control whether Draw interprets what you draw as a line or as a curve segment by clicking on Curves in the Preferences dialog box on the Special menu and changing the Straight Line Threshold value. A higher value biases Draw in favor of line segments, while a lower one encourages the creation of curves. Since you only wanted curves while you were tracing the circle, you could have reduced this value from the default 5 to 1, resulting in the creation of fewer straight segments. Raising it to 10 would have resulted in a higher proportion of straight line segments, although their incidence would still remain fairly rare. As always, experiment with this setting now if it interests you.

You can adjust the angle and length of the curve segments in a curve object on an individual basis. Select a node and note that it now displays two *control points* connected to it by dotted lines. You can modify the nature of the curve passing through a node by dragging the control points. Changing the distance of a control point from the node makes the curve larger or smaller. Changing the angle of the point alters the angle of the curve as it passes through the node. Drag the control points of a selected node to observe this.

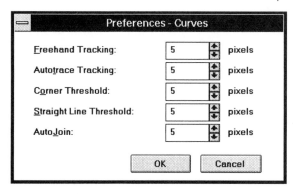

How the curve passes through the node depends on whether it's connected to a smooth, symmetrical or cusp node. As when moving nodes, the Control key constrains the horizontal and vertical movement of control points, as does Snap To Grid, Guidelines and Objects. You'll experiment with the node types, under the assumption that your tracing contains all three types of node. If not, you can easily change the nature of nodes in a curve object. For example, double-click on a cusp or smooth node to display the Node Edit menu and then click on Symmetrical to change the nature of the node.

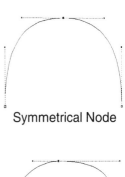

Symmetrical Node

Symmetrical nodes provide the least amount of flexibility for curve editing. Here the control points and the node lie in a straight line, the two control points equidistant from each other. When you change the relationship between a control point and a symmetrical node the other connected control point mirrors the change, ensuring the curve is the same both entering and leaving the node. Experiment with the control points of a symmetrical node on your tracing.

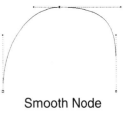

Smooth Node

Smooth nodes are a bit more flexible. True, the two control points also lie on a straight line, but they can be different lengths. Find and manipulate one of these nodes on your tracing.

Cusp Node

Finally, there are the ever-popular cusp nodes. Popular, because each control point is independent of the other in both angle and length, just the thing when you need to create an abrupt change in direction of a curve. Experiment with a few cusp nodes as well. You'll find they're the least appropriate node for the tracing, since it's harder to create symmetrical curves on both side of a cusp node.

The ideal type of node for your tracing of the ellipse would be symmetrical, assuming the ellipse was a perfect circle. Otherwise, smooth nodes would provide enough flexibility to adjust curves around softly changing angles. If there were really radical changes in angle then cusp nodes would be the ticket, although they're not needed here. They'll work, however, as long as you ensure a smooth transition between curves. Zooming in will be essential for this.

To ensure the creation of more smooth than cusp nodes while

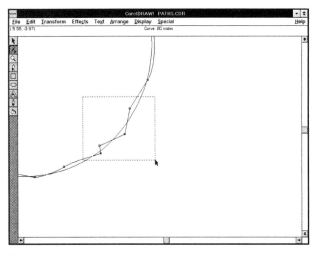

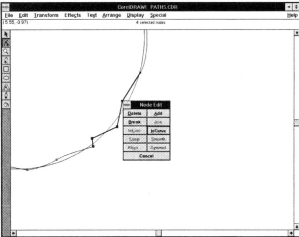

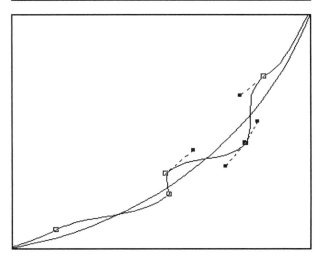

drawing with the ℓ tool, you can raise the value of the Corner Threshold parameter in the Curves sub-dialog box of Preferences. The higher the value, the more Draw will interpret what you draw as having smooth and symmetrical nodes, with correspondingly fewer cusp nodes. While not appropriate for situations where you're drawing a complex object with abrupt changes of direction, this tactic would make sense for drawing objects with smooth curves, such as your tracing.

As with object selection, you can select a group of nodes and apply commands to them in the Node Edit menu while you have the ⋏ tool selected. Hold down the Shift key and click on several nodes to select them. The Status Line keeps track of the number of selected (black) nodes. Now double-click on any node to be able to work with them as a group. You can also select multiple nodes with the selection marquee by clicking and dragging a box around them. This is the preferable approach, since it eliminates the possibility of accidentally moving nodes. Use this technique to convert all the curves in your tracing to straight lines or make all the nodes symmetrical.

Creating and Editing Outlines

The ideal to strive for when drawing with the ✑ tool is to create curve objects with as few nodes as possible. An excess of nodes often results in curve objects with a choppy, rough look. And the more nodes in your drawing the more memory will be needed to manipulate it on screen, the larger the resulting file will be and the longer it will take to print. In fact, very complex objects could keep the page from printing at all on some output devices, such as high-resolution imagesetters. Various strategies for dealing with this unhappy eventuality are covered in later chapters, such as *Service Bureau Strategies*.

Zap that Node

One way of simplifying an overly complex drawing is to delete excess nodes. This is often necessary when working with scanned images that have been converted to objects with Draw's internal autotracing feature or the CorelTRACE program. Your traced circle could probably stand a little cleaning up. In fact, only two nodes are really needed for the creation of a circle. Delete a node by double-clicking on it and choosing Delete from the Node Edit menu. You can also select and delete multiple nodes. The keyboard shortcut for deleting objects — pressing the Delete key — also works on one or more selected nodes, and is faster than using the Node Edit menu.

Unless you have either a very high resolution monitor or remarkable eye-hand coordination, you probably didn't end the tracing of the circle within 5 pixels of the first node. In other words, you've got an open path on your hands that can't be filled. Select the trace with the ➤ tool and the right-hand side of the Status Line will indicate if it's open. (For those of you who *did* create a closed path, draw a new open path in a circle shape with the ✑ tool anywhere on the page.) Select the ⤚ tool, then zoom in on the first and last nodes of the open path. The first node of a curve object is always the largest. Selecting it with the ⤚ tool reveals in the Status Line that, as expected, it's the first node of an open curve. It's also a cusp node, although it doesn't indicate that in the Status Line. Click on the last node, however, and it will be identified as cusp. Beginning and endpoint nodes are always cusp nodes. Click on the Home or End keys to quickly identify the first or last nodes in a path, respectively.

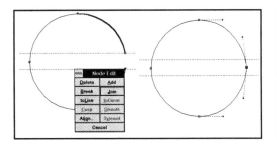
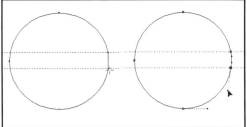

You can join the two nodes at the beginning and end of a line or curve segment as long as they're both part of the same path, which is the case here. Select both the endpoint and the first node; the easiest way is to draw a marquee around both of them. Then double-click on either node and choose Join. When you join two segments, Draw places a single new node midway between the two selected nodes. This has the sometimes undesirable effect of changing the shape and position of the segments connected to the nodes. In the series of four illustrations I've first used the Join command to close two nodes, which has distorted the shape of the ellipse.

There is currently no way to automatically add a new segment while leaving the nodes in their original location. If this is the effect you're after, you can simply use the ℓ tool to click on one node and drag a segment to the other. As long as the object to which you're adding the line is selected when you do this, and you click within 5 pixels of each node (or you use Snap To Objects), the new line will be autojoined to the existing one, and you'll wind up with a closed, fillable object. If the object wasn't selected, your new line won't be connected to it.

In the third and fourth illustrations of the circle, I've used the ℓ tool to draw a line between the two nodes, then used the ⤧ tool to convert the straight line to a curve, convert the two nodes to smooth and then adjust the control point handles. Since this situation will often arise, why not experiment by creating an object with an open path and then use the ℓ tool to close it with a new line segment. First try it with the object selected, then again with it deselected. Note what happens when you attempt to fill either object using the Color Palette at the bottom of the screen.

Creating and Editing Outlines

Finally, continue deleting and adjusting nodes until you've reduced your original tracing to a perfect circle requiring only two symmetrical nodes, as shown in the illustration.

In the previous exercise you joined nodes that were both on the same path. But you'll often find that the nodes you wish to join are on separate paths. Use the 𝒍 tool to draw two unconnected curve objects side by side. If you now click with the 𝒜 tool on first one, then the other, you'll notice that only the nodes of the object you click on are displayed. There's no way to simultaneously select both of the nodes you want to join, even when using the Shift key or a marquee. To join them, first select them both with the ▶ tool and then create a single path by choosing the Combine command from the Arrange menu. You can now select both nodes with the 𝒜 tool and join them in the usual way.

Breaking Up Isn't Hard to Do

You can break the connection between segments in much the same way, either a node at a time or en masse. Double-click on a node and choose Break from the Node Edit menu. You can now drag the topmost node to a new location. Unfortunately, there's currently no way to select the node on the bottom without first moving the one on top. If the object is an open path and your intention is to create two separate objects, you could choose Break Apart on the Arrange menu, use the ▶ tool to select the object with the node you want to manipulate and then switch back to the 𝒜 tool. You'd then be able to select the node that was previously underneath the other broken node. (If you all send a letter to Susan Wimmer at Corel Corp. in Ottawa and ask her to add the ability to easily select either node, the odds are good that this feature will appear in the next release of Draw. So don't let me down — write her today!)

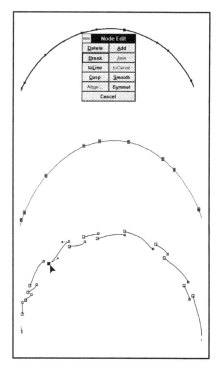

You can also break a segment anywhere between nodes. Simply double-click on the segment at the point at which you want to break it and choose Break from the Node Edit menu.

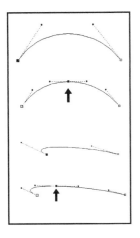

If you've cleaned up the tracing to the point where you're low on nodes, you can double-click on a node or segment and choose Add from the Node Edit menu. When you double-click on a node, Draw tries to add a new node midway along the segment. It usually succeeds unless the curve has a very sharp bend on one side. Draw will then place the new node closer to the bend, as shown in the illustration. Verify this for yourself by creating some segments of varying shape and adding nodes. You can also place a single new node with precision by double-clicking on the segment itself and choosing Add.

The ability to add nodes to the midpoint of a number of selected segments makes it easy to quickly create an octagon. Create a circle with the ○ tool and the Control key. At this point it has only a single node. Now choose Convert To Curves from the Arrange menu. This breaks the object down into its component curve segments, allowing it to be altered with the 𝆏 tool. Choose the 𝆏 tool and drag a marquee around the circle to select its four nodes. Double-click on any node and choose Add to add four new nodes. Then double-click again and choose toLine to convert the eight curve segments to straight lines. Instant octagon.

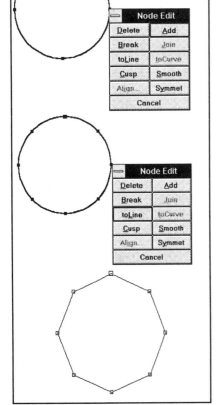

You could also use Convert To Curves to break a square down into four line segments. Deleting a node would then leave you with a triangle. You may find it easier converting circles and squares to curves and editing them than creating objects from scratch with the ℓ tool. For a good example of this, see the *Cartooning with Draw* chapter.

Hooray for Bézier

You've probably already found that the ℓ tool is inherently difficult to control in Freehand mode. It provides no way to place nodes with precision, typically resulting in a significant number of them showing up in awkward places and requiring time-consuming editing.

Creating and Editing Outlines

Version 2.0 of Draw added the ability to use the ℓ tool in Bézier drawing mode, which provides considerably more control over the placement of the nodes and segments that make up your objects. Since the lines and curves of all the objects in your drawings are represented by Bézier curves, an understanding of how these curves work is essential for productive work in Bézier drawing mode. (Since the remainder of this chapter is quite demanding, now might be the time to take a break before continuing.)

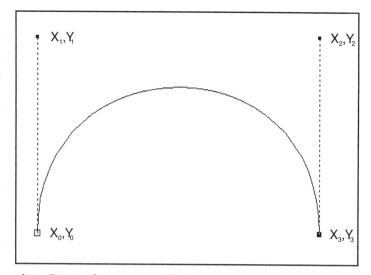

There are a number of ways to mathematically represent curves, but Bézier cubic sections are arguably the most elegant and flexible. Such a curve is defined by four points: two define the x and y coordinates of the beginning and ending of the curve, and two others define the x and y coordinates of control points that determine the angle and size of the curve. These four points are calculated for you automatically when you draw in Freehand mode. When drawing in Bézier mode, however, you have control over these by creating one segment at a time. As you've seen, in Draw terminology the beginning and endpoints of a segment are marked by nodes, while the points that control the angle and size of the curve are called control points.

Click and hold on the ℓ tool and choose the Bézier ℓ icon. The Status Line should indicate that you're drawing in Bézier mode. In this mode, as in Freehand, you can create straight line or curve segments, but the procedure for creating straight lines is slightly different than in Freehand mode. Click once to mark the beginning of a straight line, release the mouse button and move the mouse. Notice that, unlike in Freehand mode, the Status Line doesn't provide any feedback on the line segment you're creating as you drag. In fact, you can't even see it until you click a second time.

On the other hand, if you create a closed object using this technique, the Status Line tells you right away that it now has the default fill. Contrast this to Freehand mode, which forces you to select a closed object composed of straight lines with the ▶ tool before the Status Line will tell you whether it's closed.

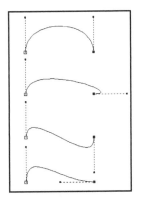

As in Freehand mode, straight line segments are really curves in disguise. Create a single straight line in Bézier mode, choose the ⚲ tool and double-click on the segment. In the Node Edit menu choose toCurve and note that the segment is now displaying its control handles. Since you'll be defining the position of the control handles for each segment you draw in Bézier mode, it's very important to understand how the position of handles affects the curve. Pull these handles to new locations and observe their relationship to the curve to which they're attached. The distance of the handle from its node determines the size, or *velocity*, of the curve. The illustration shows the same line modified by different positions of one of the handles.

Earlier, you traced over a circle in Freehand mode and were rewarded with an irregularly-shaped object studded with unwanted nodes. It's time to try it again in Bézier mode. Drag both a horizontal and vertical guide from the rulers onto the page. Check the Display menu to ensure you have Snap To Guidelines enabled. Hold down both the Shift and Control keys, then click and drag near the intersection of the two guides to create a perfect circle with the ⬭ tool.

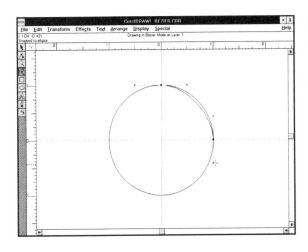

Enable Snap To Objects from the Display menu. Choose the ⚲ tool, click on the top of the circle (at 12 o'clock) and drag to the right, about half as far as the right edge of the circle, holding down the Control key while you're dragging to stay perfectly horizontal (assuming the Constrain Angle in Preferences is set to an appropriate value, such as 10° or 15°). Because Snap To Objects is enabled, Draw moved your click location to precisely that of the top node of the circle. The Status Line should verify this by indicating Snapped To Ellipse as you drag.

Now click a second time where the horizontal guide crosses the circle (at 3 o'clock) and drag straight down until the segment you're drawing matches the curve as closely as possible. Add a second segment by clicking on the bottom of the circle (6 o'clock) and dragging to the left, then a third segment by clicking at 9 o'clock and dragging straight up. The Status Line indicates that what you've constructed so far has four nodes and is an open path.

Finally, complete the curve by clicking on the first node at the top of the circle (12 o'clock) and dragging to the right. You'll notice that only the handle to the left of this node is changing size as you drag — the first curve you drew remains untouched. Since you've created a closed object, the Status Line should indicate it has been given the default fill of X when you release the mouse.

While the new circle has considerably fewer nodes than the one you created earlier in Freehand mode, it's still far from perfect. Time for the ⚲ tool. Click on the four nodes one by one and note in the Status Line that beginning at 3 o'clock you have been blessed with a symmetrical node, another symmetrical, a cusp and... what? Earlier versions of Draw indicated the nature of the first node in the Status Line, but currently 3.0 does not. Unlike closed objects created with the ℓ tool, those you construct with the ℓ tool always follow a predictable sequence. You won't find this in the Draw documentation, but when creating closed objects the first node is always smooth, followed by symmetrical nodes. The exception is the last node, which is always cusp. Thus, you may find it easier to construct a perfect circle from the four segments if you convert its smooth and cusp nodes to symmetrical with the ⚲ tool and the Node Edit menu.

When drawing open paths composed of curves, on the other hand, the first and last nodes are both cusp (as in Freehand mode), with all other nodes symmetrical. To verify this, double-click on a ruler and in the Grid Setup dialog box set both the Horizontal and Vertical Grid Frequency to 4 per inch, click on Show Grid and Snap To Grid, and then OK. Zoom in until you can actually see a grid mark for every quarter of an inch on your ruler.

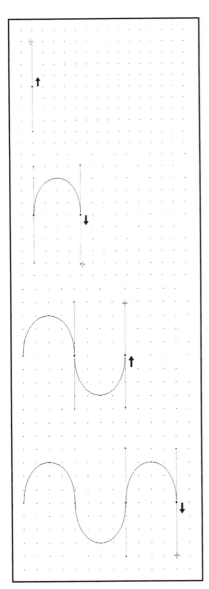

You should still be in $\wp$ drawing mode. Hold down the Control key, move your cursor near a grid point, then click and drag upwards one inch (four grid points). The Control key ensures that you drag the control point handle straight upwards. Unfortunately, Draw won't snap control handles to grid points while you drag them when creating a curve, but you *will* be able to snap the handles later with the $\wedge$ tool. Now click and drag downwards, starting at a grid point one inch to the right of the first node you placed at the beginning of the curve. Again, press the Control key as you drag down one inch. Continue this as many times as you like, alternating between a click and drag down, then up. You can end a drawing and begin another by switching to the $\uparrow$ tool and back — a quick way is to press the Spacebar twice. And if you later want to return to the current drawing tool, whether the $\wp$ or $\wp$ tool, use the F5 function key.

Switch back to the $\wedge$ tool when you're done and click on some of the nodes in your wave. As predicted, you should find the last node is cusp, the nodes in between are symmetrical and the first node is cusp, although the Status Line doesn't indicate this. As you can see, Draw creates symmetrical nodes by default when you use the $\wp$ tool to draw curves. While you can always change these nodes after the fact with the $\wedge$ tool, it would be much easier to define the type of node while you go.

While it's not currently documented, in fact there *is* a way to define node types while drawing. Move to a fresh section of the page and begin drawing as you did in the previous exercise, clicking and dragging first up and then down to create a single arc. Here comes the tricky part. Double-click on the second node you drew. Now click four grid points to the right and drag *down* again. You can see while you drag that what you're creating is a curve connected to a cusp node, since it sharply changes direction. This then is the trick. However, all is not what it should be — the second curve doesn't match the first.

Creating and Editing Outlines

So here's a variation that provides more control over the curve you're about to create. Create a wave as before, but this time *double-click* on the second node and drag the control handle up one inch, keeping the Control key down as always. Then click one inch to the right and drag down. By dragging after a double-click, you determine the angle and velocity of the subsequent curve. You can also use the same technique while you draw to create a smooth node. In this case use a single click on the end node, or click and drag, before clicking and dragging elsewhere.

If you'd like to get rid of a segment you just created don't use the Delete command, or you'll vaporize the entire curve object. Instead use Undo (shortcut: Alt-Backspace), then click, or double-click, on the last node of the curve object. Then proceed as before, clicking and dragging to place nodes and create segments.

You've now had a taste of the power of Bézier mode, but you should put it to a more rigorous test. For a good workout, follow the steps in the *Tracing a Bitmap* section of the *Working with Bitmap Graphics* chapter. Import the bitmap image discussed there and begin drawing segments with the ⌀ tool, using the bitmap as a guide. This will help you practice placing nodes and dragging out curves. Don't expect proficiency to come immediately. It

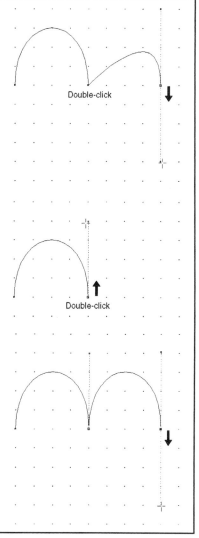

takes weeks and months to be able to quickly and accurately place curves.

Before going on, it would be worthwhile to spend some time practicing your drawing skills with the ⌀ and ⌀ tools, then editing the resulting segments with the ⅄ tool. You'll build on these techniques in the next chapter. In any case, congratulations are in order for simply completing this demanding tutorial. Well done!

Working with Clip Art and Symbols

orelDRAW is supplied with a sizable collection of ready-made, or *clip art*, images. These represent a sampling from a variety of electronic clip art vendors who have provided images in categories ranging from office or sports themes to specialized architectural, technical or medical graphics.

Clip art images are typically available in many graphics formats, such as .PCX, .PIC, .TIF, .EPS, .CGM or Draw's own .CDR. Earlier versions of Draw included clip art in a variety of these formats, while version 2.0 made the switch to supplying it in compressed libraries containing only images in .CDR format. This was an improvement, but the necessity of using the included CorelMOSAIC utility for extracting files from the libraries made for an inelegant solution. Thankfully, Draw's clip art is now all in uncompressed .CDR format. The advantage of this approach is that .CDR files can be quickly previewed and then either opened or imported, the latter approach allowing you to combine multiple Draw files on a page. This is often how you'll construct an illustration, by importing a number of images, tearing them apart to use just a few elements, modifying them and combining them.

The clip art reference book included with the Draw documentation displays all the available images, but only those that are reproduced in color are on the floppy disks — the rest of the more than 10,000 images are on the CD-ROM disk supplied with Draw. If you performed the default Draw installation, a DRAW\CLIPART subdirectory was created. This in turn has 20 subdirectories holding about 2 megabytes of .CDR files divided into such as categories as sports, money and food. If you performed a custom install and these clip art directories weren't created, you can always rerun Draw's Setup program.

Using building blocks to create illustrations

See *Customizing Draw's Defaults* for details. Conversely, if you aren't much of a clip art user, you may want to free up some disk space by deleting them.

Using Mosaic

While you no longer need Mosaic to access the clip art supplied with Draw, you'll find it can make this easier in a number of ways. Mosaic also provides some often-overlooked abilities for working with both clip art and your own files that I think you'll find useful, such as batch and thumbnail printing, file compression and keyword searching. You'll explore these and other Mosaic features in this chapter. I'm assuming you have access to Draw's clip art, either on your hard disk or CD-ROM. If not, you can still work with the .CDR files in the DRAW\SAMPLES directory.

MOSAIC

While Mosaic can be run from the Import and Open dialog boxes from within Draw, many of its most useful features are only available when it you run it from the Windows Program Manager. So if Draw is running, close it now and return to Program Manager. Double-click on the Mosaic icon in the Corel Graphics group to run it, then double-click on its title bar at the top of its window to zoom it, so it fills the screen. This simply ensures you won't accidentally send the Mosaic window behind Program Manager. (If that happens, redisplay it with Alt-Tab.)

Choose Open Directory from the File menu and move to the DRAW\CLIPART\BIRDS directory, but don't click on the OK button yet. (If you're having trouble with such Windows operations as switching directories, take a look at *Windows Survival Skills*, or the manual that accompanies Windows itself.) If you haven't installed the clip art, move instead to the DRAW\SAMPLES directory. Click on the Options button. If you click once on any file in the BIRDS directory, you'll see it's been given a number of *keywords*. These can be useful when searching for files that

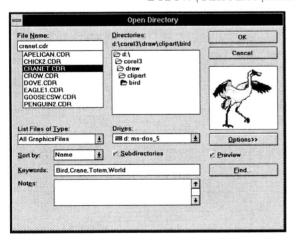

match certain criteria. You can change these, as well as add these or new ones to your own files. Among the keywords given to the Draw images is always the name of the clip art vendor, such as Artright or Totem, as well as the category, in this case Birds.

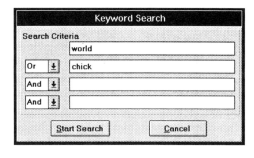

You'll typically know what clip art file you're looking for by first consulting the pictorial paperback reference supplied with Draw. So the keywords assigned to Draw's clip art aren't that useful, except for the purposes of experimenting with them here and getting a sense of how you might use them to organize your own images. For example, click on the Find button. This dialog box allows you to define multiple keyword search criteria using and/or logic. Type 'world' in the top text entry box (it's not case sensitive), then click and type 'chick' in the one below. Click on And and change it to Or, then click on Start Search.

Mosaic now displays thumbnails of the images in the current directory that match your search criteria: that is, all files that have the keywords 'world' or 'chick.' The idea is that you assign keywords to files when there are a lot of them in a directory. Then when you access them with Mosaic, only the files you're looking for are displayed. This saves you from wading through dozens or hundreds of files. If you had entered 'world' And 'chick', for example, no files would have been displayed. Or with just 'world', then four files would be displayed, since none meets this search criteria. Verify this, if you like, by choosing Open Directory from the File menu and going through the procedure again.

Click once on any of the thumbnails to select it. Then choose Keywords from the Edit menu. This dialog box lets you add or delete keywords from the currently selected file. Type in a new keyword, then click on Add and Done. You can also change the keywords

---

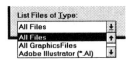

for more than one file at a time. Hold down the Control key and click on two or three thumbnails to select them. You can also select multiple thumbnails by selecting one, holding down the Shift key and clicking on a second. In this case, all the thumbnails lying *between* the two clicks will be selected. Finally, you can select all the files in a directory by choosing Select All from the Edit menu. You can deselect a thumbnail simply by clicking on it or choosing Clear All from the Edit menu.

On occasion, you'll want to add or delete keywords associated with a number of files. Select a few thumbnails and choose Keywords from the Edit menu. Note that now you can use the Next and Previous buttons to examine and work with the keywords of all the currently selected thumbnails. Click on the Update All Selected Files box. If you now enter a new keyword and click on Add, all the currently selected thumbnails will be given this new keyword. Give it a try, then check to see if it worked by using the Next button, before clicking on Done. Choose Clear All from the Edit menu to deselect all the thumbnails. Now choose Select By Keyword from the Edit menu and enter your new keyword to select just the thumbnails to which you assigned it.

You've seen that Mosaic provides flexible control over both the display and selection of the thumbnails in a directory, using such criteria as creator, client or project name. But so what? Well, now that you've selected one or more of the files that interest you, the fun can begin. For example, Draw itself provides no ability to delete files. But if you select one or more files and press the Delete key, you can quickly zap them. This

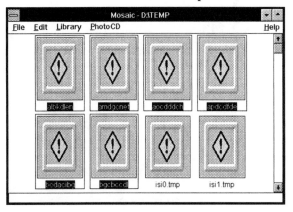

also holds true for non-Draw files. If you chose Open Directory from the File menu and at the bottom of the dialog box changed the List Files Of Type to All Files, you could display and delete any file you liked. Mosaic will prompt you before deleting each selected file; choose Preferences from the File menu to disable this, if you're the confident type.

In the illustration, I've selected a bunch of annoying temp files created by my printer, prior to blowing them off my hard disk. The exclamation marks just indicate that Mosaic, naturally enough, can't display a thumbnail of the files. Unfortunately, file deletion is one the functions that's only available when you run Mosaic from its Program Manager icon. But when the time comes to delete a lot of

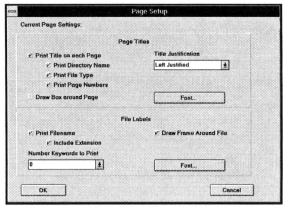

images, I find it's nice to be able to actually see them in thumbnail form in Mosaic, rather than flying blind in the Windows File Manager.

One function of Mosaic I've found very handy is the ability to print out selected thumbnails. This provides a quick way to create compact hard copy of all the files in a particular project, without the tedium of loading them into Draw and printing them out full size. For example, I supplied both the tutorial tester and the designer of this book with copies of the thumbnails to work from. Be warned, though, that the temporary file created on your hard disk during thumbnail printing can be mammoth, and print times can be lengthy.

Before creating some of your own thumbnails, choose Page Setup from the File menu and configure the look of your output as desired. Then select some thumbnails and choose Print Selected Thumbnails from the File menu. If no thumbnails are selected (for example, by choosing Clear All from the Edit menu), the command would instead be Print Thumbnails. Thumbnail away! Since you can display thumbnails of any of the graphics formats Draw supports, you could also use this feature to print thumbnails of scanned images in .TIF or .PCX format, or images created with CorelCHART. Fun stuff.

While I'm a big thumbnail fan, you can also print multiple files full size. Simply select one or more and choose Print Selected Files. If you've chosen .CDR files, they'll be opened in Draw and printed one at a time. If they're in another format, such as .BMP or .TIF, they'll be *imported* into Draw and printed.

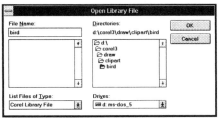

It's worth keeping in mind that you can also batch import files into Draw with Mosaic. This can prove very useful if you're constructing an illustration composed of several existing images. Select two or more files and choose Import Into Draw from the Edit menu. They'll be placed on top of each other on the page, ready to be moved, resized and ungrouped. Then return to Mosaic by holding down the Alt key and tapping Tab until its title bar is displayed.

Going to the Library

If hard disk space is tight, you might be a candidate for using Mosaic's ability to compress Draw files into *libraries*. By placing Draw files in libraries, you can typically reduce the file size by about a third. For example, choose Select All from Mosaic's Edit menu. Then choose Add Images To Library from the Library menu. Since you're not adding the images to an existing library, type in the name of a new library — I called mine 'birds'. When you click on OK, Mosaic will ask you if it should create a new library file. Of course!

The result will be the creation of a library composed of the BIRD.CLB and BIRD.CLH files. I compressed all the bird files, which originally took up about 91 Kb of space, and wound up with a library of about 69 Kb. Once you've compressed your files, you should open a file from the library to ensure the compression process worked before deleting the original .CDR files. Library files can only be accessed from Mosaic, which can be run in this case either from Program Manager or from Draw's Open and Import dialog boxes. Are libraries worth the effort? For me, the modest space saving isn't enough to bother with — but then I have 350 Mb of storage. However, if you're archiving large numbers of files, or you simply can't fit a single large .CDR file on a floppy, then libraries have their place.

As with all Windows applications, Mosaic has its own .INI (INItialization) file that contains a variety of default settings. You can run File Manager and double-click on CORELMOS.INI, in the DRAW directory, to open it in Notepad. Of the various settings, I'd suggest changing the screen size values. In the [Window] section you can change the W= and H= values to match the horizontal and vertical resolution of your display. For example, on my system I changed these to 1028 and 768, respectively. This ensures that Mosaic always runs full screen.

```
─  Notepad - CORELMOS.INI   ▼  ▲
 File   Edit   Search   Help
 [Window]                        ↑
 X=0
 Y=0
 W=1024
 H=768
 DisplayAhead=0
 ConfirmDeletes=1
 3DLook=0
 GraphicsDisplay=1              ↓
 ←                              →
```

The Clip Art Thing

In the rest of this chapter you'll be working with two clip art images that I've provided on the Utility disk included with the book. Since both of them need to be on the page at the same time, you'll import first one, then the other, directly into Draw. Close Mosaic and run Draw. Then choose Import from the File menu and click on the Mosaic button. In the Mosaic window, choose Open Directory from the File menu, set List Files Of Type to .CDR, switch to the SAMPLES directory on your floppy drive (make sure the Utility disk is inserted first) and click on OK. You should see thumbnails of several images. Double-click on FUSION.CDR to import it.

Save that File

The title bar at the top of the screen says UNTITLED.CDR, since you have yet to save the publication into which you imported the two files. If (perish the thought) your computer crashes, you would lose all your work, so before going further choose Save from the File menu. Mouse to the drive and directory in which you want to save your current publication (perhaps \DRAW\SAMPLES), type in a name using up to eight characters (Draw will add the .CDR extension) and click on Save.

You may have noticed that Draw pauses to make a temporary backup file, with an .ABK extension, every 10 minutes. It deletes these automatically when you close Draw, but if your system crashes you can at least open the most recently saved .ABK version of your file. This is great for those who forget to save their files, but it has the disadvantage of bringing work to a halt every few minutes while the save takes place.

Draw also creates .BAK versions of your file every time you save. This can be useful if you want to return to an earlier

---

version of your work, but it clutters up your hard drive with old files. I believe it's better to simply get in the habit of saving on a regular basis, especially after performing an operation that you wouldn't want to be forced to redo. It's a good idea to save periodically and avoid the sinking sensation brought on by lost work. The keyboard shortcut for saving, Control-S, is surely a mantra for the 1990s.

Both timed backups and the creation of .BAK files can be disabled by editing Draw's CORELDRW.INI file. For more on these and other defaults, consult *Customizing Draw's Defaults*.

Clip Art Groups

Clip art images are made up of many individual objects, but when opened or imported these are initially grouped together. Your imported Fusion drawing is currently selected, for example, and the Status Line indicates that it's a group. You should be in the default preview window, which means the image's fill and outline attributes are displayed. If not, press Shift-F9 to switch to preview mode.

The text object in this group needs to be deleted, so the first step is to choose Ungroup from the Arrange menu. The Status Line changes, indicating that you've now separated the object into 25 objects, all of which are currently selected. Click anywhere on a blank part of the page to deselect the objects and then click just on the text at the bottom of the fusion reactor. Then zap it with the Delete key.

You're now in a very vulnerable position. With the drawing ungrouped, you are free to select and modify its component objects, either on purpose or by accident. Click carefully on some of the objects and note their fills and outlines in the Status Line. To be on the safe side, select all the objects in the reactor by choosing Select All from the Edit menu or by dragging a marquee around all the objects. Then choose Group from the Arrange menu.

The reactor's a bit on the large side, so scale it to roughly 60 percent of its size, using either a corner handle or the Stretch & Mirror dialog box of the Transform menu. Click on it to go into Rotate/Skew mode and rotate it clockwise to about -55°. Choose

Working with Clip Art and Symbols

Undo from the Edit menu if you make a mistake while sizing or rotating. After rotating, press the Spacebar to select the reactor, then click and drag it down into the lower half of the page.

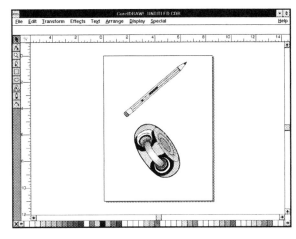

Time to import the second clip art image you'll work with in this chapter, PENCIL.CDR. Use Mosaic to import it from the Utility disk, as you did the reactor. Because you were importing rather than opening these files, you combined them on the page, instead of having just one or the other open at a time. Now rotate the pencil, keeping in mind that it has to ultimately fit through the hole in the reactor.

To create an image of a reactor impaled on a pencil you'll need two copies of the pencil, which you could create in a number of ways. The most obvious (but slowest) is to simply import another copy of the pencil. A faster approach is to select the pencil and choose Copy from the Edit menu. This makes a copy of the selected object and places it in the Clipboard, an area of memory in which Windows stores the result of the most recent copy (or cut). You could then choose Paste from the Edit menu to put a copy of the pencil on the page — it would be dumped right on top of the original. Make a copy this way and drag it off the page for safekeeping; you may need it later.

A drawback to this approach is that due to limitations in Windows itself, you can run into problems using the Clipboard to copy complex objects. You've seen earlier that a quick way to make a copy that doesn't rely on the Clipboard is simply to tap the right mouse button while moving the object, and it's the technique I recommend.

But yet another way to make copies of objects is to select them and choose Duplicate from the Edit menu, which also bypasses the Clipboard. You'll often be duplicating objects, so the Control-D keyboard shortcut is worth trying out now and committing to memory. Duplicates are currently showing up at a default offset of .25 inch

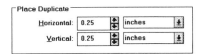

---

from the original object. To control where duplicates are placed, choose Preferences from the Special menu and specify positive or negative horizontal and vertical Place Duplicate values up to 2 inches. Click on OK and then press Control-D to make a duplicate of the selected pencil. You'll find Duplicate handy for quickly placing a number of similar objects a defined distance apart on the page.

Rearranging Objects

Now drag one of the pencils on top of the hole of the reactor's core, as shown in the illustration. Draw lets you stack objects on top of one another and provides a quick way to change the stacking order. With the pencil still selected, choose To Back from the Arrange menu. Since the reactor is composed of objects filled with solid shades, it's covering the middle of the pencil. But you also want to hide the point of the pencil.

Select the Rectangle □ tool from the toolbox, and draw a rectangle on top of the right half of the pencil, covering part of the reactor in the process. With the box still selected, choose the Fill ⬧ tool and click on white in the flyout menu. Then choose the Outline ⬧ tool and choose ✕ from the flyout menu, to give the rectangle no outline. To achieve the desired stacking order for the rectangle, select both the rectangle and reactor, then choose Reverse Order from the Arrange menu.

At this point the white rectangle will disappear. Choose Edit Wireframe from the Display menu. This view displays the outlines of all your objects, devoid of fill or line attributes. It's often easier editing objects in wireframe view than in the Preview Window, since there's less visual clutter and all objects are accessible, even if they're below other objects or have a white or no fill. I'll leave it you which view to work in as the chapter progresses — press Shift-F9 to quickly switch between the two views.

You now have a pencil on the bottom, a white rectangle on top of part of it and the reactor on top. Creating white boxes with no outline is a quick way to mask out parts of your drawing. The masked part underneath is still there, however, and will add to the size of your file and the time it takes to redraw and print, so use white boxes with discretion.

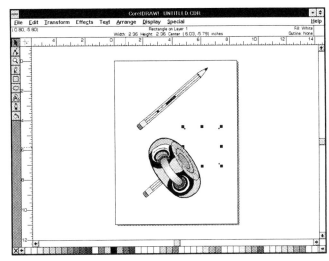

To create the effect of the tip of the pencil emerging from the reactor will take a fair amount of effort. It will involve grouping and ungrouping objects, working with line segments and converting a circle to an arc. This is typical of the actions you'll have to perform when modifying clip art images. Let me say right up front that this is picky work; I encourage you to follow my directions very closely the first time through this section. Make copies of your pencil as you go, so if things go wrong you won't have to start from scratch. If you've skipped the previous chapter, you may lack many of the fundamental object editing skills you'll need to complete this section. If you find you're struggling, you should work your way through Chapter 4, *Creating and Editing Outlines*, then return here for another try.

Groups of Groups

Select one of the copies of the pencil with the Pick ▶ tool. The Status Line indicates that it's currently a group composed of nine objects. Rather than leave the constituent parts of your images as separate entities, it's wise to group related objects so they can be easily moved and transformed en masse. You can also group groups, and ungroup them as desired.

Before you can manipulate the individual bits and pieces of the pencil, you first have to ungroup them. Choose Ungroup from the Arrange menu. The Status Line indicates that you now have nine objects selected. Click anywhere off the pencil to deselect all its objects. You won't need the pencil's eraser. Zoom in on the eraser end of the pencil and click and drag around the rectangle and lines representing the pencil's metal band, to select and then delete them. Then select and delete the text on the pencil.

You need a shorter version of the pencil to fit into the hole of the reactor. Before you go any further, select all of the pencil's objects by clicking and dragging around them, set the Place Duplicate values in the Preferences dialog box to 2 inches (to place the duplicate a safe distance from the original) and then duplicate them. Scale this duplicate by dragging a side handle and note that this is obviously not a viable approach, since it distorts the pencil as it shortens it. The use of a corner handle imposes different, but equally undesirable, distortions.

Delete the mess you just made of the duplicate pencil and make another duplicate. It's a good idea to make duplicates of objects and perform experiments on them, leaving an original for safekeeping. The area surrounding your page won't print and is an ideal place to hold parts of your drawing in various stages of development. The contents of this area are saved along with the page.

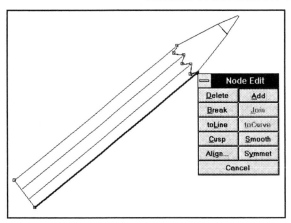

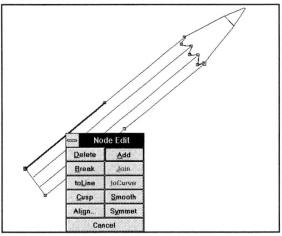

Editing the Pencil

You're going to edit the pencil not only to shorten it while maintaining its proportions, but create a rounded end that matches the curve of the hole in the reactor from which the pencil emerges. Choose the Shape ⚲ tool, which lets you modify the line and curve segments that constitute objects. Note that you now hear a warning beep if you click on the reactor and its pencil, since they're grouped objects and thus can't be edited with the ⚲ tool — you'd have to ungroup them first.

Zoom in until the pencil you're working with fills the screen. As you click on different line segments or nodes, the Status Line indicates the attributes of what you're selecting. You need to add a node in the middle of the four long lines running the length of the pencil. Start with the middle two lines, clicking once on each in turn to identify their nodes, then double-clicking on either end node and choosing Add from the Node Edit menu. Then click on the long line that makes up the lower edge of the shaft of the pencil. Remembering that each segment in an object has an associated primary node (displayed as bold when you click on a segment of the currently selected curve object), click once more on the long line to reveal its node. Then double-click on the line's node at its top-right end and add a new node. Finally, double-click on the lower-left node of the top line and add another new node. You should have new nodes in the mid-points of each of the four long lines.

Before deleting excess segments to shorten the pencil shaft, check to make sure that the remaining shaft segments are defined as straight lines, and not curves, by double-clicking on them. If toLine is ghosted in the Node Edit menu, the segment is a line. Click on toLine to convert curve segments to lines where necessary. Failing to do this could produce unwanted results when deleting connected segments, since Draw will attempt to maintain the integrity of the curve. Now double-click and choose Delete from the Node Edit menu for first the upper-left end segment, as shown in the illustration, and then the now elongated and angled end segment. Then delete the two inside end segments. Make a copy of this version of the pencil for safekeeping.

You've got a shorter pencil — but what if you want to shorten it just a bit more? When working with the ⚲ tool, you've seen that one or more nodes belonging to a curve object can be repositioned at a time. Click on an outer segment of the pencil shaft, and click and drag a marquee around the two end nodes at the bottom of the shaft. The Status Line should indicate two nodes are selected. Note that you won't be able to also select the two bottom nodes of the inner pencil shaft segments this way, because they currently belong to separate paths. To select all these nodes at the same time, you'll soon *combine* all three paths. Then you'll be able to select and resize all the straight line segments of the pencil simultaneously.

Choose the ⬆ tool, select one of the inner shaft segments, make a duplicate of it and drag it below the pencil. You'll use this for reference when you resize the pencil shaft. Now hold the Shift key down and click on the two inner lines, then on one of the outer lines of the pencil shaft. The Status Line should indicate that three objects are selected. Choose Combine from the Arrange menu to combine the three selected paths and then return to the tool. Since you'll be constantly moving between tools, try to get in the habit of toggling between the tool and the most recently used tool with the Spacebar on your keyboard.

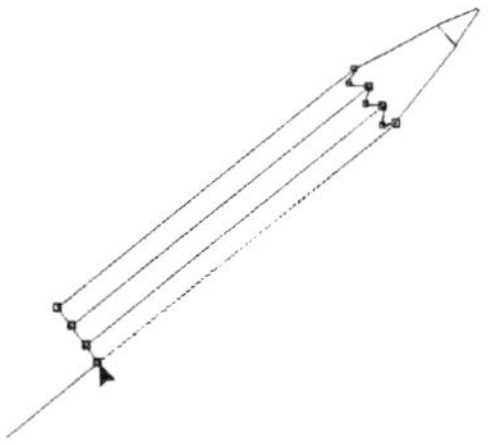

You should find that the nodes on both the inner and outer lines are displayed. They're now part of the same path, and the Status Line indicates that this object is now composed of three combined subpaths. Select the single reference line with the tool and drag it on top of the lower pencil shaft line. Select the pencil shaft with the tool and click and drag around all four end nodes of the shaft, both inner and outer. Then drag any of the selected nodes to shorten the handle a bit, using the reference line to keep it at its original angle. Before you go on, delete the reference line with the tool and make a copy of this version of the pencil. Now's also a good time to save your file by choosing Save from the File menu.

Creating Arcs

You've created a nice neat pencil, but one problem remains — the bottom end of the pencil is straight, while the hole it must project through is slightly curved. There are two ways to create a curve that matches the hole on the end of the pencil. Select the reactor with the tool and ungroup it. Then deselect it by clicking on a blank part of the page. Now select just the elliptical middle hole, duplicate it and drag the copy over to the base of the pencil you've been editing.

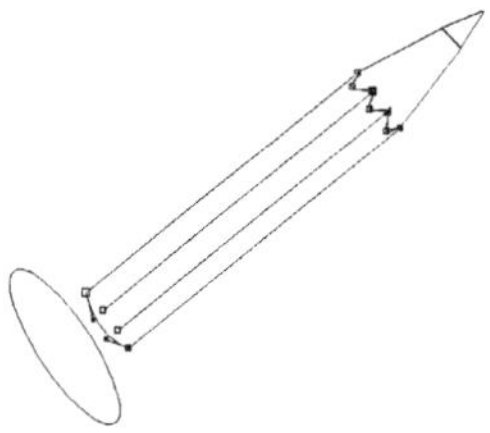

Choose the tool, double-click on the short straight line segment at the base of the pencil and choose toCurve. Drag the curve's control points to match the curvature of the hole, zooming in as necessary. You may find it easier to match the curve by dragging the copy of the hole right on top of the end of the pencil while adjusting it. In that case, the bottom nodes of the shaft may also have to be dragged slightly to meet the hole.

Hold the Shift key down and click on the lower end nodes of the two interior handle segments. Drag them to meet the new rounded pencil end. Drag the end corner nodes of the pencil as necessary.

Now that you've tried the eyeball approach, let me suggest a more precise — but slower — way to incorporate the curve of the hole directly into the end of the pencil. Select the copy of the hole with the ↳ tool and feast your eyes on the particulars in the Status Line. You're told that this ellipse is *distorted*; its creator declined to hold down the Control key when drawing it, thereby creating an ellipse rather than a perfect circle.

Drag the ellipse off the pencil with the ↰ tool and zoom in to get a detailed view of the end of the pencil and the curve segment. Double-click on the top-left node at the end of the pencil shaft with the ↳ tool and choose Break from the Node Edit menu. Do the same for the bottom-left node. Then double-click and delete the curve segment on the end of the shaft you so carefully created a few minutes ago.

Draw provides no tool for creating arcs. Instead, you draw a circle or ellipse and modify it with the ↳ tool. You can use this ability to create an arc from the ellipse representing the hole through the reactor. First, make a copy of the ellipse for safekeeping. Then select and position it over the end of the pencil.

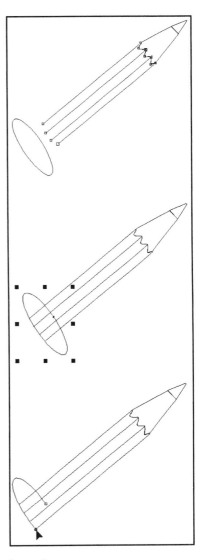

Select the ellipse with the ↳ tool and click on its single node. Now drag the node clockwise until it meets the pencil end, keeping your cursor outside the arc. If you accidentally move it inside while you drag the node, a pie shape would result — something you'll make use of in a later chapter. Then drag the other node counter-clockwise to meet the other pencil end line.

Enable Snap To Objects from the Display menu and try dragging the arc's nodes again. You'll find if you keep your cursor on the arc's path while you drag that it snaps to 90°, 180°, and so on, as well as to the nodes on the end of the line. If you move

---

your cursor off the path, however, Snap To Objects is ignored. Disable Snap To Objects when you've finished experimenting with it.

The curved end is in position, but it must be joined to the pencil lines to create a closed path that can be filled. To join line endings, the paths of the curves in question must first be combined. Click on the curve with the ↖ tool and note that its selection box is the same size as it was before you modified it. Now hold down the Shift key and select both the curve and the shaft of the pencil shaft, then choose Combine from the Arrange menu. Bounce back to the ↗ tool, select the curve and click and drag around the two nodes on the lower end of the pencil and the curve to select them. Then double-click on either one and choose Join from the Node Edit menu. Do the same for the top two nodes.

You may have noticed that a new node showed up all by itself when you combined the curve and the pencil lines. So where did it come from? You saw in the last chapter that Draw renders circles and ellipses as four connected arcs. When an arc is combined with another object, any nodes that were originally on the current section of the arc will appear. You can verify this by selecting a copy of your hole ellipse with the ↖ tool and choosing Convert To Curves from the Arrange menu.

Copying Object Attributes

By breaking open the shaft of the pencil and later closing it, it may have been given Draw's default outline and fill values. If that's the case, rather than guess at the nature of these values, you can quickly copy them from another pencil. Select the shaft of your edited pencil and choose Copy Style From from the Edit menu. In the Copy Style dialog box, click on Outline Pen, Outline Color and Fill. Your cursor will change to a From arrow. Click on the fill of the original pencil shaft to copy its fill and outline to your edited pencil. Of course, this will only work if the edited pencil is a closed path.

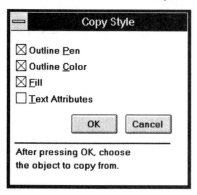

Now that your pencil is finished, drag around it with the ↖ tool and choose Group from the Arrange menu to tie all its objects together. While you're at it, create a single group from the reactor, pencil and rectangle objects. Now drag the edited pencil down and position it in its final resting place. If your nudge value in Preferences is set to a small value, such as 1 point, you could zoom in and bump the pencil exactly into position. Zoom in now and make sure the end of the pencil echoes the curve of the hole. If through some cruel twist of fate it doesn't match, you can ungroup the pencil and adjust its nodes and curve angles.

That's it. You've just performed a typical clip art session by importing several images, ungrouping, editing and then regrouping them. Save this file if you like before continuing.

Using Symbols

In this chapter you've been working with clip art files, which are typically complex graphics that can be filled with a variety of colors. Simpler in construction, but no less useful, are the approximately 3,000 symbols that are supplied with Draw. Like the clip art supplied with Draw, they're divided into libraries in such categories as buildings, bullets and transportation. But they differ from clip art in that they are less complex and can be given only one fill.

I like to think of symbols as building blocks. Rather than reinvent (or more accurately, redraw) the wheel, I often just pop a symbol onto the page that contains objects similar to what I'm trying to create, then delete what I don't want and manipulate the rest with the ▶ and ⚲ tools. I'm going to lead you through several examples of the use of symbols.

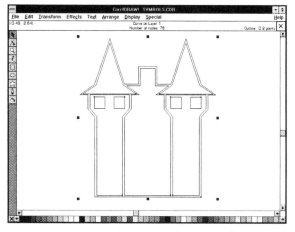

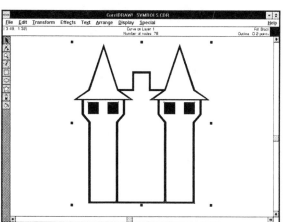

While you can find and select symbols from the dialog box, it's faster to use the clip art book supplied with Draw. Though it's not required, I recommend you keep it at hand while completing this chapter. Turn to the back of the book now and locate the Buildings section of the Symbols section. You'll begin by placing some building symbols on the page, modify them and then use them to construct a new building. This should be fun, and the actions you'll take will be typical of those you'd use to work effectively with symbols on your own projects.

Begin with a clean page, choose the 𝔸 tool and Shift-click on the page. In the Symbols dialog box choose the Buildings library. Start by entering 84 in the Symbol # area, set the size to 2 inches and click on OK. Change to the ▶ tool to select the symbol and zoom in until it fills the page. This building is a *compound* symbol, which means that instead of consisting of a simple object outline, as with some symbols, this is a collection of objects that have been bound together, as if you had selected them all and then used the Combine command on the Arrange menu. When objects are combined they lose their unique characteristics and take on just one set of fill and outline attributes. This symbol, for example, has been given the default outline (probably .003 inch) and is filled with your default fill, (probably ✕). Click on any color in the Color Palette at the bottom of the screen to fill the symbol.

Perhaps the result is not what you expected. When Draw fills a compound object that's composed of objects that overlap, as do the 10 that constitute this symbol, it fills from the outside of the object inwards, alternating between applying the colored fill and X (None, or transparent). The largest object is the outline of the entire building. It's the outermost object, so it's filled with the color. Next in are the triangular shapes at the top and the three large shapes at the bottom. Because they're the next objects in, they're transparent. Last are the two square windows. Being the third objects in the sequence, they're filled with color.

The limitation of symbols is that as long as they're combined, you can't select individual objects and fill or transform them. Choose Break Apart from the Arrange menu and the Status Line will change to indicate that you now have 10 objects selected. By breaking the symbol apart, you have given all the objects the current fill, making it rather difficult to select and work with individual objects. So click on the X icon at the far-left side of the Color Palette with the left mouse button to make

all the selected objects transparent, then click on a blank part of the page to deselect everything. You can now select any of the 10 component parts with the ▶ or ⸝ tools, and perform the usual manipulations and transformations.

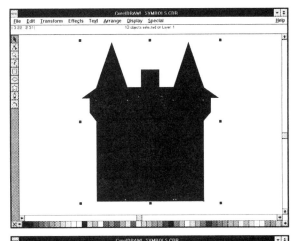

For the building I constructed, I wanted to be able to use just the two tower shapes on either side of the symbol. I'll lead you through the steps required to extract these from the symbol. You can always return to the Symbol dialog box and generate another building symbol if things get out of control.

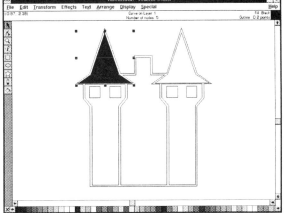

Go slow during this section of the tutorial and make sure you're clear on what I'm asking you to do. Save often and make copies of objects as you go. And don't forget the Undo command on the Edit menu if you make a mistake.

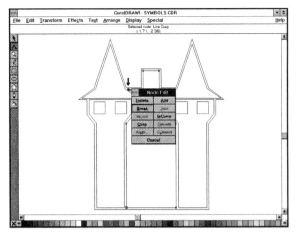

First, you need to construct the outline that will define the outer perimeter of the tower. Double-click on the lower-left node of the middle object (between the two towers) with the 𝄃 tool, and choose Break. Then double-click on the top-left node of the middle object, where it joins the tower (as shown in the illustration), and again click on Break. Now that you've broken this outline at two points, choose Break Apart from the Arrange menu and the Status Line will indicate that you now have two selected objects on your hands (although there's only one set of selection handles displayed). Deselect, then select only the right-hand object of the two you just broke apart and delete it, leaving just an outline around the tower.

Switch back to the 𝄃 tool and select the outline of the large, outer object. Double-click on the node of the outline where it meets the top of the tower and choose Break. At the lower-right side of the tower double-click on the outline itself just below the unconnected outer line of the tower and choose Break. Now choose Break Apart from the Combine menu, deselect, select the right-most of the two objects and delete it. You should wind up with something resembling the illustration. Now it's just a matter of connecting the unconnected end nodes to close the outline of the tower.

Before going on, you might want to delete the leftover objects on the right. And since you've worked so hard to get this far, it wouldn't be a

bad idea to select all the objects in
your new tower and make a copy of
them, just in case. Fastest way: drag
all the selected objects to a new location, tapping the right mouse button
as you go.

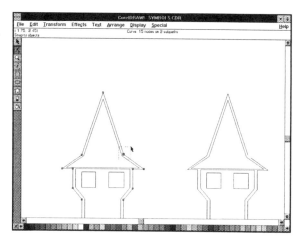

When you use the Join command to
connect two end nodes, they move
to a new position mid-way between
them. So before joining them, it's
often desirable that they be right on
top of each other. To do this, enable
Snap To Objects from the Display menu. Then zoom in on the
top of the tower and with the ⟨ tool drag the lower unconnected node up to snap on the unconnected node above it. Then
zoom in on the bottom of the tower, drag the upper node down
and snap it on the lower node. Switch to the ⟨ tool, select both
of the tower half objects and choose Combine from the Arrange
menu. Now that they've been combined into one object, choose
the ⟨ tool and click and drag a selection marquee around the
two nodes at the lower-right corner of the tower. Then double-
click on either one and choose Join. Do the same thing for the
two unconnected nodes near the top-right of the tower. That's
it — you're done!

Okay, it seems like a lot of work, I admit. I can only promise that
with practice all this bouncing back and forth between the ⟨

and ⟨ tools becomes second nature, and symbol editing proceeds
quite quickly. Now that your tower
is finished, you have two options to
bind together the five objects of
which it's constituted. If you want to
color individual elements, do so now,
then select all five objects and choose
Group from the Arrange menu. Or
you can select them all and use the
Combine command, to duplicate the
color-transparent-color scheme of
the original symbol. It's up to you.

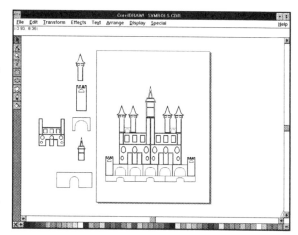

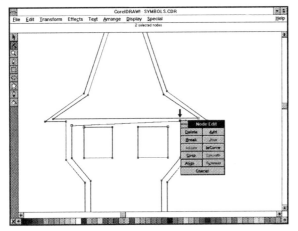

In any domain, doing something once rarely produces mastery. That's why I've recommended you go through all the tutorial sections at least twice. So my suggestion now is to practice your symbol editing skills on a few more buildings, isolating some interesting architectural elements. Symbols 69, 81, 82 and 86 are my personal favorites. And with these bits and pieces in hand, combine them with entire symbols to construct a fanciful edifice of your own devising (i.e., play). I'm sure you won't have much trouble creating something better than the architectural oddity illustrated on these pages.

Remember that the use of the Control key when dragging a node will constrain it to movement in just the horizontal or vertical axes, which you'll find very useful when editing the symbols. Something I haven't yet discussed, however, is the ability of Draw to precisely align two nodes in terms of their horizontal or vertical positions. In much the same way as you can select two or more objects and align them in terms of one another, you can align nodes horizontally or vertically. But there are some slight differences between the two procedures that I should point out.

In the illustration you can see a typical application of this feature, a node that's out of alignment with another. To make use of this, I selected both nodes with the ↗ tool following the same procedure used when aligning objects. That is, the last one I selected with the Shift key was the *control* node, the one I didn't want to move. (For some reason, the documentation currently doesn't mention the significance of which node you select last — which is why you read books like this, right?)

I clicked on Align in the Node Edit menu and then selected just Align Horizontal in the Node Align dialog box. Clicking on both Vertical and Horizontal will make both nodes occupy the same position. This is often a useful precursor to using the Join command

and creates the same result as using Snap To Objects, as shown above. (By the way, make sure you turn off Snap To Objects, on the Display menu, when you've finished using it, as it can produce unexpected results if you forget it's turned on.) I won't discuss the final option of Align Control Points here. It's used primarily for matching the outlines of two adjoining objects, as in the case of a map, but I find it very hard to control. There are easier ways to accomplish this. I'll leave it to you to find two nodes and experiment with aligning them.

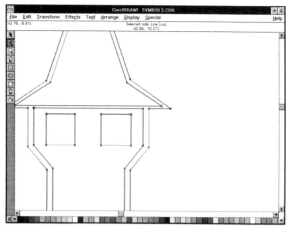

Still feeling playful? Try constructing your own instrument using fragments from symbols in the Music library. I won't lead you through this, since you're already familiar with the required techniques, but I've illustrated my own humble effort for your inspiration. I call it a French tubatrumpetphone.

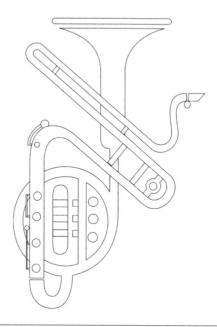

Getting Your Fill of Draw

Up to this point you've been working primarily with object outlines, exploring the many ways of creating and editing the lines and curves that constitute objects. And yet one of the strengths of CorelDRAW is its very flexible approach to object fills. It provides excellent control over not only solid colors, but fountain and pattern fills. And as is so often the case in Draw, if you need to create your own variations on any of these fills, you're free to do so.

Mastering uniform, fountain and pattern fills

While Draw's fill capabilities are comprehensive, a significant number of the more advanced features are either undocumented or simply tricky to implement. I'll follow the approach of previous chapters by leading you through a rigorous exploration of this core topic, and also provide many optional byways for further exploration by the adventurous. You'll begin your introduction to Draw's fill abilities by giving a rectangle a 3D relief effect.

Create a fresh page and drag both a vertical and horizontal guideline onto it. Make sure Snap To Guidelines under the Display menu is enabled and then choose the Rectangle ☐ tool. Zoom in on the intersection of the guidelines. Then click near the intersection and drag while holding down the Control and Shift keys, creating a box an inch square. It should be centered on the intersection of the two guidelines.

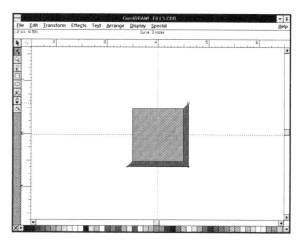

When you created the square it was given the current default fill, shown as an ✕ in the top-right corner of the

Status Line. When you first use Draw this default is a transparent fill, so objects placed behind your square would show through it. This is very different than a fill of solid white, which would cover up any object beneath it.

Select the square with the Pick ↖ tool and click on the Fill ⟨⟩ tool in the toolbox to display the Fill flyout menu. Five shades of gray can be selected from the bottom row of icons, ranging from 10% to 90%. Click on a number of these in turn and note that the Status Line keeps you informed of the current fill. Wind up with a fill of 50% black.

Make an enlarged duplicate of the square by choosing Stretch & Mirror from the Transform menu, entering 120% for both Horizontal and Vertical, selecting Leave Original and clicking on OK. Fill this new square with 70% black. Choose To Back from the Arrange menu to send the large square behind the small one and then zoom in to fill the screen with the two squares. Choose Convert To Curves from the Arrange menu, to convert the larger square into an object that can be edited. Choose the Shape ⟨⟩ tool and select any of the big square's four corner nodes. Then press the Delete key on the keyboard to create a triangle.

With the triangle selected, choose Stretch & Mirror again, click on both the Horz and Vert Mirror buttons, enable Leave Original and click on OK. Give your new triangle a fill of 30% black. Your original square should be on top of the two triangles. If not, select it and choose To Front from the Arrange menu. The effect produced is of a light source striking a square with beveled edges at a 45° angle.

The objects you created were given the default outline, which is originally .003 inch (¼ point). So you could use the Pencil ✏ tool at this point to add short lines to the two corners that currently lack them. If the objects do have an outline, zoom in closely now on the lower-left or top-right corners. Notice the

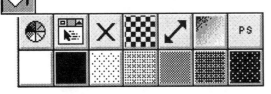

problem with the overlapping outlines. You can solve this by raising the Miter Limit value to 45° in the Preferences dialog box. (More on this in the next chapter, *Controlling Object Out-*

lines.) You could also click and drag around the square and both triangles with the ▶ tool to select them, click on the Outline ⬚ tool and then click on ✕ to give them no outline.

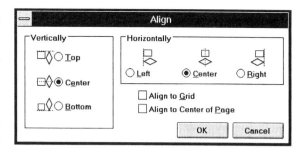

The shades on the sides of the square provide the illusion of a raised object, but you can easily create the opposite effect. Make a copy of your square and triangles (to be collectively called a *button* from now on) by selecting them all and making a duplicate by dragging them off to one side, clicking the right mouse button as you go. Reverse the shades in the two triangles of the new button (change the 70% to 30%, and vice versa), select all three objects and choose Group from the Arrange menu. Then reduce the size of the button about 50%. Now select all three objects belonging to a full-size button and group them. Select first the smaller button and then the full-size one with the Shift key before choosing Align from the Arrange menu. Click on the Center buttons for both Horizontal and Vertical, then click on OK to center align the small button within the big one. When aligning objects, the last one you select is the control object that remains fixed on the page — all others align in terms of it. If the smaller button seems to be under the bigger one, with both buttons still selected choose Reverse Order from the Arrange menu.

Taming Fill Defaults

Before heading off to more exotic fills, a final word on defaults is in order. As indicated above, objects you create are automatically given the default fill. This is a fill of ✕ (none, or transparent) when you first use Draw, but it can be changed at any time — usually inadvertently. To see this in action, click anywhere on a blank part of the page to deselect all objects. Click on the ✑ tool and then click on any of the gray fill icons. A dialog box appears which provides the ability to assign your fill to just text objects, other (non-text) objects, or all objects. What's especially significant is that this default will apply not only to objects in the

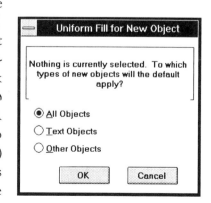

current drawing but those in future ones you create, even between Draw sessions. So click on Cancel to avoid creating a new default fill at this time. If you've inadvertently changed the default fill, you may wish to reset it to black for text objects and none (✗) for other objects. (For more on defaults, see *Customizing Draw's Defaults*.)

A brief pause is appropriate here for some background on the use of color before diving right in. Color is a very complex topic, both from the perspective of how we perceive color itself and how we react to different combinations. This is primarily physiological, but much of it is also psychological and cultural. Couple these factors with the many complex ways of defining the colors themselves and the difficulties in accurately displaying, proofing and reproducing color, and you've got a topic that can take years to master. To design effectively with color and ensure the output of your illustration is faithful to those colors will take much work and study. I'll devote relatively little space in this chapter to color theory, focusing instead on techniques for specifying color in Draw. For a solid grounding in the theory behind color practice, covering such topics as color models, color spaces and separations, you should consult the later chapter devoted to this. In addition, a number of books in the bibliography deal with this topic.

So far you've been filling objects with the shades of gray and colors provided in Draw's default palette. But you can edit existing colors, create new ones, load in new palettes and save modified ones. Draw follows the standard practice of providing two significantly different methods of defining colors: spot and process. Which method you employ when specifying colors depends on the medium in which your illustration will wind up: slides, color printer output or offset press lithography.

Process Color

This is the color specification method used for reproducing images containing many colors, via offset printing. It's based on the principle that virtually any color can be represented by mixing different amounts of three basic colors: cyan (a bright blue), magenta (a reddish color) and yellow. Black is also added to provide finer detail and improved density, resulting in the term *four-color process*.

Draw provides sets of colors, or *palettes*, defined using the process model, and you can modify them or create new ones. When using the spot model, on the other hand, you're limited to a fixed set of colors — only their percentage tint can be modified. That is, you can create a 50% tint of one of the available spot colors. Artwork containing many colors is typically reproduced by the creation of four film negatives, one for each of the process colors. Each of the films uses dots to represent one of the process colors. This is known as a halftone screen.

Draw can output color separations on any PostScript printer, although the separations created on desktop lasers are of a quality suitable only for crude proofing. Instead, a high-resolution PostScript imagesetter must be used to create color separations that can be used for offset printing, since it produces finer, more accurately placed dots than a laser and can output directly to film. The resulting four film negatives are used by an offset printer to create a printing plate for each process color. Thus the use of the spot method would not be appropriate for an image containing more than a few colors if it was going to be separated for offset printing, since a separate piece of film would have to be created for each color, resulting in excessive film and press costs.

The process method should also be used when creating an image that will be exported and later imported into another application for separation. An image you create for later import into PageMaker or QuarkXPress can be output along with the rest of the page on which it resides when creating separations from these applications. Again, the spot method would result in the generation of excessive film.

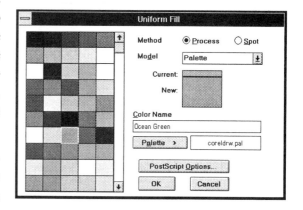

Select any object on the page (or create a new one) and fill it with a color from the Color Palette at the bottom of the screen. Choose the ✍ tool in the toolbox to display the Fill flyout menu. Then click on the ✺ icon to display the Uniform Fill dialog box with the current palette of colors. Since, as with several of Draw's dialog boxes, the Uniform Fill dialog box displays using the settings with which it was last used, I'd like you to make sure that it's set up a particular way before you continue. Make sure the Process button at the top of the dialog box is enabled. If the Model name isn't Palette, click on the current name and choose Palette. Your display should resemble the illustration.

Since literally millions of colors can be created with different percentage combinations of the four process colors, Draw doesn't attempt to provide you with immediate access to all of them. Instead, it groups different combinations of them in palettes, which can be loaded, modified and saved as desired. When you run Draw it loads the default CMYK palette, CORELDRW.PAL. The current palette name is displayed to the right of the Palette button. If you load a different process palette during a session, this will become your default palette for future Draw sessions.

The colors in the current palette are thus rather arbitrary combinations of the process colors, to which Corel has given equally arbitrary names, such as Baby Blue and Murky Green. The color with which you filled the object is currently active; its name is displayed and there's a highlighting box around the color itself in the palette.

If many of the colors are being displayed in a dotted, or *dithered*, form rather than as a solid color, don't blame Draw. The display of colors depends on your monitor and graphics card, and you may well have a combination that provides only 16 pure colors. The good news is that you may be able to upgrade your system with the addition of new *driver* software that can crank out 256 or more pure colors. Such drivers are available from the manufacturer of your graphics card or monitor. If accurate color specification is impor-

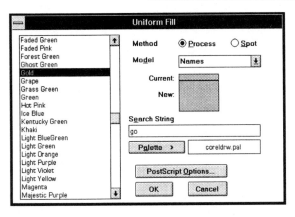

tant in your work, a 256-color or higher display is essential. In fact, many of the newer cards support 32,000 colors, once you install the appropriate driver. Even better is a 24-bit *true color* card that supports a palette of over 16 million colors.

Click on a few other colors to display their names. If you want to choose a color by name, it can be tedious clicking on color after color to find the one you're after. Click on Palette, to the right of Model, to display the menu of available models and then choose Names. A list of the color names in the current palette is displayed, with the currently active color highlighted. Scroll through this list to check out the names. Martian Green? Weird.

The second color on the list, bearing the unwieldy name of 100C100M100Y100K, is an interesting one, since it creates a black composed of 100% of all four process colors. Adding a process color to black enriches it, so this color produces a very juicy black when printed to a color printer or used in a color separation. In fact, it's a little too rich for most printers and presses. More common is to create a color that's 100% black and 40% of one of the other process colors, typically cyan. When creating colors for offset printing, avoid creating colors that use more than 250% total color.

There are many further considerations to keep in mind when creating colors for artwork that will be separated and offset printed. For example, you can virtually eliminate *moiré*, the unsightly patterns sometimes seen in offset printed images, by creating colors that use 100% of one process color and a tint (less than 100%) of just one other. Experiment to see what colors can be created using this technique.

When you're done, click on Names and choose Palette again from the menu. Click on any color and then on OK to fill the currently selected object. The Status Line will indicate your choice. Since the palette colors in the Uniform Fill dialog box are the same as those in the scrollable palette at the bottom of Draw's window, it's often faster to simply select solid colors from the scrollable palette. Only use the dialog box when you need to select a color by name, edit an existing color, create a new one or load a palette. Return to the Uniform Fill dialog

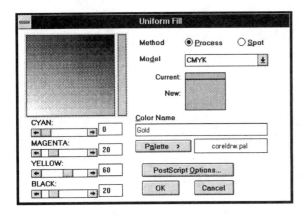

box, using the Shift-F11 keyboard shortcut.

In previous versions you could simply double-click on a color in the palette to edit it, but that ability was dropped from version 3.0 of Draw. It's still not hard to edit an existing color, although you can get bogged down in the many available options. I suggest you edit the color Gold. To save time clicking on color after color, switch to the Names model and click in the Search String area. You'll find that simply typing in the letters 'go' is enough for Draw to locate Gold.

Draw provides three process color models for editing colors or creating new ones: CMYK, RGB and HSB. Begin by choosing CMYK from the Models menu. This dialog box displays the definition of the current color both numerically, in terms of which model you've selected, as well as with a visual selector. For example, the CMYK values of Gold are defined as 0% cyan, 20% magenta, 60% yellow and 20% black. Click on the right scroll arrow of magenta repeatedly and note that as you raise its value the small dot in the square visual selector is moving upwards, providing a visual display of the relationship between cyan and magenta.

Keep clicking on the scroll arrow until magenta hits 40% and you'll find the current CMYK values are now that of Red Brown. In other words, the current palette contains no colors defined with 0% cyan, 60% yellow, 20% black and magenta between 20% and 40%. The color in the New display area represents the current CMYK values, while Current in fact represents the original Gold color.

To get a better sense of the relationship between the CYMK colors, drag the marker (the small dot) in the visual selector up to the top-left corner of the square. The numerical values will change to indicate a cyan value of 0% and a magenta value of 100%. Now drag the marker to the lower-left corner and the values will change to 0% cyan and 0% magenta. The lower-right corner will give you 100% cyan and 0% magenta. This is pretty straightforward, but the top-right corner is a little trickier. The cyan and magenta values displayed when you drag the marker here depend on the position of a second marker on the thin bar to the right, which controls the amount of yellow in the current color.

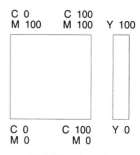

CMYK values in the Visual Selector

What's happening is that as you drag the two markers to change the amounts of cyan, magenta and yellow in your color, Draw automatically calculates the appropriate amount of black. It's using a principle called *gray component replacement* (GCR), which is a response to the problem of successfully offset printing dark colors, due to the large amount of ink required. By adjusting colors numerically, you can bypass the GCR process, if desired.

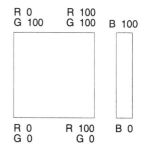

RGB values in the Visual Selector

Experiment further with the creation of new colors, keeping in mind that the thin bar on the right controls the range of colors you can create by changing just the yellow component of your color. When you've created an interesting color, type 'Gold' into the Color Name area, click on the Palette button and then on Add Color To Palette. You'll get a dialog box warning you that your new color will take the place of the existing one. Click on OK.

To me, it seems strange that the Current color name disappears as soon as you begin changing it, forcing you to retype the name when it's time to save your editing changes. It's a small thing, but pesky. So here's my workaround if you want to avoid retyping the name. Go back to Names model and click on a color name to select it, perhaps Avocado Green. Then switch to the CMYK model. Now click and drag over the name in the Color Name area to highlight it *before* you begin changing it and press Control-Insert to copy the name into the Windows Clipboard. When the color is edited, simply press Shift-Insert to paste the name back in.

So far, you've been changing existing colors in the palette. But what if you want to add a new one to what's already there? Follow the same procedure as before, but this time give your color a new name. Choose the Palette model and scroll down to the bottom of the palette to find your new color. Leaving it at the bottom means you'll later have to scroll all the way over to the far right of the Color Palette to choose it. Click on your color now, hold down the mouse button and drag the small black dot up to the very top of the palette. The color you drop it on will be bumped one down. I leave white and the shades of black at the top of my palette, followed by new colors. To remove a color, click on the Palette button and choose Delete Color From Palette.

You've been saving the results of your color edits, but sometimes you simply need a quick, one-time edit. In that case, click on OK after modifying a color and it will be applied to the currently selected object or objects without being added to the palette.

There's much more to be explored in the realm of color definition and specification. When defining colors using the CMYK model, it's a good idea to use one of the many books available that show charts of process colors, either singly or juxtaposed with others, along with their CMYK values (see the bibliography for examples). You can use these books to pick colors and then enter the CMYK values right into the dialog box.

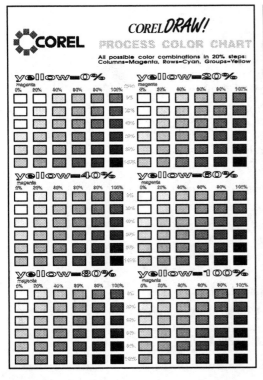

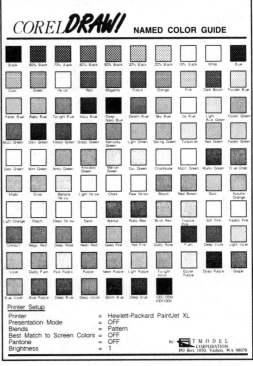

Included in the SAMPLES directory of the Draw program directory is COLORBAR.CDR, which defines combinations of process colors in 20% steps. You'll find a printed version of it on the cardboard quick reference card included with your Draw documentation. Open the file and print it out on your color printer (or send it to your slide service bureau) to create a reference between your screen and output device. Keep in mind that your final printed colors will differ from those on the reference card or in color specification books, due to variations in imagesetter calibration, printing inks and paper. I've included another color reference file, NCG.CDR, on the Utility disk. This file contains all the colors in Draw's default process palette. If you typically use these colors, rather than define your own, this should prove a more useful reference.

While CMYK is the recommended model for working with process colors, there are several alternatives. Change the model now to RGB. When you switch between the available models, the values of the current color are translated automatically. For example, the color which was currently active (New) is still displayed, along with the corresponding percentages of red, green and blue. So even though you may have defined a color using the CMYK model, you can modify just its blue component by switching to the RGB model. The visual selector now provides control over RGB values, with the square representing the amount of red and green in the current color, and the thin bar controlling the blue. Few Draw users create colors from scratch using the RGB model, since it varies from device to device; it's difficult to specify an RGB color and predict how it will print or color separate.

Change models to HSB. Again, your color is still displayed but with percentages in terms of the hue, saturation and brightness model. Colors around the outside of the color wheel are the purest in hue and can be specified in values from 0 to 360. As the marker moves towards the center of the wheel, hues become less saturated. The marker in the thin bar to

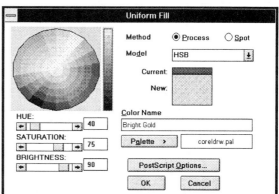

the right of the square controls brightness.

As with RGB, if you create colors with the HSB model you're forced to rely on how they display on your monitor; you won't find books of HSB colors. However, some designers find it a more intuitive model to use than CMYK, and it's handy for creating variations of colors by changing just the brightness value. In the illustration, I've increased the Brightness of Gold to 90 and saved the new color as Bright Gold. Switching to the CMYK model revealed that this had the effect of changing the original Gold values of C0, M20, Y60, K20 to C0, M22, Y67, K10.

As discussed earlier, colors are grouped in palettes. Click on the Palette button and choose Load New Palette. A dialog box will warn you that you haven't yet saved the changes you've made to the default palette. To abandon these changes, click on OK and a dialog box will display the available process palettes in the Draw program directory. Or you could first choose Save Palette, or Save Palette As if you want to retain any changes you've made. Don't worry about screwing up the original palette. The PURE100.PAL palette contains the same colors as CORELDRW.PAL, so you could always load this if necessary and then save it as CORELDRW.PAL.

Begin by loading SMALL.PAL, which contains just a few colors and shades of gray, a good base for the creation of a new palette. DITHERED.PAL contains colors defined in CMYK. Click on some of these and note that the names they've been given denote their process components. However, many of the palettes, such as PURE225A.PAL, are defined using RGB colors, which diminishes their attractiveness for most users. I've included two additional palettes in the PALETTES directory of the Utility disk, which may prove handy. GRAY.PAL contains only shades of gray, which is useful when working in black and white, while SEPIA.PAL contains a broad spectrum of sepia tints.

I'd like you to open TRUMATCH.PAL at this point, one of the lesser-known additions to version 3.0 of Draw. The TRUMATCH palette is the largest supplied with Draw, and contains more than 2,000 colors defined in CMYK. What makes it of particular interest is that it's a *swatching system*

designed with those creating color separations in mind. It takes advantage of the ability of imagesetters to produce process color tints in 1% increments. So the system lets you easily choose a lighter or darker tint of a color, and also ensures that the colors you choose will separate and print as expected. Since you shouldn't trust your monitor, to really make use of this approach to color specification you'll need to purchase the TRUMATCH COLORFINDER swatch book. Then you can simply flip through the book, pick a color and search for its name in the Uniform Fills dialog box to specify it.

If you're creating color separations, I recommend checking out TRUMATCH. (A coupon for a $20 discount on the COLORFINDER was included with your Draw documentation.) Click on OK and you'll find TRUMATCH colors displayed in the Color Palette at the bottom of the screen.

I've included an interesting variation of Draw's TRUMATCH palette on the Utility disk. Created by John Murdoch, this solves some problems you may experience with knockouts and traps when printing black type on a tinted background, especially with .EPS files imported into Ventura Publisher. Read the TRUNEW.TXT file on the disk for details on how to use this palette.

While you have the option of clicking on the Palette button in the Uniform Fill dialog box and choosing Set As Default Palette, I wouldn't bother; the documentation doesn't mention it, but the palette that's currently loaded when you close Draw automatically becomes the default for this and future sessions. You should set the palette back to CORELDRW.PAL before continuing.

Spot Color

Having explored process color, it's time to take a look at spot. Click on the Spot button in the Uniform Fill dialog box. When you run Draw, it loads the default spot palette. This is CORELDRW.IPL, unless you've loaded a different spot palette of your own creation (no others are supplied) into a Draw document in this or an earlier session. This palette contains 796 colors found in an earlier version of the PANTONE Color

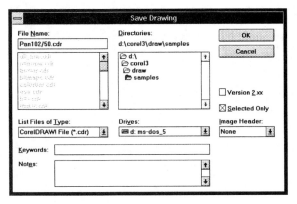

Matching System. As with the TRUMATCH system, to make effective use of these colors you should purchase a PANTONE color swatch book, available from most graphic arts supply stores. You can then pick a color from the swatch book and choose it from the dialog box, using the search function when the PANTONE names are displayed. If you then output your file to a PANTONE-certified color printer, such as a member of the QMS ColorScript series of thermal PostScript color printers, it will be reasonably close to the color in the swatch. And if you're creating spot color separations, you can instruct your offset printer to mix inks to match the PANTONE color number.

Click on any PANTONE color in the palette. One advantage of spot colors is that you can easily change their tint by typing in a percentage or using the scroll arrows. Try this out now. Although the documentation says that you can create a percentage tint of a spot color and save it with the palette, this isn't currently possible. If you have frequent recourse to spot colors with a particular percentage tint, you can resort to an old trick dating from the days before Draw provided editable palettes.

Simply fill an object, such as a rectangle, with the percentage tint and choose Save As from the File menu. Make sure Selected Only is enabled, and you might as well set the Image Header to None, to trim the file size a bit. I use names like PAN10250 to identify a 50% tint of PANTONE 102. You can then import these tinted rectangles and use the Copy Style From command from the Edit menu to quickly transfer their color to other objects.

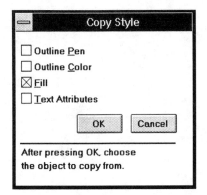

You may wind up saving sets of these colors in .CDR files, then choosing Import from the File menu to bring them into the current publication. You can then move the rectangles off to the side of the page, ungroup them and copy colors from them into objects as needed. The easiest way to do this is to select

Getting Your Fill of Draw

the destination object, choose Copy Style From from the Edit menu, choose Fill and then click on the object to be filled with the From cursor.

Some designers like a hybrid approach, in which they specify a color using the spot method and then convert it to its process equivalent. Click on any PANTONE color in the palette and then click on the Process button. Now type in a name, click on the Palette button and click on Add Color To Palette. (You can't add a color to the TRUMATCH palette.) The new color will be added to the bottom of the palette. If this seems deceptively easy, you shouldn't be lulled into a false sense of security. PANTONE supplies a special swatch book to show the process equivalents of its spot colors; some convert quite closely, others not.

A final attribute of spot colors is that they can be assigned special halftone screens, if you're outputting to a PostScript printer. Click on the PostScript Options button. A variety of screen types, frequencies and angles can be applied to spot color fills, as long as they have a tint less than 100%. These are covered in more detail in *Working with Bitmap Graphics*, but by all means experiment with them now if you have a PostScript printer available. Screens don't display — you'll have to print them to see them.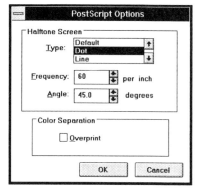

The default dotted PostScript screen is set to a frequency of 60 lines per inch, an appropriate value for 300 dpi laser printers. If you were printing to a higher-resolution PostScript device, however, you could raise this value to take advantage of its resolution. You could also lower it to create a special effect. Values between 10 and 1,000 can be entered for line frequency.

Screen angles can be changed from the default 45° to anything between +360° and -360°. Something to keep in mind here is that if you rotate an object, its screen won't rotate with it. You'll have to change its angle in this dialog box. The default value for all four PostScript Options dialog boxes accessed from the Uniform Fill, Fountain Fill, Outline Color and Two Color Pattern dialog boxes can also be simultaneously changed in the Print dialog box.

Defined screen frequency and angle values will be applied to the default screen type or any of the 10 special halftone screens you select. These special screens provide a broad range of interesting effects. A keyboard shortcut worth mentioning again here is to use the Tab key to move between fields in a dialog box. Choose a screen type and then press the Tab key to highlight the frequency field. You can now type in a new value without having to delete the existing one. The Draw manual reproduces a wide variety of these PostScript screens.

Fountain Fills

So far you've been creating solid fills, but you can also create graduated, or *fountain*, fills. Here you pick a beginning and ending color and Draw creates intermediate colors between the two. Select an object on the page, click on the ✏ tool and then on the ■ icon. You can create fountain fills using either the spot or process method.

There are two types of fountain fill: linear and radial. Begin with the default linear fountain, in which the fill sweeps across the object at the Angle value. Click on the From button and select a color from the palette. Then do the same with the To button. As you click on a variety of beginning and ending colors, the display window provides a preview of the fill. Click on OK to fill your object with the fill you've defined.

How smoothly a fountain fill displays depends on a number of factors. One is the color capability of your display system. If it's

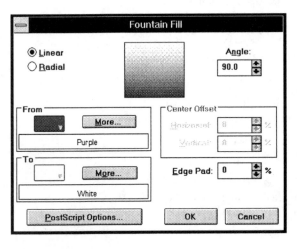

using a palette of 16 colors, for example, Windows will be forced to dither the colors between the beginning and ending colors. This is much less apparent on a display that has a palette of 256 or more colors. You can also control the number of steps, or *stripes*, that make up the in-between colors displayed by changing the default Preview Fountain Stripes value of 20 in the Display subdialog box of Preferences to a value between 2 and 256. Lowering it will speed up the screen display of fountains, while raising it will provide a slower, but more accurate, display on some monitors.

Note that this value affects only the screen display of fountains. To control the number of fountain steps on your output device use the Fountain Stripes value in the Print dialog box. The Screen Frequency setting in the Print dialog box works in tandem with the Fountain Stripes value to determine the ultimate smoothness of fountains. Higher resolution output devices let you raise both values, so you can have not only a finer halftone dot structure but more blend steps. I recommend experimenting by outputting fountains with a variety of these settings. If your file will be output on a high-resolution imagesetter, bump Fountain Stripes all the way up to 250 for the smoothest possible fountains. But there's no point doing this on a low-resolution laser — you won't see any difference, and the print file will be markedly larger.

As a final note, a limitation of fountains is that you can't set the Fountain Stripes value when exporting, only when printing. And there's no way to set the value on an object-by-object basis — it's a global setting. Where more control is needed you're better off using Draw's Blend abilities, which are covered later in this chapter.

Edge Fill: 0%

Edge Fill: 25%

Edge Fill: 45%

With an object selected, return to the Fountain Fill dialog box using the F11 keyboard shortcut. As when working with solid colors, you can choose from spot or process colors, using the current palettes for each. However, you can't mix the two, as you can when blending. To change palettes or edit colors, you must return to the Uniform Fill dialog box covered earlier, by clicking on the More button for either From or To.

Click on the up scroll arrow for Edge Pad and observe the preview box. This determines the relative amount of the beginning and ending colors. Enter a value up to 45% and then return to the page to see how this affects the object. Unfortunately, this value can't be applied to just *one* of the two colors; however, you can make use of an undocumented technique to adjust right on the page how linear fountains fill your object.

First change the Edge Pad value back to 0%. Choose the ℓ tool and draw a very short straight line (the shorter the better) slightly above an object. Then choose the ↗ tool and drag the

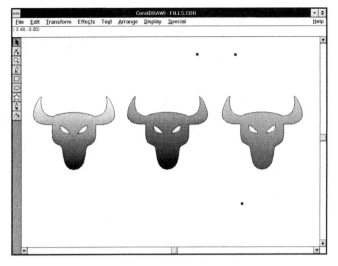

node on one end of the line you drew right on top of the other (you may have to zoom in). Adjust the control handles of the nodes, if necessary, to wind up with two nodes and no visible line. Now select both the two nodes and the object they're next to with the ➤ tool and choose Combine from the Arrange menu. Choose the ⚲ tool and drag a marquee around the two nodes that constitute the short line, to select them.

You can now control the relationship between the two fill colors by dragging the short line to a new location, relative to the filled object. What's happening is that the fountain fill area has expanded to encompass both the object and the short line. While the single line can be used to adjust the amount of one color in a linear fountain fill, the amount of the second color stays fixed. For even more control, draw a second line and combine it with the first object. Now the two sets of nodes can be used to control the amount of each color in the object. The illustration shows the original object, with two variations; the first is using one combined line to reduce the amount of pure white, while the second is using two lines to reduce both the pure white and black.

Return to the Fountain Fills dialog box and change the fill angle. As well as using the scroll arrows or typing in a numerical value, it's fun to click and drag right in the preview window in the dialog box. Hold down the Control key while you do this to snap to the default constrain angle of 15°.

Another interesting, although undocumented, use of linear fills is to employ them to keep track of the rotation of an object. If you rotate an object and later select it, there's no way to determine the degree to which it has been rotated. However, rotate an object that's been given a linear fill and you'll see that the fill rotates with it. What's even more interesting is that if

Getting Your Fill of Draw

you select the rotated object and then return to the Fountain Fill dialog box, the current angle of the fountain fill (and hence the object itself) will be displayed. If you give an object the default fill angle of 90%, for example, and rotate it 10%, the value in the dialog box will be 100% (or as close as Draw's integer math abilities permit). Since a line's fill never prints, you can safely give a linear fountain fill to a line and always be able to ascertain its current degree of rotation.

0°

You might be wondering how to determine the degree of rotation of other objects, such as rectangles and ellipses. This can be useful when you want to rotate something to match the angle of an existing object, but dont know the objects degree of rotation. While this has nothing to do with fills, I'm happy to explain this here, since the Draw documentation doesn't mention this trick.

90°

180°

To try this out, draw a rectangle and rotate it counterclockwise to 30°. Keeping the Control key down will make this easier. Now you need to draw a straight line along the top edge of the box. When you do this, the angle displayed in the Status Line will correspond to the degree of rotation of the box. Enable Snap To Objects from the Display menu. Choose the 𝓁 tool, click on the top-left corner of the box, release the mouse and drag over until the line snaps to the top-right corner. Without clicking, simply check the angle displayed in the Status Line, which should be 30°. Then click and delete the line. You could also check the angle of ellipses by first converting them to curves and snapping to their midpoints. In this case, you'd have to perform some simple math on the angle displayed in the Status Line to figure out the degree of rotation.

270°

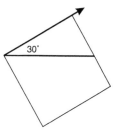

I should mention that I picked up this tip from *Aldus Magazine*, where it was applied to Aldus FreeHand. I simply adapted it for use with Draw. In fact, I've picked up all kinds of stuff in books and magazine articles about other drawing programs, such as FreeHand and Adobe Illustrator, that could be put to use in Draw. So don't limit your reading to Draw-specific publications.

While all this is interesting enough, I don't want to stray too far from the topic of fills. As discussed above, you can assign a variety of PostScript halftone screens to fountain fills using

Type: Dot
Frequency: 20
Angle: 45°

Type: Diamond
Frequency: 10
Angle: 90°

Type: MicroWaves
Frequency: 30
Angle: 180°

spot colors that are a tint (less than 100%) by clicking on the PostScript button. Some of the many possible effects are illustrated here.

Select an object, return to the Fountain Fill dialog box and click on the Radial button. You define radial fountain fills using the same techniques as for linear ones. Radial fills differ by filling the selected object in circular, rather than linear, bands. These begin from the From, or outer, color and move inwards to the To, or inner, color. Try a variety of colors and observe the results in the preview window of the dialog box. Then click on OK to apply the fill to your object.

Since fountain fills can take quite a while to redraw, it's a good idea to make sure Interruptible Display in the Preferences dialog box is enabled if your publication contains more than a few of them. Then you can click anywhere to pause the screen redraw.

Return to the Fountain Fill dialog box with F11. As with linear fills, you can enter an Edge Padding value to increase the percentage of the outer and inner colors in the fill. This is useful when filling an irregularly shaped object with a radial fountain. In such a case, very little of the outer and inner colors may be displayed unless Edge Padding is increased.

A nice feature of Draw is the ability to change the origin of the radial fill, which by default is the center of the object. Click on the up or down arrows for Horizontal and Vertical Center Offset and the preview window will show you what's happening. You can enter a value for either orientation up to plus or minus 100%. But 100% of what? The manual is silent on this, but a value of 50% in any direction will offset the origin of the fill to the edge of the object. A value of 100% will offset it twice this much, an amount corresponding either to the height or width of the object. You can also click right on the preview window in this dialog box and drag the crosshairs to change the fill origin. (You'll have to drag outside the window to create a value larger than 50%.) Hold down the Control key while you drag to snap the crosshairs to increments of 10%.

But what if you want to shift the offset even further away from

Getting Your Fill of Draw

the center of the object? The undocumented technique described earlier for controlling linear fountains will also work for radically shifting the center of a radial fill. Simply draw one or more short lines, combine them with the radial-filled object and move the lines with the ⚲ tool to a new location. Give it a try.

The Fountain Fill dialog box lets you create linear fills that move between two colors of your choice. And what if you need a complex fill that moves from blue to yellow, then back to blue? Complex fountain fills aren't currently supported in Draw, but they're not difficult to construct manually. Fill a rectangle with a linear fill. Then mirror it by selecting it with the ▮ tool and dragging a middle handle into and right through the rectangle in the direction of the fill, pressing and releasing the right mouse button as you go to leave behind the original rectangle, then holding down the Control key to constrain the new rectangle to the same size as the original. (See Chapter 3 for details on how to mirror objects.) The result is two objects that seem to constitute a single object with a complex fill. The train image reproduced in the color section of this book is a good example of this technique. Simply select the second rectangle and change its To color to create a three-color fountain.

The only drawback to this approach is that you can't give these two objects separate outlines — you'll have to construct a single outline to surround them both. To do this, make a copy of one of the rectangles and press the gray + key on the far right of your keyboard to make a quick copy. Give the duplicated object no fill (✕) and the outline of your choice. Make sure Snap To Objects

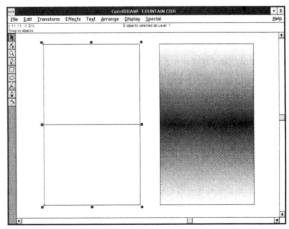

X: 0% Y: 0%   X: 100% Y: 100%

X: 50% Y: 0%   X: 100% Y: 0%

X: 0% Y: 50%   X: 0% Y: 100%

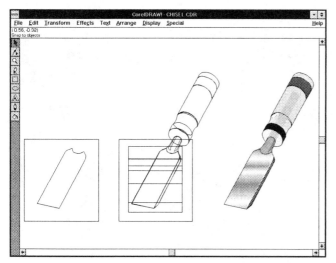

on the Display menu is enabled. Bring the duplicate to the front with Shift-PageUp and then drag an inside middle handle until it snaps to the edge of the second rectangle.

I've included several illustrations showing the type of applications to which you can put this fill effect. I continued the process of dragging middle handles of each new rectangle and created a series of connected objects of arbitrary size, by not holding down the Control key. I then selected all the rectangles and grouped them. If Draw provided a Paste Inside command, I could have then simply pasted my multiple blend inside any object. In its absence, I was forced to draw a rectangle around the group with the □ tool, select both the rectangle and the object I wished to fill, and then choose the Combine command from the Arrange menu. I gave this combined object no outline and a fill of white. It then functioned as a mask, with only the object I wanted filled displaying.

By all means try out this technique with type, a symbol or a clip art image, as shown in the illustrations. Close observation will reveal that the 'shiny' text has an outline around it. I simply made a copy of the text before combining the original with the mask rectangle. The copy was given no fill and a 2-point outline, and then brought to the front.

Getting Your Fill of Draw

Filling with Blends

As I indicated earlier, one problem with fountain fills is that you can't control the number of intermediate colors, or steps, on an object-by-object basis. Another drawback is that the steps are always either straight or round bands — they don't echo the outline of the object being filled. This lack of control can be remedied by using the Blend command, which can be thought of as just another way to fill an object, although you won't find it on the ✍ flyout menu. The Blend command is on the Effects menu and is described in detail in the *Creating Special Effects* chapter. But it's appropriate to take an introductory look at it here in the context of object fills.

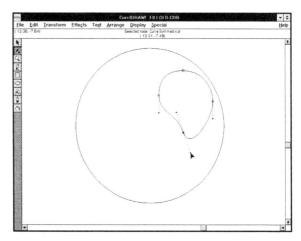

Blends are the preferred way to impart a sense of depth to objects in your illustrations. But using blends effectively is an art that requires a sound knowledge of color theory and many hours of practice. You'll begin using them in an example that imparts both a highlight and a shadow to a sphere.

Press Shift-F9 to switch to wireframe view. Draw a circle anywhere on your page by holding down the Control key and dragging with the Ellipse ○ tool. Give it a fill of 30% black, then click on the ✦ tool and give the circle no outline. First you'll create the highlight area. With the circle selected choose Stretch & Mirror from the Transform menu. Enter 40 for both

stretch percentages, enable Leave Original and click on OK. Drag the small circle up and to the right edge of the big circle. Choose Convert To Curves from the Arrange menu, choose the ✦ tool and reshape the circle by dragging its nodes and control points, as shown in the illustration.

Now return to the Stretch & Mirror dialog box and make a copy of the reshaped circle, with 40 for both stretch percentages and Leave Original enabled. Move the copy a bit up and to the right, then fill it with white. Now select both it and its larger duplicate, choose Blend Roll-Up from the Effects menu, and click on Apply. The resulting 20 intermediate objects will be created as a group, with each object being given a different shape and shade. Press Shift-F9 to switch back to the preview window and view the fill effect.

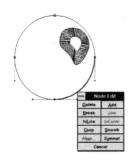

Why 20 steps? In fact, this number is quite arbitrary. The optimum number depends on the shapes and colors of the objects being blended, as well as on the output device. For example, there's no point creating a blend of 100 steps in a one-inch square object if you'll be printing it on a 300 dpi laser, which lacks the shades of gray to reproduce all those steps. On the other hand, a 1,200 or 2,400 dpi imagesetter would be able to create the illusion of a smooth blend from all those objects. Experiment by changing the number of steps to 10 or 30, each time clicking on the Apply button. Since you can't trust your monitor too far when creating blends, it would be instructive to print out these variations as you go. The objective is to specify just enough steps for a smooth blend without creating more objects than necessary, since extra objects will result in large files that print slowly.

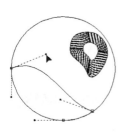

As well as highlights, you can also use blends to create the illusion of shadow. Switch to the wireframe view. Select the original large circle with the ▶ tool and choose first Copy and then Paste from the Edit menu. This places a copy of the circle right on top of the original. Now choose Convert To Curves from the Arrange menu to convert the circle into an editable object.

Choose the ⚲ tool and double-click at roughly five o'clock on the circle to display the Node Edit menu. Click on Add to add a node to the circle. Double-click on the new node (being careful to hold the mouse steady to avoid moving the node) and click on Cusp. Double-click on the node at nine o'clock and convert it to cusp as well. Then delete the nodes at twelve and three o'clock by clicking on them once to select them and then pressing the Delete key on the keyboard. You'll be left with a rather awkwardly shaped object sporting long control handles. Drag these handles to reshape the object into a thin crescent, as shown in the illustration.

Getting Your Fill of Draw

Select the finished crescent with the ➤ tool and make a duplicate using Copy and Paste. Choose the ⚲ tool and drag the nodes of the new crescent to widen it. If you seem to have lost the first crescent, press Control-W to redraw the screen (or click the scroll box in the vertical scroll bar). Select the small crescent with the ➤ tool and choose To Front from the Arrange menu, then fill it with 60% black.

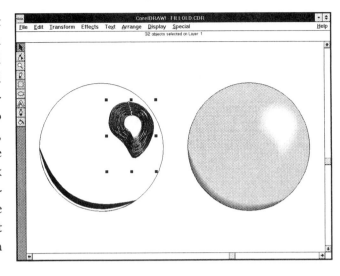

Select both crescents with the ➤ tool and blend them, using 30 steps. Switch back to the preview window. The result? A nice graduated shadow. Make sure the circle is behind the blends — use To Back from the Arrange menu if necessary. You could give your creation an outline by selecting the circle and making a duplicate with Copy and Paste. Give this new circle a fill of ✕ and a ✦ hairline outline from the ▴ flyout menu. Click anywhere to deselect everything, then select either crescent and give it a different color. The intermediate objects will automatically reblend.

As mentioned earlier, this exercise has been designed to give you a sense of how blends can be used to create graduated fills over which you have more control than simple fountain fills. For in-depth coverage of this complex topic, see *Creating Special Effects*. You won't need the Blend Roll-Up for the rest of this chapter, so double-click on the control bar in the top-left corner of the dialog box to close it.

Pattern Fills

You've seen that Draw provides considerable control over the creation of uniform, fountain and blended fills. But things get even more interesting at this point with the use of three types of pattern fills: Two-Color, Full-Color and PostScript Texture. Pattern fills can lend interesting texture to many illustrations

---

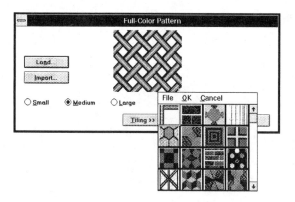

but keep in mind that their complexity can also result in slow print times if used injudiciously. In some cases, such fills can even keep a document from printing. However, while caution is advisable, pattern fills are simultaneously one of Draw's claims to fame as well as one of its most overlooked features.

Full-Color Fills

Full-color fills are typically vector in nature (although they can also be bitmaps). In this they follow the way in which Draw describes objects: as collections of lines and curves. The advantages of this approach are that these patterns are compact, output relatively quickly and are resolution independent; as with Draw objects, the higher the resolution of your output device, the less jaggy the pattern will print. A library of full-color fills is provided to get you going, but as is the case throughout Draw you can extend this collection by creating your own.

A Full-Color pattern fill

Select any good-sized object on your page, or draw a large rectangle. Choose ↗ from the ✋ flyout menu. Click on the large ✕ to display the scrollable library of fills. Explore these and then double-click on one to choose it. Then click on OK. Perform some transformations on your filled object, such as

Rotated 45°

Exported as .TIF, imported and rotated

resizing, mirroring, skewing or rotating. You'll find that such operations leave the fill unchanged. For example, if you rotate the object the

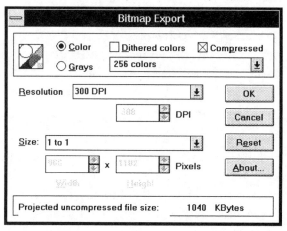

fill remains unrotated. The object outline is thus basically a window through which an unchanging fill is displayed. But what if you *need* a rotated fill?

One undocumented workaround is to export the filled object, import it and then rotate it. The problem with this approach is that Draw won't let you export a pattern fill in any of the supported vector formats, such as .CGM or .WMF — it will replace it with gray. So you'll have to export to one of the color bitmap formats, such as .TIF or .PCX, which negates the advantages of vector fills. However, if you simply must have a rotated full-color fill, this is worth a try. With the object selected choose Export from the File menu. Enable Selected Only and choose the desired export file format from List Files Of Type. Click on OK. In the resulting Bitmap Export dialog box, select the appropriate number of colors and resolution. Then import the resulting file. Keep in mind that once you rotate the bitmap it will display simply as a gray box, but it will print correctly to any PostScript printer (with the exception of some PostScript clones). See *Working with Bitmap Graphics* for more on this topic.

Return to the Full-Color Pattern dialog box. While choosing patterns from the scrollable preview is fine, an alternative method is available. Click on the Load button to display a list of the available patterns, which are saved in the Draw directory with a .PAT extension. Clicking once on any pattern file name displays a preview, much as when opening a Draw .CDR file. You'll find this way of accessing patterns faster if you create your own and give them names that place them at the beginning of the list. In contrast, the scrollable preview places new patterns at the bottom of the display. Double-click on any pattern now to choose it. Then click on the Tiling button.

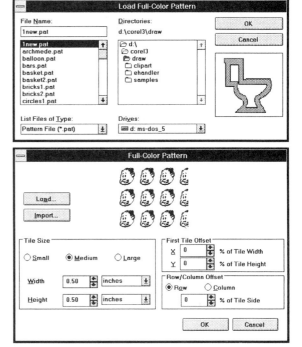

Full-color patterns are treated as a series of tiles laid edge to edge, like linoleum squares. As well as changing the size of these tiles by simply clicking on the Small, Medium or Large buttons, you can set the width or height to a custom value of up to 4 inches. Click on the Width and Height scroll arrows to see a preview of this. Now click on the First Tile Offset scroll arrows to offset the first tile that will fill your object in the horizontal (x) or vertical (y) axes. Set these back to 0, then experiment in the same way with the Row/Column Offset values. Like a spreadsheet, the rows are offset horizontally, while the columns are offset vertically. Click on OK to see the effect of your new tiling parameters on the object.

While you'll find some of the full-color fill patterns supplied with Draw useful, it's more likely that you'll want to create your own patterns. You can do this in two ways: either by importing an existing graphic file in any of the formats supported by Draw, or by taking a slice of what's on your Draw page and saving that as a pattern tile. In other words, just about *anything* can quickly be turned into a full-color pattern. This is a hot feature that's all too often overlooked by even veteran Draw users, so I encourage you to investigate it.

You'll begin exploring this feature by importing a black-and-white .TIF image. Return to the Full-Color Pattern dialog box and click on the Import button. Move to the SAMPLES subdirectory of Draw, change List Files Of Type to .TIF, select SHERMY.TIF and click on OK.

You should see Shermy's smiling face displayed as a tile pattern. You can now perform such familiar actions as changing the tile size and offset before clicking on OK to file your object with multiple Shermys. Since .TIF is a bitmap format, this fill wouldn't benefit much from higher resolution output devices. But it's handy to be able to take any scanned image in .TIF or .PCX format and quickly turn it into a pattern fill.

The ability to turn existing bitmap files into fill patterns can be used to create interesting textural effects. A nice collection of such textures is supplied with Draw for use in CorelCHART. But the documentation doesn't mention the fact that these files make great pattern fills. Choose Import again from the Full-

Getting Your Fill of Draw

Color Pattern dialog box, move to the BITMAPS subdirectory of CHART and change List Files to .BMP. There are 20 patterns in this directory and some, such as SHARKS, COARSE and WEAVE, provide very interesting effects. Double-click on any one to load it, adjust the tile as desired and click on OK to fill your object.

You'll have to zoom in to really get a good sense of what the texture looks like. Keep in mind that when printed to a black-and-white laser printer, many of these won't look too riveting with the standard 60 lpi screen frequency associated with 300 dpi lasers. On a higher-resolution printer running at 90 lpi or higher, however, they look quite nice. You might try filling some text with a texture.

There's another set of bitmap images supplied with Draw that you can use as fill patterns, with a bit more work. The PHOTOPNT\TILES directory contains 26 .PCX files that you can import, but you'll find some of them produce white lines between the patterns, as shown in the bottom Saturn symbol. If these seem of interest you'll have to fix them first in CorelPHOTO-PAINT. I don't suggest you do this now. For more on this see *Working with Bitmap Graphics*.

Finally, if you've imported a file and want to create a pattern fill that you can access more easily in the future, click on the pattern in the Full-Color Pattern dialog box and then choose Save Current Fill from the File menu. (Note that the File menu also lets you delete patterns.) Full-color patterns are saved as files with a .PAT extension in your Draw directory. Since the text in the file name box is already

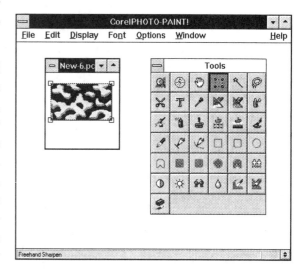

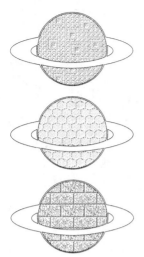

highlighted, simply type in a name up to eight characters in length and click on OK

Before leaving the import aspect of full-color fills, let me point out one more source of bitmap patterns on your system. These are the .BMP files supplied for use as Windows *wallpaper*. Again, some of these produce white borders, but as the three in the Saturn illustration show, most work quite nicely. You'll find them in the WINDOWS directory. And of course any .CDR file can be imported for use as a pattern. You could try importing one of the clip art images in the DRAW\CLIPART subdirectories, for example. The bomber image is clip art, filled with clip art doves.

If you often have to pick through directories containing large numbers of images in search of the right pattern, you could run CorelMOSAIC to display or print thumbnails of all the patterns in a directory. Unfortunately, you can't use Mosaic to actually import the graphic into the Full-Color Pattern dialog box. For more on Mosaic, see *Working with Clip Art*.

As well as importing patterns, you can create your own right in Draw. Once created, they can be used in any subsequent drawing and can also be edited. For this exercise you'll turn an image from the symbol libraries into a pattern fill. Choose the 𝔸 tool, hold down the Shift key and click anywhere on the page. Choose the library and symbol of your choice, set its size to two inches and click on OK. Fill it as desired, but keep in mind that complex fills, such as fountains or PostScript textures, can result in long print times.

Very shortly you'll be called upon to indicate the size of the pattern tile your symbol will occupy by clicking and dragging a marquee on the screen. A little preparation now will make the process more accurate. Choose the ☐ tool, hold down the Control key and drag to create a square large enough to comfortably hold your symbol. Select first the square and then the symbol using the Shift key, and then choose Align from the Arrange menu. Click on the Center buttons for both horizontal and vertical alignment and then click on OK to center align the square around the symbol. Deselect, then give the square both a fill and outline of ✕. Since it will then disappear, switch to

Clip art used as a fill

wireframe view (Shift-F9) to continue working with it.

Now you're ready to create a new pattern. Choose Create Pattern from the Special menu. Choose Full Color and note that the resolution options become ghosted. That makes sense, since unlike two-color fills these will output at the full resolution of your output device. Click on OK. Your

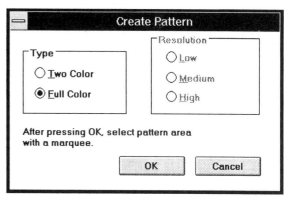

cursor now marks the intersection of the crosshairs. Position it at one corner of the square you drew. Then click and drag diagonally across to the other corner to define the tile area of the fill pattern you're creating. When you release the mouse button

Draw will prompt you, asking if you want to save the area you just defined as a pattern. Assuming that's the case, click on OK.

Name your pattern, but before clicking on OK you may want to change the default preview header, as shown in the lower-right corner of the dialog box. This defaults to a color 8 Kb header. With this setting, the palm tree pattern in the illustration resulted in a file 10 Kb in size. Set to a 1 Kb header, however, it took up only 3 Kb of space. If space is tight and a high resolution preview in the dialog box isn't significant for you, the smaller black-and-white headers are more efficient. Now select any object on the page and try out your new fill; it's been added to the list of fills in the Full-Color Pattern dialog box.

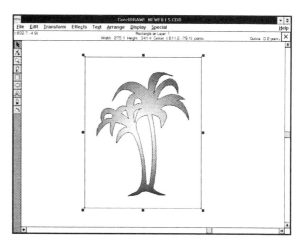

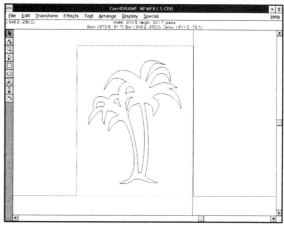

Having created a fill, what if you later want to edit it in some way? Earlier versions of Draw made you go

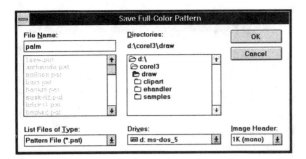

through hoops to accomplish this desirable task, but as of 3.0 it's now no more difficult than changing the colors in any .CDR file. If you have something on your page that you'd rather not part with, you should save it at this point. Then choose Open from the File menu. Change List Files to .PAT and move to your DRAW directory. You should see all the pattern files displayed. For this exercise, double-click on BRICKS2.PAT to open it. Click on any of the bricks that constitute this pattern and the Status Line informs you that you've selected a group of seven objects. You could ungroup it and work with the individual bricks, but for now you'll simply change the fill and outline of all the bricks.

Give the bricks a fill of 30% black. Then change the outline color to 70% black and its width to 2 points, using the ✎ menu. You're done. Choose Save As from the File menu and save the

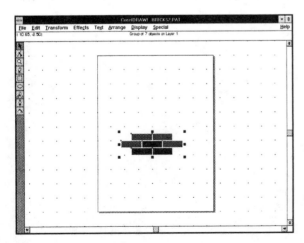

modified pattern as BRICKS3.PAT. You can test the new pattern at this point by drawing a box anywhere on the page and filling it with BRICKS3. Just make sure you delete the box if you save the pattern file again. I should also mention that while you're free to modify the objects in the pattern, it's best not to move them. That's because they're positioned inside an invisible bounding box. Move them and the tile edges probably won't line up when you later use the pattern.

If you're in the middle of a complex drawing and need to edit a full-color pattern, it's annoying to have to close your drawing, open the pattern file, edit it, close it and re-open the original drawing. The answer is surprisingly simple, although undocumented. Just Alt-Tab back to Program Manager and run a second copy of Draw to edit the pattern, leaving your drawing undisturbed. You can run as many copies of Draw as memory permits and Alt-Tab between them.

Original full-color fill

Modified full-color fill

Two-Color Fills

In earlier versions of Draw these were called *bitmap* fills, and while the name has changed, they remain bitmap in nature. Since bitmap fills can swell the size of your file, are limited to two colors and are only slightly less jaggy when output on higher resolution printers, their use should be limited to low resolution output. In fact, I never use these bitmap fills, preferring the flexibility, output quality and compact nature of full-color fills.

That said, it's worth a quick look at two-color fills, since they do provide a few unique capabilities. Select any object on your page and click on the ▓ Two-Color Pattern icon in the ◇ flyout menu. Click on the polka dots and scroll through the available patterns. Double-click on whatever strikes your fancy. You can assign foreground and background colors to your two-color pattern using the same techniques you employed for uniform and fountain fills earlier in the chapter. Simply choose colors from the current palette by clicking on the Back and Front Buttons, while More takes you to the color definition dialog box. The PostScript Options button also works in an identical fash-

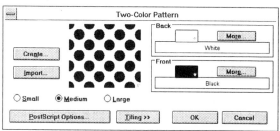

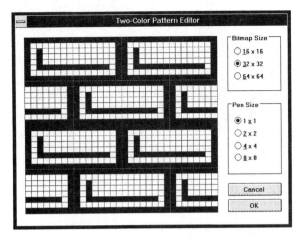

ion. Admittedly, this is a function that full-color patterns can't provide. When you've assigned the colors of your choice to the fill, click on OK.

With the object still selected, return to the Two-Color Pattern dialog box. Click on the brick pattern; it's at the left in the second row of patterns. Then click on the Create button. You can edit or create simple patterns in this dialog box. Each two-color tile is divided into a grid composed of 16 by 16, 32 by 32 or 64 by 64 pixels. The larger the grid, the more sophisticated the bitmap pattern can be, although a larger grid will also take up more disk space and take longer to print. Some of the included patterns have been created at a higher resolution than 64 by 64, and thus can't be edited.

Try modifying the brick pattern. Choose a pen size from the four available and click and drag with the left mouse button to draw with black, and with the right one to erase. In the illustration, I added some lines to give an illusion of depth to the bricks. When you've finished, click on OK and this new pattern will be added at the end of the scrollable list of fills. Double-click on it to select it and then click on OK to fill the currently selected object with your new pattern. That's it for two-color fill patterns. My suggestion is to stick with the more flexible full-color variety wherever possible.

Original bitmap fill

Modified bitmap fill

PostScript Textures

If you have a PostScript printer there's yet another pattern fill technique you can apply to objects. Select an object and click on the PostScript Textures icon on the far right of the ✋ menu.

Scroll through the extensive collection of PostScript fill routines. These are made even more useful through the ability to modify them by altering the values of their variables. Choose one of the fills and click on OK. Draw won't display these fills on the screen — no matter which texture you choose, your object will display filled simply with the letters PS. The only indication of the object's current texture is in the Status Line. Thankfully, the PostScript textures and many of their variations are illustrated at the back of the Draw section of the documentation.

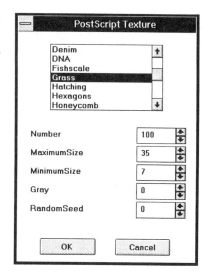

Some of these fills are transparent and some are opaque, while others can be defined either way by the use of the appropriate variable. For example, the space between the bubbles in the Bubbles fill is always transparent, while the color of the bricks in the Bricks fill is transparent if the BackgroundGray value is negative. You can create unusual effects by using the Combine command to create a mask for filling objects that have a transparent texture fill.

Prudence is advisable when using PostScript texture fills. Many of these are complex and will take a long time to print. In fact, a drawing containing numerous textures may become so complex it will fail to print at all. Raising the Flatness value in the Print dialog box may help such files output, although image quality will degrade if it's increased too much. Try bumping it up in increments of four or five until the file outputs, or enable Auto Increase.

The definitions of the texture fills are contained in USERPROC.TXT, an editable ASCII file in the Draw program directory. Existing textures can be modified and new ones added here if you have PostScript programming skills. If you're the adventurous type, you should first make a copy of USERPROC.TXT under a new name as a backup. Then load USERPROC.TXT into a text editor, such as Windows Write. The file begins with some useful information that's worth reading before beginning your hack. Then scroll down to the section below the dotted line that begins with %@Fill. You've arrived at the PostScript texture definitions.

Transparent Bricks texture fill above linear fountain fill

My personal favorite is the Motifs procedure, which is divided into a series of short routines that draw a shape and place it at a regular interval within the selected object. The checkerboard example below is one of the simpler routines you'll find in the USERPROC.TXT file and is an excellent place to start your

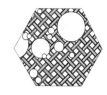

Transparent Bubbles texture fill above Basket vector fill

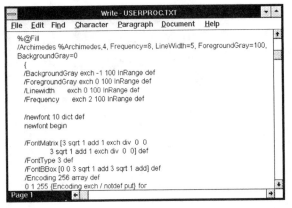

```
Write - USERPROC.TXT
File  Edit  Find  Character  Paragraph  Document  Help
%@Fill
/Archimedes %Archimedes,4, Frequency=8, LineWidth=5, ForegroundGray=100,
BackgroundGray=0
{
  /BackgroundGray exch -1 100 InRange def
  /ForegroundGray exch 0 100 InRange def
  /Linewidth      exch 0 100 InRange def
  /Frequency      exch 2 100 InRange def

  /newfont 10 dict def
  newfont begin

  /FontMatrix [3 sqrt 1 add 1 exch div  0  0
               3 sqrt 1 add 1 exch div  0  0] def
  /FontType 3 def
  /FontBBox [0 0 3 sqrt 1 add 3 sqrt 1 add] def
  /Encoding 256 array def
  0 1 255 {Encoding exch / .notdef put} for
Page 1
```

explorations in modifying Draw's PostScript fills.

```
/Checkerboard
{ 0 0 moveto
500 0 lineto
500 500 lineto
0 500 lineto
closepath
fill
} def
```

For those learning PostScript, playing with the textures code is a great way to become more familiar with the language and to generate some bizarre fills. Since Aldus FreeHand provides a simpler way to add new PostScript textures, you'll find some interesting suggestions for writing code for custom PostScript fills in such books as *Real World FreeHand* (Peachpit Press.)

I've left to the end a discussion of yet another of the ubiquitous Draw roll-ups. Choose ⊞ from the ✎ menu to display the Fill Roll-up. The roll-up doesn't provide any new controls over fills, but simply lets you make changes faster, since unlike the ✎ flyout menu and dialog boxes, it remains displayed on the screen. The only fill missing is PostScript Textures.

Using the roll-up is pretty straightforward. Simply select your object, choose the appropriate fill icon, make the desired settings and click on Apply. You can also access the full dialog box for each icon by clicking on the Edit button. To get an existing object's fill 'into' the roll-up for editing, click on Update From and then on the object. You can also use this as a way of copying an object's attributes to another object, much like the Copy Style From command on the Edit menu. With the object you want to fill selected, click on Update From. Then click on the object you want to copy the fill *from*. Finally, click on the Apply button.

Had your fill of fills? As always, it's a good idea to go back and work your way through this chapter in more detail, exploring the many byways that arise. Then it's on to outlines.

Controlling Object Outlines

7

The last chapter explored the many ways Draw provides to fill objects, but considerable control over object outlines is also available. On a blank page, begin by choosing the Text 𝔸 tool, holding down the Shift key and clicking anywhere on the page. Choose the Geographic Symbols library and click on #38 (the first starburst) to select it. Set its size to 3 inches and click on OK.

Your object was given Draw's current default fill and outline when you created it. If it isn't currently displayed in the Status Line, choose ✕ now from the ✎ menu to give the object no fill. (Clicking with the left mouse button on the ✕ to the left of the Color Palette at the bottom of the screen is another way of accomplishing this.) If the Color Palette at the bottom of your screen isn't currently displayed, choose Show Color Palette and Process Colors from the Display menu. Now click on the ✎ tool to display the Outline flyout menu. You can use this menu to specify the type, width and color of object outlines.

Arrowheads, calligraphic lines and dashes keep things interesting

By default, the width of object outlines is displayed in the Status Line in inches. Click on some of the five width icons in the top row of the menu, which range from ✚ for a hairline outline of .003 inches (.25 points, although it displays in the Status Line as .20) up to .333 inches (24 points).

As with fills, it's important to have an object selected before clicking on an icon in the ✎ menu. Choose the ⬉ tool and click anywhere on a blank part of the page to deselect all objects. Then choose the ✎ tool and click on any of the width icons on

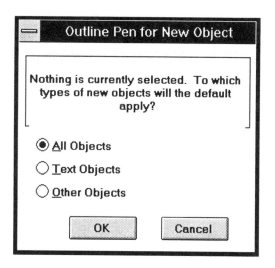

Outline Pen for New Object

Nothing is currently selected. To which types of new objects will the default apply?

◉ All Objects
○ Text Objects
○ Other Objects

OK   Cancel

---

the flyout menu. As expected, with no object selected you have the option of defining a default outline for just text, just non-text objects or all objects. Such a default will apply to all objects you create in this or future illustrations. Click on Cancel now to abort the procedure. Don't change any of the default outline attributes unless you have a good reason to do so. It's not uncommon for novice Draw users to inadvertently assign default outlines to their text that result in poor print quality.

Select your symbol by clicking on its outline, click on the ♦ tool again and choose some of the available outline fills in the bottom row of the flyout menu. They range from white and black, through 10% to 90% black. In the previous chapter you assigned fills to objects by clicking on colors in the Color Palette at the bottom of the screen with the left mouse button. Use the right button now to assign some outline colors to the selected object. Unfortunately, the Status Line provides only a rough indication of outline color — it doesn't display the name, as it does with fills.

Click on the ⊗ icon in the ♦ menu to display the Outline Color dialog box. The outline color of your currently selected object should be identified here. As with fills you can also edit spot and process outline colors and load new palettes. Outline colors function identically to the fill colors covered in the previous chapter, so I won't go into all the details of this dialog box again. If you're defining outline colors in an illustration that will be color separated and offset printed, see *Service Bureau Strategies* for recommendations on trapping. Note that with an object selected, you can display the Outline Color dialog box by pressing Shift-F12. Otherwise you'd wind up first in the defaults dialog box.

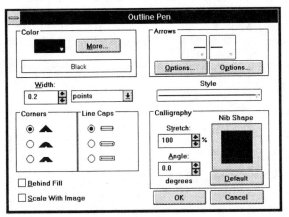

Most of Draw's outline abilities are concentrated in one big dialog box. With the starburst symbol selected, click on the ♦ icon on the ♦ menu to display the Outline Pen dialog box. Because small values expressed in inches are hard to visualize, I find it easier to specify them using points (1 inch=72 points). Click on the current Width measurement system to display a drop-down menu and choose points. You can also define a custom line thickness from .1 to 288 points (4 inches) in .1-point increments by changing the Width value. Enter a new Width value now and click on OK.

Choose the □ tool and draw a small rectangle. Since you've changed the measurement system of the outline thickness, note that the thickness of the rectangle is now displayed in points in the Status Line. In fact, this default outline measurement system will show up in all future documents you create or open. This is an exception to the rule in Draw that no object must be selected when creating a default. (For more on defaults see *Customizing Draw's Defaults.*)

Line Patterns

There's a keyboard shortcut you can use to quickly display the Outline Pen dialog box, as long as an object is selected; press F12 now to try this out. By default, outlines are given a solid line, but you can pick from a healthy selection of dotted and dashed variations, and also create your own. Click on the line below Style to display a pop-up list of line styles. Scroll through the list, pick a line type and click on OK. Now give your object a variety of thicknesses from the ♟ menu and observe the results.

In the illustration, the middle starburst has a line pattern with rounded ends. You can create rounded ends by choosing the middle of the three Line Cap options in the Outline Pen dialog box. Note, however, that some of the starburst's line endings taper to a point. When corner angles are below the current *miter limit* amount, Draw automatically bevels them, no matter what corner you've chosen. Give your starburst round line caps and choose Preferences from the Special menu. The Miter Limit can be a value between 5° and 45°.

Experiment with different Miter Limit values. As the illustration shows, when you raise this value you're instructing Draw to bevel the corners of ever-larger angles. Sometimes this can be a little tricky to see on the screen; if so, try different miter values and line widths. Unfortunately, there's no way to have Draw

Dotted and
dashed outlines

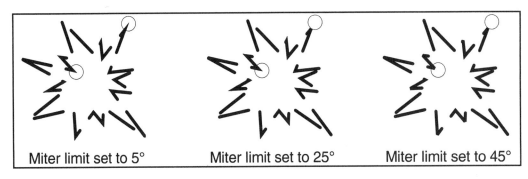

| Miter limit set to 5° | Miter limit set to 25° | Miter limit set to 45° |

create rounded corners in this case. The Miter Limit value applies to all the objects in an illustration — you can't set it on an object-by-object basis. When you've finished your experiments, return to Preferences and set Miter Limit back to the default 10°, or your new value will be saved as a default.

It's undocumented, but dotted and dashed line styles always begin at the first node of an object and follow the direction in which the object was created. The top-left corner node of a rectangle drawn with the □ tool, for example, is always the first node and therefore the origin of the line pattern. Verify this by using the Convert To Curves command from the Arrange menu on a rectangle and then selecting it with the ⸜ tool. The first node should be clearly visible. Assign a dashed and dotted line to the rectangle and observe the origin of the pattern at the first node. Note that if you assign square line caps to your line styles, the ends of the dashes will be extended a distance of half of the object's line thickness. Use the Outline Pen dialog box to try out the three available line cap options.

First node
⇓
— — — —
Drawn to the right

First node
⇓
— — — —
Drawn to the left

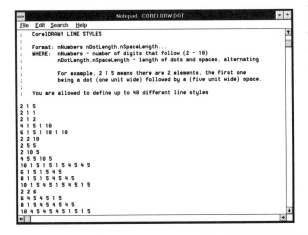

If the collection of available line styles doesn't meet your needs, you can create new ones as desired. Line style definitions are stored in the CORELDRW.DOT file in the Draw program directory. This is an ASCII text file that can be modified in a text editor, such as Notepad or Write, both of which are supplied with Windows. (It would be wise to create a renamed copy of COREL-DRW.DOT before you edit it.)

If you open this file you can edit existing definitions or add your own, for a total of up to 40. Line patterns are defined using three values. The first one specifies the number of lines and spaces, or elements, that make up the line style. So if you were creating a style that had a long line, followed by a space and a short line, the first numerical value would be three. Each line style can have up to 10 elements. The second value determines the number of units of length assigned to the first space, while the third value determines the length of the first segment. For example, a line segment defined as 2 1 1 would consist of alternating spaces and lines of an equal short length.

You might think that creating such a line style and assigning it round line caps in the Outline Pen dialog box would result in a line composed of round dots. But because the round corners extend beyond the edges of the dots you'll wind up with ovals, unless you make the values 2 1 1. (To create a true dotted line see *Creating Special Effects.*) You'll have to re-run Draw each time you make a change to CORELDRW.DOT, but you can ease the pain of the editing cycle by customizing a new Notepad icon to load the file automatically. You could also run a second copy of Draw to test new line styles, to avoid closing and opening your illustration file more than once.

You can create some interesting line styles by making copies of lines and pasting variations on top of them. I've shown several examples of the many variations possible. A simple effect would be to copy a dotted line of one color onto a duplicate of a different solid color. By changing Line Caps and creating your own styles in CORELDRW.DOT, many effects can be achieved in this way. You could then select both lines and group them, to ensure they're moved and transformed together.

Despite this ability, I find Draw's implementation of line styles limiting. As well as the annoyance of having to edit CORELDRW.DOT, the definition process lacks the precision found in programs like Adobe Illustrator, which let you precisely define dot and space values in fractional points. Another limitation is that as the point size of dotted lines is increased, the space between the dots also increases — not always a desirable effect when you have a particular effect in mind.

LAYERS
LAYERS

Yet another effect can be created by pasting multiple versions of an object on top of each other, each with different outline thicknesses and colors. These move from the bottom object, which has the thickest outline, up to the top object, which has a thin outline. You could try this out on some display type. While I won't give you specifics here, the easiest way to proceed is to give the first block of text the thickest outline and adjust character spacing if necessary with the ⟨ tool. Then make a quick copy on top of the original by pressing the gray + key on your numeric keyboard. Give the top object a thinner outline in a different color. Do this as many times as you like.

You may not have noticed, but outline thicknesses extend equally on either side of an object's path. An 8-point outline, for example, extends 4 points into the fill area of the object. You can instruct Draw to only display the half that extends outside the path. This is handy for a number of operations, including layering and trapping. With the top object selected press F12 to display the Outline Pen dialog box and click on Behind Fill. When you return to the page, only the outer half of the outline will display. This ensures that the top object displays with its shape undistorted by the outline thickness. Give the top object the fill of your choice and you're done.

Behind Fill not
enabled

Behind Fill
enabled

Original

Stretched 50%
without Scale
With Image

Stretched 50%
with Scale
With Image

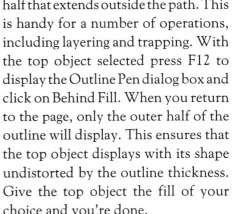

Scale with Image

When you resize an object, the outline thickness by default stays the same. But you can enable an option that will scale the outline thickness in proportion to the change in size of the object. Select an object and in the Outline Pen

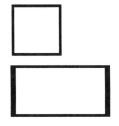

Box stretched 100% using Scale With Image

dialog box enable Scale With Image. Hold down the Control key while you drag a starburst's corner sizing handle to double its size and note in the Status Line that the outline thickness is also doubled.

The Draw manual doesn't mention it, but if you drag one of the middle sizing handles of an object that has Scale With Image enabled, the Status Line is only telling you half the truth about the resulting outline thickness. To see this, choose the □ tool, hold down the Control key and drag to create a square of any size. In the Outline Pen dialog box enable Scale With Image and set the width to 5 points, then click on OK. Now hold down the Control key and drag a middle sizing handle until the object snaps to 200% in the Status Line. The Status Line indicates the line size is 10 points, but you can see for yourself that in fact it's only increased in thickness in one axis. Display the Outline Pen dialog box.

Calligraphy

The dialog box is displaying some interesting information. The object's width of 10 points should be displayed, but the Stretch and Angle values are no longer the default 100% and 0°. In effect, you've changed the nature of the *pen nib* that renders the outlines of your object. It's no longer square, but rectangular. Click on the Default button to reset the Stretch and Angle values. When you click on OK, your object will have a 10-point outline on all four sides.out

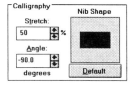

Select the starburst symbol or some text and return to the Outline Pen dialog box. You can alter the pen nib by entering new values for Angle and Stretch. The Angle value must be

Corners: Miter
Angle: 45°
Stretch: 1%

Corners: Round
Angle: 45°
Stretch: 200%

Corners: Bevel
Angle: 100°
Stretch: 25%

Miter

Round

Bevel

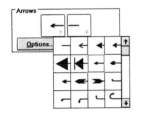

between -180° and +360°, while Stretch can be set up to 1000%. You can also click and drag on the nib shape itself to adjust it. Experiment with different combinations of these values. Note that if you rotate an object that has a custom pen nib, the nib's orientation won't change with it unless you have Scale With Image enabled. You'll find switching between the three corner options also changes the outline quality.

Arrowheads

A final outline ability of Draw is that of applying line endings, or *arrowheads*, to open paths. You can choose from a library of available arrowheads or quickly create your own from any object in the editing window. Create an open path now by drawing a short line with the Pencil ℓ tool, then give it a thickness of 2 points. Select it, display the Outline Pen dialog box and in the Arrows section click on the left box to display a scrollable list of line endings. Click on one to choose it and click on OK to apply it to the beginning of the selected line.

The size of an arrowhead depends on the width of the line to which it's attached: thin line, small arrowhead. So try giving your line a variety of widths. Return to the dialog box and click on the right-hand box to assign an arrowhead to the end of your line, following the same procedure as before. To remove an arrowhead, either choose the first line ending in the scrollable list, or choose click on the Options button and choose None from the menu. This menu also lets you delete arrowheads and swap beginning and end selections. As always, you can close these drop-down menus by pressing the Escape key.

You've probably already wondered if there's a way around the limitation of linking the size of arrowheads to the line to which they're applied. What if you need a thin line with a large arrowhead, or vice versa?

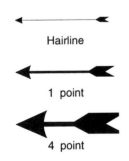

Hairline

1 point

4 point

One approach is to create a new arrowhead from scratch. Zoom out if necessary to display the entire starburst symbol. Select it and choose Create Arrow from the Special menu. Click on OK when Draw asks you if you're sure and the starburst will be added to the scrollable Arrows list in the Outline Pen dialog box. Select the line you drew earlier and in the dialog box scroll

Controlling Object Outlines

down to locate the starburst at the
bottom of the list of arrowheads. It
may look rather unimpressive at this
point, so click on it and then choose
Edit from the Options menu.

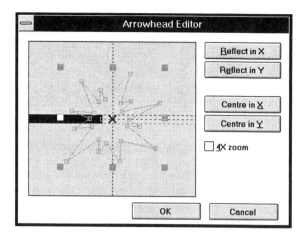

The Arrowhead Editor lets you size
and position the arrowhead relative to
the end of the line, displayed here as a
thick black horizontal line with a relative thickness of ½ inch. Begin by
dragging a corner handle to scale the
starburst up to a more satisfying size.

Once resized, you can move the starburst by either dragging one of
its nodes, or by clicking on one of the Centre In X or Y buttons. The
line itself has a node that can be dragged horizontally to alter its
relationship to the arrowhead. The Reflect buttons mirror the
current arrowhead in either axis. When all is well, click on OK and
then return to the page to see how it looks.

A final variation to try is the creation of an arrowhead that's
hollow, rather than filled with the color of the line to which it's
attached. Select the starburst with the ↗ tool and double-click
on any node. Choose Break in the Node Edit menu to create an
open path. Now follow the usual procedure for creating a new
arrowhead and you'll find it's outlined with the color and
thickness of the line to which it's attached.

As you've seen, you can resize line endings using the Arrowhead Editor, but the new size will permanently take the place of
the existing arrowhead — there's no way to save these as
variations on the original. If you're going to follow this approach you should first save the file that holds the arrowhead
definitions, CORELDRW.END, under a new name. Or you
could create a number of arrowheads of varying size by changing the size of the arrowhead object on the page before adding
it to the list. But this procedure can't be applied to arrowheads
that have already been added to the list — for example, the
default arrowheads. It also has the disadvantage of cluttering up
your arrowhead library and still limits you to the sizes you so
laboriously create.

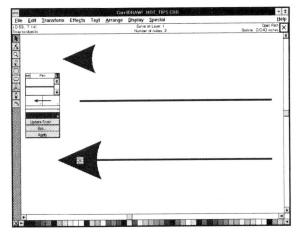

I've come up with a relatively simple way to mix line and arrowhead sizes, using two separate objects to represent the line and the arrowhead. Try the following technique first with a straight line, then a curve. Make sure Snap To Grid, on the Display menu, is disabled. Draw a short straight line with the ℓ tool by clicking, releasing and dragging the mouse to the right with the Control key held down to keep it horizontal. Use the Duplicate command (Control-D) to make a copy of it and then assign any arrowhead to one end of either one of the lines.

Now here's the tricky part. Zoom in on your lines and choose the ⚓ tool. Hold down the Control key and drag the smaller of the two nodes on the line with the arrowhead over to the larger one. Placement of the node is critical — it should be almost, *but not quite*, centered on the larger node, leaving a bit more of the larger one displayed in the direction in which you want the line to point. If you position the node incorrectly, the arrowhead will simply point the wrong way. If so, just drag the node a bit more to one side until the arrowhead points correctly.

To make use of this arrowhead, it must be positioned precisely on the end node of the original straight line. There's no need to eyeball objects when you can position them with precision using the new Snap To Objects feature of Draw 3.0. Enable Snap To Objects on the Display menu. If the arrowhead is deselected, it can be difficult selecting it simply by clicking on it. You'll find it easier to click and drag a selection marquee around it. Choose the ▶ tool, select the arrowhead with a marquee, drag it over to the straight line (being careful not to drag a sizing handle) and snap it to the end node of the line. The Status Line will indicate when it's snapped by displaying a Snapped To Curve message.

You're done. You can now select either the arrowhead or the line and independently change their size in the Outline Pen dialog box. When you've arrived at the desired arrowhead size and line width, you'd be wise to select both objects and choose Group from the Arrange menu. That will ensure you don't accidentally modify just one of them. To later modify either the line or the arrowhead, first choose Ungroup from the same menu.

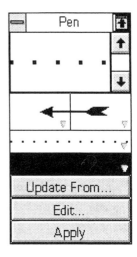

As with the ⟨🖊⟩ tool, the ⟨🖊⟩ tool also provides a roll-up that can make it faster to apply multiple changes to object outlines. Choose the 🔳 icon from the ⟨🖊⟩ menu. I'll let you click on the various parts of the roll-up to discover what they do. Don't forget to have an object selected first, make your selection and then click on Apply.

Text Creation and Alignment

CorelDRAW has always had a deservedly fine reputation in the area of text creation. One of the reasons for this is that it was the first drawing application to include a significant library of fonts, which now numbers 153 TrueType fonts. For those with access to a player, the CD-ROM disk included with Draw provides another 103 TrueType fonts and all 256 fonts in PostScript format. You can also use other TrueType or PostScript fonts installed in Windows, such as the 26 OptiFonts TrueType fonts included on the Fonts disk at the back of this book.

Artistic and paragraph text

To squeeze the most performance out of your fonts, Draw uses two modes for its creation and manipulation: artistic and paragraph text. Each mode has its unique capabilities and applications. For example, only paragraph text can be set in columns or hyphenated, while artistic text is the mode to use if you want to apply such special effects as extrusions or envelopes. The default mode is artistic, which is appropriate for tapping Draw's current typographic strength — creating and manipulating short blocks of display type. So it's here that you'll begin the exploration of this core Draw topic. (For details on the technical side of installing and printing fonts, see *Advanced Type Topics*.)

There are three tools in Draw's toolbox that you'll use when working with text in either mode: the Pick ▶ , Shape ⟨ and Text 𝔸 tools. Since their capabilities overlap in some cases, this can be a bit confusing, so I'll lead you through a complete investigation of what each tool can do when working with first artistic, then paragraph text.

Technical

Switzerland

𝕱rankenstein

UMBRELLA

Artistic Text

Begin with a blank page, choose the A tool and click to make an insertion point anywhere on the page. Then type just a single word and choose the ↖ tool. The Status Line will indicate that you've created a block of artistic text in the default font — 24-point Avalon Normal. The coordinates of the lower-left corner of the block are also displayed, as well as the default fill of black and outline of none. Although the Status Line doesn't indicate it, text is also given a left alignment relative to where you made the insertion point.

Now that the text is selected with the ↖ tool, you can do anything to it that you'd do to a graphic — Draw makes no distinction between the two. For example, enlarge the word by dragging a corner handle and note that the Status Line indicates the new point size. If you drag a side handle, you'll either compress or expand the text. Try mirroring, moving, copying, rotating and skewing the text block. If it gets really bent out of shape, choose Clear Transformations from the Transform menu.

Just as you can modify text with the ↖ tool using the same techniques as for graphics, you follow similar procedures for changing the fill and outline attributes of text. I've covered this in detail in earlier chapters, so I won't repeat it all here, but you should spend a few minutes applying different fills and outlines to your text. When you've finished, return the text to the default fill of black and outline of none.

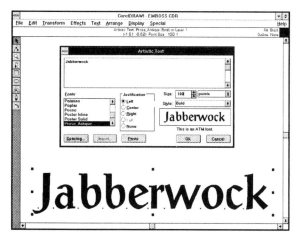

What's especially significant is that even after bending and filling the outlines of your word, the text is still fully editable. (You should know that not all drawing programs work this way, and often convert such text to a graphic.) To edit your text while it's selected with the ↖ tool, choose Edit Text from the Edit menu. The Artistic Text dialog box lets you make editing changes to your text block. While you can also do this directly on the page, as you'll soon see, there are times when it's easier or necessary to do so in the dialog box; very small text and text on a path are examples of this. Edit the text string to give yourself two lines of a few words each. You can use the Windows keyboard shortcuts to work with text in this dialog box: Shift-Delete to cut highlighted text, Control-Insert to copy, and Shift-Insert to paste.

Click on the ↓ arrow to see what's available on the Fonts menu. Then click on a new font name and you'll be treated to a preview of the first few letters of your text string. Below the preview it will identify the current font as either TrueType, WFN or ATM format. The WFN fonts used by Draw version 2 are still supported by Draw 3, although its fonts are no longer supplied in that format. The default Avalon font, however, is a WFN. ATM stands for Adobe Type Manager, Adobe Systems' popular PostScript type manager. In fact, any PostScript Type 1 font should work fine with Draw. (For more on font formats, see *Advanced Type Topics*.)

You can be forgiven for wondering about the origin of the Draw TrueType font names. While the outlines are similar to industry-standard faces, for copyright reasons they must bear other names. So Times is called Toronto and Bodoni is dubbed Bodnoff. This renaming can cause several problems. The most immediate is that you may need to specify type using the standard name and not know the Draw equivalent. You'd be wise to keep the fold-out type poster supplied with Draw handy, since this shows the full character set of all the faces, as well as the name equivalents. You can also find the name equivalents at the front of the clip art reference guide. If you find the names really irksome, they can be permanently changed with several third-party utilities, as discussed in *Advanced Type Topics*. This chapter also describes the use of Fonter, a utility I've included on the Utility disk. Use this to print out type sample pages of all your installed fonts.

Some fonts are supplied in a variety of weights, which you can access by clicking in the Style area. While the documentation currently lists the maximum point size as 1,440 (there are 72 points to an inch), in fact you can set it as large as 2,160 points. This corresponds to Draw's maximum page size of 30 inches. The left, right and center alignments (which Corel calls 'justification') apply to the alignment of the text string within its own selection box — *not* its alignment in terms of its position on the page. Initially, text will be given this alignment relative to where you made the insertion point on the page with the A tool. The full alignment option is currently ghosted; it's only available for paragraph text. And the alignment of none is a special one that you'll work with in a few minutes. Pick a new font and click on OK.

I'd like you to return to the Edit Text dialog box, this time using the Control-T shortcut (T is for type). This is one shortcut you should commit to memory, since frequent trips to this dialog box are required. Click on the Spacing button.

In typical Draw manner, you can control the amount of space between characters, words and lines either by entering values in

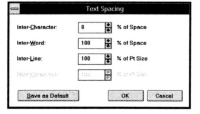

a dialog box or by adjusting them interactively right on the page. If you like the dialog box approach, you can specify spacing values in terms of the size of an *em space*. An em is a typographic unit of measurement corresponding to the size of a capital letter M in the font you're working with. So as the size of type grows, so does its em space size. Positive and minus values can both be used here. Controlling inter-line spacing — more commonly known as *leading* — is really quite difficult, since you have to specify it as a percentage value in terms of the type size. If you want 10-point type with an inter-line spacing of 12 points, it's not hard to figure out that the desired percentage is 120%. But what if the type is 11 points and you want an inter-line spacing of 13 points? Time to get out the calculator. We can only hope that the next version of Draw lets us simply specify the desired amount of leading in points, as do most page layout programs. Inter-paragraph spacing is ghosted here, an indication that it's only available when working with paragraph text.

What about the Save As Default button, you ask? Clicking on this will save all the values in this dialog box and apply them to all future blocks of text you create — no matter what font — during the current session of Draw. When you close and re-run Draw these values will still be in effect; they've been saved in the

CONFIG.SYS file as the new default spacing values. Just make sure you change these values back before you close Draw. I find this feature useful in cases where I've adjusted the spacing of a text block interactively on the screen. With the block selected, I display this dialog box and click on the Save As Default button. Then as I create new blocks of text, these values are automatically applied. If you need to permanently alter the character spacing attributes of your fonts, consult (yet again) the *Advanced Type Topics* chapter. Change these spacing values, if you wish, and click on OK.

I haven't mentioned the Paste button, which simply dumps the contents of the Windows Clipboard into this dialog box at the location of the insertion point. You can use this to move text into Draw from other Windows applications, such as word processors. (You can also choose Paste from the Edit menu to place text directly on the page.) The Import button, you'll note, is ghosted; it's yet another paragraph text-only option. Click on the OK button to return to the page.

There remain a number of dialog boxes that you can use to change the formatting of a block of artistic text. Choose Text Roll-Up from the Text menu. This is another of Draw's special roll-up dialog boxes, which in this case is handy for quickly making formatting changes. With your text block selected, choose a new font and size, then click on Apply. You can also use this roll-up to change the alignment of text within its block. An important point is that doing this not only changes the alignment of the text within the block, but also repositions the block itself, in terms of its left side. That is, if you switch from left to right align- ment, the right edge of the text will be moved to where the left edge was.

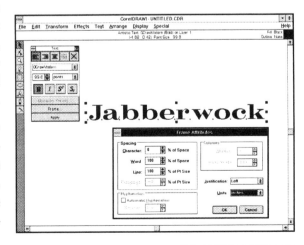

With the text block still selected, try clicking on the bold, italic, super- script and subscript buttons, if these are available for the current font. Superscripts and subscripts change a character's vertical shift and re-

---

duce its point size. Characters are placed below the baseline for a subscript, and above the x-height of the face for a superscript. Click on the Frame button to display the Frame Attributes dialog box. Most of these options apply only to paragraph text, so they're unavailable here. You can change your alignment, but it's faster to do this in the roll-up. So the only use of the Frame dialog box at this point is to access the spacing options, which are the same as those in the Text Spacing subdialog box of Artistic Text that you looked at earlier. Return to the roll-up.

Choose Character from the Text menu. This dialog box displays different options, depending on what tool you've used to select the text. With the text block selected with the ▶ tool, this dialog box is a hybrid of elements from the Text dialog box and the Text roll-up. You can preview a font, for example, as in the Text dialog box, and can alter its placement, as in the roll-up. Make whatever changes you desire here and click on OK. If you find yourself making frequent trips to the Character dialog box, you should construct a Windows Recorder macro to assign it to a keyboard sequence, such as Control-Shift-C.

So far, you've been working with the formatting of the entire text block while in the ▶ tool. If you choose a new fill or outline, this would also apply to the whole block. Naturally, you need to be able to select and format just some of the characters within a block. Time to change to the ⋏ tool.

With the text block still selected, you should notice that each character now has a small square, or *node*, at its lower-left corner. Two new icons, ⬍ and ⫴, have also appeared. Click and drag the ⫴ spacing control handle to adjust the space between all the characters in the text block. Holding down the Control key while you do this adjusts inter-word spacing, as shown in the Status Line. And if you have two or more lines of type in your block, ⬍ adjusts their inter-line spacing. You could press Control-T and add a line of text now if you wanted to test the ⬍ handle. If so, choose the ⋏ tool again when you return to the page.

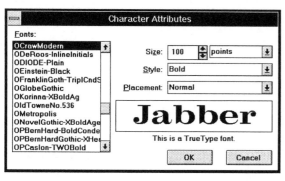

Text Creation and Alignment

Click once on any character's node and the Status Line will indicate the horizontal (x) and vertical (y) position of that node. Now click and drag the node to move the character anywhere you like. If your text has a left alignment and you drag the left-most letter to a new position on the page, you'll find the rest of the text string moves to the left to fill its position. To avoid this shifting, give your text an alignment of none in the Frame or Paragraph Text dialog boxes, or the roll-up.

Kerning Type

The most common application of the ability to move individual letters is in *kerning* display type. You'll find that large type can be set rather loosely by Draw, so tightening it up improves its fit and legibility. Holding down the Control key while you drag a character will constrain it to its baseline. You could also use Draw's nudge feature, by simply pressing the keyboard arrow keys. If you go this route, make sure the Nudge value in the Preferences dialog box is set to only 1 or 2 points. Hold down these keys to quickly move the selected character in any direction. You can also move as many characters at once as you want by selecting them with the Shift key held down, or by

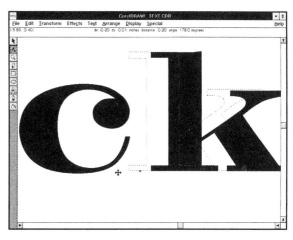

dragging a selection marquee around them. Snap To Grid, Guidelines and Objects can all be used when dragging a character node.

Specifying the degree of character movement numerically is another option. Double-click on any character's node to display the Character Attributes dialog box. This provides the same possibilities as it did earlier when you used the ▶ tool, with the exception of the newly added options of changing the selected character's horizontal and vertical position, and its angle of rotation. In fact, this dialog box provides the only

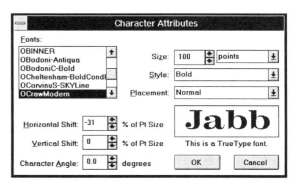

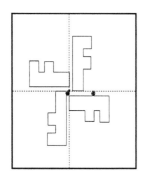

way to rotate individual characters in a text block. Entering a negative value in this field rotates characters clockwise, while a positive one rotates counter-clockwise. You can rotate between -300° and +300°. Choose a few formatting options and click on OK. If you changed the character angle, note that characters are rotating around their nodes, not their mid-points.

Return to the Character Attributes dialog box. Horizontal and vertical shift must be specified as a percentage of the point size of your type. Using proportional — instead of fixed — values for horizontal and vertical character shifts ensures they remain in proportion to the text string, if you later resize it. However, the required value is sufficiently difficult to figure out that you'll probably simply drag characters to where you want them on the screen, rather than specify movement numerically. It can be handy, however, in situations where you want to move a number of characters the same amount. In this case you'd move a character with the mouse, note the shift values in this dialog box, select all the characters to be moved, then enter the desired value and shift them all at once.

When applied to text with a straight baseline, you'll find that positive horizontal values shift the letter away from the beginning of the string, negative ones towards it, following the x and y axis principles of Draw's coordinate system. Change the horizontal shift value for some characters in the straight text block to observe this.

Positive vertical values move characters above the baseline, while negative values move them downwards. These values are always perpendicular to the baseline, even if the text string has been rotated with the ➤ tool. (This is also true when you nudge characters.) An undocumented aspect of moving characters is that the vertical shift values are defined as a percentage of the point size of the *entire* string, as specified in the Artistic Text dialog box and Text roll-up, not in terms of the selected character. This can be a bit confusing, since the size of characters within a text string may be varied. The Status Line displays the point size used by Draw for calculating this.

As when moving, you can use this dialog box to format all currently selected characters. So select a few characters and double-click on any selected node. The important principle here is that only the values you change will be applied to the selected characters. In other words, if you select several characters that are currently in two different fonts and double-click on either one, the attributes of the character on which you double-clicked will be displayed in the dialog box. If you then change just the point size, the fonts and other attributes of all the selected characters will remain intact — only their size will change.

I should add a final subtle twist to working with multiple characters. Select a number of characters and choose Character from the Text menu. This is just another (slower) way to call up this dialog box, but there *is* a slight difference: the values displayed in this manner are always those of the first selected character in the string. Okay, so it's not riveting, but now you know. Spend a few minutes experimenting with the Character Attributes dialog box before going on.

Draw provides two related commands for tidying up a text block you've modified with the ⚲ tool. Choose Straighten Text from the Text menu. This resets all values in the Character Attributes dialog box to their as-created state, so it will strip out any individual character shifts, rotations or typeface changes in the text. However, it will leave intact the inter-word, inter-character and inter-line spacing values you specified in the Artistic Text dialog box and Text roll-up, or created directly on-screen by dragging the ⠿ and ☰ spacing markers with the ⚲ tool.

The Align To Baseline command on the Text menu is easily confused with Straighten Text, but it differs by leaving intact any rotations, horizontal shifts or face changes in individual characters. It's often used for aligning the baseline of a block of text after a heavy kerning session. Verify the difference between these two commands.

If it currently isn't displayed, choose Text Roll-Up from the Text menu. You have access to the same font specification capabilities now as when using this roll-up with the ⬂ tool, but with a few twists. If the text block is selected, but no characters are,

Mixed si.es
Mixed type

Did gyre and gimble

Did gyre and gimble

Did gyre and gimble

whatever formatting you specify here will be applied to the entire block. However, if one or more characters are selected, formatting will be applied to just those characters. So it makes sense that with no characters selected, you can click on the Frame button and specify inter-word, inter-character and inter-line values for the entire block. But if you have one or more characters selected, you can click on the Character Kerning button and control the movement and rotation of just those characters. Unfortunately, Draw currently lacks _range kerning_, the ability to adjust the space between the characters of a range of selected text.

Since you can select individual characters with the ⚹ tool, you can use it to change the fills and outlines of type. However, you should know that there's no way to delete individual letters with the ⚹ tool. You can drag them off the printing area of the page, replace them with spaces, or draw a white rectangle with no outline over them as a mask, but you can't delete them.

Creating and Editing Text

Time to explore the third and final text-related tool, the Text 𝔸 tool itself. You can use this not only to change the formatting of selected characters, as you did with the ⚹ tool, but to edit existing blocks and enter new text right on the page. Try

using it the first way, by clicking and dragging over text to highlight it and then choosing formatting options from the Text roll-up or Character Attributes dialog box. Quick ways to select text include double-clicking to select a word, Control-clicking to select the entire sentence, or clicking then Shift-clicking to select all the text between the two insertion points.

As with the ⚹ tool, either the Character Kerning or Frame buttons are avail-

---

Text Creation and Alignment

able, depending on whether you've selected individual characters. And Control-T will take you to the Text dialog box. So far, then, I haven't shown you anything about the 𝔸 tool that the ↗ tool can't do. The unique capability of the 𝔸 tool is that you can edit and enter text with it. Click anywhere inside a text block, for example, and you're now in a rudimentary text-editing mode; you can type new text and use the Delete, Backspace and Spacebar keys, much as you'd expect. (Tabs, however, are something Draw currently doesn't support.)

A number of other text-oriented keys can also be used with the 𝔸 tool. The arrow keys, for example, move the insertion point in their respective directions. Home and End move the insertion point to the beginning and end of the current line of the text block. The undocumented Control-Home and Control-End move it to the beginning and end of the entire block. Since it's sometimes tricky to select small text at the beginning of a block by dragging over it, instead you could simply click anywhere in the block, press Control-Home, then hold down the Shift key and click at the place you want the selection area to end.

You can also cut, copy and paste selected text areas, either within one block or between other blocks. Text you paste in will assume the formatting of the character to the left of it in the block into which it's pasted. If you paste text into a fresh insertion point you've made on a blank part of the page, it will be given the formatting of that insertion point. Which brings us to the subject of type defaults.

Type Defaults

Click anywhere with the 𝔸 tool on an area of the page that doesn't already contain text and type a few words. Then switch to the � tool and you'll find that the text you just created was Avalon (Draw's version of Avant Garde), set at 24 points. This is the default font that shows up when you type or paste text onto an empty part of the page. It's possible to permanently change the default font, weight and size by editing the CORELDRW.INI file. For example, most of the captions for the illustrations in this book are set in 10-point Helvetica normal, a default I set in my .INI file. (I've covered this process in detail in *Advanced Type Topics*.)

You can also set the desired font for the current insertion point, as well as change the default for all future new insertion points during the current Draw session. Set the current insertion point by clicking with the tool on a blank part of the page. Then choose the desired font and size in the Text roll-up or Character Attributes dialog box and click on Apply. Now when you type, the text appearing at the insertion point will be as you specified in the roll-up or dialog box. But the next time you click to make a new insertion point, it will revert to the default. As mentioned above, that default can be either global or for the current session only.

To set the session default, choose the ↖ tool and make sure no text block is selected. Now define the attributes of the desired default text in the roll-up or dialog box. When you click on Apply or OK, a dialog box will request confirmation for the creation of this default. Click on OK and you'll find that all new insertion points will be as you specified, until you exit Draw. The next time you run Draw, however, it will have reverted to the default in the .INI file. It would thus be possible to create a number of .INI files for Draw, which differ only in the default font specification they contain. A batch file could be created to copy them over the current CORELDRW.INI before loading Draw. You could then activate these from Program Manager with a series of Draw icons, each labeled with the name of the default font.

Text on a Path

Although type is designed to be read from left to right along a horizontal surface, contemporary graphic designers and illustrators are a perverse lot. We insist on rotating type at bizarre angles and aligning its baseline along curves or even irregular paths. Such feats were long the bane of traditional typesetters, who had to work very hard indeed to coax type into performing such unnatural acts. With Draw, however, creating such effects is all part of a day's work.

Draw has always provided the ability to align text along a path, but with version 3 this was given a remarkable degree of sophistication. Before diving in, the important concept to keep in mind is that text applied to an open or closed path is linked to it *dynamically*. That is, you're free to modify either the text or path itself at any time, without the need to first detach them from each other. This provides a great amount of freedom to manipulate such text effects.

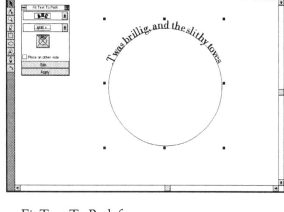

Begin by clearing off the page, then hold down the Control key and draw a large circle with the Ellipse ⬭ tool. Next, choose the 𝔸 tool, click anywhere on the page and type in a few words. Choose both the circle and the text with the ▶ tool. Then choose Fit Text To Path from the Text menu and click on Apply. The Status Line now says you have Text On A Path selected. As a default, text is center aligned along the outside and top of either a rectangle or an ellipse. Begin by clicking on the four triangles in the alignment box, each time clicking on Apply. Then try Place On Other Side to move your text inside or outside the circle.

If you're experiencing system crashes while aligning text to a path, it may indicate a problem with your fonts. You could switch to the Arial font supplied with Windows, for example, to see if the problem is with your Draw fonts. If you're running Adobe Type Manager, as well as using TrueType fonts, this could also be the cause of crashes, especially if it's an old version of ATM. Try disabling ATM and see if the problem persists. Finally, make sure you're using Revision B of version 3, with .TTF font file dates no older than August 16, 1992. If this is not the case, request free upgrade disks from Corel.

Horizontal 0°

Horizontal 15°

Horizontal 45°

The roll-up contains two sets of drop-down menus that provide a variety of alignment options. Click on the top ↓ arrow and experiment with this set of options, which affect how text positions itself vertically and horizontally in terms of the path. The default top option causes letters to rotate to follow the curvature of the path; this is the one you'll use most of the time. The bottom option keeps the type straight up and down; you can create some interesting effects with this. But the second and third options are less clear. The second option skews the text

Vertical 0°

Vertical 15°

Vertical 45°

horizontally, while the third skews it vertically, as shown in the illustration. When you've finished experimenting with these, return the text to the default rotated orientation.

Now click on the lower ↓ arrow, which displays a menu of five options that provide control over the vertical position of the text in terms of the path. From the top down, these begin with the default alignment, which aligns the baseline of text to the path; an option that allows you to define a custom distance between text and the baseline; an alignment of the top of the text's ascenders to the baseline; an alignment of the bottom of the text's descenders to the baseline, and an alignment of the midpoint of the text to the baseline.

Next to the default alignment, probably the most commonly used of these options is the one that lets you align the top of text along a path. To try this out, choose the 𝔸 tool and type another short text string on the page. Then select the new text and the circle with the ⬏ tool, choose the third alignment option from the menu and click on Apply. To get the text to align below the circle, click on the lower alignment triangle in the roll-up as well as Place On Other Side.

Click anywhere on the page to deselect the text and then click on either block of text that you've aligned to the path. The Status Line now says that you have a Compound Object Of 3 Elements selected — the path and the two text blocks. Notice that the roll-up is now ghosted; you can no longer make changes to your text. In fact, once you apply more than one text block

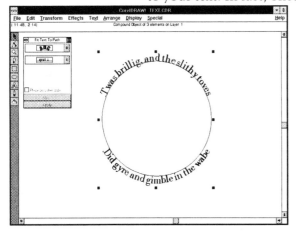

to the path, you must use a special technique to select just the block of text you want to work with. Hold down the Control key and click on just the top block of text to select it. The Status Line should now indicate that you've selected a block of Control Text. You also use the Control key when only one block of text is aligned to the path and you want to select *just* the control text, rather than the entire text on a path object.

This is significant, because with the control text selected, you can modify it with the ▶ or ⚡ tools while it's on the path. For example, drag a corner handle to resize the block. Then try dragging a side handle to condense or expand it; this can generate some pretty strange effects. You can always use the standard technique of returning to the way the text was first created by choosing Clear Transformations from the Transform menu.

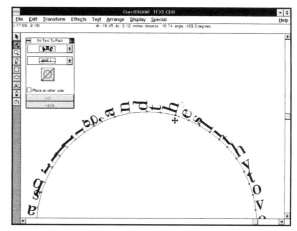

Click on the text block again to put it in rotate mode, and then rotate it. Again, interesting effects are possible here, since you're rotating each letter rather than the entire block. If you rotate 90°, you'll find the letters go end-to-end, as shown in the illustration.

While this is sometimes a desirable effect, the character spacing will no doubt need some work. Choose the ⚡ tool and you'll have access to all the usual character spacing techniques. Drag the ◄▮► handle to the right, for example, to add some space between all the characters. Now zoom in on some letters that need individual attention. If you click and drag a character's node, you'll find the character stays on the path, although it flips itself upright while you drag. Of course, you can select multiple characters with the Shift key, or by dragging a marquee, and slide the characters along the path. (This, by the way, is an essential technique when positioning text on an irregular closed path, such as a symbol.)

Assuming that you've done some terrible things to the text by now, choose Clear Transformations from the Transform menu and choose the ⚡ tool again. Character spacing on a path is important enough that I'd like you to practice it a bit more on this more normal text block. For example, use the ◄▮► handle, both with and without the Control key, to make your text go exactly halfway around the circle.

Before leaving the ⚡ tool, verify that you can double-click on one or more characters, as you did before, and change their formatting in the Character Attributes dialog box. This is also useful for rotating individual characters to more closely follow the angle of the path. You saw earlier that dragging a character's node slid it along the path, but you could change the horizontal and vertical shift values to move it in the x and y axis. The nudge keys also have the same effect. Both the Align To Baseline and Straighten Text commands under the Text menu work as before, only now they operate in terms of the new curved baseline.

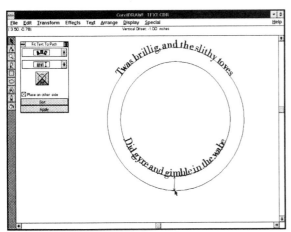

The other alignment options are pretty self-evident, with one exception. Choose the second option, the one with gray text above and below it in the roll-up, and click on Apply. Not much will seem to happen, but click on the text (note — *not* a resizing handle) and drag upwards. You'll soon be pulling out a line with an arrow on the end, and the Status Line will indicate how far you've moved from the baseline. Pause while you drag and the new text baseline you're creating will be previewed. When you release the mouse, the text will align itself to the new baseline. Now click on your text again and drag the arrow inside the curve. This is a neat feature, no doubt about it. If dragging the text isn't to your taste, however, click on the Edit button in the roll-up. Here you can type in a positive or negative baseline shift for Distance From Path. The Horizontal Offset value lets you shift the text to the right or left along the baseline, using positive or negative values. Change these values as desired and click on OK, then Apply.

Now Control-click on the lower text block and choose the same custom baseline option from the roll-up. When you click on Apply, the text will re-align itself along the inside of the path. Now either drag it or use the Fit Text To Path Offsets dialog box, as discussed above. There's currently no way to simultaneously align the baselines of two blocks of text.

What if you want to edit text that's aligned to a path? Choose the A tool and click on either text block. While you can't highlight text or edit it right on the screen, clicking on a block sometimes (but not always) takes you to the Artistic Text dialog box, where you can edit it and change the font, size or character spacing. What you can't change is the alignment, which is always set to none. If the $\mathbb{A}$ tool is proving frustrating, Control-click on some text with the ▶ tool and then press Control-T to display the dialog box.

In my earlier comments, I stressed that text aligned to a path creates a dynamic relationship between the text and the path. You've seen that text can be altered while it's on the path, but you're also free to modify the path itself. Click on just the circle, and the Status Line should indicate that you've selected the Control Ellipse. Drag a handle of the circle to resize it and the text will reshape itself to fit on the new path.

Time to get a little fancier. With the ellipse selected, choose Convert To Curves from the Arrange menu. Whoa! What happened to the text? When you apply text to a path created with the ○ or □ tools, it's easy to position text evenly around the object. But now you're faced with a common situation in which text is applied to the path of an irregularly shaped closed object. The same would be true if this was an open path. Hold the Control

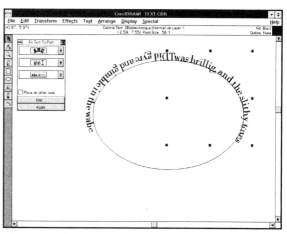

key down and click on one of the text blocks. Note that the roll-up has changed: the alignment triangles have been replaced by a third ↓, providing access to left, right or center alignment. Currently, both text blocks have been given a default left alignment. This explains their position on the path, since alignments take place in relation to the start node of a path.

If you click on the ellipse with the ⚹ tool, you should see that the path has four nodes. The start node is the largest of the four. Click and drag one or more of the nodes to radically reshape the path. All four nodes are symmetrical, so double-click on a node and use the Node Edit menu to change the node type if you need to create curves with a more acute angle. Then reposition the

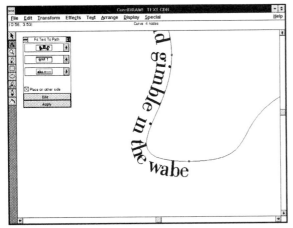

two text strings more attractively on the path, using one of three techniques. Once you've selected a block of text with the ➤ tool, using Control-click, you can choose left, right or center alignment from the roll-up. To shift the position of the text along the path, click on the Edit button and change the Horizontal Offset value. Or, more interactively, you could click and drag around all the characters in the string with the ⟆ tool, then drag any node to slide the whole string along the path. If you're dragging a lot of characters this way, you should go slowly and pause occasionally for the preview to catch up with you. Once you've finished, you should zoom in on any awkward character rotations and fine-tune them.

At this point I'll let you explore on your own some of the special effects you can apply to all Draw objects, including artistic text, such as envelopes, perspective, blend and extrude. (You'll find coverage of these procedures in *Creating Special Effects*.)

Paragraph Text

So far, you've been working with artistic text. This is appropriate when you're creating relatively small blocks of type and you want access to the broad range of features that Draw can apply to such text. However, there are some areas in which artistic text is lacking: it's limited to 250 characters per block; it can't be hyphenated or justified; it can't be divided into columns; you can't adjust inter-paragraph spacing, and text doesn't wrap automatically when edited. These are all attributes of paragraph text.

I need to stress right up front that Draw is not (yet) the ideal tool for full-page layout, mixing large amounts of text with graphics. In my view, a page layout program like PageMaker, QuarkXPress, or Ventura is more appropriate for this, due to the faster and more sophisticated text-handling these programs provide. I would not be at all surprised to see Draw move more in that direction with future releases. Meanwhile, paragraph text, when used with its limitations in mind, can prove a useful adjunct to the more common artistic text. Begin exploring this with a fresh page.

A block of paragraph text is always constrained within its *frame*. You can either create a frame by clicking and dragging with the mouse, or one can be generated automatically for you. You'll begin with the mouse approach. With the 𝔸 tool selected, click and drag diagonally anywhere on the page. As you go, the Status Line indicates the size of the frame you're creating, as well as its starting, middle and current cursor coordinates. It's undocumented, but you can hold down the Control key while you drag to create a square text block. In addition, Snap To Guidelines, Grid and Objects can all be used here.

When the text frame is the desired size, release the mouse button and you'll be left with an empty paragraph text frame. That small white bar at the top-left corner is the insertion point; one can hope that in the next release this will blink, to make its location more apparent. At this point I'd like you to pound in a few lines of type, which will appear in the default font, Avalon. (As discussed above, this default can be changed for the current Draw session, or permanently for all future documents.) You should see something significant happening right away; the text wraps to the next line when you reach the end of the frame. When you've got some text in the frame to play with, choose the ▶ tool.

The Status Line now tells you that you've got a block of paragraph text selected. Drag a sizing handle outwards and you'll find that, unlike in artistic text mode, the size and shape of the characters themselves don't change — you're simply altering the dimensions of the frame within which the text aligns itself. Speaking of resizing, here's a little undocumented tip. Choose Snap To Objects from the Display menu. Now drag a middle, top or side handle inwards to reduce the size of the block, dragging towards the center point of the frame. Keep your eye on the top-left corner of the Status Line, and when you get to the center of the frame you'll be snapped to exactly 50% of the original dimension. This tip also works with regular non-

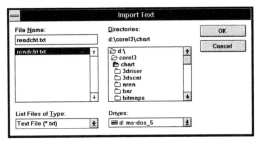

text objects, by the way. Once you've seen this work, turn off Snap To Objects.

As with artistic text, you can modify paragraph text with the ▶, ◿ and 𝔸 tools, although they work slightly differently in some cases. For example, with the block selected with the ▶ tool, press Control-T to display the Paragraph Text dialog box. You'll notice that a number of options are available that were ghosted when working with artistic text, such as the Import button and Full justification (by which Draw simply means *justified*). To give yourself more text to work with, click on the Import button and move to the CORELDRW\CHART directory. Double-click on the READCHT.TXT file to bring it into the dialog box. Scroll up to the top of the imported text file and you'll find that your original text has been replaced by the imported file.

Since you're now working with a fair amount of text, drop its point size down to a more typical body text size, such as 10 or 12 points. You might also want to pick a more legible body face than Avalon. Before leaving this dialog box, you should try out some of the new paragraph text capabilities that are available to you. Choose Full justification, for example. Then click on the Spacing button and set the Inter-Paragraph value to 200% to increase the amount of space between each paragraph. Click on OK.

If you're currently in full-page view, it's quite likely your text is now displaying as a bunch of indecipherable squares. Draw is

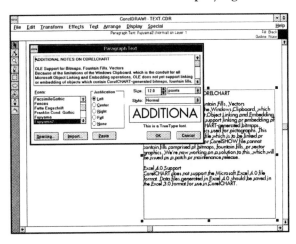

using the Greek Text Below value to speed the screen display of paragraph text in small point sizes by *greeking* it. Those of you with large, high-resolution monitors can lower the default value of 9 pixels in the Display subdialog box of Preferences to force Draw to display small type when zoomed-out. Otherwise, simply zoom in to read the type in the frame.

Drag a side resizing handle into the block to make it fairly narrow. If you make it skinny enough, the lack of hyphenation should begin to make itself known by the appearance of large spaces between words. Where these also appear between lines, an effect known as *rivers* of white space may be apparent. It's time to access a special dialog box that contains a few more options applicable only to paragraph text.

Choose Frame from the Text menu. Enable hyphenation and note that the default hot zone (more typically called the *hyphenation zone*) is set at .5 inch. This value defines an offset from the right side of the frame. A word that begins to the left of this location, but which would otherwise extend beyond the right side of the frame, will be hyphenated. So the smaller this value, the more hyphenation Draw will perform, resulting in text that takes up less space. Conversely, a larger hyphenation zone results in more words being moved to the next line down. For narrow frames, you should lower this value considerably if you want Draw to actually perform much hyphenation. Draw currently lacks such typical page layout provisions as the ability to limit the number of consecutive hyphens, or to add user-defined word breaks to a hyphenation list. Click on OK and examine the fit of your text. You might want to return to the Frame dialog box several times and try different hyphenation zone values.

Although it's not documented, keep in mind that Draw uses an *algorithmic* method of hyphenation, rather than a hyphenation dictionary. While this makes for speedy hyphenation, the linguistic rules that make up any hyphenation routine should not be trusted implicitly. So it's not a bad idea to check your hyphenated text for peculiar word breaks. You can insert a hard hyphen to break a word manually, but you'll also have to put in a carriage return.

So far, you've been using the ⬆ tool with paragraph text. Choose the ⬆ tool and you'll find that all the text manipulation procedures you explored earlier when working with artistic text also hold true for paragraph text. To make formatting easier, choose Text Roll-Up from the Text menu. This provides access to the Frame Attributes and Character Spacing dialog boxes. One severe limitation of paragraph text is that you can't apply different alignments to selected paragraphs within a frame, despite the documentation's claim to the contrary — the entire frame has just a single alignment. Give this a try using the roll-up. Finally, choose the tool and use it to both edit and format your paragraph text block.

You've typed text into an empty frame, as well as imported a text file using the Paragraph Text dialog box. But there are a couple of other ways to get paragraph text onto the page. When you import a text file into Draw it must be in plain ACSII format, containing no word processing codes. But if you've created text in another Windows application, such as a word processor or page layout program, you can bring it into a frame using an undocumented technique.

To try this out, press Alt-Tab to return to Program Manager and run Windows Write from the Accessories group. Type in a few words, highlight the text, choose Copy from the Edit menu, close Write and return to Draw. Now choose Paste from the Edit menu and your words will appear as a block of artistic text in the default font. Here's the trick. This time choose Paste Special from the Edit menu. In the dialog box choose Paragraph Text and click on Paste. Your text will be placed in a frame with a .5-inch margin on either side.

Of course, you could also use the documented technique of first creating a frame, typing in at least one character, and choosing Paste. Paste Special is something you'll have to use when pasting in text created in some applications, such as Word for Windows, into artistic text blocks. In this case, the standard Paste command results in the Word icon being pasted onto the page.

What's to be done when you want to convert text you've already created in Draw between artistic and paragraph mode? This process is undocumented, but you can convert from paragraph to artistic by selecting the paragraph text with the tool and choosing Copy from the Edit menu. If you then switch to the ▶ tool, choosing Paste from the Edit menu will create a new artistic text block. You can select a block of artistic text, clicking and dragging with the tool to create a new frame and then choosing Paste from the Edit menu. Again, for this to work you must use the tool to select the text in both cases.

Find all this undocumented stuff valuable? If these kinds of techniques whet your tips n' tricks appetite, my *Mastering Corel Draw* newsletter may prove of interest. I've provided a discount subscription coupon at the back of the book.

There remain a few last aspects of paragraph text to explore. Begin this exercise with a blank page, then choose Import from the File menu. Change List Files Of Type to .TXT and move to the CORELDRW\SHOW directory. Once you're there, double-click on READSHW.TXT to import it. You'll be treated to a message informing you that this rather lengthy file is about to be 'truncated', which is to say only the first 4,000 characters will be imported. Click on OK to acknowledge this current limitation of Draw.

Note that, as when using Paste Special, the paragraph text block has been given the height of the page, with a .5-inch margin on either side. Knowing this, you could temporarily create a new page size in the Page Setup dialog box before importing paragraph text, to precisely control the size of the block. If you do this regularly, you should create a Windows Recorder macro to quickly restore the usual page dimensions.

Set your type back to a more normal body text weight, such as 12 points. Then it's time for a final trip to the Frame dialog box under the Text menu. Here you should change the number of columns to three, set the gutter width (inter-column spacing) value to .25, set justification to Full, and enable hyphenation before clicking on OK. Now zoom in on the text. Despite hyphenation, you'll probably agree that setting justified text in narrow columns is currently not a good idea in Draw, since it doesn't adjust inter-character spacing to ensure good character fit. The result is large white spaces. Despite its current limitations, paragraph text does have its uses — just keep a close eye on the fit of the text to ensure that the quality is what it should be.

Draw now has both a spelling checker and a thesaurus, and while the latter is something of an oddity in an illustration program, the spelling checker is very useful indeed. Select your paragraph text block with the ⬏ tool and choose Spell Checker from the Text menu. Then click on Check Text to begin the checking process. The spelling checker, which uses a dictionary containing about 116,000 words, operates much like those found in most word processors and page layout programs, so I'm going to leave it to you to explore its operation. A notable feature is the ability to add words to your own dictionary (handy for those needing British/Canadian spelling).

You should also try selecting just a few words with the A tool before invoking the spelling checker, which lets you check just the highlighted text. You can also run it with no text selected and type in the word you want checked in the Word To Check area. One point I should stress is that if you click on the Cancel button after making changes with the spelling checker, those changes will remain in your text. To get rid of them, choose Undo from the Edit menu. A sizable number of foreign-language spelling dictionaries are included on the CD-ROM supplied with Draw, although British English is unfortunately absent. (For details on installing these, see *Customizing Draw's Defaults*.)

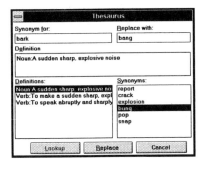

While Draw's thesaurus is currently a feature in search of a user, one can speculate that future versions of Draw may well have vastly improved word processing abilities. That being the case, the thesaurus will prove very handy. Meanwhile, why not give it a quick try. Like the spelling checker, you can use it in a number of ways. For example, double-click on a word with the A tool and choose Thesaurus from the Text menu. Draw will display any available definitions for your word. If a number of possible definitions are displayed, click once on each to see the associated synonyms. Then simply double-click on the desired synonym to replace the selected word on the page. As with the spelling checker, you can also type in words for which you're seeking synonyms.

Using Special Characters

While using the characters on your keyboard is straightforward enough, Draw lets you access the full character set of your fonts. Special characters are available in a font but are not directly accessible from the keyboard, such as accented letters, the copyright symbol and fractions. The characters available in

Text Creation and Alignment

Draw's fonts are listed on the cardboard Character Reference Chart supplied with your documentation. Armed with this, you can hold down the Alt key and press a three-digit sequence on the numeric keypad of your keyboard to generate the desired character within the Text dialog boxes or right on the page at the current insertion point. Alt-0165, for example, generates the yen ¥ symbol.

But what if (as always happens to me) the Chart has disappeared within an office awash in paper? The path to painless special character creation lies with three utilities: two supplied with Windows 3.1 and another supplied on the Utility disk included with this book.

Character Map

You'll find the Character Map program in the Accessories group of your Windows 3.1 Program Manager. This is a nicely implemented utility that lets you quickly display the Windows character set of a font and copy one or more characters to the Clipboard. They can then be pasted into any application, including Draw.

Character Map

While you can run Character Map simply by double-clicking on its icon, I find it such a handy adjunct to my word processing and graphic arts applications that I like to have it available at all times. To ensure that Character Map runs automatically each time you start Windows, drag its icon from Accessories to the StartUp group. However, running Character Map in this fashion will place its window on top of Program Manager, which is probably not what you had in mind. You simply want it quickly available from within your applications.

To load Character Map minimized, click once on its icon in StartUp to select it and choose Properties from Program Manager's File menu. In the dialog box, click on Run Minimized. While you're there, you might want to specify a keyboard shortcut for quickly accessing Character Map from within Draw. Click in the Shortcut Key area and type your desired keystroke shortcut. Click on OK and re-run Windows at this point to automatically load Character Map. You can now use it in any Windows application.

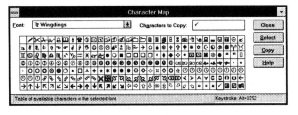

Run Draw and type your keyboard shortcut to pop up the Character Map window. While a list of fonts installed for the default printer driver is displayed, Draw currently can't make use of this font information — characters you bring into Draw via Character Map will either be in the default font, Avalon (Avant Garde), or in the font of the text block on the page into which you're pasting it. So don't bother changing fonts in Character Map itself unless you're using an application, like Word for Windows, that will make use of font information, or if you need to access one of the symbol fonts, such as Wingdings.

If you click on a character and hold down the mouse button, Character Map will display an enlarged view of that character and indicate its keyboard equivalent in the lower-right corner. Double-click on one or more characters to add them to the Characters To Copy list. Then click on the Copy button to place these characters in the Clipboard and choose Paste from Draw's Edit menu, or click on the Paste button in the Text dialog boxes. This will place the characters either directly onto the page, or into the window of the Text dialog boxes. Character Map is still running, so you can quickly access it at any time, using your keyboard shortcut or Alt-Tab. Since Draw makes you re-specify the font of characters you paste in, you may find Character Map useful simply for its ability to display the Alt-number combination of a character when you click on it.

Macro Creation

If there are certain characters you regularly use in your Draw documents, you can speed things up even more with the use of macros. While commercial macro programs provide more flexibility, the Recorder program supplied with Windows is up to the job.

To construct a special character macro, Character Map must first be running. Then double-click on the Recorder icon in the Accessories group of Program Manager. Return to Draw and use the Alt-Tab combination to display Recorder. Choose Record from Recorder's Macro menu. Now define the keystrokes that will invoke the macro you're about to construct.

Text Creation and Alignment

For example, click on the Shift box and type a 'C' in the Shortcut Key area to assign your first macro to Control-Alt-C. Optionally, you can type a name in the Record Macro Name area to identify your macro. If you want your macro to be available in other applications, and to work in the Text dialog box as well as directly on the page, change Playback to Any Application.

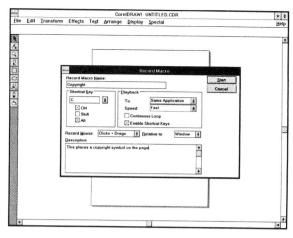

Click on Start to begin creating the macro. At this point, every mouse movement is being recorded in your macro, so don't perform any unnecessary actions. Press Control-Shift-C (or whatever keystroke sequence you assigned to this task) to display Character Map. Because Character Map remembers each character you choose during a session, it's best to clear out any accumulated characters before choosing new ones. Click in the Characters To Copy area and drag to the right. Then double-click on the copyright symbol. This has the effect of deleting any characters remaining from an earlier use of Character Map and selecting just the copyright symbol.

Click on the Copy button and then anywhere in the Draw window. Press Shift-Insert to place the symbol on the page, then press Control-Break to halt the macro recording process. Click on Save Macro and OK to finish. You're done. Click on the ⬧ tool and test out your macro by pressing Control-Shift-C. Then try it out in the Text dialog box.

So you now have a process to create macros that quickly select special characters. But before shutting down Windows, be sure to save these new macros or they'll be lost. Use Alt-Tab to display Recorder and save any macros you've created. By default they're saved in the Windows directory and given a .REC extension.

There are several ways to run your macros in subsequent Draw sessions. If you've created a number of macro files and don't know which ones you'll be using in a session, drag the Recorder icon into the StartUp group (hold down the Control key when you drag if you want to leave behind the original). Follow the

steps discussed above for Character Map to set Recorder to run minimized when Windows loads. Create a keyboard shortcut for it and you can quickly pop up Recorder on top of Draw and open the desired macro file.

But if all your macros are in a single Recorder file, as is the case on my system, just add the name of your macro file after RECORDER.EXE in the Program Item Properties dialog box. This will ensure that both Recorder and your macro file will load each time you run Windows.

Compose Yourself

Compose

If all this seems a little onerous, there is another method available for automating special character creation which would make sense for those needing access to large numbers of characters. Compose is a modest little Windows application created by Digital Equipment Corporation, which I've included on the Utility disk with this book. (See *The Draw Companion Disks* for details on installing this.)

Once you run Compose (it's a natural for the StartUp group), it's invoked in an application by pressing the right-hand Control key on your keyboard, although this key can be redefined, if necessary. You then press one or more predefined keys to access special characters or the time and date.

Compose is supplied with fairly sensible two-keystroke combinations to access special characters, and you can easily redefine these. For example, pressing E then ^ gives you Ê. Thankfully, the ability to print out all the keystroke sequences has been provided, so there's no need to memorize them.

Beyond quick access to special characters, Compose will also display your screen fonts in whatever size you specify and output a complete character set for each font, along with ANSI numbers for direct keyboard access. You can display this font window simply by pressing Control-Space-Space. Compose can't display Draw's .WFN format fonts, but it works fine with PostScript and TrueType.

Creating Special Effects

T he Envelope, Perspective, Extrude and Blend commands on the Effects menu let you alter the shape of an object, or create new objects based on existing ones. These effects can be applied to any object, be it text or a graphic, with the exception of bitmaps and paragraph text.

Envelopes

On a fresh page use the 𝔸 tool to create just a single word in a sans serif face, such as Switzerland or Fujiyama, set at 100 points. Then choose Edit Envelope from the Effects menu to reveal a selection of four envelopes. Click on the top ◺ icon to choose the Straight Line envelope. Eight handles, connected by dotted lines, have now surrounded the text, and the Status Line indicates your current envelope. Click and drag any of the four corner handles either towards or away from the text, and note that the Status Line indicates how far you're moving in the x or y axis — the Straight Line envelope constrains you to dragging in either axis. When you release the mouse button, the text will reshape itself to fit within the new envelope.

Experiment by dragging different handles, choosing Undo from the Edit menu to undo the most recent envelope as desired. If the resulting distortions get too extreme, choose Clear Envelope from the Effects menu to return to square one. As always in Draw, the keyboard comes into play when working with envelopes. Hold down the Shift key while dragging a handle to move the opposite handle away from or towards the

Enrich your drawings with Envelope, Perspective, Extrude and Blend

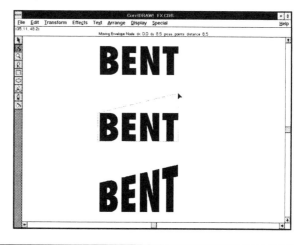

---

one you're dragging. Hold down the Control key to move the opposite handle in the same direction. And hold down both to move all four corners or sides at the same time.

You may find that the effect you want to achieve is impossible with the current envelope. Choose Add New Envelope from the Effects menu to leave the fruits of your labors intact, while adding a fresh envelope of the currently selected variety. If you've added multiple envelopes, each time you choose Clear Envelope it will step you back to an earlier version of your object. You can also choose Clear Transformations from the Transformations menu to quickly remove all the envelopes you've applied.

It's sometimes useful to copy an envelope you've created to another object. The process is similar to that of using the Copy Style From command. Draw a rectangle with the Rectangle □ tool and from the Effects menu choose Copy Envelope From. The cursor will change shape to the familiar From icon. Click on the outline of the object you want to copy the envelope from — the enveloped text — and the rectangle will reshape itself to fit in that envelope.

You may have noticed that when you apply an envelope to an object, the ⨍ tool is selected. The problem with this is that you can't node edit an object once you've applied an envelope to it. There's no good solution to this, but you can use the Copy Envelope From command to apply the envelope to another object and then get it back again. To try this, place one of Draw's symbols on the page (using the ☆ tool) and then modify it with an envelope. At this point, you're not free to select and work with the symbol's individual nodes. Create a copy of the symbol, select the original and choose Clear Envelope from the Effects menu. Now edit the outline of the symbol with the ⨍ tool. When you're done, choose Copy Envelope From from the Effects menu and click on the outline of the still-enveloped copy. It should re-apply the envelope to the original edited symbol.

Now investigate the other envelopes: Single Arc ◁ , Two Curves ◁ and Not Constrained ⨍ . The latter is the most versatile envelope, since you can drag not only handles but

control points. When using this
envelope you can also select multiple handles and move them all at
once. One thing to watch out for
when changing envelopes is that
the type of envelope you choose is
applied to all objects on the page
that have been given envelopes.

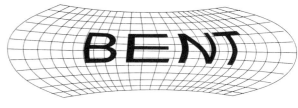

Choose Import from the File
menu, select the .CDR format
from List Files Of Type and import GRID.CDR from the
SAMPLES directory of the Utility disk. Drag your text or symbol
on top of the grid, select both objects, group them and then experiment further with the envelopes.
The grid will provide a good sense
of just what the envelope is doing
to the enveloped object.

Whatever changes you make to
text with envelopes it will remain
text, although it's handled a bit
differently than normal. For example, you can't select and work
with individual characters with the
𝔸 or 🖊 tools. However, you
still have access to the Edit Text
dialog box on the Edit menu, and

both Character and Text Roll-Up on the Text menu. The fastest
way to edit enveloped text is to simply click on it with the 𝔸
tool, which takes you to the Edit Text dialog box. If you then
make editing changes, note that additional letters you type will
remain inside the envelope, thereby condensing the type.

Before leaving envelopes, try applying a few to simple objects,
such as boxes and circles. This is often an easier way to create
fairly basic objects than drawing them from scratch. You might
also go the other route and import a complex drawing from one

of the DRAW\CLIPART directories and warp it with some envelopes.

Perspective

When you've fully explored envelopes, use Clear Transformations to return a text and grid group to its as-created state. Select it and choose Edit Perspective from the Effects menu. The result will be the addition of a dotted border very much like that of a Straight Line envelope, only with handles on just the corners, not the midpoints. Drag a handle and note that you're no longer constrained to movement in just the x or y axis, as you were when adjusting the envelope.

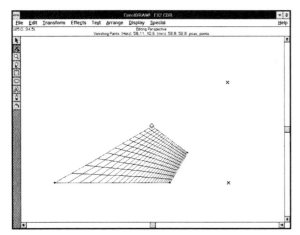

Holding down the Control key while you drag a handle constrains movement in terms of the dotted border. Drag a handle or two to alter the shape of your object, and then drag a handle with the Control key held down to see this principle in action. Holding down both Control and Shift will cause the opposing handle to move in the opposite direction, similar to holding down just the Control key when working with envelopes. The Shift key alone currently has no effect.

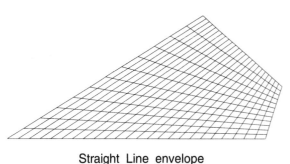

Straight Line envelope

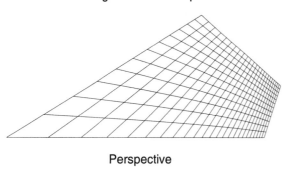

Perspective

Alter the perspective of the grid I supplied you with and it will become evident that perspective alters the object logarithmically, in contrast to the even distortion provided by the Straight Line envelope. The illustration on this page contrasts the two effects.

When you first apply a perspective to an object, the Status Line indicates that the horizontal and vertical vanishing points are both Very Far. How

Creating Special Effects

far is very far? Draw displays this when the location of the vanishing point lies beyond the borders of the editing window. Drag the handle on the top-right corner of the grid downwards and you'll see an ✕ icon representing the horizontal vanishing point, with the Status Line indicating its coordinates. Drag the top-left handle to the right and the vertical ✕ icon will appear.

Once the vanishing point icons are displayed, you can drag them to alter the perspective of the object. Note that dragging an ✕ icon moves two of the handles controlling the object. With the ✕ icon visible, hold down the Control key and drag a handle on the object to see the constraining effect of the movement of the icon. Neither the Control nor Shift keys have any effect when dragging an ✕ icon itself. And whatever you do, don't hold the Alt key.

The ability of ✕ icons and handles to snap to grids and guidelines is useful when working with objects that share a common perspective. The technique here is to first generate the desired perspective effect, then note in the Status Line the coordinates of the vanishing point. You could then place both a vertical and horizontal guide at that location by choosing Guidelines Setup from the Display menu. With Snap To Guidelines enabled, you could now snap the ✕ icon of a new object to the intersection of the guidelines, as shown in the illustration. Give this a try. It's worth adding that handles and icons can also take advantage of Snap To Objects, when that's enabled on the Display menu.

Since there's currently no way to move an ✕ icon just horizontally or vertically, another technique is to place a guideline of the appropriate orientation on the ✕ icon, enable Snap To Guidelines and then drag the icon along the guideline. The Add New Perspective, Clear Perspective and Copy Perspective From commands work just like their envelope equivalents covered above.

Extrude

The ability of Draw to project into three-dimensional space — or *extrude* — the outlines of an object provides rendering abilities usually associated with sophisticated CAD (computer-assisted design) programs. For the designer or technical illustra-

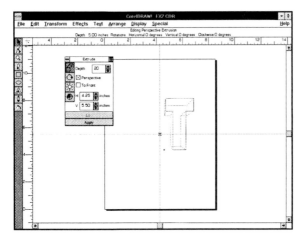

tor, the extrusion capabilities of Draw make it relatively simple to generate accurate projections of objects that before had to be laboriously constructed. For architectural and product illustrations, or simply fancy text effects, extrude is a powerful command that can greatly enhance your work with Draw.

Delete everything on your page or create a fresh one. While your first impulse might be to extrude a string of text, you'll get a better sense of how this command works if you start with something simpler. I suggest just the capital letter 'T' set in 200-point Fujiyama Extra Bold, or something similar. Then move this into the top-right corner of the page. The extrusions you create will also make more sense if you're not distracted by fills, so switch to wireframe view with Shift-F9. I'd like you to mark the center of the page, by clicking in the ruler areas and dragging both a horizontal and vertical non-printing guideline onto the page. After this small amount of setup, you're now ready to begin extruding.

Make sure your letter is selected and then choose Extrude Roll-Up from the Effects menu. When this roll-up is first displayed, it automatically gives an extrusion to the currently selected object. You should see that the letter has a perspective extrusion, with its vanishing point set by default to the center of the page. The horizontal and vertical extrude values in the roll-up indicate that the vanishing point is indeed the center of the page. These values display in terms of the 0,0 point on the page, which by default is its lower-left corner. They use the same measurement system as the rulers, which can be set as desired by choosing a different system in the Grid Origins section of the Grid Setup dialog box. Begin altering the current extrusion by clicking on the horizontal and vertical scroll arrows; you'll see the corresponding values change in the roll-up. You can also drag the ✕ icon to change these values interactively. Snap To Guidelines, To Grid and To Objects can all be employed here.

The amount the extrusion extends towards the vanishing point, its *depth*, is currently at a default value of 20, as shown in the roll-up. Change the depth to a value between 99 and -99. At 99, the extrusion tapers to the vanishing point. The use of negative values projects the extrusion forwards, with a change in color to red. Experiment with the To Front option, which by default is not enabled. This one's a bit hard to figure out at first. Take a look at the examples on this page, which show the same letter extruded with both positive and negative values, and with To Front both enabled and turned off. You should see that with this option enabled, the extrusion increases in size as it moves away from the vanishing point. Click on the Apply button after changing this option, then click anywhere on the page to see the extrusions more clearly. If the Apply is ghosted while working with extrusions, just click on the extrusion to re-select it.

A final option is turning off Perspective. Here the Depth value has no effect. The resulting parallel extrusion creates a duplicate of the original object and centers it at the horizontal and vertical coordinates in the roll-up. Try this with and without To Front selected.

Click anywhere on the page to end the extrusion process; the Status Line should indicate you have an extrude group selected. You can perform all the usual transformations on an extrude group, such as moving, resizing and rotating. Give this a try. However, you can't use the Envelope or Perspective commands; you should apply these first, then extrude. Click anywhere on the page to deselect the group, then click on the outline of just the letter. The Status Line should indicate you've selected the control text. You can now edit this as you would any text block. Press Control-T, for example, and in the Edit Text dialog box choose a new font. Note that when you click on OK a new extrusion is generated automatically.

Return to the Edit Text dialog box, this time by choosing the 𝔸 tool and simply clicking on your letter. Now type a few more letters in the text editing window and return to the page. Again, new extrusions have been created for all the letters. Switch to the 𝄢 tool and you can now either use the ⫿⊪ icon to adjust inter-character and inter-word spacing (with the Control key) of the entire text string, or you can click and drag one or

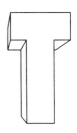

Depth 20
To Front not selected

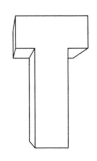

Depth -20
To Front not selected

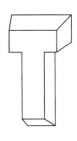

Depth 20
To Front selected

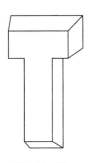

Depth -20
To Front selected

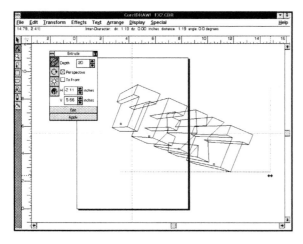

more character nodes to kern letter pairs. Pretty neat, I think you'll agree.

Return to the Edit Text dialog box and edit your text string, leaving just the original 'T'. It's important that you're clear about exactly what's happening when you extrude an object. Choose Separate from the Arrange menu. Click anywhere on blank part of the page to deselect, then click on first the text, then the extrusions. You'll find the extrusions are all in a group. Select this group and then choose Ungroup from the Arrange menu. You've now turned the extrude group into five individual objects, which can each be selected and manipulated. Return to the preview window with Shift-F9, select each object in turn and give them different fills to verify this. Initially all the extruded objects are black; by default such objects are given the fill of the control object. If you later change the fill of the control object, the extrusions also change. This makes it easy to apply fountain fills to extruded objects. To avoid this, first use the Separate command before you fill the control object.

When an object is given a fill of none (X) before being extruded, the creation of the extrusions takes place differently. Delete all the extruded objects and return to the wireframe view. Make a copy of just the large letter 'T' and fill one letter with white, and the other with none. Give them both a parallel extrusion and compare the results. You should switch back and forth between the wireframe and preview windows to see the effect of the white fill.

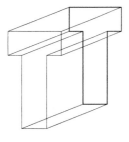

Filled with none

If you have several extruded objects on the page, to modify an extruded object just select it and click on the Edit button in the roll-up. This will display the object's current extrusion parameters and let you continue modifying them. To remove an extrusion, choose Clear Extrude from the Effects menu.

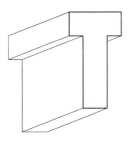

Filled with white

Select either of your extruded 'T's and click on the Edit button to return to the wireframe extrusion editing mode. Make sure the 'T' has a perspective extrusion. You've been working with the default

Depth $\mathcal{D}$ icon selected. Draw also provides the powerful ability to rotate an extrusion in three-dimensional space, which you can access by clicking on the 3-D Rotation ↻ icon. The roll-up changes to display a sphere with six arrows, two for each axis of movement. Click on any of the arrows now to rotate your extrusion in the desired axis. The Status Line provides feedback on the degree of rotation in the six axes. You can hold down the mouse button to keep the object in continual motion.

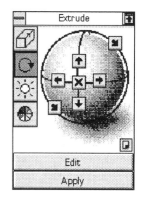

If you need to rotate with more precision, click on the ⊏ icon in the lower-right corner of the roll-up. This lets you specify the exact amount of desired rotation. You can also hold down the mouse button on the scroll arrows. I find objects rotate faster here than with the sphere displayed. Click on the ⊏ icon again to return to the sphere. If things get really out of control, you can click on the ✕ in the middle of the sphere to remove any rotation you've added.

You should click on the $\mathcal{D}$ icon now and change the extrusion type from perspective to parallel. Now try clicking on the sphere's arrows and you'll find that you're no longer rotating the extrusion; you're simply accomplishing the same thing as dragging its ✕ vanishing point icon around on the page.

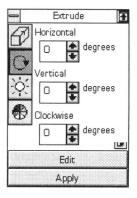

Coloring Extrusions

The Extrude roll-up provides several controls over the color and shading of your extrusion's fills. Give your extrusion a fill of white and switch to the preview window. Click on the Light Source Direction ☼ icon. The roll-up now lets you control two aspects of the lighting of your extrusion group: the direction of light striking it and its intensity. First click on the light switch icon to enable this ability. Then change the light direction by clicking on the intersection of the lines forming the grid around the sphere to move the ✕ icon to a new location. Change the intensity from the default value of 100 by typing in a new value from 0 to 200, or by dragging the slider. Click on Apply after you've made these changes. I've created a few simple examples of the shading effects you can generate with these two controls, but I think you'll find it hard to achieve exactly the effect you're after. For more complete control, you should follow the earlier procedure of using first the Separate and then the Ungroup

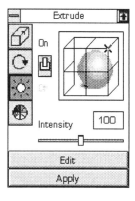

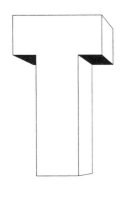

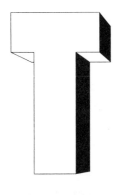

command. Give your extrusion a color fill and experiment some more before moving on.

Turn off the light switch icon to return your extrusion to its default fill color, then click on the Extrusion Coloring ⊛ icon. As you can see, normally the extrusions are given the object's fill color. But you can apply both a solid color or linear fountain fill to the extruded objects using the roll-up. This eliminates the necessity of using the Separate command. Click on the current color displayed next to Solid Fill and choose a new one from the menu. Click on Apply to display it. Then pick the desired From and To colors for a fountain fill and again click on Apply. With a fountain fill now in the extruded objects, why not click again on the ☼ icon and try changing the light intensity. In the case of fountains, I do find intensity to be a useful feature, since slight adjustments result in correspondingly subtle color changes to the fill. If you wind up with a unique color or fountain fill in the extruded objects, you can use the Copy Style From command to give the same fill to the control object.

At this point you should spend some time exploring the many possibilities of the Extrude roll-up. For example, you could create a text string, apply an envelope to it, alter its perspective and then extrude it. That's how the 'Extreme' example illustrated here was created. It was then given a linear fountain fill, with the letter 'E' on either side being filled with custom angles.

You can also extrude open paths, with sometimes interesting results. And combined objects, such as many symbols, are also fair game. But you can only extrude one object at a time, and the object can't be either grouped, a bitmap, a blend or text on a path. Why not alter the GRID.CDR graphic with a perspective effect and then extrude it? This is a good way to figure out just what extrude is doing—it's also lots of fun.

Blend Effects

You explored the use of the Blend command earlier in *Getting Your Fill of Draw* as a way of generating smooth, controlled fills that create the illusion of light and shade. However, I only touched on a few of the capabilities of this feature; Draw provides very complete control over the blending process, which I'll lead you through now.

Blending works best when the two objects you're blending between are both relatively simple shapes. While you can blend a group or combined objects, these can result in hopelessly garbled intermediate objects rendered as open paths. This is why many of the symbols in Draw's symbol libraries, which are combined objects, aren't good candidates for blending. The simpler ones, however, blend quite nicely.

Begin by giving yourself a blank page. Choose the 𝔸 tool, hold down the Shift key and click near the top-left corner of the page. In the Dixieland library choose symbol 58, set it to 1 inch and click on OK. Then drag a copy of it down to the lower-right corner of the page. Select both symbols with the ▶ tool and choose Blend Roll-Up from the Effects menu. Click on the roll-up's Apply button to generate the default 20 steps. This is one of the simplest, yet most useful, aspects of the Blend command; being able to create a defined number of equidistantly spaced

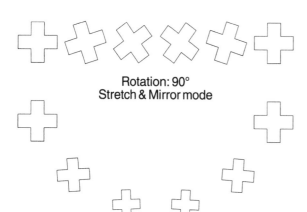

Rotation: 90°
Stretch & Mirror mode

Rotation: 90°
Rotate & Skew mode

objects. Your symbols may well be a little scrunched together, however, so why not lower the Steps value to 15 and click on Apply.

Draw provides the ability to rotate the blend steps, although it's a somewhat unpredictable feature. With your blend selected, enter a Rotation value of 90° and click on Apply. The intermediate blend steps have been rotated through 90° from the start to end object. Now click on your blend to put it in rotate mode and click on Apply. This effect is interesting, but less desirable is the change in shape of the blend objects. Experiment with different positive and negative rotation values.

Note that a single node is displayed at the lower-left corner of the start and end symbols. Closed objects always have a single beginning node, which is the orientation point Draw uses when creating the steps in a blend. By changing the nodes on the start and end that Draw uses to map the progression of steps, you can radically alter their shape. Click on the Map Nodes button and all the nodes of the end object will be displayed. Click on the one you want with the ↱ cursor. Then click on the desired node in the start object with the ↰ cursor. Click on Apply to see the effects of your node choice. You should go through the process several times, selecting different combinations of nodes. The ability to choose nodes in this manner is your only hope of controlling the shape of the steps during blending, but results remain far from predictable. The illustration shows the effect of choosing different nodes when blending between a normal and rotated version of the symbol.

As with text on a path and extrusions, the relationship between the start, end and intermediate blend objects is a dynamic one; changing any of these will affect the blend group. At this point you should deselect the blend group and then select just the start or end object. Try moving, resizing, mirroring, skewing or rotating the object and the blend steps will redraw automatically. Even more intriguing, choose the ↟ tool and adjust the nodes of the object — again, the steps will reflect the new outline.

You should be in the preview window at this point. Select the start or end node and give it a solid color fill. Then give the opposing object a different color fill. Give each object a variety of process, spot, fountain and pattern fills. There are a lot of possible combinations here, but the most significant involve solid spot and process colors. The most important principle to keep in mind is that blend steps are never given spot (or Pantone) fill colors; they're always process. This represents a handy way to quickly create a large number of color variations between two specified colors.

If you're working on an illustration that calls for a range of subtle blues, for example, you could blend between two exist-ing blues to create new shades. You'd then choose first Separate and then Ungroup from the Arrange menu. You could then use the Copy Style From command on the Edit menu to quickly copy these colors into other objects. You could also select and export them as a .CDR file, then re-import and apply them in future projects. Or you could select them one at a time and add them to the current color palette, by entering a name in the Uniform Fill dialog box, clicking on the Palette button and then Add Color To Palette.

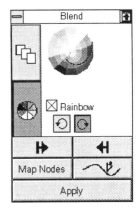

You have some control over the sequence of colors created in a blend. Click on the ✹ icon in the roll-up. The straight line on the HSB (hue, saturation, brightness) color wheel running between your start and end blend objects indicates the default color progression. Click on Rainbow and you can direct the progression to run ↻ clockwise or ↺ counter-clockwise around the color wheel, thereby including a broader range of colors than in the straight line approach. When you've finished ex-perimenting with color, click on the ⌸ icon.

While there are a lot of unusual twists packed into Draw's

implementation of blends, the ability to give one of the intermediate blend steps the same control status as the start and end
objects is a rare one. I find it's also typically poorly understood.
To see this, I'd like you to create a fresh, colored blend. Then
hold down the Control key and double-click on any one of the
intermediate blend steps. The Status Line now identifies this as
a third Control Curve. Try giving this object a different fill,
moving it or resizing it, and you'll see it affects the blend objects
on either side of it.

If you click on any of the other intermediate blend steps, the
Status Line will indicate you've selected a Compound Object
Of 5 Elements. 'What the heck's that?' was my first reaction to
seeing this. But it makes sense if you dig a little deeper. Deselect
the blend, then click in turn on the two end objects and your
new control object. That adds up to three. Then hold down the
Control key and click on any blend step on first one side of the
control curve, then the other. The Status Line will indicate in
each case that you've selected a Blend Group — which adds up
to five. In other words, the new control curve serves as the end
object for one blend group and the start object for the other.
You can create multiple new control objects per blend.

Beyond giving you more control over the progression of blend
steps, the ability to create a new control object makes it easy to
delete just some steps, while keeping a blend otherwise intact.
Just make the new control curve the last object in the blend,
Control-click on the unwanted steps and choose Clear Blend
from the Effects menu.

Blending on a Path

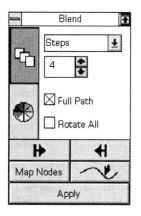

While you typically use the Blend command by specifying how
many steps you want between two control objects, you can also
use it to create a number of objects a specified distance apart.
The trick here is that this is only possible if the blend steps are
assigned to a path. To see this in action, draw a straight line with
the ℓ tool long enough to hold all the objects from one of your
blends. Select the blend group, click on the ∿ℓ icon in the roll-
up and click on New Path. With the ✔ cursor, click on the line
you drew, then click on Apply. Your blend should flow along
the line. Your blend objects may not be evenly spaced along the

path, however, so the first thing you should do is click on Full Path and Apply. The start and end nodes are now positioned with their centers aligned on the ends of the line, with the blend objects equidistantly spaced between them.

When you blend objects on a path, you have the additional capability of specifying the desired amount of space between them. Click on Steps and in the menu click on Spacing. The Draw documentation says that the Spacing value is in inches, but in fact it's whatever is currently specified as the Grid Frequency measurement system in the Grid Setup dialog box. Enter the amount of space you want between the blended objects, as measured from the left edge of the first object to the left edge of the second one. Of course, Full Path won't fill the path now, as it did before; Draw will only fill as much of the path as it can, using the current Spacing value.

You have some control over the position of the start and end control objects in relation to the path. Click on the ▷ icon in the roll-up and choose Show Start to select the start object. As well as being able to transform and color objects on a path, as you did before, you can slide a control object along its path. Try dragging the start object to see this. Now put the Start object into rotation mode by clicking on it again. If you drag the round rotation point icon to a new location, you can move the object off the path.

Here's an undocumented twist to try out: with the start object in rotation mode, enable Snap To Objects from the Display menu, hold down the Control key and drag the rotation icon until it snaps to the top of the object. When you release the mouse, this will align the object precisely to the top of the path. Snapping it to the right side of the object will snap it to the beginning of the path. To align the middle of the object back to the path, snap it to the middle. You could also rotate an intermediate object, if you first double-clicked on it to select it.

Having experimented with these options, it's time for some fun. Fun, in this case, takes the form of creating some interesting effects with the blend on a path feature. Clear your page and draw a curved line with the Pencil ℓ tool. Select the Text 𝔸 tool and Shift-click on the page to display the Symbols dialog

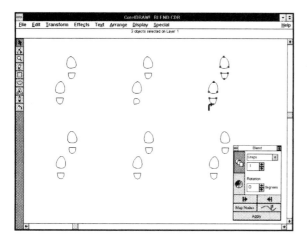

box. Choose the Tracks library and set symbol #20 at 1 inch on your page. Make a copy of it and blend between the two, with Rotation at 0 and Steps at 1. Examine the intermediate object created by blending the feet. If the intermediate object looks okay, great. But when blending compound objects such as these, some distortion may have been introduced into the intermediate object. If the lower shoe has an irregular shape, click on Map Nodes in the roll-up. Then click on the lowest node of first one shoe, then the other, before clicking on Apply. You should see that the intermediate object is now correctly shaped. When blending very complex compound objects, you may have to use the Break Apart command on the Arrange menu and blend each object element in turn.

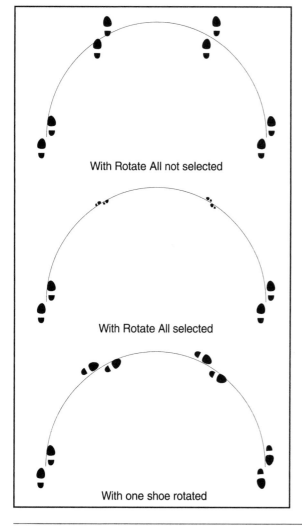

With Rotate All not selected

With Rotate All selected

With one shoe rotated

Now apply your blend to the path you drew, using the technique discussed above, then increase the Steps value to give yourself more shoes. At this point your shoes are all vertical — they're not following the angle of the path. Click on Rotate All in the roll-up. The result seems to be a step backward, but the problem is that the two sets of shoes on either end of the path are pointing towards each other, instead of in the same direction. Select either the start or end object, click on it again to put it in rotation mode and rotate it in the direction of the path, as shown in the illustration. Your shoes should now all follow the path.

Creating Special Effects

Try out some of the other symbols in the Tracks library. In the scissors example, I've blended a circle to create a true dotted outline. (While you can do this by editing the CORELDRW.DOT file and specifying a dot of zero width, then assign round line caps to it in the Outline Pen dialog box, it's hard to control the size, number and spacing of the dots.) You could also blend symbols along a closed path, such as a circle or another symbol. And for truly wild line effects, try blending several different objects along one line.

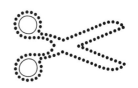

I should be candid at this point and caution you that the current implementation of blending objects on a path seems rather buggy. Strange things happen if you blend objects on a path you've created by combining paths. And controlling the spacing and position of objects blended along a closed path is very difficult indeed.

Blending Text

An interesting use for blending between objects is the creation of new weights of existing faces, or even completely new faces. Select the $\mathbb{A}$ tool, click on the page and type just a capital 'A'.

Press Control-T and set the type to 100-point Fujiyama Extra Bold. Make a copy of this letter a few inches to the right of the first and set the face to Switzerland Condensed. Then select them both and use the Blend command to create a few intermediate steps.

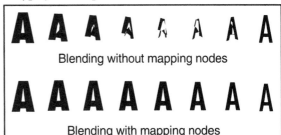

Blending without mapping nodes

Blending with mapping nodes

Disappointed by the results? In fact, a little preliminary work is typically required before you can successfully blend an 'A'. Click on Map Nodes in the roll-up and then click on corresponding nodes on each letter. When you then click on Apply, you should wind up with intermediate letters of varying weight and shape, as shown in the illustration. You could use this ability to blend letters to generate new letterforms for the creation of a new typeface, by using the TrueType and PostScript Type 1 export formats.

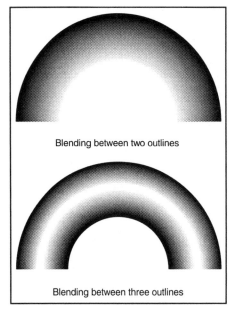

Blending between two outlines

Blending between three outlines

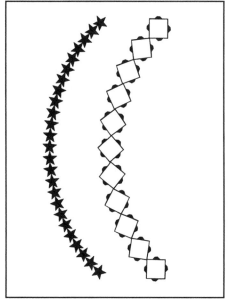

Some interesting effects can also be achieved by using Draw's Blend command in conjunction with object outlines. For example, you can blend between lines of different color, to create linear fills of varying shape. You can create much smaller files using this approach, rather than blending between rectangles, since a line only has two nodes, versus the four nodes of a rectangle. The correct line thickness depends on the length of the blend and the number of steps. The arc shapes were created by blending between two 2-point lines, using 60 steps. In the top example, I blended between black and white. In the lower example I held down the Control key and double-clicked on one of the intermediate blend objects to select it. I made its outline color white, and set the outline color of both the start and end control objects to black.

The neon effect of the hammer and sickle was created by giving one of Draw's symbols a black 8-point outline. A copy was placed on top of it by pressing + on the numeric keypad, and it was given a white hairline ✲ outline. The two were then blended using 20 steps. Conclude this section by experimenting with blending between lines. Some excellent examples of line blending can be found in *Design Essentials* (Adobe Press).

Creating Special Effects

Working with Bitmap Graphics

B itmap graphics are fundamentally different from the vector, path-based graphic objects created with Draw's Rectangle □ , Ellipse ○ and Pencil ℓ tools. Bitmap images are typically created by scanning existing artwork or drawn from scratch with a paint-type program, such as CorelPHOTO-PAINT. Four common bitmap file formats that Draw can import (most of the time) are .TIF, .BMP, .TGA and .PCX. I qualify this, since graphics file formats are known for their notoriously slippery standards. For example, there are many versions of the .TIF (tag image file format) format produced by a wide range of applications, and several flavors of .PCX. The .BMP format, on the other hand, is a solid standard with few variations.

Don't overlook this aspect of Draw

You can also bring bitmaps into Draw from Windows-based paint or scanning programs via the Clipboard; simply select and copy the image to the Clipboard from within its application and paste it into Draw's editing window. You can even use the built-in screen capture abilities of Windows itself to generate an image for use in Draw. To do this in any application simply press the PrintScreen key to copy a color bitmap image of the screen to the Clipboard. Then choose Paste from Draw's Edit menu to place it on the page. (As well, a modest screen capture program, CCapture, is in your Photo-Paint directory.) The Clipboard can only handle bitmaps of moderate size, however, so importing large ones will still be a requirement.

Why Bitmaps?

Once a bitmap is imported into Draw, it can either serve as a template for manual or automatic tracing (autotracing) before being deleted, or be kept in bitmap form and printed as an integral part of the drawing. I find imported bitmaps can add texture to illustrations that otherwise have a hard-edged quality. Bitmaps can also be autotraced in Draw's separate CorelTRACE utility, as discussed in *Converting Scans with CorelTRACE*.

Many of the operations you perform on objects can also be applied to imported bitmaps. Draw can export drawings (even those containing bitmaps) to a variety of bitmap formats, and these exported bitmaps can later be re-imported. For example, you could export your Draw image as a color bitmap and load it into Photo-Paint. There you could perform global color correction and apply special effects filters, such as blur and emboss. This altered image could then be imported into a page layout or presentations application, or brought back into Draw. Keep in mind, however, that exported bitmaps are much larger than their vector equivalents and can't be easily enlarged in an application without degrading the quality of the image.

Let me emphasize that what Draw *can't* do is create or edit drawings on a bit-by-bit basis; to actually edit bitmaps you'll need a paint-type drawing program, such as Photo-Paint or Aldus PhotoStyler.

Getting in a .TIF

Tag Image File Format (.TIF) images are created by many scanners and paint programs. In addition, bitmap clip art is often supplied in .TIF format and it's the bitmap format of choice for the Macintosh. Such files are usually *bilevel* bitmaps, in which images are represented strictly in terms of black or white. A number of these are included with Draw in its SAMPLES subdirectory. Draw can import these bilevel .TIF files and output them to any printer supported by Windows.

Some scanners and image-editing programs can also create .TIF *grayscale* files, which represent continuous tone images, such as photographs, in shades of gray. The good news is that Draw will output the grayscale information in these images when printing to a PostScript printer. The bad news is that those with non-PostScript printers will find imported grayscale images output as if they were bilevel.

Color .TIF files are also produced by scanners and some paint programs, such as PhotoPaint. Draw can import, print and color separate up to 24-bit color .TIF files containing 16.7 million colors. Such images redraw slowly in the preview window, but they open up whole new worlds to Draw users, especially for those with the fast, high capacity computers necessary for manipulating them. Working in the wireframe view displays color and grayscale images as bilevel, but provides much faster screen redraws. If you're going to stay in preview mode, make sure you have Interruptible Display enabled in the Preferences dialog box. Then you can simply click on the page to stop a bitmap from redrawing.

The .PCX format is the older of the two standards and is strictly a PC format; it's not found on the Macintosh. Draw handles bilevel .TIF and .PCX files in the same way. Less common are .PCX grayscale files. Draw can import (and trace with CorelTRACE) .PCX files created with scanners or paint programs, including color bitmaps, which it converts to objects filled with corresponding colors.

Assuming you have a graphics card that can display at least 256 colors (and many can't), experiment with the display options in the Display sub-dialog box of Preferences. If you don't have a display capable of 256 colors, these options will not be available. I should mention that in this dialog box only the Optimized Palette For Full-Screen Preview option has any effect on the display quality of bitmaps. With this option enabled, grayscale and color bitmaps will display noticeably dithered in the full-screen preview. Color bitmap images will print in color on color devices, and will be converted to shades of gray on monochrome printers.

Cropping Bitmaps

There are a number of bilevel .TIF files included in the SAMPLES subdirectory of DRAW on your hard disk. If for some reason they're not there, you can work with the ones I've provided in the SAMPLES directory of the Utility disk. Create a new publication by choosing New from the File menu. Then choose Import from the File menu, change List Files Of Type to .TIF and move to the DRAW\SAMPLES directory. The For Tracing option in the lower-right of the dialog box dates back to older versions of Draw; in 3.0 it has no effect. Double-click on

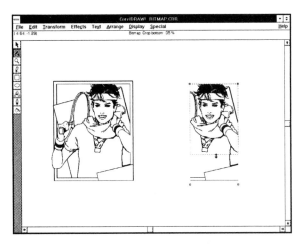

OUT_PLAY.TIF to import it. Zoom in a bit on the tennis player image to display it more clearly.

Draw has the ability to crop off unwanted parts of scanned images, a handy way to trim clip art images such as this. Let's say you only wanted the head of the tennis player and also wanted to remove the rectangular border. As is so often the case with Draw, there is no tool for cropping in its toolbox. Instead, choose the ⚲ tool and begin by dragging the bottom-middle handle up to crop off unwanted parts of the image. As expected, the Status Line provides feedback about your progress as you crop. Crop the other edges of the tennis player to eliminate as much of the excess imagery as possible, as shown in the illustration. If there were parts of the image that you didn't want that weren't accessible by cropping, such as the racquet, you could use the old trick of drawing objects over them and giving them a fill of white and no outline. I sometimes find that random garbage prints outside the frame of cropped bitmaps. Again, a white rectangle is the answer here.

Keep in mind that the part of the image that has been cropped is still there, although it's no longer visible, so you can always uncrop it. More significant is that the entire bitmap, cropped area and all, is stored in your .CDR file. Since the entire bitmap will be sent to your printer, and then cropped, you'll find a cropped image takes as long to print as the uncropped original. So try to crop your scanned images as much as possible with your scanning software, or in a paint program, before importing them. Failure to do so on a grand scale can go so far as to completely choke a high resolution imagesetter. This cautionary note also holds true for page layout programs such as PageMaker and Ventura, by the way.

Transforming Bitmaps

The familiar transformations you've performed on Draw objects with the ▶ tool also apply to bitmaps. Try moving, stretching, scaling, mirroring and duplicating (but not rotating or skewing) the lobster. Then choose Clear Transformations from the Transform menu to put the image back to its as-imported condition. The exception is cropping, which you'll have to undo manually with the ✄ tool. To select a bitmap you must click on its border, the same practice as when selecting a paragraph text block.

Now try rotating and skewing the bitmap. You'll find that Draw can no longer display the individual bits that constitute the image. Instead, it displays the bitmap as a gray rectangle with a white triangle on its lower-left corner, to help you keep track of its orientation. The only exception is a rotation of 180°, which Draw displays properly. (Choose Clear Transformations from the Transform menu to get your image back.)

The image itself will output well, as long as you're using a printer employing true Adobe PostScript. Printers with a com-patible, or *clone*, version of the PostScript page description language may not fare so well. The HP IIP in my home office, for example, is outfitted with a PostScript cartridge from Pacific Data. It prints nicely most of the time, albeit more slowly than true Adobe PostScript printers. It's also quite happy printing skewed bitmaps, but rotated ones output hopelessly garbled.

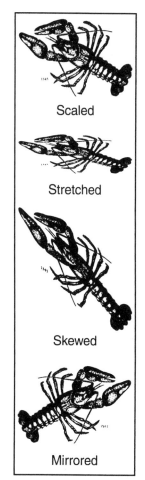

Scaled

Stretched

Skewed

Mirrored

Bitmap Fills and Outlines

You can change the outline color of a bilevel bitmap with the icons in the lower row of the ♀ tool menu. Assign different shades of gray to the bitmap and note that changing the outline color changes the bits of the image itself, but leaves the back-ground untouched. Interesting effects can be achieved by as-signing a pale gray, such as 10% or 20% black, to a bitmap and placing it behind text. You could do this in Draw itself, or export the bitmap and place text on top of it in a page layout or word-processing program.

You can also apply shades of gray or colors to the bitmap with the Color Palette at the bottom of the screen. If this is not currently displayed, choose Show Color Palette from the Display menu and click on gray shades or colors with the right mouse button. Choose ✪ from the ♀ menu to create a custom outline

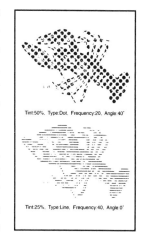

Tint:50%, Type:Dot, Frequency:20, Angle:40°

Tint:25%, Type:Line, Frequency:40, Angle:0°

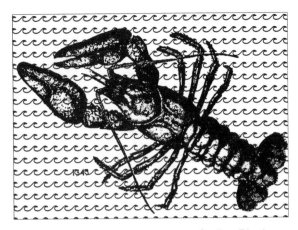

Fill:PostScript Waves Texture, Outline:Black

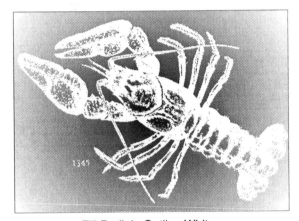

Fill:Radial, Outline:White

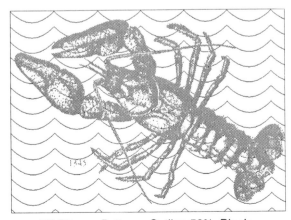

Fill:Bitmap Pattern, Outline:50% Black

color. If you're using a PostScript printer choose the Spot method, lower the tint to 50% and then click on the PostScript Options button. In the PostScript Options dialog box, scroll down to select one of the many PostScript halftone screens and drop the frequency down to about 20 per inch. This will produce a very pronounced pattern on the bits that constitute the image. Return to your page and print the tennis player to view the halftone screen. Then experiment with different tint percentages and settings in the PostScript Options dialog box before continuing on with the chapter. You can create some very unusual effects with this seldom-used Draw feature, but only if you have a PostScript printer.

Bitmap fills work much the same way as outlines, only they're applied to the entire background of the bitmap, thereby filling its frame. You can choose fills from the palette at the bottom of the screen by clicking on them with the left mouse button. All of the fills that can be applied to objects can also be used to fill the frame of bitmaps. So go wild applying two-color, full-color, graduated and PostScript fills to your lobster. You can't change the outline or fill colors of imported grayscale or color bitmaps.

Manually Tracing Bitmaps

Rather than beginning an illustration by drawing on a blank page in Draw, many designers first create a rough sketch using traditional media on paper, scan it, import it into Draw and use this as a template by drawing over it. You could also create a template by quickly sketching something in a paint program, such as Photo-Paint. You'll find more on using the bitmap images created with scanners or paint programs in later chapters, such as *Getting the Best Scan*, *Converting Scans with CorelTRACE* and *Image Editing with PHOTO-PAINT*. For now, you simply need to import one of the bitmap images supplied with Draw and use it to hone your drawing skills.

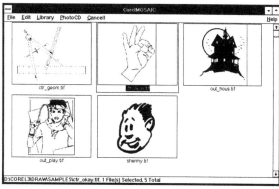

Choose the ▶ tool, choose Select All from the Edit menu and press the Delete key to clear the page. Then choose Import from the File menu. When you need to select an image to import from a directory holding many files, it's often easier to preview them with CorelMOSAIC (I cover this utility in detail in *Working with Clip Art & Symbols*.) Click on the Mosaic button. In the Mosaic dialog box choose Open from the File menu and make sure .TIF is the current format in List Files Of Type area. Then move to the SAMPLES subdirectory of DRAW and click on OK.

Click just once on CTR_OK.TIF and choose Get Info from Mosaics Edit menu. This dialog box provides some information about the file, such as its size, the color depth (1 bit per pixel in this case, or monochrome) and the image size measured in pixels. Click

on the Cancel button, then double-click on the thumbnail of CTR_OK.TIF to import it. This returns you to the Draw window, but keep in mind that Mosaic is still running. So rather than return to the Import dialog box, you can use Alt-Tab to bring Mosaic forward. Since Mosaic doesn't shut down after you import (or open) a file, its using up valuable memory. If memory is low, you should display the Mosaic dialog box and exit the program.

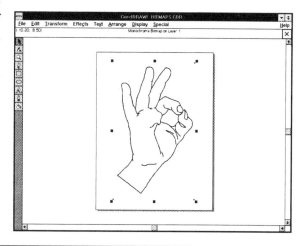

You've seen that imported black-and-white bitmap graphics, such as this TIFF image, can be assigned foreground and background colors. Since the only function of this image is to serve as a template on which to practice your drawing skills, you'll find the default black of the bitmap makes it hard to see what you're drawing.

Use the ♙ flyout menu and give the bits a color of 10% gray by clicking on the shaded box just below the ✚ icon. Another approach would be to change the outline color of the segments you draw to a contrasting color, such as red. The easiest way to do this is to make red the default outline color. With no object selected, choose the ⊛ icon from the ♙ flyout menu and choose a new color. Click on OK. In the resulting New Object dialog box, choose Other Objects and click on OK. One advantage of this technique is that as you adjust segments with the ⚲ tool, you can take better advantage of the contrasting colors Draw uses to display the segments on which you're working. Draw uses up to four colors to display the entire original object, the original segment you're modifying, the modified segment and any part of the modified segment that overlaps another object. In addition, nodes display as orange on a white background.

Make sure the bitmap is deselected by clicking on a blank part of the page, then change to the ♙ or ♙ tools; if you don't deselect it, you'll wind up in autotrace mode, which I'll cover later in this chapter. Try drawing a few lines now, using the template as a guide, then adjust them with the ⚲ tool. Zoom in as much as

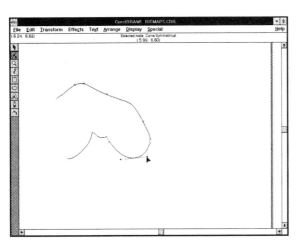

necessary to do this effectively. One thing that can quickly prove annoying is that the screen redraws every time you adjust a node. If you've enabled Interruptible Display in the Preferences dialog box, you can halt the redisplay of a bitmap simply by clicking anywhere on the page, but this will probably mean the curve object on which you're working isn't displayed.

Working with Bitmap Graphics

Zoom out to see the whole page, then press Shift-F9 to switch to the wireframe window. Bitmaps in this window display less smoothly than in preview, and their color can't be changed from the default dark gray. You also can't change the color of the lines you draw with the ✐ tool, so you give up the four display colors mentioned above. But the big advantage is speed — if you adjust a few nodes with the ⟋ tool now, you'll find that the wireframe screen rarely redraws. Note that unlike the preview window, you can't halt the redisplay of a bitmap here simply by clicking.

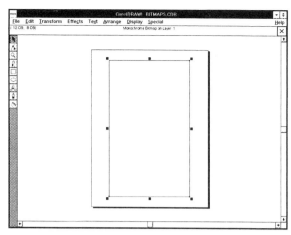

Just as you have to click on the outlines of objects when in wireframe view to select them, you must click on the selection box surrounding a bitmap with the ⟋ or ▸ tools to select it. But what if you want to see what you've drawn without displaying the bitmap itself? Choose Show Bitmaps from the Display menu. This is an option that's only available in the wireframe window, and is yet another toggle that Draw will save as a default when you close your publication. You could also create a new layer, move the bitmap there and then lock it to ensure you didn't accidentally select it. But this won't speed up screen redraws, unfortunately, so there's little benefit to this approach.

I leave it to you now to practice drawing, using the bitmap as a template and zooming in as required. The paths you construct will depend on whether you need to create closed objects — which will later be filled with a variety of shades — or open paths. Finally, zoom in and spend some time adjusting the segments you've drawn, using the Node Edit menu where appropriate. There's really no better way to master drawing, and the ⟋ tool, than this.

Autotracing Bitmaps

What if you don't want a fill to cover the entire frame of the bitmap? You can use a combination of autotracing and the

---

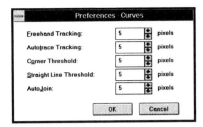

Preferences · Curves

Freehand Tracking:	5	pixels
Autotrace Tracking:	5	pixels
Corner Threshold:	5	pixels
Straight Line Threshold:	5	pixels
Auto Join:	5	pixels

OK   Cancel

Combine command to constrain the fill to just the bitmap, or everything inside the frame but the bitmap, by creating a clipping path, or *mask*.

When you autotrace a bitmap, Draw constructs a closed path of line and curve segments around one area of bits in an image at a time. The resulting object can be manipulated in the usual way with the ➤ and ⅄ tools, filled and so on. Once you've finished autotracing an imported bitmap, you typically delete the bitmap itself, leaving behind the lines and curves of the tracing. Here, on the other hand, you're going to use autotracing to create objects that will control the bitmap's fill; you'll create a hybrid composed of bitmap and vector objects.

You should still have the CTR_OK.TIF image on your screen and be in the preview window. Before autotracing the bitmap, choose Preferences from the Special menu and click on Curves. Three parameters are provided for controlling how Draw creates line and curve segments when autotracing. The default values for Autotrace Tracking, Corner Threshold and Straight Line Threshold are all 5 pixels.

The Autotrace Tracking value affects autotracing in the same way that the Freehand Tracking value affects freehand drawing with the ℓ tool. By lowering this value, Draw will more closely follow the edge of the bitmap being autotraced, resulting in a more accurate curve object but one with more nodes and a rougher, choppier look. Raising the value has the opposite effect.

Lowering the Corner Threshold value encourages Draw to treat abrupt changes of direction in the bitmap as cusp nodes. If the value is raised, Draw will be biased toward the creation of smooth nodes, which follow abrupt changes of direction less accurately.

When Straight Line Threshold is lowered, only very straight parts of the bitmap will be traced as line segments, so your autotraced object will probably be crawling with curves. As you saw in Chapter 3, the Corner Threshold and Straight Line Threshold values also apply to segments you've drawn freehand with the ℓ tool.

This is all very interesting, but the question arises: when is it appropriate to change these three defaults? Unfortunately, to coax truly useful curve objects from Draw's autotrace feature you'll often have to change the defaults several times in the course of tracing an imported bitmap. What you set these values to will depend on the image being traced and the nature of the outline you want to create.

Since you need to generate an outline that matches the bitmap hand as closely as possible, set all three values to 1. If you were creating a trace that would be used as an object on its own, these values would be inappropriate, since they will result in an object of considerable complexity. This would be virtually impossible to edit, due to its large number of nodes. Another concern is that objects with too many nodes take a long time to print, and may even fail to print at all on PostScript printers. Corel identifies 200 to 400 nodes as the danger zone for objects; very complex objects will have to be broken down with the 𝄕 tool, or your file may well be unprintable.

Select the imported bitmap and choose the 𝒍 tool to enter autotracing mode, as confirmed by the Status Line. (With no bitmap selected, choosing the 𝒍 tool simply puts you in drawing mode.) The cursor also looks a little different; it seems to be firing dots to the right. Zoom in until the hand fills the screen. Then place the cursor to the left of the hand and click once to create an autotraced outline of the bitmap. If you click and Draw can't find a bitmap to the right, it will simply display an error message.

Select the trace around the outside of the hand with the 𝄕 tool and in the Status Line note the number of nodes it contains — my traced outline had 73. Before proceeding, you may wish to make a copy of the bitmap and retrace it using different values in the Curves dialog box. How would using the default value of 5 for the three parameters affect the trace, for example? On my system, these values produced a much less accurate trace containing 50 nodes.

Adjust the autotraced outline with the 𝄕 tool, zooming in and using the Node Edit menu where necessary. The tips of the fingers, for example, could use some fine-tuning. Return to autotrace mode and trace the area formed by the thumb and index finger.

Creating a Mask

Choose the Rectangle □ tool and draw a rectangle bigger than the bitmap's frame. Select the rectangle and your two traced outlines with the ▲ tool (make sure you dont select the bitmap) and choose the Combine command. The fill you assign this object will surround the bitmap, rather than fill it. Fill this combined object with white. Assign different fill and outline values to both the bitmap and the combined trace object. I usually assign a fairly thick outline to the trace, which covers up the relatively jagged edges of the bitmap. In the first of the three hand examples illustrated here, the trace has been given a 2-point black outline, while the bitmap was given an outline color of black and a fill of 20% black. But as you've already discovered, if you assign an outline to the combined mask object, the rectangle you drew is also given an outline. So how do you give an outline to just the hand, as shown here?

The trick is to combine just the two hand tracings first and make a quick copy with the + key on your numeric keypad. Give this the desired outline attributes but a fill of ✗ (none). Now use the Tab key to select the other combined tracings below and combine them with the rectangle, as you did before. You'd then fill this object with white. The idea is that the copy of the hand is on top, with the three-object mask below and the bitmap on the bottom. If necessary, use the commands on the Arrange menu for moving objects forwards and backwards.

In the second example, the bitmap has been given no fill or outline and the mask has been given one of Draw's full-color pattern fills. A copy of the trace has a 2-point black outline and no fill. Keep in mind that the difference between a bitmap filled with none or white is significant; the former is transparent, while the latter is solid white.

Of course, you're not restricted to using a rectangle; the third object could be anything, even a complex shape drawn with the ℓ tool. The final illustration employs a trace and rectangle combo that's been given a fill of 20% black and yet another 2-point black outline. The bitmap uses the PostScript Spirals texture fill, and has been given a black outline color to display the bits.

The combination of autotracing and combining opens many possibilities for using bitmaps creatively in your illustrations. And by scanning textured images and importing them, you can add an endless variety of fills to your objects, whether bitmap or vector. There's an interesting collection of bitmap textures in .BMP format in your CHART\BITMAPS directory, for example. And check out the .PCX bitmaps in the PPAINT\TILES directory (WOOD.PCX is one of my favorites). Granted, these are bitmap fills, with all the limitations that implies: they will output with relatively jagged edges, they can't be edited within Draw and they will cause file sizes to mushroom. But they can add some interesting patterns and textures to your images and will output to any printer. They're also fine for images used in screen-based presentations. You should devote some time to investigating this fascinating set of graphic possibilities. (For more on this, see the full-color fills section of *Getting Your Fill of Draw*.)

Fun with Bitmaps

The ability of Draw to export in a variety of color bitmap formats opens up new possibilities for using your images. So I've included a few novel things to do with your bitmaps to get you going.

Digital Fuzzy Dice

Many Windows users are beloved of the ability to make any .BMP format file grace their Desktop. This can be easily done by running Program Manager's Control Panel, double-clicking on the Desktop icon and choosing one of the available .BMP

wallpaper images. While a rich array is supplied with Windows 3.1, you can create your own .BMP wallpaper files, either directly with Photo-Paint, or by exporting Draw images in .BMP format.

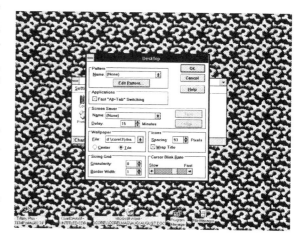

As mentioned above, a wide selection of bitmap pattern files is supplied with Draw 3.0. For example, there are 20 .BMP color pattern files in the BITMAPS subdirectory of CorelCHART that represent such

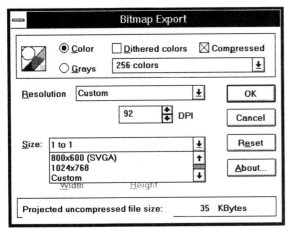

Bitmap Export

Color ☐ Dithered colors ☒ Compressed
Grays 256 colors

Resolution Custom   OK
              92 DPI   Cancel

Size: 1 to 1   Reset
       800x600 (SVGA)   About...
       1024x768
       Custom

Projected uncompressed file size: 35 KBytes

textures as cork, concrete and granite. Photo-Paint's TILE subdirectory contains 26 color .PCX format files that provide a variety of interesting patterns. And those with access to the version 3.0 CD-ROM drive will find an additional 64 .PCX scanned photographic images. You can simply copy the .BMP files into your WINDOWS directory to make these easily accessible as wallpaper, or you can enter the full path to your BITMAPS directory in the Desktop dialog box. The illustration shows the CHETAH.PCX tile from the TILE subdirectory, which was imported into Photo-Paint, exported in .BMP format and then installed as wallpaper.

Since you can now export anything on your Draw page to .BMP, you're not limited to creating wallpaper from bitmap files. For example, I imported one of the 61 vector .WMF clip art files from the VECTORS subdirectory of CHART, BULLION.WMF, and placed it on a red background in Draw. I then exported it to .BMP format, clicking on Selected Only in the Export dialog box, and then used the options shown in the Bitmap Export dialog box. The number of colors was set to 256, to match the palette of my graphics card. I chose the compressed option to generate a smaller file, which Windows has no problem installing as wallpaper. The resolution was set to 92 dpi to match that of my monitor — a higher setting would have been pointless in this case, although you can set this value up to 600 dpi for prepress applications. The size was set at 1 to 1, to keep the exported image the same size as it was created, although you can set this value up to 4,800 pixels.

When this image was installed as wallpaper, it revealed that Draw had added a thin white border around the image. Unfortunately, the current version of the export filter does this for all color bitmap formats. The solution was to import the exported .BMP file into Photo-Paint. When this file is imported into Photo-Paint, you can click and drag with the Box Selection tool to drag over just the colored portion of the image, and choose

Copy To from the Edit menu to save this selected area to a file. (Hold down the Shift key while you drag to create a square selection area.)

While this technique works, I find it tricky to drag over just the colored area. So I usually draw a square, unfilled box in Draw around the objects to be exported and export this as well. Then, as the second window in the Photo-Paint illustration shows, it's easier to select just the desired area when the image is imported. Once in Photo-Paint, you can make use of its abilities to perform global changes on your object, such as brightness and contrast, as well as apply special filters (once you convert the image to 24-bit color). You can then save the modified bitmap and re-import it back into Draw, if desired.

If you're really into wallpaper, you should be using a program like the freeware Newpaper program, which automatically picks a new wallpaper file each time you run Windows. Newpaper can be found on most online services, such as CompuServe, as NP20.ZIP.

One thing to keep in mind if you're exporting a graphic containing fountain fills is that the number of fountain steps in the exported file is the same as that of the Preview Fountain Stripes value in the Display subdialog box of Preferences. For smooth fountains, bump this up to the maximum value of 256. Happily, increasing this value has no effect on exported file size.

For the smoothest possible images you may wish to add Jaggies Are Gone (JAG), from Ray Dream, to your software toolbox. JAG is a modest utility that removes jagged edges from .BMP, .GIF, .PCX, .TIF and .TGA files. It does this by *anti-aliasing* them, a process in which bits of intermediate color and shade are added to the image, fooling the eye into seeing edges as smoother than they really are. The program is fast and it works. Those exporting bitmap images from Draw for use in an on-screen presentation — in CorelSHOW, for example — would find JAG very useful.

Bitmap Pattern Fills

The preceding technique can also be used to manipulate the full-color pattern fills supplied with Draw. First, draw a square box

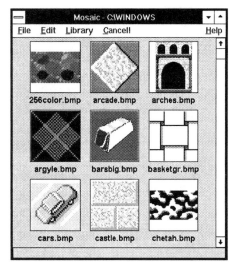

Mosaic - C:\WINDOWS

File   Edit   Library   Cancel!   Help

256color.bmp   arcade.bmp   arches.bmp

argyle.bmp   barsbig.bmp   basketgr.bmp

cars.bmp   castle.bmp   chetah.bmp

in Draw with no outline and fill it with a full-color pattern, by choosing ↗ from the ✍ menu. Set the Tile Size in the dialog box to match the size of the box you drew. Then export this box and remove the white border in Photo-Paint. You can now use this bitmap tile as wallpaper, or as a fill pattern in Chart or Photo-Paint. Or you could manipulate it in Photo-Paint and then use it as a new full-color pattern in Draw itself.

The .PCX and .BMP images supplied with Chart and Photo-Paint can also be used as fill tiles in the Full-Color Pattern dialog box. At this point, you might be wondering if the .BMP files in the WINDOWS directory that are supplied for use as wallpaper can also serve as raw material in Draw and Photo-Paint. You bet. And a quick way to experiment with these is to click on the Mosaic button in the Import dialog box. Mosaic can display color thumbnail images of files in a directory, making it easy to browse through available files before importing them. Change List Files Of Type to .BMP and move to the WINDOWS directory to see whats available for import.

Custom Startup Screens

It's well known that you can suppress the rather tedious initial Microsoft graphic when you load Windows by simply typing WIN :. But less well known is that with some fiddling you can force Windows to display a graphic of your own creation when it loads. The following procedure is adapted from Brian Livingston's excellent *Windows 3.1 Secrets* (IDG), a book no hardcore Windows user should be without.

When you type WIN to run Windows, you execute WIN.COM, a program in the WINDOWS\SYSTEM subdirectory. WIN.COM starts Windows in either standard or enhanced mode, depending on your system, then senses the type of graphics card in your computer and displays the default Windows startup screen. WIN.COM is really a combination of three files that were bound into one executable file when you installed Windows. One of these files is VGALOGO.RLE (for

VGA or higher monitors), which is the default graphic startup image in compressed .BMP format. RLE stands for *run-length encoded*, a form of file compression. Any RLE format image, up to about 55 Kb in size, can be substituted for the original VGALOGO.RLE file, with which a variant of WIN.COM can be generated to load Windows.

You can try this out fairly easily by taking advantage of Draw's new ability to export in compressed RLE format. With your image displayed in Draw, change the page size to 640 points horizontally and 480 points vertically. Then resize your image to fit this page, to ensure that the exported image will have the correct on-screen proportions. Choose Export from the File menu, choose .BMP format and click on OK. In the Bitmap Export dialog box, click on Compressed, set the number of colors to 16 (more is superfluous here), set the resolution to 92 dpi and the size to 640 by 480. The latter setting is particularly significant — using higher values will result in the startup image not being centered on the screen. Click on OK.

In File Manager rename, your exported file's extension from .BMP to RLE and copy it into the WINDOWS\SYSTEM subdirectory. Close Windows and at the DOS prompt change directories to the WINDOWS\SYSTEM subdirectory. Assuming your exported file is called SCREEN.RLE, to create a variant of WIN.COM called NEWWIN.COM type the following and press the Enter key:

```
copy /b win.cnf+vgalogo.lgo+screen.rle c:\windows\newwin.com.
```

You should see a message indicating that you copied one file. Typing NEWWIN and pressing Enter should run Windows and display your new startup screen.

Graphics for Screen Blankers

If you use a screen blanking program, you may be able to export a Draw file into a form that the blanker can use. For example, After Dark, from Berkeley Systems, can blank your screen with a color .BMP file exported from Draw. This is handy in situations where you want the company logo to display. Or you could create a series of commonly used messages at a large point size and export them, loading them into the screen blanker when appropriate.

Image Editing with PHOTO-PAINT

O ne of the most intriguing of the many new features in CorelDRAW 3 is its new-found ability to export images in a variety of color bitmap formats. With these capabilities it's possible to add new life to your Draw-created illustrations or clip art images. Although not every drawing will lend itself to this kind of transformation, there are many instances in which you might consider using all or part of an illustration created in Draw as a bitmap image.

Many times one hears the complaint about the "stiffness" of computer-generated artwork, but it takes a great deal of effort to soften object outlines in Draw; in spite of its many sophisticated blending and vignetting features, most illustrations give away their computer heritage with just one look. By combining the vector-based abilities of Draw and the bitmap-oriented approach of CorelPHOTO-PAINT, you can find many creative ways to overcome this and extend the capabilities of Draw itself.

What is possible in Photo-Paint that's not possible in Draw? You can, for example, change the overall contrast or brightness of your artwork. You can make it blurry. You can splatter the whole thing (or just parts of it) into small dots. Or airbrush some irregular shapes and make the surface appearance less smooth. Since you're working with the bits that constitute your image, you can select parts of the image with a variety of marquees, as well as by color or tonal value. Then you can apply a number of image processing filters to modify the nature of those selected bits. This contrasts with the approach in Draw, in which you would select and work with complete objects, rather than the bits in the image.

Once you've modified the image as desired, you could either print it directly from Photo-Paint or import it into Draw,

Discover a world of textures

CorelCHART, CorelSHOW, CorelTRACE or a broad range of page layout or graphics applications.

This chapter is not strictly tutorial in nature. I won't lead you through Photo-Paint by asking you to perform actions, but instead will demonstrate some of its capabilities as it's used to modify a variety of images. (Photo-Paint is also covered in *Converting Scans with CorelTRACE*. Coverage of bitmaps in general can be found in *Working with Bitmap Graphics* and *Getting the Best Scan*.) You could, of course, try out this material as you go by running Photo-Paint and opening a bitmap file. You'll find a number of color .PCX files in the CORELDRW\PHOPNT\SAMPLES directory. You could also create your own using the technique described below.

Softening Draw Images

The first illustration, of a man loading a truck, was created by Pawel Bodytko in Draw 3 for his client w.w. Grainger, Inc. Later, wanting to modify it with Photo-Paint, Pawel opened the file in Draw and exported it as a 24-bit color .TIF file. As a 24-bit file, such an image can make use of a color palette of more than 16.7 million colors. This is a requirement for being able to use many of the special effects in Photo-Paint.

You always need to calculate the size of your image while performing such an export, so it's important to know the size of the final printed image, the screen resolution it will be printed at and how grainy you want it to look. As a general rule of thumb, if the bitmap resolution (in pixels) is more than twice the resolution of the

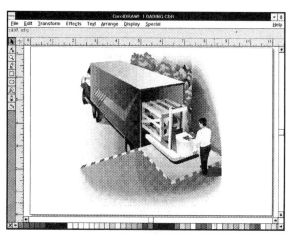

halftone screen used for printing (in dots per inch, or *dpi*), the bitmap file might be unnecessarily large. In other words, if the halftone dots of the output device are larger than the image's digital cells, the extra detail won't be used.

When exported at a resolution of 150 dpi, the image had a size of 973 by 1,055 pixels. Had a larger image been desired, either the output resolution or the size of the illustration itself within Draw could have been

Image Editing with PHOTO-PAINT

increased. This, of course, would have required more disk space to store the bitmap file, and as well would have slowed down all operations performed on the drawing in Photo-Paint.

After the file was opened in Photo-Paint, the first step was to enlarge a portion of the image to see the amount of detail that was generated during the export process. Having the image displayed at a zoom level higher than 100% helps to see the *raster* — the bits that constitute the image. A 100% zoom level means that every pixel in the image is displayed with a single screen cell, while at 200% it takes four cells for each pixel, at 400% it

takes 16 cells, and so on. With the zoom level less than 100%, the program randomly drops pixels from the screen display. Pawel chose Filter and Blend from the Edit menu, and then applied 100% blending five times. The goal was to blur the illustration more than just the single 100% setting would allow.

Pawel wanted a slightly different effect, so he applied another filter from Photo-Paint's Edit menu. Add Noise changes the value of neighboring bits, or *pixels*, creating a grainy, mezzotint-like effect. The Variance option in the dialog box lets you determine how much difference there will be between the original pixel values and those changed by the filter. The maximum setting is 255, which lets the program choose any color or

grayscale value. (The Flat option makes the shifts much more pronounced than the shifts created by Bell.) After the filter was applied, the image now looked like a soft pencil drawing created on grainy paper. When output at the right size and screen resolution, the computer origins of this image would be almost imperceptible.

Another option at this point is to convert the image to a 1-bit file that could be used in Draw as a transparent pattern, which can either be black or be given a different color with the ⬠ tool. To accomplish this, choose Brightness and Contrast from the Filters submenu of Edit. You need to maximize the contrast, leaving only black or white pixels, and then use the brightness slider to determine how dark or light you want it. Click on Screen Preview as you go, then OK when you're satisfied with the effect. You can then convert the image to a 1-bit line art file by choosing Convert To Black And White Line Art from the Edit menu. No halftone screening is necessary; this enhanced mezzotint effect can be used effectively in Draw, or imported directly into other page layout applications.

By using Blend you can create a very soft background for the main objects in your illustration, an effect similar to a low depth of field in photography. The accompanying illustration by Pawel shows both the original creation in Draw and the Photo-Paint-modified version. To make use of this effect in Draw, simply export the background areas of your illustration, delete them (or export them to a separate file for safekeeping),

Image Editing with PHOTO-PAINT

blur the resulting bitmap in Photo-Paint with the Blend filter, import it back into Draw and move it to the lowest layer in your illustration. Since bitmap screen redraws are much slower than those of Draw's regular outline objects, it's a good idea to create a separate layer just for the bitmap. You can then display or hide it as desired.

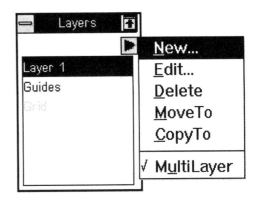

To do this, first choose Layers Roll-Up from the Arrange menu. Click on the right-pointing arrow at the top of the roll-up and choose New. In the resulting Layer Options dialog box, change the default layer name to Background and click on OK. You now have a new Background layer displayed in the roll-up, but it's currently the top layer. Click on Background in the roll-up and drag it down on top of Layer 1. This will make Background your bottom layer. With this layer

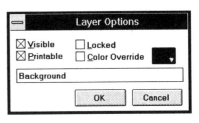

still selected, when you import the background bitmap it will be automatically placed on this layer. When the bitmap is positioned as desired, double-click on Background in the roll-up and disable Visible to eliminate bitmap redraws. Since this makes the bitmap disappear, you may first want to draw a rectangle around it to mark its location. (You could also work in wireframe mode to speed bitmap redisplay, and optionally disable Show Bitmaps under the Display menu.)

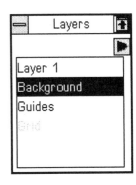

Modifying Scanned Images

Retouching and manipulating scanned photographs is probably what Corel Corporation had most in mind when it decided to include Photo-Paint as part of the Draw graphics toolbox. Although Photo-Paint is missing many important features in comparison to higher-end image editing programs, it still offers a vast array of tools, which if used with skill can produce high-quality results. However, it's important that your display system deliver enough fidelity that you can work with some accuracy right from the screen. Your graphics card should be able to display at least 256 colors, especially if you'll be working with scanned images. (For more on this, see the Hardware Considerations section of *Optimizing Windows*.)

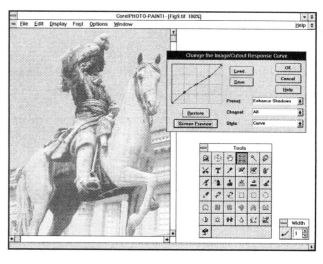

In the original photograph, the sculpture of Louis XIV had lost some of its majestic presence, due to the partly visible Versailles palace in the background. The scan of the photo also required some changes in the grayscale values. Since the shadow areas needed special attention, Pawel decided to adjust the grayscale balance first. He chose Filter from the Edit menu, then Color/Gray Map. In the Response Curve dialog box he changed the Preset to Enhance Shadow and clicked on Screen Preview to see the result. Since the resulting balance shift of the gray tones was too great, he changed the Style to Curve and modified the response curve by dragging its nodes, clicking on Screen Preview as he went.

To remove the palace from the background, he selected the primary outline color of the sky using the Eyedropper tool.

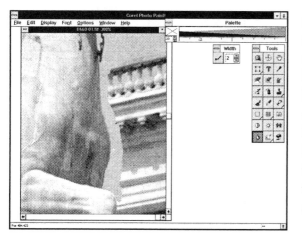

With the Fountain Pen tool he then started outlining the sculpture with the sky color. The resulting jagged outline edge of the sculpture could later be blurred with the Blend Paintbrush tool. When working with small detail he outlined using a smaller brush, while when painting over larger areas he increased its size to a full 40 pixels. He used the Local Undo tool if he removed too much of the sculpture while outlining it.

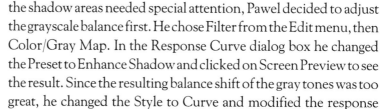

Once the building was removed, something had to be done about the unnatural flatness of the sky. It would have been difficult to use the Airbrush tool, since Photo-Paint doesn't allow you to mask areas for airbrushing. (This lack of a masking feature is a very serious handicap, and one that needs addressing in future versions of the program.) The Gradient Paint Roller tool was chosen, even though it works only on a single boundary area (with adjustable

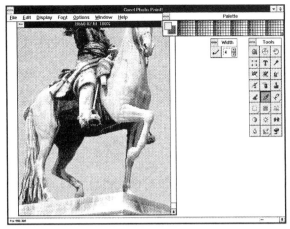

color sensitivity parameters). There are two ways to overcome this boundary shortcoming. The first method is to fill all the different areas separately. This requires that you adjust the beginning and ending colors of the gradient, or *blend*, in each area by picking the right colors from parallel areas of the first blend. This method is possible only if there is a single area long enough to accommodate the full length of the intended color blend.

Pawel used a different technique by connecting all the separate areas with lines one pixel wide. This way, a single blend 'flowed' through all the connected boundaries to the different areas. Later, using the Clone tool, he was able to smoothly close all the paint 'channels' and the sky was done.

Applying 256-color Palettes

One of the unique features of Photo-Paint is its ability to save and open palettes holding 256 colors. By saving and opening 256-color palettes, you can transfer colors from one image to another in a semi-random fashion. This provides an opportunity to quickly create endless graphic variations of any image that is converted to 256-color (8-bit) format. You can convert an image — even a grayscale scan such as the sculpture — by choosing Convert To 256 Color from the Edit menu. This creates a 256-color copy of the image. Then click on Palette under the Options menu and choose Open Palette. Simply double-click on any of the .PAL files in the PALETTES subdirectory of PHOTOPNT to load them.

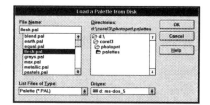

These colors can be individually adjusted with the help of the Eyedropper tool. Clicking on a color in the bitmap selects it on the floating color palette. If you then double-click on the selected color in the palette, the Adjust Individual Palette Color dialog box will let you redefine the color. Using this simple technique, it took only seconds to change the sky behind the sculpture to white. The palette files take only a small amount of the disk space. It's therefore a good habit to save the more interesting color sets you create for future use. Even if they'll never be used again, playing with new palettes is fun and can sometimes help you see a graphical problem in a different light.

Fading Out with Motion

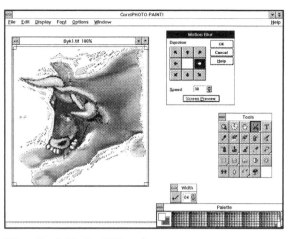

There are a number of different special effects filters on the Edit menu, and I encourage you to experiment with them on your 24-bit images. Applying the filters in different combinations can create so many different effects that it's possible to cover only a few of them here. Most of them can be applied to either the entire image or just a selected portion of it. However, if your image contains white (in grayscale mode described as value 255, in 24-bit RGB as R=255, G=255 and B=255), you can't select those areas. In this case, you can apply the filters only to the entire image. This isn't a problem most of the time, unless your background color happens to be white.

Pawel discovered this problem when trying to select a portion of the bull illustration and apply the Motion Blur filter to all the areas, with the exception of the head. The selection tools would drop white areas from the boundaries he tried to select. From looking at the preview, it was evident that the blur was not extending from the image areas into the white area beyond. This created a very unnatural result, since it did not blend into the background as expected. The easiest solution would have been to simply use the Paint Roller tool to fill the white areas with some other color. Pawel, however, wanted a free-flowing shape that faded out into the background, and a background color other than white would have created a box-shaped illustration when printed.

Photo-Paint contains an unusual feature that allows you to use the Clone tool to copy not only from one area to another within an image, but also from one image to another. The program also lets you quickly open a copy of a file without the need to save and rename it. You can even clone between images in different file formats, with the small limitation that your target file has to be able to accommodate the information from your source file. A file that is only black and white (1 bit per pixel) can't, for example, hold the information from a grayscale (8 bits per pixel) or a full color (24-bit) file. You can, however, copy image data

---

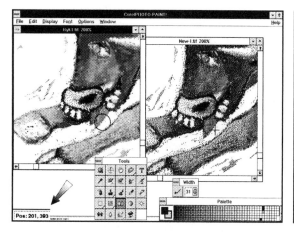
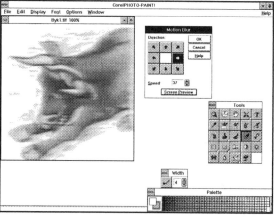
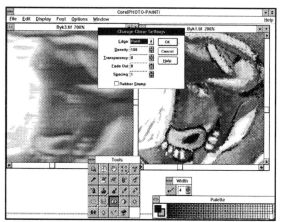
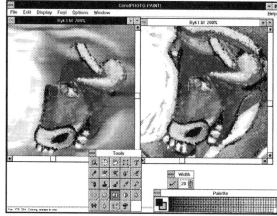

from a grayscale image to your 24-bit color image, or from black and white to grayscale.

Unable to create the motion effect around the head by applying it only to the selected areas, Pawel was forced to put the whole image in motion. Once this was done he saved the file under another name, to avoid overwriting the original image. With the two versions of the image displayed side by side, he had to make sure that the part he was going to clone from the original was properly aligned within the blurred version. To do this, he checked the lower-left corner of the screen. The values displayed there refer to the cursor location within the bitmap and not the location on the screen. This made it possible to align the images simply by making sure that the corresponding numbers from both bitmaps matched. After the unblurred head was

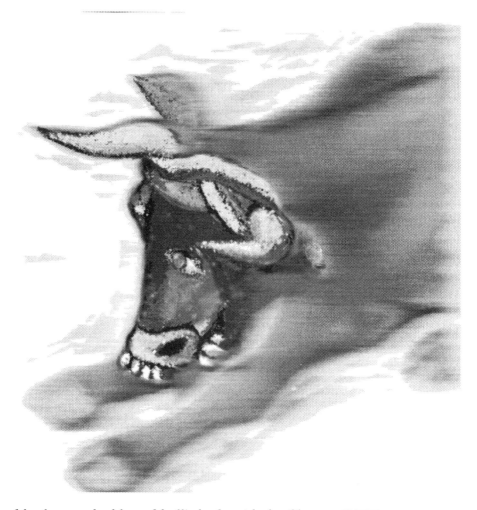

transferred back onto the blurred bull's body with the Clone tool, the Smear tool was used to further integrate the cloned parts.

CD-ROM and PhotoCD

Ever since the arrival of CD-ROM drives for personal computers, many have questioned their usefulness in the graphic arts. Because of their great storage potential, CDs have found the greatest acceptance as a medium for commercial reference libraries, databases and multimedia software. Corel has promoted CD technology by including a disc with every package of Corel Draw 3. It contains a vast number of clip art images, fonts in both Adobe Type 1 and TrueType formats, Chart templates, Show animations and backgrounds, foreign language spelling dictionaries and a few other goodies. In addition, every year Corel publishes an ArtShow disc containing hundreds of entries to the annual Draw design

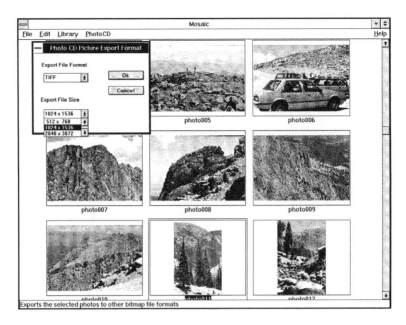

Photo CD Picture Export Format

Export File Format

TIFF   Ok

                Cancel

Export File Size

1024 x 1536
512 x 768
1024 x 1536
2048 x 3072

photo005   photo006

photo007   photo008   photo009

photo010   photo011   photo012

Exports the selected photos to other bitmap file formats

contest. This was reason enough for many Draw users to take the plunge and acquire a CD-ROM drive.

But the last few months have seen a major development in CD technology that will make it almost invaluable to many Draw users . Thanks to Kodak's new PhotoCD technology, you can not only have your photographs scanned at high resolution by a high-quality scanner, but also stored on a CD disc in digital form, all for a price 20 to 50 times lower than other high-end options. Each disc can store more than 500 megabytes of compressed images. The next time you have your film developed at your local Kodak Photo Center, you can also order a PhotoCD disc containing those photographs.

If you already own a CD-ROM drive, check with the manufacturer to determine if it is PhotoCD-compatible. The older models are less likely to support the Extended Architecture (XA) that is required to read those discs. However, sometimes all you need is to add an /XA switch to the CD drive line in your CONFIG.SYS file.

If you plan to purchase a CD-ROM drive, make sure it is XA-compatible. The newer drives also provide multi-session capabilities, which allow you to read images that have been written to the disc at different times. When a conventional CD-ROM drive accesses the disc it looks for the root directory that will list all the files on the disc. Since it is impossible to change anything on a CD once the data has been written, it is also impossible to change the root directory of the disc, and as a result the files that were added at a later time would not be listed there. Discs with images added at different times contain multiple root directories, and multi-session drives — unlike the traditional ones — read all of them without stopping after the first one. So unless you own a multi-session CD-ROM drive, it is a good idea to order a new CD disc each time you have some images you want scanned.

Since PhotoCD is still such a new technology, it is only the most current version of Draw 3 — revision B — that supports it. You can use CorelMOSAIC to preview the .PCD thumbnail pictures stored on the disc and then export the condensed Kodak .PAC files to one of the three bitmap formats supported by Mosaic (.BMP, .PCX and .TIF), as well as the .EPS vector format that can be used in page layout programs like Ventura or PageMaker (although the .EPS file will not contain the image header). Each file is in full 24-bit format at one of three resolutions and file sizes: 512 by 768 (over 1 megabyte), 1,024 by 1,536 (over 4 megabytes) and 2,048 by 3,073 (almost 18 megabytes). Once the file has been exported, it is ready to be used in Photo-Paint, Draw and your other applications.

The techniques covered here represent just a few of the many possibilities created by moving your images back and forth between Photo-Paint and Draw. The addition of the textures made possible by Photo-Paint considerably extends your Draw toolbox. And don't forget that one of the prize categories for the annual CorelDRAW Design Contest is for Draw illustrations containing bitmaps.

Getting the Best Scan

12

T his chapter is called *Getting the Best Scan*, but it's really about much more than that. It's about all the interrelated factors that combine to provide you with the optimum scanned image; whether you're going to trace it or output it from CorelDRAW to a laser printer, high-resolution imagesetter or film recorder. Those factors range from the type of image you want to scan, through to the method you'll be using to reproduce the output generated with Draw. The focus here is on the use of black-and-white scans with Draw, but this chapter will prove equally valuable for those working with scans in other applications.

While Draw can also import, print, color separate and trace color images, color scanning is a complex topic that won't be covered here. For more on the intricacies of color scanning, image manipulation and output, consult the reference works in the bibliography at the back of the book.

Getting the best scan is not simply a matter of slapping artwork on the scanner, choosing some canned settings and hitting a button. There are a number of factors to consider when you set up the scan, and the process requires some judgment. Below are the most important considerations.

- Type of image (black-and-white or gray).
- Scanning mode (line-art, dithered halftone or grayscale).
- Contrast and brightness of the source image.
- Resolution and scaling.
- Brightness and contrast settings.
- Screen frequency.

The decisions you make in each of these areas are interdependent. You'll probably scan at a higher resolution, for instance, if you're capturing a gray image and want to print it with a high

You say dither, I say grayscale

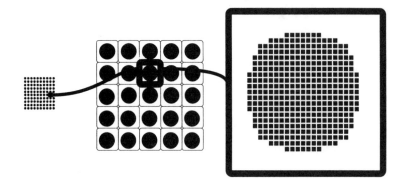

screen frequency. And if you use a high screen frequency, and will be offset printing the image, you'll probably want to set the brightness a little higher to compensate for dark areas filling in on a printing press.

How well you control the process of scanning depends to a great extent on the software driving your scanner. It should run under Windows, for example, so you can have your scanning software, Draw, CorelTRACE, CorelPHOTO-PAINT and your page layout or word processing applications all running at once. That way you can move raw scans for touchup into Photo-Paint (as described in *Converting Scans with CorelTRACE*), into Trace for conversion into a vector .EPS image, into Draw for manipulation and finally into the layout program for output. If at that point the image needs to be re-scanned or edited, the necessary applications are only an Alt-Tab away. Of course, your system will need the necessary resources for this kind of intensive work — don't attempt serious multitasking without at least 4 Mb of RAM, a fast defragmented hard disk (18 Ms access time or faster) and an 80386 processor. As a multitasking junkie, I use an 80486-based system with 16 Mb of RAM.

Your first decision is whether to scan in line art, dithered or grayscale mode. The choice between line art and the two other modes is usually pretty easy. Simply look at the image you want to scan and decide whether it has grays in it. If it does, you'll want to use dithered or grayscale scanning. If it's all black-and-white it's line art, and you'll generally use that mode for scanning it. There's line art, though, and then there's line art.

Scanning Line Art

With some line art you may run into a gray area (ha, ha) where very fine lines get so close together that the scanner can't pick them up very well as distinct lines. This is often the situation, for instance, with the finely crosshatched pen-and-ink drawings that are so common in public-domain clip art books. For that type of image, even though it looks like simple black-and-white art to the human eye, you may be able to get better quality (or the look you want) by treating it as a gray image, using either dithered or grayscale scanning.

You may find that by using a dither, instead of a line-art scan, you can pick up details in dark areas without losing fine lines. You do end up with an image that looks like a halftone, though; areas of closely spaced lines will resolve into a more uniform gray.

You can also scan line art that has closely spaced lines in grayscale mode, if your scanner has this capability. Some scanner software lets you adjust the *threshold* (changing the thickness of lines and darkness of areas with closely-spaced lines) after you've captured the image. You don't have the same control over the halftoning that you get with dithered images, though, unless you adjust the halftoning parameters in a page-makeup program, such as PageMaker, or an image-editing program. (You can also change these parameters in Draw, but the image will display the same on the screen.) And with grayscale, you pay the price of file size — they'll be four times as large for 4-bit, 16-level images as a bilevel file (there's no reason to scan with 256 levels for line art).

If you'll be autotracing the scanned image, either in Draw itself or with Trace, scan at a resolution of 300 dpi or higher. Higher is better when autotracing, since it will give Draw a more accurate original to work from. Just remember that higher resolution scans will result in larger file sizes and slower screen redraw times in Draw. I find that 400 dpi produces

better autotracing results but higher resolutions, such as 600 dpi, take forever and don't produce noticeably better traces. If you're scanning images with very fine lines, however, you may have to scan above 400 dpi when autotracing to ensure that lines don't break up.

In the illustration, a page of clip art is being scanned at 400 dpi with an HP ScanJet Plus scanner. Although the ScanJet has a physical scan capability of only 300 dpi, it can scan up to 1,500 dpi through *interpolation*, a fancy word for guessing where it thinks the dots between the 300 dpi scan points should be. The page has first been quickly scanned at low resolution to provide a preview and just one image has now been selected for a final scan at 400 dpi. While you can crop scans in Draw with the ⚒ tool, crop as much as you can before importing the image to cut down on file size and print times. The next illustration shows

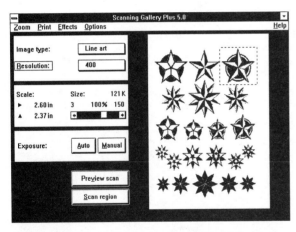

the difference in smoothness between the image scanned at 300 and 400 dpi. The extra resolution will make Trace's work easier.

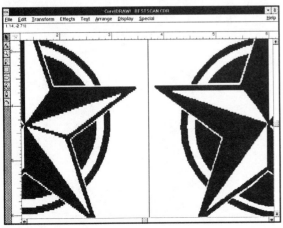

Keep in mind that Trace can only handle images up to 3,000 by 3,000 pixels (roughly 1 Mb). At 300 dpi this is a healthy 100 square inches, but at 600 dpi the maximum size drops to about 25 square inches. Larger file sizes may produce "unpredictable results", in the words of the Trace manual. Most scanning programs let you scan a user-defined portion of the page, or you can choose Trace Partial Area from the Preferences menu in Trace. In addition, simplify the image as much as possible with a paint program, such as Photo-Paint, before tracing it. There's no doubt a very fast, powerful system is required for tracing large complex files or you'll be sitting on your hands for interminable periods.

Getting the Best Scan

When scanning anything, ensure you're working with a clean, reasonably-sized original; don't expect good results from a tiny logo scanned from a business card. Bump up the size if necessary on a photocopier and ensure that the artwork is aligned straight on the scanner. If the artwork is on a scrap of paper, a good practice is to first tape it straight onto a sheet of grid paper and place the entire page on the scanner.

If your scanner can save line art scans in .PCX, .TIF, .TGA, .GIF or .BMP format, Draw can import or trace them. Of these, .PCX and .TIF are the most common. While there's little difference in file size between the two, Draw and Trace can use the compressed .TIF files created by many scanners, which do take up less space than their .PCX counterparts.

Happily, there's not much more to know or say about line art scans. They work very well and are easy to capture with good quality. With a little experimentation you can learn to get relatively fast, top-notch output, without using up your whole hard disk or waiting forever for printouts. Gray images, on the other hand, pose more difficult trade-offs, and require more judgment and experimentation.

Scanning in Dithered Modes

For gray images, such as photographs and shaded drawings, many scanning programs let you choose between *dithered* half-tone and grayscale modes. A dithered image is one in which the scanning software has represented shades of gray with one of many possible black-and-white patterns. Dithered halftones have the advantage of small file size (they're black-and-white, so they use only 1 bit per sample, as with a bilevel scan), and they can come out just as well on a laser printer as a grayscale image, as long as you're careful to ensure that your image resolution has an integral relationship to your printing resolution.

Dithers also often reproduce better than grayscales printed at 300 dpi, and some are designed specifically to be photocopied. Your choice will depend to a great extent on your output device, since grayscales will output better on PostScript than non-PostScript lasers. If you're printing to a non-PostScript printer like an HP LaserJet, you are probably better off letting

---

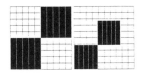

the scanner do the dithering at scan time. Again, be careful with scaling and resolution, or you'll end up with ugly patterns.

Halftoning Halftones

Sometimes you may want to scan an image that's already been halftoned. This includes anything that is printed — in a book, a newspaper, a brochure — anything. The problem here is that you end up halftoning a halftone and the result is interference patterns, much like the plaid patterns you get when you size dithered halftones.

Dithered images degrade when enlarged but grayscales maintain their quality

If the image is halftoned with a coarse screen frequency — say 75 lines or so — you might try scanning it in line art mode. The scanner will then simply *steal* the halftoning from the original

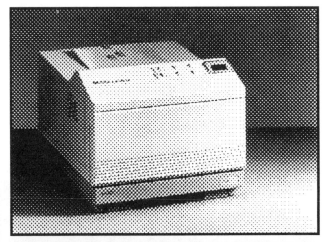

image. However, if the screen is much finer than 75 lines (if you can't see the dots easily without getting very close), you'll end up with big areas of black where there should be grays. There's no very good solution here, aside from using grayscale scanning and messing with the resolution until you get the best results possible.

If you decide to go with a dithered halftone, you have another decision to make: which dither? Most scanning programs offer several. Each is appropriate when you want different looks, or when you're working with different types of images, output devices and reproduction methods.

Grayscale Scanning

If you absolutely must have the flexibility to scale an image in a page-makeup program, if you want to retouch an image with a grayscale editor, or if you want high-quality output from a PostScript imagesetter, go for a grayscale scan. For laser output, the difference between 16- and 256-level scans is not very great, though it is discernible. For imagesetter output, definitely go for 256 levels. The imagesetter has the resolution to take advantage of that much information, so give it everything you can.

If you're printing to a PostScript device, you can choose the ✒ tool, click on the ✪ icon, set the outline color to Spot and click on the PostScript Options button. Then you can use the PostScript Options dialog box to change the screen frequency and angle of the scan, or assign a different screen for special effects, such as Microwave or Star.

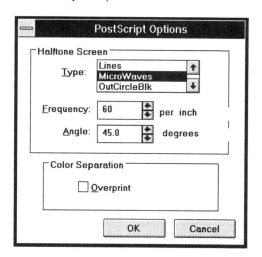

GRAYSCALE PHOTO

SAMPLED (SCANNED) PIXEL MAP

PIXEL DEPTH

PAPER SURFACE

Resolution and Scaling

In the best of all possible worlds, you would scan every image at the highest possible resolution. High resolution makes for smooth line-art scans (without jaggies) and sharp, detailed halftones. You pay for that quality, though, with file size. Consider that an 8 ½ by 11 inch, 150-dpi, 8-bit (256-level) grayscale scan comes to almost two megabytes. A 300-dpi, full-page black-and-white scan (line-art or dithered halftone) requires about one megabyte. The formula to figure file size is:

$$\frac{(\text{dots per inch2} \times \text{bits per sample} \times \text{width} \times \text{height})}{8192 \ (\text{the number of bits in a kilobyte})} = \text{kilobytes}$$

Keep in mind that when you double your resolution, your file size quadruples. Triple your resolution and your files will be nine times as large. You'll need a lot more disk space to store the scans, Draw's screen display will slow, it may display out of memory messages and printing times will climb. The printing slowdown is due to transmission bottlenecks, and for grayscale scans the reason is the processing time in the computer or PostScript printer to convert the image into a halftone.

Happily, you don't need to scan at such a high resolution with grayscale scans, so you can save a lot in file size. The general rule of thumb is to use an image resolution that is twice the halftone screen frequency. So if you're going for a 100-line screen, the image should have a 200-dpi resolution. The screen frequency of a 300-dpi laser is 53, so there's no point scanning at over 150 dpi, and you may be able to achieve good results at even lower resolutions.

While higher-resolution scans definitely result in sharper images, you need much higher resolution to get significant improvements.

Getting the Best Scan

Even a small drop in scanning resolution, however, can save a lot of space without a significant degradation in image quality. Go from 300 to 250 dpi with a grayscale scan, for instance, and the quality difference will be negligible, even on a high-resolution imagesetter. You'll save better than 30 percent in file size, though.

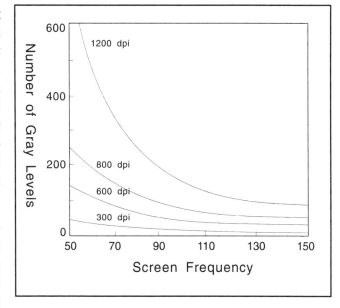

You know your quality requirements and how much disk space you have available, so the best bet is to run some tests and figure out what trade-offs you can live with. Try scanning the same image at different resolutions, and see how big the files are and what comes out of the printer (and how long it takes).

Remember to bear scaling in mind when you set your resolution. If you're going to enlarge the image once you've imported it into Draw, you'll need a higher scanning resolution to achieve the same quality. Specify the final resolution and size (if you know it) when you scan, and let the scanning software do the arithmetic.

Brightness and Contrast

It requires a good deal of judgment and experience to use the contrast and brightness controls of your scanning software effectively. With line-art scans, zoom in as close as you can in your scanning software on your on-screen selection. Then set the brightness control (which in line-art mode is working as a threshold or line thickness control) so that thin lines almost disappear, and closely-spaced lines are distinct and separate. Then darken it a little bit so thin black lines come through as lines, rather than strings of dots. This is especially critical if you'll be autotracing, since gaps will result in objects being created unpredictably, often with open paths.

This approach is only applicable to scanning programs that display changes on the screen as you make them. Most will force you to print out your scan to see the effect of different parameters. So try a printout to see how the scan looks, and judge it using the same areas of the image — thin lines should be solid, and thin areas between lines should not fill in. You'll want to adjust the parameters to what looks best, but the rule is to judge by thin lines and closely-spaced lines.

With dithered scans, your choices are more subjective, the screen representation is far less useful and you have two controls to deal with — brightness and contrast. The goal on your printout is to have a few black dots in the white areas, and a few white dots in the black areas. This may be impossible, because scanners simply cannot capture the full dynamic range of a typical photograph. Nevertheless, that is the goal.

The manuals accompanying scanning software usually recommend specific brightness and contrast settings when you're scanning an image for use with different application programs, but I've yet to find a reference to Draw. And although these are good guidelines, you'll always run into situations where they don't give you the best scan for the image you're working with, no matter what the application.

Bear in mind that if you're going to reproduce the image using a photocopier or offset press it will tend to darken slightly, particularly with fine screen frequencies (more on screen fre-

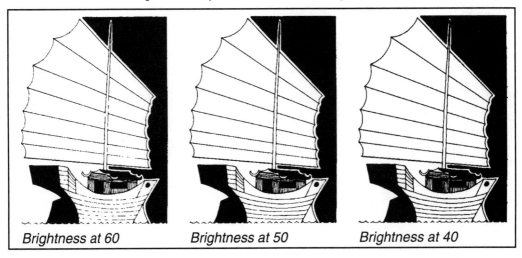

Brightness at 60   *Brightness at 50*   *Brightness at 40*

Getting the Best Scan

quencies below). Set your brightness a bit lighter than you would otherwise to allow for darkening on the press, while trying to avoid image white-out.

Things get even more subjective with grayscale scans, because the tonal gradations are so subtle on screen, and (assuming you're going for high-resolution output from your grayscale scan) because it's hard to know what high-resolution output will look like until you see it. Laser proofs provide only a crude approximation. Since output from imagesetters allows for much finer halftone screens, you'll need to be more careful to keep the image pretty light. When you get into printing fine screens (90 lines or above), the whole thing can clog up and go dark on you.

Screen Frequency

Screen frequency, as much as any other factor, can make the difference between an indistinct, washed-out, muddy, dark or blurry image, and a crisp rendition with a wide range of gray values. When producing halftones on laser printers and imagesetters you have to consider the trade-offs between output resolution, screen frequency and the number of gray levels. Put succinctly, the trade-off goes like this.

- If you want a fine screen frequency, you sacrifice the available number of gray levels.
- If you want many gray levels, you sacrifice screen frequency.
- The higher the resolution of your output device, the less you need to worry about the trade-offs.

With a 2400-dpi imagesetter, for instance, you can achieve a very fine screen frequency and still get more gray levels than the human eye can discern (256 levels is beyond human discrimination, and it's also the limit of what a PostScript imagesetter can produce). With a laser printer or other 300-dpi device, though, you have to face the music.

Several factors affect your choice of screen frequency for halftone output. Those factors are laid out in the accompanying table, along with several publishing scenarios. The factors that constrain how high you can go with the screen frequency for each scenario are in bold, and the various factors are discussed below.

Output and Reproduction

Even if your output device has the resolution to give you the frequency and grayscales you want, the output medium and reproduction method need to be able to hold that fine halftone screen without the darker areas getting clogged up. Papers created specifically for laser printing, for instance, tend to do better than normal copier bond, because the laser dots (and

Output and Reproduction Methods

Output Device Resolution	Output Medium	Reproduction Method	Reproduction Paper Stock	Screen Frequency	Approximate Number of Gray Levels
300	Laser paper	Laser printer	Laser paper	53	**35**
300	Laser paper	Photocopier	Bond	53	**35**
600	Laser paper	Offset	Coated stock	75	**65**
1000	Laser paper	Laser printer	Laser paper	100	**100**
1000	Laser paper	**Photocopier**	**Bond**	75	180
1270	RC paper	**Photocopier**	Coated stock	85	225
1270	RC paper	Offset	Coated stock	100	**160**
2540	RC paper	Offset	**Newsprint**	75-85	More than enough
2540	**RC paper**	Offset	**Uncoated stock**	90-100	More than enough
2540	Film	Offset	Coated stock	120-150	More than enough

The factors that determine how high a screen frequency you can use for each scenario are in bold.

therefore the halftone cells) are sharper and more distinct. Your best bet with most laser printers is to set the darkness/density control as low as it will go.

There is a limit to how well even laser papers can hold a screen, though. And if you go with too high a frequency on a 300-dpi device, you end up with very few gray levels. When you hit those limits, you need to use photographic paper on a high-resolution imagesetter. Since imagesetters use light and very fine-grained photographic emulsion rather than toner, which is relatively coarse, they can generate much finer detail, which is what you need for fine halftone screens.

However, you start running into problems with photographic paper when you want to reproduce an image with a fine screen. Photocopiers have trouble reproducing more than about an 85- or 90-line screen without clogging up the image, and you'll have similar problems with offset printing. Stat cameras (which are used to make the film to create plates for offset printing) just don't do very well if you go above about a 100-line screen. Darker areas will fill in. Combine that with *dot gain* on press — the tendency for ink to spread slightly, especially on absorbent paper — and you've got a dark, muddy image in your final printed product.

If you want a finer screen, you have to take the final step; outputting to film. The film that comes off the imagesetter is the actual film the printer will use to *burn* the printing plates, so there's no intermediary camera work to gum things up. Make sure you talk to your printer early in the process to find out how they want the film and work with your imagesetting service bureau to get set up for film output.

Printing Paper

You'll also need to consider your final printing stock when you're adjusting brightness, contrast, and screen frequency. If you're printing your final copies straight to laser paper, and you have some kind of halftoning board to go beyond normal laser capabilities, you can get pretty good 100-line halftones (the resolution of a normal 300-dpi printer will limit you, more than the paper itself, to about 75-line screens). You have the advantage here of seeing exactly what will come out of your *printing press*, so judging contrast and brightness is much easier.

If you're printing on a photocopier, you probably won't get good reproduction of halftones with more than about an 85-line screen. Images will usually get slightly darker when you copy them (and much darker if you use too fine a screen), depending on the copier you use and how the brightness control is set.

If you're printing offset, paper stock makes all the difference. Newsprint, for instance, absorbs a lot of ink, resulting in dot gain that makes it impossible to print more than a 75- or 85-line screen. Print with a 100-line screen to newsprint and you'll just get a splotch. Because of that dot gain you have to be especially careful in setting contrast and brightness when you'll be printing to newsprint.

With higher-grade uncoated stock, depending on how smooth and absorbent it is, you can go to a 100- or 120-line screen, and with good coated stock you can go as high as 150 lines (though you'll need film output to make it work without clogging up at the camera stage). Make sure you talk to your printer before you do final output for offset printing, and determine the preferred screen frequency for the press and paper it will be using. You'll still have to pay attention to brightness with coated stocks since you're printing at such a fine frequency. Even a little bit of dot gain fills in the dark areas quickly.

Converting Scans with CorelTRACE

CorelTRACE is a very useful utility that allows those with scanners to quickly convert scanned images, such as logos, into a format that can be imported into CorelDRAW and edited. But I'll tell you right up front that to get consistent results with Trace you need to be clear on some of the fundamental distinctions of graphic file formats. So resist the temptation to skip the following explanatory section and jump to the tutorials or you'll find yourself floundering later. At some point, you should also read the *Getting the Best Scan*, for details on the scanning process.

There are several ways to bring bitmap images, as produced by scanners, screen shots and paint programs, into Draw. The simplest is to import these images directly into Draw in their native format. For some uses this is not only acceptable, but preferable. Draw includes import filters for many popular bitmap formats, and if the bitmap is to be used as a page element without enlarging it, this is often the fastest and most direct route. Draw provides the means to add color to monochrome bitmaps. It also allows you to resize, crop or rotate them.

However, a bitmap's resolution is fixed at the time of creation, and if the image will be modified, resized for printing at significantly smaller or larger sizes, or if it must be 'improved' from a bitmap of questionable quality and clarity, it can be advantageous to convert it into a vector graphic before importing it. This is especially true if it will be rotated.

The Trace program is one of three bitmap to vector conversion methods available to you. In some cases, the fastest way to convert simple bitmaps — especially those composed primarily of text — is to import the bitmap into Draw for use as a template, set text in as closely matched a font as you have

The options make all the difference

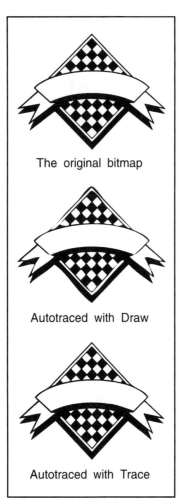

The original bitmap

Autotraced with Draw

Autotraced with Trace

available, convert the text to curves and node edit it to match the bitmap. You'd hand-draw or manually trace the remaining objects and then delete the bitmap template. Artists also like to follow this approach by sketching freehand with traditional media, scanning the sketch and then manually drawing over the template in Draw.

In previous chapters, you also employed Draw's internal autotracing feature to convert a bitmap to a vector outline. This process suffered from a number of shortcomings, the most serious of which were slowness and a lack of accuracy. However, it can be useful in 'one off' situations. In some instances, Draw's autotrace feature can also be an effective aid to the Trace utility.

It's in the area of complex drawings and situations requiring groups of bitmaps to be brought into Draw that Trace really earns its hard disk space. Trace allows the import of bitmap graphics into Draw as vector files by first creating an .EPS (Encapsulated PostScript) file. There are many good reasons to convert bitmaps to vector (traced) .EPS format. Bitmap images are much smaller when converted to .EPS, so they take up less disk space and print faster. Because they now describe the image using curve and line segments, rather than a fixed number of bits, such files are resolution independent — that is, they'll print out at the resolution of the PostScript output device. (If you don't have a PostScript printer, you can import the .EPS traces into Draw and export in another format, such as .WMF, .CGM or .GEM, or print directly from Draw.)

This resolution independence is especially important when using printers, such as imagesetters, that have output resolutions higher than the scanner or paint program that created the bitmap. But it's also applicable to the growing number of publishers with laser printers that have output resolutions higher than their scanners. In this case, the effect of using the lower resolution scanned image results in a waste of the laser's capabilities.

Converting Scans with CorelTRACE

Once traced, the resulting .EPS files can be brought directly into layout programs like PageMaker or Ventura, or be imported into Draw for manipulation. Brought directly into an application, only the bounding box surrounding the image will be displayed. However, you could import the image into Draw and export it in .EPS format to create a *header* that the application can use to display the image.

While its task may be simply defined, achieving proficiency with Trace can present a rather formidable challenge. A bitmap's inherent inaccuracies are attributable to the limitations imposed by the size and shape of the dots, or *bits*, of which it's composed. This inaccuracy introduces problems when converting in either direction between bitmap and vector formats. For example, a vector image of a straight line on a 15° angle is a perfect representation of that line. But on your video screen, where that perfect image is converted into a bitmap of approximately 100 dpi (depending on screen size and resolution), the line will appear jagged.

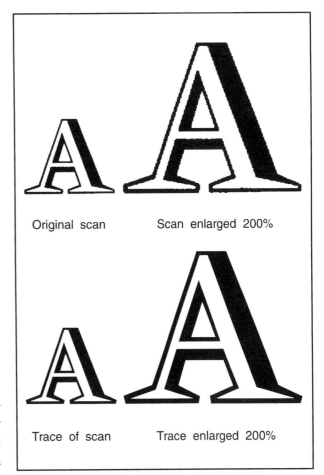

Original scan   Scan enlarged 200%

Trace of scan   Trace enlarged 200%

Take a screen shot of that display, and you have a roughly 100 dpi bitmap of the line, complete with jaggies. Print that bitmap actual size at 300 or even 2,400 dpi, and you'll print a 300 or 2,400 dpi representation of that jagged image; it will still look jaggy, even at the higher resolution. In contrast, print the vector file of the same line and you'll have a 300 or 2,400 dpi representation of a straight line. If the dots that constitute the line are fine enough their shape may not be apparent to the naked eye, but they exist none the less. You're now printing the line at the resolution of the *printer*, not the *bitmap*.

In converting from vector to bitmap, the higher the resolution of the output, the fewer decisions the program will have to make in rendering its version of the image. However, converting in the other direction, as Trace does, requires more decisions. Every dot along a line or edge in the image represents a shape, and the program must decide where the 'real' image is in relation to that shape. Fewer dots, fewer decisions. Also, unfortunately, less accuracy.

Printing a vector, or *outline-based*, font to a *raster-based* device (such as a laser printer) is basically the opposite of converting a bitmap to a vector. It too is a process in which the program must make numerous decisions, each of which basically amounts to: "What do I do with this dot that falls partially inside and partially outside the line I'm following?"

Font makers use *hinting* to control these decisions when output will be sent to a low resolution output device. But font makers are dealing with a known entity — the character shapes of their own font — and hinting it for a known output resolution. Trace, on the other hand, is forced to make judgment calls. Given that a bitmap is an inherently inaccurate representation of an object, the decisions that must be made in converting it into a vector graphic revolve around how accurate or inaccurate the bitmap is, how often the program should 'guess' when translating the bitmap into a vector graphic, what biases will influence those guesses and how strong those biases are.

If Trace did no interpretations at all and simply traced the shape of the bitmap precisely, all the inaccuracies of the original scan would be included in the vector file and nothing would be accomplished. Additionally, the resulting .EPS file of all but the simplest bitmaps would contain a plethora of nodes that would make object editing difficult and create lengthy print times.

Instead, Trace *interprets* the shape of the object. Guided by the tracing options you've set, it makes judgments about how carefully it should examine the bitmap, how closely it should trace the shapes in the bitmap, and whether to lean towards lines or curves and points orbends when it estimates where a line segment should go.

Converting Scans with CorelTRACE

The Four-Step Process

There are four steps in creating a vector graphic file with Trace: creating the scan; preparing the bitmap for tracing; adjusting tracing options (setting the biases by which it makes its interpretations) and tuning or adjusting the resulting .EPS file after importing it into Draw.

The first three steps are crucial to the production of a vector file that won't make you spend more time on the fourth step than it would have taken to create the image from scratch in Draw. A well-*prepped* bitmap reduces the number of decisions Trace must make, and tracing options properly configured to reflect the dominant characteristics of a particular bitmap guide it in making the correct decisions.

To illustrate how important the effort involved in getting a good scan, prepping the bitmap and finding the right tracing options can be, run Draw and import SPORTCAR.EPS from the SAMPLES directory of the Utility disk included with this book. This is an .EPS file produced with the default tracing options on a 'raw' bitmap scanned from a hand-rendered drawing. The jumble of garbage displayed on your screen is proof enough of the importance of prepping the bitmap and finding the right output options.

Later, you'll work with the bitmap from which this .EPS was created to discover the steps required to actually get something usable out of it. For now, though, choose Ungroup from the Arrange menu, zoom in on it in wireframe view (Shift-F9) and

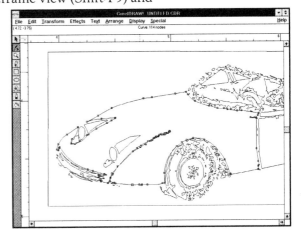

take a close look. Select the relatively clean line along the hood of the car with the ✦ tool. Note the node count in the Status Line. It should be well over 100! You could edit this vector file all day and never achieve a satisfactory result. Feel free to exit Draw now without saving (after first switching back to the preview window with Shift-F9), so you can get on with covering the techniques for avoiding having to edit such a poor graphic.

Getting the Scan

A bitmap image might come from a clip art collection, a screen capture, the output of a bitmap editing package like CorelPHOTO-PAINT, or from a scanner. Scanners — both hand-held and full-page versions — are typically used to bring printed or hand-drawn artwork into a computer. The vast majority of the artwork and other graphics most users convert into vector files comes from scanners, because such images are created on paper and a scanner is the most logical way to bring it into the computer, or *digitize* it. The list of frequently scanned graphics includes signatures, logos, maps, schematics, cartoons, technical illustrations and clip art.

Trace will convert pure monochrome (black-and-white line art), grayscale and color bitmaps into vector files. However, attempting to work with grayscale or color images before mastering the use of Trace with line art is a sure and short road to frustration. Also particularly important when working with color or grayscale bitmaps is Trace's use of memory. TIF and .PCX format bitmaps containing grayscale or color information can be quite large. The memory overhead of keeping that large file, along with the output file, the Trace program itself and other associated files open at one time can send Windows on frequent and time-consuming binges of virtual (disk-based) memory usage — even on systems with lots of RAM.

There are a few things to keep in mind when scanning artwork for conversion in Trace that will result in faster, better output. Black-and-white (line art) bitmaps should be scanned at the highest possible resolution — depending, of course, on their size. For the most part, that means a 300 or 400 dpi scan resolution. In theory, artwork scanned at higher resolutions, such as 600 or 800 dpi, can produce better results, although the node count in the output file might be excessive in the case of anything but the simplest artwork. The large size of such a file also slows the tracing process considerably. And higher resolutions can exceed Trace's capabilities when working with larger image areas. The maximum image size for tracing is 3,000 pixels square (3,000 by 3,000), which means an image of 10 by 10 inches at 300 dpi. At 600 dpi, that's only a 5 by 5-inch image, and less than 4 by 4 inches at 800 dpi.

Converting Scans with CorelTRACE

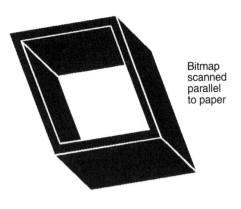

Bitmap
scanned
parallel
to paper

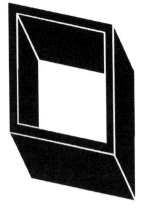

Bitmap scanned
parallel to dominant
line direction

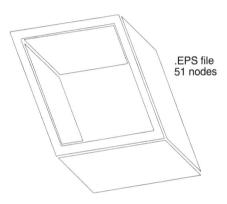

.EPS file
51 nodes

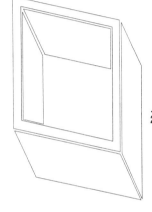

.EPS File
26 Nodes

For the sake of clarity, I've used a simple graphic to show the advantage of scanning the bitmap parallel to the dominant straight edges in the image. With this simple graphic, the difference between rotating the graphic prior to scanning is evident in the node count, but certainly wouldn't render the first scan useless. Apply that same difference to a more complex image, though, and you could be cutting a thousand node .EPS file down to a few hundred.

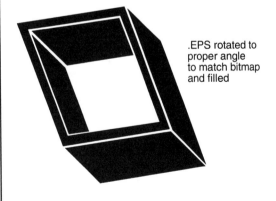

.EPS rotated to
proper angle
to match bitmap
and filled

If the artwork to be traced includes fine lines — either straight or curved — set the scanner resolution to at least twice the resolution of the thinnest line in the image. In other words, if the thinnest line in your original artwork is $\frac{1}{150}$ inch (about $\frac{1}{2}$ point), then set your scanner to 300 dpi ($\frac{1}{300}$ inch), or higher. If this is impractical or impossible, increase the scanner's intensity or sensitivity. What you're trying to avoid is the creation of bitmap lines one *pixel* in width, which Trace can easily overlook. (For more on scanning techniques turn to *Getting the Best Scan*.)

Because of the squared shape of the pixels into which the artwork is converted when scanned, purely horizontal or vertical lines will invariably have fewer jagged edges than those on even a slight angle. When it's applicable, turning the artwork on an angle to scan it, so that as many of the straight lines or edges contained in it are on the 0°/180° or 90°/270° bias, will produce a bitmap that is much easier to trace accurately, as shown in the full-page illustration.

If you're using a hand scanner, you should look for the dominant line direction in the graphic and lay a rule parallel to that line to act as a scanner guide. If you're using a flatbed scanner, fix the image to a sheet of paper on the necessary angle to accomplish the same feat.

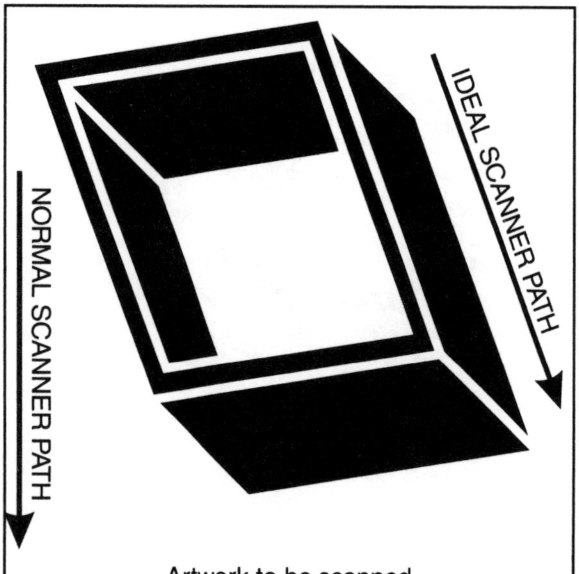

Artwork to be scanned

This precaution isn't as important if the image contains little in the way of curved elements and fine detail, because Trace's tracing options can be set to force the creation of straight lines. But if the image characteristics are such that forcing straight lines via the tracing options will produce unacceptable results in other sections of the bitmap, then getting as many of the straight line elements as possible aligned parallel or perpendicular to the scan direction can make the job of producing an acceptable vector image much easier.

Prepping the Bitmap

It's also sometimes possible to use Photo-Paint's Deskew feature to correct slight errors in scanner alignment and to make it easier to produce cleaner and more accurate .EPS output from Trace. To try this out, run Photo-Paint from its icon in the Corel Graphics group in Program Manager and open the SKEWBOX.TIF file from the SAMPLES directory of the Utility disk. Double-click on the Box Selection tool to select the entire image area, choose Transform from the Edit menu and then Area. Then select Deskew in the dialog box and enter a figure in degrees between -5.00° and 5.00°, with positive numbers rotating clockwise.

PAINT

Because you may have to find the correct adjustment angle by trial and error, and deskew is a fairly slow process, when working with large images you'd use the Box Selection tool to select a small representative area on which to experiment. If the total adjustment needs to be more than 5°, you'll have to do it in sequential steps, so it's best to work with a copy of the sample area. After clicking and dragging to select the area, choose Copy and then Paste from the Edit menu, and move the copy to a suitable area of white space (but do not anchor it by clicking). In this way, you'll only be working on a copy of your representative section.

Unless the angle to be deskewed is very slight, start with a 5° deskew in the appropriate direction. If it's not enough then deskew again, keeping track of how many degrees in total you've moved the sample section. Repeat as necessary until the largest number of straight lines possible is on the purely horizontal or vertical axis. If the first deskew went too far, press Alt-Backspace to undo it, display the Change Area dialog box again and enter a smaller deskew figure. By sequentially splitting the difference between too far and not far enough, you'll soon come upon the right figure to deskew your artwork. Since you may have to go

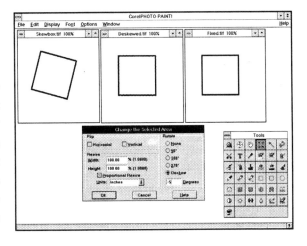

through this process several times, you could automate your deskewing sessions by the creation of Windows Recorder macros. (For details, see *Optimizing Windows*.)

When you've found the right value to align the lines along the horizontal/vertical axes, delete the sample area copy and perform the deskew on the entire bitmap. You'll still have unsightly jaggies along the edges of the lines, as shown in the illustration, but now that you've got them on horizontal and vertical planes you can easily remove them by using the Shift key to constrain the Fountain Pen tool's path to either horizontal or vertical. The Spacebar toggles it between the two constrain axes.

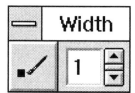

Choose Zoom from the Display menu, zoom in on the horizontal lines in the image and choose the appropriate drawing width from the Width & Shape floating workbox. You can draw with black or white by simply clicking on a black or white area of your scan with the right mouse button. Position the drawing tool along the edge of a line, hold down the Shift key, and click and drag to wipe away any extraneous bits. Do all the vertical lines first, switch the tool to black (by clicking the right mouse button with the tool in a black section) and do the same to fill any gaps along the edge. Then press the Spacebar and repeat the process for the horizontal lines.

Increase the Fountain Pen's width and use it to wipe clean any area of the drawing that shouldn't be traced. While all this might seem like donkey work, fixing these slight errors now will help make the job of tracing and later tuning the vector file in Draw much easier.

If there's any extraneous space around the edges, whether it's empty or filled with unnecessary parts of the original bitmap, you can use the Box Selection tool to crop the image to the minimum size. Not only does this give you less area to clean up, but it will reduce the size of the bitmap that you'll be tracing. Unlike vector files, the white space in bitmaps takes up room on disk and in memory. (Even though .TIF compression formats reduce the file size on disk, once you've brought the file into Trace it's expanded to its full size.) To crop, click and drag the Box Selection tool to select the desired section of the bitmap, then choose Copy To from the Edit menu, and copy it to a new name in your dedicated Trace temp directory. Then close the SKEWBOX.TIF file.

As the first step in producing a usable vector file of the sportscar drawing you looked at earlier, open the file SPORTCAR.TIF in Photo-Paint. You'll use the Magic Wand tool to eliminate the streaks of gray in the background. Gray streaks like this are typical of the output of a poorly calibrated scanner with a dirty lens. A clean background in the bitmap means fewer extraneous objects to be examined for tracing, so Trace will have fewer decisions to make.

Photo-Paint's Magic Wand tool is invaluable for cleaning up the background and eliminating unnecessary clutter. It can be used to remove contiguous, extraneous image sections from a bitmap regardless of their shape. It's especially valuable in eliminating 'confusing' background shades from maps scanned in grayscale format.

If you have the Photo-Paint toolbox *grouped*, the Magic Wand isn't currently visible. If this is the case, click on the Control Box of the toolbox (the bar at the top-left corner) and choose Layout and then Ungroup. Place the tip of the star that's on the end of the Magic Wand cursor in the area you want to remove, such as the gray background. Then click and all connected pixels of the same shade will be selected. Now you can simply press the Delete key. Repeat the selection and deletion process in other areas that should be white, but aren't.

In grayscale or color images, the Magic Wand tool removes all pixels of a contiguous group that fall within a certain color value range. It should be noted, however, that color and grayscale bitmaps containing *blended* areas are poor candidates for tracing. For consistent results, tracing of grayscale or color bitmaps should be confined to those in which gray levels or colors are clearly defined and uniform.

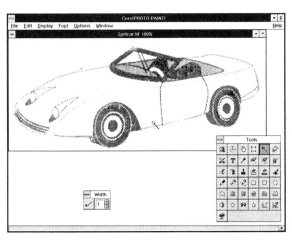

Because the car's interior has acquired a moiré pattern in the scan and the grays in it are too disparate to select with the Magic Wand, use the Lasso Area selection tool to roughly outline the area of the interior, and from the Edit menu choose Filters, then Blend.

Set the Blend amount to 100% and choose OK (you might want to preview it first). Before anchoring the selected area (making your edit permanent by clicking), repeat the blend procedure a few more times and you'll adjust the grays to a more uniform range of levels. Anchor the area by clicking, then use the Magic Wand tool to pick out and delete the gray areas in the interior, leaving the adjacent black or dark grays alone. You may want to zoom in to select some of the smaller areas. Don't worry if the resulting edges are somewhat jaggy — you'll explore a number of ways to smooth these. If you inadvertently delete something while using the Magic Wand, just press Alt-Backspace to undo.

Use the Lasso Area tool to select the car interior again. Choose Remove Spots from the Edit/Filters menu, set the size to Large and click on OK. This will smooth out the rough edges of the lines surrounding the areas from which you just removed the gray. Like Blend, this filter can be run several times on the same selected area, but with diminishing results.

As you've just seen, Photo-Paint's Remove Spots filter will

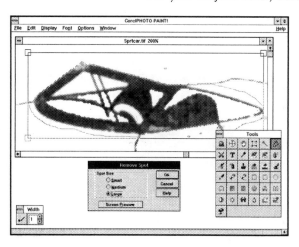

eliminate clusters of pixels that are attached to sections of the drawing, as well as free-standing pixels and groups of pixels. This aspect of the filter is useful for cleaning up the edges of hand-drawn artwork (covered in additional detail in a later exercise on tracing signatures). But when those little jags and jogs along the edges of the graphic really *are* a necessary part of the graphic, rather than noise or dirt, removing them will prevent Trace from doing its job correctly, so proceed with caution when filtering out pixels. If in doubt, use the filter's screen preview box to see how it will change the bitmap before committing to it with OK. This will avoid lengthy screen redraws.

If the need to retain uneven edges of the actual image prevents you from using the Spots filter to remove spurious dots in Photo-Paint, Trace's Noise Filter can be set to ignore small patches of dots that aren't connected to the main image. But if you plan to rely on Trace's Noise Filter, be sure to 'hint' any small patches of dots that are a desired part of the drawing while you're still in Photo-Paint, or Trace will assume they're junk and ignore them. Setting Photo-Paint's Fountain Pen tool width to a size greater than Trace's Noise Filter setting (which has a default of 8 pixels) and simply clicking on the 'real' dots does the trick. The idea is to beef up doubtful areas that Trace may otherwise drop out, a process that can be thought of as manual hinting.

Just as font makers use hinting to direct the decisions a low resolution output device, such as a 300 dpi printer, must make when printing a character at small point sizes, it's sometimes beneficial to add hints to a bitmap when the conversion is in the opposite direction.

A line of just a few pixels, for instance, is likely to be missed during the tracing operation. If the rest of the bitmap looks good, instead of rescanning the whole thing at a higher density or finer resolution you can use Photo-Paint's Line and Curve drawing tools with the width set to at least 3 pixels, to emphasize the line segment.

Choose white or black as your line color, then click and drag with either tool. If you're using the Curve tool, you first draw a straight line with it, then drag the circles and squares to adjust the line before clicking. For example, use this technique along the thin and broken lines defining the shape of the car you're now working on. Set the Curve tool to white and use it to solidify the lines around the tire edges. Use the Fountain Pen and line drawing tools to clean up the edges of the grill and anything else that doesn't look quite up to snuff.

You can also use the Box or Lasso Selection tools to select specific areas of the drawing — around each tire for instance —

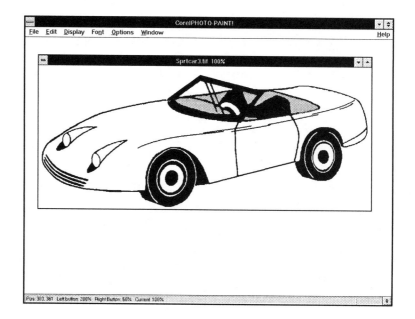

and use the Brightness & Contrast filter to convert them to pure black and white, by increasing the contrast to 100% in the selected area.

You can now choose the Paint Roller tool and select an appropriate gray to fill the interior areas of the car, or you can leave them white and fill the areas later in Draw, after you've finished prepping this bitmap and traced it. I've reproduced a touched-up version of the car, but I don't expect you to spend the time it took to complete it at this point.

Not every bitmap you plan on tracing will need this much preprocessing in Photo-Paint. Still, it's not a bad idea to open scans for a quick look to spot anything obvious that might make Trace's job more difficult. Because the shape of the bitmap will always reflect the scan resolution, images scanned at low resolution and small bitmaps, or bitmap sections that have been enlarged, can usually benefit the most from a Photo-Paint session before being traced.

Once you have a bitmap optimized for tracing and saved in .TIF, .PCX, .BMP, .GIF or .TGA format, you're ready to run Trace. If you typically favor a particular bitmap format, edit the filters list in CORELTRC.INI (in the DRAW directory) with Notepad to put that one first, since Trace's default input filter is simply the first one it finds in its .INI file — by default, .BMP.

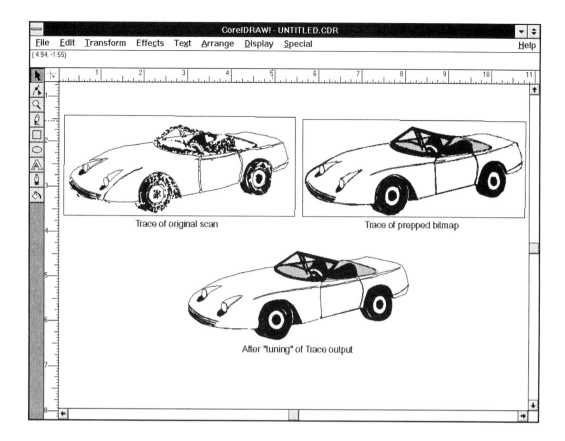

Trace of original scan

Trace of prepped bitmap

After "tuning" of Trace output

Use the Save As command now to save the edited sportscar file to your hard disk. How much have you actually accomplished by editing the bitmap of the sportscar? After familiarizing yourself with the operation of Trace itself in the next section, you should trace your car to create an .EPS file. If you've done a good job prepping it, this file should trace fairly well with either of the Normal option sets. Don't forget to open Draw and import both versions of SPORTCAR.EPS, the trace of the bitmap you just finished and the completed one on the Utility disk, so you can compare them side by side, as shown in the illustration.

Adjusting Tracing Options

Close Photo-Paint now and run Trace from its icon in Program Manager. The main Trace screen is not a true application window, since it doesn't have a border and its size can't be adjusted. So if you have more than one application open, it's

TRACE

easy to lose Trace by accidentally clicking to one side of it. In this case, press Alt-Tab to bring it forward.

While the .EPS files created by Trace can be imported directly into page layout programs, more typically you'll import them into Draw for fine tuning, then export them or save them in .CDR format. These .EPS files thus have a short lifespan and in most instances they should not be given a permanent home on your hard drive. The first time you use Trace, the initial order of business should therefore be to redirect the output path from the default setting (the main Windows directory) to a more appropriate location. Most users simply set it to the Windows TEMP directory, but there are advantages to creating a dedicated temp directory for Trace.

Some speed-hungry users have tried tracing from and to a temp directory set up on a *virtual disk*, or RAM drive. Other than ensuring that your hard disk won't become a collecting bin for overlooked .EPS files, there is little to be gained by this strategy. Except in the case of extremely complex traces, .EPS output files are rarely large enough that writing to RAM saves much time in tracing or in importing them into Draw. And if they *are* that large, the memory you would need to allocate to the RAM drive might be better used by Windows and other applications to speed general operations, rather than devoting it specifically to a RAM drive. Trace doesn't perform well when its available memory is limited, and its reaction to running out of room for its output in mid-operation is not particularly pleasant. System crashes in this case are not uncommon.

Your best bet is to set up a separate temp directory for Trace input and output on your hard drive. This could be either a subdirectory of your DRAW directory or a uniquely named directory off the root, such as TRACETMP. Move or copy bitmaps to be traced into this directory. Using a common directory for all Trace files proves especially valuable when a number of bitmaps will be traced, since when they're in the same directory Trace can be set to batch process them all in sequence.

Like all temp directories, this dedicated temp should be emptied regularly — but with some common sense precautions. If you have a decent macro utility or Windows batch language processor, it's not hard to devise a simple program to erase .EPS files after they've been imported into Draw. Just be sure that the .CDR file is suitable before deleting the intermediary .EPS. And despite any urgency you may feel to wipe those space-eating bitmaps off your hard drive as soon as they've been converted, it's good practice not to do so until the .CDR file is completely adjusted. Importing the actual bitmap into Draw along with the .EPS trace for use as a template when adjusting the final output can be a great time saver.

Choose Output Options from the File menu. The dialog box allows you to choose the output path, and to specify whether Trace should prompt you when it's asked to create an .EPS file with a name that already exists. You have two choices; Always Prompt or Always Replace. Turning on either turns the other off. Trace always attempts to give its output file the same name as that of the bitmap from which it was produced, and simply adds an .EPS extension. At least until you become fluent enough with Trace to predict the viability of the output from the status information and the view of the .EPS file it provides, it's

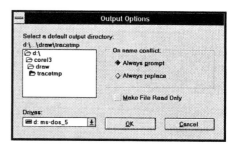

wise to let Trace prompt you instead of overwriting the file. Then you can store traces made with alternate Trace option settings under unique names.

The Output Options dialog box also offers you the opportunity to make its output read only. Choose this option and the Prompt/Replace option becomes moot, since you will be prompted by a much less friendly message box should you try to retrace a graphic using the same output name.

Despite the fact that it seems to indicate a problem with the system, in this case the message just means that the file you are trying to overwrite has been tagged as read only. For practical use, there's little need to set this option to anything other than Always Prompt.

The File menu also contains Open and Move. Other than maintaining a degree of conformity with the standard Windows

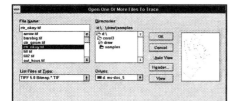

interface there's no real need for either, as it's rather inconceivable that you would be using Draw without some type of pointing device for moving the non-resizable window. There's also an Open button in the main window that accomplishes exactly the same thing as choosing Open from the File menu. Follow either approach now to display the Open One Or More Files To Trace dialog box.

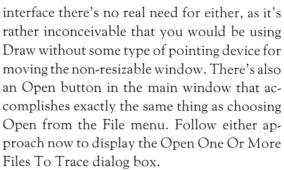

You'll find four items unique to Trace in this dialog box. To be able to try out these and the options discussed below, move to your DRAW\SAMPLES directory to display the .TIF files there. (Make sure List Files Of Type is set to .TIF.) An Auto View checkbox allows you to automatically display a thumbnail view of files in a small preview box as you select them, to make searching through your bitmaps a little easier. If you have many complex bitmaps in the current directory — particularly grayscale or color — Auto View can really slow things down, but in some cases it's still the most convenient way to find what you're looking for. As an alternative, there's a View button that allows you to selectively view files. In most cases, this is a more practical approach than choosing Auto View.

In addition, a Header button displays a dialog box of arcane technical information about the selected file. This information can be of use in determining the suitability of a bitmap for tracing and whether or not color reduction should be used. It also provides its own View button. When you've finished exploring, select one or more files using the Control key and click on OK.

On the Preferences menu you'll find two toggles — Trace Partial Area and View Dithered Colors — along with a selection for Color Reduction, which displays its own dialog box. The View Dithered Colors option displays images that contain more color depth than your graphics card can manage, and does this more smoothly on the screen by simulating the in-between colors, or *dithering* them. If you were working with 256-color images on a 16-color display, for example, this might be useful.

The Trace Partial Area option causes Trace to open the bitmap for viewing and cropping of the area to be traced before actually starting each trace. A frame with standard resizing handles appears around the bitmap, and any or all sides can be moved to select the area to be processed. The obvious advantage is that you can now isolate and trace just the desired

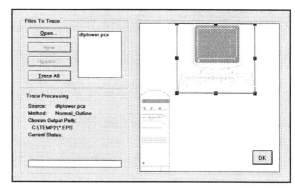

parts of a scanned image. But equally significant is that graphics too large or complex for Trace to handle can be processed in pieces that are easier for the program to digest. Each of the sections can then be imported into Draw and combined into one picture. In this case, you should make sure that you've selected Always Prompt in the Output Options, or the only section you'll wind up with is the last one you traced.

Another use of this feature is to select a small representative area of a bitmap to work on when testing tracing options. Then when you've arrived at suitable settings, you trace the entire image.

The primary drawback to having Trace Partial Area turned on is that it defeats the program's ability to process multiple images in a batch sequence, as this option must be tended to before each individual tracing operation starts.

Choosing Color Reduction from the Preferences menu displays a dialog box that allows you to specify the number of colors and grayscales (separate values may be assigned to each) that Trace works with when tracing the corresponding bitmaps. The maximum value for either is 256, but for all practical purposes if there are that many colors in the artwork, it's probably not going to produce a very good trace. However, this function permits the tracing of 256-shade grayscale graphics or color files as if they were 4 (grayscale only), 8, 16 or 64-level files. In general, choose the lowest number of colors that you can get away with.

This dialog box also offers a choice to create black-and-white art from grayscale or color bitmaps. The results are the typical, high contrast look similar to that achieved by converting a color

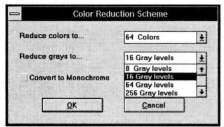

or grayscale bitmap to black-and-white line art or increasing its contrast dramatically in Photo-Paint. You can achieve some interesting effects this way, but they're hard to predict.

You'll note that I skipped right over one menu item: Tracing Options. Since the most important aspects of controlling Trace are in that menu selection, I'll save it until you've looked at the rest of the Trace main screen.

The main screen is separated into three areas: Files To Trace, Trace Processing and the Viewer. The View and Header buttons duplicate those of the same name found in the Open One Or More Files dialog box; however, until one of the files in the list box is selected, the View and Header buttons remain ghosted. The View button on the main screen provides a considerably larger view area than the thumbnail-sized perspective in the Open One Or More Files dialog box.

In the view area, as already noted, you adjust the portion of the bitmap to be traced if you have Trace Partial Area enabled. It's also where you'll eventually see Trace's interpretation of the bitmap as it's converted to .EPS format. Between what you see in the view area after completing a trace, and the object and node information in the Trace Processing section of the screen (which is not yet displaying anything), you should be able to develop some idea of whether or not Trace produced acceptable results. That's where editing the Tracing Options comes in; so, having covered all the fundamental aspects of Trace, you'll now dig into the area many users find bewildering.

Tracing Options

The tracing options affect the judgments Trace makes by controlling how far it will draw before resampling the bitmap, how tightly it will adhere to the contours of the bitmap, how sharply a line must bend before Trace considers it a corner rather than a curve, and so forth. Keep in mind that what you're attempting to convey accurately is the shape of the original object, not necessarily the bitmap's inherently inaccurate representation of that object.

These adjustments can be difficult to decipher. Often, changing one parameter — Sample Rate, for instance — doesn't seem to produce the desired or expected result. But adjusting both Sample Rate *and* Curve Fit might do the job. The end result is a matter of how well all the options are tuned to the characteristics of the bitmap and to each other. All of the options are interrelated to a certain extent, and those interrelationships are dependent on the characteristics and resolution of the bitmap being traced. It's a complex area and the nuances will only start to become clear with considerable practice.

Click on Tracing Options to display its menu, which offers access to two preconfigured sets of options — Normal Outline and Normal Centerline — along with Edit Options and eight blank tracing *option sets* (represented as three dots). The preconfigured option sets are meant to be suitable for tracing 'average' bitmaps. Like most average settings, however, they rarely fill real-world needs.

You can choose Edit Options with either of the Normal choices checked and Trace will display the Edit Tracing Options dialog box. Any changes you make in the dialog box will be in effect only as long as the current Trace session lasts, even if you rename Normal Outline or Normal Centerline to something else. The next time you run Trace, the default options will be in place again. The problem with this approach is that much effort and experimentation goes into finding viable combinations of options. Those that work — particularly if they work well on types of graphics that you'll be tracing frequently — are too valuable not to save.

Saving Option Sets

Once you begin experimenting with the tracing options, you should choose one of the sets of dots instead of Edit Options. Try this now. This approach is awkward, in that you don't know whether you'll want to save the options you create until after you've tested them, but Trace forces you to anticipate the possible need to do so. Type a name in the Option Name area and click on OK to create a new set. Note that it's been added to the Tracing Options menu.

Once you've created eight sets of tracing options and filled up all the choices, the only way to get to the Edit Options dialog box is to select a set that's reasonably close to what you need and then choose Edit Options to modify it. Having done that, remember that it's the act of renaming the set of options that saves it. You have the choice of saving it or letting it revert to its former state, but you can only save it by replacing the one that was selected when you opened the dialog box.

If all that seems a bit confining, bear in mind that eight sets of tracing options (ten, counting the Normal sets) can cover a lot of ground, and even those who use Trace daily with a wide variety of artwork rarely have as many as six or seven sets they use regularly.

Choose Normal Outline from the Edit Options menu and display the Tracing Options dialog box again. Here's where the real work is done. It's here that you'll instruct Trace how to convert your bitmap into a usable .EPS vector graphic. You'll employ the tracing options to adjust Trace to the characteristics of the specific bitmap being traced and, more importantly, to create and save sets of tracing options optimized to the characteristics of the types of bitmaps you're likely to process frequently.

There are eight areas in the Tracing Options dialog box. You'll put many of the options available here to work in the tutorial sections that follow. But first, a brief overview of their operation is in order. If you can't wait to try out some of the options discussed, feel free to experiment as you go by using the sample .TIF files in the DRAW\SAMPLES directory.

Tracing Method

The **Follow Outline** method traces the edges of each element in the bitmap image, no matter how thin, and fills the resulting outline. In the case of black-and-white line art, the fill will be either black or white. Trace does not create combined objects, so a letter O would be represented by an ellipse filled with black, overlaid with a smaller ellipse filled with white. For color and grayscale images, Trace attempts to match the color or shade of gray of each object in the bitmap, within the parameters you've specified in the Color Reduction setting on the Preferences menu.

The **Follow Center Line** method assigns a width to thin lines based on the thickness of the bitmap line and the options set for line width. Lines beyond a user-defined width are traced as if the outline method were selected, thereby turning them into fillable objects, not lines.

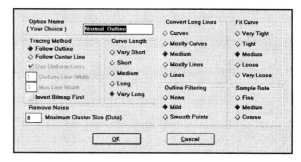

Outline or Center Line: which of these two schemes works best? To a large extent that depends on the properties of the graphic being traced, but it's also affected by the ultimate use of the resulting trace. For a hand-drawn sketch or cartoon that will be used pretty much the way a well-tuned Trace generates it, Outline tracing is usually preferable. The variations in line thickness that are part of any hand-drawn work will then be captured in the output file. The same rationale applies to signatures, but on a more pragmatic basis. In this case, the need for a faithful reproduction is more a matter of necessity than artistic purity. A signature graphic that doesn't capture the stroke weight and steadiness of hand that went into the original doesn't get the job done.

On the other hand, if the work is meant only as raw material for later completion with the tools available in Draw, then Center Line tracing can often be much more useful. In this case, individual lines are defined as lines, rather than as objects created with closed paths. If the **Use Uniform Lines** option is chosen, all the lines will carry the same width setting; however, regardless of the uniform line setting, the thickness of each *individual* line is uniform. The thickness and attributes of the lines can be adjusted once the .EPS file has been imported into Draw, so calligraphic effects can be added after the fact, although this technique certainly isn't a substitute for capturing the natural calligraphic qualities of a traced signature.

If you choose Follow Center Line, Trace will either assign a uniform line width to all lines in the drawing, or will calculate the appropriate line width. The results depend on how you've set the line width in the Tracing Method section. If you've chosen Uniform Line Width, Trace offers you the option to set the

---

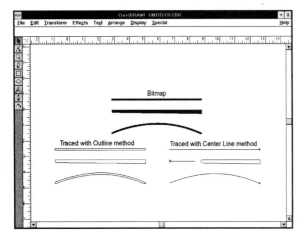

width of the line it assigns. (This option is only available when Follow Center Line and Uniform Line Width are both checked.)

A straight line four pixels wide and 100 pixels long traced with the Outline method will import into Draw as a closed path, much like a skinny rectangle that's been converted to curves. Of course, if that line isn't quite straight or uniform (and bitmaps are rarely either), it will be a much more complex closed path. Editing a graphic in which each line is actually an object with nodes and control points along each of its sides can be a major headache.

To make the editing job even tougher, if the traced bitmap contains lines of varying thickness, then narrow sections will be perceived as gaps in the line. A hand-drawn or otherwise uneven line might actually be represented as a series of unconnected, closed path curves that can be even more confusing once editing commences.

It's possible for the Center Line tracing method to create broken lines by misinterpreting very narrow sections as gaps, or even (if Uniform Line Width is disabled) to decide that a sudden and substantial change in line width should be two lines with different properties, or even a line and an outlined object. Still, this can be far easier to edit in Draw than a series of closed paths representing a line. Bumping the **Max Line Width** setting higher (it defaults to 3, with valid values from 2 to 99) will usually help in this regard by producing continuous lines, rather than a series of line segments or outlined objects. The importance of this setting is dependent to a certain extent on how much time and effort went into bitmap preparation before opening Trace.

Using the Center Line tracing format, lines with very sharp corners have a tendency to become rounded corners with a separate line pointing at the true corner or a filled object sitting

Converting Scans with CorelTRACE

in the true corner. This typically happens when lines intersect at an angle of less than about 45°. You can see this clearly in the illustration of a corner of one of the stars. This can usually be repaired fairly easily in Draw, but if such corners are numerous the Max Line Width can be adjusted and the image retraced. In keeping with the interrelated nature of the Tracing Options mentioned earlier, the **Outline Filtering** option setting can also have an effect on this phenomenon. Setting it to None helps alleviate corner distortion.

Original bitmap

The **Uniform Line Width** option — available when you select Center Line as the tracing method — allows you to specify a weight from 1 to 99 pixels for all the lines in the image. The default of 1 pixel, in a 300 dpi bitmap, will result in all lines in the image being given a hairline thickness (.25 point) when it's imported into Draw.

Outline traced

When capturing the artistic differences in line width is important, the Uniform Line Width option is self-defeating. But when clarity of the image and ease of editing are higher on the priority list, and the graphic contains numerous intersecting lines with varying angles (as with technical drawings and maps), then choosing Uniform Line Width is almost always advisable.

Center Line traced

If you do choose this option, be sure to set its value at least as high as the widest line in the image. Since this setting is dependent on the resolution of the bitmap being traced, there is no way to make a hard and fast recommendation. However, you can always zoom in as much as possible on a section of that narrow line in Photo-Paint, and simply count the pixels.

The Tracing Methods section of the Edit Options dialog box also provides a choice to invert the bitmap before tracing. **Invert Bitmap First** can be used to make a negative image of a black-and-white line drawing, with white lines separating objects filled with black.

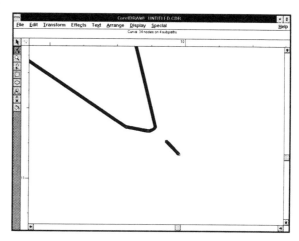

Curve Length

The Curve Length section of the Edit Options dialog box provides some control over the length of the curves in the output file. Unfortunately, as with the settings available for most of the other tracing options, a series of vague ranges is provided rather than actual values. Creating segments with a shorter curve length will more accurately reflect the shape of the bitmap, but they'll contain correspondingly more nodes. The default value (as found in the Normal tracing option sets) is Very Long.

You'll find that changing this particular value has almost no effect unless the Sample Rate and Fit To Curve values are also adjusted. For very detailed images, particularly those you expect to use with minimal tuning of the output in Draw, you will need to shorten the Curve Length, as well as increase the Sample Rate and tighten the Fit To Curve. Shortening the Curve Length beyond what's necessary, however, simply adds extra nodes to the file, which can create problems with complex shapes that would normally have a high node count anyway.

Sample Rate

The Sample Rate setting controls how far Trace will set off in one direction, or follow one arc, before it checks how close it is to the bitmap. The Fine setting will typically result in a more accurate trace (but with lots more nodes), since each time it checks and makes a correction Trace will create a node.

Like most of the tracing options, this has more effect on low resolution (that is, very jaggy) bitmaps, and its setting interacts to a great extent with others — particularly Curve Length and Fit Curve. If your bitmap is 300 dpi or higher, and is made up primarily of straight lines on the 0/180° or 90/270° bias, setting the sample rate to Coarse can give quality results more quickly and produce an easier to edit vector file. Graphics with lots of curves, but not with a very small radius, trace better at Medium, while a Fine sample rate becomes necessary for bitmaps with many sharp corners and tight curves. The general guideline, though, is that a lower Sample Rate will produce a more easily edited file.

Fit Curve

The best setting for Fit Curve is also heavily dependent on the resolution and the physical characteristics of the bitmap being traced. Just as Sample Rate controls how frequently Trace checks to see where it should be, the Fit Curve option controls how sharply it will turn to get back on track and how far it allows itself to be off track before making a correction.

Convert Long Lines

Even the curves of a bitmap are made up of straight lines — that's what gives it the jaggies. So despite the fact that those square pixels are arranged in a broad curve, what Trace really 'sees' is a series of tiny, straight lines. But you don't want to trace a circle as if it were composed of a huge number of straight lines, with each corner a 90° bend.

Convert Long Lines controls how freely Trace uses curves to approximate the shape of the image represented by that conglomeration of straight-edged, right-angle bound pixels. As you'd expect, if the drawing is made up completely of straight lines, as many technical drawings are, setting Convert Long Lines to Lines will result in an accurate trace. If, on the other hand, the bitmap contains a lot of curves, setting this option to Lines will result in a poor quality trace that can be difficult to edit. It will look much like a Draw object displayed with Curve Flatness (in the Display subdialog box of Preferences) set low for speedier display updating. Unfortunately, in this case you can't round the curves by merely changing the flatness in Draw; you'd have to convert the line segments in your imported .EPS file into curves to let you edit the shape of the objects with node control handles.

Perhaps more than any of the other tracing options, Convert Long Lines is a judgment call. If there are neither curves nor straight lines, the choice of one or the other of the two extremes (Lines and Curves) is easy. But if the bitmap is made up of both types of elements, which of the intermediate settings will do the best job is a decision that may require some experimentation. You may be tempted to use the default (Medium) setting and let it go at that. But the differences in accuracy, file size and ease of editing between the right setting for one bitmap and another can be dramatic. It's well worth the effort to spend some time running a few trial traces with different values assigned to this setting.

Outline Filtering

Just how accurate does the conversion from bitmap to vector need to be? Outline Filtering will have a major effect on the output by limiting the creation of sharp corners. In the Normal option set the middle of the road Mild is the default. If a bitmap is fairly rough, and especially in the case of bitmaps that contain few sharp corners (most signatures, for instance), setting this to Smooth Points will result in a more accurate trace, or at least one that is considerably easier to edit.

If the image to be traced contains a lot of sharp corners, particularly on the thin lines found in some maps and most technical drawings, then setting the Outline Filtering to None will produce a more accurate representation of the image — albeit one that may require more thorough checking and tuning in Draw to repair the corners that Trace will invariably 'see' in bitmap irregularities.

You should also be aware of a relationship between Outline Filtering and Maximum Line Thickness; either can result in broken lines in the traced output if the bitmap contains very thin lines. Sometimes that means you can make up for emphasizing one of these options to achieve a desired result, while using the other to offset the negative effects (such as gaps in thin lines) of the other. Other times it means you end up tracing and retracing the file to eliminate a glaring inaccuracy, all the while making adjustments to the wrong option while trying to eliminate it.

Remove Noise

Noise in a graphic file is simply stray extraneous pixels that have nothing to do with the image. This is especially prevalent in bitmaps that were scanned from dirty or poor quality originals. Typically, the scanner intensity has to be cranked up pretty high to get a good scan from such originals, and this usually picks up dirt in the background. Similar dirt invariably shows up in files scanned from photocopies — especially second and third generation photocopies. Trace's noise filter can be set to eliminate most of the noise or dirt in the background, but if you prepped the bitmap in Photo-Paint you probably ran it through that application's own noise filter, removing most of the random pixels.

Trace's Remove Noise filter setting is a value between 2 and 99, and it represents the number of pixels in the largest cluster that the filter will be allowed to ignore. With detailed artwork it's difficult to completely remove noise without also losing some detail, but the default value of 8 typically works fine for all but poor quality originals. In the case of very dirty bitmaps, if there's not a lot of fine detail to lose, then a cleaner output file can often be achieved by raising the noise value to 20 or 30. And in some cases, even if it will result in a loss of detail, it's worth it to get something you can more easily edit.

If you applied manual hints to the bitmap to embolden tiny drawing elements that you wanted preserved while tracing, be sure to take that into account when setting the maximum noise removal cluster size.

Option Name

Arriving at a suitable set of tracing options for any specific bitmap or type of bitmap requires some degree of understanding of what each option does, familiarity with how they're interrelated and a lot of time-consuming trial and error. When you get it right and Trace produces exactly the results you had in mind... you *did* save those option settings, didn't you? Too often the answer to that is no. All that switching in and out of Draw to import the .EPS file and check it out, then trying an adjustment with one option or another; who remembers to save every combination, especially when most seem too far off base?

Many users keep both Trace and Draw running at the same time, and flip back and forth with Alt-Tab. However, it's usually not necessary to import the file into Draw to get a good idea of whether or not it's an improvement over an earlier effort. Between the preview and the node and object count in the Tracing Process section at the lower-left of the Trace screen, you can usually tell if an .EPS file you create is usable. If the particular combination appears to have produced a successful trace, then save it.

Don't worry about using up your eight namable option sets. You can always overwrite an unneeded set, or one that didn't live up to your expectations, simply by renaming it. Or you can rename any of the option sets (except the two Normal options) with an ellipsis (...) and return it to an unsaved state that will automatically open the Edit Options dialog box when you select it. You'll get a message saying the name hasn't been changed when you do this, but just choose OK and you're back to square one as far as that option set is concerned.

Since the values for these option sets are saved in the CORELTRC.INI file, another strategy is to create multiple versions of this .INI file, which differ only in containing different option set definitions. You could give these a variety of names and create batch files to be run from icons in Program Manager that simply copy GRAYSCAL.INI (which could contain option sets for grayscale images) to CORELTRC.INI, for example, before loading Trace.

You can name an option set anything you like, but there are two basic naming conventions that make sense. Luckily, you're not limited to an eight character DOS-based filename, so more descriptive names are possible. You *are* limited to the physical space in the text window. This is character-size dependent, so you can be much more specific and descriptive with lowercase alpha characters and numerals than with uppercase alpha.

One naming scheme is to use the type of graphic being traced: signature; block logo; detail logo; grayscale logo; schematic, etc. This is fine if all your bitmaps come in at the same resolution and at comparable quality. The options arrived at for one signature, map or technical drawing will likely do a passable job on most similar artwork at the same resolution. Logos, though, are by nature unique and if you do a lot of logo conversion you might find it advantageous to keep a hard copy log with a photocopy of each logo you work on and the best set of tracing options you came up with for it.

An alternate naming scheme, which grows more sensible as you become familiar with the Tracing Options dialog box, is to assign alpha or numeric values to the selections and stick with them. For example, the Normal Outline method might be o/-/8/1/3/2/3/2 or Normal Center Line c/u/1/3/-/8/3/2/3/2. In both of these examples, the first letter indicates the method and the hyphen indicates no inversion of the bitmap. In the Center Line method, the line width selections become available, so they precede the inversion marker. Following the hyphen, it's just a series of numeric values assigned to the selections. It could as easily have been vl/m/m/m/m, except that a combination of the Center Line method with two-digit values for line width settings and noise could conceivably produce something like c/u/10/15/30/i/vs/mc/sp/vl/m, which won't fit in the allotted space, while its numeric equivalent — c/u/10/15/30/i/1/4/1/1/2 — will.

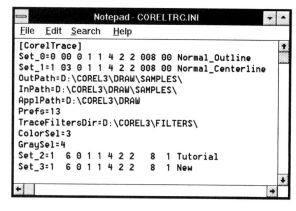

```
                Notepad - CORELTRC.INI
 File   Edit   Search   Help
[CorelTrace]
Set_0=0 00 0 1 1 4 2 2 008 00 Normal_Outline
Set_1=1 03 0 1 1 4 2 2 008 00 Normal_Centerline
OutPath=D:\COREL3\DRAW\SAMPLES\
InPath=D:\COREL3\DRAW\SAMPLES\
ApplPath=D:\COREL3\DRAW
Prefs=13
TraceFiltersDir=D:\COREL3\FILTERS\
ColorSel=3
GraySel=4
Set_2=1  6 0 1 1 4 2 2   8  1 Tutorial
Set_3=1  6 0 1 1 4 2 2   8  1 New
```

The whole point is to devise a scheme for naming tracing options that tells you what the options are or what types of images they are best suited to trace. The most important aspect of the code you use is that it makes sense to you and conveys the information you need to quickly select an appropriate tracing option set directly from the Tracing Options menu, after you become familiar with the effects of those options.

One of the primary reasons to use Trace, instead of autotracing the imported bitmap in Draw, is that it can be set up to trace a batch of files consecutively. A cartoonist working on paper, then tuning his work and adding lettering in Draw, can render and scan an entire strip and let Trace do the conversions later. Similarly, when a company converts to electronically signed documentation, all the signatures or groups of newly added signatures can be converted in batches.

It's important to remember, though, that when you choose a Tracing Options set, you're assigning it to the entire batch of bitmaps to be processed, so they should all have similar attributes. You can't effectively mix technical drawings, signatures and grayscale renderings in one batch and expect the same set of tracing options to do an adequate job on all of them.

Cleaning Up the Output

Sometimes Trace's output is usable just as you get it from the program. Depending on the type of bitmaps you scan, and on the intended use of the resulting vector graphics, this might happen frequently or almost never. In either case, your ability to clean up and adjust Trace's output will have a strong influence on how useful the utility is to you.

At first glance, it would seem that anyone with decent Draw skills could clean up a bitmap trace with relative ease. In practice, some of the best Draw users find tuning Trace's output hopelessly confusing. For one thing, there are differences between the way objects are constructed when manually drawing versus tracing them. The circle on the grid illustration clearly shows this. Note that the graphic appears essentially the same in the preview window, whether it was created from scratch in Draw or traced from a bitmap in Trace. However, the wireframe views beneath each version show a dramatic difference in the way they are constructed.

The placement and type of node is the result of automated tracing options, rather than common sense. As Trace adjusts its path to capture the bitmap's shape, the gyrations it must sometimes go through often result in strange path constructions. At times, deleting what seems to be an unnecessary node will send the line between the two adjacent nodes completely off the screen! This is fixable, of course, but the fact that it happens illustrates how differently Trace draws than we do.

The goal, as always, is to achieve maximum accuracy with a minimum node count. Depending on the qualities and resolution of the original bitmap, as well as the tracing options used, either of these desired aspects may be sacrificed to the other. Cleaning up or tuning the output is then basically an effort to bring it back into line. If both accuracy and simplicity are lacking, retracing with a more appropriate set of tracing options — even perhaps rescanning or re-prepping the bitmap — might make more sense than laboriously trying to salvage a poor trace.

Most users find that for complex editing it's simpler to work in wireframe mode and switch to preview mode occasionally for reference, using the Shift-F9 shortcut to toggle back and forth. It's also a good idea, especially when it's evident that a traced vector graphic will need more than a slight touch up, to import the original bitmap for use as a template. You can simply import it and send it to the back using the Arrange menu or, better yet, move either the bitmap or the trace to a new layer. The Visible option found in the Layers roll-up, accessed via the Arrange menu, can be used to toggle the layer contain-

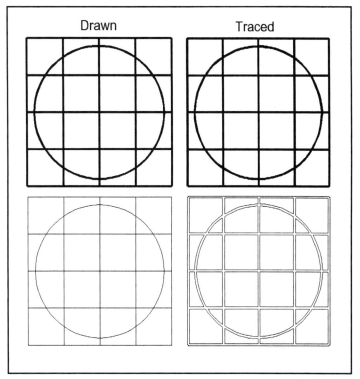

ing the bitmap on or off as needed. Be sure you have Show Bitmaps in the Display menu enabled. (For more on layers see *Working with Bitmap Graphics*.)

In the case of complex drawings that were traced with very fine settings, it's often advisable to select all the nodes and convert the associated curve segments to straight lines. Then you can edit the drawing by removing as many nodes as possible and selectively converting the remaining line segments back to curves as needed.

It's also possible to use Draw's autotrace feature to quickly retrace individual objects or shapes within the imported bitmap graphic. This is a good way to replace sections of the imported .EPS graphic that are unworkable because they were so far out of whack with the dominant characteristics of the rest of the bitmap, the Tracing Options were in conflict with them. In addition, slight editing mistakes have a tendency to compound themselves, and it's far from impossible to edit an object right out of the realm of "almost right" and into the area of "what is

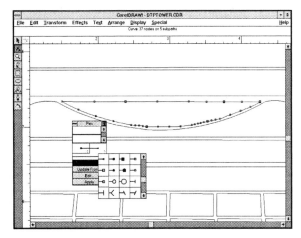

that thing?" In this case, rather than importing an entire second copy of the .EPS file, just autotrace the affected curve object using your bitmap template.

Broken line segments commonly need attention, especially in the case of files produced with the Center Line tracing method. Using the ⬆ tool, marquee select or Shift-click to select the problem segments, then combine them into a single object by choosing Combine from the Arrange menu. Then, using the ⤝ tool, select adjacent end nodes (again using either a marquee or Shift-click to select multiple nodes) and double-click on a selected node to access the Node Edit menu. Choose Join and the two nodes become one.

If Join is ghosted (unavailable) you either have more than two nodes selected, or one of the nodes isn't an end node. This is not entirely unlikely, since Trace often ends up putting adjacent nodes almost atop one another, and the larger end node often hides the smaller nodes underneath. Zoom in to select only the end node and drag it slightly to peek underneath. If there's a node under there, press the Delete key. The end node you just dragged will be removed and the formerly hidden node will become the new end node.

Sometimes you'll be faced with so many broken line segments that finding the end nodes seems almost impossible. This is especially troubling when you've opened what should be a closed path and need to rejoin all the various ends to allow the path to be filled. There are several ways to approach this.

One is to zoom in and select a segment with the ⤝ tool. You can then press the Home key to select the first node of the segment (the End key selects, as you might expect, the last node). With Snap To Objects enabled on the Display menu, you could snap the first node to the last node of the other segment. You'd then select both segments with the ⬆ tool, combine them and join the two nodes with the ⤝ tool.

A second technique is to select all the line segments with the ▶ tool, give them a fill of ✕ and combine them into one object. With the ◮ tool, assign a line width of two points (click on the icon to the right of ⚊). Then click on the ◮ icon in the ◮ menu and in the Outline Pen dialog box choose the arrowhead that looks like an empty circle surrounding the end of the line (as opposed to being tacked *onto* the end). Apply it to one end of your line and apply a small filled box or dot to the other end.

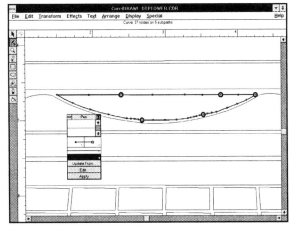

If you are in wireframe view, use Shift-F9 to go into preview view so you can see the line attributes. Closing a path with numerous openings now becomes a simple task, since each matching pair is displayed as a circle and a small block, as shown in the illustration. Line each block up in a circle, marquee select two nodes at a time with the ⋏ tool, double-click and choose Join from the Node Edit menu.

Converting Specific Graphics

Logos are among the most frequently traced artwork. Since they are often registered trademarks, an accurate rendition is important. Careful analysis of the original is vital to producing a vector graphic with minimal problems.

If any text components of the logo are recognizable as a common font it's often better to set the Trace options based on the characteristics of the logo's non-text elements. You can then eliminate what will undoubtedly be poorly traced text elements from the .EPS file and replace them with text in the appropriate font in Draw. Keep in mind, however, that Draw's fonts do not exactly match their industry-standard counterparts. Where a client expects a particular cut of a font, you may need to purchase that font or output your file at a service bureau.

The non-text-based artistic elements can usually be traced very accurately if the text elements are ignored when choosing

---

tracing options. Then, using the imported bitmap as a template, the new text can be positioned, stretched, distorted and snapped into proper alignment. If necessary, the text can be converted to curves so that it can be exactly matched to the bitmap original with the ✗ tool.

Signatures are much like freeform logos: each is unique, and accuracy is paramount in both cases. But the geometric shapes and symmetrical designs common to typical business logos are absent in signatures. Instead you might encounter neat, flowing curves, choppy, angular lines or a freehand artistic flourish that trails off into a gently waving line representing the rest of the signer's name. It may or may not look like handwriting, but it's up to you to create trace option settings that capture its detail without requiring a lot of tuning in Draw, because it's almost impossible to tune a freeform shape without losing some of its unique characteristics. Is the little hook in the O a scanning aberration, or an element of the actual signature? It's a good idea to have a photocopied enlargement of the original, handwritten signature available for comparison purposes, as well as the scanned bitmap from which the trace was created.

Technical drawings, maps, schematics and similar graphics have much in common, so a few general rules apply. Such drawings are typically a series of straight lines, with text and geometric shapes added. It's often advisable to trace each twice — once with trace options set for the straight line elements (Curve Length to Very Long, Convert Long Lines to Lines, Coarse Sample Rate, no Outline Filtering), and then again with the options set for the characteristics of the geometric shapes (Curve Length Short, Convert Long Lines to Mostly Curves, Fine Sample Rate, Mild or Smooth Outline Filtering). Import both of the .EPS files and the bitmap into Draw, move one .EPS to each side of the screen and ungroup each of them. You could then combine the line and shape elements from the two .EPS files, erase the traced text and use the bitmap as a template for text creation in Draw.

Sooner or later when using customized trace options, Trace is going to warn you that a bitmap may not trace correctly. It may be that the settings you've selected, combined with the size or resolution of the drawing, will in fact cause Trace to skip over parts of the graphic. But in most cases the algorithm Trace uses to determine the complexity of the combination it's

faced with is on the conservative side and the bitmap will trace just fine. In any case, you've got nothing to lose by choosing OK and letting Trace have a shot at it despite its misgivings.

If the bitmap does come up short, you'll have to either simplify it, change the options, or use a series of partial area traces to bring it into Draw. Those are the same options you would have to choose from if you had canceled the trace in response to the warning message, so nothing's been lost except a few minutes' time.

A Simple Exercise

For this exercise, you'll eliminate the need to take scanner-produced inconsistencies and dirty or poor quality bitmaps into consideration. You'll deal strictly with the effects of the various tracing option settings by tracing a simple bitmap exported from Draw.

Run Draw and display the Symbols dialog box (press F8, then Shift-click on the page). In the dialog box choose Shapes2 from the category list. Enter 96 in the symbol # box, change the size to 2 inches and click on OK. Select the symbol and give it a line width of .003 inch (hairline) and a fill of black.

Choose Export from the File menu, enable Selected Only and choose the .PCX format from List Files Of Type. Name the file PIE.PCX and export it (preferably to your Trace-dedicated temp directory). When the Bitmap Export dialog box appears, choose Grays, Black and White, and 300 dpi. Now repeat the export procedure, this time naming it PIE2.PCX and choosing 75 dpi in the dialog box. Press Alt-Tab to leave Draw running and return to Program Manager to run Trace.

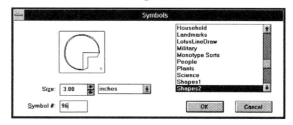

Click on the Open button, set List Files Of Type to .PCX and, if necessary, move to the directory to which you exported the two files. Select both PIE.PCX and PIE2.PCX with Control-click and click on OK. Now click on PIE.PCX and the View button to display it. Then do the same for PIE2.PCX. You can clearly see the difference in image quality between the 300 and 75 dpi bitmaps. Choose the Normal Outline tracing method from the Tracing Options menu and click on Trace All.

It should take Trace only a few seconds to process these simple graphics. When it's done, click on the Open button again and reselect the same two files. From the Tracing Options menu choose an open options set (...) and in the Edit Options dialog box change Tracing Method to Follow Center Line and the Max Line Width to 6, which should be enough to clearly illustrate the Center Line tracing method's tendency to distort corners, and the effect this setting can have on lines — particularly curved lines.

Before choosing OK, name the option set. Any name you choose is fine, but this might be a good time to start practising a naming code, as described earlier in the Trace Options section of this chapter. Choose Output Options from the File menu and ensure Always Prompt is enabled. Click on Trace All, choose No from the overwrite warning dialog box and assign the names PIE3.EPS and PIE4.EPS to the respective outputs.

When the operation has finished, return to Draw with Alt-Tab and move the original symbol to the top-left corner of the screen. Then import the two .PCX and four .EPS files you created, changing the List Files Of Type as necessary. Note that there is another .EPS file type listed in conjunction with the Adobe Illustrator .AI filter. Don't choose

Original   300 DPI   75 DPI

Outline Trace

Center Line Trace

this one. The one you want for importing from Trace is the second choice on the list, immediately following .CDR. Using the Directories list box, locate your designated Trace temp directory and import one file at a time. Unless you change Trace's output path, you should only have to find the directory in Draw's import box once for each file format. The second time it will automatically move to that directory when you choose the appropriate import format.

Arrange and resize the files as you import them. Then zoom in and scroll around to examine the imported files up close. Look at them in both preview and wireframe views, using Shift-F9. You'll note that in the case of the outline trace, the 300 dpi bitmap produced much better output than the 75 dpi image. These extremes exaggerate the difference resolution makes, but on more complex drawings the difference between even 200 and 300 dpi can be significant.

Also note that for this simple graphic, the default Normal Outline settings produce acceptable results when using the 300 dpi bitmap. In the Center Line traces, notice the differences attributable to the resolution and how the corners of the outlined portion of the drawing are distorted, especially at 75 dpi. In particular, note the broken line and object arrangement that Trace "saw" in the curved line that makes up most of the image.

This is directly related to the Maximum Line Width setting in the Tracing Options dialog box. Seeing the typical result of an inappropriate value for that option here should help you quickly identify the problem when this situation turns up in your real-world use of Trace. Understanding how and why this particular example of bad Trace output occurs should help you get a feel for the importance of matching tracing option settings to a bitmap.

In this particular bitmap the width of the curved line is 12 pixels. This should be enough to prevent Trace from tracing any portion of the line as a Center Line, just as its 3 pixel width in the 75 dpi version of the bitmap prevents it from seeing any portion of the line as a closed object. But as Trace's output of this 300 dpi file proves, it's not always that straightforward. When dealing with a curved line shape made up of square

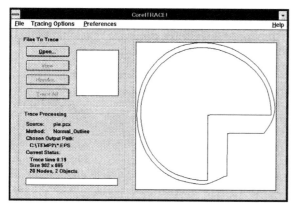

pixels, Trace must go through digital acrobatics to determine the size and shape of the line. This will cause it to see a very distorted picture of the line, the interpretation of which is reflected in its output.

The solution for the 300 dpi bitmap is to change the Maximum Line Width tracing option. Double it, and Trace will see the whole arc as a line. Cut it in half, and Trace will see it as an object to be outlined. You may want to retrace this image using different Maximum Line Width settings to further familiarize yourself with its effects.

Most of the differences in output between the two Tracing Option methods we used in this example were obvious enough in the Trace view window that in real-world use you would have easily recognized the usable conversion when you saw it. Unless you're doing a sizable batch trace, taking the time to examine the appearance of the output in Trace and watching the object and node count in the Trace Processing section of the Trace window can tell you whether adjustments you make to the Tracing Options are improvements or actually worsen things. Remember that the general goal is to minimize the node count while maximizing the accuracy.

Sometimes those two criteria conflict and you'll be forced to make a choice between accuracy and node count. As the next exercise will illustrate, the factor that helps you make that choice is often the vector file's likely ease of editability. Before going on, it would be instructive to print out the page with all your imported images from Draw, to see how your printer handles both the bitmaps and the traces. Then enlarge the images and print again, to get a clear picture of that aspect of a vector-based image's advantage over a bitmap.

Additionally, switching to Draw's wireframe view and ungrouping the .EPS traces so you can use the ⚲ tool to examine where Trace placed nodes will prove valuable. You might also want to check the sizes of the .EPS and .PCX files with the Windows File Manager. You'll find the 300 dpi .PCX file is about 8 Kb, versus less than 3 Kb for the .EPS Trace. The proportional difference in size is for a line art (monochrome) bitmap; the difference in file size between raster and vector files becomes even greater when dealing with grayscale or color images, the bitmap versions of which contain color information for every dot.

Before moving on to the next exercise, feel free to reopen Trace and retrace PIE.PCX and PIE2.PCX with different tracing options. Of course, you may now be wondering why you should bother with Center Line tracing at all, since it was so much easier to get an accurate trace with the Outline settings. The next exercise should help to illustrate the value of Center Line tracing.

A Little More Complex

Copy the COPIER.TIF file from the SAMPLES directory of the Utility disk included with this book to your dedicated Trace temp directory. Click on the Open button in Trace and bring COPIER.TIF into the list box. Choose Normal Outline from the Tracing Options menu and click on Trace All. Note the resulting object and node count, and the appearance of the trace in the view window. Choose Normal Centerline from Tracing Options and name the second output file COPIER2.EPS. Again, note the object and node count, and the appearance of the traced file.

Often, .EPS files imported into Draw are easier to edit if they are Center Line traced, but in this case the Center Line output would obviously need much more editing than the Outline trace you created earlier. By making some adjustments to the options, you can try to achieve the best of both worlds.

Load COPIER.TIF into Trace again, but before tracing choose a blank (...) option set from the Tracing Options menu and set the options as shown in the dialog box illustrated here. Don't forget to name the option set before leaving the Options dialog box. (If all your blank selections are filled up, choose Edit Options directly from the Tracing Options menu and don't name the options

Original .PCX

Normal Outline

Normal Center Line

c/4/8/4/5/1/3/5/3

when exiting the Edit Options dialog box.) Trace the file and name the output file COPIER3.EPS. Note that the output is a more accurate rendition of the copier than the previous Center Line trace, but the node count has also gone up substantially.

If it's running, switch to Draw with Alt-Tab or simply click in its window, which should be visible behind Trace's smaller window. Otherwise, run Draw from the Program Manager. Import all three of the files you just traced (COPIER.EPS, COPIER2.EPS and COPIER3.EPS) into Draw, and arrange them so they aren't piled on top of each other. Look them over to get an idea of just how Trace constructed each of them. Most of what you do from here on will be easier in wireframe view, so if you normally work in the preview window, switch now by pressing Shift-F9.

Close examination of the three different versions of the copier graphic illustrates how Outline Tracing can make for an overly complex vector graphic when converting images that consist primarily of straight lines. If you're thinking of schematics, road maps and certain technical illustrations, you're definitely on the right track.

At this point, the outline trace has served its purpose of illustrating how poorly suited it is for this type of image. Select it and delete. Now compare the two different Center Line traces more closely. Ungroup each one, so you can see the node arrangement by clicking on an object with the ⚡ tool. Be careful not to move them atop each other, or it'll be difficult to separate them later.

The difference between the two, as shown in the illustration, is significant. The primary reason behind the high node count in one of the images is the Curve Length setting of Very Short. This forced Trace to be more accurate by drawing only a very short distance before placing a node. Consequently, it also drove the node count through the roof. As you'll see, though, in the case of a drawing made up primarily of long, straight lines, such as this one, this does not necessarily result in a major increase in editing difficulty, and it's usually well worth trading the increase in node count for a corresponding increase in

accuracy, particularly if many of
those lines are not on the 0°/180° or
90°/270° axis. If they *are* on the horizontal or vertical planes, you can get
an accurate trace without resorting
to a Very Short Curve Length setting, because the edges of the pixels
and the line they are indicating are
on the same angle.

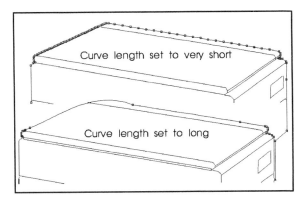

Marquee select and delete the .EPS
file that resulted from the Center Line trace and you're ready to
work on the other one—the one with too many nodes. Choose
the ↗ tool and select its top line. Click and drag around a string
of nodes along one of the long, straight sections of this curve to
select them. Ideally, you'll select all but the very last node on
each end of the straight line. Normally, just getting most of
them is fine, and you definitely don't want to grab one of the
nodes at the end of the straight section.

Once they're selected, simply press the Delete key and that
series of short straight line segments will be replaced by a
longer, more or less straight, curve. Double-click on that curve
to select it, and from the Node Edit menu that pops up choose
toLine.

Setting Trace's Curve Length to Very Short produces loads of
nodes, but they're so easily removed in Draw that it's not a great
concern. Just repeat the preceding sequence on all the other
long lines overpopulated with nodes. If you missed a few near
the end of a long straight section, just zoom in and go through
the same process.

Zoom in on sharper bends to edit individual nodes and smaller
groups of nodes. You can usually eliminate nodes that Trace
left on curved lines shorter than a quarter of a circle, although
you'll likely have to make control point adjustments, move
nodes slightly or change node types among curve, cusp and
symmetrical to maintain accuracy. While you node edit curved
sections of the drawing, eventually you're bound to delete a
node and have the result "go crazy."

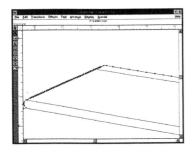

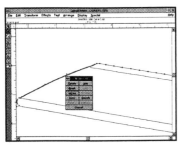

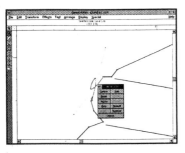

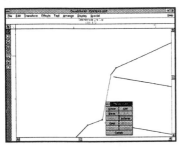

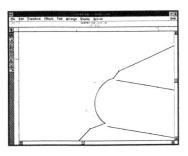

The reasons for this are discussed earlier in the chapter, but it can be disconcerting, to say the least, especially if you're zoomed in on a small area of the drawing. At times, the loop itself will expand completely out of view, while at other times the loop is in view but the control point handles are completely off the screen, seemingly necessitating a zoom-out to find them. Don't panic. Double-click on any visible part of the offending line and in the Node Edit menu choose toLine to bring the line segment back under control. Then double-click on it again and choose toCurve, if necessary, to allow you to adjust the line segment, as shown in the illustration.

Zoom out every now and then to check for areas that need more adjustment. Use the ⚲ tool to lengthen or reposition straight lines as necessary. Delete unnecessary nodes and adjust curves with Node Edit. For example, the left vertical edge of the copier obviously needs attention, as do the areas of grillwork on its front panel. In a case like this, it's often easiest to zoom in on one object (in this case, one of the slots in the grillwork) edit it to perfection, and then duplicate it to simply replace the others, rather than spend time adjusting each of a group of identical objects. Fix one now, then use your choice of Draw's selection of methods to replace the others with a copy of the one you fixed. No need to copy the same object 12 times. After replacing the second one, select both finished objects before doing the next step in the move, or duplicate, so you replace two. Then select all four new ones and replace the next four. You could also use the Blend command to specify how many copies you wanted.

When you've adjusted the vector graphic to your satisfaction, save the .CDR file you and Trace have created in an appropriate directory. The demands of deadlines and work schedules don't always permit it, but it's a good idea to set aside any heavy editing job for a day or so when you think you're done with it, and return to it for a final edit after you've had a chance to clear your mind of nodes and control points. You could print out

Converting Scans with CorelTRACE

your adjusted copier trace at this point before moving on to the next tutorial section.

A Signature Exercise

Thanks to the increased popularity of graphical word processors and the increasing affordability of computers powerful enough to handle scanning and graphics-oriented programs in a practical fashion, PC-generated form letters, faxes and legal documents are becoming commonplace. Computers, with growing frequency, are also being called upon to sign those documents, as well as to verify signatures.

The finished copier

Among commonly scanned and traced graphics, signatures are perhaps as far removed as you can get from the straight lines of even weight found in maps, schematics and technical illustrations, as exemplified by the previous exercise. The graphical properties of signatures are typically freeform curves with calligraphic qualities inherent in the varying width of the lines. The criteria for image quality are also different. Appearance, clarity, consistent line thickness and similar concerns don't apply here.

You'll naturally want to lean towards increased accuracy when you set Trace's options for signature tracing, but accuracy must be defined as fidelity to the original signature, not the bitmap. Keep that in mind when prepping the bitmap for tracing. Setting Trace's Curve Length to Short, Curve Fit to Very Tight and Sample Rate to Fine will contribute to an accurate trace — accurate in terms of the bitmap, that is. The rough edges, and especially any seemingly spurious 'barbs' projecting off or into the curve, will create node editing nightmares. You'll get a lot of nodes that send their associated curves off in odd directions and create loops when deleted, as discussed in the previous exercise.

Depending on the quality of the scan, how smooth a surface the original signature was created on and even how well the pen worked, there may be plenty of these barbs that are not really a part of the signature. They also show up in the scans of all sorts of hand-written or drawn work, so learning to eliminate them will save you a lot of editing time.

Because flowing curves are a major element of signatures and the pixels of a bitmap are straight-sided, most scanned signatures are rather poor renditions of the originals. That's the primary reason for converting them to vector files in the first place. But it also means that Trace will start with an inaccurate model, so by controlling and 'hinting' those inaccuracies manually, you can direct Trace's efforts more toward the signature's true shape.

Copy ASAMPLE.TIF from the SAMPLES directory of the Utility disk to your dedicated Trace temp directory. But before opening this graphic in Trace, open it in Photo-Paint for preprocessing. It's a good idea when making any changes to the bitmap of a signature to make them on a copy and save the original until the final product is okayed by the signer. So be sure to save your Photo-Paint work as ASAMPLE2.TIF.

Photo-Paint's Remove Spots filter will, if set properly, clear up the majority of any extraneous pixel formations, even though they are contiguous to the body of the bitmap image, rather than self-contained spots. Click on Filter from the Edit menu and choose Remove Spots. In the dialog box choose Large and click on Screen Preview. This will show you what the result of the filter will look like before you commit to it with an OK. This is an important consideration when the output must remain true to the original signature.

If spot removal doesn't appear to have removed anything it shouldn't have, click on OK to have it repeat the procedure on the actual image. If on closer inspection it *does* smooth a line that shouldn't have been smoothed, choose Undo from the Edit menu. Then use the appropriate area selection tool (the Box or the Lasso) to select the area you want to protect and choose Copy from the Edit menu. Then return to the Remove Spots filter and repeat the

procedure. When it's done, choose Paste from the Edit menu and move the 'patch' onto the area that shouldn't have been smoothed. Click anywhere outside the patch to make it permanent.

Alternately, you can save the bitmap under a new name before processing, and then open both win-

---

Converting Scans with CorelTRACE

dows to Copy and Paste as many sections as you need from the original into the cleaned-up version. Or you could take the opposite approach and use either the Box or Lasso Selection tools to select specific areas on which to run the spot filter, and leave areas where sharp jags are to be left as-is, unfiltered. The point of all this is that when Trace is set to trace very closely, as it should be for signatures, all those little extraneous protuberances in the pixel layout will be traced. This will make your editing session in Draw a most unpleasant one. The spot filter makes it easy to get rid of the unnecessary ones now and saves a lot of time later.

Once you have the bitmap in satisfactory condition, store it to the dedicated temp directory for Trace, naming it ASAMPLE2.TIF, as described earlier. Close Photo-Paint, run Trace and open the prepped version of Mr. Sample's signature into the list box. If you haven't been doing the Trace exercises in sequence, go back to the last section for detailed directions on loading files.

As already pointed out, you'll want to set the Tracing Options (Choose Edit Options from the Tracing Options menu) to achieve maximum detail. Ideally, filtering as much of the rough edges as possible from the bitmap will have left you with something that won't create a node editing nightmare when closely traced.

Because the line width — and particularly the dynamics of the width — is a major identifying factor in signatures, you must use an outline tracing method for conversion. From the Tracing Options menu choose either a blank (...) or Normal Outline then Edit Options, depending on whether you want to save the options you're about to use. As a suggested starting point for most signatures, the options shown in the illustration of the dialog box are recommended (o/-/8/4/5/1/4/3, according to the naming code described earlier).

Choose Trace All, and when Trace finishes its magic act exit the program, run Draw and import the .EPS file of the signature, using the procedures outlined in the last exercise. When working with signatures, it's a good idea to import the .TIF file as well to serve as a template. For convenience's sake, I like to put it on

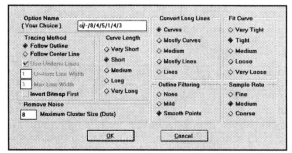

a different layer than the vector image. Choose Layers Roll-Up from the Arrange menu, click on the Layer right-pointing arrow, choose New from the menu and then OK to create Layer 2. Then import ASAMPLE2.TIF and it will be placed on the current layer, Layer 2. If the bitmap displays only as a box, enable Show Bitmaps from the Display menu.

Assuming that you have not moved either file, they should be aligned directly atop each other in the center of the screen. Since you last used Layer 2, that should be the active layer. On the Layers roll-up, click on Layer 2 and drag it on top of Layer 1 to reverse their order on the page, so the .EPS file is above the bitmap. If they are not correctly aligned with each other, select them both and align them to the center of the page, by choosing Align from the Arrange menu and checking the Align To Center Of Page option in the Align dialog box.

With both objects selected, hold down the Shift key and drag a corner handle diagonally to resize both graphics to fill the page. The larger you make the drawing, the farther apart the nodes will be and the easier it will be to select the right one from a group of closely spaced nodes. This is not the same as simply zooming in. By working with a larger graphic, you're actually increasing the distance between the nodes and you can still zoom in for increased clarity. In fact, when editing very complex drawings with lots of nodes and objects, you'll find it faster to work zoomed in as closely as possible. But for maximum clarity of small detail, stretch the graphic as large as possible before zooming in. You can easily fine tune the alignment between the bitmap and vector graphics at this point, by setting the Nudge amount in the Preferences Dialog box (Control-J will access Preferences) to a

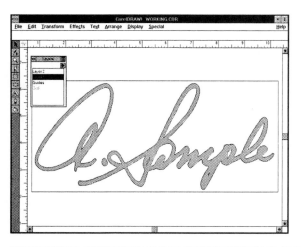

minimal amount, such as 1 point. You can then select only the vector object and use the cursor arrows on the keyboard to move it in very small increments.

You'll find it much easier to maintain the required faithfulness to the original by using the template you imported earlier, but it will definitely slow down screen rewrites, and at times it can cause confusion. By leaving the Layers roll-up open (you can roll it up when it's not needed), you can double-click on Layer 2 and toggle Visible on and off as desired. (Since you don't want to edit the bitmap, it would be a good idea to choose Locked for that layer as well.) Another approach would be to toggle the bitmap display on and off by choosing Show Bitmaps from the Display menu.

A side benefit of using the template when you're zoomed in tightly on an expanded combination of vector and bitmap images is that it really provides an understanding of how Trace created the vector image. After you've been faced with making each of the decisions about where the image really should be in relation to the bitmap version of it, it's a little easier to understand what you want Trace to do. Eventually, that knowledge will help guide you in making adjustments to the tracing options.

Switch to the layer the vector file is on, Layer 1, and with the ➤ tool select the object by clicking anywhere on its outline and ungroup it. With the tracing options you used on this signature, the only places likely to need much attention are the sharpest bends, which are usually at the ends of characters. As with the last exercise, choose the ⚲ tool and zoom in on an area that seems overly thick with nodes. Use a marquee to select a group of nodes and delete them. If the resulting curve looks like it will be easy enough to bring into line with the underlying bitmap, then go to it using the bitmap template as a guide. Otherwise, use the Undo command to reverse the change (Alt-Backspace), select a smaller group of nodes or a single node and try again.

On the general principal of lowering the node count, you may also want to remove some of the nodes on the long, sweeping sections of the signature, like the loops of the A, S and L. This is very similar to removing the nodes on the long straight lines in the previous exercise, except, of course, you don't convert to lines after deleting a series of nodes. You will have to readjust the control points of the curves though, so unless there's a real node overload the extra work is not usually necessary.

When you're satisfied with the editing, switch to the layer with the bitmap, unlock the layer if it was locked and delete the bitmap. There's no harm in deleting the layer itself at this point. Once back on Layer 1, you should make the objects in your signature graphic into a single entity before saving to a file. If the signatures you digitize will be printed directly from Draw, sent to other applications via Object Linking and Embedding (OLE), or exported for import into other applications, combining them is the easiest way to do this. Use the ▶ tool to marquee select all the elements in the signature, and Control-C to combine them into a single curve.

If they will be exported, run a test export and import with the signature combined into one curve, to check for *construction lines* in the exported output. If you do find construction lines, you may be better off breaking the curve apart, assigning a white fill to all the 'holes' and a black fill to the main body section, arranging the holes on top, and grouping rather than combining.

Ready, Set, Trace

By now you should be familiar enough with Trace, and with the means of editing a traced bitmap, that you might want to tackle a grayscale image. Remember SPORTCAR.EPS, the file you created earlier in this chapter? You've got nothing to lose by importing it into Draw and using it to review and practise the traced vector editing techniques covered in the exercises you've just finished. You could also import one of the color clip art images from your DRAW\CLIPART directories and export it as grayscale or color, as raw material for further Trace experiments.

Graphing with CorelCHART

14

C orelCHART may be a new addition to the applications included with CorelDRAW, but it acts like a seasoned veteran when it comes to creating eye-catching, professional-looking charts. While you can construct impressive charts right in Draw, it makes more sense to use a program like Chart that's been created specifically for this purpose. These can be output directly to any Windows-supported printer or moved into documents created by other Corel applications, such as CorelDRAW and CorelSHOW, as well as most word processing or desktop publishing programs.

Turning numbers into graphics

What's more, Chart takes full advantage of the ability of some Windows 3.1 applications, such as Word for Windows, to embed, link or automatically update an imported chart when the original file is modified. To make this possible, Chart supports both DDE (Dynamic Data Exchange) and OLE (Object Linking and Embedding). Because Chart uses these Windows technologies to provide integration with the full suite of Corel graphics applications, you can easily incorporate charts into illustrations you create in Draw. You can just as quickly incorporate graphics made in Draw or pictures retouched in CorelPHOTO-PAINT into the charts you create with Chart.

In this tutorial chapter, you'll get a hands-on chance to explore the formidable abilities of Chart by creating a variety of charts and modifying them in a number of ways. But first I'll lead you through a brief overview that outlines the program's organization and provides some key concepts you should know before working with it. My assumption here is that Chart is your first presentation graphics program. If you're a veteran, you can move quickly through sections explaining common charting concepts.

CorelCHART!

Quick Tour

In this overview you'll quickly create a basic chart and then enrich your work with some of Chart's more impressive design tools. Run Chart now by double-clicking on its icon in the Corel Graphics group of the Windows Program Manager.

Chart's initial display is minimalist. The toolbox running down the left and the text ribbon at the top are ghosted, while the menu shows only File at the left and Help at the right. The Color Palette, at the bottom of the window, is the only part that doesn't seem lifeless. In a moment, though, you'll get Chart moving. Depending on the size and resolution of your display, Chart may not be running full screen. If that's the case, double-click on its title bar at the top of the window to maximize it. To force it to always run full screen, see the *Advanced Chart Topics* section at the end of this chapter.

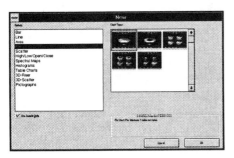

Choose New from the File menu and Chart immediately displays a colorful catalog of chart designs for your browsing pleasure. Click on some of the chart types in the list at the left and Chart displays thumbnails of several variations on the right, the Gallery area. In this quick tour you'll create a pie chart, so choose Pie from the list and then click on Use Sample Data, below the list. This helpful feature will give you a sample pie with sample data that you can then modify as desired. This is often easier than beginning with a blank screen. From the gallery of samples, click on the first thumbnail in the upper-left corner.

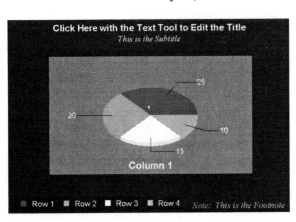

At the bottom it should indicate that you've chosen PIE0001.CCH, one of the pie templates supplied with Chart. (Many more of these templates are on the CD-ROM disk supplied with Draw.) Now double-click on the pie template to open it.

Take a moment to examine this chart before you go on. Try selecting some of the titles and numbers within the graphic portion of the chart by clicking on them. As you do, you'll see the text ribbon (the horizontal area below the menu bar) display the formatting of each text object. Changing the formatting of a selected object is simply a matter of changing the settings on the text ribbon. Try selecting the title and making it 18 point Bangkok bold. Click on the down arrows to access the scrollable list. As in Draw, click on the large B to bold selected text. Note that in the case of numbers, changing one will reformat all of them.

Now click on each of the pie slices in turn, click on the dark blue frame that surrounds the pie and click again on the medium blue chart background. As you select each object, notice that the Color Palette at the bottom of the screen indicates the color of the object. As in Draw, changing the color of a selected object is just a matter of clicking on a different color in the Palette. Select the dark blue rectangle and then click on one of the dark grays in the Palette. Next, select some text and choose light blue from the Palette.

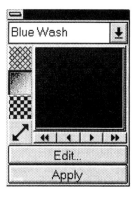

You also can fill any of the graphic objects onscreen with a fountain fill, a color gradient that runs smoothly from one color to another. Click on the chart background (anywhere outside the gray frame and away from the titles and legend). Then click on the Fill ✋ tool and choose the Quick Pic 🖼 icon. You'll explore the many Quick Pic fill options a bit later. For now, choose Blue Wash from the pull-down list of fountain fills and click on Apply. Click once on the close button at the upper-left corner of the Quick Pic window to close it.

Your chart looks better already, but it's still displaying somebody else's data. It's time to enter your own titles and numbers. As the current title says, you could click on the title with the Text 𝔸 tool and edit the text. And you could do the same with the subtitle and footnote. But Chart provides a way to let you more easily change multiple data elements of your chart. Click on the Data Manager icon at the intersection of the toolbox and the text ribbon (above the currently selected ↖ tool).

The Data Manager window and the Chart View window provide two different ways of viewing your chart. Note that the Data Manager icon has changed its look to that of a chart. Click on it now to return to the Chart View. The Chart View window

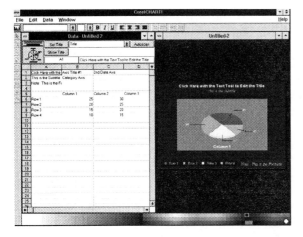

is labeled Untitled-1. You can also switch views using the Window menu. Choose Untitled - Data from the Window menu. Both windows can also be open together on the screen. This is useful when you're making many changes to the data and need to see how it looks. Choose Tile Horizontally from the Window menu to see this. Then double-click on the Data Manager title bar to fill the screen again with its window.

The Data Manager looks just like a spreadsheet grid; columns have letters at the top and rows have numbers. As with other Windows spreadsheets, you can select any *cell* in the grid by clicking on it. You can select a group of cells by dragging across them, and you can select an entire column or row by clicking on the column letter or row number, respectively. Try out all of these selection techniques.

Take a look at how the sample data is organized in the Data Manager. The title is in cell A1. The subtitle is below, in cell A2, and the footnote is in cell A3. The data is arranged in a rectangular region a little farther down. Each column has data for a different pie, but only the first pie is displayed in the chart at the moment.

You'll be replacing the column headings with something a little more meaningful than Column 1 and Column 2. And you won't overlook the row headings, either. But first you must replace the current titles with ones of your own. Click on the title in cell A1 and type in 'Sarah Gets the Lion's Share.' As you type, the text will appear to the right of A1, above the grid area. Then select the subtitle in cell A2 (or press the Enter key) and type in 'Breakdown by Salesperson.' Finally, select cell A3 and press Delete on your keyboard to delete the current footnote. Footnotes are optional, as are all titles.

Next, click on cell B5 and replace Column 1 with 'Newborn.' Replace Column 2 with 'Infant.' Then replace Column 3 with 'Toddler' and 'Column 4' with 'Baby.' Use the same technique to replace the row headings (Row 1, Row 2, etc.) with the names Sarah, Andrew, Susan and Aaron. You're now ready to enter new numbers.

Click and drag across all the cells that contain numbers — B6 to E9 — to select them. This is a shortcut for entering numbers quickly. Then type the following five numbers, pressing Enter after each: 42, 24, 8, 17 and 62. Notice that the cursor moves down from cell to cell but jumps to the top of the next column when it reaches the bottom of the selected range. As long as you've first highlighted the range, you can simply type the columns of numbers one after another without positioning the cursor manually.

This technique would also have worked when you changed the row and column names. Of course, you can also select each cell in turn and type in a number. Continue entering numbers until you've fully reproduced the data shown below:

	Newborn	Infant	Toddler	Baby
Sarah	42	62	83	58
Andrew	24	37	65	47
Susan	8	12	58	52
Aaron	17	20	26	30

Switch back to the Chart View window and double-click on its title bar to enlarge the window, if necessary. The chart now shows the first column of data you entered (soon you'll display the other rows) and the legend keys of each of the slices in the lower-left corner.

The chart might be more easily understood if the names were adjacent to the slices. Forcing viewers to match the colors in the legend with the pie slices is counter to your goal of making the chart easy to interpret. The whole reason for presenting information in a chart, rather than simply as a table of numbers, is to make it easier on the viewer. Later in this chapter you'll learn how to move the slice names

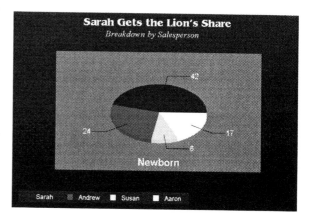

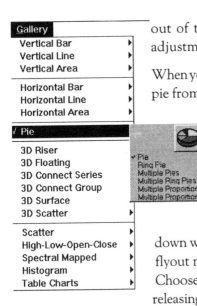

out of the legend and next to the slices, and perform other adjustments to the pie .

When you started the pie chart, you selected a thumbnail of a single pie from the Chart Gallery. But even after you've chosen a chart design and modifed the resulting chart, you're not locked into your decision — you can access the templates that were displayed in the Chart Gallery by using a different technique. Click on the Gallery menu and take a look at the available chart types. Click on Pie, and then click and hold the mouse button down while you slowly drag down each of the options on the Pie flyout menu. A preview shows how each chart design will look. Choose Multiple Pies from the list by dragging down to it and releasing the mouse button. Now your chart displays four pies representing the four columns of data in the Data Manager.

To present a different take on the numbers, you can quickly represent the information in the Data Manager with a completely different chart design. A pie chart shows how a total breaks down, while a stacked bar chart shows how totals add up. From the Gallery menu, choose Vertical Bar and then pick Stacked from the flyout menu. The chart now shows the total of sales for all four salespeople in each product category. It also shows how each category breaks down.

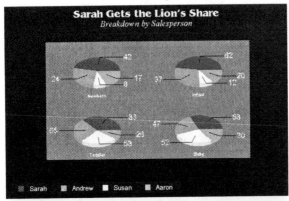

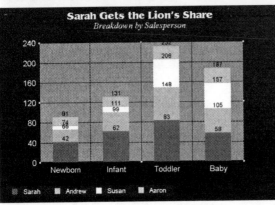

The function of this quick tour was to give you an overview of the fundamentals of Chart, and to give you a sense of both its structure and charting abilities. Chart provides a wide range of chart types. Try out some other formats from the Gallery menu before going on. The rest of this chapter provides a comprehensive look at Chart's capabilities.

Creating a New Chart

Unlike Draw, which currently only lets you open one file at a time, Chart can open multiple files, which you can then switch between using the Window menu. But it would be simpler to proceed at this point with just one file open. So choose Close from the File menu to abandon the chart you created in the quick tour, or choose Save to save it.

Now choose New from the File menu. You've probably already been taken by the sexy, futuristic look of the 3D styles. Resist the temptation. These may be stunning to look at but they can be difficult to comprehend, and easy comprehension is the name of the game in charting. The primary task is always to analyze the message your numbers bear and then design a chart to convey that message quickly and efficiently. The goal of a chart is thus to visually represent groups of numbers by making variations in the data and trends (or even the lack of any change)

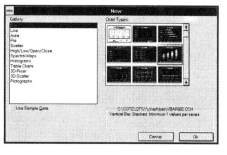

obvious at a glance. If viewers must struggle to interpret a chart, they may as well look at the raw numbers.

Choose a vertical, stacked bar chart by clicking once on Bar at the left and clicking again on the thumbnail in the third column and second row. Confirm that you're about to choose the correct thumbnail by checking the description in the lower right. You should see 'Vertical Bar; Stacked. Minimum 1 values per series', with a file name of VBAR002.CCH

What the Chart Gallery does is really very simple. Each thumbnail it shows is a miniature view of an actual chart file stored on your hard disk in one of the subdirectories under the CHART directory. When you click on Bar, for example, the Gallery shows all the charts in the BAR subdirectory. Click on Line instead, and you see all the charts in the LINE subdirectory. As you click once on each thumbnail, you see the pathname and filename for each chart in the description box at the lower-right corner of the Gallery. To add a new chart design to the Gallery, you can simply save or copy the file into one of the subdirectories under CHART. In fact, to have your custom chart designs show up immediately when the Chart Gallery opens, simply copy them into the BAR directory, since its contents are displayed in the Gallery first.

Where you end up after choosing a chart type depends on whether you click on the Use Sample Data checkbox before you exit the Gallery. If you leave Use Sample Data unchecked, then Chart takes you to the Data Manager window, where you'll enter or import the numbers to be graphed. As you saw earlier, if you check Use Sample Data you'll be shown your chosen chart type plotted with some sample numbers. From this display, you had to go to the Data Manager window to replace the sample numbers with your own. Working with sample data simply provided an on-screen example of how to enter your own text and numbers. This time, double-click on the thumbnail without choosing Use Sample Data.

Entering the Data

Double-click on the title bar of Chart if the Data Manager window isn't currently filling the screen. Before you can begin working on the appearance of the chart, you'll need to enter the chart's data. Most of the Data Manager window is reserved for the numbers that the chart will show. Besides providing space for data, it also gives you room to enter a chart title, subtitle, footnote and titles for the graph's axes. You enter these titles in cells of the Data Manager window and use the controls at the top of the window to specify which cell holds which title. However, it's faster to place the titles in a specific arrangement so that Chart can automatically determine the titles.

In general, you'll place the title in the first cell at the upper-left corner (cell A1), the subtitle in the cell below (A2) and the footnote below that (A3). You'll begin entering the content of the chart by typing the title, subtitle and footnote for the chart into the Data Manager window. Click on the first cell in the first column (A1) and type 'Lola's Privileged Pets' for the chart's title. Then press the down arrow key to move to the cell below (A2). Don't worry if the whole title doesn't fit into cell A1. Type 'Sales Subtotals' for the chart's subtitle. Move down one more cell and then type 'Dogs only' for the chart's footnote.

Now skip down to cell A5 by clicking on it with the mouse or by pressing the down arrow key twice. Cell A5 will be the top-left corner of a rectangular area of data. Move one cell to the right (cell B5) and type 'Walks.' Move again to the right (you can use the Tab key) and type 'Grooming.' Move one more cell to the right and type 'Food and Supplies' and then press Enter. You'll see that 'Food and Supplies' is so long that it doesn't fit in the D column. You can make the column wider by placing the cursor on the vertical separator line that is between the letters D and E at the top of the data area and then dragging the line to the right. You may also want to make the first column wider. Changing the width of columns has no impact on the appearance of the chart; it's just helpful to see your numbers more clearly in the Data Manager window.

Walks, Grooming, and Food and Supplies are the names of the three groups of data you'll be graphing. Along the left edge of the data area, you'll enter the types of dogs you want to compare. Click on cell A6 and type 'Terriers.' Then type 'Spaniels' and 'Retrievers' into the two cells below (A7 and A8). With the framework for the graph created, you can now enter the numbers.

To enter the data, you can move the cursor to each cell with either the arrow keys or the mouse and key in numbers. Or you can select the entire area where numbers will go and then simply begin typing. Use this second method by putting the cursor in the upper-left corner of the data area (cell B6) and then clicking and dragging across two columns and down two rows until a 3 by 3 rectangle of cells is highlighted. Notice that the upper-left corner cell is still selected. Type '34' and it will fill this cell. Then press Enter and the cursor will jump to the cell below. Continue entering numbers and pressing Enter until you've reproduced the following set of numbers, as shown in the illustration. Make sure you press Enter after typing the '78', or it won't appear in the cell.

	Walks	Grooming	Food and Supplies
Terriers	34	45	65
Spaniels	76	87	98
Retrievers	56	76	78

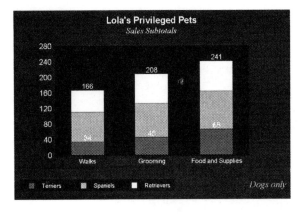

Lola's Privileged Pets

Sales Subtotals

To see the graph this group of numbers creates, click on the Chart View button or choose Untitled from the Window menu. As you'll see when you examine your new chart, it compares the totals of the three sales categories you entered. Secondarily, it provides a snapshot of the breakdown of each category (though a pie chart is a better way to display a breakdown, if that's your main objective).

How you enter the information to be graphed in the data window — whether you arrange it down columns or across rows — and which chart type you select depends on the comparison or change in the data you want to show. Generally, if you want to compare numbers, choose a bar chart and arrange the numbers in rows in the Data Manager window. In the chart, the column headings will appear across the bottom (x) axis. If you want to show how numbers change over time, use a line or area chart and again arrange the numbers in rows. For column headings in the Data Manager, enter intervals of time (month or year names, for example). These will appear along the x axis. If you want to show breakdowns, use pie charts. In the Data Manager window, you'd put the name of a pie at the top of a column, and arrange the data for the slices in the column below.

Choosing Chart Parts

Chart is smart enough to determine which cells in the Data Manager contain the chart title, subtitle and footnote, and which cells contain the data area, but you can also designate other cells.

Now you'll create a variation of the first chart. In the Data Manager, select the entire rectangular region into which you've entered numbers, from cell A1 to cell D8. Then choose Copy from the Edit menu (or press Control-Insert) to copy the data to the Windows Clipboard. Click on cell F1 and then choose Paste from the Edit menu (or press Shift-Insert) to paste a copy of the data back into the window.

Now you can modify the numbers and graph this data. Begin by clicking on the cell with 'Dogs only' and replace it with 'Cats only'. Then replace Terriers, Spaniels and Retrievers with Siamese, Calico and Persian.

Because cat walking is not part of your business, you need to delete the contents of column G, Walks. Click on the letter G at the top of the column to highlight the entire column and then choose Delete from the Edit menu. (Clicking on Insert would have inserted a blank column at this position.) Delete is only available after you select an entire row or column. To delete a single entry, press the Delete key or choose Clear from the Edit menu. To cut an entry, but place a copy on the Windows Clipboard, choose Cut from the Edit menu or press Shift-Delete. After you Cut an item, you can Paste it somewhere else. Finally, replace the existing Grooming and Food and Supplies numbers with these:

	Grooming	Food and Supplies
Siamese	36	75
Calico	25	123
Persian	16	88

Although you've entered a second set of information, Chart is still set up to display the original data. To instruct Chart to display the new data instead, you need to *tag* it. Click on the cell containing 'Cats only' and then pull down the list of chart parts at the top of the Data Manager. Click on the down scroll arrow to the right of Title (or click on Title itself) to display the list.

Choose Footnote from the list and the chart thumbnail at the left shows the footnote highlighted in red. The red highlighted items in the chart thumbnail provide a visual explanation of the selected chart part. Click on the Set Footnote button to assign the selected cell as the new footnote. Next, select the two column headings (Grooming, and Food and Supplies), choose Column Headers from the chart parts list and then click on the Set Column Headers button. Notice again that the column headers in the chart thumbnail at the left are depicted in red. Using the same procedure tag

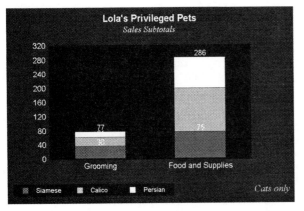

Lola's Privileged Pets
Sales Subtotals

Siamese, Calico and Persian as Row Headers. Finally, select the 2 by 3 rectangle of numbers and tag it as the Data Range. When you click on the chart preview icon your revised chart will be displayed. Choose Save from the File menu and give your chart the name PETS1. In the description field, you can type a multi-line description of the chart.

By the way, you can make the text in the Data Manager considerably easier to read. Select any cell that contains text and then choose another font, such as SerpentineBold, from the font list and choose 16 points from the list of font sizes. This is especially useful on large, high resolution monitors. You can also bold, italicize or underline text by clicking on the appropriate buttons. You can't apply these settings to just selected text — you're formatting all the text in the Data Manager window. However, you *can* select individual cells and give them one of the four standard alignments. Of course, all this has no effect on the text formatting in your actual chart.

Importing from Abroad

If the numbers you need to graph are in an Excel or Lotus 1-2-3 worksheet, you can avoid retyping them by employing Chart's import abilities. On the Utility disk accompanying this book, I've included a sample Excel 3.0 file for you to work with that contains additional sales data for Lola's pet store. (At the time of this writing, Chart didn't support Excel 4.0 files.)

Choose Import Data from the Data Manager's File menu. Under List Files of Type, select Excel (*.XLS). Under Drives, select the drive in which you've placed the diskette. Then change directories to SAMPLES and select PETS1.XLS from the file list. Immediately, the contents of the Excel worksheet replace all the existing data in the Data Manager. Keep this in mind, because in the future you'll want to be sure to save a chart that contains important data before importing a data file.

Graphing with CorelCHART

Switch to Chart View and you'll see data for Afghans, Schnauzers and Beagles properly graphed, but the titles will be incorrect. That's because Chart assumes that the first cell that has data in row 1 is the chart title, and the two cells underneath are the subtitle and footnote. You must insert space above the data for real titles.

To do so, return to the Data Manager and click on the row number 1 button and then drag down over row numbers 2, 3 and 4 to select four entire rows. Then choose Insert from the Edit menu to insert four blank rows. Now you have space for the chart titles. In cell A1 type 'Lola's Privileged Pets.' In A2 type 'Sales Subtotals.' In A3 type 'Dogs only.' Now click on the Autoscan button to have Chart automatically scan the grid for the location of titles, headers and data. Finally, switch to the Chart View and take a look.

If you've already graphed your numbers in Harvard Graphics, you can easily pull in the data directly from a Harvard chart file, so you can use the powers of Chart to further enrich existing presentations. After you choose Import File from the Data Manager's File menu, choose Harvard (*.CH?) from the List Files Of Type pull-down list. Then navigate to the directory in which you've stored your Harvard Graphics charts and select the Harvard file you need. Chart imports the Harvard data into the Data Manager window just as it imports an entire Excel or Lotus 1-2-3 for Windows worksheet.

Chart recognizes files made with the DOS versions of Harvard, but not those made with Harvard Graphics for Windows. If the data you need is in a Harvard Graphics for Windows chart, you can copy and paste data from the Harvard Data Manager to the Chart Data Manager through the commands on the Edit menus of both programs. You can also paste in tab-delimited text created in any Windows word processor using the same technique.

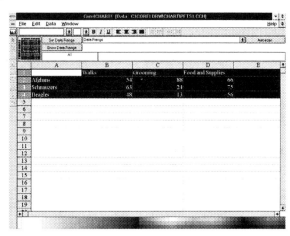

Changing its Appearance

You've supplied the content of the graph by working in the Data Manager window. But to modify the chart's appearance, you must work in the Chart View window. Switch to it now by clicking on its icon or using the Windows menu. (If the Chart View is already open underneath the Data Manager, you can click on any part to bring it forward.)

As with Draw, in the Chart View you first select an object with the ▶ or 𝔸 tools and then modify it with another tool or a menu command. The stacked bar chart you selected from the Gallery served as a model for the new chart you've created. All of its formatting — its text formats, bar colors, background shading and so forth — is reflected in the new chart design. But you can quickly change any aspects of the default formatting.

Tempting Titles

To format the title, subtitle or footnote, you can click on them in turn and then select text styling options from the text ribbon at the top of the screen. For example, change the font and increase the size of the chart title by clicking on it, then select Timpani from the font list and 24 points from the size menu. You should also change the subtitle and footnote to Timpani for consistency.

If the title text is now large enough to require two lines, use the handles surrounding the text box to stretch the left and right edges all the way out to the left and right sides of the chart. The text is centered in the box, so it will also now be centered across the top of the chart. (You could also choose Center On Page from the Arrange menu and then choose Center Horizontal.) You can use the same text formatting techniques to change the styling of the data point values that appear at the top of each bar segment. But as you discovered in the quick tour, changing any one value will alter all of them.

The remainder of the text — the entries along the axes and in the legend — requires an extra step to modify. The size of this text is *autofitted* to the size of the chart. Try increasing the size of the legend area by clicking on it and then dragging out a corner handle, for example, and you'll see that the size of the legend text increases proportionately. To modify the size of text along the axes and in the legend, you must first turn off autofitted text. Click on 'Walks' along the x axis with the *right* mouse button. (If you've switched the functions of the right and left mouse buttons, then use the left mouse button). When you use the right button to select an object, a pop-up menu appears containing only those options that apply to the object. This is an unusual and very handy feature.

The Column Header pop-up menu contains commands that let you display the column headers on the top or bottom of the graph, and a Show Grid Lines option to turn on or off the vertical grid lines that appear on the graph's background. The two other commands on the menu determine how the text along the axes will appear. Autofitted Text sizes the text so it fits properly along the axis or within the legend. Staggered Text staggers the text along the axes so more of it fits. Try out some of these options now.

You can get a better idea of how autofitting works if you select the graph's dark blue frame and then drag the right edge to the left about a third of the way across the page. Notice that the autofitted x-axis text has automatically reduced in size. Resizing a chart in this way makes room for a paragraph of text at the right, for example, which you could add with the 𝔸 tool or an imported graphic. Restore the chart to its normal shape before continuing by choosing Undo from the Edit menu or by manually resizing it.

The Legend command, available on the Legend pop-up menu when you right-click on the legend box in the lower-left corner, displays a dialog box with a set of options for fine-tuning the legend text and a second set for the legend layout. Try out these options to see their effect, but return the settings to Text To Right Of Marker and Automatic Legend Orientation when you're done.

A Graceful Graph

Now you'll turn your attention to formatting the graphic portion of the chart, including the frame and the graph's bars. You'll use a combination of the Color Palette at the bottom of the screen and the toolbox at the left. You'll also use pop-up menus to display only those options that apply to the object you've selected. You've displayed these so far by clicking on an object with the right mouse button, but there's a second technique.

Choose the pop-up menu tool, located under the ▶ tool in the toolbox, then click on any bar in the graph to display the Bar Riser pop-up menu. You can immediately click on another object, such as the dark blue frame in the background of the graph, and a different pop-up menu appears. With the pop-up menu tool you can move quickly from object to object, happily formatting as you go. Personally, I prefer the right mouse button approach. If you agree, return now to the ▶ tool. As in Draw, you can always return to this tool by pressing the Spacebar.

The effects of many of the commands you'll be trying out will be more apparent on a side-by-side vertical bar chart, so choose Vertical Bar from the Gallery menu and then choose Side-By-Side from the list of vertical bar charts.

Click on the furthest left red bar with the right mouse button to redisplay the Bar Riser menu. This provides commands that change the appearance of the bar, such as Bar Thickness. Choose Bar Thickness. The current setting, Default, is checked. Hold the mouse button down as you drag down across each of the five options. Wherever possible, Chart takes the guesswork out of choosing settings by showing you a preview of the result of each option. Choose Major for the Bar Thickness setting.

Click on the red bar again with the right mouse button, but this time choose Bar-Bar Spacing. As you drag across each option on the Spacing menu, you'll see the effect it would have on the graph. Choose Minimum to bring the bars for each category of service as close together as possible. This makes it clearer that the graph displays three groups of data.

Click on the first bar again and choose Marker Shape from the menu. The default Bar setting is the most familiar shape, and therefore makes for a clear and easy-to-interpret chart. But you may also want to try choosing Triangle from the list to create a message that's a little more pointed. Note that the symbol for the bar in the legend has automatically changed to a triangle.

Intelligent features like this take much of the drudge work out of modifying graphs.

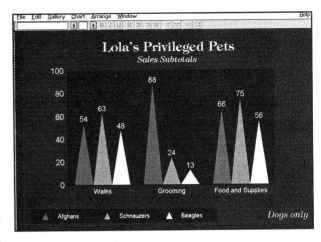

Changing the color of a set of bars is easy. With the ▶ tool select the orange bar in the first set (the number of walks of Schnauzers) and click on bright green in the Color Palette to change all three of the bars for Schnauzers. Using this same technique, click on the dark blue chart frame and then choose a dark gray from the Palette. You can even select the grid lines in the graph's background. Click on any of the horizontal grid lines (this may require a few attempts) and then select a medium gray. All the lines will change simultaneously.

You can create an impressive effect by filling the bars of a chart or the frame with a fountain fill, rather than a solid color. Select the bar on the far left and then choose the ✍ tool. From the flyout menu choose the Quick Pic ▦ tool, which in many ways resembles Draw's roll-up dialog boxes.

In the Quick Pic window click on the Fountain Fill ▦ icon. Then click on the Forward button (the single right-pointing arrow) to advance to the next fill in alphabetical order. Now, click on the Fast Forward button (the two arrows pointing to the right) to automatically advance through the fills. Click on the same button to stop advancing when you get to Yellowing. Finally, click on the Apply button to apply Yellowing to the first set of bars.

If you click on Edit in the Quick Pic window you'll display the Fountain Fill Effect dialog box. This lets you manage fountain fills, using a procedure that's quite different from that in Draw. The big difference is that in Chart, as with chart types, you begin by choosing a preset fountain fill and then modify it. Notice that the current Fill Type is A-B Regular. This linear fill blends smoothly from the Start to the End color. Change the Fill Type to A-B-A Regular. This fill blends from the Start color (A) to the End color (B) and back to the Start color (A), something that's not possible in Draw.

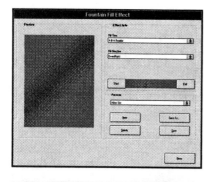

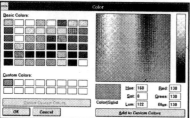

Now try various Fill Direction settings and examine the results in the preview at the left. Finally, click on the two buttons labeled Start and End. Each leads to a Color dialog box that lets you choose a color or define a new one. Unfortunately, color definition in Chart is much more limited than in Draw; there's no support for process or Pantone spot colors, for example. Keep in mind that you're free to create objects with fountain fills in Draw and bring them into Chart by simply copying and pasting.

When you've finished experimenting with the Fill Effect dialog box, click on Save As, name your effect and click on Apply in the Quick Pic window. Then set the fill of the first set of bars back to Yellowing, choose Blue Wash for the second set and the oddly named Palace Of The Brine for the third. Notice that you've chosen three of the more subdued fountain fills. If you plan to use more than one fountain fill, be subtle in your choice of colors to prevent a garish effect.

Fun with Frames

You can also fill frames with fountain fills. Select the graph's frame (the rectangle holding the grid) and choose the ■ icon from the ⌥ menu. This takes you directly to the Fill Effect dialog box. For the Fill Type, choose A-B Regular. For the Fill Direction, choose Downward. For the Start color, choose the navy blue in the Color dialog box and then click on OK. For the End color, choose the fourth red in the first column, a deep red. If you simply want to use your new fountain fill once, click on Apply — in this dialog box you don't have to save it first.

As a finishing color touch, click on the background of the chart (outside of the frame) and choose black from the Color Palette at the bottom of the Chart window. Then click on the legend frame and select a very dark gray from the Palette.

Another interesting effect is to fill the frame of a chart with a texture. This is especially effective if you'll be generating color slides or printouts. Select the chart's frame and then choose the ▤ icon from the ⌥ menu. Click on the Bitmap ▒ icon and then click on Apply to use the first bitmap from the drop-down list, Blue Swirls. To remove a bitmap fill or fountain fill, choose ✕ from the ✋ menu.

As alluring as bitmap fills are, be sure that you have sufficient contrast between the background bitmap and the foreground bars. If the bitmap is light, use dark bars — and vice versa. If the bars are difficult to distinguish against the background, your message may not be clearly understood. You can also fill the bars of a graph with a bitmap fill, but this would be appropriate only when graphing a single series. Two or more sets of bars with contrasting bitmap fills are typically less than attractive.

The documentation doesn't mention it, but the Chart bitmaps are simply files in .BMP format. So you're free to create your own bitmap fills by exporting anything from Draw as a .BMP file to the CHART\BITMAPS directory. You could also bring the existing Chart .BMP textures into CorelPHOTO-PAINT to perform color correction or apply its filters, such as Motion Blur and Emboss. (For details on this see *Working with Bitmap Graphics*.)

Legendary Legends

You have several possibilities for changing the appearance of the chart's legend. First, you can change its size and position on the screen by dragging a resizing handle or dragging the entire legend. You've seen that as you change the size of the legend the text inside resizes proportionately, provided Autofitted Text is enabled. To check this, click on any of the legend text with the right mouse button. If you turn off Autofitted Text, you can adjust the size of the text manually using the text ribbon.

Here's something to try. Click in the legend area with the right button and then choose Legend from the menu. Under Legend Layout, choose Vertical Legend and then click on OK. Now drag in the sides of the legend frame so there isn't too much space around the legend contents, and resize the legend frame so the text inside is easily readable. Then drag the legend inside the graph, above the bars but within the frame. This makes more space available around the graph, so you can make the graph larger and more easily read.

Formatting the Data Axis

The vertical axis of the graph — the data axis — has its own special set of formatting options. To see these, click on any of the numbers along the data axis with the right button or with the Pop-up menu tool. The Data Axis Scale pop-up menu that appears shows four sets of options.

The first set lets you display the axis information on the left, the right or on both sides (for both sides, make sure both options are checked). For now, leave the axis information on the left.

The second set of options gives you the choice of a linear or logarithmic scale. Along a linear scale, the numbers increase in equal increments. Along a logarithmic scale, the numbers increase by powers of 10. You'll probably want to use a linear scale unless you're graphing numbers with huge variations.

The third set of options lets you define the end limits of the data axis, change the formatting of numbers along the axis and determine whether to show grid lines that start at the axis and run horizontally to the right. Choose Scale Range from these options and then choose Exclude Minimum from the Scale Range dialog box to remove the zero from the bottom of the data axis. Then select Manual Scale under Range Method and enter 0 next to From and 120 next to To. This will provide a little extra space above the bars for the legend. Although it's often not done, you should always plot bar charts with a minimum of zero. Your viewer can only judge the relative heights of bars accurately if the entire lengths of the bars can be seen. Click on OK to view the adjustments.

To format the numbers, right-click on any number and choose Number Format. As you click on each of the number format options, a sample below displays the result. Choose the $0 option, which places a dollar sign at the beginning of the number and displays the number without any decimal places. Then click on OK.

When you choose Grid Lines from the pop-up menu, you're given the option to display Major or Minor grid lines. Major grid lines are horizontal lines that start at each of the numbered points along the data axis. Minor grid lines are additional evenly spaced lines lying between major grid lines. Ticks are the tiny marks along the axis, the same type you'd find along a ruler. You can choose grid lines alone, grid lines with ticks, or ticks alone. If you choose to manually determine the number of Major grid lines, Chart will take the upper limit of the axis and divide it by the number of divisions you enter. Select Manual under Major Divisions and enter 4 for Number Of Divisions. Under Minor Divisions, select Show Minor Grid Lines, Inside Ticks and enter 3 as the Number Of Divisions. Then click on OK to see the result. You'll see four 'major' numbers along the data axis and three 'minor' divisions between each number.

The last set of options gives you three choices for the scale: ascending, autofitted and staggered. Selecting Ascending Scale creates a data axis that starts at the lowest value at the bottom of the axis and runs up. Turning off Ascending Scale places the lowest value at the top of the axis. The bars of a vertical bar chart thus run down from the top, as shown in the illustration. A chart like this might

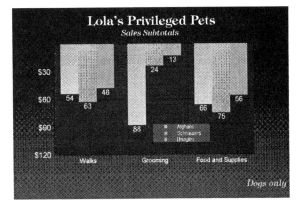

show losses effectively, but I hope you'll never have to use one.

Selecting Autofitted Scale automatically adjusts the size of the numbers so they fit nicely along the axis. Turn off Autofitted Scale and you can manually resize the numbers using the text ribbon. Staggered scale will stagger the numbers along the data axis so more of them will fit.

Adding Emphasis

Chart provides two automatic ways to emphasize a set of data, or even just a single bar. First, you can display one of the series of data as a line, rather than a bar. This distinguishes that series from the others and says "this is the series to compare the others against." To display the second series in your chart as a line, click with the

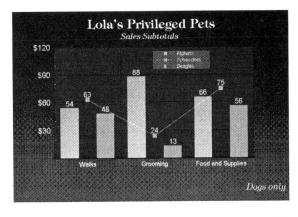

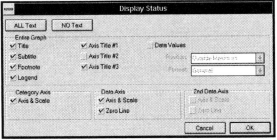

right button on the middle bar above 'Walks' and then choose Display As Line from the pop-up menu.

Chart is now displaying the numerical data point values immediately above the line. To turn off the data point values, click on one of them with the right button and then click on Data-point Values. With the data point values removed, you can select the line with the ⬉ tool and change its color with the Color Palette, or its width with the ✒ tool. Try this now. To bring them back, choose Display Status from the Chart menu and then click on Data Values. The Display Status dialog box lets you centrally control all of the text in the chart. Before proceeding, select the line with the right button and click on Display As Line again to get rid of it.

To emphasize a particular bar, click on the bar with the right button and then choose Emphasize Bar from the pop-up menu. Select it with the ⬉ tool and the bar can now be colored independently of the rest of the series.

Chart comes with the capability to perform and display a surprising number of analytical calculations on your data. You can have Chart plot not only mean and trend lines, but also logarithmic progression, moving average and polynomial fit lines. What's more, after Chart plots the line it can display the formula it used and the correlation coefficient it calculated.

If none of this means anything to you, you can safely skip this section and move right on to Changing Chart Types. But if numbers are your game, you'll appreciate the ease with which you can add statistical information to a chart. Try adding a trend line by right-clicking on one of the bars in the chart. Then choose Data Analysis. Just check off the lines you'd like to display and whether to show the formula and correlation coefficient. You can turn off the trend line by clicking again on its name.

The most important options for most people's use will be Connected Line, which connects a straight line from data point to data point, and Linear Regression, which plots a best-fit straight line among all the data points in a series. A linear regression (also called a *trend line*) shows the general direction of change in your data. Those who really need the other, more complex calculations will understand what they mean.

Changing Chart Types

You meant well when you chose a vertical bar chart to display the sales data. Bar, line and pie charts are the most often used and therefore the most familiar chart types. But Chart's gallery of charts includes some impressive designs that pick up in sizzle where they leave off in precision.

Not sure which chart design you want? You can switch from one type to another at will until you've found the chart that suits you best. The Gallery menu lets you quickly choose from a huge visual catalog. You should save the current chart before proceeding as PETS2, by choosing Save As from the File menu.

With the vertical bar chart still on the screen, choose the Gallery menu and click on Vertical Bar. The flyout menu shows

Side-by-Side checked and a thumbnail of a side-by-side chart. Click on Side-by-Side and hold the mouse button down while you drag down across the other charts on the list, inspecting each thumbnail as you go. Choose Absolute Line from the Vertical Line group of charts.

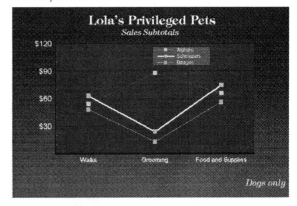

Colored markers help to distinguish among the lines in this chart, but they aren't enough. Select each line in turn (this may take a few tries) and then select a bright color from the Color Palette. You may also need to increase their thickness. The markers themselves can also be selected and colored independently.

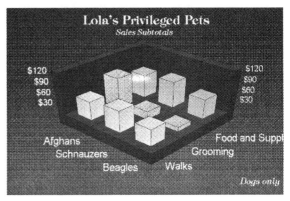

Return to the Gallery menu and choose 3D Riser. Then choose Bars from the flyout menu. 3D Riser charts are visually striking, but less than

---

impressive in the precision department. Take a look at the chart and determine how much Lola's Privileged Pets made from grooming Schnauzers, for example. While the precision required to easily answer such a question is lost in 3D Riser charts, the dazzle you gain may be more important when your goal is to make a strong impression. If you're running Chart on an older or memory-starved machine, you may find that the 3D formats slow it down considerably. Removing any fountain fills or bitmaps should speed things up.

Special 3D Formatting

Your 3D Riser chart is indeed impressive, but the fun has only just begun. On the Chart menu you'll find a host of options for changing the appearance of the chart. The first of these, Preset Viewing Angles, is particularly helpful. Choose this and then drag across each of the preset angles (California Special?) and see the effect on the thumbnail before choosing Column's Eye. In addition to the preset angles, you can select an angle of your own by using the totally wild 3D View tool. Choose this now from the Chart menu.

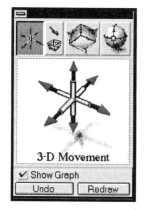

3-D Movement

The 3D View tool appears in its own persistent window, much like the Quick Pic tool. The four buttons across the top let you change different aspects of the 3D view. Click on the left button at the top of the 3D View Tool, which lets you move the graph left, right, up, down, front or back in 3D space. Try moving the graph up by clicking on the red up arrow several times (you can also hold down the mouse button.) As you do, you'll see a superimposed wireframe of the walls and base of the graph move up. When you click on Redraw, the graph is redrawn at the new position of the wireframe.

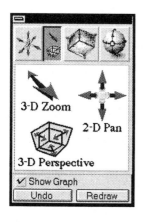

3-D Zoom
2-D Pan
3-D Perspective

Click on the second button, which lets you change the zoom, pan and perspective of the graph. The current graph is so large that some of the text runs beyond the edge of the page. If it won't fit on the screen, it won't fit when it's printed. To reduce the size of the graph, click a few times on the 'rear' portion of the 3-D Zoom double-arrow (the arrow facing upper left). To see only the wireframe, click on Show Graph to uncheck it. Click once or twice more on the rear arrow and then click again on the Show Graph control to make the new graph appear. Use the 3-

D Zoom control to make the graph small enough so there's plenty of white space around its edges.

The 2-D Pan control simply moves the graph left, right, up or down within the chart. Click on the right arrow of the 2-D Pan control a few times and then click on Redraw to redraw the graph in the new position.

The 3-D Perspective tool moves the walls of the graph to change their degree of perspective. Click on any of the red arrowheads to move a wall.

Now select the third button at the top of the 3D View Tool. The diagram below should read 3-D Box Proportions. The three double-arrowheads in the picture change the length, width and height of the graph. The three double-arrowheads at the edges of the picture change the thicknesses of the two walls and the base. Try these out.

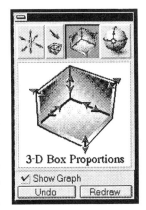

3-D Box Proportions

When you click on the fourth button at the top of the 3D View Tool, the diagram shows a sphere labeled 3-D Rotation. This is the button that's selected by default when you first open the View Tool. Click on any of the red arrows to rotate the entire graph. When you've finished with the View Tool, click once on the button at the upper-left corner to close it.

By default, the text and numbers along the edges of the graph are resized in proportion to the graph itself. Right-click on the row header 'Beagles', for example, and then choose 3D Text Options from the pop-up menu. Because Autofitted Text is on, and All Headers Same Size is selected, Chart makes all the row headers a size that will fit the graph. Click on Headers Change Size With Perspective and then click on OK. Because the left edge of the graph appears to come directly towards you, the headers along the edge should now get larger as they come closer.

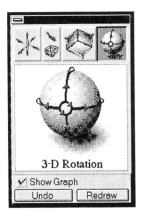

3-D Rotation

The numbers next to the back walls of the graph run along the vertical z axis. Right-click on any of the numbers and then choose 3D Grid Lines from the pop-up menu: you'll see a control for changing the Z-Axis Divisions. Choose Automatic, rather than Manual, and click on OK. The graph will revert to the original scaling it had before you changed the y axis on the vertical bar chart.

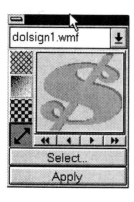

3D Risers have two options that are not shared with standard bar charts. Right-click on the 3D Riser bars in your chart and choose Riser Sizing from the pop-up menu. This leads to a flyout menu that lets you choose from a variety of the preset choices. Then click again on the bars and choose Riser Colors. Try Color By Series. All the risers for Schnauzers are now the same color. Switch back to Color By Group and you'll see that now the bars are color-coded by income category.

You've now finished with the 3D chart, but feel free to experiment with the many additional options. Before continuing on, you may want to save it using Save As from the File menu.

Creating a Pictograph

A pictograph uses pictures of objects, rather than bars, to give a chart a little fun and extra meaning; however, you must start with a bar chart to create a pictograph. From the Gallery menu choose Vertical Bar and then pick Side-By-Side from the flyout menu. From the Chart menu, choose the new option that has appeared: Show As Pictograph. The chart doesn't change much because you haven't yet chosen pictures for the pictograph.

Click on the ✎ tool and then select the ▣ icon from the flyout menu. Now click on the ↗ icon in the Quick Pic window to be able to access files in .WMF (Windows Metafile) format. A selection of these is provided in the CHART\VECTORS directory, but you can also create your own pictograph images by exporting from Draw in .WMF format to this directory. If you do so, say yes when prompted to include a placeable header. You may also have to change the aspect ratio of the objects in Draw before exporting them, to avoid having them looking squashed when loaded into Chart. I find that many of the images in Draw's symbol libraries are good candidates for .WMF export. And the existing images in the VECTORS directory can also be imported into Draw, if desired.

After you select one of the bars in the chart, you can use the control arrows of the Quick Pic window to scan through the available files for a suitable image, but let me suggest DOLSIGN1.WMF for the first set of bars, BUNDLE.WMF for the second set and COINSTK2.WMF for the third. Chart will stack as many copies

of the image as it needs to approximate the heights of the bars. If you
create a pictograph chart, make sure
the legend is large enough to distinguish the tiny pictures inside it.

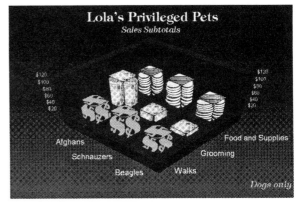

Try out some of the other Vertical
Bar and Line styles on the Gallery
menu. Then venture into undocumented territory by choosing other
styles, such as the 3D variations, to
see your .WMF images used to represent the data. (To remove
the .WMF images from your chart, select an object on the page and
choose a color from the Color Palette to replace it.) If you like, save
your chart as PICT01.CCH before continuing. Then use the File
menu to close it.

Creating Pie Charts

Pie charts serve a prime purpose far different from that served
by bar, line or 3D riser charts: a pie chart shows the breakdown
of a total. Stacked bar charts also show breakdowns, but their
prime purpose is to add measurements together and compare
several totals.

Entering the Data

To create a pie chart, select New from the File menu and Pie
from the list of chart types. This time you don't want to use the
sample data, so double-click on the first pie thumbnail in the
upper-left corner.

In the Data Manager window, type
'Lola's Privileged Pets' in cell A1
again, and 'Breakdown by Product' in
cell A2. Move the cursor to A5 and
type the first pet food name, 'Canine
Delight.' In the cell to the right, type
the sales quantity for Canine Delight,
which is 64. Continue entering sales
figures until you've reproduced this
table:

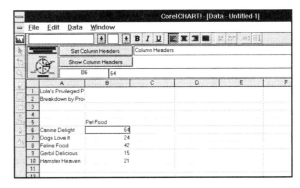

Canine Delight	64
Dogs Love It	24
Feline Food	42
Gerbil Delicious	15
Hamster Heaven	21

Then, at the top of the column of numbers, enter a name for the pie, Pet Food, in cell B4. Now click on the change view button at the upper-left corner to switch to the Chart View window and display the pie.

Decorating a Pie

Changing the appearance of a pie chart is just like working with a bar chart; you use a combination of main menu commands, pop-up menus and the Color Palette. In fact, the Palette is the tool you'll use first to assign a different color to each of the pie slices.

Select any slice with the left mouse button and click on bright red in the Palette. Then select the next slice and pick orange. Continue with the rest of the slices, using the 'beach ball' colors: yellow, bright green and bright blue.

You should now attend to the legend. Legends are helpful in bar charts, where it would be inappropriate to try to label 15 or 20 bars. But when you've got a pie with only a handful of slices, you can directly label each slice and save the viewer from playing the color match game ("If they're red, these must be the figures from our East Coast office.") Remove the legend by choosing Legend from the Chart menu and click on Display Legend to disable it. Click on OK and the chart redraws without the legend.

It's time to label each slice. Right-click on any of the numbers attached to the slices and choose Show Slice Names from the pop-up menu. You're getting there, but the slice names and numbers are too distant from the pie.

Each of the slice names and slice values is connected to a slice with a two-segment line called a *slice feeler*. If you reduce the length of the line segments, the slice names will move closer to the slices. Right-click on a slice and then choose Slice Feeler Size from the pop-up menu. On the sample diagram in the dialog box, click on the circle at the middle of the line and drag it just next to the edge of the pie. Then click on the circle at the end of the line segment that extends out from the pie and drag it close to the pie. As you move the circle, you'll see that the Horizontal measurement changes. Move the circle until the measurement reads 15%, then click on OK.

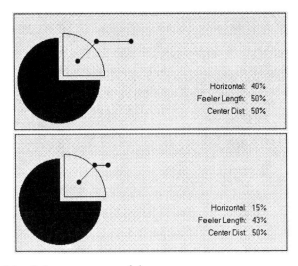

You'll see the black slice feeler lines within the pie, but you may have difficulty making them out against the blue frame behind the pie, so change the feeler line color to white to ensure the feelers will be easily visible. Select any one of the feeler lines and pick white from the Color Palette. You can emphasize the feelers a bit more by increasing the width of the lines. With the feeler still selected, click on the ♦ tool in the toolbox and then click on the ♦ icon. Specify 1 point for the line width and press Enter or click on OK.

Slice feeler lines are helpful when you have many slices, but pies that have only a few slices (five or less) can do without them. Even this pie would be perfectly intelligible without feelers, so right-click on any slice and click on Slice Feeler Lines to uncheck it. Even though you've removed the slice feelers, you still can use the Slice Feeler Size control to change the distance between the slices and their names.

Finally, you may want to remove the slice values (the numbers next to the slice names) so they are not confused with the product names. Right-click on any slice name and click on Show Slice Values to uncheck it. Now only the names appear near the slices. You could put the numbers back inside the pies manually using the 𝔸 tool from the toolbox. Unfortunately, Chart will not do this for you automatically.

Other Pie Options

You can emphasize a single slice by detaching it from the rest of the pie. To accomplish this, simply right-click on the 'Dogs Love It' slice and then choose Detach Slice from the pop-up

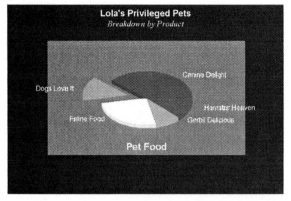

Lola's Privileged Pets
Breakdown by Product

menu. Take a look at each of the options on the flyout menu by dragging across them and then select Default.

When you right-click on the pie chart frame, you'll find several other options at the top of the pop-up menu for refining the appearance of the pie. (You could also access these with the Chart menu.) Pie Tilt, Pie Thickness and Pie Size all provide a number of variations. Drag across the flyout menu for each of these options and experiment with the options.

Pie Rotation, also on the pop-up menu for the pie chart frame, lets you select from pre-determined rotation angles for the pie. The previews on the Pie Rotation flyout menu are a little deceiving, though. The default pie — the pie you get when No Rotation is chosen — actually starts the slices at the 3 o'clock position and fills in the pie counter-clockwise, rather than beginning at the 12 o'clock position shown in the thumbnail picture.

Side-by-Side Pies

By entering more than one column of numbers in the Data Manager window and choosing Multiple Pies after picking Pie on the Gallery menu, you can display two or more pies on the screen to compare breakdowns. You'll use this technique to create two side-by-side pies. One will show the breakdown of pet foods sold in summer and the other will show the same breakdown in winter.

Begin by switching to the Data Manager window, then change 'Pet Food' in B4 to 'Pet Food - Summer.' Add 'Pet Food - Winter' to cell C4 and enter the following numbers in the column below: 74, 36, 54, 25 and 43. Click on Autoscan to have Chart include the column in the revised data range.

Switch back to the Chart View and choose Pie from the Gallery menu, and Multiple Pies from the Pie flyout menu. One pie's slice names fit just fine, but try to put two pies with slice names on the same screen and you'll run out of room. Instead, it looks as though you'll need a legend to represent the names. First,

remove the slice names by right-click-
ing on either pie and turning off Show
Slice Names on the pop-up menu.
Then right-click on the chart's frame
and choose Legend from the menu.
Click on Display Legend, make sure
Autofit Legend Text is on and choose
Vertical Legend from the Legend
Layout group of options. Set Num-
ber Of Markers Per Column to 5.
This will ensure that all five slice
names fit in a single column within the legend.

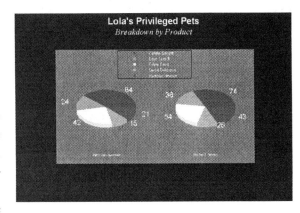

When you click on OK, you'll see a legend with a single column. Left-
click on the legend and drag the handles
surrounding it until the legend is neatly
positioned squarely above the two pies.
You may now want to turn on Show Slice
Values when you right-click on either pie.

To place the two pies above one another, right-click on the chart frame
and change Pies Per Row to 1. Now you
can bring in the left edge of the frame,
slide the entire frame to the left, and
reposition the legend to the right of the
pies — perhaps hanging outside of the
frame on the right, as shown in the illustration.

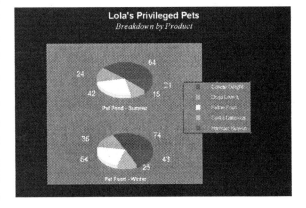

Other Pie Types

The other flavors on the Pie menu are
Ring and Proportional. Ring pies are
just like regular ones except they show
data as segments of a ring, rather than
slices of a pie. You can have a ring pie
display the total of all the values of the
pie in its center.

Proportional pies are only meaningful
when you have more than one pie.
They depict the relative totals of the

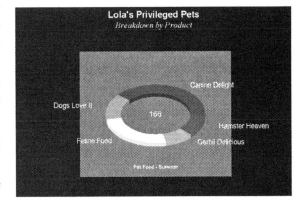

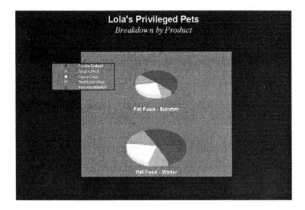

pies by changing the pie sizes. The larger the sum of the slices, the larger the pie. Try both these pie types out now, if you're curious.

Uncommon Chart Types

Although bar, line and pie charts are so popular that they appear daily in virtually every newspaper and magazine, Chart's other types serve very select purposes. If your needs are scientific, educational, financial or presentation-oriented, you may find one of the special chart types on the

Gallery menu to be appropriate. I'll leave it up to you which ones to try out now. Since many of these require you to enter data into the Data Manager in a particular sequence, it's often easier to begin by enabling Use Sample Data in the New dialog box.

These charts display points on an x-y grid. Each point represents the intersection of an x and y value. A typical scatter chart might have a point on the grid for each model of sports car, as shown in the Price-Performance Comparison chart. Each point is plotted against both a vertical (y) axis that measures unit cost and a horizontal (x) axis that measures performance. By seeing

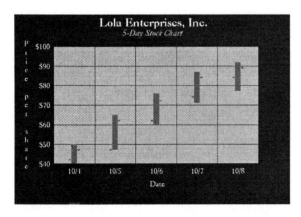

where the points fall, you can quickly judge which car has the highest performance at the lowest price.

To create a scatter chart, you must enter data into the Data Manager window according to a particular arrangement. Unless you do a lot of scatter charts and thus will always remember the pattern for data entry, you're best off selecting Use Sample Data when you choose a scatter chart from the

Chart Gallery. You'll then see that names for the measurements you've made should go into the Data Manager window's column A. The x measurements should go into column B, and the y measurements should go into column C. You can place labels that you'd like to have appear on the chart's data points in column D.

Hi-Lo-Close

These charts display the high, low and closing prices of a stock or other financial instrument for a day, week, month, or other time period. The chart for Lola Enterprises is an example of this. Hi-Lo-Close charts can also display any other data that has a measurable high and low during a given time period, such as temperature, humidity or even traffic density on a highway.

Replacing the sample data provided with Chart is the best way to remember the organization of data in the Data Manager. If you've chosen New from the File menu, be sure to select the correct Hi-Lo-Close chart from the Chart Gallery dialog box. If you want to plot only Hi and Lo numbers, then select the first chart thumbnail, which plots only Hi-Lo numbers. The chart's description on the Chart Gallery tells you which data the chart plots. If you plan to create a chart with Hi, Lo, Close and Open, make sure to select either the third or fourth thumbnail.

Generally, the figures for stocks are entered across rows in this order: Hi, Lo, Open, Close. For each day, add another four numbers in the same row. To plot more than one stock, use more than one row. To have dates appear along the x axis, replace the word 'High' above each set of four measurements with the date.

Spectral Mapped charts

These charts represent numbers by coloring the blocks of a grid. Spectral mapped charts are especially useful when you want to show a spatial relationship among the numbers. For example, a spectral mapped chart would be well suited for displaying the average daily temperatures of a geographic region, as shown in the illustration.

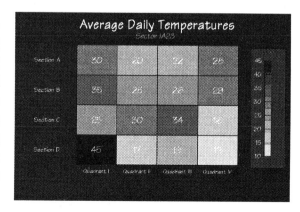

The data layout in the Data Manager for a spectral mapped chart is the same as that for a standard bar chart. Place the chart titles in the first few cells in the upper-left corner, and set up a grid of data arranged in columns and rows. In the spectral mapped chart, each cell of the grid will be represented by a rectangle of a color determined by the cell's contents. The cells that hold the lowest values have one color and the cells with the highest values have a second color. Cells with intermediate values have intermediate colors.

For example, if the cell with the lowest number is yellow and the cell with the highest number is red, cells with intermediate numbers will be shades of orange. To specify the range of colors, right-click on any cell and then choose Spectrum from the pop-up menu. Then choose Spectrum again from the flyout menu. Click on the Start button to choose a starting color and on the End button to choose an ending color. The number in the box above the color range determines the number of intermediate color steps. The more color steps in the example above, the more possible shades of orange you'd find in the chart.

When you select Use Sample Data after choosing a Spectral Mapped chart from the Chart Gallery, be aware that a mistake in the sample data has Row 6 defined as Column Headers rather than Row 5. You may want to fix this by reassigning row 5 as the column headers for the chart.

Histograms

These charts are like vertical bar charts, except they show a y axis (called the *interval* axis) that displays the highest and lowest values,

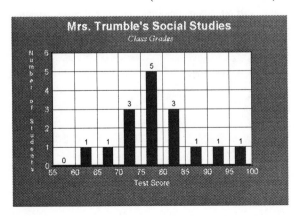

and is segmented into equal intervals. Horizontal bars extend from the y axis, showing the number of measurements that fall into each interval. For example, a histogram might show the number of days the temperature fell in the following ranges: 50° to 60° Fahrenheit, 60° to 70° and 70° to 80° (if the highest and lowest measurements were 50° and 80°). Mrs. Trumble's Social Studies shows an example of a histogram.

Graphing with CorelCHART

Data points for a histogram are plotted in a group of contiguous cells in the Data Manager. Chart counts the number of occurrences of each value automatically. When you right-click on a histogram chart's frame, you'll see two options for setting the Interval axis (the y axis) and the Data axis (the x axis). These options are similar to those for bar charts. The Intervals options let you enter a designated number of intervals or have Chart automatically create appropriate ones.

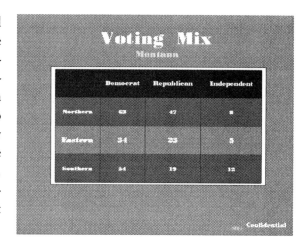

Tables

Table charts show data that cannot easily be represented with a graphic chart. Sometimes the trend in a group of numbers is so clear that a graphic isn't required; other times, the actual values of the data are more important than a comparison or display of trends. Voting Mix is a typical application of a table chart.

Because table charts simply display the raw data in the Data Manager in tabular format, they have the least number of settings. Nevertheless, when you right-click on any cell in a table chart, you'll see options that let you determine how to display colors in the chart and how to display the grid lines and borders surrounding the cells and chart.

The row and column headers act as two groups. For example, when you format the text of one column header, the rest of the column headers pick up the same formatting.

Embellishing Charts

Chart provides a number of ways to embellish your charts. You can type text directly on the chart; draw lines, arrows, boxes and other simple graphics, and import complex graphics in a variety of file formats.

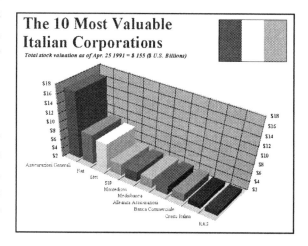

Using the Toolbox

The ready-to-roll charts you select from the Chart Gallery are colorful and attractive. And when you use fountain fills and bitmaps in the chart frames and backgrounds, you can create some dramatic effects. To see finished examples that use some impressive designs, take a look at the charts in the SAMPLES subdirectory of CHART by choosing Open from the File menu. You can modify these as desired, if one of them meets your needs; many more are on the CD-ROM disk supplied with Draw. These provide a good example of what your completed charts might look like. And some of them go a step beyond standard Chart output.

A chart called IT_STOCK incorporates the Italian flag, for example, while NET_TV uses an image of a television set. The Italian flag is a piece of clip art that was pulled from the Draw clip art library, while the TV set was hand drawn using the tools in Chart's toolbox. You'll now learn how to draw upon and annotate charts, and how to incorporate clip art images from Draw's vast library of existing images.

You can add drawn objects and text to your chart at any time. Just remember that the chart remains a background on top of which you add objects created with the tools in the toolbox. Why is this so important? Because you can select the objects in the background part of the chart — the bars of a bar chart or the lines of a line chart, for example — and you can choose a fill or line width for them, but you can't move them freely around the screen or control them with the commands on the Arrange menu. The only objects you can move freely are the chart text and the graphic portion of the chart — the chart's frame and legend areas, the contents of which move as a single unit.

Remembering that the chart is a backdrop is also important because, although you can rearrange the layering of objects placed on top of a chart, you can't even partially place an object behind it. With this in mind, you'll use the Rectangle □ and 𝔸 tools to annotate a chart.

Close the chart currently displayed on the screen and open the one you saved earlier as PETS2.CCH (or another, if that's not available). Then choose the ☐ tool and draw a small rectangle in the very center of the graphic portion of the chart. With the rectangle still selected, choose the ✍ tool and choose the solid black fill from the flyout menu. Choose Duplicate from the Edit menu to make a copy of the rectangle. Choose the ✎ tool and click on the X icon to remove the white outline from the duplicate. Choose

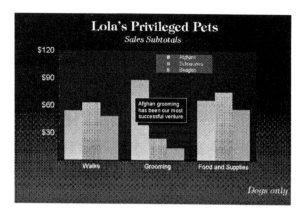

To Back from the Arrange menu to send the duplicate behind the original. Notice how the copy goes behind the first box, while a bit still remains on top of the chart background.

Choose the ▶ tool and move the top box until the duplicate is only slightly offset to the lower-right of the first box. Now choose the 𝔸 tool and click within the first box, at its upper-left corner, and drag over to just inside the right corner. You're defining the width of the text box into which you'll type. Choose a face and point size from the text ribbon, click on the center alignment button and then type 'Afghan grooming has been our most successful venture.' If the text goes below the box's border, switch to the ▶ tool, select the text and lower its point size to fit. Then change its color to white.

Like Draw, Chart provides an Align command. You may remember that in Draw the *last* object you select with the Shift key is the one that doesn't move when you align — it's the control object. Well, just to make things interesting, in Chart it's the *first* object you select that's the control object. Select the top box with the ▶ tool, then hold down the Shift key and click on the text you typed. Choose Align from the Arrange menu, then Align Center Vertical. Choose Align again and this time Align Center Horizontal.

Using text and graphic objects like this is just one example of the many ways you can annotate charts with the tools in the toolbox. You can add explanatory notes and point with arrows to significant bars, pie slices or spikes in lines. To add arrowheads to

lines, simply draw a line with the Pencil ℓ tool, then right-click on it and choose the arrowhead of your choice. Or you could use the Ellipse ○ tool to call attention to an important result.

While the tools in the toolbox work much as they do in Draw, they're not identical. And some menu commands are missing, such as Group. But for complex drawings, you'd be wise to do the work in Draw, copy it to the Clipboard and then paste it into Chart. To incorporate a bitmap image or scanned photo, create the object in CorelPHOTO-PAINT, then copy and paste it into Chart.

Using Clipart

The Corel graphics applications come with a vast amount of clip art you can use to take the hard edges off a chart, while hopefully also giving it a little extra meaning. If the clip art is in one of the formats supported by Chart, you can import the file directly. Choose Place from the File menu and change the List Files Of Type to Windows Metafile. Move to the CHART\VECTORS directory and double-click on any .WMF file to import it. You can then move and size it as desired.

Unfortunately, Chart can't import Draw's .CDR files. So to use one of the files in the clip art directories, you must first import the file into Draw and then copy and paste the image from Draw into Chart. For example, a chart about vacation travel might be more fun with an image of a golden sun in the corner. You could run Draw and open SUN062.CDR from the DRAW\CLIPART\MISC directory, and then copy and paste this into Chart.

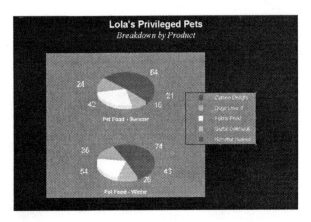

The best way to find a clip art file is to use CorelMOSAIC (see *Working with Clip Art*). The Corel CD-ROM is loaded with thousands of clip art selections that you can use in Chart, which can be quickly browsed through and opened with Mosaic. In fact, there's a whole group of images in the PET directory that would be perfect for the sample chart you created earlier in this chapter.

Advanced Topics

The Chart Gallery is supplied with a selection of common chart types, but you can delete or move the obscure ones and add types that you'll use frequently.

Modifying the Chart Gallery

To add a chart type, simply create the chart and save it into the appropriate subdirectory under the CHART directory, such as BAR or PIE. For example, to create your own custom pie chart design with custom title settings, pie slice colors, slice feeler settings, a particular frame color and a background fountain fill, create a sample chart with all of the settings just the way you want, then save it in the CHART\PIE directory. Be sure to enter a description when you save the file, so you'll see the description when you click on the chart in the Chart Gallery window.

To delete charts you'll never need, you must make a note of the chart's name and then delete the file from the appropriate subdirectory. The easiest way to do this is to click on the chart once in the Chart Gallery and note the full pathname to the chart, including the chart's filename. Then use the Windows File Manager to delete the file. You can also use Mosaic to do this, with the added advantage of being able to see thumbnails of the files you're deleting.

By adding to and deleting from the Chart Gallery, you can create your own custom assortment of frequently used chart types. You can have at hand charts already containing your company's colors and logo, for example. You can also have two versions of each chart: one for color slide output, and one for printing on a black-and-white printer.

After entering data into one chart, simply copy the data to the Windows Clipboard and then paste it into the Data Manager for the second chart. You can have only one Data Manager open at a time, so you must switch charts to get to the second chart's Data Manager.

Because the charts in the BAR directory are the group that appear when you first open the Chart Gallery, you may want to place the charts you create most frequently in this directory.

Working with Templates

Even after you've completely formatted a chart, you can still quickly change its design by applying that of a second chart. The second chart is called a *template*, and its chart type, colors, text styles and other settings are instantly transferred to the first chart.

To try this technique, load the file you created earlier called PETS2.CCH. Then choose Apply Template from the File menu. Select the file you created called PIE2. In a moment, the PETS2 bar chart will become a pie chart with the same color selections, text fonts, legend placement and other design attributes as PIE2; only the data has remained unchanged. Rather than graphing all four series in a bar chart, the chart now graphs only the first series in a pie chart. To graph the other three series, you'd need to choose a Multiple Pie chart.

By using templates, you can quickly convert existing charts in a variety of designs into a uniform set for a new presentation. Your viewers will never know the charts they see were not custom designed for the new presentation.

Printing and Exporting

Printing charts requires the same considerations you use when printing illustrations you've made in Draw. If you're using a black-and-white laser printer, for example, you can't use dark colors in bars or pie slices against a dark chart frame. You're best off setting the frame color to solid white and using gray shades to fill the bars or pie slices, so your printed output will have the same gray shades you see on the screen.

If you must print a colorful chart that was created for slide output or for inclusion in a Draw illustration, you should make a duplicate of the chart and spend a moment removing its colors before printing to a black-and-white printer. Another technique is to apply a template you've already created that uses shades of gray.

Printing a colorful chart to a color printer or slide maker presents no such problems. (For details on using the Autographix slide service software supplied with Draw, see *Alternate Output Devices*.) As long as you use the correct Windows driver for the color output device, your printed colors should approximate the onscreen colors. When you print directly from Chart to a color device, you can't expect the type of exact color matching that Draw provides, because Chart does not include support for process or Pantone color models. If precise colors are important, you must export a chart into Draw and modify the colors there.

To properly export a chart that you can edit in Draw, you must observe this rule: Do not use fountain or bitmap fills in the bars of a bar chart, the slices of a pie chart, the chart frame or the chart background — use solid colors, instead. If you use fountain fills, the position of these elements when exported may be unpredictable. You can always add these fills in Draw.

You must also modify a special line of the CORELDRW.INI file that tells Draw to import a Chart file as a group of editable objects, rather than as a single object that can only be resized or moved. The CORELDRW.INI file is an ASCII text file that's located in the Draw directory (usually C:\CORELDRW\DRAW). Use the Windows Notepad or another ASCII editor to open CORELDRW.INI and then add or edit the line in the section headed with [CDrawConfig] to read OLEConvertObjectsToDraw=1, as shown in the illustration.

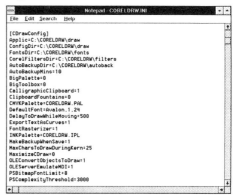

Now save the file, and close and restart Draw if it's currently running. Open the file in Chart that you want to transfer to Draw, then choose Copy Chart from the Edit menu. Run, or move to, Draw and use the Paste command to place the chart on the page. Choose Ungroup from the Arrange menu. You can now select each of the bars and choose just the color you need. Edit and print is as desired.

You can also export charts using the Export command on the File menu. When you choose Export and display the List Files Of Type list, you'll see a broad range of both vector and bitmap file types. Select the appropriate file type and enter a name for the file before clicking on OK.

Linking and Embedding

Windows gives you the ability to easily copy a graph from Chart into Draw. Object Linking and Embedding (OLE) in Windows 3.1 automatically updates the copied graph if the original is updated in Chart. But in order to take advantage of OLE, you must copy the chart from Chart to Draw with a specific procedure.

First, create the graph in Chart. Then copy the chart to the Windows Clipboard by selecting it and choosing Copy Chart from the Edit menu. Now switch to Draw and choose Paste Special from the Edit menu. In the Paste Special dialog box, select CorelCHART 3.0 and then click on the Paste button. A copy of the chart appears in Draw.

You can try this by opening any of the charts created earlier in this chapter, copying them to the Clipboard, then using Paste Special in Draw to make a duplicate appear and to create an OLE link. In this case you've *embedded* the pasted chart. After the chart appears in Draw, you can double-click on it at any time. This opens the chart in Chart, where you can edit it as desired. When you close Chart, the chart in Draw will be updated automatically.

A second way to embed a chart can be initiated from within Draw. To accomplish this, select Insert Object from Draw's File menu. Then in the Insert Object dialog box, select CorelCHART! 3.0. This runs Chart, where you can create the desired chart. When the chart is finished, select one of the two commands on the File menu that let you either Update And Return to the Draw file or Exit And Return to the Draw file. The chart will be placed on the Draw page, where it can be edited in Chart by double-clicking. The limitation of this technique is that it can't be used to paste in an existing Chart file, just to create a new one.

If you click on the Paste Link button in Draw's Paste Special dialog box when pasting in a chart, you also establish a *link* with the original chart file. So this button will be ghosted if you're pasted in an untitled chart. By establishing a link with a Chart file, you can ensure that you're always working with the latest version of it, since Draw will automatically import it again if it's edited in Chart.

While in Draw, you can also use the Links command on the Edit menu while your chart is selected. In the Link Properties dialog box, make sure Update is set to Automatic to make sure that the copy of the chart will be updated automatically if the original is modified. You can also manually update the chart in Draw by clicking on the Update Now button. Note that if you ungroup a chart in Draw, you sever any OLE connections.

OLE will update a chart in Draw that you created in Chart, but if you create a graphic in Draw and copy it to Chart, the copy won't update automatically through OLE. Technically, this means that Chart may be an OLE *server*, but it is not an OLE *client*. If you modify the object in Draw, you must copy the modifications into Chart manually.

OLE also plays an important role when you want to maintain a link between spreadsheet data and a chart. Using Import File brings in an entire Excel worksheet file. The same command also works when you import a Lotus 1-2-3 worksheet. But using Import File creates no link between the data in Excel or 1-2-3 and the chart. If you change the numbers in Excel or 1-2-3, graphs in Chart that depend on these numbers don't change.

When you use Excel, Lotus 1-2-3 for Windows or Quattro Pro for Windows, there's another method you can employ to preserve an active link between the original data and the chart. You can try this procedure now if you have Excel or 1-2-3 for Windows. This would also work if you have a Windows word processor that supports OLE, such as Word for Windows. Run either spreadsheet and open the Excel or 1-2-3 worksheet called PETS.XLS or PETS.WK1 from the SAMPLES directory of the Utility disk. If you're running a word processor, type in the following sample data, separated by tabs:

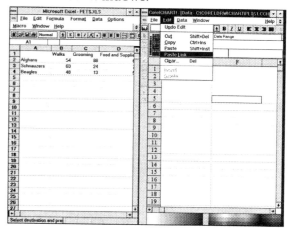

10	20	30
40	50	60
70	80	90

Select the rectangular block of cells

that's filled with data and choose Copy from the Edit menu.

Switch back to Chart and position the cursor in cell F5 of the Data Manager window, just to the right of the existing data. Choose Paste Link on the Edit menu and you'll see that the data from Excel, 1-2-3 for Windows, or your word processor appears in blue to indicate that a link has been established. Be sure to select the 3 by 3 grid of blue numbers, choose Data Range from the Chart Parts list and click on Set Data Range. To see this link in action, switch to the Chart View window and arrange the Excel, 1-2-3, or word processor window and the Chart window side by side on the screen.

Now add 100 to any of the numbers in the spreadsheet or word processor and watch the graph change in the Chart View window. Any change you make to the original data flows through to Chart, thanks to the link you've established. If you close and later make changes to the data in the spreadsheet or word processor, when you later open the linked chart, the data link will be automatically re-established.

Before leaving this topic, switch to the Data Manager window in Chart and try altering one of the blue numbers. You'll find that Chart prevents you from altering linked data to avoid a discrepancy between the original data and that in Chart. Linking allows you to update data in just one application and have the updates occur automatically in all other applications that depend on the data. (For more on OLE, see the following chapter on CorelSHOW.)

Windows Recorder

The Windows Recorder provides a quick way to automate many functions in Chart. Chart's menus are notoriously short on keyboard shortcuts. You could create a macro in Recorder that both center and vertical aligns objects, for example, saving several multi-menu trips. Another way might be to quickly display the fill or outline dialog boxes, using the same function key shortcuts as Draw. (For details on using Recorder, see *Optimizing Windows*.)

Presenting with CorelSHOW

You can use CorelSHOW to create presentations composed of images created in CorelDRAW, CorelCHART and CorelPHOTO-PAINT. The presentation you come up with can be as simple as a slide show of graphic images, displayed on the screen one after another. Or it can be as complex as a contemporary video production, complete with slick, TV-like transition effects between images. Show even gives you the power to incorporate graphic images, animation sequences and sounds created in other Windows applications.

Integrate your graphics, sounds and animations

Show also fulfills another equally important purpose. It acts as the home base from which you can head out and create all the graphic elements of a project. You produce the backgrounds of presentation pages in Show, but you then launch other Windows applications to take advantage of their capabilities. You always return to Show, where you organize the bits and pieces you've formulated elsewhere. After the entire collection of graphics is complete, you can use Show to print all the components you've amassed in one huge batch, create a file for printing on a high-resolution imagesetter or slide device at a service bureau, or create a screen-based presentation.

Linking and Embedding

The ability to move graphics easily from one application to another is one of the great advantages of the Windows environment. After creating a graphic in Draw, for example, you can move it easily into PageMaker. You simply copy the just-completed object with the Copy command, and then Paste it into the application where it's needed. Windows has always provided this capability. But an important new feature added in Windows 3.1, object linking and embedding (OLE), takes this concept a step further.

Not only can you copy and paste graphics, text and other objects between applications, but you can create an active link between the applications that changes every copy in every application when you change the original object. With OLE, for example, you can create a company logo in Draw and link it to a report in a word processor, a form in a forms-generating application and a chart created in Chart. Change the logo in Draw and the logo changes in the documents of the three other programs.

This active link, called *object linking*, lets you change an object once, where it was originally created. The same change then flows through to every copy of the object, no matter where it resides. You no longer need to worry about discrepancies between copies you're using and the original. And you don't need to go around trying to find and update every instance of a logo when you need to make a minor change.

OLE is the name of the game in Show. Every object, whether it's text, a drawing, a scanned picture or a chart, is created in its own application and can then be incorporated into a Show presentation via OLE. No objects are created in Show itself; they're pulled in from other applications and used in building a Show presentation. The one prerequisite is that the applications must be capable of acting as OLE servers.

Object linking has one role in Show and *object embedding* has another. Object linking lets you copy objects from multiple Windows applications to a screen show. Once the items are copied, they'll be updated in Show if any of the originals are changed. The second aspect of OLE, object embedding, allows you to temporarily launch a second application from within a Windows program and use it to create a new object. When you finish the object and close the second program, the object you've created is embedded in the file of the first program. To edit the object, you can later double-click on it. The original application in which the object was created then opens to permit you to make changes. You can also embed an object by copying it from one application and choosing Paste Special from the second application's Edit menu.

The benefit of object embedding is that anyone can give you a document that contains objects created in a variety of applications. If one of the objects needs editing, you can simply double-click on it and the original application in which it was created will open the object, ready for editing (as long as you have that application installed on your system, of course). You don't need to know the file name or the program in which the object was created, since there's no file involved and Windows keeps track of the application that created the object.

For example, while you're working in a document you can record sounds with the Windows Sound Recorder (if you have a microphone and a sound board). These will become embedded objects in the destination document and be represented on the page by a sound icon. Anyone with a sound board (or the Windows speaker driver) can play the sound by double-clicking on the sound icon. With this technique, you can embed a spoken message, or even music, in a Show presentation that will play automatically when the page is displayed. Similarly, you can embed a video clip if you have the proper hardware.

With object embedding, you can incorporate objects from different Windows applications on a single Show page. On one page, for example, you can embed text created with Draw and a chart with Chart, while on another page you can create and embed an image with Photo-Paint and a sound with the Windows Sound Recorder.

If both object linking and object embedding let you create a show that contains objects from other applications, which technique should you use? Use object linking if you want to maintain a link to an existing file, and optionally update it in Show if the original file is modified. Use object embedding if you need to create new objects for a presentation as you go. You'll launch an application, such as Draw, to create a new object and close it when you're done. Or you'll embed objects by running Draw and Show at the same time, and pasting in objects copied from Draw.

Of course, like all rules of thumb, this one has exceptions. You can embed an existing object in a Show file, for example. And while you're working in a second application that was launched from within Show, you can save the object you've created so you can load it separately later.

Starting a New Presentation

Double-click on the CorelSHOW icon in the Corel Graphics group of the Windows Program Manager to start Show. The Welcome To CorelSHOW! dialog box appears in the middle of the Show window. It offers the choice starting a new presentation or opening an existing one.

If you're having trouble running Show, or it crashes while you're creating a presentation, the problem is probably related to your graphics card and screen driver. Make sure you're using a Windows 3.1 driver. And check with Corel technical support to find out if there are any known problems running Show with your card and driver.

Click on Start A New Presentation and then examine the Options For New Presentations area just below. Notice that the number of pages is set to 5. You can always add more pages later, but that number is fine for now. In fact, all of these options can be easily

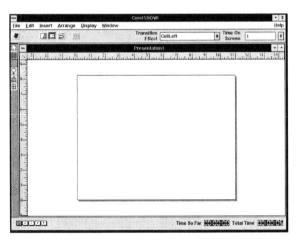

changed later, but click on the Page Setup button to check the page settings. The Page Setup dialog box lets you choose a page orientation and one of 10 preset page sizes. You can also choose Custom and enter your own page height and width. You'll create a standard on screen presentation, so make sure Landscape is selected and choose Screen as the Page Size. Then click on OK. In the Welcome dialog box click on OK to begin the presentation with the chosen settings.

Exploring the Show Screen

The Show screen now becomes active and a window labeled Presentation1 appears in the center. If Show isn't filling the screen, double-click on its title bar, then do the same for the presentation's window.

Below the standard Windows menu bar in the Show screen, a ribbon contains icons for playing a screen show and selecting page views, and provides a menu for specifying transition effects between pages. The toolbar at the left has tools you'll be using in a moment. The status bar at the bottom of the screen shows five page icons in the lower left (your presentation currently has five empty pages). Two clock counters indicate that you're at the beginning of the presentation and that it has five seconds in total running time (one second for each of the five pages).

Your first task will be to choose a background for the screen show. After that, you can move from page to page, building your presentation with objects from other applications.

Creating a Background

To work on the background you must be in Background view, which displays only the page background. Click on the Background View icon in the ribbon, the one to the right of the movie icon. The title bar for the presentation window now displays the word 'Background' in parentheses, and it also appears at the bottom of the screen.

You can now either create a new background in Draw or another graphics application, or you can select from a library of existing presentation backgrounds. If you paste in a graphic while you're in Background view, it will become the background on every page in your presentation. Selecting from the library is easier, so begin by clicking on the Background Library tool (the tool that shows a grid, just under the Pointer ▸ tool). In a moment, the default library of backgrounds appears in its own window.

Click on Change Library, which displays a dialog box that lets you open different libraries of backgrounds. Click once on the SAMPLE.SHB library in the \CORELDRW\SHOW\BACKGRDS directory. (The .SHB extension stands for Show Backgrounds.) Then click on the scroll arrows to preview the backgrounds in the library. When you've taken a look, click on OK to open SAMPLE.SHB. While this is the only background library supplied on the floppy disks, there are many more on the CD-ROM included with Draw. Select the background that looks like the figure in the illustration and then click on Done. The background automatically fills the page.

To confirm that the background is now on every page, click on the second of the three view icons in the ribbon, the Slide View icon. Then press the PageDown key on your keyboard repeatedly to advance from page to page (or click on the page icons at the bottom of the page). The highlighted page icon tells you which page is displayed. Click on the third of the three view icons, the Slide Sorter View icon. You'll see all five pages with the same background. Double-click on the first of the pages to view it back in Page View. Now you're ready to begin copying and pasting objects onto the presentation's pages.

 I should point out here that you can turn off backgrounds on a page-by-page basis by displaying the page in question and choosing Omit Background from the Edit menu. You could then switch to the Slide View and paste in a graphic copied from another application, such as Draw, to serve as that page's background.

Here's another technique that will let you mix different backgrounds from an .SHB library in the same presentation. With your background displayed, switch to Slide View, click on the background to select it and choose Copy from the Edit menu. From the same menu, choose first Omit Background and then Paste. Now click on the Background Library tool and choose a new background. You'll find it's applied to every page *except* the one on which you pasted the previous background.

Inserting a File

As discussed above, there are several ways to bring objects into your presentation. To begin, leave Show running and return to Windows Program Manager by pressing Alt-Tab. Then run Draw by double-clicking on its icon.

You'll use several files found on the Utility disk supplied with this book. All of these files are in its SAMPLES directory. Choose Open from Draw's File menu, move to the SAMPLES directory of drive A or B and open RESORT.CDR. Select the 'Water Mill Resort' text that appears on the Draw screen and choose Copy from the Edit menu. This copies the text to the Windows Clipboard. Close Draw and return to Show by holding down the Alt key and tapping on the Tab key until the Show title bar is displayed, then release it to switch back to Show. Choose Paste Special (not Paste) from the Edit menu. Select CorelDRAW! Graphic and then click on the Paste Link button. The Draw text will appear on the Show page. Drag the upper-left corner handle to reduce the size of the object until it fills the right two-thirds of the page, but stays within the blue frame. Use the illustration here to judge the proper placement.

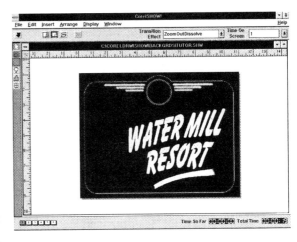

Note that you could have simply chosen Paste, instead of Paste Special. This would have also placed the graphic on the page, but it wouldn't have created a link to the original .CDR file on your floppy. Of course, if you don't plan on later editing or updating the pasted file from the original, then you can simply choose Paste.

If you're using a 256-color SuperVGA system, you'll notice that the smooth fountain fill (from red to orange) now looks coarse. The reason is that Show has a limited range of available display colors. In fact, it displays using a palette of just 16 colors. To create the additional shades of red and orange necessary for the fountain fill, Show must use various mixtures of red and orange dots — a process called *dithering*.

Because of this dithering, the text would look better in a solid color. It's easy to change, because you've linked the object. Double-click on the text. Windows automatically opens the application in which the object was created, in this case Draw, and the original file. Click on the text and select bright red from the Color Palette at the bottom of the screen. When you save the revised file, the text in Show will also be updated. Choose Save from Draw's File menu, close Draw and then switch back to the Show window to take a look. If the update isn't displayed, choose Links from the Edit menu and click on Update Now to force Show to read the edited file from the floppy. Now you'll try linking an object a second way.

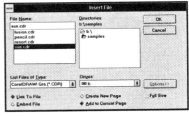

Choose File from Show's Insert menu. In the Insert File dialog box, click on the Options button. Two new buttons at the bottom-left let you either link or embed the file. Click on Link To File. Make sure Add

To Current Page is also selected, otherwise the linking process will add a new page and place the embedded file on it. List Files Of Type should be set to CorelDRAW Gra (*.CDR). Now move to the SAMPLES directory on the Utility disk and select SUN.CDR from the list of files. The cursor becomes a crosshairs on the Show screen. Click and drag to draw a box to the left of the text. When you release the mouse button, the sun image will appear. You'll also get a message advising you that the file to which you're linking is on removable media. This warning makes sense, since you're establishing a link to a file that may not be there in the future. Proceed in this case, but be aware that normally you wouldn't create a link to an image on a floppy, you'd embed it.

Choose To Back on the Arrange menu to move the sun to the rear. Notice that the sun remains on top of the page background. Stretch the lower-right handle of the sun frame so that it extends just a bit behind the text.

Now it's time to create the second presentation page. Press the PageDown key or click on the second page icon at the lower-left corner. On this page you'll link another existing file from the Utility disk. Choose File from the Insert menu, click on Options again and make sure Link To File is selected. Then set List Files Of Type to CorelCHART 3.0 (*.CCH) and pick the file ADVANCE.CCH from the SAMPLES directory. This image will take noticeably longer to place. You've now linked a Chart file to the second page, as shown in the illustration.

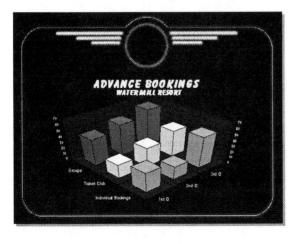

Drag the handles surrounding the chart until it nearly fills the blue frame in the background. Show comes with several aids you can use to precisely place objects on the page. On the

Display menu, make sure Show Rulers is selected (a checkmark should be next to it). If the checkmark is not displayed, click on Show Rulers to enable it. Notice that the rulers indicate the page is indeed 11 inches wide and 8 ½ inches high. Click anywhere within the vertical ruler at the left and drag out a guideline onto the page. Place the guideline at exactly 5 ½ inches on the horizontal ruler, halfway across the page.

Now you can align the middle frame handles of the chart with the guidelines to exactly center the chart. If the guidelines are being covered up by the background, choose Omit Background from the Edit menu while you're aligning the chart, then choose it again to display your background again. Since there's no keyboard shortcut to toggle backgrounds on and off, this might be a candidate for a Windows Recorder macro. (See *Optimizing Windows* for Recorder details.)

Rather than pull guidelines out from the rulers, you can also use the Guidelines Setup command on the Display menu. The Guidelines dialog box, which works much like the one in Draw, lets you position a vertical or horizontal guideline precisely on the page. The measurement units start at the left side of the page if you're creating a vertical ruler, and at the bottom of the page if you're creating a horizontal ruler. As in Draw, you can double-click on a guideline to display this dialog box.

The ruler displays distances from the lower-left corner of the page, but it can also be used to measure the distance across the page from any other point. To measure the width of the chart you just inserted, for example, click on the icon at the intersection of the two rulers and drag the zero point crosshairs for the rulers to the left edge of the chart. Then release the mouse button and move the mouse to the right edge of the chart. A dashed line within the ruler moves in conjunction with the cursor, so you can easily read the distance measurement on the ruler.

Using Show as Home Base

Up to now, you've linked only files that you happened to have on hand to the screen show. But you can't always count on the readiness of every chart, drawing and text block that you'll need. Often, you must create the bits and pieces you need on the fly, as you build the presentation. Even if all the charts and graphs are prepared in advance, you may want to call upon the capabilities of Draw when it comes time to make an introductory slide, or special graphic slides that begin each segment of the presentation.

Show is ideally prepared for such a method of working; in fact, it includes special capabilities that let you launch another application, create the graphic object you need, and then place it back in Show. You can repeat the process for each page, even dipping into several different applications to create different objects for the same page.

 Switch to the third page of the presentation. On this page, you'll place a pie chart created from scratch in Chart. The toolbar at the left side of the screen shows a group of three icons below the ⬉ and Background Libraries icons. These three icons launch Draw, Chart and other Windows applications that can take advantage of OLE.

Click on the second icon, which runs Chart. Then, with the new crosshairs cursor, click and drag a horizontal rectangle that fills much of the blank space within the blue outline on the page. When you release the mouse button Chart will run, ready for you to create a new chart. Click on Pie in the Chart Gallery, click on Use Sample Data and then click on OK. This chart could certainly use a lot of prettying up, but for this exercise it will do as is. Now choose Close And Return To CorelSHOW on the File menu, and click on Yes when you're asked whether to update the file in Show.

You'll be returned to Show and the new chart you created will be embedded on the page. To edit the chart double-click on it now, just as you would with a linked chart. Make changes to the chart in Chart, and choose Update on its File menu to see those same changes made to the chart in Show. For example, select one of the pie slices and choose a new color from the Color Palette at the bottom of the Chart screen. When you're finished, choose Close & Return To CorelSHOW.

You may find all this switching back and forth is taking quite a while. This is especially true on 386-based systems, or those low on memory. I'm afraid there's not much you can do about this except beef up your system.

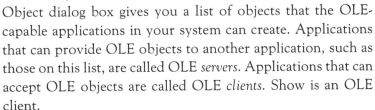

Move to page four, where you'll use another method to embed an object. To embed an object on this page, choose Object from the Insert menu. The Insert New Object dialog box gives you a list of objects that the OLE-capable applications in your system can create. Applications that can provide OLE objects to another application, such as those on this list, are called OLE *servers*. Applications that can accept OLE objects are called OLE *clients*. Show is an OLE client.

From the list, choose CorelPHOTO-PAINT! Picture and click on the Insert button. Use the crosshairs cursor to click and drag a large horizontal rectangle in the center of the page. When you release the mouse, Photo-Paint will run and you'll be ready to paint an object. I won't ask you to hand paint a masterpiece expressly for this presentation. Instead, in the Create A New Picture dialog box enter 3.00 inches as both the width and height. Then choose Paste From on the Edit menu and select the file PAINTWAY.PCX from the CORELDRW\PHOTOPNT\SAMPLES directory of your hard disk (It's also in the SAMPLES directory of the Utility disk). Then choose Exit And Return To CorelSHOW from the File menu, clicking on Yes when you're asked to update. You'll be returned to Show and the embedded image will be on page four. Use the handles to center the image on the page.

Turn to page five so you can try still one more way of embedding an object. Choose File from the Insert menu. Then click on the Options button in the Insert File dialog box. Click on Embed File rather than Link To File and make sure Add To Current Page is selected, rather than Create New Page. Set List Files Of Type to CorelCHART 3.0 (*.CCH) and select WM-BNFTS.CCH from the SAMPLES directory of the Utility disk. Draw a box for the object on page five with the crosshairs cursor. In a moment, Chart will open with the file you selected already loaded. Make any changes you'd like to the chart and choose Close & Return To

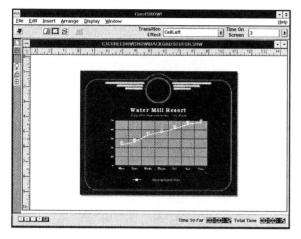

CorelSHOW from the File menu. Click on Yes when asked if you want to update Show.

Updating Links

Show provides a way for you to manage the OLE Links you've established between pages of the presentation and objects in other applications. Choose Links from the Edit menu to investigate this feature.

The Link Properties dialog box lists each of the objects you've linked to the presentation. Notice that Automatic appears next to each of the objects to confirm that the object in Show will be updated automatically if the object changes in its source application. You can select any one of the objects and change this to Manual. This causes the object to be updated only when you click on the Update Now button, and lets you prevent changes in the original objects from flowing through to your presentation until you're ready for them.

Selecting an object and then clicking on Open Source will open the original application in which the object was created, so you can make edits. This is the same as double-clicking right on the object. Clicking on Cancel Link will break the link to the original object. The word Static appears next to the object on the list. Use this command when you'll never want an object to change in Show, even if it changes in the source application. Clicking on Change Link lets you choose a different object to link in place of the selected object.

Adding an Animation

Show can display animations created with Autodesk Animator, or other applications that can generate .FLI files, in a screen show. To place an animation in your presentation, you must either run an animation program to create one or use any of the three dozen animation files that you'll find on the Draw CD-ROM.

A few animation files have also been supplied with Show.

First add a new page to your presentation by choosing New Page from the Insert menu. Now add an animation by choosing Animation from the Insert menu. Then click once on NENTEED.FLI in the FLICS subdirectory of the SHOW directory. The Preview control lets you advance through the frames of the animation by clicking repeatedly on the right-hand scroll arrow.

Clicking on the Options button gives you more control over how the animation will run. You can repeat the animation a specified number of times, or even *ad infinitum*. You can also choose to stop the animation on its last frame until you advance to the next page of the show. The speed of the animation can be controlled by entering a different value for Frames Per Second. Set these as options as desired, then click on OK.

Show has placed the animation on a new page inserted before the current page. It also updated the Total Time counter to include the run time of the animation. You'll see the animation in a few minutes when you run the screen show.

Rearranging Pages

Just as you can rearrange the slides of a slide presentation on a light table before inserting them into a projector, you can rearrange the pages of a presentation in Slide Sorter view.

Click on the Slide Sorter View icon to display the pages of the presentation in miniature thumbnail versions. In this view, you can change the sequence of the presentation by simply dragging any page to a new position. Try dragging the animation page to the right of the current last page, for example. Then drag the page holding the Photo-Paint object to between the first and second pages. A black vertical bar appears to indicate where the page will be placed when you release the mouse button.

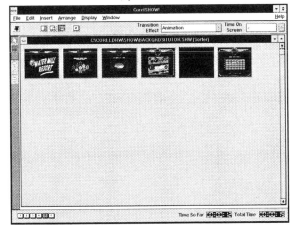

While you're in this view you can also accomplish a few other things. For example, you can delete any page by selecting it and pressing the Delete key. You can duplicate a page and its contents by selecting the page and choosing Copy and then Paste from the Edit menu (or by pressing Control-Insert and then Shift-Insert). And you can also go to a full screen view of any slide by double-clicking on it. Experiment with some of these possibilities.

The Numbering Tool

Another way to rearrange the order of slides is to use the Slide Numbering tool in the ribbon, which is identified by a number sign. Choose this tool, then click on the pages in the order in which you want them to appear in the presentation. When you've clicked on all the desired pages, click again on the Slide Numbering tool and they will automatically be rearranged in the proper order. The Numbering tool does not actually place numbers on the pages. You'd have to manually place a number on each page that you had created with Draw.

Adding Transition Effects

When you intend to display a presentation on a computer screen, you can add slick television-like transition effects between successive pages. Each new page can fade in, for example, or wipe across the screen from top to bottom.

The fastest place to add transition effects is in Slide Sorter view. Click on the Slide Sorter View icon in the ribbon and then click on the first slide in the presentation. Select Curtain Open from the drop-down Transition Effect menu and 2 seconds as the Time On Screen (the duration the slide will remain on the screen before the show advances to the next slide). Then click on each of the other slides and select a different transition effect, with 2 seconds for each slide's Time On Screen. You'll see that Animation is automatically selected for the slide that contains it. At this point, use the File menu to save the show you've created with the name WATERMIL.SHW.

Displaying a Show

Before you display the show onscreen, you should check Presentation Options on the Display menu. If Automatic Advance To Next Slide is selected, the show will use the Time On Screen settings for each slide. If Manual Advance To Next Slide is selected, then you can double-click with the left mouse button or use any of the following keys to advance to the next slide: Down arrow, right arrow, PageDown, F6, Enter or Spacebar.

To return to the previous slide, you can double-click with the right mouse button or use any of these keys: Up arrow, left arrow, PageUp or F5. To return to the first slide, press Home or F9. To jump to the last slide, press End or F10. To end the show, press Escape.

When you're running the show automatically, the F2 key will pause the show. Press F2 again to continue the show. F3 will play the show backward, while F4 will play the show forward. Home returns to the first slide and End jumps to the last. Escape ends the show and returns to the Show window.

Other options in the Presentation Options dialog box let you run the show continuously until the Escape key is pressed (ideal for unattended presentations in store windows or at trade show booths), display a cursor on the screen (good for pointing to objects with the mouse) and generate the slide show in advance, so the transitions between slides occur more smoothly.

To begin the show, click on the Screen Show icon at the upper-left corner of the screen.

The Screen Show Player

CorelDRAW 3.0 Rev B comes with a special Windows program called SHOWRUN.EXE that you can copy and distribute freely along with your screen shows. This lets others display a screen show and even change transition effects for slides, but not add or delete objects from the show.

To distribute a screen show, copy both the SHOWRUN.EXE file and your .SHW screen show file to a diskette (the SHOWRUN.EXE file is in the SHOWRUN subdirectory of the SHOW directory).

Then SHOWRUN could be run on another computer, either directly from the floppy or the files could first be copied to the system's hard drive to speed up the presentation. To run it, choose Run from the File menu of the Windows Program Manager and then type either A:SHOWRUN or B:SHOWRUN, depending on whether the diskette is in drive A or B.

The Run-Time Player works just like Show; it simply lacks the tools and menu commands required to insert or delete objects. If you've incorporated an animation in the screen show, make sure you also copy the CAAPLAY.DLL file in the SHOWRUN directory to the floppy diskette.

Printing a Show

To print a show, you must use the proper settings for Page Setup. When you started the current show, you selected Screen as the page size. Now that you're about to print the show, choose Page Setup from the File menu and select Letter. Then click on OK. You'll see that the letter-size page is a bit wider (it appears a little taller on the screen because of its landscape orientation). You may want to stretch the background so it fills the page. To do this, click on the Background View button so that only the background appears. Then select the background object. On the Arrange menu, select Fit Object To Page. The background will stretch to fit all the pages.

To print the show, choose Print from the File menu. The option Don't Print Background can come in handy when you want to print only the objects on the page. You might want to create handouts to accompany a slide show, for example. Since only the contents of the pages are important, you'd select Don't Print Background before printing. Note that you can also print to disk, creating a .PRN file of PostScript code. This could then be output on any PostScript device. For example, you could use the included ToAGX utility to send the presentation via modem to an Autographix service bureau for output. (For details on ToAGX see *Service Bureau Strategies*.)

You're now ready to start creating your own presentations. You can click on the remaining two buttons in the toolbar to create links to Draw or other OLE-aware applications. You could also try placing a .WAV sound file in a presentation. I've included a PC speaker driver and some sample sounds in the SPEAKER.ZIP archive in the UTILITY directory of the Utility disk included with this book. Choose File from the Insert menu to place these on a page. See *The Draw Companion Disks* for details on extracting files from the disk and installing the speaker driver.

As with Draw, you can access context-sensitive help by pressing Shift-F1 and choosing an item from any menu. Use this to obtain explanations of some of the features I haven't had room to cover here, such as the ability to add imported images to your background libraries. Because of its modest number of tools, Show is at first deceptively modest in its capabilities. However, its OLE support provides an open-ended way to integrate a wide range of images, sounds and animations created not only with other Corel tools, but a wide range of Windows applications as well.

Advanced Type Topics

16

Earlier versions of CorelDRAW supported only its proprietary .WFN font format, and required the use of the included WFN BOSS utility to convert these fonts into formats usable by other applications. With Draw 3.0 all this has changed. Draw now supports three type formats: its proprietary .WFN, PostScript Type 1 and TrueType. Forty-eight symbols and three fonts are supplied in .WFN format, 155 TrueType fonts are provided on floppy and 256 fonts are provided in both TrueType and PostScript Type 1 format on the CD-ROM supplied with Draw.

Your fold-out type chart lists these 256 fonts using Corel's name and the "similar to" industry standard name, along with specimens of each font. The included clip art reference book also supplies both font names and indicates whether they are on floppy or CD-ROM. And the included Character Reference Chart shows you what keystrokes to use with these fonts. You should keep these three resources handy when you're working with type.

In this chapter you will examine the three type formats supported by Draw and learn how they work within both Windows and Draw itself. If you currently use only TrueType or PostScript fonts, mix the two together, or use both formats along with .WFN fonts, this chapter will help you better understand how these formats compare and work together. You will discover which format is appropriate for the type of work you produce, as well as how to optimize your system. You'll master the intricacies of Draw's unusual method of font handling. And you will also explore the capabilities of third-party programs — many of which are included on the Utility disk included with this book — that enhance your productivity when working with type.

Taming PostScript, TrueType and .WFN fonts

The material I'll cover here applies not just to Draw, but to all your Windows applications. Most of this is not tutorial in nature, but is a distillation of all I've been able to learn about font installation and use in the Windows environment. Much of it has never been documented. All of it is quite technical. You may want to go through this chapter several times until all the pieces fit together.

Overview

The TrueType font format was developed by Apple Computer and optimized for Windows by Microsoft. The Type 1 PostScript font format was developed by Adobe Systems and has become the standard for PostScript fonts. Deciding which of these font formats to use can be a perplexing decision, since each has its advantages and disadvantages. I'll begin by briefly comparing these two formats.

Both formats use outline font technology to *rasterize* a character in a chosen font and size from a single outline. An outline font contains a mathematical description of the outlines of all the characters in the font. Rasterization is the process of converting the outline to display on your screen and print on your output device. This produces a size-specific *bitmap*, which is a collection of dots (pixels) that define the letter form. Outline fonts eliminate the need to permanently install large numbers of bitmap fonts, each created for a given size.

TrueType fonts occupy more disk space than their PostScript equivalents, but PostScript fonts require Adobe Type Manager (ATM) and its associated files, which occupy about half a megabyte of disk space. Support for the installation and removal of TrueType fonts is built into Windows, and is easier to use than the same procedure for PostScript fonts and ATM. TrueType fonts use just one file from which both screen and printer fonts are generated. PostScript, in contrast, uses two.

There is at present a larger selection of PostScript fonts, because this format has been in use since the dawn of desktop publishing on the Macintosh. TrueType fonts were first available for the Macintosh platform in March of 1991, and for Windows 3.1 in April of 1992. The availability gap has already started to close.

Major foundries, such as Bitstream, Agfa, Linotype-Hell and Monotype, are already selling fonts in both formats. Boutique foundries like Treacyfaces and Giampa TextWare are embracing the Windows platform, delivering type collections in both PostScript and TrueType format. Many of these vendors, and even Microsoft itself, are providing aggressively priced collections of TrueType fonts. Even Apple recently joined in with a collection of its own for the Macintosh. Additional individual TrueType fonts are also generally less expensive than similar PostScript fonts.

A big difference between the two formats is that TrueType is a font technology and not a language. PostScript is both a font technology and a page description language, that provides device independence and supports Encapsulated PostScript (EPS) graphics and print-to-disk files (PRN) across multiple platforms.

PostScript fonts are still the standard in service bureau work, with most major bureaus providing access to hundreds or thousands of fonts. If your job specifies Adobe's Helvetica (which it licenses from Linotype-Hell), you can be confident that your service bureau already has it on hand. If you specify the TrueType Arial font included with Windows 3.1, your service bureau (unless it's PC-based) will likely not be able to output your file without some extra preparation on your part. This support at the service bureau level is not likely to change for the near future, since the majority of bureau work comes from the Macintosh platform, where TrueType users are still a very small segment of the population.

Both formats support *kerning pairs*. Kerning pairs are collections of spacing information for particular combinations of letters, such as AW or To. Most TrueType fonts include a maximum of 512 pairs (Arial-Roman contains 105 pairs), but this will change as developers capitalize on the new kerning features for TrueType fonts in Windows 3.1. Contrary to popular opinion, both formats can support up to about 16,000 kerning pairs.

Both formats also employ *hinting* to improve your screen display and printed output at specific sizes and resolutions.

Hinting is the process of arranging dots (pixels) on your screen or printer to produce higher quality type at small sizes (4 to 10 points) and low resolutions. At 300 dpi, 6-point type may have only two or three pixels available to produce the vertical stroke of a letter. Hinting arranges these dots to produce better-looking type. At 1,200 dpi or higher hinting is of no value, since the output device can produce all the necessary dots in the characters.

TrueType and PostScript also both support the new Windows ANSI (American National Standards Institute) Plus character set (130 to 159). These new characters include the OE ligature (œ), trademark ligature (™) and ellipsis (…). Most fonts, including Draw's, provide some or all of these characters. Even your three-year-old PostScript fonts already contain these characters. Corel has changed the mapping of its proprietary .WFN fonts to support this new feature. Consult your Character Reference Chart for the specific characters and numbers.

Fourteen TrueType fonts are included in your Windows software package (Arial, Times New Roman, Courier New, Wingdings and Symbol). Since support for PostScript fonts is not built into Windows, it requires the purchase of the base 13 Adobe fonts as well as ATM for both screen display and printer output to equal the TrueType support built into Windows.

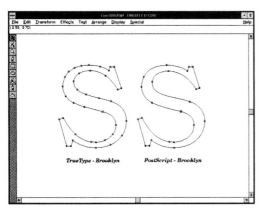

TrueType fonts use Quadratic B-splines to construct outlines, while PostScript fonts use Bézier curves. Examine the Draw screen shot reproduced here, in which both formats have been converted to curves using Draw's Brooklyn font. The TrueType character has 39 control points (or *nodes*), while the PostScript has 23. The additional nodes make the TrueType character more difficult to manipulate with the ✎ tool, and it consumes more memory.

Keep in mind that the base 13 PostScript fonts are *not* the same as the TrueType fonts bundled with Windows. Examine the screen shot from Draw and it's apparent that TrueType Arial and Times New Roman differ from PostScript Helvetica and Times.

Installing a large number of either font format will dramatically slow down Windows and all your applications, including Draw. You will start to notice this when you reach about 50 fonts in either format. For every additional 50 fonts you install, your system will become noticeably slower. When you reach 200 or more installed fonts, Windows turns to mush. With 163 fonts installed, I find Word for Windows takes 18.21 seconds to load. But with 59 fonts installed it only takes 8.97 seconds to load.

Draw is not as sensitive to this issue, since it does not read or use your PostScript font entries in the WIN.INI file. However, it still takes longer to load, because Windows itself is affected by the installation of fonts, and Draw reads the ATMFONTS.QLC file created by ATM (discussed later in the PostScript section).

This slowdown is caused by the archaic architecture of Windows and DOS. All your font entries are held in a single segment of memory, which has a documented limitation of 64 Kb. This means that all your font entries listed in WIN.INI reside in this segment, and Windows loads these entries every time you launch it. As this segment fills up with font entries, you run slower long before you reach the documented limitation. The commonly accepted rule that your WIN.INI file can't be larger than 64 Kb is true, but when it comes to fonts, noticeable performance penalties appear when this file reaches 25 Kb. Later in this chapter I'll cover ways to work around this performance penalty.

While there are significant differences between PostScript and TrueType fonts, keep in mind that you can create jobs in Draw or any Windows application using both formats. However, Windows must work harder to display both formats in the same document, so your system will run slightly more slowly set up this way.

The following sections of this chapter are organized by font format (TrueType, PostScript and .WFN) and begin with a system-level discussion of the format from a Windows perspective. They then cover how Draw handles each format, provide optimizing suggestions and conclude with a discussion of useful third-party applications.

TrueType Fonts

When you choose a TrueType font in Draw, or any Windows application, the characters displayed on your screen and later sent to your printer are generated from a single outline stored in a .TTF file. TrueType also employs a small .FOT file for each font, the purpose of which is to tell Windows where the .TTF file is located on your system. When you choose a TrueType font, the characters are stored in an area of memory known as a *cache*, to improve the speed of screen display and printing. Draw, however, does not use this feature, but relies on its own proprietary rasterizer.

The cache is dynamic in nature and forms part of the global memory pool that most Windows applications use. (Draw is one of the few programs that doesn't.) This pool is composed of the physical memory (RAM) installed on your system plus the size of your swap file, if any. As you specify more fonts, Windows uses this global memory to store the fonts in the cache. As your jobs print, the fonts are stored in this cache. When you close your document, this memory is returned to the global pool for other applications to use. If you use a large number of fonts in a document on a system with only 4 Mb of RAM, you will notice a lot of disk activity as Windows enlarges the cache using your swap file after it runs out of RAM.

Windows allows TrueType fonts to be *embedded* in a document, enabling it to be read or printed on another system, even if the fonts used in the document aren't installed on that system. This ability is implemented by the type foundry or font conversion software when the font is created. There are two variations of embedding.

Using *read-only* embedding, fonts in a document can be read or printed from another system, but not edited. *Read-write* embedding permits the document recipient to permanently install the font on his or her system to use in other Windows applications. All the TrueType fonts supplied with Windows and in the Microsoft TrueType Font Pack are read-write. But most foundries produce TrueType fonts that support read-only embedding.

FontMonger, a font conversion utility from Ares (covered later), supports both types of embedding. At the present time, the only publishing application that supports embedding is Microsoft

PowerPoint, but Corel, Aldus, Micrografx and other software developers have announced support in upcoming versions of their applications. Corel plans to release a version of the 256 TrueType fonts supplied with Draw that will permit embedding. PostScript fonts do not currently support embedding.

TrueType Windows Font Installation

TrueType support is automatically enabled when you install Windows and is controlled with the Control Panel in Program Manager's Main group. When working with TrueType, the only time you'll have to restart Windows is when you turn TrueType on or off. To ensure that TrueType is currently turned on run the Control Panel and double-click on the Fonts icon.

In the Fonts dialog box click on the TrueType button and then click on the Enable TrueType Fonts check box, if it currently *doesn't* have a check mark. If you had to enable the TrueType fonts, click on OK and the Restart Now button to rerun Windows. The 14 TrueType fonts supplied with Windows will now be available to all your applications, as will any of the Draw TrueType fonts you've installed. If TrueType was already enabled, click on Cancel and return to the Fonts dialog box.

To install the 26 OptiFonts TrueType fonts on the Fonts disk included with this book, click on the Add button in the Fonts dialog box. In the Add Fonts dialog box move to your A or B drive to display a list of all the fonts on the Fonts disk. Unfortunately, Windows provides no way to preview a font before you install it. But you can check the inside back cover of this book for a display of the fonts. Hold the Control key down to choose more than one font, or click on Select All to highlight them all. The Copy Fonts To Windows Directory check box should be enabled; this will ensure Windows copies the fonts to your hard drive. (The installation procedure will also create a .FOT file for each typeface located in your WINDOWS\SYSTEM directory.) Then click on OK to install the fonts. You'll be returned to the Fonts dialog box, where you can click on one

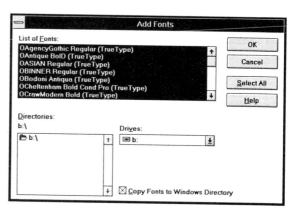

of your newly installed fonts to preview it. All the OptiFonts fonts begin with an O.

Follow the same procedure to install the extra 101 TrueType fonts from the FONTS\TTF subdirectory of the Draw CD-ROM. Make sure the disc is Revision B, however — there were problems with the fonts on the Revision A CD-ROM.

Whether you're installing from a floppy or CD-ROM, you should now click on the Close button and then close the Control Panel. Your new fonts are immediately available for use in all your Windows applications (unlike the installation of PostScript fonts via ATM, which requires restarting Windows). Some applications, such as Windows Write or Word for Windows, recognize your newly installed fonts if the programs were running when the fonts were installed. Draw, unfortunately, must be closed and restarted to recognize newly installed TrueType fonts.

Return now to the Fonts dialog box for some more font configuration. Click again on the TrueType button. If you like, you can instruct Windows to display *only* TrueType fonts in your applications. This is a dynamic configuration that affects some running applications (although Draw isn't one of them). That is, even if ATM is turned on, your PostScript fonts will disappear from the font menus of your applications. You would click on the Show Only TrueType Fonts In Applications check box to enable this feature, although I don't advise doing this now. Click on Cancel to return to the Fonts dialog box.

You may have TrueType fonts installed on your system that you never use. Perhaps your system is operating slowly because you selected a large number of fonts during your Draw install. Simply accepting the default would have installed more than 150 of them. You have the option of temporarily or permanently removing them. To temporarily remove TrueType fonts, click or Control-click, on the desired names in the Installed Fonts list and then click on the Remove button.

The Remove Font dialog box offers you the option of enabling Delete Font File From Disk. If you leave this disabled, the only file deleted will be the .FOT file; the .TTF file remains on your system. This lets you temporarily remove fonts, a technique you should employ if you are reorganizing the location of your fonts, anticipate using a font again, or if the performance of your Windows applications has suffered because you have too many fonts installed.

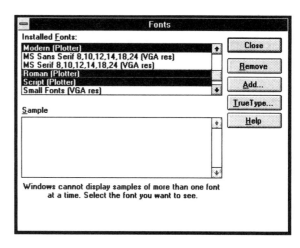

If you wish to permanently remove a font from your system, click on the Delete Font File From Disk check box. This will delete both the .TTF and .FOT files, and is the option to use if you never anticipate using the selected fonts or you wish to increase your available hard disk space. Whether you click on this option or not, the reference to the font is removed from the [Fonts] section of your WIN.INI (Windows INItialization) file.

You probably have a few other types of fonts installed on your system that you never use, but which consume hard disk space and memory every time you run Windows. Most publishing applications don't use plotter fonts, for example. If this is the case on your system, you can safely delete three plotter fonts. In the list of installed fonts, Control-click on Modern (Plotter), Script (Plotter) and Roman (Plotter). Click on the Remove button, select the Delete Font File From Disk check box and click on the Yes To All button in the Remove Font dialog box. This action removes the plotter fonts from your type menus, and from the [Fonts] section of your WIN.INI file.

You've probably noticed that the list of installed fonts contains a number of entries like MS Sans Serif 8,10,12,14,18,24 (VGA res). If you are running Windows in another video mode you would see something else — (8514 res), for example. These listings point to a screen font with an extension of .FON (for font). These fonts are *bitmaps* (a collection of bits) optimized for a specific point size and video mode. All Windows applications use these fonts in dialog boxes, menus, rulers and sometimes in text display. Because they are optimized for specific sizes and video displays, they look much better than any TrueType or

PostScript font. So leave these screen fonts installed on your system, or your menus and dialog boxes may become populated with illegible fonts.

If you wish, you may remove just the .FOT files for some or all of your installed fonts and use File Manager to move the .TTF files to a single subdirectory, such as DRAW\TTFONTS, rather than cluttering up your WINDOWS\SYSTEM directory with them. You could then use the Control Panel to reinstall them. Keeping them in a separate directory would also prove useful when installing an updated version of the Draw fonts. You could then easily remove the old ones before installing the updated versions. This de-install and reinstall procedure also corrects problems with fonts that may not display or print properly. If you are still using Revision A of Draw you should upgrade to Revision B, since these fonts have been revised to eliminate these problems. Check your version by choosing About CorelDRAW from Draw's Help menu.

When you install or reinstall fonts, your .FOT files by default reside in the WINDOWS\SYSTEM directory and contain the paths to your .TTF files. These .FOT files *must* reside in a directory listed in your PATH statement for Windows to use them. Alternatively, you can move these files to the same directory as your .TTF files and then edit your WIN.INI to point to these files. To accomplish this, open WIN.INI (in the WINDOWS directory) with Notepad or SysEdit and scroll down to the [fonts] section. (If you're new to WIN.INI editing, it might be wise to make a backup of it first, in the unlikely event you alter it to the point where Windows won't load.) Change the path for each of Draw's TrueType font entries to point to your DRAW\TTFONTS directory. Save your changes and restart Windows. If you ever move these files to a directory not in the PATH statement, you will have to edit the WIN.INI file again or reinstall the font.

There are two other sections in the WIN.INI file used by TrueType that you should know about. The [TrueType] section contains two switches: one enables or disables TrueType; the other displays only TrueType fonts in the type menus of your applications. Both of these options are more easily set using Control Panel, as you saw earlier. If you experience problems printing or displaying complex TrueType fonts at larger point sizes, try adding OutlineThreshold=X to this section. Draw does not use this setting, but it *is* used by most Windows applications. The X default value is 256 and represents the number of pixels per em (about 60-point type on a 300 dpi device or VGA screen) below which you want Windows to use bitmaps to render TrueType fonts for your printer and screen. Type set at 60 points and larger uses a somewhat slower type outline filling method, utilizing curves rather than bitmaps, which can be more successful when handling large, complex characters. Windows assumes there are 72 points to an inch when working with type. In traditional typography, however, one inch equals 72.2752 points. This explains the use of "about 60-point type."

If you're experiencing problems, start with a value of 70, which is roughly 17-point type on a 300 dpi printer or VGA screen. In this case, all type set at 17 points or higher will use outlines to display and print your job, requiring less memory than bitmaps. Keep in mind that raising this value too high (Microsoft recommends not setting this value over 300) can cause degradation of the character outlines, while dropping it too low may cause a dramatic slowdown in printing. Save your changes to the WIN.INI file and restart Windows for the new settings to take effect.

Windows uses another section of your WIN.INI for managing TrueType. The [FontSubstitutes] section lists screen fonts (.FON) that were supported in version 3.0 of Windows but may not be installed on a version 3.1 system. An example is a document that specifies Times, which is not installed on your system. In this case the Times=Times New Roman entry tells Windows to automatically substitute the Times New Roman TrueType font. All the existing entries in this section were automatically created when you installed Windows 3.1. If you exchange documents with co-workers and your systems don't contain the same screen fonts, you can edit this section to control exactly which screen fonts (.FON) or printer fonts (.TTF) are used. But on the whole, this is a rarely used aspect of TrueType.

There is one final option you can set with the Control Panel if you're using an HP LaserJet-compatible printer. Double-click on the Printers icon, click on the Setup button and then on the Options button to display the Options dialog box. The Print TrueType As Graphics check box should be left unchecked if you're printing documents that normally contain only a few fonts and graphics. This tells Windows to render your fonts as bitmaps, which print significantly faster than outlines but require more printer memory. In my tests, a three-page Windows Write document took 20 seconds to print with this option not checked and two minutes to print when it was checked. This setting does not affect Draw, however.

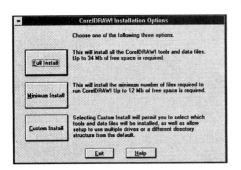

If your documents specify lots of graphics and fonts, or your printer is starved for memory, then turning this option on uses less printer memory, since font outlines are printed rather than bitmaps. You pay a performance penalty for this, but if it's the only way to output your job then you don't have much choice. You should experiment with this option using a variety of documents to determine when to turn it on.

TrueType Draw Font Installation

Draw provides a selective install in the form of Full, Minimum and Custom. You run the install program from the floppy disk or CD-ROM version of Draw using SETUP.EXE. I've provided an icon to let you subsequently rerun it easily from Program Manager. (See *Optimizing Windows* for details on installing it.) You can run Setup at any time to add additional Draw fonts to your system, but before you do this you should consider a number of factors.

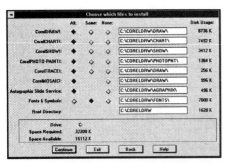

The floppy disk installation of Draw lets you install 155 hinted TrueType fonts, while the CD-ROM install provides access to another 101 fonts, for a total of 256. But do you really need this many fonts? And can you afford the hardware requirements for installing them? The

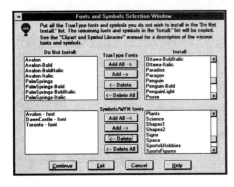

performance of all Windows applications (including Draw) will be dramatically slower with all of these fonts installed. You'll notice this when launching Windows or its applications, and when specifying fonts. If you select the Full install, all of these fonts are placed in your WINDOWS\SYSTEM directory and are automatically installed for all your Windows applications. If you select the Minimum install from the CD-ROM or floppies you'll wind up with 104 fonts.

If you already have ATM and its base 35 fonts installed on your system, there's no point to installing the 31 Draw equivalents. The BASE-35.TXT text file in the REGISTER.ZIP archive, included in the FONTS directory of the Utility disk, lists the 31 Draw fonts and four Windows TrueType fonts that should not be installed on your system if you've already installed PostScript versions of these 35 fonts. It also includes instructions for those of you who have already unknowingly installed these duplicate fonts. A far wiser procedure for installing Draw's TrueType fonts is to select the Custom install and use your clip art reference book or font chart to determine exactly which of the 155 or 256 fonts, 48 symbols, and three .WFN fonts you actually need. You can always install more fonts later by running Setup again.

If you are using the Draw CD-ROM, you can install any of the 256 TrueType fonts located in the FONTS\TTF directory and leave their .TTF files on your CD-ROM. Just make sure your CD-ROM is always turned on and the disc is inserted before you run Windows. This configuration saves almost 9 Mb of space on your hard drive, as the only new files installed on your system are the 256 .FOT files, which occupy about 330 Kb. While this saves space, there is a noticeable decrease in performance when you specify fonts in Draw using the Artistic Text or Paragraph Text dialog boxes. However, at print time there is no performance penalty, since these fonts are not downloaded to your printer. As discussed, these bitmaps print faster than curves but require more printer memory. Draw automatically *rasterizes* all your text at all sizes. (The process of rasterization, you'll recall, is a conversion from outline to bitmap.) This rasterizer is proprietary in nature, so none of your other Windows applications rasterize type in this manner.

Other applications may not fare as well as Draw when using TrueType fonts installed on a CD-ROM. For example, Windows Write will rasterize the specific characters you used from the .TTF font as bitmaps or outlines. It uses the Windows TrueType rasterizer to accomplish this. In this case you pay an initial performance penalty, based on the speed of your CD-ROM and your system. Since Windows uses the global memory pool to cache TrueType fonts, your second print job will be much faster with no performance penalty. Watch the access light on your CD-ROM to determine when your font is initially rasterized and when it's stored in the cache.

Editing Your CORELDRW.INI

Every time you run Draw, and on occasion during your session, it reads numerous settings in its CORELDRW.INI file (located in your COREL\DRAW subdirectory). For example, Draw's internal Font Manager examines your system to determine which fonts are available. First it looks at your installed TrueType fonts, then at your PostScript fonts and finally at your .WFN fonts.

If you have a TrueType and PostScript font installed with identical names, the PostScript font will be ignored. If you have a .WFN font with an identical TrueType or PostScript name, it too will be ignored. There are four areas of CORELDRW.INI that pertain to TrueType.

As discussed, if your Draw document specifies a large number of TrueType fonts, your job may not print. In this case, the fonts are sent to the printer as bitmaps. These require more memory than the usual font outlines, and can exceed the available memory of your printer. To fix this, open the CORELDRW.INI file in your DRAW directory with Notepad and find the FontRasterizer=1 line in the [CDrawConfig] section. This switch controls the rasterization of type for LaserJet-compatible printers — it has no effect on PostScript devices. However, it *does* affect the rasterizing of type for your screen display, regard-

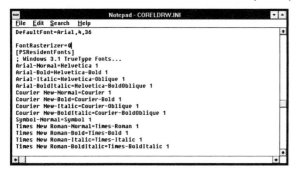

less of your output device. Setting this option to 0 will turn off Draw's rasterizer and slow down your screen redraw speed by about 500 percent.

Only change this switch with LaserJet printers when absolutely necessary. Setting the value to 0 instructs Draw to use the Windows PCL driver to rasterize type, rather than its own internal rasterizer. As a result, you'll find that text printed as a curve does not look as crisp as it does when printed as a bitmap. Even 20-point type looks thicker and less sharp. Examine the print samples reproduced here, which used Draw's TrueType Brooklyn, to see the difference. These were printed at 300 dpi with an HP LaserJet Series II.

6 Point ABCDEFGHIJK abcdefghijk

8 Point ABCDEFGHIJK abcdefghijk

10 Point ABCDEFGHIJK abcdefghijk

12 Point ABCDEFGHIJK abcdefghijk

14 Point ABCDEFGHIJK abcdefghijk

18 Point ABCDEFGHIJK abcdefghijk

20 Point ABCDEFGHIJK abcdefghijk

TrueType, Brooklyn, rasterizer off

6 Point ABCDEFGHIJK abcdefghijk

8 Point ABCDEFGHIJK abcdefghijk

10 Point ABCDEFGHIJK abcdefghijk

12 Point ABCDEFGHIJK abcdefghijk

14 Point ABCDEFGHIJK abcdefghijk

18 Point ABCDEFGHIJK abcdefghijk

20 Point ABCDEFGHIJK abcdefghijk

TrueType, Brooklyn, rasterizer on

You also pay a performance penalty in print time with the rasterizer turned off: your jobs will take about twice as long to print. A better solution might be to convert artistic text to curves and see if the job prints before you resort to turning off Draw's rasterizer.

On high resolution laser printers, you may find that text in sizes 10 points or below looks very grainy. The driver setup in Windows probably doesn't have a resolution setting that matches the printer. This causes Draw to think it's printing to a lower resolution (300 dpi) device. Find the line PSBitmapFontLimit=8 and change the 8 to 0 (zero). I find this makes a big improvement to my LaserMaster WinPrinter text when outputting at 800 dpi. This setting may also have to be changed if documents containing a lot of text set at small point sizes fail to output. Here the printer's memory is being used up by all the bitmap text being sent to it. Again, set the PSBitmapFontLimit= value lower or to 0 to disable it.

New text created with the Text g tool in Draw, or an imported text file, is automatically set at 24 points using the first available .WFN font, by default Avalon. If none is present, then the first TrueType font is used; on PostScript systems, the first PostScript font is used. You can change this by editing the DefaultFont= entry in the [CDrawConfig] section. To the right of the equal sign, enter the family name (sometimes called a 'menu name') exactly as it appears in your CORELDRW.INI, WIN.INI or ATM.INI file. The next entry is the style (1 for normal, 2 for bold, 4 for italic and 8 for bold-italic). The final entry is the point size, with a legal range of 0.7 to an undocumented 2160. No spaces are permitted, and each entry is separated by a comma. Contrary to Draw's online help, any one of the following are legal entries:

```
DefaultFont=Avalon,1,24
DefaultFont=Aardvark,2,72
DefaultFont=Michele,1,56
DefaultFont=Arial,4,36
DefaultFont=NewCenturySchlbk,2,48
```

The first three examples are all properly installed .WFN fonts. Their names appear in the [CorelDrwFonts] section to the left of the equal sign and must be entered exactly this way. The next example is a TrueType font, and this family name (not the weight) must be entered exactly as it appears in the [fonts] section of your WIN.INI. Remember, only the family name must be listed. The final entry is a PostScript font and this family name (not the weight) must be entered exactly as it appears in the [Fonts] section of your ATM.INI file, to the left of the equal sign.

As an example of where this might be useful, all the illustration captions in this book are set in 10-point Helvetica. By setting this as my default font, I could simply click with the 𝔸 tool and start typing, without having to reset the font each time.

The final edits to perform on your CORELDRW.INI file, from a TrueType perspective, are located in the [PSResidentFonts] section. At the end of this section you will see ; Windows 3.1 TrueType Fonts... and below this 13 TrueType font entries. These entries are Draw's attempt to override the Windows PostScript driver if TrueType and ATM are both turned on and you are printing to a PostScript device. Unfortunately, a problem occurs because of this. If you have told the PostScript driver to download Arial and not substitute Helvetica, this is what happens: in Draw you specify Arial and it displays properly, but when you print, the job uses Helvetica. In this case Draw has overridden the PostScript driver setting, but can't override the TrueType screen display. You probably won't like the results, so it's best to remove all these entries and use the PostScript driver's substitution table. I'll be discussing the substitution table at length in the PostScript section of this chapter.

Corel supplies additional documentation that refers to a TTFOptimization=1 entry in your CORELDRW.INI file. This entry was used with version 3.0 Revision A, in the event that TrueType support failed in Draw. Setting the 1 to 0 would sometimes fix this problem by handing back the rasterizing of TrueType fonts for your screen display to Windows. This switch is not functional with Revision B or later.

Changing Screen Fonts

Draw normally uses your MS Sans Serif .FON screen font for displaying the type in Draw's roll-ups, menus, rulers, Status Bar and other interface elements. It's listed in the [fonts] section of your WIN.INI and is located in your WINDOWS\SYSTEM subdirectory. Here are the entries from this section for a typical VGA system:

```
[fonts]
MS Sans Serif 8,10,12,14,18,24 (VGA res)=SSERIFE.FON
MS Serif 8,10,12,14,18,24 (VGA res)=SERIFE.FON
Aachen Bold (TrueType)=C:\DRAW\TTFONTS\AACHE1.FOT
Arial (TrueType)=ARIAL.FOT
```

If your Draw sessions display different fonts for your roll-ups, rulers and other screen elements, you can resolve this issue by understanding the order in which it selects font entries in this section of the WIN.INI file if SSERIF.FON is not present on your system. In this case, Draw uses SERIFE.FON, and if neither of these .FON files are present it uses the first TrueType font listed in this section. Unfortunately, other Windows applications may not follow this convention. If you wish to experiment with different fonts to suit your taste (or eyesight), run Notepad or SysEdit to open your WIN.INI file and insert a semicolon (;) in front of the entry, save your edit and re-start Windows and Draw. For example, here are the edited entries that would force Draw to use Aachen Bold:

```
[fonts]
;MS Sans Serif 8,10,12,14,18,24 (VGA res)=SSERIFE.FON
;MS Serif 8,10,12,14,18,24 (VGA res)=SERIFE.FON
Aachen Bold (TrueType)=C:\DRAW\TTFONTS\AACHE1.FOT
Arial (TrueType)=ARIAL.FOT
```

Kern Me and Space Me

Most of the TrueType fonts bundled with early copies of Draw 3.0 Rev B are without kerning pairs. This was caused by an anomaly in the conversion software. Some of these fonts behave strangely in other applications, with letter forms that are chopped off or a hollow rectangle displaying rather than the desired character. Call Corel to receive free replacement font disks, with new TrueType fonts that resolve these issues. The file date on these new fonts is August 16, 1992. Unfortunately, you will have to remove your old fonts and install the new ones with the Control Panel.

TrueType Service Bureau Output

If you send your jobs to a PostScript-based service bureau for output, you can still use TrueType fonts. If you don't have a PostScript printer, however, this procedure will require extra work, larger files and careful planning. In this example, let's say you are using a LaserJet-compatible printer and have finished a job that used Draw's Alto in TrueType format. You have proofed your work and are ready to prepare the file for your service bureau.

The easiest way to complete this step is to use a service bureau with Draw installed. In this case, you would simply give it your .CDR file and ensure it had the same TrueType fonts installed on its system. Unfortunately, finding service bureaus that can do this will prove very difficult. Their work is driven by PostScript fonts and the Macintosh platform, where TrueType has not enjoyed much success. Failing a stroke of luck, you must use the following procedure.

Install the most current Windows PostScript driver and the Linotronic L530 variant of this. While other imagesetters are supported by the driver, the L530 supports the largest selection of extra and user-defined media sizes. Open your Draw job and choose Print from the File menu. Click on the Print Setup button, change the current Specific Printer to Linotronic L530 and click on OK.

At this point ensure that the Print To File option is selected. Do *not* select the All Fonts Resident option. Draw will now convert the characters in any TrueType font you use to curves. Deliver the resulting .PRN file to your service bureau and you will have completed this procedure. You'll find that your print file will be about five times larger than if you had used ATM and PostScript fonts.

Another variation of the first procedure involves using a TrueType font that is listed in the [PSResidentFonts] section of your CORELDRW.INI file. In the previous example, Alto is not listed in this section. To get a better understanding of what Draw is doing here, open your CORELDRW.INI file with Notepad and scroll down to the [PSResidentFonts] section. This section lists 153 Draw fonts (TrueType and PostScript) and their Adobe PostScript equivalents to the right of the equal sign. The numbers (0, 1 or 3) after the names signify whether the font is resident in the printer (1 or 3) or not resident (0).

The purpose of this section is to provide a font substitution table. This job uses Draw's TrueType Brooklyn-Normal, which is listed in this section (Brooklyn-Normal=Bookman-Light 3). Because this TrueType font is listed in this section, your .PRN file will not contain curves; it will require your service bureau to have Bookman-Light and use this font for your output. Follow the same procedure discussed in the first example to create your .PRN file, except in this case it makes no difference whether you select the All Fonts Resident option in the print dialog box.

The reason for this is that Draw first looks at the target device, and since support for the base 35 fonts are built into the L530 driver, it always inserts a call for Bookman in the .PRN file. What Draw is doing is just ignoring your request for curves, because it sees that the font is supported by the L530 driver. The good news is that your .PRN file will be five times smaller than the Alto job.

You must determine if substituting the Adobe font Bookman-Light for your specified Draw Brooklyn-Normal font is satisfactory. Examine the screen shot, which shows Brooklyn sitting on top of Bookman. There is a very slight difference in the letter forms. Deliver your .PRN file to your service bureau and tell it that the job uses Adobe's Bookman-Light.

If your job specified Draw's TrueType Switzerland Condensed Black-Normal, which is also listed in the [PSResidentFonts] section as SwitzerlandCondBlack-Normal=Helvetica-Condensed-Black 0, follow exactly the same procedure you used with Brooklyn-Normal. However, here it *does* make a difference if the All Fonts Resident switch is turned on. In this case, if the switch is turned on the service bureau must have Helvetica-Condensed-Black. If the switch is not turned on then curves are created for the .PRN file.

The [PSResidentFonts] section also contains 13 Windows TrueType fonts (Arial, Courier New, Symbol and Times New Roman) along with their PostScript equivalents. These TrueType fonts don't look like their PostScript cousins, so remove all these entries.

Chances are you already have the base 13 fonts in Draw TrueType format installed on your system. Refer to BASE-

35.TXT in the REGISTER.ZIP archive on the bundled disks for the exact names. All of these names (Toronto-Normal=Times-Roman 1) are already listed in this section with their nearly identical PostScript equivalents. Other .TXT files in this archive provide the entries for all 256 Draw PostScript fonts, volumes 1 to 127 of the Adobe Type Library and the OptiFonts TrueType fonts supplied on the Fonts disk, should you convert them to PostScript.

TrueType Utilities

There are many useful freeware, shareware and commercial utilities available for managing your here, a number of which are included in the FONTS directory of the Utility disk. Others can be found on many online services, such as CompuServe. (For complete decompression and installation information, see *The Draw Companion Disks*.)

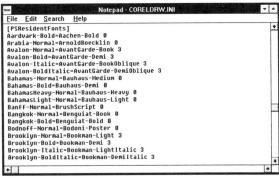

Fonter

This Visual BASIC Windows shareware application ($15 registration) from OsoSoft is included on the Utility disks. Fonter supports both

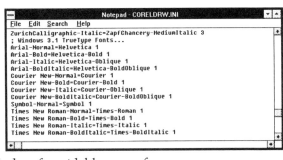

TrueType and PostScript fonts, and includes a formidable array of features. You can view fonts and print font lists, specimens, character sets and font books, as well as copy and paste characters from your installed fonts.

You can even run this application at the same time as FontMinder (covered later) to install and remove TrueType fonts with FontMinder and examine them with Fonter, without ever restarting Windows or closing down either application.

Use the Re-List Fonts command to have Fonter list your new fonts. You can view all the ANSI codes in a font, copy these characters to the Clipboard and paste them into Draw or another Windows application. This feature is very helpful for accessing characters mapped to 130 through 255. If your clients or co-workers are always asking you what fonts are available for jobs, you will appreciate the Print Font Books feature. Select your fonts and Fonter will automatically print a font list and then a sample for each font. Printing a font book for 100 TrueType or PostScript fonts can take hours, however, so it's best to schedule this activity at night or when you don't need your computer or printer.

ANSIPLUS.CDR

Included on the Utility disk is a version Draw 3 Rev B file that you can use to view and print the Windows 3.1 ANSI Plus character set. Re-specify the paragraph text in this file to determine exactly which characters are mapped to positions 130 through 159 in any font. You will discover that version 2.x .WFN fonts, version 3 .WFN fonts, Draw's bundled TrueType and PostScript fonts, and third-party fonts map these characters differently. Use your printout to determine exactly what numbers to enter with your specified font to produce a desired character.

TrueType Info

This clever shareware ($10 registration) Windows application is included on the Utility disk, and is written by Herb Chong of Shady Tree Software. This application permits you to determine the TrueType family name (menu name) and full name to resolve conflicts when either of these names is identical to a PostScript font or .WFN installed on your system. If either of these names conflicts, use RENAMETT (see below).

RENAMETT

This DOS application is freeware and can be downloaded from many bulletin boards, including the DTP Forum of CompuServe (GO DTPFORUM) in Data Library 6. Unfortunately, the creator of this utility won't permit authors to include it on disks bound into books such as this one, or I'd have provided it for you. RENAMETT permits you to change the name of any TrueType font and avoid missing fonts in Draw or other Windows applications. Remember that when installed PostScript, .WFN and TrueType fonts have exactly the same name, the TrueType font is available while the other formats are ignored. This can easily happen when using your old .WFN fonts in Draw. Or you might want to have available both the TrueType and PostScript versions of one of Draw's fonts. This is important enough that I'd like to provide two examples.

Let's say you install your .WFN font properly for use in Draw. You use it to create jobs and all is well. Later on, you create a TrueType font with the exact same name and install it. Both fonts may have the same name, but the letterforms are different. The next time you open the job that used the .WFN font, Draw will substitute the TrueType font, with probably undesirable results. On top of this, your .WFN font will no longer be available and Draw will issue no warning when the file using it is opened.

The second example involves a properly installed PostScript font that you've used in your Draw jobs. Some time later, you create a TrueType font with the same name as your PostScript font. When you open your job that used the PostScript font, Draw substitutes the TrueType font and skips the PostScript font. No warning is issued and Draw no longer lists your PostScript font. In this example, Windows will always use the TrueType font and drop the PostScript font.

To fix these problems, you will have to change the name of your TrueType font; this permits Draw and all your Windows applications to use both fonts. A TrueType font contains three *names*: the family name, font subfamily name and full name. You can use RENAMETT to examine an existing font to see what these names are. In the following exercise, I'm assuming that you have a copy of RENAMETT available.

Double-click on the MS-DOS icon in Program Manager to launch a DOS session. Move to your working directory that contains RENAMETT.EXE. You might want to keep this handy utility in the same directory as your TrueType fonts (WINDOWS\SYSTEM or COREL\TTFONTS). I suggest you begin by examining Windows' Times New Roman Italic, which is located in the WINDOWS\SYSTEM directory. At the DOS prompt, enter

'RENAMETT TIMESI.TTF' and press Return. In this case the font family name is Times New Roman, the font subfamily name is Italic, and the font full name is Times New Roman Italic. RENAMETT can change all three of these names, but it's only necessary to change the family name and full font name.

Say the TrueType font that had to be renamed was called Michele (MICHELE.TTF), which conflicted with a .WFN font also called Michele (MICHELE.WFN). Start by making a backup of the TrueType .TTF font file as a safety measure. It's unlikely that anything unexpected will happen, but backing up is a wise precaution. Next, at the DOS prompt, enter 'RENAMETT MICHELE.TTF RENNICKW.TTF', which specifies both the existing .TTF file name and the new name you wish to create, and press Return. This will run RENAMETT in interactive mode. Enter 'Rennick Wow' (spaces are allowed) and press Return when prompted to Enter New Font Family Name. The next prompt asks for the new subfamily name, which you don't want to change, so press Return. The final prompt asks for the full font name, so type 'Rennick Wow' and press Return to create your new .TTF file. If you get stuck you can enter RENAMETT /? for a screen of instructions or read the complete documentation included in the .ZIP file.

The final procedure is to launch the Control Panel and double-click on the Fonts icon. Remove your conflicting TrueType font (Michele) and then install your new .TTF font (Rennick Wow). The next time you open your Draw file, both your custom .WFN font (Michele) and your new TrueType font (Rennick Wow) will be available.

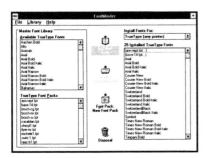

FontMinder

If Windows has turned to mush because you have 200 fonts installed, go directly to the coupon section of this book and order this essential Windows application. Written by Dennis Harrington, and published by Ares Software, this utility permits you to install and remove TrueType or PostScript fonts using 'font packs', with no need to use the Control Panel or edit your WIN.INI.

Font packs are collections of fonts that you create and name. FontMinder lets you keep only the fonts you actually *need* installed in Windows, and you can easily install other fonts present on your system any time you wish. This approach provides dramatically faster performance for all your Windows applications.

The FontMinder interface features an intuitive 'drag and drop' approach, as well as employing the seldom-used right mouse button. All your installed TrueType fonts are immediately recognized by Draw the next time you launch it in the same Windows session, and some applications (Write and Word for Windows) will even recognize your new fonts while the applications are running. Single-click on a TrueType font and you can display a sample or information on where it's located on your system. To install only the fonts you need for a project, just drag your custom font packs to the Installed TrueType Fonts list box.

To install individual fonts, click on the name in the Available TrueType Fonts list box, or Control-click on two or more and then drag them over to the Installed TrueType Fonts list box. Save your configuration and you are finished. If you accidentally install a font you don't need, just drag and drop it on top of the Disposal (trash can) icon. This program is very easy to use and should save you many hours, thanks to increased system performance and significantly faster font management.

PostScript Fonts

In this section I'll cover how to install, manage and fine tune the setup of your PostScript fonts. Earlier in this chapter I mentioned that support for PostScript fonts is not built into Windows. To use PostScript fonts with Draw, or any Windows application, you must first install Adobe Type Manager (ATM) version 2.0 or later, and then use this to install your fonts.

The information needed to manage PostScript fonts in Windows is contained in two text files. Use Notepad to open your WIN.INI file, located in your WINDOWS directory, and print it out. Do the same thing for your ATM.INI file, which is also located in your WINDOWS directory. Make a backup of both these files and keep the printouts handy as you read this chapter.

Windows makes use of two files to manage PostScript fonts. A small .PFM (printer font metrics) file contains the PostScript *printer font name*, which the printer looks for, and the PostScript *family name*, which is used in the type menus of Windows applications. It also contains kerning pair, weight and metrics information. The PostScript outline used by your printer is contained in a .PFB (printer font binary) file. The Draw fonts are also supplied with an .AFM (Adobe font metrics) file. This file contains kerning pairs, character mapping and PostScript font names. If you have a .PFM file for a font, you don't need the .AFM file to install or use the font with Windows. By default, ATM creates a C:\PSFONTS directory which contains all your installed .PFB files, and C:\PSFONTS\PFM which contains all your .PFM files.

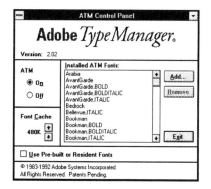

I'm assuming that you have already installed ATM 2.0 or later (Draw requires this for proper operation), using its default directory structure. If you're using an earlier version, you should update it before proceeding. Double-click on the ATM Control Panel icon (the red 'a') to run it now. The Font Cache setting in ATM's Control Panel may need to be adjusted to improve performance. ATM uses a *static* memory cache. In this case, the cache is a specific size and only uses the physical memory (RAM) installed on your system (not disk-based virtual memory). The memory allocated to this cache is reserved and may not be used by other Windows applications, even after you close down your document. This cache setting has no effect on Draw, since it uses its own font manager. However, applications such as PageMaker or QuarkXPress do use this cache every time you redraw the screen.

If your documents specify a large number of fonts, then raise this number in 50 Kb increments until you don't notice any improvement in screen redraw speed. Most publishing and graphics applications, including Draw, do not require the Use Pre-Built Or Resident Fonts setting enabled, so leave this option unchecked. This setting applies only to non-PostScript printers. Draw does not make use of this setting, but many Windows applications do. Pre-Built fonts are point-specific soft fonts that are automatically downloaded to your LaserJet if this option is turned on. Resident fonts are cartridge-based fonts or fonts built into your printer.

Advanced Type Topics

If this option is turned on, ATM will use these fonts for your print job, rather than creating bitmap fonts from the appropriate .PFB file. Your print jobs may be faster, but some problems may arise. If your application supports auto-kerning, such as PageMaker, the fonts printed with ATM will be kerned. But if you turn on the Use Pre-Built Or Resident Fonts option, these fonts will not be kerned.

Another potential problem is that your print job may not exactly match your screen display. Here ATM uses your .PFB and .PFM data to render your screen display, but your print job uses the Pre-Built or Resident Font. These fonts, alas, are not exactly the same. Fortunately, you can turn this option on and off to test the results without restarting Windows.

Every time you launch Windows, ATM reads your ATM.INI file and creates a special file called ATMFONTS.QLC, which is located in your C:\PSFONTS directory. Because ATM is not built into Windows and needs to create this file each time Windows runs, using the ATM Control Panel to add and remove fonts or change the font cache requires you to restart Windows.

If you accidentally turn off ATM none of your PostScript fonts will be available in Draw, and the only ones you'll be able to use will be properly installed TrueType or .WFN fonts. Once Draw's Font Manager has a list of your PostScript fonts, it uses this information to rasterize your fonts for the screen and printer. Draw's rasterizer is proprietary in nature and does not rely on ATM to perform these tasks.

Installing and Removing Fonts

In this exercise you will install the PostScript version of OptiFonts Bernhard Gothic Extra Heavy, which is in the FONTS directory of the Utility disk. If you have other PostScript fonts available, you could also use these — for example, those on the disk included with earlier editions of this book. You could convert a Draw font from TrueType to PostScript using a program such as Ares FontMonger. Or you could work with one of the many freeware or shareware PostScript fonts found on online information services like CompuServe. If you have a CD-

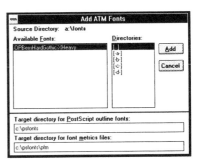

ROM drive, you could also install one of the 256 PostScript fonts on the CD included with Draw. But due to the way these have been created, they require a slightly different installation procedure, which I'll cover a bit later on.

Click on the Add button in the ATM Control Panel. In the Add ATM Fonts dialog box, click on the scroll arrow to display the end of the list of Directories. Make sure the Utility disk is properly inserted in your floppy drive and then double-click on [-a-] or [-b-] to access this disk. Double-click on the FONTS subdirectory name to move to this directory. You should see OPBERNHARDGOTHIC-XHeavy displayed in the Available Fonts list box. Single-click on this name to select it. If you are installing two or more fonts, you can Control-click on them. Once all the fonts to be installed are selected, ensure that the target directories for PostScript outline fonts and font metrics are accurate. On most systems, this will be \PSFONTS and \PSFONTS\PFM.

Click on the Add button and ATM will copy your font files (.PFM and .PFB) to the target directories and install the fonts on all of your active ports in WIN.INI. It also adds these fonts to the [Fonts] section of your ATM.INI file. Unfortunately, ATM always installs fonts to be downloaded automatically with documents. Later in this section, you will learn how to fix this. Once all your fonts are installed, click on the Exit button and the Restart Windows button so your new fonts will become available to all your Windows applications.

In this exercise you will install four weights of Draw's Timpani. I'm assuming that you selected these four fonts during the CD-ROM installation of Draw, which copied these fonts to your WINDOWS\SYSTEM subdirectory. Click on the Add button in the ATM Control Panel. In the Add ATM Fonts dialog box move to your WINDOWS\SYSTEM subdirectory. All four fonts will appear in the Available Fonts list. Ensure that the target directories for PostScript outline fonts and font metrics are accurate, as discussed above. Hold down the Control key and click on all four weights of Timpani. Click on the Add button to finish installing these fonts.

The final procedure involves some house-cleaning. Your four

fonts are still in your WINDOWS\SYSTEM directory. Run the Windows File Manager, locate the 12 Timpani .PFB, .PFM and .AFM files in the WINDOWS\SYSTEM directory, and delete them.

But what if you need a font from the CD-ROM that you didn't install with Draw? In the next exercise, you will install four weights of Draw's Euromode directly from your CD-ROM. Ensure that your CD-ROM is turned on and Draw's CD-ROM disk properly inserted. In the Add ATM Fonts dialog box, move to your CD-ROM and then to the \FONTS\ATM subdirectory. At this point you need to be patient, while ATM reads all 256 fonts in this subdirectory. Depending on the speed of your system and CD-ROM drive, this procedure could take three minutes or more. From this point on, the installation procedure is exactly the same as the OptiFonts Bernhard Gothic Extra Heavy exercise above.

To remove installed fonts, return to the ATM Control Panel and click on the font you wish to remove. You will use Draw's Bedrock in this exercise. Use Control-click to select two or more fonts and then click on the Remove button. Click on Yes when asked for confirmation, click on the Exit button, then restart Windows for your changes to take effect.

Unfortunately, this procedure does not remove the .PFB or .PFM files of the removed font from your hard disk, does not renumber your soft font entries in your WIN.INI, and sometimes forgets to remove the soft font entry for your deleted font. So the next time you launch Windows, your applications' type menus may still list the deleted font. If you accidentally specify this deleted font, ATM will render a jagged bitmap. That's your cue that something is wrong.

Since both the installation and removal of fonts often involves editing your WIN.INI, use Notepad to open this file (or construct a custom Notepad icon to quickly open it, as discussed in *Optimizing Windows*). Scroll down to the section that says [PostScript,LPT1]. Your system might have Com 1 or LPT2. If you frequently install or remove fonts you can move this section to the first line of your WIN.INI and reduce your scrolling. Study the screen shot and you will notice that the

```
                      Notepad - WIN.INI                    ▼ ▲
 File  Edit  Search  Help
[PostScript,LPT1]                                               ↑
feed1=1
feed15=1
orient=1
softfonts=22
softfont1=c:\psfonts\pfm\arabia.pfm,c:\psfonts\arabia.pfb
softfont6=c:\psfonts\pfm\eosb____.pfm,c:\psfonts\eosb____.pfb
softfont7=c:\psfonts\pfm\eosbi___.pfm,c:\psfonts\eosbi___.pfb
softfont8=c:\psfonts\pfm\gdi____.pfm,c:\psfonts\gdi____.pfb
softfont9=c:\psfonts\pfm\gdrg____.pfm,c:\psfonts\gdrg____.pfb
softfont10=c:\psfonts\pfm\gdsb____.pfm,c:\psfonts\gdsb____.pfb
softfont11=c:\psfonts\pfm\gdsbi___.pfm,c:\psfonts\gdsbi___.pfb

softfont13=c:\psfonts\pfm\cas_anti.pfm,c:\psfonts\cas_anti.pfb
softfont14=c:\psfonts\pfm\cas_antn.pfm,c:\psfonts\cas_antn.pfb
softfont15=c:\psfonts\pfm\casablcb.pfm,c:\psfonts\casablcb.pfb
softfont16=c:\psfonts\pfm\casablci.pfm,c:\psfonts\casablci.pfb
softfont17=c:\psfonts\pfm\casablcn.pfm,c:\psfonts\casablcn.pfb
softfont18=c:\psfonts\pfm\casablct.pfm,c:\psfonts\casablct.pfb
softfont19=c:\psfonts\pfm\timpanin.pfm,c:\psfonts\timpanin.pfb
softfont20=c:\psfonts\pfm\timpanib.pfm,c:\psfonts\timpanib.pfb
softfont21=c:\psfonts\pfm\timpanit.pfm,c:\psfonts\timpanit.pfb
softfont22=c:\psfonts\pfm\timpanii.pfm,c:\psfonts\timpanii.pfb
ATM=placeholder
◄ ▮                                                          ► ▼
```

softfonts=22 line does not match the number of installed fonts. Count the softfont entries and you will find just 18 fonts listed.

ATM only requires that the softfonts=22 entry be the same number as your softfont22 entry at the end of this section. If it's not, fonts won't appear on your type menus. This explains why it fails to renumber your entries, but it makes it difficult to determine how many fonts are actually installed. Note that the softfont12 entry still appears for the Bedrock font you removed (softfont12=c:\psfonts\pfm\bedrockn.pfm, c:\psfonts\bedrockn.pfb) and points to the .PFM and .PFB files still present on your hard disk. You can click and drag across this line to highlight it and press Delete to remove the entry. Then use the Windows File Manager to delete the font's .PFM and .PFB files.

Softfont19 through 22 point to the four Timpani fonts you installed from the CD-ROM. Let's say you want to permanently download these fonts to your printer and not download them every time they are used in a job. This procedure means faster print times and is a good practice for frequently used fonts. To do this, remove all the entries to the right of timpanin.pfm, starting with the comma. Do the same thing for the other three entries. If you have an imagesetter installed on your FILE: port for service bureau work, these same edits must also be performed in that section. Typically this section will say [PostScript,FILE]. If you install fonts that your service bureau does not have, then the .PFB entry must be listed for each softfont. If you use fonts that your service bureau already has, then only the .PFM entry is required in this section.

Removing the .PFB entry requires you to permanently download these fonts to your printer before you specify them in a job. Use WinPSX for this (covered later in this section). Make sure none of your standard 35 fonts (.PFM and .PFB) are listed in either section of your WIN.INI; earlier versions of ATM would accidentally install these fonts. These entries are built into the Windows PostScript driver for your local laser printer and imagesetter. Listing them in either section wastes memory and enlarges the size of your WIN.INI. (They still must be listed in your ATM.INI file to produce screen fonts.) Save your changes and restart Windows for your changes to take effect.

Resolving PostScript Font Problems

Your ATM.INI and WIN.INI files must contain *exactly* the same soft font entries. If they don't, a variety of problems can occur. One example is a properly listed font in your WIN.INI that does not appear in your ATM.INI. In this case, Draw does not warn you and will not display the missing font in the Text roll-up or the Style list box in the Artistic or Paragraph Text dialog boxes. PageMaker, on the other hand, permits you to specify and print the missing font. However, sometimes PageMaker will substitute another family member for screen display (italic for roman, for example), despite printing the font properly.

A second example is a properly listed font in your ATM.INI that is not listed in your WIN.INI. Let's call this problem a mismatch. Here, Draw will permit you to specify and print this font as long as the .PFM and .PFB files are located in the proper directory and you have registered the font in the [PSResidentFonts] section of your CORELDRW.INI file. This procedure is covered later in the section. The following entry from ATM.INI illustrates this unusual procedure:

CopperPot,BOLD =C:\PSFONTS\PFM\COPPRPOB.PFM, C:\PSFONTS\COPPRPOB.PFB.

Other Windows applications can behave differently. PageMaker, for example, permits you to specify the font but will substitute another member of the same family for screen display and printer output. As you can see, this issue is confusing, due to each application handling a mismatch differently. To resolve these problems, you must audit your ATM.INI and WIN.INI files. The best way to do this is to open both files with Notepad and use your printouts to audit each entry. All the entries starting with your drive letter (C) in the [Fonts] section of your ATM.INI must be *exactly* the same as the softfont entries in the [PostScript,LPT1] section of your WIN.INI starting with the same drive letter (C). When you find a missing font, copy and paste the entry between the two .INI files to correct the mismatch, or reinstall the font with ATM. Here is an example of a correctly installed font. The second WIN.INI entry is a legal one *only* if you edit your CORELDRW.INI file, as discussed in the section below.

ATM.INI entry: CopperPot,BOLD=c:\psfonts\pfm\copprpob.pfm, c:\psfonts\copprpob.pfb
WIN.INI entry: softfont16=c:\psfonts\pfm\copprpob.pfm,c:\psfonts\copprpob.pfb
or: c:\psfonts\pfm\copprpob.pfm

If you have installed your PostScript driver for an imagesetter, the [PostScript,FILE] section of your WIN.INI must also be edited to solve this mismatch. If you don't correct this section, your .PRN files may not specify or contain the correct fonts for your service bureau work. This is not a problem with Draw, however, which creates its own .PRN files independent of assigning a driver to FILE: with Control Panel.

TrueType Fonts with PostScript Printers

In the Overview section of this chapter, I stated that TrueType and PostScript fonts may be specified in the same document and printed to a PostScript printer. Later, I pointed out that if your system contains both a TrueType and PostScript font with identical family names the TrueType font will be available, while the PostScript font can't be used. There is no way to override this preference, since it's built into the Windows environment.

Before you create documents that contain both TrueType and PostScript fonts, some options should be set in the PostScript driver. (Draw does not use any of these options, but your other

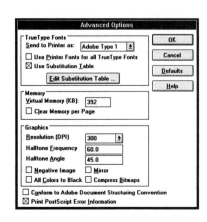

Windows applications do.) Run Control Panel from Program Manager and double-click on the Printers icon. With a PostScript driver selected, click on the Setup button, then the Options button and finally the Advanced button.

Unfortunately, the TrueType Fonts Send To Printer As list box setting does not work properly in Windows 3.1. When printing TrueType fonts to your local laser, for example, it makes no difference whether you set this option to Adobe Type 1 or Bitmap (Type 3). In either case, your TrueType font

is always rasterized at all point sizes (as opposed to being sent to
your printer as curves) and it looks crisp and identical. If you set
this option to Type 3, your print jobs will take 25 percent
longer, because the PostScript driver will now convert all the
characters in a font to bitmaps. If you set the option to Type 1,
the driver only converts the characters you actually used in
your document to bitmaps — a much faster approach.

If you are creating .PRN files using the FILE: port for your service
bureau or co-workers, this setting contains some additional surprises. In this case, setting the option to Type 1 will convert your
TrueType font to a Type 1 PostScript font containing only the
characters used in your document. The results at 300 dpi can look
thick and jagged when rendering type at body copy sizes. Setting
this option to Type 3 creates a bitmap font for every size of type you
specified using the entire character set. The resulting .PRN file, not
surprisingly, is significantly larger and will take longer to print. For
example, a Windows Write document that contained eight sizes of
Arial was a slim 34 Kb when Type 1 was selected and a gigantic 5.1
Mb when Type 3 was selected. If you are producing files for your
service bureau, set the option to Type 1. At 1,200 dpi or more your
type will look crisp and your job will run much faster. If you are
creating .PRN files for co-workers, convert your TrueType fonts
to PostScript using FontMonger (covered later in this section).

The Use Printer Fonts For All TrueType Fonts check box permits
you to automatically substitute all your printer-resident PostScript
fonts for any specified TrueType fonts. If this check box is selected,
specifying Arial will automatically use Helvetica, providing faster
print jobs. This setting is automatically recognized by most running applications (Write, for example), and all applications
launched after you enable it.

The Use Substitution Table option permits you to selectively
substitute a resident PostScript font
for a TrueType one, or to convert your
TrueType font to curves or bitmaps
and download it. Make sure its check
box is selected and then click on the
Edit Substitution Table button. Then
click on Arial in the For TrueType

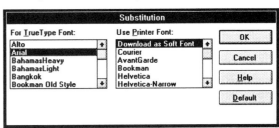

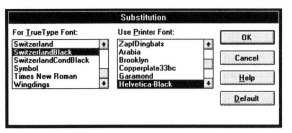

Font list box. All your installed PostScript fonts are displayed in the Use Printer Font list box. Notice that the default is Helvetica. If you leave it set this way, the resident PostScript font Helvetica will be used instead of Arial when you print. Your print jobs will be about twice as fast this way, but you might not like the results. Earlier in this chapter, I pointed out that none of the TrueType fonts are exact matches of their PostScript cousins, so your typographical taste and thirst for speed will dictate the use of this feature.

With Arial still selected in the For TrueType Font list, click, scroll up and click on Download As Soft Font in the Use Printer Font list box. This procedure instructs Windows and the PostScript driver to automatically rasterize Arial and download the bitmap to your PostScript printer. Remember, you get the same crisp results with either a Type 1 or Type 3 setting in the Send To Printer As list box for your local laser printer, but faster print jobs if Adobe Type 1 is used. Now click on Draw's Switzerland Black in the For TrueType Font list and then scroll down to Helvetica Black in the Use Printer Font list and click on the name. This tells the driver to substitute this PostScript font for your Draw TrueType font. Click on the OK button to finish this procedure.

In the Advanced Options dialog box, ensure that the Clear Memory Per Page check box is not selected. Draw does not use this setting, but your other applications do. This tells the PostScript driver to hold your specified fonts in memory until the job is finished, so printing is faster. If you create a job with such a large number of fonts that you exceed the memory capacity of your printer, you can turn this switch on and the driver will flush printer memory after each page. This may permit such a job to print. Printing is slower this way, so only enable this feature if you need it. To save this configuration to your WIN.INI file, click on OK four times and then on the Close button.

The [PSCRIPT] section of WIN.INI contains the names of the 13 bundled TrueType fonts and their PostScript equivalents. It also contains the names of the 22 TrueType fonts that Microsoft includes in its TrueType Font Pack, along with their PostScript equivalents. This matches the 35 fonts resident in most PostScript printers sold today. This section also lists any other TrueType fonts that you have chosen to substi-

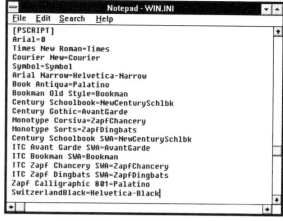

tute for a resident PostScript font. If you chose to download Arial as a soft font in the previous exercise, for example, the entry Arial=0 will appear in this section. If you decide to substitute Helvetica for Arial, then the entry will be Ariel=Helvetica.

Given the anomalies of the current Windows PostScript driver when using TrueType fonts, you may wish to stick to PostScript fonts, especially if you're sending files to service bureaus. The cost of FontMonger, using the coupon included with Draw, is $75 for the full version and only $25 for the limited version (covered later in this chapter). Use either version to convert all your TrueType fonts to PostScript format.

Draw and PostScript Fonts

The bundled 256 PostScript fonts that are supplied on the Draw CD-ROM are hinted Type 1 fonts compatible with ATM version 2.0 or later. The CD-ROM install copies these fonts and related files (.AFM, .PFM and .PFB) to your WINDOWS\SYSTEM directory but does not install them, as discussed above. An easier way to install these fonts is to deselect all the Type 1 fonts during the installation of Draw. After Draw is installed, use the ATM Control Panel to install the

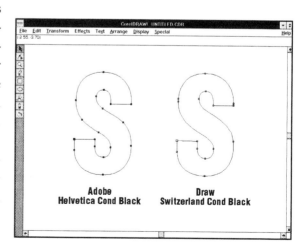

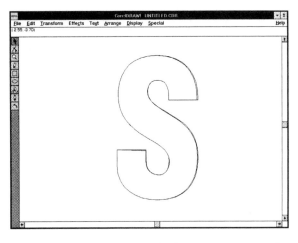

Draw fonts directly from your CD-ROM. This procedure eliminates deleting the duplicate Draw fonts from your WINDOWS\SYSTEM directory after they're installed.

Draw's Type 1 fonts are not exact copies of their "similar to" names, but for the most part are very close. Examine the screen shot from Draw shown here. In this example, Adobe's Helvetica Condensed Black is displayed next to Draw's Switzerland Condensed Black. As you can see, the number and position of the nodes on the letter S are not identical; the Adobe font has 18 nodes, while the Draw font has 16. The larger number of nodes in the Adobe font theoretically means better-looking output at 300 dpi, but in reality this small difference has little effect.

The respective letter forms of these two fonts are very close in appearance, as the illustration of two overlapped Adobe and Draw letters clearly shows. But there are structural differences beyond node placement. For example, an examination of the respective .PFM files using PFM Editor (covered later) shows that the Adobe version has 115 kerning pairs, while the Draw version has 155 pairs. So while the fonts are very similar, they differ in significant ways.

Editing Your CORELDRW.INI File

After your PostScript fonts are properly installed in Windows, actually using them in Draw for some tasks can require a non-standard, complicated procedure. Let's say you have installed the printer-resident Adobe PostScript Bookman font with the ATM Control Panel. You've checked to make sure that the respective .PFM and .PFB entries for Bookman do not appear in your WIN.INI file. This is the case because Bookman is ROM-resident in your PostScript printer and the Windows PostScript driver already contains the necessary .PFM data to use this font.

---

6 Point ABCDEFGHIJK abcdefghijk

8 Point ABCDEFGHIJK abcdefghijk

10 Point ABCDEFGHIJK abcdefghijk

12 Point ABCDEFGHIJK abcdefghijk

14 Point ABCDEFGHIJK abcdefghijk

18 Point ABCDEFGHIJK abcdefghijk

20 Point ABCDEFGHIJK abcdefghijk

Draw rasterized Bookman

6 Point ABCDEFGHIJK abcdefghijk

8 Point ABCDEFGHIJK abcdefghijk

10 Point ABCDEFGHIJK abcdefghijk

12 Point ABCDEFGHIJK abcdefghijk

14 Point ABCDEFGHIJK abcdefghijk

18 Point ABCDEFGHIJK abcdefghijk

20 Point ABCDEFGHIJK abcdefghijk

Draw rasterized disabled

6 Point ABCDEFGHIJK abcdefghijk

8 Point ABCDEFGHIJK abcdefghijk

10 Point ABCDEFGHIJK abcdefghijk

12 Point ABCDEFGHIJK abcdefghijk

14 Point ABCDEFGHIJK abcdefghijk

18 Point ABCDEFGHIJK abcdefghijk

20 Point ABCDEFGHIJK abcdefghijk

Resident Type 1 Bookman

You run Draw and create some 8-point Bookman type. Much to
your surprise, this type looks lumpy on the screen and many
letterforms are poorly rendered in your printout. If you look
closely at the bottom of each letterform in the first print sample
reproduced here you should be able to spot the problem. In this
case, Draw is using its own rasterizer to render Bookman. This

rasterizer sends artistic or paragraph text set under 18 points on a 300 dpi device to your printer as a bitmap. Text set at 18 points and above is not rasterized; this text is sent to your printer as curves.

Draw determines the resolution of your printer by examining the PostScript driver. In those cases where you are using a higher resolution device, the printer manufacturer typically supplies a .WPD (Windows Printer Description) file. This file is used by the PostScript driver and permits your jobs to print at the higher resolution.

In either case, Draw does not use your Type 1 Bookman outline or any entries in your WIN.INI. Even if you disable Draw's rasterizer by editing your CORELDRW.INI entry to read PSBitmapFontLimit=0 (more on this later), Draw will use curves to render your 8-point type, which won't look as good as when the hinted Type 1 Bookman font is used. Compare the print samples which used curves for all the type to the Type 1 outline. The curve-rendered text prints heavier and is not as crisp. If these results don't suit you (and they don't thrill *me*), then the second way to use PostScript fonts with Draw requires a significant amount of setup.

The key concept here is that all your PostScript fonts must be *registered* with Draw. Even the base 35 fonts found in most PostScript printers must be registered. So you must perform the following procedure to register any PostScript font, in this case Bookman.

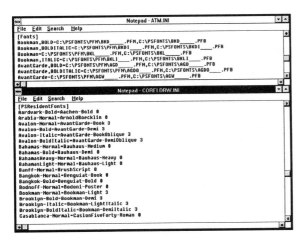

Open first your CORELDRW.INI and then your ATM.INI file by running Notepad twice from Program Manager. In the CORELDRW.INI file, scroll down to the [PSResidentFonts] section. In this section you'll register all your PostScript fonts. The syntax for all the entries in this section must be:FamilyNameweight=PrinterFontName #. The Family Name (menu name) does not include the weight. The weight must be expressed as Normal, Bold, Italic or BoldItalic. The PrinterFontName must be the actual name that your printer looks for (not the family name), and is often referred to as the printer font name. This name is usually different than the family name entry.

Thirty-one of the standard 35 PostScript fonts are already listed in this section, along with 122 other fonts that are supplied with Draw. These 153 listings use Draw's name (Brooklyn) for the family name and the Adobe name (Bookman-Light) for the printer font name. The existing entries in this section are a substitution table. In the TrueType section of this chapter I discussed this feature, and in the .WFN section I'll return to it. You will use parts of these entries to register your fonts. Later in this section I'll show you how to determine other PostScript font names from their respective .PFM files. The # value is a number (0, 1 or 3) with a space before it. A 0 indicates the font is temporarily resident in your printer, and 1 or 3 means it is permanently resident in your printer. No exceptions to these rules are permitted, and if any part of your entry is incorrect or missing your text will look lumpy, since Draw will rasterize your type and not use the resident font.

If you edit this section frequently, then move it to the beginning of your CORELDRW.INI file to reduce scrolling. Locate the line that says Brooklyn-Normal=Bookman-Light 3 and remove everything to the left of the first hyphen (-). At this point your entry will read -Normal=Bookman-Light 3. Alt-Tab to your ATM.INI file and locate the line that says Bookman= c:\psfonts\pfm\bkl____.pfm,c:\psfonts\bkl____.pfb. in the [Fonts] section. Click and drag to select Bookman (just the family name) and copy this name to the Clipboard. Alt-Tab back to your CORELDRW.INI file and paste this entry into the line in front of the hyphen (-) to finish this edit. This entry should read Bookman-Normal=Bookman-Light 3. Save your file and Alt-Tab back to Draw.

Re-run Draw and the next time you print your job it will use the Adobe Bookman font resident in your printer, with a corresponding increase in quality. Studying the print samples reproduced here, it's apparent that 8- and 10-point type look much crisper. Even 20-point type looks finer and lighter when using the Type 1 outline rather than curves. Consult the .TXT files in REGISTER.ZIP, included in the FONTS directory of the Util-

---

ity disk. These files list a variety of font entries that you can make to this section simply by cutting and pasting the entries into your CORELDRW.INI file.

You'll find that Courier does not appear in this section of CORELDRW.INI, so follow this procedure to register this font. Locate the Courier line in your ATM.INI file. In this exercise it reads:

Courier,BOLD=c:\psfonts\pfm\cob_____.pfm,c:\psfonts\cob_____.pfb

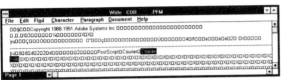

Alt-Tab back to your CORELDRW.INI file and start the entry on a new line by typing 'Courier-Bold=.' Notice that your ATM.INI points to the .PFM file. You will use the .PFM file to determine the proper printer font name. Open the Courier .PFM file in the PSFONTS\PFM subdirectory with Windows Write and click on the No Conversion button when prompted. Five lines from the top you will see an entry that reads PostScript Courier Courier-Bold. Every .PFM file follows the same syntax. Courier is the PostScript family name (Windows menu name). Courier-Bold is the actual name your printer looks for (printer font name). This is the name you want to use. Another way to remember this confusing issue of "names" is that a family name *may* contain spaces, as in Cantoria MT. A printer font name *never* contains spaces and is *never* more than 32 characters long, as in Cantoria-MTExtraBold.

Study the screen shot with the printer font name selected. Don't let the squares bother you — they represent spaces in this file. Click and drag across Courier-Bold and copy this entry to the Clipboard. Return to your CORELDRW.INI and click your cursor after the equal sign and paste in the entry. Press your Spacebar once and enter '3' to finish this procedure. Your entry should read: Courier-Bold=Courier-Bold 3. Follow this procedure for the other three members of this typeface family.

A more complicated procedure involves using fonts that you want downloaded to your printer which are not listed in the [PSResidentFonts] section. This procedure even applies to some of Draw's own fonts that aren't listed in this section. In this example, the WIN.INI and ATM. INI files list the two members of Draw's Scribe family. Your ATM.INI entries are:

```
Scribe=C:\PSFONTS\PFM\SCRIBEN.PFM,C:\PSFONTS\SCRIBEN.PFB
Scribe,BOLD=C:\PSFONTS\PFM\SCRIBEB.PFM,C:\PSFONTS\SCRIBEB.PFB
```

Most Windows applications — with the notable exception of Draw — will automatically download these fonts to your printer and then flush them from memory at the conclusion of the job. As described in the previous section, you can even tell the PostScript driver to flush fonts after every page to free up memory. Since Draw does not download PostScript fonts, some problems can occur here.

You must manually download these fonts to your printer, where they will consume memory until the printer is manually reset. (In the utilities section, I'll discuss a PostScript font downloader called WinPSX.) After you do this, a complex Draw job may not print because of a lack of memory in your printer. This later job may not even use any of the permanently downloaded fonts that still reside in the printer. Because of this problem, not only will you have to edit the [PSResidentFonts] section, but you may have to reset your printer to free up needed memory.

The first step is to copy the two Scribe entries from your ATM.INI file to the Clipboard. Open your CORELDRW.INI file and start a new line in the [PSResidentFonts] section, then paste your two entries into this section. Run Write and open SCRIBEN.PFM. Quickly select the printer font name, which is Scribe-Normal, by clicking in front of the first letter (S) and Shift-clicking after the last letter (l), and then copy this to the Clipboard.

Return to your CORELDRW.INI file and click your cursor to the left of the equal sign in the first entry. Type a hyphen and then the weight, which is Normal. Move your cursor to the right of the equal sign and paste the printer font name you copied from this font's .PFM file. Press your Spacebar once and enter a 0. Deciding whether to enter 3, 1 or 0 is a confusing affair, thanks to the unusual way Draw manages PostScript fonts. One or 3 in fact mean the same thing: the font is permanently resident in your printer, unless you're using a very early Apple LaserWriter, or a similar museum piece.

If you enter 0 and Draw's rasterizer is turned on (which it normally is), the following occurs: if you *do not* select All Fonts Resident in the Print Options dialog box, the job prints with clipped (partially formed) letterforms below 18 points on a 300 dpi printer. This is very noticeable at typical body text sizes of 6 to 10 points. Draw is rasterizing the font, and the results at small sizes don't look nearly as sharp or well-formed as the same job using the hinted font.

If you *do* select All Fonts Resident, the job uses your downloaded font, creating crisp text at any size. However, if you forgot to download the font, the job prints using Courier — just what you don't need.

In the heat of production it's easy to forget to check the All Fonts Resident box, download your fonts, or carefully examine your job to ensure the downloaded font is used. In this case you may wish to use 1 or 3, which always prints Courier if the font is not downloaded to your printer and always uses the downloaded font, regardless of the All Fonts Resident check box status. Follow the same procedure for the other font in the Scribe family. The two correct CORELDRW.INI entries for this typeface are:

```
Scribe-Normal=Scribe-Normal 0
Scribe-Bold=Scribe-Bold 0
```

Don't forget to save your editing changes. The next time you launch Draw you can specify this font and print using the hinted version. If any part of your entry in CORELDRW.INI is wrong, however, your job will either print in Courier or crash. While edits to the [PSResidentFonts] section are a pain, at least they are immediately recognized by Draw the next time you print. This means Draw can be running if you wish to change these entries.

If a Draw font is already listed in the [PSResidentFonts] section, and you are using this Draw PostScript font and not the Adobe equivalent, you can use parts of the entry to register your fonts. In this example the following entries already appear:

```
SwitzerlandBlack-Normal=Helvetica-Black 0
SwitzerlandBlack-Italic=Helvetica-BlackOblique 0
```

Use the same technique described above for the Scribe fonts to determine the printer font name. Open each SwitzerlandBlack .PFM with Write, then copy and paste the entry to the right of the equal sign. Remove the Adobe name and save your changes. Your new entries should read:

```
SwitzerlandBlack-Normal=SwitzerlandBlack-Normal 0
SwitzerlandBlack-Italic=SwitzerlandBlack-Italic 0
```

The REGISTER.ZIP archive contains 542 completed entries from Volumes 1 to 127 of the Adobe typeface library. It also contains 256 completed entries to register all the Draw PostScript fonts. I'd like to acknowledge Steve Shubitz's dedication to compiling this material for the user community. Thanks, Steve.

Still More Edits

If your jobs fail to print because you run out of printer memory, the following undocumented entry may help. Insert a new line in your [CDrawConfig] section that reads: PSBitmapFontSizeThreshold = XX where XX is a value between 75 (the default) and 1,000. This entry determines at what point size Draw will render text as bitmaps (rasterize it) or use curves, and is resolution-specific. This setting only affects text that meets the following criteria:

- The font is not registered in the [PSResidentFonts] section of your CORELDRW.INI.
- No scale or skew has been applied.
- No Envelopes have been applied to the text.
- The text object has a uniform fill.
- The Fit To page and Scale print options are disabled.

Draw determines the resolution from the driver for your default printer. The formula to compute this for your system is:

$$\frac{\text{PSBitmapFontSizeThreshold} \times 72}{\text{Resolution of selected device}}$$

An example is

$$\frac{75 \times 72}{300}$$

In this example, any text that is set smaller than 18 points at 300 dpi is rasterized. As you learned in the previous section, this procedure is faster but requires more printer memory. For a 600 dpi printer, text set under 9 points is rasterized. If you have installed the Lino 530 on your local port (LPT1:, for example) or FILE: port, and set the resolution to 1,270, the formula would be:

$$\frac{75 \times 72}{1270}$$

In this case, text set under 4.25 points is rasterized. If your job won't print and contains text set between 12 and 18 points, then lower the number. Your entry would be 'PSBitmapFontSizeThreshold=50', so all text set smaller than 12 points with a 300 dpi printer will be rasterized and all text above 12 points will be sent as curves. Depending on the amount of text, your job could take two or three times longer to print, but at least it prints. Experimentation may be necessary, and in some cases it's easier to convert some of the artistic text to curves rather than editing the CORELDRW.INI file and restarting Draw.

If your jobs use a large number of fonts, you can alter the PSBitmapFontLimit=8 entry. This entry controls the number of fonts (with a default of 8) that Draw will rasterize. If your printer runs out of memory and your job uses more than eight fonts, then lower this number till the job prints. In this case you could also convert your artistic text to curves to get your job out. If your printer has plenty of memory and your jobs use more than eight fonts you can raise the number, which provides faster printing.

You can also disable Draw's PostScript rasterizer by setting the entry to 'PSBitmapFontLimit=0'. This will force all non-resident typefaces to be rendered as curves, but body text won't look as crisp this way and print jobs will be slower. This setting has no effect on the rasterizing of type for your screen display. If you are using a 600 dpi printer, or the popular LaserMaster WinPrinter at 800 dpi, disabling Draw's rasterizer with 0 may produce better-looking text at small sizes. Experiment with your frequently used fonts to determine if this procedure works for you.

6 Point ABCDEFGHIJK abcdefghijk

8 Point ABCDEFGHIJK abcdefghijk

10 Point ABCDEFGHIJK abcdefghijk

12 Point ABCDEFGHIJK abcdefghijk

14 Point ABCDEFGHIJK abcdefghijk

18 Point ABCDEFGHIJK abcdefghijk

20 Point ABCDEFGHIJK abcdefghijk

Draw's PostScript Brooklyn, unregistered

6 Point ABCDEFGHIJK abcdefghijk

8 Point ABCDEFGHIJK abcdefghijk

10 Point ABCDEFGHIJK abcdefghijk

12 Point ABCDEFGHIJK abcdefghijk

14 Point ABCDEFGHIJK abcdefghijk

18 Point ABCDEFGHIJK abcdefghijk

20 Point ABCDEFGHIJK abcdefghijk

Adobe PostScript Bookman, registered

Draw's internal rasterizer for PostScript fonts is designed for speed, at the expense of output quality. Study the print samples reproduced here, which were produced with a QMS 810 PostScript printer at 300 dpi. The first sample uses Draw's Brooklyn in Type 1 format, set up as a non-resident (unregistered) font. The second print sample used the Adobe PostScript Type 1 outline with a registration entry of Brooklyn-Normal=Bookman-Light 3. This resident font looks much sharper at all sizes. Unfortunately, it took twice as long to print. The slower print time for the resident font is caused by a number of factors. The QMS 810 is a PostScript Level 1 printer, and this version of PostScript is not very efficient. The same can be said for the Windows PostScript driver. Finally, remember that the print sample was mostly composed of type set under 18 points. In this case, Draw's efficient rasterizer produced the majority of this job with point-specific bitmaps, which print much faster than PostScript outlines.

What can you learn from these print samples and performance figures? Given the fact that the most severe performance penalty is printing speed, leave Draw's rasterizer turned on for 300 dpi printers. Convert your TrueType fonts to PostScript and properly install them in your CORELDRW.INI file. If your printer should run out of memory, then convert as much text as necessary to get the job to print.

PostScript Service Bureau Output

Creating Draw jobs for your service bureau with a .PRN file is now more complicated than it was in previous versions. Draw never downloads your PostScript fonts, so they can't be imbedded in your .PRN file. In the utilities section I'll discuss FontPRN, which solves this problem. Start here by ensuring that all your PostScript fonts are properly installed (registered) in the [PSResidentFonts] section of your CORELDRW.INI file. In the first example you will use Scribe, so the entry is:

Scribe-Normal=Scribe-Normal 0

If you now create a job for your service bureau, the .PRN file will contain the printer font name (not the actual font bitmaps or curves) should you select the All Fonts Resident option in the Printer dialog box. So your service bureau must have this font downloaded to its imagesetter to properly output this job. Bring the appropriate .PFB file to your service bureau, along with your job, if it's a PC-based service bureau. If you *do not* select the All Fonts Resident option your .PRN file will be about four times larger, since it contains bitmaps or curves for your text and does not require the printer font. This file will also take longer to output. At 1,200 dpi and above there is little or no difference in the quality of your service bureau output between these two methods of creating .PRN files.

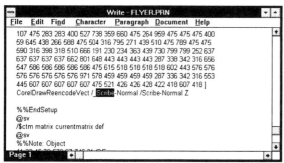

If the entry in the [PSResidentFonts] section is Scribe-Normal=Scribe-Normal 1 or 3 it makes no difference whether you select the All Fonts Resident option. In either case your .PRN files will always contain the

---

printer font name and require your service bureau to download this font to its imagesetter. In the heat of production it's often helpful to determine if your .PRN files are created properly. In this example, the .PRN file only contains the name of the printer font (Scribe-Normal). Create a .PRN file, open it with Write and click on the No Conversion button when prompted. Choose Find from the Find menu and enter Scribe, then click on the Find Next button. Study the screen shot reproduced here; notice that Scribe is highlighted, and its line reads:

```
CorelDrawReencodeVect / Scribe-Normal /Scribe-Normal Z
```

This is the entry which indicates that a printer font is required to properly output this file. If the .PRN file does not contain this reference to a printer font, but does contain bitmaps and/or curves, this entry would not appear. In this case you would see the following entry:

```
%%FONT / Scribe-Normal 333.00 z
```

You can use this same technique to audit the .PRN files created by your other applications. For example, if a PageMaker .PRN file contains your PostScript font you will find a section that starts with:

```
%%BeginResource: font SwitzerlandBlack-Normal
%!PS-AdobeFont-1.0%%CreationDate: Tue, Feb 18, 1992 12:38
```

If the .PRN file does not contain your PostScript font, and requires your service bureau to download it to its imagesetter, you will find the following entry two or three lines from the end of the .PRN file:

```
%%DocumentNeededResources: font SwitzerlandBlack-Normal
```

I Want a Transfer!

Moving documents between the Windows and Macintosh platforms remains a challenging proposition. In this section, you will focus on the typographical aspects of these procedures. Each platform has its own method for character encoding and font specification.

The problem is that PostScript fonts contain character encoding for a specific platform. The first 128 characters are the same on both platforms. These 128 character slots contain the stan-

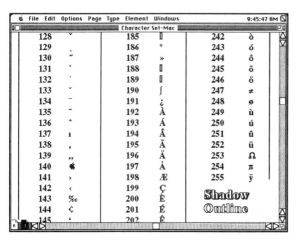

dard roman alphabet, numerals and simple punctuation. The problem lies in the encoding from 130 to 255. Each platform treats some of these character slots differently.

Examine the two screen shots and notice the difference in how some characters are arranged in their respective slots. The majority of applications on both platforms use the menu name (family name) when specifying fonts, which is different on each platform. An example is the Windows menu name FrGothHeavy and the Macintosh name H Franklin Gothic Heavy. This difference can produce font substitution problems when documents are transferred.

The vast majority of applications do not use the printer font name (AGaramond-Regular), which is identical on both platforms. At the application level, all the major multi-platform applications (PageMaker, QuarkXPress, FreeHand and Adobe Illustrator) have problems in properly transferring documents. These screen shots were taken from PageMaker 4.0 under Windows and 4.2 on the Macintosh. PageMaker is unusual in that it contains an internal data base, or *lookup table* , for 31 resident PostScript fonts. This lookup table translates names (menu names) to prevent font substitution.

Given the fact that there are thousands of PostScript fonts available for both platforms, it's not unusual to experience font substitution when documents move between platforms. Another area to be aware of is that of type effects. Notice that the Macintosh version of PageMaker is capable of producing shadow and outline type, which is not supported in the Windows version.

With this in mind, you have a number of solutions and work-arounds available. If you are using a service bureau that has

Macintoshes driving its imagesetters, provide it with a Windows
.PRN file to avoid character and font substitution problems. If you
must transport application files (PageMaker's .PM4 files, for
example) across platforms to co-workers or service bureaus, check
the application's type menu to determine the available fonts after
the document is transferred. If font substitution occurs under
Windows, you will see something like ?Galliard on the menu in
PageMaker. If font substitution occurs on the Macintosh, the
menu name will be grayed out.

To resolve this issue, and handle some of those pesky characters
that change in character slots 130 to 255, use the search and replace
feature available in some applications before the job is printed.
Unfortunately, not all the major multi-platform applications have
this feature. FreeHand is a perfect example. In this case you have to
develop your own list of characters that change when the document moves across platforms, such as the Windows Bullet (149).
Once your list is completed you must edit the text and replace the
character with the proper one (Option-8) on the Macintosh. In all
cases you should try out some test files and record your most
frequently used characters and fonts. With this data, you can
develop standards and rules that apply to your specific jobs.

The Macintosh version of Draw was not yet available when this
book was written, so I can't comment on how well Draw files can
be moved between platforms. But it's likely that much of the
material I've discussed here will be applicable.

PostScript Utilities

There are many useful freeware,
shareware and commercial utilities
available for managing your PostScript
fonts. I'll discuss some here, a number
of which are included in the FONTS
directory of the Utility disk. (For decompression and installation information, see *The Draw Companion Disks*.)

Fontographer 3.5

Since 1988, Macintosh typographers
have used this professional-level tool

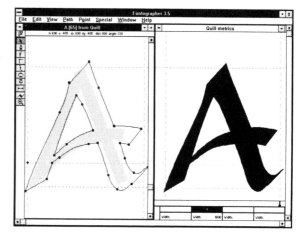

to create and modify typefaces. If you read *Business Week*, *The Washington Post* or *Rolling Stone*, you have already seen some examples of its handiwork. After two years of development, Altsys recently delivered Fontographer for Windows. The Windows incarnation has the same features as the Macintosh version, plus drag and drop using Object Linking and Embedding, as well as support for .BMP format graphics.

With Fontographer you can create hinted PostScript Type 1 or TrueType fonts for either platform. It provides a rich set of drawing features, including a pen, tangent point, corner point, curve point and freehand drawing tool. The freehand tool features a calligraphic pen and pressure-sensitive mode for use with drawing tablets, such as that from Wacom. You can autotrace your scans of a letterform, or use them as a template to revive the thousands of fonts that are not available in digital format. When it comes to production and precise control, Fontographer includes eight levels of undo, scale, rotate, skew, overlapping path merge, interpolation between two existing typefaces and the creation of kerning pairs.

The screen shot provides a taste of what can be done with Fontographer. In this case the letter A was created in Draw using Scribe and set at 70 points. This character was exported as a 72 dpi black-and-white .BMP bitmap graphic and imported into Fontographer to serve as a rough template. I then used the calligraphic pen tool to create a new letterform. As sometimes happens in the creative process, the end result bears little resemblance to the original typeface. Like all professional-level tools, Fontographer won't make you an overnight typographer — mastering this craft requires creativity and dedication. But Fontographer *will* provide you with the necessary tools to create great-looking typefaces, which you can use with Draw and all your Windows applications.

FontMonger

The limited version of this application is discussed in the .WFN fonts section of this chapter. The full version is just $75, using the discount coupon supplied with Draw. Don't let this low price fool you; FontMonger converts fonts in any direction between PostScript (Windows and Macintosh) and TrueType (Windows and Macintosh). It also converts Draw's .WFN fonts and Agfa Intellifonts to the other formats. PostScript Type 1 and TrueType fonts are hinted and look very crisp. A rich set of drawing tools includes pen, scissors and a combination tool called a gizmo. This single tool permits you to slant, rotate, skew and merge outlines. Also valuable is its ability to import art created in Draw and exported in .AI or .EPS format, and add it to existing fonts.

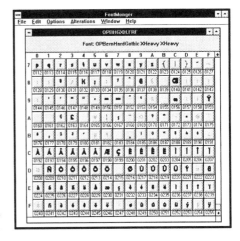

Most PostScript and TrueType fonts do not include fractions. Sure, you can create a 'pseudo' fraction in Draw or PageMaker, but it always requires time-consuming extra work. However, creating fractions for your typefaces in FontMonger is quite easy. In this exercise, you will be working with the CastCraft OptiFonts OPBernHardGothic-XHeavy font, which is on the Utility disk included with this book. Run the full version of FontMonger and open OPBernHardGothic-XHeavy from the FONTS directory of the Utility disk. Ensure that the Character Chart is displayed.

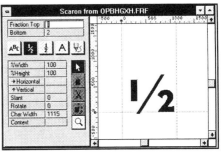

Study the screen shot that shows the Character Chart. It's not unusual to find empty character slots, and *mapping* (character placement) that doesn't strictly adhere to the ANSI Plus character set. Included on your bundled disks is ANSIPLUS.CDR, in the ANSIPLUS.ZIP archive, which you can use to determine exactly which characters in a font are mapped to positions 130 to 159. For example, slot 138 is empty. This slot would normally contain the Š character, but it's a perfect place for a fraction. Double-click on this slot to open the Alter Character window and then click once on the Diagonal Fraction button, to have FontMonger automatically assign the ½ fraction to this slot. Additional fractions only require edits to the Fraction Top and Bottom fields. Double-click on the Control menu bar in the top-left corner to finish this procedure.

The final modification to this font is to change the name that appears in Draw's font list boxes and all the type menus of your Windows applications. This name (the menu name) is always the family name of a given typeface. Since you can use keyboard shortcuts to navigate to your desired font, these Windows menu names should be as descriptive as possible, rather than referring to a vendor. For example, the OptiFonts fonts supplied with this book begin with O or OP. Draw displays the first 19 characters of a menu name, while other Windows applications typically display from 15 to 25 characters. PageMaker's Type Specifications list box displays 24 characters.

Use FontMonger's Set Font Information dialog box to change the family name (menu name) to BernhardGothic-XH-O. This modification permits you to press B (for Bernhard) to jump to this font in Draw, which is much faster and easier to remember. The O at the end reminds you that it's an OptiFonts font. Use the Build Font option to complete your new typeface. Your new PostScript Type 1 font is finished and ready to be installed in Windows. FontMonger is easy to use and powerful. I believe it will prove invaluable to most Draw users.

FontMinder

I discussed this application earlier in the TrueType section. But because FontMinder is such a significant tool for increasing productivity, and many use both TrueType and PostScript fonts in their Draw jobs or other Windows applications, it bears additional discussion here from a PostScript perspective.

If Windows has turned to mush because you have 200 PostScript

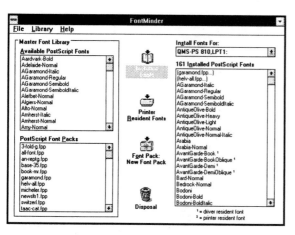

or TrueType fonts installed, then go directly to the coupon section at the back of the book and order this marvelous Windows application. Written by Dennis Harrington and published by Ares Software, this utility permits you to install and remove TrueType or PostScript fonts using font packs and never use the ATM Control Panel or edit your WIN.INI again. You only keep the fonts you need installed in Windows and can easily install other fonts present on your hard disk anytime you wish. You'll find that Windows runs dramatically faster with 50 fonts installed, versus 200.

Font packs are collections of fonts that you define by project, such as NEWSLTR1.FPT, or by typeface, such as SWITZERL.FPT. The interface features a drag and drop procedure, as well as the seldom-used right mouse button. Click on a PostScript font and you can display information on where it's located on your system, the font name (printer font name) used by your printer and the family name (menu name) used on your type menus. FontMinder lets you manage fonts on your local port (LPT1:, COM1:, etc.) or your FILE: port (for service bureau work with applications other than Draw).

The Print Library Font List feature is a valuable tool for Draw users. This printout lists the family name and the font name for every PostScript font on your hard disk. You can use it to verify the accuracy of your entries in the [PSResidentFonts] section of your CORELDRW.INI file. If you have not registered your fonts with Draw, you can use Print Library Font List to save yourself some editing. Run Control Panel from Program Manager and double-click on the Printers icon. Then install the Generic/ Text Only printer on your FILE: port. Run FontMinder and print your Library Font List to your FILE: port, which has the Generic/ Text Only printer installed.

This procedure creates a text file, which you can open with Notepad and copy your entries to the Clipboard. Study the screen shot and notice that FontMinder lists the family name 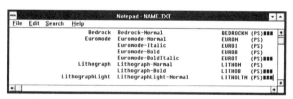 (menu name) in the first column and all the printer font names for each member of the family in the second column. Paste these entries into your CORELDRW.INI file and edit them as required.

FontMinder can manage up to 2,000 fonts, which should satisfy nearly every font fanatic. To install only the fonts you need for a project, drag your custom font packs to the Installed PostScript Fonts list box. To install individual fonts, just click on the name in the Available PostScript Fonts list box, or Control-click on two or more and then drag them over. If you accidentally install a font

---

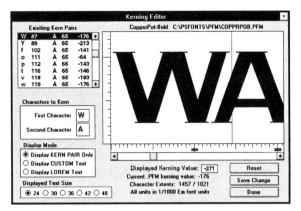

you don't need, just drag and drop it on top of the Disposal icon. FontMinder is a 'must have' tool for Draw users.

PFM Editor

This clever Visual BASIC Windows application is included in the FONTS directory of the Utility disk. It's written by the prolific Dennis Harrington and distributed as freeware. You can use this application to create your own kerning pairs for any Type 1 PostScript font that's compatible with ATM.

Kerning is the adjustment of space between specific letterforms, like the WA pair in the illustration. Each kerning pair is stored in your .PFM file and used by Draw or any Windows application that supports kerning. All your jobs use the same set of kerning pairs, whether the document is output at 300 or 1,200 dpi. Most kerning is performed on headline type, although many purists also kern body copy and some even kern for a specific resolution. Since type looks lighter at 1,200 than 300 dpi, your pairs will indeed produce a slightly different look. Creating proper kerning requires experience and lots of testing. Real aficionados of type often manually kern specific characters in a headline, rather than relying on the existing kerning pairs from the font's .PFM file. Draw and most major publishing applications support this feature.

Despite the importance of kerning, the average PostScript font contains only 200 pairs in its .PFM file. Included on the bundled disks is CastCraft's OptiFont OPBernHardGothic-XHeavy, which contains a more generous 358 kerning pairs. Some of the smaller type foundries may include up to 3,000 pairs. Most of Draw's PostScript fonts have about 300 kerning pairs but some, such as Arabia, have none.

Run PFM Editor and click on the Kerning menu. In the Available ATM Fonts list double-click on the font you'd like to kern. Notice the Existing Kern Pairs list box displaying the kerning pairs that have already been defined. You want to adjust the kerning of the WA pair, so enter 'W' in the Characters To Kern box and press the

---

Tab key to move to the Second Character box. Enter 'A' in this box and your kerning pair will appear in the kerning window. Although this pair has already been kerned, it's still a little loose for satisfying headline text.

Click on the left horizontal scroll arrow to begin the kerning procedure. Every time you click on this arrow the value is shown in the Displayed Kerning Value box and your pair is kerned more tightly. If you accidentally kern the pair too much, then click on the Reset button or right scroll arrow. Once the pair is kerned to your satisfaction, click on the Save Change button and OK in the Modify Kerning dialog box. When you have completed all your kerning pairs, click on the Done button and then the OK button in the Save All Changes dialog box. You've created a new .PFM for your font and a backup file with the extension .MBK. If you ever need to revert back to your original .PFM, then copy the .MBK file over the modified .PFM. You must restart Windows to use your new kerning pairs.

If you want to create kern pair data for an .AFM (Adobe font metrics) file, click on the Yes button when prompted in the Create Kern Pair Data For .AFM dialog box. AFM files are not used by Windows, but GEM Ventura Publisher and some DOS applications, such as Word, require them. If you click on Yes, an ASCII file is created with a .KPX extension. This file contains all your existing pairs and any new ones you created for use in applications that require an .AFM file.

Examine the screen shot displaying WAVE after kerning all the pairs in the word, which is set in Draw's CopperPot Bold. The word is now much more dramatic. Draw uses your kerning pairs at any size of specified Paragraph or Artistic text. Included in the bundled disks is KERN.ZIP. This archive contains a text file that lists 500 kerning pairs. Use a printout of this file as a model for your new pairs. Consult PFM Edit's help file for additional feature information.

Pi fonts, such as ZapfDingbats, contain pictures or symbols. PFM Editor permits you to use your properly installed PostScript pi fonts as symbols in Draw. This undocumented behavior is caused by an anomaly in Draw's Font Manager. Open the .PFM for ZapfDingbats (Z_.PFM) with the Properties menu. Change the character set from ANSI to Symbol by clicking on this button. Notice that the family is already set to Decorative. Most of your pi fonts are set this way. However, Draw's PostScript Dixieland and Geographic are incorrectly set to Don't Care. Change this to Decorative if you wish to use these as symbol fonts and the .WFN is not installed on your system. Click on the Save Changes button and restart Windows.

The next time you open the Symbols dialog box in Draw, you can view and use all the characters in ZapfDingbats. No editing is required in your CORELDRW.INI file and you don't have to convert these fonts to the .WFN format used by the other symbols. You can still use this font in your other Windows applications, just as you did before this procedure. This trick only works for those fonts that are really pi fonts and have the family style set to Decorative. Other examples of pi fonts are Wingdings converted to PostScript format, or the popular shareware font called Bill's Dingbats.

WinPSX

This freeware Windows application, written by Costas Kitsos, is included on the Utility disk. Every PostScript publisher

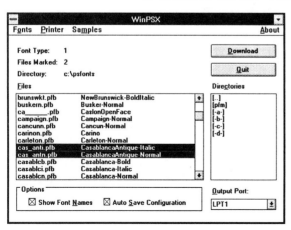

should make use of this application to solve the serious limitations of the Windows PostScript driver and tame Draw's non-standard PostScript font handling. Once it's decompressed and installed, double-click on the WinPSX icon and move to the directory on your system where your .PFB files are stored. Make sure the Show Font Names and Auto Save Configuration check boxes in the Options area are enabled.

All your sorted .PFB file names and the corresponding PostScript printer font names are displayed in the Files list box. Select the Print Files ListBox option from the Printer menu. This printout can be used to eliminate unnecessary fonts that still reside on your hard disk, and also aid the installation of fonts in your CORELDRW.INI file. Locate the printout of your ATM.INI file that you created earlier and compare the font names listed in the [Fonts] section with the font names listed in your WinPSX print-out. If you find a font name listed in the WinPSX printout that does not appear in your ATM.INI, you can safely delete the .PFB and .PFM files from their respective directories.

However, if a softfont entry in your WIN.INI specifies a font that must be manually downloaded to your printer, follow this proce-dure. Locate the name of your font in the Files list box by scrolling down or press the first letter of the PostScript name to jump to that section in the list. Click on the font names you wish to download. Once all your fonts are selected, click on the Download button and a Sending status bar will appear while the fonts are downloaded to your printer. All downloading is accomplished as a background task, so you can continue working with other applications while your fonts are being downloaded. Of course, you can't use them until the download procedure is completed.

It's often helpful to know which fonts have been downloaded to your printer before you send a job. Choose Device Info from the Printer menu and WinPSX will produce a printout that lists all your ROM-resident and downloaded PostScript fonts in the Available Fonts section. This printout also tells you how much available memory is left for your jobs or fonts, as well as a page count.

You can use WinPSX to batch download fonts for specific jobs using the Job List feature. You'll have to run Notepad and type in a few lines of material, using exactly the following syntax. The first line to enter is your output port, so the entry is 'Port=LPT1' (without a colon). On your system it might be LPT2 or COM1. Press Enter and type in the path to the first font (.PFB) you wish to download. In this exercise all your .PFBs are assumed to be in the default C:\PSFONTS directory, so your first entry is 'C:\PSFONTS\SCRIBEB.PFB'. Then press Enter. On separate lines enter the path and .PFB names for each additional font you wish to download in this Job List. Use your Font Listing printout to determine the correct file names, or you can open ATM.INI and copy and paste the path for each .PFB. Note that the Windows convention of inserting a comment with a leading semicolon (;) is not permitted in this file.

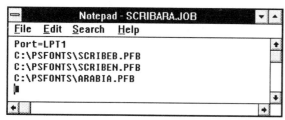

The Notepad window illustrated here is specifying three fonts from Draw's PostScript collection. You may specify up to 25 fonts in each Job List. When you've finished entering your fonts, save the file with a .JOB extension. Your file name can describe the fonts in the Job List (SCRIBE.JOB), or you can name the file by task (NEWS-LTR.JOB). You can store these Job List files in any directory on your system, but it's simpler if you keep them in the same directory as your .PFB files.

Close Notepad, return to WinPSX and select Job List from the Fonts menu. The Files list box now displays all your Job Lists, which must have an extension of .JOB. Click on each Job you want to download (to deselect a file, click on it again). Click on the Download button and the Job dialog box will appear for each selected Job List. Click on the Print Device Info Following Download check box and then click on the Download button. WinPSX will display a status bar as it automatically downloads each of your fonts and will then print the Device Information page. You can abort this downloading procedure by pressing your Escape key or clicking on the Cancel button.

You can also automate downloading Job Lists from Program Manager. One way to make use of this handy feature is to run the Windows File Manager. Move to your PSFONTS directory and click once on a .JOB file to select it. Choose Associate from the File menu. In the Associate dialog box, click on the Browse button and move to the directory on your system that contains WINPSX.EXE. Double-click on this file and click on OK to finish this procedure. Press Control-Escape to display the Task List and click on Tile to display File Manager and Program Manager side by side. To install this Job file in Program

Manager, click and drag it from File Manager and drop it in your Corel Graphics group to generate an icon. The next time you want to use this Job List, double-click on its icon and you'll go directly to the Job dialog box. If you drag the icon into your StartUp group, you automatically launch WinPSX and go directly to the Job dialog box when Windows loads. WinPSX automatically closes down at the end of this procedure. Consult the well-written help file for additional features.

While few users are aware of it, Adobe Systems includes a Windows font downloader with its typefaces, which provides many of the features of WinPSX. Two unique features of this application are its ability to format a hard disk connected to your printer and to download a PostScript .PRN file. Downloading your .PRN files from Windows eliminates the need to open a DOS session and use the 'COPY FILENAME.PRN LPT1' command.

I wish I had room to include every utility that I find useful on the Utility disk bound into this book. One that didn't quite make it is Dumper, a shareware Windows program that simply *dumps* (downloads) a PostScript .PRN file to your printer. Unlike the Adobe utility discussed above, Dumper lets you multitask with your other Windows applications while it performs its magic. Additionally, you can drag and drop a job, cue it, suspend and cancel it. You'll find its archive on bulletin boards as DUMP31.ZIP.

FontPRN

This Visual BASIC Windows utility, by the prolific Costas Kitsos, is included on the bundled disks. A freeware application, it was written especially for this book. It permits you to embed your PostScript fonts in a .PRN file for your service bureau or co-workers. Since Draw does not download fonts, this application will prove very handy for service bureau work. Start by creating your .PRN file in Draw, writing down the name of all the fonts you used. Then run WinPSX (covered above), click on the down arrow in the Output Port list box and select FILE. Click on the fonts you used in the Files dialog box and then

download them to your FILE port. This procedure creates a .PSX file in your C:\PSFONTS directory for each downloaded font. Each file contains a downloaded font and has the same eight-character name as your .PFB file, but with a .PSX extension.

Run FontPRN and choose Select PRN from the File menu. Move to your working directory and select your .PRN file. Then choose Select PSX from the File menu. In the Select PSX dialog box, double-click on each .PSX you want to include in your .PRN file. If you accidentally insert one you don't want, just double-click on the name in the Selection list to remove it. Click OK when all your

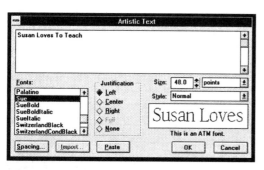

.PSX files are selected. The final procedure is to choose Create PRN from the File menu. In the Output PRN dialog box enter your path and a new file name, and click on OK. This .PRN contains your Draw job and all the specified fonts., ready for output.

wPFMfix

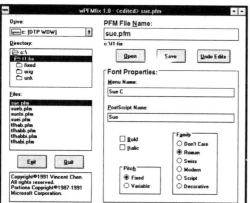

This handy Windows Visual BASIC shareware application written by Vincent Chen ($5 registration) is included on the Utility disk. Some font converters do not properly name fonts, so they all appear in the same family. This results in four entries in all your Windows font menus, rather than one. wPFMfix lets you group four fonts in a single menu name (family name). Some font converters also fail to properly set the bold and italics attributes in a .PFM file, which also results in unnecessary font entries.

In the example shown here, all four fonts in the Sue family appear on Draw's font list. To correct this, you'd begin by copying the four .PFM and four .PFB files for this font to your working directory. Launch wPFMfix and move to your working directory. Double-click on your font name (in this case SUE.PFM) in the Files

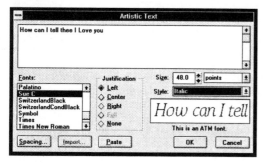

list box. The menu name in the Font Properties section must be exactly the same for all four fonts. This is the name that will appear in all your Windows applications. The PostScript name (printer name) does not need to be changed. If you do ever change this name, you will also have to change the name in the .PFB file to match it exactly. Change the menu name from Sue to Sue C (spaces are fine, but a parenthesis is an illegal character). The C signifies a custom font that must be delivered to your service bureau or embedded in your .PRN file. The Bold and Italic attribute check boxes are not checked, which is correct. Click on the Save button to complete this procedure.

Double-click on SUEB.PFM. Notice that there are two things wrong with this .PFM: the menu name reads SueBold and the Bold attribute is not set. Change the menu name to Sue C and click on the Bold attribute check box and then the Save button. You still need to fix the bold-italic and italic .PFM files. Open each one and change the menu name to Sue C and select the Bold and Italic attributes for the bold-italic .PFM and the Italic attribute for the italic .PFM. Don't forget to click on the Save button after each edit. Run the ATM Control Panel and remove your four incorrect Sue fonts. Then use ATM to install your new .PFM files. This procedure overwrites your old .PFMs and completes the process. Restart Windows and notice that the only Font menu entry you have in Draw is Sue C, which contains all four weights.

A Heavyweight and Lightweight Match

Unfortunately, Draw only supports four type weights in PostScript or TrueType typeface families: normal, bold, bold-italic and italic. However, many typeface families today contain more than four weights. An example is Adobe's ITC Kabel, which contains five members: book, medium, demi, bold and ultra. FontMonger and Fontographer are both capable of producing 10 weights for each family. You may purchase a vendor's typeface family, or create your own, and discover that only four weights are available on your menu — you have lost the use of the other fonts.

To illustrate this point, I used Fontographer to create a light and heavy weight from Draw's Euromode family. This family now

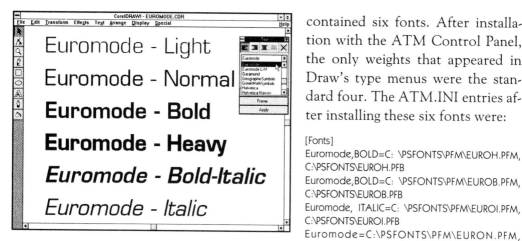

contained six fonts. After installation with the ATM Control Panel, the only weights that appeared in Draw's type menus were the standard four. The ATM.INI entries after installing these six fonts were:

```
[Fonts]
Euromode,BOLD=C: \PSFONTS\PFM\EUROH.PFM,
C:\PSFONTS\EUROH.PFB
Euromode,BOLD=C: \PSFONTS\PFM\EUROB.PFM,
C:\PSFONTS\EUROB.PFB
Euromode, ITALIC=C: \PSFONTS\PFM\EUROI.PFM,
C:\PSFONTS\EUROI.PFB
Euromode=C:\PSFONTS\PFM\EURON.PFM,
C:\PSFONTS\EURON.PFB
Euromode,BOLDITALIC=C:\PSFONTS\PFM\EUROT.PFM, C:\PSFONTS\EUROT.PFB
Euromode=C:\PSFONTS\PFM\EUROL.PFM, C:\PSFONTS\EUROL.PFB
```

To resolve this problem I used wPFMFix to create a new family name (menu name). The tricky part here is setting the weight switches, and remembering which ones to use. The family name (menu name) for the light weight was changed to Euromode L/H and the Bold or Italic check boxes were not selected. The heavy weight family name was changed to Euromode L/H and the bold weight check box was selected. This procedure created a new typeface family and type menu entry with two weights. Once this procedure was completed, I removed the Euromode fonts with ATM and re-installed them. The ATM.INI entries after this procedure looked like this:

```
[Fonts]
Euromode,BOLD=C:\PSFONTS\PFM\EUROB.PFM, C:\PSFONTS\EUROB.PFB
Euromode,ITALIC=C:\PSFONTS\PFM\EUROI.PFM, C:\PSFONTS\EUROI.PFB
Euromode=C:\PSFONTS\PFM\EURON.PFM, C:\PSFONTS\EURON.PFB
Euromode,BOLDITALIC=C:\PSFONTS\PFM\EUROT.PFM, C:\PSFONTS\EUROT.PFB
Euromode L/H,BOLD=C:\PSFONTS\PFM\EUROH.PFM,C:\PSFONTS\EUROH.PFB
Euromode L/H=C:\PSFONTS\PFM\EUROL.PFM, C:\PSFONTS\EUROL.PFB
```

It's a good idea to use a similar family name (menu name) and indicate the supported weights in the name (L\H).

REFONT

This shareware DOS application, from Acute Systems, is included on the Utility disk. A font converter's dream, it supports four types of conversions:

- Macintosh PostScript Type 1 outlines to Windows PostScript Type 1 outlines (.PFB).
- Macintosh TrueType outlines to Windows TrueType outlines.
- AFM files to .PFM files
- INF files from .AFM files

A registration fee of $20 will get you Wrefont, a Windows application that does everything its little brother does, plus:

- Generate .AFM or .PFM files from Macintosh or Windows outlines, including any kerning pairs present in the Macintosh screen font.
- Convert .PFB outlines to Macintosh MacBinary files.
- Decrypt and encrypt .PFB files. Decrypt turns the outline into an ASCII file that can be edited. Encrypt turns this file back into a .PFB.
- Change the encoding of a PC or Macintosh outline.

REFONT is a handy application for those of you who frequent online bulletin boards or CompuServe. These resources provide a large selection of PostScript fonts for the Macintosh that are not available for Windows. Use REFONT to convert these fonts for use in Draw and all your Windows applications. The author provides a very detailed and well written help file. If you need a powerful font converter, this is an excellent place to start.

WFN Fonts

Converting your Draw version 2 files containing .WFN fonts to version 3 is a tricky procedure, fraught with surprises. In the first example, I've opened a version 2 file that specified the standard Aardvark font. I'm assuming that you have not installed Draw's TrueType or PostScript version of this font. Version 2 of Draw is still installed on my system. What a pleasant greeting the Bad Or Missing Font File dialog box is! If you ignore this warning, your .CDR file will open but your specified font will change, as will the spacing in your text. This is caused by the new font architecture of version 3.

Previous versions of Draw used only .WFN fonts and referenced these fonts by their actual DOS filename. Font references in Draw 3, however, are based on the font name (the name you see in the Fonts list or Text roll-up). The benefit of this architecture is that Draw is no longer dependent on a specific font technology. Rather, it uses fonts that all Windows applications recognize — all your installed TrueType or PostScript fonts — as well as its own .WFN fonts.

To resolve the Bad Or Missing Font File message, you must perform several modifications to your system. Start by making a backup of your version 3 CORELDRW.INI file, located in your COREL\DRAW subdirectory. Next, open this file with Notepad. In the [CDrawConfig] section of this file you will see an entry that points to the location of all your standard and custom .WFN files. Typically, this would read FontsDir=C:\COREL\FONTS. If it does not appear, or is not correct, you must edit this line to point to the directory on your system that contains all your .WFN fonts and symbols. Next, move your version 2 font, in this case AARDVARK.WFN, to your version 3 fonts directory using File Manager. If you have followed these steps, AARDVARK.WFN is now located in your C:\COREL\FONTS directory.

Now Alt-Tab back to Notepad, which still has CORELDRW.INI open. Scroll down to the [CorelDrwFonts] section. This section lists all the .WFN fonts and symbols provided with version 2 of Draw, with a semi colon (;) in front of each entry. Look for a line in this section that says ;Aardvark=2 aardvark.wfn and remove the semicolon beginning this line. This procedure makes the font available for use in Draw. In this case Aardvark is already listed in the [CORELDRW20FontMap] section lower down.

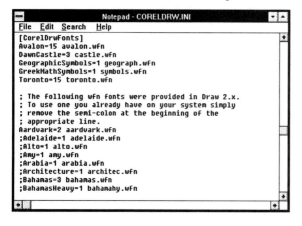

This section of your CORELDRW.INI contains all your version 2 .WFN fonts and symbols. They must be properly listed in both sections to use them in Draw. If you ever change the name (not the file name) of any fonts in either section, you can use spaces in the name. A correct entry is My-Font or My Font. These names must be exactly the same in both sections. Save your changes and close down Notepad. Your Draw 2 file can now be opened in 3 and the font specification is correct.

Now that I've told you how to fix this situation, there are instances when you may not have to. This procedure is undocumented. In this first example, the version 2 Draw file contains the name of the .WFN font used (aardvark.wfn). Later in this section, I will show you how to determine exactly which fonts are used in your version 2 .CDR files. If you have installed Draw's PostScript or TrueType version (Aardvark) of this font, here is what happens.

When you open your version 2 file Draw's Font Manager reads the [CORELDRW20FontMap] section of your CORELDRW.INI file. In this case the entry aardvark.wfn=Aardvark 0,606,0,0 already appears in this section. If Draw finds a PostScript or TrueType font installed on your system with a menu name of Aardvark, it uses the existing entry in your [CORELDRW20FontMap] section to automatically substitute the PostScript or TrueType font for your .WFN font. Draw is using the entries in this section as a substitution table. The version 2 file opens and no substitution warning is issued. No editing of your CORELDRW.INI file is required. And if it's a PostScript font, you don't have to register it.

As neat as this may sound, I'm not thrilled about this automatic substitution for a number of reasons. TrueType and PostScript fonts have different kerning values that sometimes don't match your .WFN fonts. So you may have to fine-tune your text to match your version 2 job. If you want to use your version 2 .WFN fonts and a PostScript or TrueType font with the same menu name, you are forced to change the name of the TrueType or PostScript font. You may want to read the review of RENAMETT again in the TrueType section of this chapter to refresh your memory about the order in which Draw permits you to use fonts if the menu names are identical.

The Bad Or Missing Fonts message will also display if you specified a custom .WFN font in your version 2 file and open it with 3. This occurs if you used WFN BOSS to convert a non-Draw font to .WFN format. If version 2 of Draw is still installed on your system, it may be easier to open the job and convert

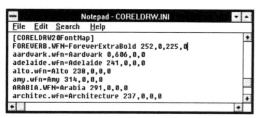

your text to curves using the Convert To Curves command on the Arrange menu. But in many cases this is not feasible.

Failing this, the first step is to move Draw's WFNSPACE.EXE DOS utility, which is currently located in your COREL\DRAW directory, to your C:\COREL\FONTS subdirectory. Then open your version 2 CORELDRW.INI file with Notepad, locate the [CorelDrwFonts] section and scroll down to your custom font entry. In this example, you will use ForeverExtraBold=5 FOREVERB.WFN 0 and copy this line to the Clipboard. Run Notepad again, open your version 3 CORELDRAW.INI and paste this entry into the [CorelDrwFonts] section on a separate line. Then move this custom .WFN file (FOREVERB.WFN) to your COREL\FONTS subdirectory.

Open a DOS session in Windows, move to your COREL\FONTS directory, type 'WFNSPACE FOREVERB.WFN' and press Enter. You will see a screen of instructions, but most importantly a line that reads WFNFilename=FONTName 252,0,225,0. Write the four numbers down, including the separating commas, exactly as they appear on your screen. You will use these numbers later. These numbers are font-specific calibration values that attempt to maintain visual accuracy and spacing when using your old .WFN fonts with Draw 3. In the majority of instances this works quite well, but you may encounter a few files in which the text needs to be fine-tuned to match the 2 file. Each number is weight specific (normal, bold, italic, and bold-italic).

Return to your 3 CORELDRW.INI file, locate the [CORELDRW20FontMap] section, insert a new line and enter 'FOREVERB.WFN=ForeverExtraBold 252,0,225,0'. Double-check your entry for accuracy. None of the existing font and symbol entries or the four numbers in this section should be edited. They list all your version 2 .WFN fonts and symbols, along with the proper calibration values. Save your CORELDRW.INI file and your version 2 file should open properly in 3.

Advanced Type Topics

If you've used WFN BOSS to convert Bitstream fonts to custom .WFN fonts, some additional problems occur. WFN BOSS sometimes converts bold fonts to a .WFN font that's roman (normal). This means that WFNSPACE reports incorrect values for this font, and your old Draw files won't contain the specified font. The work-around is cumbersome and requires you to re-convert your Bitstream font with WFN BOSS and specify the bold weight in the bold field. Then open your version 2 files with version 2 of Draw and re-specify the new font in all your files. Finally, run WFNSPACE on your new custom .WFN and install it using the procedures in this section.

Given the complexity of these procedures, it's important to summarize the key points and offer some recommendations. If you have a large number of version 2 files on your system that use standard or custom .WFN fonts and symbols, you should move all the .WFN files to your COREL\FONTS directory. To determine exactly which .WFN fonts you used in these jobs, open the .CDR file with Write and click on the No Conversion button. Use the Find command to search for .WFN. The name of each .WFN font is contained in the file. (You can use this same procedure to examine version 3 files and determine which fonts are used. You can also scroll through the file and look for names if you think you used TrueType or PostScript fonts.) Write these names down and follow the procedures outlined in the examples above. If you open a version 2 file and the Bad Or Missing Fonts message does not display, the first thing you should do is determine which font format (TrueType, PostScript or .WFN) Draw has used for the substitution.

If opening your old .CDR files is not practical, ensure that the following is completed. There are three critical entries in your version 3 CORELDRW.INI file. The first is FontsDir= C:\COREL\FONTS, which must point to the directory in which all your standard and custom .WFN fonts are located.

Second, the [CorelDrwFonts] section must list your standard or custom .WFN font without the semicolon. Only remove the semicolon for .WFN fonts actually installed on your system. Study the screen shot and notice that the Artistic Text dialog box lists (Not Found) Adelaide. The semicolon was accidentally re-

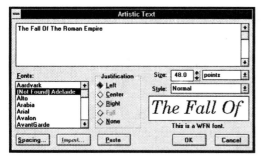

moved from the Adelaide=1 adelaide.wfn entry in this section, but this font was not present in C:\COREL\FONTS, thus generating an error message.

You may wish to use this feature as a shortcut for the installation of your version 2 .WFN fonts (standard — not custom). Remove the semicolon for all the .WFN fonts listed in the [CorelDrwFonts] section. Move all your standard version 2 .WFN fonts to the FontsDir=C:\COREL\FONTS subdirectory. Run Draw and write down any .WFN fonts that have a (Not Found) in front of the name in your type dialog boxes or roll-up. Finally, close down Draw, open your CORELDRW.INI file and insert a semicolon in front of those .WFN entries that were listed as (Not Found). Save your changes to complete this procedure.

Third, the [CORELDRW20FontMap] section must list your standard or custom .WFN font and include the four calibration values. It already lists all the standard .WFN fonts and symbols bundled with version 2. Don't forget that this section also acts as a substitution table. The existing entries instruct Draw to substitute your installed TrueType or PostScript font for the .WFN font used in your version 2 jobs.

The .WFN format is still a viable solution for many jobs. WFN fonts print just as crisply as properly registered PostScript Type 1 fonts and I found print times to be almost identical. Surprisingly, 8-point type in the .WFN format looks much crisper at 300 dpi than the same print job using a PostScript Type 1 font that was not registered (so Draw rasterized the type). In this case, .WFN fonts take three times longer to print. If you convert your PostScript type to curves in Draw, the .WFN font looks much crisper at all sizes. Print times were identical. TrueType fonts print crisper at 8 to 14 points than the same font in .WFN format, and typically output five times faster.

If you use PostScript fonts, and Draw's unusual procedures and editing requirements take too much effort, continue to use your .WFN fonts. If you use TrueType fonts with Draw and other Windows applications, use FontMonger (covered below) to convert your .WFN fonts to TrueType for new jobs. This format provides better-looking type, is available to all your Windows applications, and eliminates font substitution problems caused by duplicate menu names (family names). Once all your version 2 .WFN fonts are converted and the jobs are finished, remove your .WFN fonts by editing each reference — add a semicolon and 'REMOVED' in front of the name in the [CorelDrwFonts] section of your CORELDRW.INI file. Commenting out each reference with a semicolon provides you with a 'trail' in case you ever need to reinstall these fonts to finish an old job. Finally, copy the .WFN files to floppies and delete them from your hard disk.

WFN Service Bureau Output

Preparing your Draw job for service bureau output is easy if all your .WFN fonts are properly installed. If you are using a PostScript printer, select the Print To File option in Draw's Print dialog box to create your .PRN file. If you are a LaserJet user, install the Windows PostScript driver and the Lino 530 on your FILE: port using the procedures discussed in *Service Bureau Strategies*. Select the Print To File option in Draw's Print dialog box to create your .PRN file. If your job only uses .WFN fonts, it makes no difference whether you select the All Fonts Resident switch or not. In either case Draw always converts text set in a .WFN font into curves. Deliver this .PRN file to your service bureau to complete your job. At 1,200 dpi or higher your text looks just as crisp as the same job using a PostScript or TrueType font, although the character outlines of commercial-grade fonts can be of better design than those in .WFN format.

Converting .WFN Fonts with FontMonger

If you have read this chapter straight through from the start, it should be apparent that you need to try and standardize on one font format — either TrueType or PostScript — and convert your .WFN fonts at the appropriate time. A limited version of FontMonger is only $25 using the discount coupon included with the Draw package and would be money well spent. This limited version does one thing very well; it permits you to convert all your .WFN fonts or symbols to TrueType or PostScript format. You can also convert your fonts between TrueType and PostScript Type 1. It does an excellent job of hinting your fonts during the conversion, using a proprietary procedure. The full version is covered in the PostScript section of this chapter, but the conversion procedure is the same in either case.

Let's say you currently have a properly installed custom .WFN font (Michele) and a TrueType font installed with the exact same name. You can use FontMonger to convert your custom .WFN font to TrueType and eliminate the substitution problem. Start by double-clicking on the FontMonger icon in Program Manager. Choose Convert Batch from the File menu. In the Convert Batch dialog box ensure that the New Format list box says TrueType, and click on the Add button. In the Add To Batch dialog box move to your COREL\FONTS directory, in which all your .WFN fonts are located. Scroll down the list of fonts and click on MICHELE.WFN. Click on OK and you are returned to the Convert Batch dialog box with Michele (Corel) listed in the Fonts In Batch list. If you want to convert other .WFN fonts at the same time, click on the Add button to move back to the Add To Batch dialog box. This time, just double-click on your .WFN font. You'll be returned to the Convert Batch dialog box, where your second font is added to the Fonts In Batch list.

Another method to select two or more fonts is to use the Find button in the Convert Batch dialog box. Click on this button to navigate to the Choose Directory dialog box and select the directory on your system that contains your .WFN fonts. Click on OK and FontMonger will display a count for the number of fonts it locates and list all of them for you in the Add To Batch dialog box. At this point you can deselect a font for conversion by Control-clicking on its name or names.

Once your list is accurate, click on the Add Selection Button to return to the Convert Batch list. Check your list again and if there is still a font in the list you don't wish to convert, Control-click on the name or names and click the Remove button to remove them. Then click on the Convert button. In the Choose Directory dialog box, move to the directory on your system in which you keep all your TrueType fonts. Click on the OK button to begin the conversion.

The time necessary to convert your .WFN fonts to TrueType depends on the complexity of the .WFN fonts and the speed of your system. Using a 50 MHz 486 with 16 Mb of memory, a text face like Aardvark took two minutes and 10 seconds. A very complex symbol font, such as Animals, required six minutes and 25 seconds; the less complex Geograph symbol font took three minutes and 20 seconds, and a basic symbol font like Starsout converted in just one minute and 45 seconds. It's best to plan this conversion for a time when you don't anticipate using your machine. Since this is a batch conversion, you could select all 42 of your .WFN fonts and convert them automatically in one step.

You still have a few things left to do once FontMonger has created a new .TTF file. You must first install this font with the Windows Control Panel. The next procedure involves removing the .WFN font from your disk and editing your CORELDRW.INI file. Use File Manager to delete the font, in this case MICHELE.WFN, and then open your CORELDRW.INI file. Scroll down to the [CorelDrwFonts] section and remove the line that says Michele= 1 MICHELE.WFN 0. Then scroll down to the [CORELDRW20 FontMap] section and remove the line that says MICHELE.WFN=Michele 301,0,0,0. Don't forget to save your changes before closing Notepad. Your future Draw sessions will no longer list the .WFN font but will list your new TrueType font, thereby eliminating conflicts and font substitution.

Conclusions and Recommendations

Before you decide which format, or combination of formats, is best for the type of work you produce, it's helpful to compare the speed and output quality of TrueType and PostScript fonts in a number of contexts. I'll start with printing speed, since this can be a major bottleneck in the production cycle.

Printing Benchmarks

All tests were conducted on a 50 MHz DX 486 ISA clone with 16 Mb of Memory and a Pro Designer IIS video card running in 16 color SuperVGA mode (800 by 600). No print cache was used. A LaserJet Series II with 1.5 Mb of memory was used for the first series of tests. The Windows Universal Printer Driver version 3.1 and HP LaserJet Series II Driver version 1.1 were used. Windows 3.1 was running in Enhanced mode using ATM version 2.02. No modifications were made to the CORELDRW.INI file. The Draw document specified Casablanca - Normal in each format and contained paragraph text set in 24- and 26-point type, and artistic text set in 10- and 11-point type. The "Time with" means only one format was present in the document. Each test was run twice, with the average time listed.

Document	Time withTrueType	Time with PostScript/ATM
Draw	53.2 seconds	54.1 seconds

The small difference in time between these two tests is insignificant. What *is* significant is that in both cases Draw's proprietary rasterizer does an excellent job with either type format. This contrasts sharply with the following tests run on the same system and also printed with a LaserJet Series II.

Document	Time with TrueType	Time with PostScript/ATM
Write	1 min. and 20 sec.	8 min. and 35 sec.
Word	50.5 sec.	5 min. and 56 sec.
PageMaker	3 min and 19 sec.	27 min. and 30 sec.

The Windows Write and Word for Windows documents were eight pages long and specified 10-point Casablanca in each format. The PageMaker document was 20 pages in length and specified Casablanca in normal, bold and italic in each format. There were no differences in print times if ATM and TrueType were both turned on, versus having just one or the other enabled.

The second tests clearly show that the support for TrueType in Windows can provide significantly faster output than that of ATM from some applications when printing to a non-PostScript device.

The benchmark tests were then run using the same system, files and fonts, but outputting to a standard QMS 810 PostScript printer and version 3.53 of the Windows PostScript driver. Even though it's not identical to the LaserJet, this printer is similar in engine speed and represents a typical printer in use today. The PostScript driver was set up to rasterize the TrueType font and not substitute a resident font. The PostScript version of Casablanca was permanently downloaded to the printer before the tests were run.

Document	Time with TrueType	Time with PostScript/ATM
Write	1 min. and 50 sec.	1 min. and 17 sec.
Word	1 min. and 2 sec.	1 min. and 8 sec.
PageMaker	3 min and 3 sec.	3 min. and 7 sec.

What's significant here is how well the TrueType rasterizer works with a LaserJet — as shown in the previous tests — compared to the resident font in a PostScript device. In this case you can see that Microsoft has optimized TrueType printing speed for non-PostScript devices, as the print times for TrueType with a LaserJet demonstrate in two of the examples. (Remember, Microsoft also wrote both of these applications.) In the case of PageMaker, it's unclear why the tests are slightly faster with TrueType fonts to a PostScript device. But in the test of the downloaded PostScript font, it's not surprising that these times are dramatically faster with a PostScript device. Rasterizing PostScript fonts for a LaserJet requires significantly more work by the ATM software, as compared to the same procedure using a printer-resident outline and the printer's PostScript interpreter.

Some conclusions can be made from these printing tests. If you use a LaserJet printer and primarily work in Draw, then either format works fine. However, if you venture outside the domain of Draw and use the Windows TrueType rasterizer or ATM with other publishing applications, then TrueType is significantly faster than ATM.

The tests run with the QMS PostScript printer illustrate some interesting points. The similar print times clearly show that in this case PostScript is not very efficient when contrasted to the TrueType rasterizer built into Windows. Keep in mind that the PostScript fonts were permanently downloaded — there was no time lost downloading them. TrueType fonts work very well with a PostScript device, although non-Adobe interpreters may cause problems. Mixing the two formats is a viable solution for jobs that are finished at 300 dpi.

Screen Display Quality

The screen display quality of TrueType versus PostScript is often difficult to determine. To test this, I specified Draw's Brooklyn in PostScript/ATM format and then below it the TrueType version. Some of the 6-point type displayed in PostScript/ATM was slightly sharper than that of the TrueType version. But some of the 8-point type in TrueType was slightly sharper. This indicates that both formats display about the same, as no consistent pattern for relative screen quality emerges.

Screen Display Speed

Determining which format displays faster on your screen is a challenging proposition. Differences between the two formats must be large enough for you to notice and must be a real-world measure of the type of work you do. Complicating this equation is that after a very short while you don't notice any difference, since you become accustomed to working with a particular format. My subjective opinion is that TrueType displays slightly faster in the majority of Windows applications, including Draw. To confirm these beliefs I ran *PC Magazine*'s Windows benchmark tests. Version 2.5 of the WINBENCH application was run on the same system used for the printing tests discussed earlier. The tests incorporated into WINBENCH are recognized standards and are very thorough. Only significant differences will be listed here. Times are given in characters per second.

Video Benchmarks

Test	TrueType	ATM
Image Times Roman	20,513	3,783
Scroll Times Roman	15,401	5,741
Mixed Fonts	14,276	6,541

WINBENCH's image test repeatedly fills a window with 21-point Times New Roman and Times Roman. The scroll test repeatedly scrolls a window upward and fills the bottom of the screen with text using the same fonts. The mixed fonts test displays Courier New and Courier in normal, italic, underline and bold. These tests validate the subjective opinion that TrueType display is faster.

To confirm the belief that Draw displays TrueType fonts slightly faster, the same system and single-page Draw document was used from the printing tests. No modifications were made to the CORELDRW.INI file. The figures below represent the time needed to display all the type in full page preview mode at a zoomed-in view (to ensure no greeking occurs). Each test was run twice, with the average time listed.

Document	Time with TrueType	Time with ATM
Draw	11.4 seconds	13.1 seconds

The slight speed improvement with TrueType is barely noticeable as you run this test, and it's certainly not dramatic.

Standardize or Mix?

Draw clearly favors the use of TrueType fonts, because it conforms to the Windows architecture and uses them in the same manner (as a system resource) as all Windows applications. Once they are installed with the Control Panel, no special procedures are required to use them. Using .WFN fonts is not as efficient, but is still a viable solution for many users, especially those with older devices that support neither TrueType nor PostScript. In both cases, these two type formats can even be used for occasional service bureau work.

The use of PostScript fonts with Draw is non-standard and time-consuming to manage. Draw does not rely on these fonts as a system resource by reading your WIN.INI, as do most Windows applications. After they are installed for the use of all your other Windows applications, you are faced with the daunting task of special edits and procedures to properly use PostScript fonts with Draw. I've saved you hours of font name editing by providing 859 PostScript entries in REGISTER.ZIP. However, with more than 10,000 PostScript fonts available today, you may still have to spend a significant amount of time registering new fonts. If most of your final output is at 300 dpi, these reasons alone justify the use of TrueType and/or .WFN fonts, rather than PostScript.

If you currently output the majority of your jobs on an imagesetter, and use PostScript fonts and a PostScript printer to proof your work, there is no compelling reason to switch to

TrueType. You do have the option of mixing the two formats, or using FontMonger to convert your TrueType fonts to PostScript format.

If your system contains a significant number of jobs that specified standard or custom .WFN fonts, you may wish to continue to use both version 2 and version 3 of Draw until you can safely archive these files. This gradual procedure permits you to integrate version 3 into your production cycle without causing you unnecessary work in the form of edits and fine-tuning of type. If Draw 2 is removed from your system, spend the time to install your standard and custom .WFN fonts and continue to use them along with TrueType and/or PostScript fonts. Your new jobs should use PostScript and/or TrueType fonts. Gradually convert your standard or custom .WFN fonts to either format as you need them.

If your business contains a mixture of Macintosh and Windows publishing workstations, you should standardize on either PostScript or TrueType. Mixing platforms is challenging enough without introducing new variables into the equation.

This chapter has presented you with a very detailed discussion of type management. In many instances, some of the information is undocumented or rarely discussed in print. If you are still confused about how to use type with Draw after reading this chapter, you're not alone. The subject is complex, due to Draw's unusual support for three font formats and the way it manages them. Even veteran Draw users are challenged by this subject. If this is the case, spend the time to read this chapter again in its entirety.

Cartooning
with CorelDRAW

17

J im Phillips is the art director for Loblaw International Merchants. L.I.M. is the company that develops and markets President's Choice™ NO NAME™ and President's Choice G.R.E.E.N. products for supermarkets in North America and abroad. Jim Phillips works for David Nichol, the president of L.I.M. and helps produce Dave Nichol's Insider's Report®, among other things. A significant number of Mr. Nichol's television commercials contain graphics created with CorelDRAW.

A lighter approach to illustration

Jim is also the creator of SUNtoons©, which appear on the editorial pages of both the Toronto and Ottawa Sun. SUNtoons is created with a mixture of Draw and traditional hand rendering techniques and is faxed to the papers. Jim was one of the first cartoonists to develop a proven quality method of faxing cartoons for newspaper reproduction in Canada.

The Social Butterfly

Jim had seen so much 'stiff' computer illustration that he wanted to create a Draw image with a little emotion, and nothing is as emotional as a crying baby. He also wanted to impart his illustration with some humor, a goal he undoubtedly achieved.

The key to The Social Butterfly was to create all the elements separately and combine them later into a final image. Jim first created the main elements — the head, mouth, body and the teddy bear — without worrying about the color. As his primary drawing technique

---

he used the Convert To Curves command to convert a circle into four arcs and copied it to the Clipboard. He then simply pasted circles from the Clipboard onto the page as needed and modified them with the ⬥ and ⬥ tools, adding nodes where required.

After the shapes were completed the color was added using flat color, blends and fountain fills. The color was done last because of the need to keep it consistent in each of the elements, since they would be combined later. Having a body with one set of fleshtones and a head with a different set would have produced an undesirable effect and would probably have required time-consuming changes. Planning ahead is important for keeping the creation of a complex drawing as simple as possible.

Jim used a process color book to specify the colors, using hot to faded pinks in the baby elements. Some were already available in Draw's default palette, and he mixed new ones as required. He placed solid CMYK colors (no fountain fills) first to assess their suitability and to quickly give the drawing shape. At this point he wanted an impression of what the final image would eventually look like. He considers this a 'painterly' approach, much like the one he would have employed if he had been creating a painting in acrylics. Jim added the fountain fills only after he was satisfied with the color placement — a process similar to the 'glazing' technique he uses in a traditional painting. Fountain fill angles, blends, highlight colors and highlight x and y coordinates were his main concern at this stage.

One of the strengths of Draw is that it allows you to export selected objects. Since Jim kept the pieces for the final image in separate files, he used the Import command to assemble them into a new file, with each file placed on the page as a group.

Once they were in position Jim simply exported the elements back to overwrite their original files by choosing Selected Only in the Export dialog box. He could then adjust an element and import it again into the final image without the need for any complicated repositioning of the changed element. Using the Clipboard to move elements to and from your final drawing is appropriate for simpler drawings. However, when you have a more complex drawing using fountain fills and blends it becomes important to minimize screen redraw time.

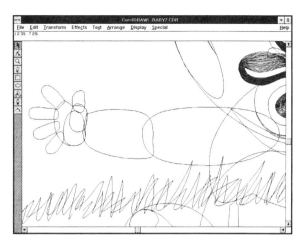

Exporting and importing provides an easy way to move elements back into the main file, while keeping the exact position and size. Jim finds altering areas of a complex drawing in a separate file avoids confusion with the other parts of the drawing. For example, he had a separate file for the mouth of the baby and updated it several times by exporting it from the final drawing which, due to the large number of blends, looked like a tangle of fishing line in the wireframe window. He could change it without fear of losing control of the whole drawing by importing the mouth along with the other elements (the body, the bear, the butterfly, the right arm and the grass) into the final drawing, which already contained the sky and the background grass.

Once he had everything sized and in the position he wanted Jim exported each element, overwriting the original file in which they were created. This resized and positioned the mouth elements in the MOUTH.CDR file in exactly the same location as they appeared in the final drawing.

Therefore, if a change or adjustment to the mouth was needed he did it in the MOUTH.CDR file (being careful not to move or resize it) and then saved it. Then Jim opened the final drawing file and moved the old mouth to the side of the page, but didn't yet delete it. He then imported the MOUTH.CDR file with the latest changes, and it appeared in exactly the original position of the old mouth. He then selected both the old and the new mouth and chose Reverse Order from the Arrange menu. This moved the new mouth into the same stacking

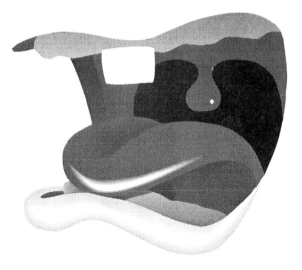

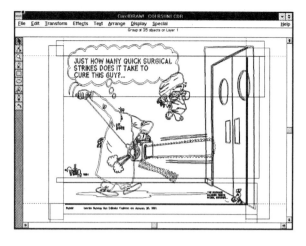

order as the old mouth, which could then be deleted.

If Jim wanted to resize or reposition the mouth he did it in the final drawing, since these changes would need to be compared with the rest of the design. He would then immediately export the mouth element back to overwrite the original or create a new file, such as MOUTH2.CDR, to preserve the possibility of returning to the original version.

When Jim was comfortable with all the elements he added the grass and the butterfly (a radically altered clip art image supplied with Draw), which was also created in a separate file. In the interests of having the file output from the office QMS ColorScript PostScript thermal printer in less than an hour, Jim resisted the urge to give each blade of grass a fountain fill. Printing time turned out to be about 50 minutes.

Jim planned most of the drawing on paper first using a fine-line magic marker to mimic the object outlines. Throughout its creation careful organization was vital to avoid mixing up different versions of the elements. For example, at one point Jim had three different versions of the mouth, two of the baby's body, two butterflies, four baby heads and two right arms.

To keep track of the various versions of each of the baby's elements, Jim created a directory called BABY and gave the files such names as HEAD.CDR, HEAD2.CDR, HEAD3.CDR, MOUTH1.CDR, MOUTH2.CDR and so on. Jim has the habit of not discarding anything, since he often returns to a previous drawing after becoming dissatisfied with the current version and then proceeds in a new direction. After doing the baby's forehead one way in HEAD3.CDR, for example, he decided that while he didn't want to discard what had been done so far, he wanted to try an alternative route. So he opened HEAD2.CDR and saved it as HEAD4.CDR, and then carried on with the new approach. This made possible some mixing and matching in the final drawing.

Jim used a PC-compatible 40 MHz turbo 386 with 4 megabytes of RAM and a 14-inch high resolution monitor to create the cartoon. He printed the proofs to a 300 dpi QMS ColorScript thermal printer from a Dell 33 MHz 486 with 8 megabytes of RAM and a 20-inch NEC MultiSync XL high resolution monitor.

The Editorial Cartoon

The Toronto Sun asked Jim to fill in and supply a color Sunday cartoon because the regular cartoonist was unavailable. This was the opportunity he had been looking for to test Draw's capabilities in a deadline-intensive project. Not only did he intend to deliver a finished cartoon, he was intent on giving the Sun final separated film created with Draw.

A DFI hand scanner made it possible for him to complete the cartoon in about the same time (four hours) as if he had done it the 'old-fashioned' way. Purists may blanch to hear that this cartoon was done on the computer, but actually it was initially

drawn by hand. The method of scanning a drawing into a computer and coloring it is not new. But just try to get it to print when some of the objects have more than 800 nodes. Oh, sure, you can break them apart and spend the night editing nodes with the ⚊ tool. But then there goes your sleep, and you may still miss your deadline. The tough part about doing cartoons this way is making sure that the elements are not so complicated as to not allow the final art to print.

The secret to success is to simply draw the cartoon in pieces, scan it in pieces and then construct the cartoon from the autotraced elements. Organization is important and a good hand-drawn rough is essential. The actual pieces of the cartoon were first drawn on layout paper and inked with a brush. Jim made an effort to avoid open-ended objects for the sake of efficient color application later — it takes time to close curves with the ⚊ tool, so it's best to take a little care in the traditional drawing stage.

All the pieces were scanned at 300 dpi and converted into .EPS format with CorelTRACE (being careful to avoid creating excess nodes). Color was added to each piece in a separate file, and each file was then imported into the background art, which was also a separate file.

Once the editorial cartoon was finished, Jim sent a QMS color proof to editor Glen Woodcock for final approval. The one change Glen requested was accomplished in five minutes. Had it been a watercolor cartoon rather than a 'computoon', Jim reports that he might have jumped from the nearest bridge. The next step was to send the file by modem to Jim's service bureau to be output at 1,270 dpi with a 100 line screen frequency, using a Scangraphic imagesetter. The service bureau delivered the film directly to the newspaper.

Although Jim toyed with the idea of using Draw's color trapping, he decided that given the questionable registration of most newspapers it would probably be a waste of time. In fact the Sun provided excellent registration and he vowed to make use of Draw's trapping abilities next time.

The Cartoon Font

Jim created the cartoon font he uses in his daily cartoon panel with Draw. This font has saved him countless hours of labor, and the few hours it took to create have been more than worth it. He can now simply type his captions (and quickly edit them) into a ready-made Draw template that includes the cartoon title, borders for three separate SUNtoons, Jim's signature, the year and a box for fax information at the bottom.

The captions are typed in, the page is output, the cartoon figures drawn by hand and the page is then popped into the fax machine. Jim uses premium quality Sharp faxes set to fine mode on both ends of the transmission, and sends the image 33% larger than final size.

To create your own font Jim suggests using a brush or marker to hand draw an alphabet (following a font from a type book or catalog helps) and scanning it. Trace the letters with CorelTRACE and save them in separate .CDR files. Then import them into Draw and export them as TrueType or PostScript font characters (see Advanced Type Topics for details). Jim provides a tip — import a letter from another font as a guide when touching up the letters of your new font. He node-edited his letters using Swiss Narrow as a guide. And don't forget to delete this guide letter before exporting the new letter to your custom font.

 Another tip — keep all the letter .CDR files in one directory and back it all up, including your final font file. Otherwise, if disaster strikes your hard drive you'd have to start from scratch again. Ouch.

I've included a few other samples of Jim's work here, along with a President's Choice piece on which he and Peter Trollope collaborated.

Essential Concepts in Color Publishing

18

CorelDRAW provides a rich assortment of tools for publishing in color, but to effectively use these tools you must understand the fundamentals of color itself. This chapter provides a succinct overview of the crucial concepts in color theory, with an emphasis on applying these principles while using Draw. Among the topics explored are color models, differences between spot and process color, how color separations are made, color calibration and the properties of various kinds of color output.

An overview of color theory

Color Models

A color model is a way of representing colors as numerical information — as data that can be manipulated inside a computer. Color models are necessary for the communication of colors between application programs, computer platforms and color publishers. When people match colors visually, they are often trying to transform the additive colors produced on a computer screen into the subtractive colors produced by the printing process. (I will explain these terms further on.) Therefore, it is important for color publishers to know something about the most commonly used color models — RGB, CMYK, HSB and CIE (and its variations).

I will begin by exploring the RGB color model on which color scanners and displays are based, then discuss the CMYK model used by color printers and printing presses, and finish by looking at the CIE model that forms the foundation for color calibration systems. First, there's one important distinction you need to be clear about. In any computer system, you can specify 256 different values by using eight bits (binary digits) of data. For example, an eight-bit graphics board and monitor can display up to 256 colors. On the other hand, with 24 bits of color data you can specify 16.7 million colors.

Don't automatically assume that 24-bit color is better than eight-bit color — indeed, all other things being equal, it will take three times as long to display on your screen. If you're working with simple drawings, presentations and position-only photos, eight-bit color is all you need. However, if you need to see photorealistic color on screen, invest in a 24-bit graphics board and monitor, such as the Radius TwoPage Display. Also, keep in mind that you can scan your images as 24-bit color and view them on an eight-bit display system, then output them to a 24-bit color printer, or as color separations to an imagesetter, without any loss of quality.

The RGB Color Model

For many people, the most familiar color model is the RGB (red, green, blue) system used in virtually all color television sets, computer monitors and slide film recorders. In the RGB system, the red, green and blue components of each picture element, or pixel, in the image are assigned a number, usually an integer between 0 and 255. Inside a color monitor, the numbers are fed to digital-to-analog converters, which produce a voltage proportional to each number, and the voltage is used to drive the monitor's electron gun or guns. The electrons strike colored phosphors on the inside of the screen, resulting in the emission of red, green and blue photons (bundles of light energy).

Although it is widely utilized, the RGB system is device dependent, meaning that a given set of RGB values will be interpreted differently by every monitor, resulting in different colors on screen. Even two brand-new monitors from the same manufacturer will exhibit slightly different responses, a variation that can only increase as their phosphors fade over time.

A partial solution to this problem has been available in the Macintosh environment for some time, in the form of display calibrators from Radius, RasterOps, SuperMac and Barco. Unfortunately for users of Draw and other Windows-based graphics products, these color calibrators are taking a long time to migrate to the Windows platform.

Even when Windows-based display calibrators arrive, they will only partially solve the problem of color calibration. Although they help ensure that a given set of RGB values produce the "correct" color on screen, they do not address the larger problem of system-wide color correspondence.

The problem of system-wide calibration requires a CIE-based color management system, such as EfiColor from Electronics For Imaging (EFI), or the Precision Color Management System from Kodak Electronic Printing Systems (KEPS). These systems are based around device profiles that describe the color gamut and bias of individual types of scanners, monitors and printers with each profile expressed in terms of the CIE color model. A set of mathematical transforms is used to convert color values between these device profiles, so that the colors displayed on screen will, as closely as possible, match those from the scanner and the printer.

Color scanners also make use of the RGB system, however there is a major difference between the way color information is handled by the expensive drum scanners used in a color trade shop and the economical flatbed scanners found on the desktop. Color scanners work with the fact that the RGB system is an additive color model — equal amounts of red, green and blue light add up to white. Therefore, by scanning a color original through successive red, green and blue filters, the scanner can capture virtually all the color information in the original scene, and represent it as RGB values.

Desktop scanners typically capture these RGB values and send them directly to your computer. On the other hand, the high-end scanners found in a color trade shop contain specialized hardware, called a color computer, that converts the RGB signals into CMYK values. The color computer in a high-end scanner also sharpens the scanned image, and applies color corrections according to the settings selected by the scanner operator.

One of the major problems when using Draw and other color publishing programs is that the colors displayed on an RGB screen often cannot be reproduced with CMYK inks on a page. There are three main reasons for these differences:

- The human eye perceives the radiant light emitted by monitors differently than the reflected light by which we view printed pages.
- The colorants in a monitor (phosphors energized by an electron beam) are different from colorants (inks, dyes, waxes, and toners) used in desktop printers, color proofers, and printing presses.
- The gamut, or range of achievable colors, of an RGB color monitor is different from that of a CMYK color printer.

A gamut map can show how the gamut of the human eye is much larger than that of a typical RGB monitor, meaning that there are many colors you can see in nature that cannot be displayed on a color monitor. Even more significant for users of Draw or other color graphics programs is the fact that monitor gamuts do not match those of a typical CMYK printer.

This means that there are many colors that can be displayed on the monitor but not reproduced on the printed page with any combination of cyan, magenta, yellow and black. Conversely, there are some colors that can be printed with process inks yet not be displayed on screen.

The CMYK Color Model

The CMYK (cyan, magenta, yellow, black) color model is used in the printing process, which relies on light reflected from the image on the page to the eye, as determined by the light-absorbing properties of the ink. In other words, the color of the object is established by the frequencies of light that are absorbed or subtracted.

The CMYK system is called a subtractive model: a white surface reflects all the wavelengths of visible light, a black surface absorbs all of them, and a green surface, for example, absorbs (subtracts) all but the green wavelengths.

Practically speaking, the CMYK model is among the most important color models, because it is the basis of almost all color reproduction processes. Combining percentages of the four process color inks on a press produces the appearance of millions of colors — enough to reproduce even color photographs.

In a perfect world, we would not need the CMYK model; we would simply print onto paper with the same RGB values captured by scanners or defined in Draw and displayed on computer screens. Unfortunately, combining red, green, and blue inks only produces a few thousand possible colors, nowhere near the million or more colors needed to adequately represent color photographs or specify colors precisely.

The solution is to print with the colors that are exact opposites, or complements, of red, green and blue. The complement of red is a greenish-blue color called cyan, the complement of green is a bluish-purple color called magenta, and the complement of blue is yellow. In theory, then, it should be possible to print full-color images by combining various percentages of cyan, magenta and yellow.

It doesn't quite work out that way though, because of the impurities in all printing inks. Even the best and most expensive magenta inks, for instance, are contaminated with minute amounts of cyan. This is due, not to an error in the ink factory, but to the fact that it is impossible to create any ink whose spectral signature is totally isolated in one portion of the spectrum. The spectral curve for magenta inks, for instance, always shows that some yellow light is being reflected.

The result is that combining equal proportions of cyan, magenta and yellow inks produces a dark muddy brown, instead of a solid black. To compensate for this deficiency, process color printing adds black ink, not only to produce a solid black (especially for type), but also to add some depth and 'snap' to the printing. The addition of black ink also adds contrast to the images, and provides better detail in the shadows, or darker areas.

For this reason, many desktop thermal wax transfer printers are available with both CMY and CMYK ribbons. The CMY ribbons provide faster (and lower-cost) output when producing pages without black type or graphics with lots of dark tones, but they let you insert a CMYK ribbon when you want to print pages combining color graphics with black type.

By the way, the black ink in the CMYK model is represented by the letter 'K' for two reasons: it avoids confusion with the 'B' for blue in RGB, and the black plate is usually the 'key' on which all other aspects of a color separation depend. I'll return to the subject of color separations a little later.

The HSB Color Model

In addition to RGB and CMYK, Draw supports the HSB (hue, saturation, brightness) model. The HSB model provides one major benefit to illustrators and designers — it is a relatively intuitive way to specify colors. It doesn't make it any easier to ensure that the colors selected on screen match those that appear on the printed page.

However, it makes it easier to look at a color that isn't quite right, and know whether the overall color itself is wrong (you need to change the hue), whether it needs to be more vibrant or more pastel (change the saturation), or needs to be lighter or darker (change the brightness).

The CIE Color Model

All computers, software and peripherals must use a color model internally for specifying color. Therefore, the ultimate goal of many researchers has been to find a color model independent of any particular scanner or monitor, based on the way color is interpreted by a scientific instrument called a spectrophotometer.

The concept of device-independent color calibration was developed in the 1920s by an international scientific commission on illumination, the Commission Internationale de l'Eclairage, or CIE. Its 1931 model is based on the notion of a 'standard observer' whose color vision is described in terms of the spectral sensitivity of the red, green and blue receptors in his or her eyes.

Unfortunately for users of Windows-based computers, Microsoft has been somewhat lax in providing support for device-independent color calibration systems. Such operating system-level support for color is promised for future versions of Windows. In late 1992 Apple Computer shipped ColorSync, an extension to System 7 that provides support for third-party color calibration systems.

To date, the first vendors to provide such systems are Kodak, with the Precision Color Management System, and Electronics For Imaging (EFI), with EfiColor. Both systems are based on the

CIE color model, and enable you to achieve a close match between the colors seen on screen and those printed on paper, with built-in capabilities for mapping the out-of-gamut colors into the closest possible alternative colors.

Another important part of the color calibration puzzle is also starting to fall into place with the increasing acceptance of PostScript Level 2, which uses the CIE model as its internal representation of color information.

As most desktop publishers are aware, the PostScript page description language was an enabling technology that helped give birth to the desktop publishing revolution (the others being the Apple Macintosh computer and LaserWriter printer, plus Aldus PageMaker software). Adobe Systems' latest version of this page description language, PostScript Level 2, provides a number of features important to color publishers. In addition to CIE support, other significant aspects of PostScript Level 2 include:

- greater speed in printing than the original version of PostScript;
- support for the JPEG (Joint Photographic Experts Group) standard for compressing and decompressing photographic images, which allows you to reduce the size of an image file by 90% or more without any visible degradation in picture quality;
- the ability to download fonts, forms and other resources to your printer, which can significantly increase printing speed;
- support for a variety of other color models, such as the PhotoYCC model on which Kodak PhotoCD is based, plus the ability to add conversions to any other color model;

Spot Color

An essential distinction in color printing is between the two different ways color can be added to a document.

- Spot color involves printing a specific color, often in addition to black, in which the spot color has been mixed prior to printing, and has been specified according to some standard color specification, such as the Pantone Matching System.
- Process color involves separating the original image into its cyan, magenta, yellow and black components, then printing the four together to recreate all the original shadings of color.

One useful way to think about the difference between spot and process color is that spot colors are like overlays — each color is placed by itself on the page — whereas the process color method creates different hues through combinations of the four process ink screens.

The important thing about spot color is that it has made it possible for many people to create colorful documents for which the cost of full four-color printing would be prohibitive. For example, if you currently print your newsletter in black and want to give it some zing, you can specify spot color printing for certain headlines, ruling lines, logos and other elements. As long as documents are reproduced on multi-color printing presses — as opposed to running the job several times on a one-color press — in many cases it will be cheaper and easier to use spot color, rather than process.

The Pantone Matching System

The Pantone Matching System is based on a series of books of color swatches, printed on coated and uncoated stock, and a set of ink formulations for creating such colors on a printing press. Using this system, a graphic designer can specify that the logotype on a client's letterhead be printed as PMS 314, and be reasonably sure that the resulting color will be the same deep forest green shown on the Pantone Matching System swatch — whether it's printed in Peoria or Paris.

However, if your company logo is always printed in a specific PMS color, running an ad in a full-color magazine could be a problem. Although some Pantone spot colors can be reasonably well-matched by combining cyan, magenta, yellow and black, other PMS colors simply can't be duplicated in CMYK. Also, Pantone Matching System inks include colors that are impossible to reproduce with process inks, including silver, copper and creamy, saturated slate blue.

If your company color can't be approximated with process inks, you can always get the printer to run the entire magazine one extra time to add your spot color (or use a press with one additional color tower), but because this can be prohibitively expensive, it often makes more sense to change the design.

Some applications, such as high-quality maps or product labels, may involve ten or more spot colors, in addition to the four process inks.

A great many ink manufacturers and software developers (including Corel) advertise their products as complying with the standard PMS colors, thereby providing publishers with some measure of certainty that color graphics and documents will print in the desired shades. In practical terms, it means that you can specify a colored graphic element within a desktop program such as Draw, knowing the on-screen representation need not exactly match the sample in the swatch book, yet secure in the knowledge that the printed piece will come reasonably close to the intended color.

You must exercise caution when using the word Pantone — it doesn't automatically mean spot color. Although the Pantone Matching System is synonymous with spot color, Pantone Inc. also publishes a variety of other color specification tools, including many for working with process colors. The Pantone Process Color Imaging Guide, for example, gives the closest cyan, magenta, yellow and black equivalents for each of the Pantone spot colors, and shows at a glance which PMS colors can and cannot be closely approximated with process colors.

Process Color Guides

The major limitation of the original Pantone Matching System is that it is based on specially mixed inks, rather than on the four process inks. This made it difficult to specify colors that were being reproduced with process color, until the recent release of three new matching systems, all based on CMYK inks. The advantage of all three systems is that they enable designers to select colors efficiently, without ever choosing a color that falls outside the range of four-color process reproduction.

Pantone Process Colors

Pantone has also released a CMYK-based color specification system, designed to fill the gap for those working with process rather than solid colors. The Pantone Process Color System specifies more than 3,000 colors in CMYK percentages. All screen values are specifically chosen to perform within the quality control tolerances and capabilities of today's printing presses. The new system is also available in Pantone-licensed software applications, and has been formulated in both SWOP (Standard Web Offset Press) and Euroscale versions for international use. The Pantone Process Color System Specifier is a two-book set that presents the same process color values in a tear-out chip format. Each chip is identified with its corresponding CMYK percentages.

The Focoltone Color System

The Focoltone Color System is an innovative way of selecting and matching process colors. Focoltone is designed to help everybody involved in process color reproduction: print buyers, designers, prepress houses and printers. Although the Focoltone system is not supported directly from within the current version of Draw, you can take advantage of it simply by specifying colors according to the CMYK percentages shown in the Focoltone swatch kit and charts.

The Focoltone color range consists of 763 four-color combinations which contain single tints of all four process inks from five to 85%. By selecting colors from this palette, you can be confident that the specified colors will be closely approximated on press. The Focoltone colors are printed on swatches, specifier sheets and charts, showing not only the specified color but all the (process) colors which make it up. This enables the printer to follow the progressions in the charts, matching them to the press sheet as each new process color is added.

Unlike the Pantone process color system, which was designed to work with the traditional mechanical screens available only in five-percent increments, the Focoltone system was created with PostScript technology, using screens accurate to one-percent increments. There are two main advantages of working with the Focoltone system. The first is that it provides your commercial printer with a set of progressives, charts that show how each color is constructed step-by-step as the cyan, magenta, yellow and black inks are laid down on the paper during the printing process. The second advantage is that the Focoltone charts are organized so that you easily see which two-color and three-color combinations are part of each four-color composite — all such combinations are shown on a single line in the Focoltone color charts. This makes it very easy for designers to consciously choose colors that will require little or no color trapping on press. (Trapping is the process of shrinking or expanding adjacent color areas — making chokes or spreads — to compensate for misregistrations on press.)

Focoltone specifications refer to colors printed on sheet-fed (as opposed to web) presses with industry-average dot gain and ink density levels. From these conditions, the standard specification lets you quickly match to the reference color by normal press adjustments. Different printing conditions, such as web offset, will print different colors from the standard specification. Focoltone uses a software program to recalculate each of the color percentages every time a new dot gain is entered, thereby changing the specification so that the color remains the same. A special set of charts is available for printing color newspapers.

The Trumatch Swatching System

The Trumatch Swatching System, from Trumatch, takes a similar approach and is also designed specifically to improve the accuracy of color specifications for process color. It offers more than 2,000 computer-generated colors that specify exact percentages of cyan, magenta, yellow and black for process inks.

Typical commercial printers' process tint guides display colors as combinations of cyan, magenta, yellow and black in five- or ten-percent increments. Trumatch provides proportional gradation of color using the computer's ability to produce CMYK increments of one percent. This results in smooth steps of color without color gaps, and without changing color cast.

Creating Color Separations

Throughout this book, there are frequent references to the process of color separation and to the separated film that is the end product of the process. Therefore, a thorough understanding of the principles governing color separation is essential.

Full-color printing is based on an illusion: that a few colors in combination appear to contain all the colors of the rainbow.

This illusion occurs in reverse when a colorful original is separated with the purpose of creating four pieces of film, one for each of the process colors, so they can be combined during the printing process to create all the other colors.

Screen Angles

Screen angles are an essential, behind-the-scenes technology at work whenever you include a photograph or color in a publication. During the early days of desktop publishing, color output often looked blotchy due to unsightly patterns — moiré — caused by interference between the cyan, magenta, yellow, and black halftone screens. In the past few years, however, a number of new technologies for controlling screen angles have come to market, thereby solving the moiré problem.

The new screening tools — HQS Screening from Linotype-Hell, Accurate Screens from Adobe Systems, Balanced Screening from Agfa, and others — produce desktop color output that looks great when compared side-by-side with output from high-end color systems. Today virtually all the major imagesetter vendors make use of one or more of these techniques.

Screen angles are easy to understand, and even easier to work with, once you understand three basic facts:

- All electronic devices, such as laser printers and imagesetters, create halftone dots by grouping together many individual picture elements, or pixels.
- Unless the output device produces film separations with halftone dots at precisely correct screen angles, many images will be ruined by ugly moiré patterns.
- Under the control of a clever screening program, an imagesetter can activate the appropriate pixels to create virtually any screen angle imaginable, thereby eliminating the moiré problem.

The key to reproducing tones is the halftone, which creates the illusion that a black-and-white photograph contains many shades of gray by breaking the image into a pattern of varying sizes and shapes of dots.

Extensive research has shown that when two or more screens overlap, the moiré effect is kept to an absolute minimum whenever the screens are precisely 30° apart from one another. But the screens can only be rotated through 90°, which works fine if you're only printing two or three colors, but doesn't work with four-color process reproduction. The next best thing is to have one of the screens precisely 15° from another, so the traditional color separation angles are 15°, 75°, 0° and 45°, for cyan, magenta, yellow and black respectively.

Digital Halftoning with PostScript

Unlike the dots of varying size that make up a traditional halftone, the pixels comprising the recorder grid of an electronic output device, such as a PostScript imagesetter, are all the same size. Electronic screening makes use of the fact that each digital halftone cell can be made of many individual pixels. By turning on and off specific pixels, the PostScript spot function tells the imagesetter how to create areas of varying density.

Selecting a particular screen angle affects how the halftone cell interacts with the recorder grid. At some angles, such as 0° and 45°, the corners of each halftone cell intersect the pixel grid at the corners of a pixel. These are the rational angles, so-called because their tangent can be expressed as the ratio of two whole numbers: that is, as the ratio between the number of pixels horizontally and the number of pixels vertically.

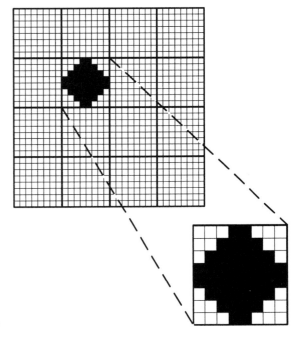

(The tangent of an angle is the ratio between the length of the opposite and adjacent sides. A rational number is one that can be expressed as the ratio of two whole numbers, or integers. It follows then that an irrational number is a number such as pi, which begins with 3.14159 and continues for millions of decimal places without a repeating pattern.)

At other angles, such as 15° and 75°, for example, the corners of each halftone cell do not precisely fit on the recorder grid, resulting in halftone

---

dots with variable shapes and number of pixels. These irrational angles pose a serious problem. If you select a screen based on an irrational tangent angle, each dot description must be calculated individually, which requires a substantial amount of computing power.

The first attempt from the desktop — rational or RT Screening — sought to minimize moiré by using screen angles and frequencies that more or less approximate those desired. Instead of generating the precise screen angle, RT Screening rounds the irrational tangent angle up or down to the nearest rational tangent angle. This ensures that all halftone cells are identical, and need only be calculated once. Although rational screening is relatively fast, rounding up or down to the nearest rational angle also forces you to modify the screen frequency; both actions can result in moiré and other quality problems.

The New Screening Technology: Supercells

The solution to the moiré problem, which was discovered more or less simultaneously by a number of researchers, is to work with supercells containing hundreds or thousands of conventional digital halftone cells. Although this does not enable them to precisely obtain the irrational (15° and 75°) angles, it lets them get much closer than was possible with previous kinds of rational screening.

With RT Screening, for example, the 75° angle is typically rounded to 74.9°; with Accurate Screens it is rounded to 74.9998°. The screen angles created through the supercell method are still rational, but they are much closer to the desired irrational angles, which is why moiré is almost — but not totally — eliminated. Naturally, you pay a price in performance for the greater angular accuracy of a supercell; describing a supercell containing many halftone cells requires more calculations than a single halftone cell.

But an interesting phenomenon has occurred in conjunction with the new screening software advances. The hardware in which screening takes place (the RIP) has also improved recently, in particular through the use of integrated RISC (reduced instruction set computing) chips to significantly speed the rasterizing process. The increased speed of the new RIPs appears to more than compensate for any additional calculation required to handle the supercells. (The color separations you create with Draw use Adobe Accurate Screens. For more on these, turn to Service Bureau Strategies.) But keep in mind that these can be overridden, so you can take advantage of the superior screen angle technology of newer output devices that use the supercell technology.

Color Proofing

In the printing industry, where million-dollar print runs proceed on the basis of the client's signed approval of a Cromalin or other pre-press proof, there's another old saying: "The chrome is the contract." In other words, if the printed piece looks pretty much like the proof you approved, you have very few grounds for complaint.

Indeed, the standard printing trade customs that govern most commercial printing in North America do not require that the printed piece exactly match the original or the proof. According to the Graphic Arts Council: "Because of differences in equipment, processing, proofing substrates, paper, inks, pigments and other conditions between color proofing and production pressroom operations, a reasonable variation in color between color proofs and the completed job shall constitute acceptable delivery." The question remains as to what a reasonable variation might be.

To be precise, one should distinguish between an actual proof, from which the client is expected to evaluate and approve colors, and a composite, or comp, used only for layout and design approval.

Leading Proofing Technologies

Color proofing is an excellent example of the perennial trade-offs between time, money and quality. If you can wait and aren't particularly fussy about matching colors, a proof can be obtained for a few dollars, which is about all its worth. But even if the client hasn't requested a proof, most printers will create one for their own use, rather than take a job on press without some kind of proof.

There are six main kinds of proofs in commercial use today, each with its own relative advantages and deficiencies. Ranked from cheapest to most expensive, they are: thermal, overlay, integral, digital and press. (That doesn't even take into account the so-called soft proof, which is a fancy name for staring at the colors on the screen and guessing about how they will look when printed.)

Thermal proofs, such as those from QMS, Tektronix, Seiko, Calcomp, Océ Graphics, and others, are relatively quick and cheap, but will not match the results from the print shop. Their 300 dpi resolution is far too low to reveal detail in a color photograph, but for vector-based art, such as that created by Draw, they're more appropriate. Such color comprehensives give an approximation of the assigned colors, and permit you to correct any obvious mistakes before you incur the expense of color printing. But you should watch out for color shifts with problem colors, such as blue. Basically, these should be considered as comps, rather than proofs.

Overlay proofs, such as 3M Color Key and Du Pont Chromacheck, combine four pieces of colored film (cyan, magenta, yellow and black) in register over a single white sheet. This makes it easy to check details on each separation negative, but produces a proof in which the density of the overlays adds a yellowish-gray tone.

Integral proofs, such as Du Pont Cromalin, 3M MatchPrint, Polaroid Spectra, AgfaProof (illustrated here), and Fuji Color-Art are photographic prints created by exposing each of the four separations to a primary-colored, thin-pigmented emulsion layer, which is laminated in register to a sheet of white paper. Integral proofs, though more expensive than most overlays, provide a much better indication of how the four separation halftones will print.

Digital proofs, such as the 3M Digital MatchPrint and Kodak Approval, are created directly from digital data. Dye sublimation printers, such as the Kodak XL7700 and the Mitsubishi printer illustrated here, output continuous-tone proofs on photographic paper directly from color-separated digital data, without the creation of separation negatives. The prints are excellent and have the look, feel and stability of conventional photographs. High-quality inkjet proofers, such as the Iris color inkjet printer, use CMYK pigments and can produce 256 distinct dot sizes directly from digital separation data.

Although still in their infancy, digital proofs are expected to become a dominant force during the next few years, despite the fact that they are not made from separation films. Color copiers, such as those made by Canon, Kodak and Xerox, can also be used as proofers, especially when outfitted with continuous-tone controllers.

Press proofs, using the separation negatives, press, paper and inks intended for the actual job, offer the best possible quality. The cost, however, is very high, because of the time and expense of the press make-ready process. In fact, there are special little presses that some printers use exclusively for making proofs.

Evaluating Color Proofs

To evaluate a color proof, you need to look at it closely. Start by purchasing a good magnifying glass with a minimum eight-power magnification, and preferably 15-power or higher. A magnifier may also be called a loupe, glass or linen tester. Most professionals prefer a swivel-arm design, because it can rotate to any position and is relatively free of distortion. You may find that the more expensive fold-up version is better value if you carry a regular magnifier with you to the separators and printers, and are concerned (quite reasonably) that, sooner or later, the lens will get scratched and become effectively useless.

When looking for quality, whether in a proof or a reproduction, let your eyes be the judge. In some market segments, such as merchandising catalogs and advertising, if you can tell the difference between the original and the printed piece, the quality isn't acceptable. The growing exception to this rule is the emergence of 'good-enough' color produced on the desktop, where the lack of quality is more than compensated for (in the opinion of the observer) by the reduced cost and turnaround time.

You don't have to work with color for long before you're able to recognize that the brilliant colors displayed in a proof can be difficult or impossible to accomplish on press. Many factors can contribute to unsatisfactory results, from subjective color perception to paper and ink densities. Color proofs can help you avoid unpleasant surprises before they occur, but only if you know what to look for. Here, too, some factors apply to drawings, while others are relevant only to photographic images.

- Sharpness — use a strong magnifier to ensure that detail areas are crisp and clean.
- Color accuracy — compare the proof to the original under a standard 5,000K color-correct light source.
- Neutral areas — make sure they are completely free from green or blue casts, all the way from white to gray to black.
- Registration — confirm that all elements are properly registered to eliminate fuzziness, shadows and color changes.
- Size — all photos, art, type and pages must be exactly the right size.
- Borders — these should be correct size, color and position.
- Captions — these must be correct in content, size and position.
- Pagination — all pages and folios must be placed correctly, with crop marks and scores indicated where necessary.
- Spots and scratches — along with pinholes and dust, these must be removed from film and plates.
- Broken type — there should be no white specks on type, no sections partially or completely covered.

To identify potential press problems, many printers use color control bars, such as those sold by the Graphic Arts Technical Foundation. The entire control bar series is usually printed on progressive proofs, with various specific elements included on the production run, depending on available trim space.

When publishing in color, it is easy to make very expensive mistakes. Before giving the go-ahead for a color printing job, forget intuition and don't depend on a five-dollar thermal print. The few extra dollars spent on proofing are your best insurance against the horrendous cost of reprinting a botched job. I've listed a few good color books in the bibliography. For more comprehensive information on color output, contact the San Francisco-based The Color Resource. It provides a wide variety of color-related publications.

Service Bureau Strategies

19

T he cost of high-resolution toner-based printers has dropped dramatically since the last edition of this book. The LaserMaster WinPrinter 800, for example, which I used to proof all the illustrations for this book, retails for well under $2,000. Even the tabloid-format LaserMaster Unity 1200XL with which the camera-ready pages for this book were created comes in at under $10,000.

But there will always be those who simply want to proof their pages at relatively low laser resolutions, and then use photo-based devices to get the highest possible output quality. Although prices are falling, such devices are still quite expensive, with the result that most of them find their way into high-volume in-house installations and service bureaus. The latter category provides the possibility of generating higher quality hard copy of Draw images than we can with our own personal printer.

Service bureaus employ high-resolution PostScript printers from vendors such as Agfa, Varityper and Linotype, all bearing the generic name of *imagesetter*. Imagesetters differ from one another in the resolutions at which they output, their 'repeatability', the quality of their halftone dots, output speed and the maximum media size they can handle. High repeatability is critical for the creation of quality color separations, since it dictates the accuracy of the film handling and dot placement of the imagesetter.

Of all the imagesetters you're likely to come across, Linotype's Linotronic L300 (or Lino, for short) is still the most common. Able to output at resolutions up to 2,540 dpi and image an area 70 picas (11.6 inches) wide, the L300 is the workhorse of the service bureau industry. The RIP (Raster Image Processor) of an imagesetter makes a difference not only in speed but in the

Using high resolution output devices

ability to output complex files. The RIP30 driving an L330, for example, is a vast improvement over earlier models, and the L330 is a color-capable imagesetter. Beyond its sluggish speed, the L300 just doesn't have the repeatability to create quality color separations.

If you're creating simple black-and-white paper or film output, the type of imagesetter isn't that vital. But if the files are quite complex, they may take an inordinate amount of time to output, sometimes resulting in extra costs. And if you're creating color separations, be picky about the imagesetter you use. The Linotronic L330, BirmySetter 300, Scitex Dolev, Scangraphic Scantext 2030 PD, Varityper 5300, Optronics ColorSetter or Agfa SelectSet 5000 can all produce quality separations.

Just as important is finding a competent service bureau. Anyone can lease an imagesetter and go into the service bureau business. But those with a solid knowledge of computers, applications software, film processing chemistry, PostScript programming and color theory are few.

When to Use a Service Bureau

A number of situations might call for the use of a service bureau. If you reproduce your publications via offset printing, the sharper output of text, line art and halftones at high resolution may well be worth the modest extra cost. Service bureaus typically charge a base price per page and some charge an hourly rate if the page takes longer than five or ten minutes to print. The latter could easily happen if you have a very complex image containing hundreds of objects, multiple fountain fills or bitmaps. Always provide the service bureau with a hard copy proof of your drawing and ask for advice before committing yourself to printing complex files.

If you have only a non-PostScript device available as your personal printer, a service bureau provides a way to make use of the PostScript-specific features of Draw. In addition, if you create documents larger than the paper size of your printer, you must tile such drawings on a laser and then assemble the tiles. This is tolerable when proofing, but it's awkward for creating finished artwork. The larger paper sizes of service bureau imagesetters let you create large-format output without tiling.

Many service bureaus provide access to expensive color printers, such as thermal printers, film recorders and sublimation devices. Some have color plotters that can create billboard-sized output, while others can image your illustrations on garments, mugs and other three-dimensional objects. Finally, if you reproduce your publication via offset printing, you can create film negatives on an imagesetter directly from your Draw files. Go the film route to create color separations, or if your drawings contain grayscale bitmaps.

Preparing Your Files for Output

Using service bureaus isn't overly complex, but there are some things to look out for. The first comes during the creation of the Draw image itself. When filling an object with a tint using the Fill ⬧ tool, for example, keep in mind that these are relative values that vary between output devices. In other words, the 10% gray on a 300 dpi printer will be different (heavier and coarser) from that produced on a service bureau's imagesetter, while the imagesetter will render an 80% gray darker than that of the laser printer. As another example, if you set your line thickness to 0.001 in the Outline Pen dialog box, you'll get the thinnest line that your printer can output. Of course, this will be much thinner at 1,200 than at 300 dpi.

To avoid unpleasant surprises, your best bet is to prepare a test page loaded with different line thicknesses, calligraphic outlines, fills, PostScript textures, bitmap images and text in different formats at multiple sizes, and run it through the imagesetter long before an actual job is due. In the area of color specification, the TRUMATCH palette included with Draw is recommended if you'll be creating process separations. You should also check out the modified TRUMATCH palette included in the DRAW directory of the Utility disk (TRUNEW.ZIP), since it provides a workaround to trapping problems. If you'll be using a service bureau's color output device, such as a film recorder or dye sublimation printer, you should first output the NCG.CDR file (in the NCG.ZIP archive) as a reference. This file contains samples of all the colors in

Draw's default palette. You could also output this to your own color proof printer.

As well as creating test pages, you could go further by testing your output files before sending them to the service bureau. LaserCheck, from Systems of Merritt, is a useful tool for doing just this. You download the LaserCheck software to your printer and then send it a PostScript print file. (You can dump .PRN print files to your laser at the DOS level by typing COPY FILENAME.PRN LPT1:, assuming your printer is attached to the parallel port. Adobe Systems also supplies a file downloading utility with its PC fonts.) LaserCheck's output lets you check crop and registration marks, and provides special error-handling capabilities, as well as generating a list of printer memory usage, font requests, page processing time and other useful information. The included documentation also provides debugging tips for problem files. A discount coupon for the purchase of LaserCheck is included at the back of this book.

Your choice of service bureau may be limited by geography, although many do accept files sent to them on disk or via modem. If at all possible, try to find one that understands PCs; many are Macintosh-specific and while these *may* be able to handle your files with some fiddling, weird glitches can show up in your output. I've experienced randomly scattered quote marks in text, and parts of drawings — as well as entire files — not outputting. This is not a limitation of Draw, but just the reality of exchanging files of any kind between hardware platforms.

Output Format Alternatives

If a service bureau uses PCs and has your version of CorelDRAW installed, simply copy your .CDR file to a floppy — the bureau can then output it directly from Draw. This approach has the advantage of allowing the service bureau to make adjustments to your drawing, if for some reason it isn't outputting properly. But be sure to specify just how the options in Draw's Print dialog box should be set. I usually supply a printout of the Print dialog box, just to be sure. To create one, set up the Print dialog box as desired and hold down the Alt and PrintScreen keys on your keyboard. Click on Cancel, then choose Paste from Draw's Edit menu and print out a copy of the dialog box.

While this sounds simple enough, you may still experience problems if you've installed fonts not present on the service bureau's system, or have renamed Draw's fonts. If there are just small blocks of text causing problems, choosing Convert To Curves from the Arrange menu will eliminate the problem. Just be sure not to save your file after performing this, or you'll lose the ability to edit the text.

If the bureau doesn't have Draw, you'll have to create a PostScript version of your .CDR file by either exporting your drawing as an .EPS (Encapsulated PostScript) file, or by printing it to disk as a pure PostScript file. You should ask your service bureau which format it prefers.

Exporting to .EPS

An exported .EPS file can be imported into another application, like PageMaker, and printed from that application. This lets the service bureau view the image on the screen before printing (if you've exported the drawing with a 'header') and alter its size and page position. However, you have fewer options in Draw when exporting than when printing to disk. You can't export when creating color separations, for example, or specify fountain fill stripes or object flatness.

To create an .EPS file of a currently open Draw image, choose Export from the File menu and choose Encapsulated PostScript *.EPS format from List Files Of Type. You have the option of exporting just part of your graphic by enabling Selected Only. Clicking on OK displays an Export EPS dialog box that provides several output options. You should click on All Fonts Resident if you want to use the service bureau's versions of the fonts in your illustration. If you go this route, don't forget to tell the bureau to download the fonts required by your file to its imagesetter before printing, or the fonts will output in (ouch) Courier. While this much is straightforward, the setup procedures you need to go through to ensure that your fonts actually output as specified differ for Draw .WFN, TrueType or PostScript fonts. This is poorly documented, so I've covered it in obsessive detail in *Advanced Type Topics*.

The Convert Color Bitmaps To Grayscale option works much as you'd expect: Draw converts color bitmaps — such as scanned images — into grayscale format to ensure they'll output to Level 1 PostScript printers. (Newer black-and-white Level 2 printers have no problem outputting color bitmaps.)

The Image Header section of this dialog box creates a low-resolution .TIF-format version of the exported image that displays for positioning purposes when the file is imported into another application, such as Ventura or PageMaker. You have a choice of header resolutions; the higher it is, the more clearly it will display, but the larger your file will be. In fact, for a complex drawing the size of this header may make the difference between success and failure when importing the exported .EPS file into an application. If you're receiving error messages when you try to import exported .EPS files, then lower or dispense with the header entirely. Corel recommends the lowest resolution, but I usually use the highest one that will import, since I prefer a sharper screen image. Your choice of header only influences screen display — the quality of printed output is not affected.

It's worth noting that if you include a header and import the resulting file into a Macintosh application, such as PageMaker, the header displays perfectly. However, some Macintosh applications perversely refuse to even acknowledge the existence of .EPS files created with PC applications. You'll have to use ResEdit, or a similar Macintosh utility, to edit the resource name of the file to let such applications import Draw .EPS files.

As an example of how important it is to remain current with Draw updates, WordPerfect users have until recently been experiencing problems importing Draw-generated .EPS files. It seems WordPerfect expects such images to use an older version of the TIFF header than that generated by Draw. To work around this, Corel recently modified the TIFF export filter to export to TIFF version 4.2 for those programs, such as WordPerfect, unable to accept TIFF 5.0. This filter also affects the image header on .EPS files exported from CorelDRAW. With the new filter installed, you can add the following line at the end of your CORELDRW.INI file:

Here x is a value of 1 or 0, with 1 creating TIFF 4.2 and 0 generating version 5.0 headers. This filter, along with similar updates and bug fixes, can be found on the Corel forum of CompuServe (GO COREL), or can be obtained directly from Corel.

Printing to a File

Printing to a file is a little more involved, but it provides more control over the resulting PostScript file. To print to a file you must have a PostScript printer driver installed. If you're not currently using a PostScript printer, first install one as discussed in *Windows Survival Skills*. The process of adding new printers is also well-covered in the Windows documentation.

The important point here is that you should be using a current version of the PostScript driver. You can determine the version by running the Windows Control Panel, double-clicking on Printers, clicking on Setup and then on About. The current version of the Microsoft-supplied driver is 3.53. If you have an earlier one, you may experience limitations in its support for imagesetter media sizes. Earlier versions also caused problems when creating print files of documents using TrueType fonts. The current version of the driver can usually be found on CompuServe (GO WINADV) or it can be obtained from Microsoft. Recent versions of the driver come with Windows PostScript Definition (.WPD) files for a variety of imagesetter models.

As an example of how different versions of the Windows PostScript driver perform, consider the notorious case of the rotated .EPS image. When an .EPS image exported from Draw (or any application) is imported into a landscape-orientation page in some Windows applications, such as PageMaker, the image may output rotated. The problem here was that a bug in the Windows 3.0 PostScript driver caused such images to rotate, so applications worked around this by rotating the images again; this way they wound up correctly oriented. With Windows 3.1, Microsoft fixed this bug but — you guessed it — applications that have not been made 3.1-aware are still expecting the bug and are blindly rotating away.

The fix is to add the following line to the [ModelName,Port] section of your WIN.INI file (where ModelName is the name of your PostScript printer model):

```
LandScapeOrient=270
```

There are a number of such modifications you can make to your WIN.INI file. For example, if you selected the Print PostScript Error Information check box in the Advanced Options dialog box when you configured your printer, and your printer is issuing timeout messages, try increasing the printer's timeout value. Add the following setting to the [ModelName,Port] section in the WIN.INI file :

```
timeout=<number-of-seconds>
```

A value of 600 would set the timeout value to 10 minutes. On the other hand, I heard of one case recently where setting this value to 0 solved a problem printing a file containing lots of fountain fills. In this case the imagesetter gave a timeout error but kept trying to process the file, remaining in printing mode until the power was switched off.

With the PostScript driver installed and selected, quit Control Panel and choose Print from Draw's File menu. You could simply choose Print To File, click on OK, then name and generate a print file, but some of the available options in the dialog box should not be overlooked. Of course, these can also be used when printing directly to a PostScript printer, not just to a disk file.

As when exporting, for example, you can print just selected portions of your image to disk by choosing Selected Objects Only. Fit To Page will enlarge all the objects on the page, or just the currently selected objects, as large as possible within the page boundaries. You should choose Tile when printing an

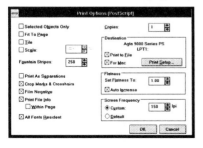

image that's either too big to fit on the media size of your output device, or if you enlarge your image at print time beyond the limits of the media size by entering a value in the Scale box larger than 100%. Tiling is usually used when proofing oversized drawings on a laser printer, and less so when using the larger media capabilities of imagesetters. Scale lets you proportionately shrink or reduce your entire image when printing (or just selected objects, if used in conjunction with Selected Objects Only).

Print As Separations is used for creating color separations, and is discussed later in this chapter. Clicking on this option automatically selects Crop Marks & Crosshairs, Film Negative and Print File Info. Choosing Crop Marks & Crosshairs causes these to be printed if the page size you've created in the Page Setup dialog box is *smaller* than the paper (or film) on which the image is being printed. For example, if you defined your page in Page Setup as being smaller than the 8 ½ by 11-inch paper size to which you're printing, you'd get crop marks and crosshairs. Crop marks and crosshairs are useful when creating undersized pages, and critical when creating color separations.

Printing your image as a film negative simply saves a step in the platemaking process, since the offset printer no longer has to create film from your paper original. Although film negatives cost more than paper positives, the cost savings of creating negatives directly and the improvement in quality, especially for halftones, makes this a desirable option. Don't forget to turn this off when proofing, unless you like black pages.

Choosing Print File Info prints the name of the file as well as the current time and date alongside the image. This information is handy for archival purposes, but Draw also prints the name of each spot or process color when creating separations, as well as the separation angle and screen frequency. This is printed outside the page area, if there's room on the output media. If your defined page size is the same as the output media, you can choose Within Page to force Draw to print the information inside the page borders. This is handy when proofing 8 ½ by 11-inch pages on a laser printer.

As when exporting, you can choose All Fonts Resident to use imagesetter or other remote printer fonts, rather than those supplied with Draw. I recommend a thorough perusal of the service bureau sections of *Advanced Type Topics* before you choose this option.

Fountain Stripes is significant when printing to higher-resolution PostScript devices, since it controls the number of steps in fountain fills. Corel recommends a setting of 128 for 1,270 dpi output and 200 for 2,540. The images on the last three pages of the color section of this book were output at 2,400 dpi with Fountain Stripes set to 200. This value can be set at up to 250, but there's no point in raising it so high that the resulting fountain fill has more steps than the output device can render. The result will be overly large files that take too long to output. You have more control if you use blends, rather than fountain fills, for creating shading effects, since these can be defined on an object-by-object basis.

It's important that you have the correct printer selected in the Destination area. If you've installed the Agfa or Linotronic versions of the driver, all you have to do is click on Setup and select them. However, you don't have to choose the output media size at this stage and the imagesetter doesn't have to be assigned to your FILE: port in Control Panel, as with some other Windows applications. Instead, simply click on To File. If you'll be sending the resulting file to a Macintosh-based service bureau, you should also click on For Mac. This will eliminate the Control-D characters that PCs normally place in print files, which cause Macs to cough and die.

The ability to change the Flatness value is significant if your drawing contains complex objects that the output device may have difficulty rendering. (I discuss this in more detail in the limitcheck error section later in the chapter.)

You can also change the Screen Frequency value, which will affect color separations and graphics using halftones. This value is the one that's used if you choose the default PostScript Halftone Screen Type in either the Fill or Outline dialog boxes. Normally it's set to Default in the Print dialog box, which means that Draw lets the output device use its own default screen frequency. This default value is based on the currently selected driver. For example, with a 300 dpi laser selected the default is 60 lines per inch (lpi), while for the Agfa 9000 imagesetter it's 121. The images on the last three pages of the color section were given a screen of 133. (See *Getting the Best Scan* for details on the relationship between resolution and screen frequency.)

You can override the default screen frequency by choosing Custom and entering a new value. Do this for creating special effects or fine-tuning your output on an imagesetter. In the latter case, it's best to first get recommendations from your service bureau on changing screen frequency from the default device value. Sometimes, the service bureau will prefer to set the resolution itself right on the device. Raising this value will also let you create better-quality halftones on laser printers that output at 400 dpi or higher, but that use a generic 300 dpi driver.

Click on OK and name your file when prompted. Use this dialog box to specify the final output media size. For example, you could use one of the transverse options provided by some imagesetter drivers to rotate your output and save media.

If your files are relatively modest in size, you can simply copy them onto a floppy. But what if they're too big for a floppy — how can you get them to the service bureau? Your best bet, for all but the largest files, is to simply compress them. If the service bureau uses Draw, you could use CorelMOSAIC to compress the file by about one-third. If they're PC-based but don't use Draw, your best bet is to use the shareware PKZIP program, which can be downloaded from most bulletin boards. You could use the WinZip program I've included on the Utility disk as a Windows-based shell for your file compression and decompression.

You'll find .PRN files of 8 Mb or more will usually fit on a 3.5-inch floppy using this technique. To decompress the files, there are both PC and Macintosh versions of the shareware PKUNZIP utility. WinZip will also decompress these without the need for PKUNZIP. StuffIt, the popular Macintosh compression utility, can also decompress .ZIP files. If your files are too big for PKZIP to handle, then you'll have to invest in some additional hardware, such as a removable hard drive, or send your file via modem.

Limitcheck Errors

Limitcheck errors are caused by creating a page with art or text that exceeds the capabilities of the PostScript output device. This is actually surprisingly easy to do with an illustration program like Draw, as anyone who has output complex files at service bureaus has probably already discovered.

Two recent articles in *timeout*, the journal of The Association of Imaging Service Bureaus, provided a much-needed discussion of limitcheck errors and supplied solid strategies for avoiding them. I've adapted them here, with permission, for Draw users, and have added my own output tips. The first section, by Bob Hires, a computer-based illustrator and designer, covers the issue from a designer perspective. After all, as a designer you can't just toss whatever you want onto your Draw page and expect the service bureau to magically output it. It's essential that the designer take some responsibility for successfully outputting files. As Bob points out, that responsibility begins with a thorough understanding of what's going on 'under the hood' of the PostScript output device.

Tips for Designers and Illustrators

Keep things simple. It only takes two nodes to create any single curve (a complete path consists of multiple curves and lines). If you draw a curve that has more than two nodes along its length, some of them are unnecessary. Look the curve over closely, determine which points aren't needed, delete them and then adjust the control handles attached to the remaining nodes to reshape the curve into the desired shape.

Avoid long paths. Very long paths can create limitcheck errors. Keep paths short, and where possible avoid combining two or more paths into one longer path with the Combine command.

Split paths when possible. Some drawing programs have an option that automatically splits long paths into shorter paths. For example, Adobe Illustrator has a Split Path Resolution command in its Preferences dialog box. Draw provides the same functionality when you output to a PostScript printer, using the PSComplexityThreshold= setting in the [CDrawConfig] section of the CORELDRW.INI file in the DRAW directory.

When printing an object that passes the complexity setting threshold, set by default to 3000, Draw will automatically carve up an object into smaller pieces, thus increasing its chances of rendering successfully. The value corresponds to the number of segments in an object. When working with complex objects, such as those created with CorelTRACE, or long text strings converted to curves, you may need to lower this even further. Note that this value applies both when printing and exporting. The palm tree illustration shows an example of path splitting.

Control flatness. If you find you have to make some extremely long paths, you can avoid printing problems by adjusting the *flatness* of the curve (how smoothly the imagesetter draws a curve). The more straight line segments the imagesetter has to create to approximate the curve, the more likely it is that you'll have limitcheck problems. For example, you can decrease the flatness of a circle to the point that it will print out looking like a stop sign; this, however, is too extreme. Even a modest increase of the Flatness value in the Print dialog box can greatly improve the speed and efficiency of the imagesetting device.

Avoid masks. Masks (PostScript clipping paths) are notorious for creating PostScript problems. Avoiding these isn't always possible when you are trying to create a desired effect, so if you must use masks keep them simple. For example, when creating masks out of a headline or logo, mask each letter form individually, rather than masking a whole word or sentence.

Convert fonts to curves. Convert the font used in a logo to curves if it is to be exported and then imported into a page layout application. This will speed up printing, but do this only if you're printing at a higher resolution than 300 dpi, otherwise you lose the font's built-in hinting. (Hinting helps you get better printing results on lower-resolution printers.) Other reasons for converting fonts to paths: you avoid font conflicts and, with some service bureaus, extra charges for outputting fonts not in their current library.

Learn how to use your tools. The most abused is the Pencil tool when used in Freehand ℓ mode. Be aware that when drawing in this mode, Draw is deciding where to place nodes, rather than you. The problem with this approach is that it often creates way too many nodes to describe a path, which can in extreme cases cause limitcheck errors. Yes, you can go back and edit the path once it's been created. But a better solution is to adjust the Freehand drawing tolerance. If you must use Freehand mode, at least set the drawing parameters in the Curves subdialog box of

Preferences, as discussed in *Creating and Editing Paths*. Better is to create curves with fewer nodes by using Draw's Pencil tool in Bézier ⌀ , rather than Freehand ⌀ , mode.

Be careful of autotracing. In general, I don't like the idea of letting the computer make decisions that you, as an artist, should be making. However, I do realize that there are times when using these tools is necessary. Whether tracing a bitmap with Draw's internal autotrace capability or the separate Trace utility, caution must be exercised to avoid the creation of objects with excessive node counts. (For a complete discussion of autotracing, see *Converting Scans with CorelTRACE*.)

Don't scale and rotate .EPS files in another application. For example, you can bring an .EPS logo into a page layout program and scale it 58.5% and then rotate it 18.25 degrees. This will slow your output time significantly and could cause printing errors. A better solution is to design your page, then go back and make the transformations to the logo in Draw. You'd then go back into the page layout program and re-import the transformed art. This is an extra step, but it can avoid many problems. Some service bureaus attach a surcharge on jobs based on the time it takes for the job to output, so the few minutes it takes to do this could save you a great deal of money.

One way to make moving back and forth between Draw and the page layout program easier is to use Object Linking and Embedding (OLE). If you embed the logo in your page layout program, you can simply double-click on it to load Draw and open the logo file. After making changes, you simply close Draw and the updated logo is automatically brought into the page layout program. (If you're not familiar with OLE, it's covered in the chapters on CorelSHOW and CorelCHART.)

 Print a laser proof. If it's crashing on your PostScript laser printer, it most likely will crash at the service bureau. However, the reverse isn't necessarily true; just because you can run out a laser print doesn't mean it will print on an imagesetter. If you decrease the flatness setting in Draw's Print dialog box, you can create curves of greater complexity and, in effect, simulate your files being output at higher resolutions. Flatness can be set from

.01 to 100, but when set to .25 it roughly simulates an imagesetter outputting at 1,200 dpi, in terms of curve complexity. This is a good way to test problem files before sending them to the service bureau. To the average illustrator or graphic designer this may seem too technical to bother with, but this really isn't the case. Designers must assume the responsibility for making sure that their files print correctly.

Talk to your service bureau. Good communications with your service bureau can make the difference between a successful project and a nightmare. Get to know the people you're working with. When in doubt, call them for advice before submitting the job. A few minutes on the phone can save you both headaches and money. Keep up with changes in the technology and understand what is happening when you send a file out to be printed. Most problems are the result of not understanding how things work.

Handling Limitcheck Errors

Frank Braswell is well-known as an expert in the area of trouble-shooting PostScript output problems. His firm, Systems of Merritt, supplies a variety of products and services in this area, including books, seminars, an advanced PostScript error handler and the LaserCheck software discussed above. The article by Frank in *timeout*, which I've adapted here, approaches limitcheck errors from a technical perspective.

A limitcheck error simply means that the PostScript code for an illustration has exceeded a limit built into the PostScript interpreter. With Level 1 PostScript machines, a limitcheck error (indicated by the limitcheck error message) can happen during one of four types of operations: path-building, rendering, masking and memory management. The fixes are different for each of these. The error message itself is not displayed by Windows, however, so you have to get it by using a communications program or PostScript error handler.

The Adobe Systems EHANDLER.PS error handler is supplied in your DRAW\EHANDLER directory. To install it, generate a Program Manager icon for it by attaching the included PSERROR.ICO icon to either the PSSEND1.BAT or

PSSEND2.BAT batch files. These copy EHANDLER.PS, and the related PSINFO.PS file, to either the LPT1: or LPT2: ports, respectively. If you're using another port, you'll have to edit the batch file with Notepad. Once downloaded, if a subsequent file dies in the printer, the error handler should print out the PostScript error message, which can help you track down the problem.

Path-building Problems

```
Error  message:  %%[Error:  limitcheck;
OffendingCommand: lineto]%%
```

The offending command can be any of the path-building PostScript commands, such as lineto, curveto, rlineto, arc and arcto.

Cause: An illustration created with a drawing program is made up of numerous PostScript *paths*. A path is a mathematical collection of lines and curves. Each path can be used for stroking (applying a line) or filling (filling the letter or graphic with a color, etc.) during rendering (rasterizing). In PostScript Level 1, there is limited memory allocated for the description of any path. If this memory is exceeded with too many lines or curves, a limitcheck error occurs.

To find the problem path, run Draw and with the illustration on the screen select one of the many lines and curves that make up the drawing with the Shape ⚲ tool. The object you select must not be grouped. Each of the nodes on the path designate individual curves or lines that make up a single path. If the total number of these, as shown in the Status Line, is larger than what can be held in allocated printer memory (typically 300 to 400 lines and curves), a limitcheck error occurs. That may sound like a generous amount of curves and lines to work with, but because Draw quickly generates a large number of lines and curves (especially if you've imported an .EPS file created with CorelTRACE), the path memory limit can be easily exceeded.

How many nodes can be used before a limitcheck error occurs? That depends on which PostScript interpreter you're using. Some have more *path space* (memory allocated for paths) than others. Those with lots of path space (some Hyphen RIPs, for example) experience few limitchecks. Old imagesetters have very limited amounts of path space and constantly have problems. More recent imagesetters fall between the two extremes.

If you only have the PostScript print file, you can still use a PostScript error handler to locate the problem path, although this requires knowledge of the PostScript language. Sometimes the PostScript code can be modified to run. However, you may still need the .CDR file to fix a problem path so that another print file can be generated.

Fix: Cut the offending path into smaller paths, so that each of the smaller paths fits within the path limit. You can also delete unnecessary nodes if they have no effect on the shape of the path.

Rendering Problems

```
Error    message:    %%[Error:    limitcheck;
OffendingCommand: stroke]%%
```
(or the OffendingCommand can be 'fill'.)

Cause: To render a curved path, the PostScript interpreter first *flattens* it by converting the curves of the path into a sequence of line segments. If the number of line segments required by a flattened path exceeds the path limit, a limitcheck error results. The amount of flattening is device-dependent — the PostScript interpreter uses more line segments (and dots) to create the same path at a higher device resolution. That's why some files only output on low-resolution devices.

Fix: Most application programs have menu options that allow the flatness to be adjusted. Raise the flatness so that fewer line segments are required by the flattened path. Draw only allows you to set flatness on a global basis, by adjusting the Flatness value in the Print dialog box. Others, such Aldus FreeHand, can operate on a curve-by-curve basis. Be careful — if you raise this value too high, the curves start to look choppy. Corel recommends raising this value in increments of four or five, until the file prints. You can also enable Auto Flatness, which provides a more sophisticated approach. Here flatness is automatically raised one increment at a time for the object that won't render. When this value hits 10, the object is simply skipped and the next object in the drawing is rendered.

Masking

Error message: %%[Error: limitcheck; OffendingCommand: clip]%%

Cause: Masks are used to hide parts of a graphic or text object, using invisible clipping paths to crop unwanted portions of images and other objects. A typical application in Draw would be the creation of a mask to fill an object with an imported bitmap, as described in *Working with Bitmap Graphics*. Besides dramatically increasing print time, clipping paths can generate limitcheck errors if too many nodes are used.

Fix: Open the application and simplify the clipping paths by reducing the number of nodes along each clipping path. Text is a particularly notorious offender, especially if it's in TrueType format. In this case, substitute a PostScript or .WFN font.

Memory Management

Error message: %%[Error: limitcheck; OffendingCommand: save]%%

Cause: Memory used by a PostScript program must be managed properly, so that it can be reused. This ensures that each successive page in a job doesn't use up more and more memory until all available program memory is consumed.

The PostScript 'save' operator is used for this purpose in virtually all application programs. Memory for .EPS files and embedded fonts is also managed using the save operator. Trouble arises when too many embedded fonts are included in a print file, or when .EPS files are *nested* too deeply.

For example, say a clip art image in Adobe Illustrator .EPS format is imported into an existing Draw illustration. The resulting image is then exported and imported into another illustration, which is then imported into a page layout program, which is then processed by a separation program. Each of these steps increases the amount of nesting of underlying .EPS files. The result is an exceeded save limit. Note that unlike the other three error types discussed here, this problem exists on both Level 1 and Level 2 devices.

Fix: Reduce the number of fonts used in the document, or instruct Draw to use fonts resident on the printer's hard disk or in the printer's memory (see *Advanced Type Topics*). This dramatically reduces the print file size, which also makes the job output faster. You should also reduce the nesting of .EPS files by breaking nested elements into separate files before including them in the final illustration file.

What about Level 2?

Level 2 devices eliminate limitcheck errors from paths and rendering. When a Level 2 printer or imagesetter reaches the path limit, it dynamically allocates additional path space in memory and merrily continues on its way. However, keep in mind that when using Level 2 devices, you can still get the save limitcheck if you have excessive nesting, overly long paths, and so on. It's still highly recommended for a designer to strive to eliminate potential limitchecks, so that a service bureau has the option of printing on a Level 1 device when required.

Creating Color Separations

So far, I've been discussing general output topics. But Draw also possesses the ability to create both spot and four-color process separations. You must have a PostScript printer driver installed and selected to create a separation file, but you don't actually need a PostScript printer connected to your system. If you *do* have a PostScript laser printer, you can use it to create process proofs and spot separations. But you'll have to output your four-color process separations on a high-resolution imagesetter to create film negatives.

Unless you're lucky enough to have access to a service bureau that uses Draw, you'll have to print the separations to disk and give the resulting text file to the bureau. While Draw can create process separations, it currently has some limitations in this area. It does a less-than-professional job if your image contains scanned images, for example, and there are few controls provided for the separation process. There are a number of PC-based separation programs, such as HiJaak ColorSep, from Inset Systems, that provide much more control over the separation process. To use these, you create a PostScript print file from Draw (or the page layout program into which you im-

---

ported a Draw-generated .EPS image) and load it into the separation program. In the case of HiJaak ColorSep, you then have control over gray component replacement and removal, black type surprinting, global trapping, dot shape and other separation parameters.

Process Color Separations

If you're creating an illustration for eventual color separation and offset printing, there are some things you should keep in mind. One is the number of steps, or intermediate colors, in fountain-filled and blended objects. If you fill objects with radial or linear fills, Draw provides no way to specify the number of intermediate colors in each object. As discussed earlier, you can change the Fountain Stripes value in the Print dialog box, but it applies to all objects containing fountain fills. A large number of steps will produce smooth blends on a printer that has the resolution to render them, but it will also create a larger file that takes longer to output. When proofing separations on 300 dpi lasers, I usually drop this value to 50 or lower to speed up output.

A big advantage of using Draw's Blend roll-up instead of fountain fills is that you can control the number of steps on an object-by-object basis. But just what is the optimal number of steps? The answer to this is a complex one that depends on such factors as output resolution, screen frequency and the two colors being blended. There are no rules for the creation of blends, but a general consensus is beginning to emerge about what works (most of the time).

For example, use the highest-resolution device possible. You'll create smoother blends at 2,400 than 1,200 dpi, because of the greater number of gray shades available at the desired screen frequency. At lower resolutions you may have to decrease the screen frequency to provide more shades and avoid *banding* (visible steps). Draw outputs to the default screen frequency of the output device, but you can set this in the Print dialog box by clicking on the Custom button. Keep in mind that when you create process separations, Draw ignores any special screens that you've assigned to object fills or outlines in the PostScript Options dialog box.

Beware of long blends that use only a few steps. A blend from 70% to 80% black spanning six inches will exhibit more noticeable steps than one spanning two inches. Similarly, if the six-inch blend was between 20% and 80% black it would display less banding than one from 70% to 80%, due to the greater number of steps — and subsequently smoother transition — between shades. A rule of thumb is to use 256 steps for a 100% change in color, or one step for every point of distance (there are 72 points in an inch) — whichever is fewer.

OUTPUT RESOLUTION	1626 DPI		2540 DPI		3252 DPI	
MAXIMUM SCREEN FREQUENCY	EASY BLENDS	DIFFICULT BLENDS	EASY BLENDS	DIFFICULT BLENDS	EASY BLENDS	DIFFICULT BLENDS
LINES PER INCH	110	100	170	150	200	180
10	20	26	23	30	30	35
20	40	52	44	56	56	64
30	60	78	65	80	80	93
40	80	104	86	106	106	122
50	100	127	106	131	131	150
60	120	153	126	157	157	180
70	140	179	147	183	183	210
80	160	216	168	208	208	240
90	180	230	189	234	234	270
100	200	250	210	260	260	300
For blends over short distances	One blend for every 3 point distance	One blend for every 2 point distance	One blend for every 2 point distance	One blend for every 1 point distance	One blend for every 2 point distance	One blend for every 1 point distance

percentage change in color

Some process colors seem to produce banding more than others. Yellow is generally regarded as the worst culprit, followed by cyan, magenta and black. Blends that cover a small area and use colors other than black are usually considered a safe bet — call them easy blends. But those that cover a large area and use black can be problematical — call them difficult. Blends that have the same orientation as the screen angle or have tints greater than 50% also fall into this category. See the accompanying table for suggestions on settings to minimize banding when working with both easy and difficult blends at a variety of resolutions and screen frequencies.

To sum up, you can minimize banding by reducing the size of the blended or fountain-filled area, increasing the percentage between the two colors, decreasing the screen frequency or raising the output resolution. You should always create film-based proofs before going to press if your drawing contains blends.

Trapping

When offset printing either spot color overlays or process separations, you may encounter thin white areas appearing between adjacent colors in your final printed piece. This is caused by slight misregistrations on the offset press and can range from the virtually undetectable to the glaring. Modern presses have reduced the registration problems that require *trap* — the slight overlap of objects of different colors — but for critical work it's wise to play it safe and create a trap for objects filled with colors that will draw attention to misregistration.

When you overlap objects containing different fills, only the fill in the top one prints; it replaces whatever is beneath it, an effect known as a *knockout*. To create a trap, you must specify a certain amount of an object's outline to actually print on top of the color adjacent to it, a process known as *overprinting*. This is yet another feature only available to those with a PostScript printer.

You can also use Draw's overprint abilities to mix colors right on the printed page. By overprinting two spot colors in various percentage tints of each, for example, you can create a variety of effects on a modest printing budget. But overprinting is more often used to provide trap.

Draw lets you create the two types of traps traditionally used in offset printing: *spreads* and *chokes*. An object that has been given an outline that will overprint on the object surrounding it has been given a spread. If an object has been given an outline that overprints on the one it surrounds, it's a choke. You can go even further and combine both a spread and a choke.

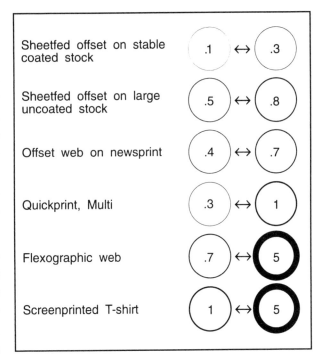

Sheetfed offset on stable coated stock	.1 ↔	.3
Sheetfed offset on large uncoated stock	.5 ↔	.8
Offset web on newsprint	.4 ↔	.7
Quickprint, Multi	.3 ↔	1
Flexographic web	.7 ↔	5
Screenprinted T-shirt	1 ↔	5

There are a few rules of thumb to go by when creating traps. In terms of trap thickness, the table on this page provides some guidelines by recommending values from .1 point to 5 points. Thick traps are necessary if you're trapping a spot color with a process one, so in this case use the higher values in the table. Since outline thickness extends equally inside and outside an object, double these values to achieve the desired trap thickness. You should then enable Behind Fill in the Outline Pen dialog box, to make sure that only the outer half of the outline overprints.

Choosing the color of traps is a little trickier. As a general rule, you should trap the least visually dominant color; that is, the lighter color should overlap the darker. Depending on the objects, this may require either a spread or a choke. If objects have similar brightness but different hues, both a choke and a spread may be required to create a composite color that straddles both objects. This is often appropriate for type, since the resulting trap will minimize changes to the perceived shape of letters. For a composite trap, give both the spread and the choke the desired trap thickness, rather than doubling it. The outline color of the spread and choke of a composite trap should be made up of elements of both.

The first trap example on this page shows an L filled with 40%

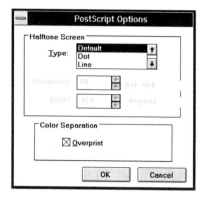

magenta on top of an object filled with 100% cyan and 100% yellow (green). Since magenta is the least dominant color, you would give the letter a spread by creating a 40% magenta outline for it and clicking on Overprint in the PostScript Options subdialog box of Outline Color.

In the second example, a D filled with 100% cyan and 100% magenta (purple) is on top of an object filled with yellow. Since yellow is the least dominant color, it should be choked. To accomplish this, you could create a quick copy of the D by selecting it and pressing the + key on your numeric keyboard (on the far right of your keyboard). This places a copy of the selected object on top of it. You could give the selected letter a fill of white and an overprinting yellow outline and then choose Back One from the Arrange menu. This would sandwich it between the purple D and the yellow background object.

Unfortunately, it's difficult to gauge the effectiveness of your chokes and spreads until your image is on the press; neither the monitor nor your printer will reveal them if you output the image. Digital proofs, such as those created with the Kodak XL7700 printer, also won't show them. Short of creating plates and printing the illustration, you'll have to use a film-based proofing method, such as a Cromalin, to create proofs from your high-resolution film negatives. You could also get a rough sense of your traps by using the clear acetate designed for laser printers to create low-resolution separations, as described below.

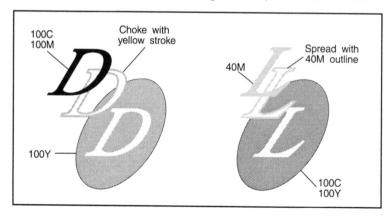

Creating Separations

To see Draw's separation abilities in action, open a file containing objects filled with color, such as one of the images in the SAMPLES subdirectory of your Draw directory. EYE.CDR is a good one — just ignore the warning message about the font mismatch (see *Advanced Type Topics* for an explanation of this error message.) Failing that, simply give any object on the page a process fountain fill.

Choose Print from the File menu. The many options in this dialog box have been discussed earlier in the chapter, so I won't go into them again here. To create separations on your own PostScript laser printer, click on Print As Separations and disable Film Negative. Crop Marks & Crosshairs, as well as Print File Info, will only be generated if the page size defined in the Page Setup dialog box of the File menu is smaller than the media size to which you're printing. Set the Scale value to 60%, to shrink down the image and leave lots of room for these, and then click on OK. (If you don't have a PostScript printer connected to your PC, but have installed and chosen the PostScript driver, click on To File and print your separations to a disk file.)

The Color Separations dialog box appears, listing all process and spot colors used in your image. A number of options are available to you at this point. The default is to automatically print one page for each of the process and spot colors listed. You can also click on Selected Colors and print one or more colors by simply clicking on them to choose them.

Draw also displays — and allows you to change — the screen angles and screen frequencies for each of the process colors. The values Draw displays here are those of the Adobe Accurate Screens. The first illustration, for example, displays screen angles and frequencies with the Agfa 9000 driver selected. I left the default screen frequency in the Print dialog

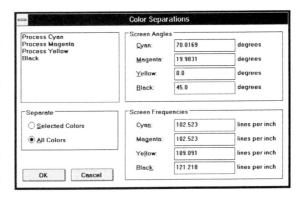

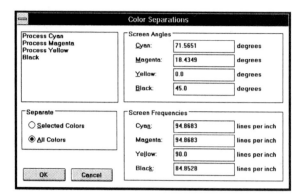

box set at 121 lpi. In the second illustration, I lowered the screen frequency in the Print dialog box to 85 lpi. Note that a quite different set of values is now displayed.

It's not discussed in the documentation, so if you're wondering where Draw is getting these values, they're all stored in the Color Separations Information section of the CORELDRW.INI file. As you can see from the illustration, these are based on the resolution of the output device, which Draw obtains from the current driver. In the case of the Agfa 9000, it assumes I'm outputting at 1,200 dpi (in fact, too low a resolution for process color separations).

You're free to edit any of these values, if you want easy access to different sets of them from the Print dialog box. (It would be wise to first make a backup of your CORELDRW.INI file.) However, these values are best left alone unless your service bureau advises you to change them. And, in fact, whatever screen angles and frequencies you use to create your separations can be overridden by your service bureau. In some cases this gives you access to device-specific values that create separations with less visible artifacts, or *moiré*. Click on OK now and one page will print for each selected spot or process color in your graphic.

If you use fairly translucent paper, you can place the resulting separations on top of each other and hold them up to the light to get a good idea of how Draw is separating the image into its various components. If you apply thick traps to some of the objects in the EYE illustration and create another set of separations, you'll be able to see Draw's trapping abilities in action.

```
┌─────────────────────────────────────────────────────────┐
│ ═  Notepad - CORELDRW.INI                           ▼ ▲ │
│ File  Edit  Search  Help                                 │
├─────────────────────────────────────────────────────────┤
│ [1200dpi]                                              ↑  │
│ Default=121lpi                                            │
│ 85lpi=71.5651,18.4349,0,45,94.8683,94.8683,90,84.8528    │
│ 90lpi=71.5651,18.4349,0,45,94.8683,94.8683,90,84.8528    │
│ 106lpi=70.0169,19.9831,0,45,102.523,102.523,109.091,121.218│
│ 110lpi=70.0169,19.9831,0,45,102.523,102.523,109.091,121.218│
│ 121lpi=70.0169,19.9831,0,45,102.523,102.523,109.091,121.218│
│                                                        ↓  │
│ ←                                                      → │
└─────────────────────────────────────────────────────────┘
```

Spot Color Overlays

When your graphic will be reproduced by offset printing but contains only a few solid colors, you don't have to go the process route. If you'll be outputting to a PostScript printer, simply specify each color using the Pantone method — when you create separations, each color will be printed on a separate piece of paper or film.

If you're unlucky enough to be outputting to a non-PostScript device, the only way to create spot color overlays in Draw is to select all the objects that have a similar spot color and print a separate page for each color, by choosing Selected Objects Only in the Print dialog box. You'll also have to create your own registration marks and print them on each page, since these are generated automatically only on PostScript printers. Note that this technique will not knock out overlapping colors.

Actually, there is one more way to create spot separations on a non-PostScript device. You could assign all the objects of each color to their own layer, and then simply print out one layer at a time. But again, you'd forfeit the ability to create knockouts.

Creating quality process color separations is fraught with technical difficulties, especially if your image is complex. Again, let me urge you to work as closely as possible with a competent service bureau.

Optimizing Windows

One of the strengths of Windows is the ease with which it can be customized to reflect the production needs of the individual user. The ability to make it work *your* way begins with different techniques to load Windows itself and leads to personalized configurations of, enhancements to, and even replacements for, Program Manager and File Manager.

There is also a variety of ways to run Windows applications — such as Draw — and optionally open data files at the same time. Finally, there is a multiplicity of third-party utilities that extend the capabilities of Windows. Some simply display the current time and date. Others locate files, provide enhanced task switching or add advanced macro capabilities.

In this chapter I'll discuss a number of ways to customize the configuration and operation of Windows and your applications. I won't, however, wade into the technical arcana of tweaking DOS and Windows. For that, I'll refer you to *The Microsoft Guide to Managing Memory with DOS 5*, by Dan Gookin (Microsoft Press) and *Windows 3.1 Secrets*, by Brian Livingston (IDG Books). But really, all you need is a careful study of the surprisingly good *User Guide* supplied with Windows itself; check out its *Optimizing Windows* section.

Windows itself can be run from the DOS prompt simply by typing WIN. But perhaps your computer, like mine, is set to run Windows automatically when you turn it on; in this case the WIN command has been placed in the AUTOEXEC.BAT file. Running Windows automatically makes sense, since you're probably either running Windows applications, such as Draw, or grungy old DOS applications while Windows is running. But what if you want to stop Windows from loading automatically?

Making Windows work your way

In the Utility directory on the disk included with this book you'll find WINLOA.ZIP. As with most of the files on the disk, this is a compressed file. Complete instructions for decompressing .ZIP files are provided in *The Draw Companion Disks*. That chapter also provides contact information for the developers of the programs on the disk. If you encounter problems installing or using the programs that can't be solved by the accompanying documentation files, you should contact the developers for assistance.

Once WINLOA.ZIP is decompressed to WINLOAD.EXE, simply copy the file to any directory included in your PATH command (such as WINDOWS or DOS) and replace WIN with WINLOAD in your AUTOEXEC.BAT file. The next time you turn on your computer, WINLOAD will pause for a default two seconds before going on to run Windows. If you press any key during that time, Windows won't load and you'll wind up at the DOS prompt. You can change the pause length by adding a value; WINLOAD 5, for example, will pause for five seconds.

When running Windows from the DOS prompt, you can be more specific if you know with which program and data file you'll be working. At the DOS prompt you can type 'WIN CORELDRW', for example, if the location of Draw's program file, CORELDRW.EXE, is listed in the PATH command of your AUTOEXEC.BAT file. If not, you'd have to type 'WIN C:\CORELDRW\DRAW\CORELDRW', assuming Draw was installed in the suggested default directory. You can also load a Draw file at the same time by adding its name and location to the command line. An example would be 'WIN CORELDRW C:\FILES\TEMPLATE.CDR.' Since Windows knows .CDR is the extension of Draw's files, in fact all you'd have to type in this case is the complete location and name of the file: 'WIN C:\FILES\TEMPLATE.CDR.'

When Windows loads, it first runs Program Manager. This is simply a default, however. The SYSTEM.INI file in the WINDOWS directory has a SHELL= line that determines the first program to load when Windows runs. You could change this line from SHELL=PROGMAN.EXE to SHELL= WINFILE.EX if you want Windows to run File Manager instead. You could even change it to SHELL=MSDOS.EXE to run the creaky old MS-DOS Executive shell used by Windows 2. More realistic is to run one of the many shareware or commercial Program Manager enhancements or replacements, such as Aporia (shareware from NewTools) or The Norton Desktop for Windows (from Symantec).

WinEZ

WinEZ

I've included a Program Manager enhancement that I find useful on the Utility disk. During a typical Draw session you may also be running CorelCHART, CorelPHOTO-PAINT, CorelTRACE, scanning software, a word processor or a page layout application like PageMaker or Ventura. A simple method for switching between currently running applications is to pop up the Windows Task List by pressing Control-Escape. You can then double-click on the application which you want to display. Or you could hold down the Alt key and tap on the Tab key until the title bar of the desired running application is displayed. But if you want to run a new application you'll have to return to Program Manager and double-click on the application's icon. And Alt-Tabbing can get pretty slow if you have a lot of applications running at once.

WinEZ, from New Generation Software, is a shareware ($29.95 registration) application that simplifies switching between currently running programs or launching new ones. Decompress the WINEZ3.ZIP archive and generate an icon for WINEZ.EXE. Once installed and run, WinEZ displays two buttons on your menu bar. One pops you quickly back into Program Manager or displays a menu of all the Program Manager groups. Each group then further expands into a submenu of the applications under it and lists their contents. You can use this to quickly run CorelCHART, CorelTRACE and the other applications included with

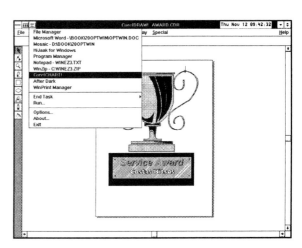

Draw. The other button displays a menu of currently running tasks, with the most recently used arranged at the top. You can then switch to an application simply by choosing it, as well as close it. The included WINEZ3.TXT file should be read for a detailed feature discussion.

If you find yourself enamored of the capabilities of WinEZ, you'll probably want it running every time you use Windows. There are two ways you can ensure that it loads automatically when Windows first runs. One technique, which dates back to earlier versions of Windows, is to add the name of the program and its path to the LOAD= line at the beginning of your WIN.INI file. But there's an easier, mouse-driven way that I recommend.

Autoloading Applications

Once you've generated an icon for WinEZ in Program Manager, locate your StartUp group window. If you can't find StartUp, look for it on the Window menu. If it's been deleted, create a new one by choosing New from the File menu, choosing Program Group, clicking on OK, typing StartUp in the Description text box and clicking on OK. Now drag your WinEZ icon into the StartUp group. This is all you have to do to make WinEZ run automatically when Windows loads.

With other applications that you want to autoload but not display their windows, such as File Manager, a final step is in order. In this case, with the program icon still selected, press Alt-Enter to display the Program Item Properties dialog box. Click on Run Minimized and OK. This ensures that the program will run in the background, out of harm's way until you need it. I have several icons in my StartUp group for programs that I like to have running at all times. However, keep in mind that loading programs uses memory. Don't load large programs such as Draw this way unless you need regular access to them.

Autoloading Templates

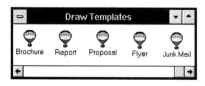

Another twist to running an application like Draw is Window's ability to load a data file at the same time. Experiment with this in Program Manager by holding down the Control key and dragging the Draw icon to a new location inside its group. This creates a duplicate of the icon. Choose Properties from the File menu, insert a space after the .EXE in the Command Line box and add the location and name of one of your .CDR files. Change the Description to that of your .CDR file and click on OK. Double-clicking on this new icon will run Draw and then open the specified .CDR file.

You could have several of these icons linked to commonly used files, such as templates — a procedure that would also work well for CorelCHART. You could go even further with this and have each Draw icon run a batch file that first copied a previously saved program configuration set — from BROCHURE.SYS to CDCONFIG.SYS, for example — to load Draw not only with a particular data file but a broad spectrum of defaults. (For more on this, see *Customizing Draw's Defaults*.)

Automating with Macros

Recorder

It's often overlooked, but one of the easiest ways to make Windows (and Draw) work your way is with the Recorder program in the Accessories group of Program Manager. Recorder lets you quickly create a sequence of keystrokes and mouse actions, or *macros*, and play them back at a later time. Macros are a great way to automate recurrent mousing around.

For example, when I'm working on a complex drawing with lots of fountain fills, I like to keep the Preview Fountain Stripes setting low to speed up screen redraw. But sometimes I like to quickly get an accurate look at the fountain fills before switching back to the faster display. Since Preview Fountain Stripes is in a subdialog box of Preferences, it requires a lot of clicking to move back and forth. Time for a macro. Use the following procedure to create two macros for switching between high and low quality screen display of fountain fills.

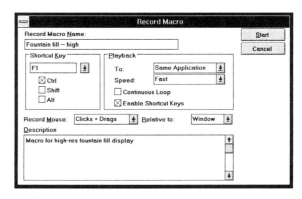

First double-click on the Recorder icon in the Accessories group to run it. Then run Draw and display Recorder by using Alt-Tab or Control-Escape. Choose Record from Recorder's Macro menu. You can ignore most of the options in this dialog box for now, but type 'Low Quality Fountains' in the Record Macro Name box. You must also specify the keystroke sequence that will activate your first macro.

Draw doesn't use Control-Shift sequences, so these are fair game for your macros. Click on the Shift button, so that both it and Control are now enabled. Then click in the text box below Shortcut Key and type in an L. Control-Shift-L will be the keystroke sequence that chooses the low resolution display of your fountains. It's optional, but you can also type in a short description of what your macro does in the Description area, if you like.

Click on Start. Recorder is now keeping track of all your mouse and keyboard actions. Choose Preferences from the Special menu and click on the Display button. Since the Preview Fountain Stripes value is already highlighted, simply type in 20. Then click on OK twice to return to the page. That's all you want to record, so end the macro by pressing the Control and Break (or Pause) keys simultaneously. In the dialog box that appears, click on Save Macro and OK to save the macro.

Bring Recorder forward with Alt-Tab and go through the process again, this time assigning the second macro to Control-Shift-H (for 'high', natch) and setting the Preview Fountain Stripes value to 100 (or 200, if you have a really top-notch display system). You're done.

Try out your high quality display macro now by pressing Control-Shift-H, and sit back to watch the performance. Set it back to low with Control-Shift-L. Nifty, or what? To preserve your macros, choose Save from Recorder's File menu and give your collection of macros a name, such as DRAW. You can open this saved macro file at any time by double-clicking on the Recorder icon and choosing Open from the File menu. But more elegant is to make a copy of the Recorder icon and add the file name and path of your macro to the Command Line of the Program Item Properties dialog box, as described above in Autoloading Applications. This will load the macro file automatically when you run Windows. Don't forget to click on Run

Minimized in the dialog box, or Recorder will run full screen.

I've included a collection of Draw macros in the UTILITY directory of the Utility disk. Simply extract MACROS.REC from the MACROS.ZIP archive — a suite of macros created by Diane Byrd and used here with her permission — and copy it to any directory on your hard drive. To try these out, run Recorder and open MACROS.REC. If you find them valuable you may want to add them, along with your own macros, to your StartUp group.

Macros are a great way to customize an application like Draw or even Windows itself. If they appeal to you, investigate one of the commercial macro programs available for Windows. These offer many capabilities beyond the rather rudimentary Recorder, such as the ability to edit macros and have them work between applications.

Using Custom Icons

I really like the ability of Windows to let me quickly assign a different icon to an existing application. While I usually use the icons supplied with programs, sometimes I either edit the existing icon or create an entirely new one.

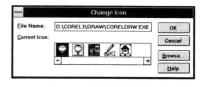

For example, several icons are included in the .EXE files for each of the Draw suite of programs. To see this, click once on your Draw icon in Program Manager, press Alt-Enter and click on Change Icon. You'll find there are five icons available that could be assigned to Draw. Besides the usual balloon, you've got a balloon in a button, a version that looks a bit like the cover art on the Draw box, a weird 'magic pencil' and a little guy with a mustache who dates back to early versions of the program. Double-click on any of these to assign the new icon to Draw.

Early versions of Draw 3.0 had problems with its icons. Some had solid backgrounds, which looked poor if Program Manager itself was given a colored background. Some of the Draw applications were installed using the button version of the icons, others not. Some, such as the CCapture screen grab program, had really ugly icons. And still others, such as the Setup program and the help files, had no icons at all.

Using the highly recommended shareware Icon Manager program, I extracted the desired icons from the .EXE files of Draw, Chart and the other applications, and gave them all transparent backgrounds. I created a new icon for CCapture by exporting an image of a monitor from one of Draw's symbol libraries as a bitmap, importing it into Photo-Paint, coloring it, and saving it as an icon with Icon Manager (whew!). I also used Icon Manager to add the Draw balloon to the standard Windows Setup icon, for use as Draw's Setup icon. Then I added balloons to the icons of all the Draw applications, so I could run their help files directly from Program Manager. As you can see in the two illustrations, I keep the help files in a separate group.

Having found these useful, I've included all these icons, in standard .ICO format, in the ICONS.ZIP archive in the DRAW directory of the Utility disk. To use them, extract and copy the .ICO files into any directory on your hard disk. Select the program icon you wish to change in Program Manager, press Alt-Enter, click on Change Icon and browse to the directory holding your icon. Make sure List Files Of Type is set to *.ICO. Simply double-click on the desired .ICO file to attach it to your program.

To generate the icons for the help files, choose New from the File menu, choose Program Item, click on OK, click on Browse, change to the Draw directory, change List Files Of Type to All Files and click on CORELDRW.HLP, then OK. Now click on Change Icon and browse to your new Draw help icon, HDRAW.ICO. You're done. Follow the same procedure for the remaining help files, CCapture (which is in the Photo-Paint directory) and the Setup program, in the latter case first inserting the Draw Installation Disk 1. Note that it's currently not possible to install Setup on a hard disk, as in the case of most Windows apps.

Tiny Perfect SysEdit

SysEdit

When it comes to system configuration, I find I often need to edit one of four DOS or Windows configuration files: CONFIG.SYS, AUTOEXEC.BAT, WIN.INI or (to a lesser extent) SYSTEM.INI. These are small ASCII files you can load into the Windows Notepad editor (it's in the Accessories group). But the SysEdit program included with Windows makes the job a lot easier. When

Ernest Hemingway

Two artworks by
Pawel Bodytko

Running Elet
from his children's book
Animals of Earth 2

Steam Engine by Douglas Gennetten

Jukebox

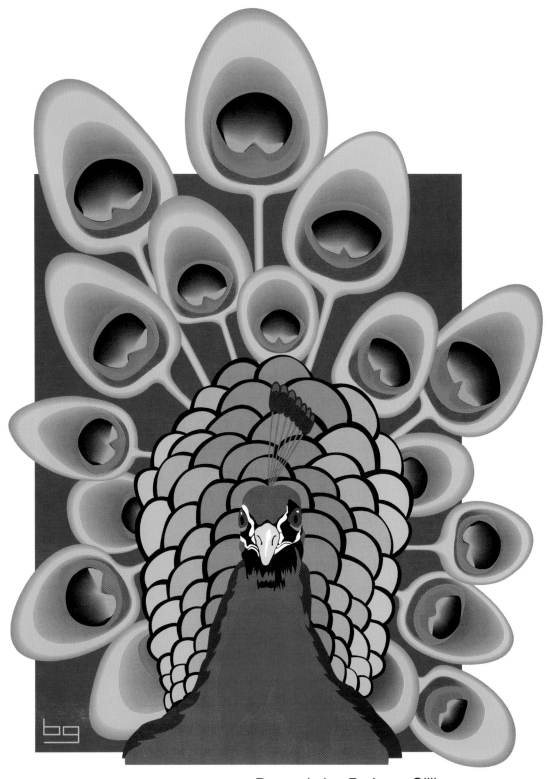

Peacock by Barbara Gilligan

Clock by Keith Donally

my Draw students contact me with system problems, for example, I often ask them to print out these four files with SysEdit and fax them to me. A careful study of these files can often reveal the cause of a wide range of anomalies.

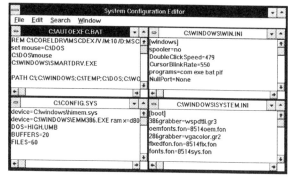

SYSEDIT.EXE can be found in the SYSTEM subdirectory of the WIN-DOWS directory, but no icon is created for it when you install Windows. If you can't locate an icon for SysEdit, then generate one by choosing New from the Program Manager File menu, clicking on Program Item, OK, then moving to the WINDOWS\SYSTEM directory and double-clicking on SYSEDIT.EXE before returning to Program Manager with OK.

File Search

No matter how well organized your hard disk, sooner or later you won't be able to find one of your files. You can use the search abilities of File Manager, but it only hunts through a single drive at a time — going through a large hard disk or remote server this way is painful. File Search, from the FSEARCH.ZIP archive, is a shareware ($19 registration) file finder that can be run from its icon in Program Manager.

Fsearch

First create an icon for it. Then run it and enter DOS wildcards, such as *.CDR to find Draw files, and it will search either the current drive or the entire disk, displaying a list of files that match your search criteria. File Search is simple and effective — essential criteria for a truly useful utility. If you're always searching for files, add it to your StartUp group, so you can get to it quickly from Draw.

Time

There are many modest utilities to keep track of the time, date, free memory and disk space. TM-WIN3.ZIP, which you'll find in the UTILITY directory of the Utility disk, decompresses to TIME.EXE. Time is an elegant little utility that, when run, simply displays the time and date in a small box. What makes it particularly valuable is that it always pops to the front when

Time

---

you switch applications, so you never have to go hunting for it. You can click and drag it to a new location and double-click on it to change its configuration or close it. The Time program is a natural candidate for inclusion in the StartUp group. If Time is displaying inaccurate information, you can reset your system's date and time by double-clicking on the Date/Time icon in Program Manager's Control Panel.

Hardware Considerations

The recommended hardware configuration for Windows is: the largest capacity, fastest, highest-resolution system you can afford. That said, there are some specifics worth keeping in mind when purchasing a system — or using an existing one — to run Windows and Draw.

Four aspects of your system determine its effectiveness as a platform for running graphics and publishing applications such as Draw: the computer's processor; hard drive capacity and speed; extended memory, and the monitor/graphics card combination. These factors become increasingly significant as your graphics and publishing projects become more sophisticated. If you'll be regularly creating large, complex illustrations, specifying exact colors and working close to deadline, a powerful system is in order. For those simply extracting and modifying the occasional piece of clip art or creating a type effect, a considerably more modest system will fill the bill.

The processor, or CPU, affects not only the speed of your computer but how Windows itself loads and runs. (Speaking of processors, a math co-processor will currently do nothing to speed up Draw.) An 80486-based computer will run Draw faster than an 80386, which in turn will blaze by an 80286. I was reminded only recently that an 80286 with 1 Mb of memory can, in fact, run Windows and Draw, when a student of mine revealed that he was using just such a system at home, albeit at painfully slow speeds. If you pack in 2 Mb or 4 Mb of memory (and have a lot of patience), you could use Draw to create simple illustrations on this type of system. Such tasks as displaying fountain fills or working with paragraph text will still be very slow, however. If you're stuck with an 80286, there are 80386 add-in boards available from a variety of firms, such as Intel. But since Windows is often finicky about the hardware on which it runs, it would be wise to purchase these with a money-back guarantee firmly in place.

A more reasonable platform for running Draw (and all Windows applications) is a PC equipped with an 80386 processor. With 4 Mb or more of memory Draw will come alive, performing in a reasonably snappy fashion for all but the most complex files. Of course 8 Mb is even better, and with RAM chips currently very affordable this amount makes a lot of sense. My own system uses 16 Mb, but then I often have a ton of apps running at once.

The current versions of Draw and CorelTRACE are thankfully much less disk-intensive than they used to be, but a fast hard drive is still a necessity to keep up the speed of Windows itself, especially on machines low on memory. Start with a capacity of around 100 Mb and go up from there as your projects warrant. If you'll be working with large, complex files or scanned graphics, something around 180 Mb is appropriate. Large drives are also fast drives, so shoot for an access speed of 18 Ms or less.

There are a few things you can do to speed up any hard drive. You should be regularly running a disk defragmenting program, for example, to put your files back in contiguous order. Such defragmenters are typically included with utility collections such as Norton Utilities and PC Tools Deluxe. My personal favorite is Vopt, from Golden Bow Systems. This runs from my AUTOEXEC.BAT file, so it quickly defragments the drive every time I turn on my computer.

Since a generous amount of memory reduces disk accesses, thereby speeding your system up considerably, you should also check your CONFIG.SYS file to see how much memory Windows has assigned to SMARTDRV.SYS, its disk caching program. On a 2 Mb to 4 Mb system, 1,024 Kb (1 Mb) is a good bet, but with more memory available you should raise this value. Third-party substitutes for SMARTDRV.SYS are available, such as Super PC-Kwik, from Multisoft, which claim improved performance. I used to advise allocating memory for use as a

RAM drive, but with Draw's more efficient use of memory this is no longer worth the bother.

The display system you use with Draw is a function of both your wallet and the nature of the illustrations you will be creating; however, on most systems it's this that forms the biggest stumbling block to increased performance. Most Windows users currently rely on a straightforward display consisting of a 14-inch color monitor running at VGA (640 by 480) resolution, with a palette of 16 colors. While this is an adequate base configuration, larger monitors, faster graphics cards, increased resolution and an expanded palette of colors can provide enhanced ease of use, productivity gains and a more accurate display of objects and colors.

Your current graphics card may also support a palette of 256 or more colors. Find out if suitable driver software (usually free) is available for your card from the manufacturer. Current drivers for most devices can usually be found in the Windows Forum on CompuServe (GO WINADV). More and more graphics cards are being supplied with High Color capabilities, which lets them display 32,768 colors. With these installed you'll see an immediate improvement in the fidelity of the colors displayed in Draw, Photo-Paint and the other Corel applications (with the exception of CorelSHOW). Again, your card may already have High Color capabilities — you simply haven't installed the correct driver. But even with a 256-color palette, Draw can display more pure, rather than dithered, colors. This makes the screen display of color much more accurate — a Pantone guide then becomes a more useful way to specify color.

Color is important, but so is resolution. A graphics card and monitor that supports Super VGA (800 by 600 or higher) will really make Draw sparkle. With such a display you'll find it easier working with the Shape ⚟ tool, since objects and their nodes are displayed more clearly. Currently, one of the best display systems you could put together for use with Draw would consist of a 21-inch color monitor, such as the NEC MultiSync 6FG, with a high-performance graphics card to drive it. The Impression Ultra, from Matrox, can crank out 24-bit color (16.7 million colors) at resolutions up to 1,600 by 1,200.

Graphics cards are appearing that push resolutions ever higher, with correspondingly lower costs. There's never been a better time to optimize your display system. If you do move up to a large display running at high resolutions, you may want to make Draw's Color Palette and toolbox larger. (See *Customizing Draw's Defaults* for details on this.)

How do you keep up with the rapidly growing capabilities of publishing hardware and software? You should be reading publishing magazines, such as *Publish*, *PC Publishing & Presentations* and *The Seybold Report on Desktop Publishing*, as well as general computer publications such as *PC Magazine*, *Windows Magazine* and *Windows User*. Check the bibliography for details on these and other resources.

Customizing Draw's Defaults

21

T he first time you used CorelDRAW, its dialog boxes and menus were set to certain defaults — Show Status Line on the Display menu was enabled, for example, while Show Rulers was not. After using Draw for a while, you may have noticed that the program is remembering some of the choices you've made in its menus and dialog boxes: objects you create may fill or be outlined with non-standard colors or thicknesses, the rulers may always be displayed, or Snap To Grid might be enabled. When you select an import format, you will be taken to the last directory from which you imported a file of the same format.

Making Draw work your way

These are all examples of Draw defaults that can be set from within the program. For example, say that while working on a drawing you enable Show Rulers. The next time you open a document or create a new one you'll find that the rulers are still enabled; Draw has made Show Rulers a new default.

A 'Seedy' Configuration

If you enable or disable a 'toggle' on the Display menu, such as Show Rulers, you have changed one of a number of defaults that will apply to all new drawings you create. Draw saves these defaults in the CDCONFIG.SYS file in the Draw program directory. Other examples of these defaults are any changes made to the Page Setup, Grid Setup or Preferences dialog boxes.

If you select an object (or objects) and then choose a new outline or fill from the flyout menus, that new choice applies only to the selected object. But if no object is selected when you specify a new outline or fill, a dialog box will give you the choice of making the outline or fill a default for just text, just non-text objects, or both text and non-text objects.

Uniform Fill for New Object

Nothing is currently selected. To which types of new objects will the default apply?

◉ All Objects
○ Text Objects
○ Other Objects

OK   Cancel

If things get really out of control, you could simply delete the CDCONFIG.SYS file; when you then exit Draw it will create a new CDCONFIG.SYS holding the defaults set in the current session, which it will apply to the next drawing you open or create in subsequent Draw sessions. Sometimes this file gets corrupted, so deleting it is something you should try if Draw begins acting strangely. On the computers in the classroom in which I lead Draw classes, the batch file that loads Windows also copies a pristine set of defaults from the file DEFAULT.SYS (a renamed version of the original CDCONFIG.SYS file) to CDCONFIG.SYS, thereby ensuring students always begin their Draw sessions with the original defaults.

The ability to save defaults in the CDCONFIG.SYS file presents some interesting opportunities for customizing the way Draw loads. You could set up a commonly used page size, choose your measurement system, define a grid, choose fills and outlines, enable various display options and save all this in CDCONFIG.SYS automatically when you close Draw. You could then rename this to BROCHURE.SYS, for example, and create a DOS batch file that would begin with the command: COPY BROCHURE.SYS CDCONFIG.SYS and then follow with C:\CORELDRW\DRAW\CORELDRW.EXE (using the appropriate path to your own Draw directory) to run Draw. You could create duplicates of the Draw icon and link each one to a different configuration file. This would be useful in an environment in which a number of people used Draw on the same workstation. There's nothing more annoying than getting stuck with someone else's defaults.

A few defaults are only in effect during a Draw session. Say that with no text selected you choose Bodnoff in the Text roll-up or Character Attributes dialog box. Not only will this be the default face as long as you work on this document, but any new documents you create or existing ones you open before exiting Draw will also have Bodnoff as the default face. This will revert to the usual default font, Avalon, when you exit and rerun Draw.

Customizing Draw's Defaults

Modifying CORELDRW.INI

Draw stores a wide variety of defaults relating to program operation, font names and separation screen angles in the CORELDRW.INI file in the Draw program directory. You can edit this file with Windows Notepad and, in fact, I've made a copy of the Notepad icon on my system and linked it to CORELDRW.INI. I can now edit the file quickly by double-clicking on the new Notepad icon. I've done the same thing for the CORELDRW.DOT file, so I can quickly change dotted and dashed line definitions. (See *Optimizing Windows* for details on creating and linking icons.)

Coreldrw.ini

When you open CORELDRW.INI with Notepad, you'll find it begins with a section of comments, marked by semicolons. This explanatory text provides a brief description of the many available settings, but you'll find a more detailed discussion of them in the Software-Related Information area of the Reference section of Draw's online help. Since there's no point duplicating information you already have, I'll confine my discussion of these settings to a few of the most commonly changed, then follow with undocumented entries. Some of these are toggles that are enabled by entering 1 after the equal sign, or disabled with 0. Others use a range of numerical values, a file name or a directory name. If you've opened CORELDRW.INI, scroll down to the [CDrawConfig] section.

AutoBackupMins

This has a default value of 10, which instructs Draw to save your file every 10 minutes. If Draw crashes, you can rename .ABK autobackup files to .CDR and open them. Since these are temporary files, Draw deletes them when you close your .CDR file. To disable autobackup, simply change the value to 0.

BigPalette and BigToolbox

Running Draw full screen on a large monitor at high resolution results in a small toolbox and Color Palette. Change both values from the default 0 to 1, if you want them displayed larger.

DefaultFont

The default font is Avalon, Draw's version of Avant Garde. You can set this to any TrueType, PostScript or .WFN font, in the format =Avalon,1,24. The font name is followed by a number for weight, with 1 for normal, 2 for bold, 4 for italic and 8 for bold italic. The last value is the desired point size. For example, both of the following entries are valid: =Arial,4,36 and =NewCenturySchlbk,2,48. (For more on this, see *Advanced Type Topics*.)

MakeBackupWhenSave

As you'd guess, this determines whether Draw makes a backup of your file when you save it, adding a .BAK extension to the duplicate. Set this to 1 to enable backups, and to 0 to disable them. Backups provide a measure of safety, and can be renamed to .CDR and opened, but they quickly eat up hard disk space. The default is 1.

MaximizeCDraw

Set this to 1 to have Draw fill your screen area when it runs. Set at the default value of 0, Draw will use the default window size. But the bigger the better, so I keep this at 1.

OLEConvertObjectsToDraw

Setting this option to 1 lets you manipulate linked and embedded objects in your Draw files using the rotate, skew, envelope, perspective and blend commands. After such manipulations, you can still double-click on them to launch their originating application. As a default, however, this is set to 0. This is no doubt to avoid conflicts with applications that don't support this ability; you'll have to try this out for yourself. It works fine with CorelCHART.

PSComplexityThreshold

This setting addresses problems that arise when printing complex objects to PostScript printers, especially imagesetters. The value equals the number of line segments in an object. If an object exceeds it, Draw will slice it up into smaller segments. The default is 3000. (For more on this, see the limitcheck section of *Service Bureau Strategies*.)

ShowObjectsWhenMoving

If you routinely have to move complex groups of objects around on the page, you may not want the screen to redraw when you pause while moving. However, I find it handy to preview objects when I pause, so I set this value to 1, rather than the default 0.

3DLook

The so-called 3D Look of Draw's dialog boxes, rulers and Status Line are not to my taste; I find it especially difficult clicking on the little triangles in the dialog boxes. So I've changed the default setting of 1 to 0 to disable this. Once disabled, you can make use of the interface colors defined in the Windows Control Panel.

SpellLanguage

By default you spell-check in English, but those with access to the CD-ROM supplied with Draw can install the foreign-language dictionaries found in the SPELDICT directory. The following files are available:

Hyphenation dictionaries

hdnry141.dat	Danish
hdurs241.dat	Dutch
hecrp301.dat	English comprehensive
hfnry141.dat	Finnish
hfrrs241.dat	French (accented/unaccented)
hgrrs141.dat	German (Doppel/Scharfes)
hitrs141.dat	Italian comprehensive
hsprs141.dat	Spanish comprehensive
hswrs241.dat	Swedish comprehensive

Spelling dictionaries

idnf9111.dat	Danish
iduf9121.dat	Dutch
ienm9150.dat	English comprehensive
ifnf9110.dat	Finnish
ifrf9121.dat	French (accented/unaccented)
igrf9112.dat	German (Doppel/Scharfes)
iitf9110.dat	Italian comprehensive
ispf9110.dat	Spanish comprehensive
iswf9111.dat	Swedish comprehensive

English thesaurus files

COM_THES.DIS   American English with definitions
The available entries for SpellLanguage= are English, French,

German, Swedish, Spanish, Italian, Danish, Dutch, or Finnish. The online help says Portuguese and Norwegian are also available, but this is not the case. Change the SpellDict= and HyphenateDict= entries to the appropriate file names. There are no other possible entries for ThesaurusDict=. Keep in mind that language files you specify should be resident in your Draw program directory.

Undocumented Revision B entries

ExportToTiff42

Draw's TIFF export filter has been modified so that you can export to TIFF version 4.2 for those programs currently unable to accept TIFF 5.0, such as WordPerfect. Significantly, this also affects the image header on .EPS files exported from Draw. First, acquire the filter from Corel Corp.; it's available for download via modem from its bulletin board in Ottawa (613-728-4752), or the Corel forum on CompuServe (GO COREL). Install the EXPTIFF.DLL filter file by copying it to the CORELDRW\FILTERS directory. When you now export to TIFF format, click on the About button; the version number displayed should be Rev B3. Add the ExportToTiff42= line to the [CDrawConfig] section. A value of 0 exports to TIFF version 4.2, while 1 exports to version 5.0.

UseResolution

This is a new option that makes use of an updated version of the Draw .PCX import filter, IMPPCX.DLL. You can also obtain this filter online. You need to add a new [CorelPCXImport] section to CORELDRW.INI, followed by UseResolution=.

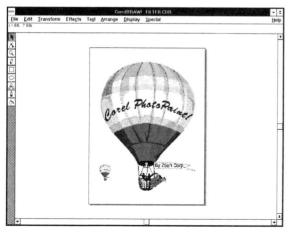

With the default value of 0, Draw will ignore the x and y values in an imported .PCX file, maintaining its aspect ratio but typically enlarging the file substantially. Set it to 1 and the x and y scaling values in the file will be used, although the aspect ratio may be distorted in some cases. As you can see in the illustration, there's a big difference in the results. The smaller balloon was imported with this value set to 1.

PSBitmapFontSizeThreshold

This value controls the type size at which Draw sends characters as bitmaps — as opposed to curves — to the printer. This can have a dramatic effect on type quality and output speed. (I cover this in detail in the Editing Your CORELDRW.INI File section of *Advanced Type Topics*.)

EPSImageHeaderHighResolution

If you're not happy with the display quality of exported .EPS files when you import them into another application, you can increase their screen quality by raising this value from the default 75 (dpi). When you then click on High resolution in the .EPS Export dialog box, you take advantage of this custom header resolution. The permissible range is 30 to 1000, although the latter value will create huge files.

UseClippingForFills

Some of the new breed of Windows accelerator graphics cards have trouble handling Draw's fountain and pattern fills. There are four values for this setting, which determine whether Draw will use the current, or an older, approach to fills. With it set to 0, Draw never uses the new method; set to 1, only for preview; set to 2, only for printing. With the default value of 3, Draw always uses the new method.

TTFOptimization

Draw uses a unique method to optimize the display of TrueType fonts. While this is faster than the standard Windows approach, it can cause problems on certain systems. Change the default value of 1 to 0 to use the Windows approach.

Corel is constantly adding to and modifying the settings in CORELDRW.INI. To stay current, you should become a regular visitor to the Corel forum on CompuServe, or Corel's own bulletin board in Ottawa.

The Draw Companion Disks

T he Utility and Fonts disks bound into this book represent a considerable resource of fonts, Draw files and useful Windows programs. The latter category includes font management utilities, file decompression and conversion programs, a sound driver, several configuration programs, a task switcher, a special character generator and much more. These will provide more control over your Windows sessions and let you use Draw more effectively. The Draw-specific material includes files used in the tutorial sections of this book, additional color palettes, icons, color printer test files and macros.

Fonts and utility programs aplenty

Since I use much of this material daily, I feel confident that you'll find it of value. Of course, all the files have been scanned for viruses, but as with all software, you do use this material at your own risk.

The Fonts Disk

This represents what I believe to be a first in computer book publishing: the inclusion of a disk of commercial-quality fonts bearing no registration fee of any kind. This disk contains 26 TrueType fonts that I've chosen from the thousands in the OptiFonts library, produced by Castcraft Industries.

Castcraft was founded in 1936 as a manufacturer of printers' spacing material, such as slugs and leads. It soon acquired two type foundries and began building a library that now totals more than 20,000 faces. Over the years, Castcraft provided

Metropolis Bold

OPTI BINNER

AGENCY GOTHIC

NEULAND

Similunatix Heavy

Runserif Regular

Franklin Gothic Triple Condensed

Globe Gothic

these faces in a variety of media. Recently it began the process of converting them to TrueType and PostScript format, and now markets them under the OptiFonts name. I believe you'll find the faces I've picked form a nice complement to the generous library supplied with Draw itself. If you like them, you'll find a special offer at the back of the book for readers of *Mastering Corel Draw* to purchase additional OptiFont faces at special prices.

Installing the Fonts

The fonts are stored in uncompressed form on the Fonts disk in standard .TTF files. To install them, run the Windows Control Panel (it's in the Main group of Program Manager), double-click on the Fonts icon and click on Add. Move to your Fonts disk, click on Select All and then OK. Windows will copy the fonts from the floppy and install them for use in all your Windows applications. It's as simple as that. You'll find that all the OptiFonts fonts are preceded by an O, as in OCrawModern. (For more details on installing and managing fonts see *Advanced Type Topics*.)

The Utility Disk

Much of the material on the Utility disk has been carefully selected from the vast cornucopia found on electronic bulletin boards. I have prowled through large online resources, such as CompuServe, as well as many smaller boards in search of the pick of the digital crop. If you're not already doing so, I recommend you get in the habit of haunting the boards through the use of a modem and communications software. CompuServe itself is a wonderful resource, providing many areas of interest to Windows publishers. It's bulging with conversations between users and is packed with files you can download to your computer. Corel itself maintains a forum on CompuServe (GO COREL), as well as a bulletin board in Ottawa that you can access directly free of charge (613-728-4752).

The Draw Companion Disks

Unlike the fonts on the Fonts disk, the material on the Utility disk is either freeware or shareware. That is, it was created by a variety of authors and placed on bulletin boards for distribution. Freeware is just that — free software that's yours to use as you see fit. Shareware, however, is offered to you on a trial basis. If you find a shareware program on the Utility disk useful, you should honor the request of its creator for the usually modest payment.

In addition, you won't find detailed instructions for using the contents of the disk in the following pages, since the authors of the programs have themselves provided accompanying text files. To make the best use of the contents of the disk, I recommend opening the explanatory .TXT or .DOC text files in Windows Notepad or Write, and printing them out. Many of them also have extensive online help files that can be accessed from their Help menus. Contact information for the authors of these programs is provided at the end of this chapter. If you're having difficulty installing or using the material on the Utility disk, you should contact them directly.

Installing the Utility Disk

With a few exceptions, such as the text and graphics files in the SAMPLES directory supplied for use in the tutorial chapters, the material on the Utility disk is all in compressed form, in standard .ZIP format archives. To decompress these archives, I've included the excellent Windows decompression application, WinZip, with the generous permission of author Nico Mak.

WinZip is shareware, and its license agreement allows you to try it out for 21 days. This should be plenty of time to decompress the material on the Utility disk. If after 21 days you're still using WinZip (and I find it a useful addition to my toolbox), you should ante up the modest $29 registration fee. Choose Ordering Information from its Help menu for details. Nico will also provide support for unregistered users (an unusually generous offer) if you send mail to him on CompuServe at 70056,241.

The first step is to install WinZip on your system. Then you can begin the process of decompressing, installing and using the

Winzip

material on the disk. WinZip, and its associated files, are in the WinZip directory of your Utility disk. You could create a new directory on your hard drive and copy all these files into it. But I'm going to lead you through the process of simply installing and running WinZip right from the Utility disk itself.

At this point, you should be in the Windows Program Manager. Choose Run from its File menu and type in A:\WINZIP\WINZIP, as shown in the illustration, and click on OK. WinZip will run and display a few dialog boxes, in which you should simply click on OK. It will ask you if you want it to add a WinZip icon to your Accessories group, for example. You should say yes to this, so that the next time you use WinZip you can simply double-click on its icon to run it. Then in the next dialog box, click on I Agree. When WinZip loads, double-click on its title bar at the top of its window to zoom it to fill your display.

WinZip has quite extensive archive management capabilities. Some of these, such as creating new archives or scanning for viruses, rely on other shareware programs that I have not included on the disk. As supplied, WinZip will simply decompress your .ZIP files. For details on WinZip's advanced features, consult its Help menu.

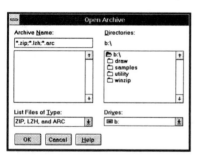

Now that WinZip is installed and running, I'm going to lead you through the process of decompressing and installing one of the applications on the Utility disk. You'll follow the same procedure for the other .ZIP archives. Click on the Open button and move to your Utility disk (on A or B), and then double-click on the UTILITY directory to display a list of the available .ZIP archives.

Double-click on TM-WIN3.ZIP to display the three files in this archive. Most archives contain explanatory text files, typically with .TXT, .DOC or .WRI file extensions. There are two ways to read these files before unarchiving them: you can click on the text file to select it and then click on the View button. Or if that fails, try double-clicking on it. The latter approach tries to load the

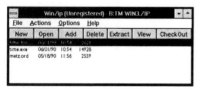

document into the Windows word processor on your system that's linked to the text file extension. In this case, click on TIME.DOC and then the View button to read it. You can resize this View dialog box as desired. When you've finished looking at the document, click on OK.

Let's say you read this text file and decide you want to decompress and install the program it discusses. Click once on TIME.EXE and then click on the Extract button. In the Extract dialog box, move to the WINDOWS directory on your hard drive and click on Extract. WinZip will quickly extract TIME.EXE from its archive and copy it to your WINDOWS directory. To run it from Program Manager you need to first generate an icon for it. (If you're not sure how to do this, see the section at the beginning of the *Windows Survival Skills* chapter. Or use the second extraction technique described below, which automatically generates an icon.) The Time program is so handy that I like to have it running at all times. To accomplish this, in Program Manager you'd simply drag its icon into the StartUp group.

While extracting the single TIME.EXE file in the previous example was simple enough, sometimes archives contain numerous files. In this case, you may want to keep them in their own subdirectories, rather than mix them in with existing files. Simply type in the name of a new directory, and WinZip will create it for you and place the extracted files in it.

In addition, it can create a new program group in Program Manager and generate icons for all the program and data files Windows recognizes. With the Time archive still selected, click on the CheckOut button. In the dialog box, type in the name of the new directory into which you want to copy the extracted files. Note the warning message at the bottom. If you type in the name of an existing directory *all the files in it will be deleted*. So simply type in the name of a *new* directory, one that doesn't exist. For example, C:\CHECK. But *don't* type in WINDOWS or DRAW.

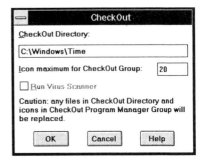

WinZip will then create this directory, extract all the files from the archive and copy them to this directory, create a new

Program Manager group called CheckOut and generate icons for the files. It will then display Program Manager, and you can run the Time program or double-click on the icon for the TIME.DOC text file to read it. You'll find WinZip minimizes the Program Manager window; just double-click on its title bar to enlarge it.

After you've tried out decompressed files in this way, you should drag the program icons you want to retain to a different group, such as Accessories, because any icons left in the CheckOut group will be deleted the next time you use the CheckOut feature. And remember to always decompress your CheckOut files to a *new* directory — such as C:\CHECK2 — each time you use this feature, or the existing files will be erased if you use the same CheckOut directory name.

That's really all you need to know about WinZip to decompress the files on the Utility disk. And remember, if you use it past the 21-day trial period, you should register it.

The DRAW Directory

The DRAW directory holds a number of files that can be used directly in Draw. NCG.ZIP, for example, is the archive file for NCG.CDR, contains all the colors in Draw's default palette. Opening this in Draw and printing it out to your color printer will help you specify colors with more accuracy. The directory also contains three color palettes. Simply copy these palettes to your Draw program directory, then load them as you would any palette (as described in *Getting Your Fill of Draw.*)

SEPIA.ZIP decompresses to SEPIA.PAL and the text file SEPIA.TXT. This palette provides sepia tones in single-step increments, as well as pure black and white, for creating drawings with that old-time feeling. The author suggests that fountain fills look best in the range of Sepia 98 to Sepia 3. The negative values of Sepia are light warm tones, closer to yellow than Sepia. You'll need a 256-color display to really appreciate the subtle differences of tone possible with this palette.

GRAY.PAL contains a palette defined in shades of gray, from black to white in 1 percent increments. This palette may prove useful for illustrations that will be output in monochrome, since you can easily make use of a broad spectrum of grays.

TRUNEW.PAL is based on the TRUMATCH palette supplied with Draw, which has been supplemented by John Murdoch to provide an interesting way to trap colors when creating images that will be offset printed. It's designed to eliminate the problem of black type's being knocked out of the tinted backgrounds on which it's placed. The TRUNEW.TXT file provides details on the palette's construction and use.

The MACROS.ZIP file decompresses to MACROS.REC, a collection of Draw macros created by Diane Byrd and used here with her permission. Decompress this file to your Draw directory. You can test the macros out by running the Windows Recorder program from the Accessories group in Program Manager and opening this file. Then run Draw and try out the macros. The included text file explains what each one does. (For details on how to autoload these macros each time Windows runs, see *Optimizing Windows*.)

The ICONS.ZIP archive contains a number of Windows icon files in standard .ICO format. I've extracted the icons from Draw and its companion programs, modified them in some cases, and created new ones for the Setup program, Capture and all the Help files. (For details on installing and using these, see *Optimizing Windows*.)

Finally, I've also included two recycling symbols in the RECYCLE.CDR file, since I have yet to come across these among Draw's many symbols and clip art images.

The FONTS Directory

This directory includes a number of handy utilities for installing and managing your fonts, as well as a number of text files. Most of these are discussed in more detail in *Advanced Type Topics*.

Composing Special Characters

You can create text containing special characters, such as accented letters, by pressing Alt key combinations: Alt-0-165 on the numeric keypad, for example, generates ¥, the Japanese

Compose

---

yen symbol. Remembering these is next to impossible, however, and the special character reference card supplied with Draw always seems to go missing when you need it. As discussed in *Text Creation and Alignment*, you can also use the Windows Character Map program to generate special characters. But there is yet another method available for automating special character creation, which would make sense for those needing access to large numbers of characters.

Compose is a modest little Windows application created by Digital Equipment Corp. and made available free of charge. Its archive is CMPKIT.ZIP, which you should decompress to the directory of your choice. Then generate an icon for it, so you can run it from Program Manager. First, click in the Program Manager group in which you want the icon to appear — for example, Accessories. Then choose New from the File menu. Assuming you placed the Compose files in a WINDOWS\COMPOSE directory, mouse to that directory now and double-click on COMPOSE.EXE. Then click on OK to return to Program Manager and the icon should appear.

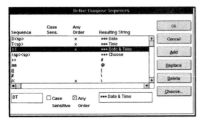

Once you run Compose, it's invoked in an application by pressing the right-hand Control key on your keyboard (the one to the right of the Spacebar), although this key can be redefined, if necessary. You then press one or more predefined keys to access special characters, or the current time and date.

Compose is supplied with fairly sensible two-keystroke combinations to access special characters, and you can easily redefine these. For example, pressing Right-Control, E then ^ gives you Ê. Or pressing D and T places the date and time on the page. Thankfully, the ability to print out all the keystroke sequences has been provided, so there's no need to memorize them.

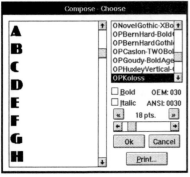

Beyond quick access to special characters, Compose will also display your installed fonts in whatever size you specify and output a complete character set for each font, along with ANSI numbers for direct keyboard access in Draw. You can display this font window simply by pressing Right-Control-Space-

Space. If Compose is something you'd like to use in most of your Windows sessions, install it in the StartUp group. Then it will load in the background each time you run Windows. (For details on this, see *Optimizing Windows*.)

Fonter

Fonter lets you create printed lists of all your fonts, with a text sample of each font. You can also print sample sheets displaying your font in all of its weight variations, and a character set chart showing what characters are in every font, along with the keys to press to access that character. I find the sample sheets useful to quickly see what a face looks like at a variety of sizes. And the character set chart lets me know what special characters are in a font. You can quickly put Fonter to work by diving into its menus, but the excellent online help is worth a look.

Installing Fonter is as simple as decompressing the FNTR50.ZIP archive to its own directory with WinZip and generating a Program Manager icon to run it, as discussed above. Since Fonter was written in the Visual BASIC programming language, you'll also need the VBRUN100.DLL runtime library, which I've included in the UTILITY directory. Simply decompress this to your WIN-DOWS directory before you run Fonter. A number of other programs on the UTILITY disk also require the runtime library to be resident in your WINDOWS directory.

The first time you run Fonter, it will create a list of your TrueType and PostScript fonts, and save the list in a file. This process can take a minute or two. You'll see a window telling you what's going on. On subsequent loading, Fonter will use its own font list, letting you know if there are changes in your fonts and offering to create a new list at your option.

Fonter is shareware, with a registration fee of $15 if you continue to use it past a 30-day trial period.

wPFMfix

Wpfmfix

This shareware ($5 registration) Windows application lets you alter the weight attributes and names in a PostScript font's .PFM file. This solves the problem created by font converters that don't properly name converted fonts, making them all appear in the same family. This is a Visual BASIC application, so the VBRUN100.DLL file (included in the UTILITY directory) must be extracted and placed in your WINDOWS directory. The PostScript Utilities section of the *Advanced Type Topics* chapter contains detailed information on using wPFMfix. Its archive is WPFMFIX.ZIP.

REFONT

This is a handy utility for those of you who frequent online bulletin boards or CompuServe. These resources provide a large selection of PostScript fonts for the Macintosh, which are often not available for Windows. Use REFONT to convert these fonts for use in Draw and all your Windows applications. The author provides a very detailed and well-written help file. Decompress the REFONT4.ZIP archive and run it from the DOS prompt. This is also covered in the PostScript Utilities section of *Advanced Type Topics*. While REFONT is freeware, registering it (for $20) will get you the more advanced Windows version.

WinPSX

winpsx

For downloading PostScript fonts, this freeware Windows utility is a must. It lets you download predefined batches of fonts, as well as print out printer status pages. Simply extract it from the WINPSX.ZIP archive, generate an icon in Program Manager and run it. Check the PostScript Utilities section of the *Advanced Type Topics* chapter for information on getting the most out of this utility.

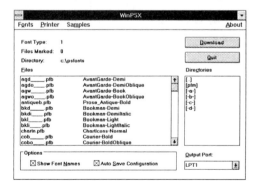

FontPRN

This clever freeware Visual BASIC Windows application has been written especially for this book by the prolific Costas Kitsos, the author of WinPSX. Draw does not download fonts, so the ability of FontPRN to embed your PostScript fonts in a .PRN print-to-disk file for your service bureau or co-workers is a useful one. Its archive is FONTPRN.ZIP. No special installation is required, but the VBRUN100.DLL file must be resident in your WINDOWS directory.

fontprn

PFMedit

This freeware Visual BASIC Windows application lets you create your own kerning pairs for any Type 1 PostScript font that is compatible with Adobe Type Manager. This would be useful for those who want to tighten up the Draw PostScript

pfmedit

fonts, or have converted fonts from TrueType format. Extract it and its text file from the PFMEDIT.ZIP archive. No special installation is required, other than the requirement for VBRUN100.DLL on your system. (Its use is discussed in *Advanced Type Topics*.)

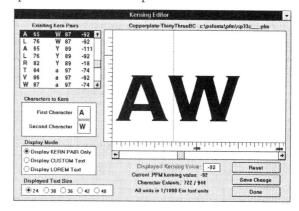

FONTINFO.ZIP contains three text files providing tips on working with .WFN, TrueType and PostScript fonts in Draw.

ANSIPLUS

The ANSIPLUS.ZIP archive contains ANSIPLUS.CDR and a short text file. Open this file in Draw 3.0 (revision B) to view and print the Windows 3.1 ANSI Plus character set. Re-specify the paragraph text in the desired font to determine exactly which characters are mapped to positions 130 through 159. You will discover that version 2 .WFN fonts, version 3 .WFN fonts, Corel's bundled TrueType and PostScript fonts, and third-party fonts map these characters differently. Use your printout to determine exactly what numbers to enter with your specified font to produce a desired character.

Other Stuff

There are also a number of font-related text files in the FONTS directory. KERN.ZIP contains more than 500 kerning pairs, which can be used as a guide when modifying a font's kerning with PFMedit. REGISTER.ZIP contains a number of text files that you'll want to use to modify your CORELDRW.INI file, if you're using PostScript fonts and sending files to service bureaus. A-1-127.TXT lists font volumes 1 to 127 of the Adobe Typeface Library; BASE-35.TXT lists the base 35 fonts resident in most PostScript printers; CASTC-26.TXT lists the 26 fonts on the FONTS disk supplied with this book, and CD-256.TXT lists the font names from the PostScript fonts on the CD-ROM disk supplied with Draw. (Details on using these files can be found in the Service Bureau Strategies section of *Advanced Type Topics*.)

The UTILITY Directory

Since there are many useful text, graphics and font files to be found on bulletin boards in Macintosh format, you'll find the included utilities handy for decompressing downloaded Macintosh files. I've also included a program that can read Mac floppies for direct file transfer.

Unsit, in the UNST30.ZIP archive, is a simple freeware program that decompresses files compressed with the Macintosh StuffIt utility. As this is a non-Windows program, you should run it from the DOS prompt. Either exit Windows or run a DOS session by double-clicking on the MS-DOS Prompt icon in Program Manager. Simply type UNSIT for a screen of basic help. The accompanying text file explains its use in detail.

ExtractorPC is a freeware utility for expanding the files in archives created by the Macintosh Compact Pro program. Like UnSit, you run it from the DOS command line. Its EXTRACT.ZIP archive also has an associated text file explaining its many options and some of the mysteries of Macintosh file formats.

The final Macintosh-related program I've included is Mac-ette, found in the MACETTE.ZIP archive. A shareware DOS program (registration is $20), this one has the ability to copy files directly from a Macintosh 1.4 Mb floppy onto your PC. It has an easier-to-use interface than the other two, but I still recommend reading its text file before running it.

Cubit Meister

Cubit Meister, in the CUBT102.ZIP archive, is a simple little Visual BASIC shareware application designed to convert decimal and fractional inches, millimeters/centimeters, picas/points and points into all the other available formats simultaneously. It also provides an electronic proportion scale which can calculate proportions, even when different measurement systems are entered for the original and target sizes. Installation is as simple as extracting it and clicking on OK when it asks for a registration number. You can use Cubit Meister for 30 days, after which you'll need to register it ($15) for the program to keep running. The online help is all you'll need, but you may also want to read the included text file for more details.

cubit

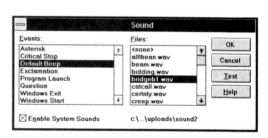

Speaker Files

The SOUND.ZIP archive contains a speaker driver, which when installed will add modest sound capabilities to your PC. Not only will you be able to assign digitized sounds in .WAV format to various Windows system events, such as the default beep, but you can also play these in sound-capable applications, such as CorelSHOW. Read the SPEAKER.TXT file for installation information, then run the Sound program in Windows Control Panel to assign these sounds to system events. I've also included a few .WAV files in this archive to get you going.

WinLoad

This freeware program couldn't be much simpler to use, but it performs a useful task. If you've set up your computer to load Windows automatically, but sometimes would rather simply go to the DOS prompt first, you know what a pain it can be. Simply replace WIN with WINLOAD in your AUTOEXEC.BAT file and WinLoad will pause for two seconds by default before running Windows. If you press any key during the pause, Windows won't run and you'll wind up in DOS. Read the WINLOAD.DOC text file for details.

File Search

Fsearch

Always losing track of where your files are? Yes, you can use the search capabilities of the Windows File Manager, but it's a bit awkward to access these. File Search is an easy-to-use file finder that you can run from Program Manager. Extract the FSEARCH.ZIP archive, copy FSEARCH.EXE to your hard drive, generate an icon for it and you're in business. The included text file is worth a look, but you can figure this simple program out for yourself. Registration for this shareware application is $19.

WinEZ

WinEZ

I'll close this section with one of the handiest utilities on the disk. WinEZ, from New Generation Software, is a shareware ($29.95 registration) application that simplifies switching between currently running programs or launching new ones. Once installed, WinEZ displays two buttons on your menu bar. One pops you quickly back into Program Manager or displays a menu of all the groups in Program Manager and lists their contents. You can use this to quickly run CorelCHART, CorelTRACE and the other applications included with Draw. The other button lets you switch between currently running tasks, as well as close them.

Decompress the WINEZ3.ZIP archive and generate an icon for WINEZ.EXE. Run the program by double-clicking on its icon or drag it into your StartUp group to ensure it loads automatically when Windows first runs. The included WINEZ3.TXT file should be read for a detailed feature discussion. I also cover WinEZ in *Optimizing Windows*.

Technical Assistance

If you are experiencing difficulty installing or operating one of the programs included on the Utility disk, you should contact its developer for assistance, using the following mail and CompuServe addresses. If the program is shareware, the developers may (quite reasonably) request that you register the program before providing technical assistance. Please don't phone the folks at Peachpit Press, the publisher of *Mastering Corel Draw*, since they won't be able to help you.

The WINZIP Directory

Program: WinZip
Contact: Nico Mak
PO Box 919
Bristol, CT 06011-0919
CompuServe: 70056,241

The FONTS Directory

Program: Compose
Contact: Digital Equipment Corp.

Program: Fonter
Contact: OsoSoft
1472 Sixth Street
Los Osos, CA 93402
CompuServe: 71571,222

Program: FontPRN
Contact: Costas Kitsos
PO Box 64943
Los Angeles, CA 90064
CompuServe: 73667,1755

Program: PFMedit
Contact: Dennis Harrington
CompuServe: 76216,3472

Program: REFONT
Contact: Acute Systems
PO Box 37
Algonquin, IL 60102.
CompuServe: 71355,470

Program: WinPSX
Contact: Costas Kitsos
PO Box 64943
Los Angeles, CA 90064
CompuServe: 73667,1755

Program: wPFMfix
Contact: Vincent Chen
3083 Rasmus Circle
San Jose, CA 95148
(408) 270-6024
CompuServe: 76636,415

The UTILITY Directory

Program: Cubit Meister
Contact: John Shanley
Phoenix Creative Graphics
5 Clyde Road, Suite 101
Somerset, NJ 08873
CompuServe: 76535,3443

Program: ExtractorPC
Contact: Bill Goodman
109 Davis Avenue
Brookline, MA 02146
Compuserve: 71101,204

Program: File Search
Contact: Mike Sax
Callaertstraat 23
B9100 Sint-Niklaas
Belgium
CompuServe: 75470,1403

Program: Mac-Ette
Contact: Paul E. Thomson
Acute Systems
PO Box 37
Algonquin, IL 60102
CompuServe: 71355,470

Program: Time
Contact: METZ Software
P.O. Box 6042
Bellevue, WA 98008-0042
(206) 641-4525
CompuServe: 73567,1637

Program: Unsit
Contact: Brian K. Uechi
CompuServe: 72330,155

Program: WinEZ
Contact: New Generation Software
PO Box 9700, Dept. 271
Austin, TX 78766
(713) 283-6760
CompuServe: 70312,127

Program: WinLoad
Contact: Thomas Software
1375 Beasley Rd.
Jackson, MS 39206
CompuServe: 71071,2166

Choosing a Training Firm

If you've worked your way carefully through the tutorial sections of this book, you're not only clear on what CorelDRAW can do, you know the actions to take to perform useful work with it. You're already far beyond the material covered in not only the typical two-day introductory course in Draw, but most advanced ones. Still, there may be others in your organization who can benefit from the capabilities of Draw but need to master it in the structured environment of a training firm.

As a potential consumer of training in the use of computer-based publishing tools such as Draw, what do you expect to get in return for the money and time that you or your company invests?

Most of us would base the answer to that question on the model of education we all grew up with. That is, you'd expect the trainer to be someone who knows something you don't know, and transfers that knowledge to you so you can apply it in your own life. Based on that model, logic dictates that you hire a computer expert who knows intimately the software that you want to learn. After spending a day or two with such an expert you would expect to be competent in using a program such as Draw for your own work.

If you analyze that model, however, you begin to realize that the expert's competence with the software is hardly the issue. If it was, it would be equally effective to have the typical in-house software whiz spend a day with a novice user. Anyone who has attempted to learn software that way knows what a frustrating experience it can be. Competent users take a lot of the basics for granted, move too quickly and present material in an erratic sequence. Worse, they tend to concentrate on the software, not the student. As a result, little or no learning takes place.

In search of the perfect trainer

So there's more to successful training than software competence, or the ability to show and tell. If those are the only standards you apply when choosing a trainer or training firm, you're definitely not getting your money's worth. You need to set higher standards, so you can make better choices in the future.

Beyond a complete mastery of both Draw and Windows, a successful trainer must be familiar with the capabilities of a wide variety of other software applications, since Draw provides such rich import and export abilities. He or she must also be aware of current input and output devices, including high-resolution printers, to anticipate the needs of students. Knowledge of color theory and typography is also appropriate, as is a good grounding in graphic design and print production. But all this still isn't enough.

Taking Responsibility for Learning

The question too rarely asked is: Whose responsibility is it that learning takes place? Trainers fall into three camps; those who believe the responsibility rests entirely on the student, those who share the responsibility and those who take total responsibility.

Surprisingly, the first camp gets the most support in our society. Since we're raised with the concept of grades, we conclude that the 'A' students are naturally 'smarter'. Even the students themselves believe this. Given that the teacher is experienced and can cover the material with ease, then it's the students' intrinsic level of smartness that determines whether they learn or not. Or is it? In fact, this shared cultural belief is the most significant cause of insufficiently exacting training standards.

What kinds of actions do these trainers take in the classroom? How can you identify them? Those who take no responsibility for learning teach by the book. They have a set structure and pacing from which they rarely deviate. They discourage questions. They form quick judgments about who the smart ones are and gear the course to them, displaying no compassion for those who are obviously not keeping up. On the contrary, such trainers often adopt a tone of contempt or irritation when speaking with the 'slow learners'.

Trainers who take no responsibility for learning often speak monotonously and without passion. You can't help but feel that they'd rather be somewhere else. Their boredom and aloofness soon spreads to the students, creating a mood of tension and discomfort in the classroom — you just can't wait to get out of there. If you find yourself in such a situation, immediately ask for your money back and don't take no for an answer.

Trainers who are willing to share the responsibility for learning appear better, since they act in an accommodating manner. They stop to cheerfully answer questions and slow down if you make the request. They repeat things ten times if you insist. However, they're not proactive. Sure, they reason, it's their responsibility that you learn, but it's yours too. So if you don't speak up, well then, it's not their fault. Only outgoing, assertive students fare well with this kind of trainer. However, accept this kind of training environment if you haven't paid much money for it. After all, you can only expect to get what you pay for.

Worth Their Weight in Gold

Trainers who take full responsibility for their students' learning are the only ones really worth rewarding. Their middle name is flexibility — the course is different every time they teach it, because the students are different. Regardless of the number of people in the class, they are always alert to the needs of the individual.

In their interaction with each student, they're consistently proactive. Are you having a problem? they prod, when you struggle stoically. They seem to know that you have a question, but are too shy to ask. When you get comfortable enough to ask, they delve further. Is that clear? Is that what you really meant to ask? It's as if they know what you mean, even when you don't.

Such trainers take your learning style into account. If they notice that you learn better by watching, they adopt that method with you. On the other hand, they may simply verbally coach another student who seems to more easily grasp material that way. They repeat material as often as necessary, even if you pretend that you understand it. They definitely listen to your body language and facial expressions, not just your words.

These trainers sense when you're in dire need of some reassurance or encouragement, and offer a kind or humorous comment to provide perspective. If you're bored, they invent a challenge for you on the spot. Because this kind of trainer is so completely involved in your progress, and cares about your moods and concerns, you really feel like the course was tailored to you. You feel competent and confident to tackle the work waiting for you back at the office.

The atmosphere created by these trainers is fun and relaxed. Even if you went into the classroom with doubts about your ability to learn, a reluctance to use computers or some reservation about whether learning this software would be useful to you, you leave with a different attitude. It's a kind of euphoria, as if you could go out and conquer the world — or at least your little computer-dominated portion of it.

A trainer like this generates an optimism in you about the future and the part you can play in it. In years to come you'll remember him or her fondly as a person who changed your life.

Now that's worth paying for.

Canada

Alberta

Humana Training Centres
Calgary, 403-262-4004

Humana Training Centres
Edmonton, 403-428-3286

N.A.I.T Distribution Centre
Edmonton, 403-963-1035

PBSC Computer Training Centres
Calgary, 403-234-8087

PBSC Computer Training Centres
Edmonton, 403-424-3710

British Columbia

BCIT Industrial Education
Burnaby, 604-432-8274

Drake Computer Training
Vancouver, 604-669-8789

Humana Training Centres
Vancouver, 604-681-3110

PBSC Computer Training Centres
Vancouver, 604-682-5615

Pearson Computer Centre
Vancouver, 604-327-3795

Resolutions Enterprises
Vancouver, 604-683-1599

Manitoba

PBSC Computer Training Centres
Winnipeg, 204-694-0970

New Brunswick

Caltech Computer Specialists
Moncton, 506-859-1088

Newfoundland

Western Community College
Stephenville, 709-643-7718

Nova Scotia

Drake Computer Training
Halifax, 902-429-4357

Henson College
Halifax, 902-494-2375

Software Experts
Halifax, 902-429-4357

Ontario

Ashley Computer Systems
Waterloo, 519-746-7111

Bradson Education Services
Ottawa, 613-782-2333

Chris Dickman
Toronto, 416-924-0759

The Computer Coach
Kingston, 613-384-3114

Computer Support Services
Kingston, 613-546-6420

The Computer Training Centre
Ottawa, 613-230-6614

Computerland Learning Centre
Toronto, 416-922-9292

Corel Corp.
Ottawa, 613-728-8200

Creating With Technology
Toronto, 416-694-8842

The Desktop Printshop
Oakville, 416-829-2200

Desktop Publishing Associates
Toronto, 416-480-1376

Durham Business
Comp. College
Pickering, 416-427-3010

Lexus Computer Training
Toronto, 416-964-3466

PBSC Computer Training
Centres
Toronto, 416-971-6920

Micann Business Training
Ottawa, 613-739-9898

PBSC Computer Training
Centres
Ottawa, 613-230-2902

PC Etcetera
Ottawa, 613-235-3277

PC Etcetera
Mississauga, 416-972-0644

Ouellette Computer
Consultants
Markham, 416-470-6475

Power Presentation Systems
Ottawa, 613-230-0609

Priority 01
Computer Education Services
London, 519-679-5550

Seneca College Of Applied
Arts And Technology
North York, 416-491-5050

Soft Train Institute
Scarborough, 416-297-1945

Quebec

Cinq and Quart
Lemoyne, 514-445-0561

Computerland Training Center
Montreal, 514-393-9950

Saskatchewan

ATC
Regina, 306-522-7827

Earle Associate Training
Lloydminster, 603-825-1924

Spectrum Advertising
Nipawin, 306-862-4200

United States

Alabama

A&B Company
Talladega, 205-362-2175

Microtrain
Birmingham, 205-942-9104

Technologies Tomorrow
Mobile, 205-456-7937

Arizona

Advanced
Communications Technologies
Phoenix, 602-493-7691

Executrain
Phoenix, 602-234-0406

Laser Works
Phoenix, 602-230-1752

The Resource
Scottsdale, 602-423-8222

California

Act Inc.
Los Angeles, 213-388-0551

Act Training Services
San Diego, 619-280-9933

ATI Inc.
Sacramento, 916-363-2500

Award Software
Los Gatos, 408-370-7979

Bottom Line Sales
Huntington Beach, 714-898-2300

Client Centred Training
Walnut Creek, 510-939-9569

The Dublin Group
San Francisco, 415-227-4777

Elliott Blatt
Long Beach, 213-431-6000

The Express Train
Santa Clara, 408-243-5955

Fox Computers
Big Bear Lake, 714-866-5700

Go Promotions
Laguna Beach, 714-494-0959

Graphic Word Systems
Fremont, 415-656-7297

Hexagon Computer Center
Los Angeles, 213-478-5510

New Horizons Comp. Center
Santa Ana, 714-556-1220

Ohlone College
Fremont, 415-659-6000

PC Etcetera
Los Angeles, 213-683-1944

PC Etcetera
Sacramento, 916-291-8585

PC Etcetera
San Francisco, 415-291-8585

PC SOS
Whittier, 213-945-6899

The Productivity Center
Cerritos, 213-865-8290

The Perfect Page
Anaheim, 714-758-8957

Re-mark Computer
Pomona, 714-594-3375

Scher-voit
San Diego, 619-453-0505

Shore University
Long Beach, 213-494-8781

Silicon Valley Computer Society
San Jose, 408-293-5201

Soft Scribe
Mountain View, 415-968-9800

Southern California Ventura Users Group
Burbank, 818-955-5830

Systems Consulting
Cupertino, 408-252-5448

Technical Marketing Communications
Torrance, 213-533-4964

The Thornhill Group
Woodland Hills, 818-596-2320

The Training Alternative
San Francisco, 415-442-0101

U-Publish
San Diego, 619-292-8066

Univar
Glendale, 818-546-1600

Ventura Training Centers
Oakland, 415-636-2036
Santa Clara, 408-562-2312

Xerox Corp.
Santa Clara, 408-562-2312

Xoma Corp.
Berkeley, 415-644-1170

Colorado

Training Access
Denver, 303-752-5006

University Of Colorado
Boulder, 303-492-5148

Words And Pictures
Lakewood, 303-969-0311

Connecticut

Cimtech CAD-CAM Solutions
New Haven, 203-874-8340

Delaware

On-line Consulting
Wilmington, 302-658-3018

Florida

Computer Training Group
Miami, 305-559-9488

Diane Mines
Marietta, 404-565-7641

Designs N' Type
Sunrise, 305-742-7272

The Micro Training Centre
West Palm Beach, 407-640-9168

Seabreeze Systems
Jacksonville, 904-737-6796

Sigma Business Systems
Hollywood, 305-987-1830

Georgia

Atlanta Desktop Publishing Center
Atlanta, 404-873-4357

Computerland Business Centers
Atlanta, 404-392-2629

Customized Computer Training
Marietta, 404-933-0476

Discovery Unlimited
Athens, 404-354-1339

EDG
Atlanta, 404-952-3030

KBM Alphatech
Atlanta, 404-435-8417

Iowa

Computer Graphic Center
Des Moines, 515-282-0000

MPC Computer Graphics
Council Bluffs, 712-325-8717

NS Industries
Des Moines, 515-255-3012

Illinois

AACTT
Rolling Meadows, 708-590-9500

Computer Support Centers
Schaumburg, 708-330-1390

Computer Workshop
Downers Grove, 708-971-0004

Hawkey and Associates
Chicago, 312-915-0695

Personal Comp. Ed. Services
Maywood, 708-338-0338

Xerox Corp.
Des Plaines, 708-635-2592

Indiana

Executrain
Indianapolis, 317-574-7057

Ivy Tech
Fort Wayne, 219-480-4219

PC Solutions
Indianapolis, 317-849-7486

Massachusetts

Common Sense Computing
Huntington, 413-667-5797

Professional Development Group
Framingham, 508-872-1499

Maryland

Capital Presentations
Silver Spring, 301-588-9540

Chesapeake Graphics
Sykesville, 301-795-5689

Entre Computer Center
Hagerstown, 301-797-7850

United Information Systems
Beltsville, 301-595-7194

Michigan

Presidential Training Center
Troy, 313-649-2222

Presidential Training Support
Birmingham, 313-647-3333

TBA Career Tech Center
Traverse City, 616-922-6294

Minnesota

Able Computers
St. Cloud, 612-252-3237

Dunwoody Institute
Minneapolis, 612-374-5800

Inacomp Computer Centers
Eden Prairie, 612-828-6792

Inacomp Educational Services
Minneapolis, 612-828-9550

Missouri

Software Plus
St. Louis, 314-434-3311

Nebraska

National Printers Network
Omaha, 402-334-7271

Nevada

PCT
Reno, 702-829-8300

Starburst Designs
Las Vegas, 702-453-3371

New Jersey

Compu Color Services
Union, 201-686-6464

Corporate Support Assoc.
Hackensack, 201-487-7180

Inst. for Manage. & Tech.
Dev.
Edison, 201-417-0690

Ocean Computer Group
Spring Lake Hts, 201-974-9191

PC Etcetera
Iselin, 201-548-4800

Upstart Services
Cherry Hill, 609-428-1331

New Mexico

Microsage
Los Alamos, 505-662-7244

New York

American Training Center
Forest Hills, 718-544-8100

Applied Technical Systems
Syracuse, 315-455-6179

Computer Design Center
Buffalo, 716-896-7601

Electronic Publishing
& Design Center
Schenectady, 518-374-3132

Irwin Desktop Solutions
Westbury, 516-334-6763

Microtrek Enterprises
New York, 212-398-6410

PC Etcetera
New York, 212-736-5870

Publishing By Computers
Westbury, 516-333-4171

North Carolina

2B Creative
Matthews, 704-882-2823

Catawba Valley
Community College
Hickory, 704-327-9124

CCI Computer Corp.
Huntersville, 704-394-8213

Practical Systems
Durham, 919-544-2828

Ohio

American Logistics Group
Solon, 216-349-5555

Edge Computer Systems
Cleveland, 216-696-7310

IRD Training Services
Columbus, 614-885-2909

Progressive Computer
Services
Zanesville, 614-455-3753

Oklahoma
Auto Exec
Tulsa, 918-492-2952

Oregon
DP Printing
Portland, 503-281-7222

GBA International
Beaverton, 503-646-1027

Kinetic Computer Solutions
Beaverton, 503-620-0678

MicroAge Branch Office
Klamath Falls, 503-773-9989

University Of Oregon
Portland, 503-725-3055

Pennsylvania
Compusult
Philadelphia, 215-864-0300

Professional Training Service
King Of Prussia, 215-337-8878

Volt Information Sciences
Blue Bell, 215-825-7720

South Carolina
Wilkinson & Nichols
Mauldin, 803-297-6341

Tennessee
Training Systems
Oakridge, 615-481-0963

Texas
BYTE Management
Fort Worth, 817-624-1900

Capstone Communications
Dallas, 214-746-4855

CBM Education Center
San Antonio, 512-224-9834

Desktop Consultants
San Antonio, 512-694-5059

Ideas To Image
Houston, 713-864-4785

Micro Design Systems
Garland, 214-530-0214

Squier Computer Services
San Antonio, 512-828-9000

Vermont
Community College Of
Vermont
Montpelier, 802-229-9490

Virginia
Editorial Experts
Alexandria, 703-683-0683

Jim Elmore Illustration &
Design
Woodbridge, 703-590-4074

Your Options
Fairfax, 703-352-0944

Washington
Bellevue Community College
Bellevue, 206-246-7433

Executive Presentation
Systems
Seattle, 206-343-2202

Lee Sylvester Designs
Seattle, 206-323-2620

Levine & Associates
Redmond, 206-882-3481

Pacific Office Equipment
Port Angeles, 206-457-7987

Software U Corp.
Vancouver, 206-693-2322

Glossary

A sizes

Paper sizes more commonly used in Europe. Draw lets you choose A3, A4, A5 and B5 sizes from the Page Setup dialog box under the File menu.

Arrowheads

Draw's term for line endings. A wide variety is provided and you can create new ones by choosing Create Arrow from the Special menu.

Ascender

The part of a letter that stretches above the main body (x-height) of the character, as in k and h.

Autotrace

The ability of Draw to automatically trace imported bitmap images, the result being editable curves and lines. You can also use CorelTRACE to do this.

B sizes

Paper sizes more commonly used in Europe. You can choose the B5 size in the Page Setup dialog box.

Baseline

The imaginary line along which characters are horizontally aligned.

Batch printing

The ability to print multiple documents in quick succession. You can perform batch printing with CorelMOSAIC.

Bézier curve

Draw represents all curve objects, including text, as Bézier curves. These have the advantage of maintaining image quality when resized. The Pencil ℓ tool can be used in Bézier ℓ mode, or a Freehand ℓ mode that converts what you draw to Bézier curves.

Bitmap

An image stored as a series of bits, typically created with a scanner or a 'paint' type graphics program. Draw can import and export a wide variety of bitmap formats. To edit these, use CorelPHOTO-PAINT.

Black printer

The black plate used in printing four-color process separations. Its function is to increase the contrast of dark tones.

Bleed

Part of a drawing that runs off the edge of the printed page. You'll need a page size smaller than the media size you're printing to.

Blend

Draw can generate a user-specified number of objects 'in-between' two selected objects. Essential for creating smooth transitions of color and shade. Choose it from the Effects menu.

.CGM

File extension for Computer Graphics Metafile, a vector graphics file format. Draw can import and export to this format.

.CLB

File extension for the compressed file libraries you can create with CorelMOSAIC.

Clip art

Images available either commercially or in the public domain that can be imported in applications and edited or used as-is. They may be bitmap or vector based; Draw is supplied with vector clip art in .CDR format.

Clipboard

An area of memory set aside by Windows for storing one Copy or Cut at a time. The contents of the Clipboard can be pasted onto the Draw editing window as well as transferred to or from another Windows application.

Color palette

The on-screen display of the current palette. Choose Show Color Palette from the Display menu to enable it.

Color separation

The separation of the colors of an image into the four process colors: cyan, magenta, yellow and black.

Color transparency

A positive color image created by photographic means on clear film. These range in size from 35mm slides to 8 by 10 inches.

Comprehensive

Sometimes called a 'comp', this is a preliminary version of a design, often created for client approval. Color comps are often created on devices like the QMS ColorScript thermal PostScript printer.

Condensed type

A narrow weight of a typeface, such as Fujiyama Condensed. You can condense any face with Draw by negatively stretching it.

Constrain

Holding the Control key down while performing a transformation on an object, node or control point limits your possible movements. For example, pressing it while rotating constrains motion to 15° increments.

Continuous tone

Images that are not represented simply in black or white, as in a halftone or line art, but as a series of even, graduated tones as in a photograph.

Contrast

The variation between the darkest and lightest areas of an image.

Control Panel

A Windows program used to change your current target printer settings and system environment.

Control point

A node has one or two control points, revealed by clicking on it or its associated curve segment with the ⚲ tool. Nodes associated with straight lines don't have control points.

CorelTRACE

A separate program included with Draw, used for converting bitmap .PCX, .TIF, .GIF, .TGA and .BMP images to vector .EPS format. Run it from Program Manager.

Cromalin

A film-based proofing system for viewing color separations prior to printing.

Crop

Reducing the displayable area of a bitmap imported into Draw, using the ⚲ tool.

Crop marks

Used for indicating the four corners of the page defined with Page Setup when creating pages smaller than the paper size of the printer. Selectable in the Print dialog box when using PostScript printers.

Curve

Describes both an individual curve segment as well as any number of line and curve segments that make up a single path or combined subpaths. Also referred to as a 'curve object'.

Defaults

You can set object Fill and Outline defaults by making selections from their flyout menus or dialog boxes with no object selected. Use the same principle when setting text. New Draw publications start up using the settings you used in your last session.

Descender

The part of a lower case letter that falls below the baseline, as in the letter p.

Digitize

To convert into a digital bitmap format, as when scanning.

Dingbat

A decorative or graphic character, one collection of which is contained in the Dixieland font supplied with Draw. The Wingdings font is supplied with Windows.

Dirty proof

A proof marked up with many corrections.

Display type

Type set in a larger point size than the body text.

Dither

A method of representing colors by a mix of pixels of varying colors. Displays and output devices must dither to create the illusion of a specified color.

DPI

A measure of the resolution, in dots per inch, of an output device. See Resolution.

.DXF

Vector graphic file format used by AutoCAD. Draw can import and export to .DXF format.

Driver

Software that lets an application or operating system know the nature of the device it's accessing. It's important to use current drivers for displays and printers.

Edge padding

Altering the percentage of the beginning and end colors in fountain fills.

Editing window

This includes both the printable page and the area surrounding it. The editing window constitutes the available drawing area in which objects are displayed in outline form.

Em

A unit of measurement corresponding to the point size of the type being used.

Embedding

When speaking of TrueType, the ability of some fonts to be included with a document, enabling them to be read, printed or used to create new documents on other systems. When speaking of OLE (object linking and embedding) the ability to embed data in a document, making it easy to edit by simply double-clicking.

Emulsion

A light-sensitive coating on film used to create offset printing plates. Draw can print separations as negatives to PostScript imagesetters if Film Negative in the Print dialog box is chosen.

En

Half the width of an em.

Envelope

A frame with handles that can be dragged to reshape an object. Choose from four envelopes under the Effects menu.

.EPS

Extension for Encapsulated PostScript, a vector graphic file format. Draw can import and edit Adobe Illustrator .EPS files, and those created by CorelTRACE. Draw can also export to .EPS format, but the resulting file can't be edited.

Extract

Use this command to write text from a Draw illustration to an ASCII text file. This could then be edited and brought back into Draw with Merge-Back. Both commands can be found under the Special menu.

Extrude

The ability of Draw to render an object three-dimensionally. Choose it from the Effects menu.

Film stripping

Bringing together all the elements of a page or pages at the film stage.

Film

Clear plastic sheets covered with an emulsion used to create positives or negatives of original artwork, either through traditional camera-based techniques or directly with an imagesetter. These are then used to create printing plates. You can specify the creation of film negatives in the Print dialog box when printing to a PostScript imagesetter.

Font

A collection of type characters of similar design. A font 'family' would include italic and bold variations. Some of the fonts supplied with Draw are in families, such as Brooklyn. Others, such as Banff, are not.

Fountain fill

Also called a graduated fill. A fill which is not consistent in color or density but changes gradually from one part of a filled object to another. Linear and radial fills can be created in Draw by choosing the ■ icon from the ✍ menu.

Four-color process

Reproducing original colored artwork through the creation of four film separations representing cyan, magenta, yellow and black.

GEM

A graphics environment used by such applications as the old version of Ventura. Also a vector graphics file format used by GEM applications, such as Ventura and Artline. Draw supports .GEM import and export.

.GIF

A color bitmap file format used by the CompuServe online service. Draw can import and export these.

Gray component replacement

Draw automatically calculates the amount of black when you create or edit a color, by reducing large overlapping percentages of the process colors with black.

Grayscale image

In scanning artwork, the result of digitizing and saving as a file continuous tone artwork in a number of shades of gray. Draw can import and print .TIF images containing up to 256 shades of gray.

Guidelines

Non-printing guides you create by dragging from the rulers onto the editing window. Use in conjunction with Snap To Guidelines under the Display menu.

Halftone

The process of rendering a continuous-tone image as a series of dots of various size but uniform density. Draw can print grayscale images as halftones.

Halftone screen

When printing to a PostScript device you can specify the halftone screen type, frequency and angle of an object by choosing PostScript from the Outline Color, Uniform Fill or Fountain Fill dialog boxes from the ♟ and ✍ flyout menus.

Header

An optional Image Header created when you export Draw graphics to .EPS format. The header enables an application into which the resulting file is

imported to display a representation of it on screen. Also, the
device initialization header sent
by Draw to a PostScript printer.

Highlighting box

Refers to both the sizing handles
that appear when an object is
selected and the dotted outline
that appears when it's transformed in some way.

Hints

Algorithms contained in some
PostScript and TrueType fonts,
which increase type quality at
low resolutions in small point
sizes. Most of Draws fonts are
hinted.

HSB

A color model in which colors
are defined using values for hue,
saturation and brightness. You
can define colors in Draw using
this method.

HPGL

Acronym for Hewlett-Packard
Graphics Language, a vector
graphics file format used primarily by plotters. Draw can import
and export HPGL files with a
.PLT extension.

Imagesetter

Generic term for a high-resolution (typically PostScript)
printer capable of rendering
both type and graphics.

Kerning

Adjusting inter-character spacing, typically for pairs of letters
that need special spacing treat-
ment, such as OT and AV.
Interactive kerning of individual
letters in Draw is possible with
the ⚲ tool.

Layers

The ability to organize objects
by grouping them in separate
layers. Handy for complex illustrations. Choose this from the
Display menu.

Leading

The amount of space between
the baselines of text. You control this in Draw either in terms
of percentage of point size using
dialog boxes, or interactively
with the ⚲ tool.

Lino

Common contraction for
Linotronic, a line of PostScript
imagesetters manufactured by
Linotype. The term is now synonymous with any imagesetter
used by service bureaus.

Macro

A series of actions recorded by
an application, such as the Windows Recorder, and later
invoked with a user-defined keystroke sequence.

Mark-up

To indicate on illustrations or page layouts directions for reproduction. Often used to specify spot color and tint percentages.

Marquee

The dotted box created when dragging around a number of objects with the ▶ tool, or a number of nodes with the ⚲ tool.

Mask

Using the Combine command from the Arrange menu to form a 'hole' in two combined objects, through which underlying objects are displayed.

Merge-Back

See Extract.

Metafile

An intermediate vector graphic format used by Windows for moving images between applications. Such files have .WMF extensions.

Miter Limit

The angle below which corners will be beveled, not pointed. Change this value in the Preferences dialog box.

Moiré

A pattern that appears on off-set-printed material when the halftone screen angles of the separations are set to the wrong angles. The angles can be changed in Draw when printing to a PostScript printer or can be changed by your service bureau.

Mosaic

A utility included with Draw, used for performing a variety of file management tasks. Run from within the Import or Open dialog boxes or from Program Manager.

Node

The beginning and endpoint of a line or curve segment. Also refers to the eight 'handles' on the corners and midpoints of objects when selected with the ▶ tool.

Nudge

The ability to move an object a user-definable amount by pressing the arrow keys on the keyboard. Define the nudge value in the Preferences dialog box under the Special menu.

Offset

When using vector or bitmap fills, change the offset values to control the positioning of the fill 'tiles'.

Overprint

Used when creating color separations to compensate for poor

registration on the printing press. See Trap.

Page frame

You can quickly draw a rectangle around your page by choosing Add Page Frame from the Page Setup dialog box under the File menu.

Palette

You can save collections of colors in named palettes and reload them as required.

Pantone

The Pantone color matching system is a common standard in the graphic arts for specifying solid (spot) colors using sample color swatch books. This is supported in Draw.

Paragraph text

A way of working with text blocks up to 4,000 characters long. Click and drag with the 𝔸 tool to enable this, or import an ASCII text file.

Path

Paths may be open or closed and are composed of one or more line or curve segments. Subpaths are two or more paths that have been combined into a single path.

Patterns

You can fill objects with existing or user-definable bitmap ▓ or vector ↗ fill patterns. Choose these from the ✋ menu.

.PCX

Color bitmap graphic file format which Draw can import and export. You can also trace and separate color .PCX files.

Pen

The shape of the pen determines how object outlines will be drawn. Define this by choosing ♦ from the ♦ flyout menu.

Perspective

You can add one- and two-point perspective to objects by choosing Edit Perspective from the Effects menu and dragging handles on the resulting envelope.

Pica

A unit of measure composed of 12 points, used to describe elements on a page. There are approximately 6 picas in an inch.

PICT

Draw can import and export Macintosh PICT vector graphics files. They should be given a .PCT extension prior to import.

.PIF

File extension of IBM mainframe vector graphic file format. Draw can import and export to .PIF format.

Pixel

The smallest 'picture element', or dot, visible on the screen. Its actual size depends on your monitor.

Point

A unit of measurement used to describe type sizes, in which roughly 72 points equal an inch, and 12 points equal a pica. Draw can create type in sizes from .7 to 2,160 points, including fractional sizes.

PostScript

The industry-standard page description language used to drive a wide range of printers. A PostScript printer is necessary to use a number of Draw's advanced features.

Print merge

The ability of Draw to print multiple copies of a document, each time replacing text on the page with new text from an ASCII file. Great for certificates and similar documents. You'll find the Print Merge command under the File menu.

Process color

See Four-color process.

Proof

The creation of hard copy using a low-quality printing technique to provide a sense of how the graphic will look prior to outputting it in its final form. A monochrome image might be proofed on a laser printer before being printed on an imagesetter, while a color graphic might be proofed on a color thermal printer before separations are made. High-quality color proofs of separations can be made with Cromalins.

Rasterizer

Draw has its own rasterizer for both displaying and outputting TrueType fonts. This can be easily disabled in the CORELDRW.INI file.

Register marks

Marks on paper or film used when creating color separations, so that the various pages or pieces of film will all line up 'in register'. Register marks (crosshairs) can be chosen in the Print dialog box when printing to PostScript printers.

Resolution

In terms of output devices, a typical laser printer has a resolution of 300 dpi, while a typical imagesetter has roughly 1,200 or 2,400 dpi. The more dots per inch, the less 'jaggy' the output.

RGB

A color model in which colors are defined using values for red, green and blue. You can define colors in Draw using this method.

Rough

A very preliminary but full-size design or publication layout, often executed in pencil.

Sans serif

Typefaces designed without 'serifs', the small ending strokes on individual letters.

Scale

In Draw this refers to two processes. You can scale an object in your drawing directly by dragging a corner handle or by using the Stretch & Mirror dialog box under the Transform menu. When printing you can enter a scaling value in the Print dialog box to scale the entire image up or down by the desired percentage.

SCODL

Draw can export to SCODL (.SCD) format, which is used by many film recorders for the creation of slides.

Screen angle

When printing color separations, each of the four process colors are printed at a different angle to avoid moiré. These angles can be adjusted with Draw.

Serif

The small ending stroke of the characters of some typefaces, such as Toronto. Sans serif faces, such as Switzerland, do not have these strokes.

Set solid

Type set without any additional leading. Ten-point type set solid, for example, would be represented as 10/10, and described as 'ten on ten'.

Snap To Object

The ability to snap the current pointer location to parts of objects on the page. This is useful for alignment. Enable with the Display menu.

Spot color

A solid color other than black, applied during the offset printing process. Also refers to the method of specifying color, usually with Pantone numbers.

Status Line

An area below the menu bar that displays information about the currently selected object, node or control point and any transformation in progress. Enable the Status Line with the Display menu.

Steps

The intermediate objects created when using the Blend command.

Stripes

The intermediate shades created when using fountain fills.

Subscript

The same as superscript but with the text positioned below the baseline.

Superscript

Characters that are smaller than the point size of the rest of the text string and are positioned above the x-height of the type. In Draw, double-click on a character's node with the ⚲ tool and select Superscript from the dialog box.

Swatching system

A color specification system in which you can pick defined colors from a printed swatch book. Draw supports the Pantone and TRUMATCH swatching systems.

Symbols

Draw is supplied with libraries containing thousands of symbols. Activate by holding down the Shift key and clicking the Ⓐ tool cursor on the page.

.TGA

A color bitmap file format standardized by AT&T. Typically used by high-end paint packages, such as RIO. Draw can import and export these.

Textures

A range of user-modifiable fills that work only with PostScript printers. Choose the PS icon from the ⬧ flyout menu. Examples are reproduced in the Draw manual.

.TIF

File extension of Tag Image File Format files, a bilevel, grayscale and color bitmap graphic format which Draw can import and export. It does not currently support JPEG-compressed TIFF files.

Tile

Draw's ability to instruct an output device to print a drawing that's bigger than the available paper size on multiple pages, which you can then assemble.

Tint

A halftone area made up of dots of even size. These can be created by Draw or can be manually applied to printed artwork in the form of films of various density. Spot colors can be given percentage tints.

Trap

Sometimes referred to as spreads or chokes. The need to create overlapped areas where two colors meet in an image, to ensure that slight press misregistrations don't produce white areas between them when printed. Create traps in Draw when generating separations on a PostScript printer by choosing Overprint in the PostScript Options dialog box.

Transformation

Modifying an object by moving, mirroring, stretching/scaling, rotating/skewing.

True color

An overly optimistic term for 24-bit color, whether displayed on the screen or printed. Such devices work from a palette of over 16 million colors.

TrueType

A font format supported by Draw. 155 TrueType fonts are supplied on floppy, with an additional 101 on CD-ROM.

TRUMATCH

A swatching system for specifying process colors. A TRUMATCH palette is provided with Draw, as well as a discount coupon for purchasing the swatch book.

Vanishing point

In perspective drawing, the apparent point in space where objects seem to converge. Significant when using the Extrude and Perspective commands.

Vector graphics

A method of representing images in terms of lines and curves, used by such applications as Draw and Micrografx Designer. Differs from the bitmap approach of paint programs and scanners.

VideoShow

A vector graphic file format (.PIC) used by presentation graphics hardware such as General Parametrics Corporation's VideoShow. Draw can export to VideoShow format.

Wallpaper

Files in compressed .BMP format can be used as Windows wallpaper, to cover the desktop. You can export to this format from Draw.

WFN BOSS

A typeface conversion utility supplied with Draw 2.0 for converting fonts in other formats to Draw's native font format. Also used to convert from Draw to Adobe PostScript format. No longer useful.

WPG
Graphics file format used by WordPerfect. Draw can export to .WPG format.

X-height
The height of a character with no descender or ascender, such as an x or o.

Zero point
The origin of the rulers and grid. Define in Grid Setup under Display or click and drag onto the page from the spot where the two rulers meet.

Bibliography

Collier's Rules for Desktop Design and Typography.

David Collier: Addison-Wesley, 1990.

A funky little book that touches on most aspects of design and production from the desktop.

Color and its Reproduction.

Gary G. Field: Graphic Arts Technical Foundation, 1988.

Technical but comprehensive exploration of color perception and reproduction. A must-have if you're just getting into color.

CorelDRAW 3.0: Advanced Design & Production.

Daniel Will-Harris: Learnkey, Inc., 1992.

The inimitable Will-Harris takes you through the production cycle from start to finish via video. Covers Photo-Paint, layers, clip art, bleeds and tips for re-using design elements.

CorelDRAW 3.0: Special Effects.

D. Will-Harris: Learnkey, Inc., 1992.

Another Will-Harris video — collect them all. Covers outlines, shadows, blends, neon effects, text to path tricks, color prepress, using export and combine, and more.

Design Essentials.

Edited by Tanya Wendling: Adobe Press, 1992

Tips on using Adobe Illustrator and Photoshop, many applicable to Draw.

Designer's Guide to Color 1 and 2.

James Stockton: Chronicle Books, 1984.

Great little books filled with different color combinations. Useful for defining process colors in Draw.

Designer's Guide to Color 3.

Jeanne Allen: Chronicle Books, 1986.

In the same vein as volumes 1 and 2 but with colors displayed in complex patterns.

Desktop Publishing in Color.

Michael Kieran: Bantam Books, 1991.

The first comprehensive book on this complex topic. Technical editor for this was yours truly.

Inside PostScript

Frank Braswell: Peachpit Press, 1991

An insider's look at the workings of PostScript.

PC Secrets.

Carline M. Halliday: IDG Books, 1992

Everyone should have one fat DOS book, and this is the latest and greatest, complete with two disks of utilities.

Pocket Pal.

International Paper, 1989.

A great little paperback crammed with essentials for those new to graphic arts production techniques.

PostScript Language Tutorial & Cookbook.

Adobe Systems, 1985.
Solid introduction to the PostScript language.

PostScript Language Reference Manual.

Adobe Systems, 1985.
The classic reference guide to PostScript and its operators.

PostScript Language Program Design.

Adobe Systems, 1988.
Meaty stuff for advanced PostScript programmers.

The Art of Lettering.

Albert Kapr: K.G. Sauer, 1983.
Hard-to-find but charming book on the history and aesthetics of Roman letterforms.

The Little Windows Book.

Kay Y. Nelson: Peachpit Press, 1992.
The recommended book for learning Windows. Small, concise, easily digestible.

The Print Production Handbook.

David Bann: North Light, 1985.
Handy reference about offset printing processes, from prepress to binding.

Typefaces for Desktop Publishing.

Alison Black: Architecture Design and Technology Press, 1990.
Solid information on type design and usage.

Typography.

Ruari McLean: Thames & Hudson, 1980. Good overview of typographic fundamentals.

Typography & Typesetting.

Ronald Labuz: Van Nostrand Rheinhold, 1988.
Typographic history and usage fundamentals. Don't stretch or condense type without it.

Windows 3.1 Secrets.

Brian Livingston: IDG Books, 1992
The one huge Windows book you need, comprehensive and supplied with three disks of utilities.

Periodicals

Before&After

1830 Sierra Gardens Drive
Suite 30
Roseville, CA 95661
(916) 784-3880

Chris Dickman's Mastering Corel Draw Newsletter

16 Ottawa St.
Toronto, ON M4T 2B6
(416) 924-0759
Fax: (416) 924-4875!

Computer Graphics World

One Technology Park Drive
PO Box 987
Westford, MA 01886
(918) 831-9400

Corelation

1309 Riverside Drive
Burbank, CA 91506
(310) 452-5637

Computer Pictures

701 Westchester Ave.
White Plains, NY 10604
(914) 328-9157

Desktop Communications

PO Box 941745
Atlanta, GA 30341
(800) 966-9052

High Color

21 Elm St.
Third Floor, PO Box 1347
Camden, ME 04843
(207) 236-6267

New Media

901 Mariner's Island Blvd.
Suite 365
San Mateo, CA 94404
(415) 573-5170

PC Publishing & Presentations

PO Box 941909
Atlanta, GA 30341
(800) 966-9052

PSsssst!

ColoRip Pre-Press
130 Bridgeland Ave.
Toronto, ON M6A 1Z4
(416) 784-1234

Publish

501 Second St.
San Franciso, CA 94107
(800) 274-5116

Seybold Report on Desktop Publishing

428 E. Baltimore Pike
PO Box 644
Media, PA 19063
(215) 565-2480

Step-By-Step Electronic Design

Dynamic Graphics
6000 N. Forest Park Dr.
Peoria, IL 61614-3592
(800) 255-8800

Timeout

166 Laurel Rd., Ste. 205
E. Northport, NY 11731

Verbum

PO Box 12564
San Diego, CA 92112
(619) 233-9977

Windows Magazine

600 Community Drive
Manhasset, NY 11030
(800) 284-3584

Windows User

25 West 39th St.
New York, NY 10018
(800) 627-9860

WUGNET Windows Journal

1295 N. Providence Rd.
Suite C107
Media, PA 19063
(215) 565-1861

Resources

Adobe Systems
1585 Charleston Rd.
PO Box 7900
Mountain View, CA 94039
(415) 961-4400

Agfa
200 Ballardvale St.
Wilmington, MA 01887
(508) 658-5600
(416) 240-7323 (Canada)

Ares Software
PO Box 4667
Foster City, CA 94404-4667
(415) 578-9090

The Association of Corel Artists & Designers
1309 Riverside Drive
Burbank, CA 91506
(310) 452-5637

The Association of Imaging Service Bureaus
5601 Roanne Way
Suite 605
Greensboro, NC 27409
(800) 844-2472

Pawel Bodytko
65 East Palatine Road, Ste. 119
Prospect Heights, IL 60070
(708) 459-0520

Chris Dickman
16 Ottawa St.
Toronto, ON M4T 2B6
(416) 924-0759
CompuServe: 70730,2265

The Color Resource
708 Montgomery St.
San Francisco, CA 94111
(415) 398-5337

ColoRip Pre-Press
130 Bridgeland Ave., Ste. 100
Toronto, ON M6A 1Z4
(416) 784-1234

Corel Corp.
1600 Carling Ave.
Ottawa, ON K1Z 8R7
Phone: (613) 728-8200
Fax: (613) 728-9790

Peter Dako
698A Queen St. W.
Toronto, ON M6J 1E7
(416) 366-8570
CompuServe: 71542,1601

Desktop Publishing Associates
1992 Yonge St., Ste. 301
Toronto, ON M4S 1Z7
(416) 480-1376

Delrina Technology
1945 Leslie St.
Don Mills, ON M3B 2M3
(416) 441-3676

Sherwood Fleming
16 Ottawa St.
Toronto, ON M4T 2B6
(416) 968-3103

Golden Bow Systems
2665 Ariane Dr., Ste. 207
San Diego, CA 92117
(619) 483-0901

Bob Hires
HiRes Graphics
Sutton Towers, Ste. 808D
Collingswood, NJ 081187
(609) 858-4770

Inset Systems
71 Commerce Drive
Brookfield, CT 06804-3405
(203) 740-2400

InSight Systems
10017 Coach Rd.
Vienna, VA 22181
(703) 938-0250

Michael Kieran
1992 Yonge St., Ste. 301
Toronto, ON M4S 1Z7
(416) 480-1376

LaserMaster
7156 Shady Oak Rd.
Eden Prairie, MN 55344
(612) 944-9330

LearnKey
93 So. Mountain Way Dr.
Orem, UT 84058
800-937-3279
(801) 224-8210

Linotype-Hell
425 Oser Ave.
Hauppauge, NY 11788
(508) 369-1441

Lupin Software
P.O. Box 4009
Davis, CA 95617-4009
(412) 341-5601

Michael Lee
Advertising & Design
2615 Calder, Ste. 150
Beaumont, TX 77702
(409) 835-7564

Micrografx
1303 Arapaho
Richardson, TX 75081
(214) 234-1769

Panacea
Post Office Square, Ste. 4
24 Orchard View Drive
Londonderry, NH 03053-3376
(603) 434-2461

James Phillips
PO Box 1017,
Station Q,
Toronto, ON M4T 2P2
(416) 923-5737

Ray Dream
1804 N. Shoreline Blvd.
Mountain View, CA 94043
(415) 960-0765

Steve Roth
Open House
4021 Aurora Avenue North
Seattle, WA 98103

Steve Sagman
CMM, Inc.
140 Charles St., New York,
NY 10014
(212) 691-4200
CompuServe: 72456,3325

Steve Shubitz
Published Perfection!
7486 La Jolla Blvd. #552
La Jolla, CA 92037
(619) 546-9309
Fax: (619) 546-9309-33
CompuServe: 72047,3402

Systems of Merritt
2551 Old Dobbin Dr. E.
Mobile, AL 36695
(205) 660-7740

UserLand Software
400 Seaport Ct., Suite 202
Redwood City , CA 94063
(416)369-6600

Virginia Systems
5509 W.Bay, Ct.
Midlothian, VA 23112
(804) 739-3200

Rich Zaleski
169 Cottage Street
PO Box 3
Stevenson, CT 06491
(203) 268-5544

Zenographics
4 Executive Circle
Irvine, CA 92714
(714) 851-1314

The Mastering CorelDRAW Team

Chris co-founded Blue Heron Printing in 1980, a successful offset and silkscreen printing firm. His involvement included all aspects of the print process, from marketing and project design to production. In 1983 he began publishing *Johnson's Index to Art Auctions*, a quarterly journal subscribed to by art collectors, galleries and libraries across Canada. The *Index* was entirely created and published using personal computers.

Chris has published articles on computers and publishing in many magazines, including *Desktop Communications*, *PC Publishing & Presentations*, *Windows User*, *Business Publishing*, *Computer Shopper* and *Corel Magazine*. For three years he was editor-in-chief of *Electronic Composition & Imaging* magazine.

Chris Dickman

In addition to *Mastering Corel Draw*, Chris is a co-author of *ScanJet Unlimited* (Peachpit), a contributor to *Real World PageMaker: Windows Edition* (Bantam) and the technical editor of *Desktop Publishing in Color* (Bantam).

Chris is the senior trainer for Desktop Publishing Associates, a Toronto firm specializing in electronic publishing training, for which he conducts Draw classes. He's in demand as a speaker and moderator at such industry events as Comgraph, VICOM, the International Prepress Color Conference and MACWORLD Expo. Chris is currently organizing a series of one-day seminars, to be held across Canada and the U.S. in 1993, and has begun the publication of a *Mastering Corel Draw* newsletter. His goal is to make the use of small computers for publishing and graphics a possibility for the widest possible audience.

Pawel Bodytko

Pawel, who contributed *Image Editing with CorelPHOTO-PAINT*, founded Pawel Bodytko, Inc., in 1991, as an illustration and design firm specializing in packaging design. In 1990 he began a series of calendars on the theme of Great Artists of the 20th Century. Issue number three, saluting Frank Lloyd Wright, won an award in the 1991 Corel Design Contest. The most recent issue on Ernest Hemingway was the monthly contest winner in April 1992. (It's reproduced in the color section of this book.) Pawel also recently created a series of books with a focus on the wild animal world, called Earth 2, for "children of all ages." These were produced with Draw and other Windows-based graphics applications. You'll also find one of these in the color section.

Peter Dako

Peter Dako designed and produced the pages of *Mastering Corel Draw* with Aldus PageMaker. Peter creates publications and illustrations for a wide variety of clients, with a focus on the arts and entertainment industries. Most of his work is done with the Macintosh versions of Aldus PageMaker and Aldus FreeHand, but he's also known for his typographic designs, which he renders in Altsys Fontographer. Thanks to Chris Dickman's expert guidance as his editor during the *EC&I* years, Peter now has a blossoming career writing about desktop technology for such publications as *Desktop Communications*, *Business Publishing* and others.

Sherwood Fleming

'Communicator' is an apt description for Sherwood's diverse activities — design, writing, training, singing and song writing. Sherwood trains for Desktop Publishing Associates in Toronto, conducting seminars in PageMaker and Ventura. So her chapter on *Choosing a Training Firm* is written from experience. Years ago she saw the need for training desktop publishers in graphic design skills and her Design for Desktop Publishing course has been an ongoing hit with both novice and seasoned users of the technology. Computers have followed her into her singing pursuits as well. Coming from a traditional background of cabaret and musical theater, she was recently bitten by the

MIDI bug. She's currently co-producing and co-writing an album of New Age songs, with MIDI wizard Steve Sauvé. Whether it's the printed page or a song lyric, Sherwood has always been a communicator.

Michael Kieran

Michael Kieran is the author of *Desktop Publishing in Color*, from Bantam Books, and the author of numerous technical articles on color publishing. He is widely sought after as a consultant and speaker on desktop color technologies and their implementation. Michael contributed *Essential Concepts in Color Publishing*.

Steve Roth

Steve Roth is a *Macworld* contributing editor and the author, coauthor and/or editor of more than a dozen books on desktop publishing, including *Real World PageMaker*, *The QuarkXPress Book* and *Real World PostScript*. Steve contributed *Getting the Best Scan*.

Steve Sagman

Steve Sagman is the author of the best-selling *Using Harvard Graphics* and *1-2-3 Graphics Techniques*, both published by Que Corporation, and *Getting Your Start in Hollywood*, from Peachpit Press. He writes about personal computers, particularly presentation graphics and desktop publishing, in *PC/Computing*, *PC Week*, *Computer Shopper*, and *PC Magazine*. Steve was a natural for the creation of the *Presenting with CorelSHOW* and *Graphing with CorelCHART* chapters. His company, CMM, creates courseware and user documentation, and provides training and consulting services in the New York area.

Steve Shubitz

Steve Shubitz is President of Published Perfection!, a La Jolla, California electronic publishing and consulting company providing production, training and integration for the Windows and Macintosh platforms. Steve is a contributing editor for *Electronic Composition & Imaging* magazine, for which he authors the Publishing in Windows column, and he recently coauthored *Inside CorelDraw-4th Edition* (New Riders Publishing). Steve is a faculty member at The Advertising Arts College, where he teaches desktop publishing. Steve is also a senior instructor for a Microsoft Authorized Training Center, for which he teaches Windows and Draw. He has lectured extensively throughout the United States. His expert knowledge of both the Windows and Macintosh platforms in a real-world production environment provides his clients and students with a unique perspective of the technology. Steve contributed the mammoth *Advanced Type Topics* chapter.

Rich Zaleski

Rich has had thousands of magazine articles published in the outdoor markets to which he directs most of his efforts, and his work has won numerous awards. He provides detailed, Draw-produced illustrations for his articles, and also does catalog, brochure and packaging graphic layouts for several companies in the outdoor sports industry. Rich's computer expertise was acquired prior to becoming a full-time freelance writer/illustrator, when he earned his living managing the Service and Support Department for an office equipment/computer dealer. His *Converting Scans with CorelTRACE* chapter represents the first in-depth examination of Trace in print.

Production Notes

Text for this book was created in Word for Windows, typically running at the same time as Draw and the screen grab software. I made good use of Word's glossary and macro capabilities to automate recurrent tasks. For example, to format the tool icons used throughout the book, I typed in the letter corresponding to the desired tool and ran a macro that applied the special tool font to it, moved one space to the right and entered the word 'tool', followed by another space. Since page layout was performed in Aldus PageMaker, I embedded the formatting style codes right in the text, using glossaries to save typing. For example, to embed <SUB> in the text, I had only to type an S and press the F3 function key. I also used this technique to mark where the tips and secrets icons should be placed.

How dey do dat?

One feature of Word that I subsequently regretted using was its SmartQuotes macro. A few chapters into the book I enabled this macro, which automatically converts the usual inch and foot marks to proper opening and closing curly quotes. They looked great on the screen and printed out nicely on my printer, but when imported into Mac PageMaker they were nowhere to be found. Luckily, this was caught after only a few chapters and I then reverted to the boring old inch marks and let PageMaker perform the conversion.

The system I used for running Word and Draw was a ZEOS 33 MHz 486 with 16 Mb of RAM. The monitor was an NEC 5D, an older 20-inch model that has served me well over the years — big monitors are the only way to publish. My graphics card was the Trident SuperVGA supplied with the ZEOS, running at a resolution of 1,024 by 768 with a palette of 256 colors, using the WinSpeed drivers from Panacea. (I've been holding out for the arrival of affordable 24-bit color cards.)

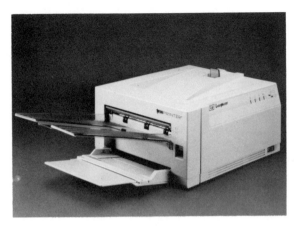

An applications-oriented book such as this inevitably uses innumerable screen shots. I've tried a lot of screen grab programs over the years and used Collage Plus, from inner media, and for Windows, from Inset Systems, to capture the ones for this edition. HiJaak was the workhorse program I used most of the time, since it let me define and save exactly the screen grab format I needed — LZW G compressed grayscale .TIF. This reduced the size of an uncompressed full-screen .TIF grab from 700 Kb to 30 Kb, with no loss in quality. Compressed .TIF files and .EPS images exported from Draw were the two formats I standardized on, since they could both be easily moved to the Mac for production.

HiJaak performed a variety of other valuable tasks. For example, I used its batch conversion abilities to quickly convert .PCX files used in the previous edition to .TIF. And its color-replacement feature let me convert the background tints in some of the screens created by contributing authors to white. I also liked its ability to very quickly grab part of a screen by simply clicking and dragging. In my view, HiJaak is currently the hands-down king of Windows screen capture and file conversion.

However, HiJaak lacked one critical ability — it had no time-delay feature that would let me begin performing an action before the grab took place. This kept me from grabbing the various cursors Draw uses when you perform an action. The solution was Collage Plus, which has just such a feature. I then converted these to compressed .TIF with HiJaak. I used Photo-Paint to edit screen shots where necessary, again saving in compressed .TIF.

For outputting text and testing images created in Draw, I used a WinPrinter 800, from LaserMaster. This proved a fine match with Draw, creating crisp output at remarkable speed. For low-cost, high-resolution PostScript-compatible output, the WinPrinter is tough to beat. For example, I used Mosaic to print out thumbnails of the illustrations for each chapter, which I then gave to both the tutorial tester and designer. These thumbnails would have been illegible at lower resolutions and have taken forever to output from most printers, since the print files generated during this process were sometimes as large as 15 Mb.

PlaceCorelChapter

I made use of the abilities of Delrina's WinFax Pro software to fax chapters directly from Word to Rosalyn Wosnick for copy editing. It also proved handy for faxing many of the letters involved in coordinating a project like this, as well as Draw-created illustrations. If you're not currently using a fax modem and Windows-based fax software, such as WinFax, you should check it out.

After using pen, brush and ink on paper, Peter turned to a number of Macintosh graphic programs including Adobe Photoshop, Adobe Illustrator, Fractal Design Painter, Satellite 3D and DeskPaint to amass about two dozen variations of the icons that line the book margins. The winning "Hot Tip" and "Secret" icons were redone in FreeHand with a Wacom 510c graphics tablet, and saved as .EPS files. The fonts used were Goudy Old Style and Kabel. Peter converted the Draw Waldo Icons font to Macintosh format with Altsys Fontographer.

UserLand Frontier and CE QuicKeys played an important role in the PageMaker production process. Peter automated tasks wherever possible, sending high-powered commands to PageMaker from Frontier via AppleEvents.

Peter wrote a "PlaceCorelChapter" Frontier DeskScript which launched his PageMaker template file, with dialog boxes prompting him for chapter name and number. With this script, new master page items and the reformatted replaced text were saved in a new PageMaker document for each chapter. Peter wrote other Frontier scripts to extend PageMaker's functionality: formatting, drawing boxes, proportionally resizing placed screen shots and aligning objects, to name a few examples.

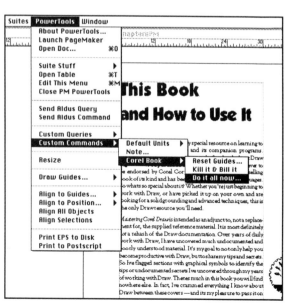

The index was compiled laboriously by the author with a back-breaking amount of manual labour and considerable assistance from the Sonar Bookends Aldus Addition for PageMaker from Virginia Systems.

Final camera-ready pages were created on a LaserMaster Unity 1200XL. This is a 1,200 dpi tabloid printer that outputs pages from PCs or Macs. From a production perspective it proved to be a treat, thanks to its high rendering speed and a built-in hard drive that held the downloaded fonts used throughout the book. The Unity 1200 is geared for design studios, quick-printers, in-plant operations and publishers. You can judge for yourself the quality of its output. I was impressed enough with it that I've provided a coupon at the back of the book worth $1,000 off its purchase price (as well as discounts on other LaserMaster printers.)

Lupin Software's Let'erRIP!, an IAC-aware scriptable PostScript server/downloader, was a workhorse, downloading completed pages to the Unity quietly in the background.

The first page of the color section was output by Pawel Bodytko, who also created the two images on the page. Pawel used an Itek IGX 9000, creating film separations at 1,600 dpi. The last three pages in the color section were output by Agfa Canada, which created the separations on a SelectSet 5000 at 2,400 dpi. Some of the print files were quite large, weighing in at over 4 Mb. I used the PKZIP program to compress the files to fit on a 3.5-inch floppy and provided the imagesetter operators at Agfa with the

public domain Macintosh UNZIP program. They then converted them back into PostScript print files that could be dumped to the SelectSet 5000.

Index

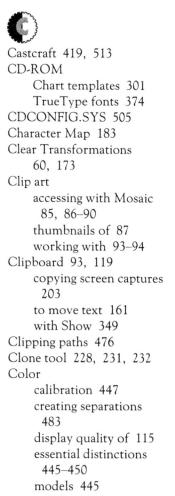

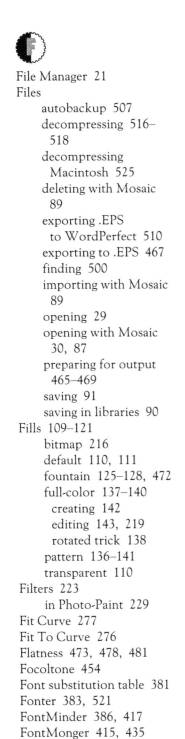

Survival Gear for the Windows Professional

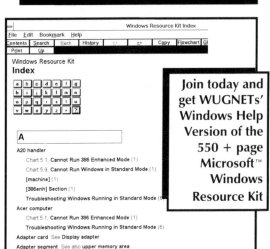

Had enough of
Chris Dickman?

No?

You mean you've found his approach to presenting hardcore Draw tips and secrets in an affable, reader-oriented manner valuable enough that you're ready for more of the same? In that case, the good news is that no longer do you have to wait a year for the next edition of Mastering Corel Draw. In fact, there are now two possibilities available for those who crave more from Chris and his merry band of contributing authors: the Mastering Corel Draw newsletter and seminar series.

The Newsletter

The newsletter contains 16 pages of the latest, hottest, most essential tips and secrets for maximizing your use of Draw and its applications. Stay abreast of bug fixes and updates, add to your repertoire of undocumented features, learn about new software to make your Draw sessions more productive, build your Windows skills, and incorporate seemingly endless font effects into your documents. You'll get more of the candid, clearly-written material you've encountered in this book. Chris and his editorial team are Draw insiders: join them ten times a year, as they explore the inner recesses of Draw and provide you with essential information to use it more effectively.

The Seminars

Chris has also put together a one-day seminar on Draw, Show and Chart. Spend the day with Chris and his team of presenters, exploring the inner workings of your favorite applications. Call, write or fax for more information.

Yes, plug me into the loop. Send me one year — 10 issues — of Chris Dickman's Mastering Corel Draw newsletter for the special price of $60, a savings of $15 off the regular price. I understand that I can cancel my subscription at any time for a full refund.

Name _____ Title _____

Company _____

Address _____

City _____ State/Province _____ Zip/Code _____

☐ Check/MO enclosed   ☐ Please bill me   (Overseas add $30)

☐ I don't want to subscribe just yet. Send me more information about the newsletter.
☐ Send me information about the seminars.
☐ Let me know when the next edition of Mastering Corel Draw is available.

Chris Dickman's Mastering Corel Draw, 16 Ottawa St., Toronto, ON M4T 2B6, Canada
Phone: (416) 924-0759 Fax: (416) 924-4875

More from Peachpit Press...

101 Windows Tips and Tricks
Jesse Berst and Scott Dunn
Compiled by the editors of *Windows Watcher* newsletter, this power-packed, user-friendly survival guide gives you tips and tricks to make Windows faster, easier, and more fun. *(216 pages)*

Desktop Publishing Secrets
Robert Eckhardt, Bob Weibel, and Ted Nace
This is a compilation of hundreds of the best desktop publishing tips from five years of *Publish* magazine. It covers all the major graphics and layout programs on the PC and Macintosh platforms, and valuable tips on publishing as a business. *(550 pages)*

The Little Windows Book, 3.1 Edition
Kay Yarborough Nelson
This second edition of Peachpit's popular book explains the subtle and not-so-subtle changes in version 3.1 as it gives the essentials of getting started with Windows. Additionally, each chapter includes a handy summary chart of keyboard shortcuts and quick tips. *(144 pages)*

The Little WordPerfect Book
Skye Lininger
Teach yourself the basics of WordPerfect 5.1 in less than an hour. This book gives step-by-step instructions for setting page margins, typing text, navigating with the cursor keys, and more. *(160 pages)*

The Little WordPerfect for Windows Book
Kay Yarborough Nelson
This book gives you the basic skills you need to create simple documents and get familiar with WordPerfect's new Windows interface. *(200 pages)*

PageMaker 4: An Easy Desk Reference
Robin Williams
At last—this highly acclaimed reference book is available for PC users. Here's the book that made Kathy McClelland of *The Page* say, "The book is so superbly indexed and cross-referenced that even if you only halfway know what you're looking for, you'll find it." No serious PageMaker user should be without it. *(768 pages)*

PageMaker 4: Visual QuickStart Guide
Webster &Associates
This highly visual reference guide is all you need to get started using PageMaker for the PC. Using actual screen shots as examples, the book shows you how to set up a publication, work with text, import and manipulate graphics, use style sheets, create an index, and more. *(176 pages)*

The PC is not a typewriter
Robin Williams
PC users can now learn trade secrets from author Robin Williams, whose best-selling *The Mac is not a typewriter* introduced tens of thousands of Mac users to the secrets of creating beautiful type. In less than 100 pages, the book explains why Typing 101 rules such as "two spaces between sentences" don't apply when using a keyboard. Covers punctuation, leading, special characters, kerning, fonts, justification, and more. *(96 pages)*

The QuarkXPress Book, Windows Edition
David Blatner and Bob Weibel
The Mac version of this book has been a bestseller for two years—so useful that Quark's own support staff uses it. It tells you everything you need to know about QuarkXPress—importing and modifying graphics, creating large documents, printing, and much more. *(542 pages)*

Ventura Tips and Tricks, 3rd Edition

Ted Nace and Daniel Will-Harris

Described by Ventura president John Meyer as "the most complete reference for anyone serious about using Ventura Publisher," this book is packed with inside information, speed-up tips, tricks for reviving a crashed chapter, ways to overcome memory limitations, and more. *(790 pages)*

Windows 3.1 Bible

Fred Davis

Compiled by one of America's leading Windows experts, this book is a wall-to-wall compendium of tips, tricks, warnings, shortcuts, reviews, and resources that will inform, entertain, and empower Windows users of every ability level. *(1,152 pages)*

Windows 3.1 Font Book

David Angell and Brent Heslop

This book is the first hands-on font guide for Windows users. It explains managing, choosing, and using fonts to enhance all kinds of documents, with instructions for working with TrueType and PostScript fonts. Additionally, it contains suggestions for building a font library, with a comprehensive listing of font vendors and over 100 font samples. *(216 pages)*

Word for Windows Essentials

Geoffrey Mandel

This book is a handy reference to Word for Windows 2.0, loaded with useful tips and tricks. It explains both basic and advanced features, and you'll learn how to customize your program and use the math and graphics features. Now you can master this popular and sophisticated program! *(232 pages)*

WordPerfect: Desktop Publishing in Style, 2nd Edition

Daniel Will-Harris

This popular guide (over 90,000 in print) to producing documents with WordPerfect 5.0 or 5.1 opens with a simple tutorial and proceeds through 20 sample documents, each complete with keystroke instructions. Humorous, informative, and fun to read, this book is invaluable to people who desktop publish with this software program. *(672 pages)*

WordPerfect for Windows with Style

Daniel Will-Harris

This generously illustrated handbook gives step-by-step instructions for creating good-looking business documents using WordPerfect for Windows. The book shows a variety of documents and provides the exact commands, codes, and keystrokes used to create each one. Includes valuable insights into styles, graphics, fonts, tables, macros, clip art, printers, and utilities. Daniel Will-Harris combines technical accuracy, detailed and easy-to-understand explanations, and a sense of just plain fun. *(528 pages)*

Works for Windows: Visual QuickStart Guide

Webster & Associates

This is a highly visual reference guide to help you get acquainted—quickly—with Microsoft Works for Windows. The book explains, through examples, all three parts of the Works integrated package: the word processor, the spreadsheet, and the database. You'll be ready to jump right into your next project after consulting this handy guide. Available with or without a tutorial disk. *(208 pages)*

Order Form

(800) 283-9444 or (510) 548-4393 or (510) 548-5991 (fax)

#	Title	Price	Total
	101 Windows Tips & Tricks	12.95	
	Desktop Publishing Secrets	27.95	
	The Little Excel 4 Book, Windows Edition	12.95	
	The Little Windows Book, 3.1 Edition	12.95	
	The Little WordPerfect Book	12.95	
	The Little WordPerfect for Windows Book	12.95	
	Mastering Corel Draw 3 (with disks)	38.00	
	PageMaker 4: An Easy Desk Reference (PC Edition)	29.95	
	PageMaker 4: Visual QuickStart Guide (PC Edition)	12.95	
	The PC is not a typewriter	9.95	
	The QuarkXPress Book, Windows Edition	28.00	
	Ventura Tips and Tricks, 3rd Edition	27.95	
	Windows 3.1 Bible	28.00	
	Windows 3.1 Font Book	12.95	
	Word for Windows Essentials	14.00	
	WordPerfect: Desktop Publishing in Style, 2nd Edition	23.95	
	WordPerfect for Windows with Style	24.95	
	Works for Windows: Visual QuickStart Guide (with disk)	24.95	

SHIPPING:	First Item	Each Additional		
UPS Ground	$4	$1	Subtotal	
UPS Blue	$7	$2	8.25% Tax (CA only)	
Canada	$6	$4	Shipping	
Overseas	$14	$14	**TOTAL**	

Name		
Company		
Address		
City	State	Zip
Phone	Fax	
❏ Check enclosed	❏ Visa	❏ MasterCard
Company purchase order #		
Credit card #	Expiration Date	

Peachpit Press, Inc. • 2414 Sixth Street • Berkeley, CA • 94710
Your satisfaction is guaranteed or your money will be cheerfully refunded!

AGENCY GOTHIC

Diode Vogue

Antique Bold

Einstein Black

OPTI ASIAN

Novel Gothic XBold Agency

Bauer Bodoni Bold

Globe Gothic

Runserif Regular

Goudy Bold Agency

Bernhard Gothic XHeavy

HUXLEY VERTICAL

BINNER

NEULAND INLINE CAPS

Bodoni Antiqua

Korinna XBold Agency

Caslon No. 2 Black

Latin Bold

Cheltenham Bold Condensed

Franklin Gothic Triple Condensed

Corvinus Skyline

Metropolis Bold

Craw Modern Bold

Koloss

Radiant Bold Condensed

Similunatix Heavy